The Last Ghetto

The Last Ghetto

An Everyday History of Theresienstadt

Anna Hájková

OXFORD
UNIVERSITY PRESS

Oxford University Press is a department of the University of Oxford. It furthers
the University's objective of excellence in research, scholarship, and education
by publishing worldwide. Oxford is a registered trade mark of Oxford University
Press in the UK and certain other countries.

Published in the United States of America by Oxford University Press
198 Madison Avenue, New York, NY 10016, United States of America.

© Oxford University Press 2020

First issued as an Oxford University Press paperback, 2024

All rights reserved. No part of this publication may be reproduced, stored in
a retrieval system, or transmitted, in any form or by any means, without the
prior permission in writing of Oxford University Press, or as expressly permitted
by law, by license, or under terms agreed with the appropriate reproduction
rights organization. Inquiries concerning reproduction outside the scope of the
above should be sent to the Rights Department, Oxford University Press, at the
address above.

You must not circulate this work in any other form
and you must impose this same condition on any acquirer.

Library of Congress Cataloging-in-Publication Data
Names: Hájková, Anna, author.
Title: The last ghetto : an everyday history of Theresienstadt / Anna Hájková.
Description: New York, NY : Oxford University Press, [2020] |
Includes bibliographical references and index.
Identifiers: LCCN 2020012854 (print) | LCCN 2020012855 (ebook) |
ISBN 9780190051778 (hardback) | ISBN 9780197696323 (paperback) |
ISBN 9780190051792 (epub)
Subjects: LCSH: Theresienstadt (Concentration camp)—History. |
Concentration camps—Czech Republic—Terezín (Ústecký kraj)
Classification: LCC D805.5.T54 H35 2020 (print) |
LCC D805.5.T54 (ebook) | DDC 940.53/1853716—dc23
LC record available at https://lccn.loc.gov/2020012854
LC ebook record available at https://lccn.loc.gov/2020012855

Paperback printed by Marquis Book Printing, Canada

For those who did not come back

Contents

Introduction: The Well-Known, Poorly Understood Ghetto	1
1. The Overorganized Ghetto: Administering Terezín	16
2. A Society Based on Inequality	59
3. The Age of Pearl Barley: Food and Hunger	100
4. Medicine and Illness	132
5. Cultural Life	168
6. Transports from Terezín to the East	201
Conclusion	239
Acknowledgments	243
Notes	247
Archives Consulted	323
Bibliography	327
Index	347

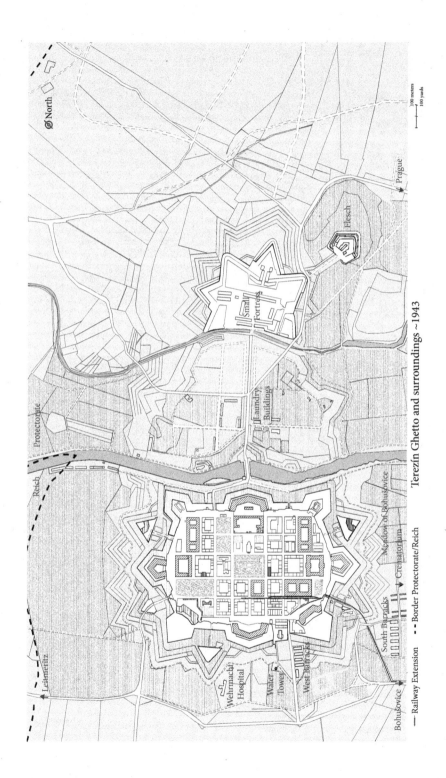

Terezín Ghetto and surroundings ~1943

Terezín Ghetto ~1943

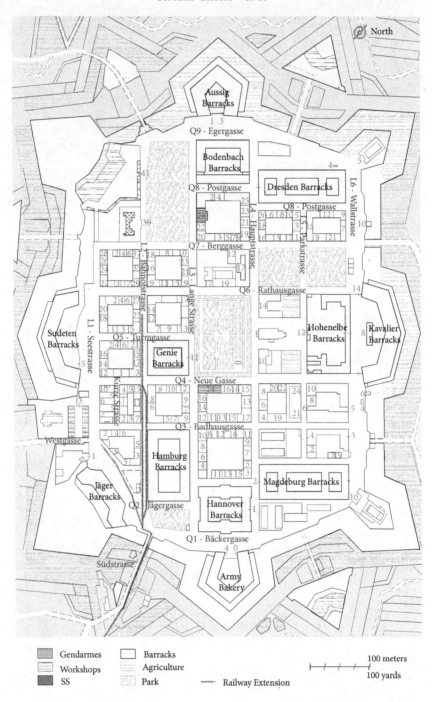

Introduction

The Well-Known, Poorly Understood Ghetto

In his diary, written while he was an inmate in Terezín, a prematurely aged young man named Gonda Redlich recorded a series of bizarre moments. Here is one:

> A small child shouts at an old man, "Stinky Jew!" A man walks up to them and says, "What are you doing? You should be ashamed of yourself! You are a Czech and you talk in such a vulgar way." This occurred in the ghetto in the year 1944. The child, the old man, and the man—all of them were Jews. It happened in the city of Terezín, which was only recently named: "ghetto Terezín."[1]

This scene was one of many in which Redlich criticized the numerous Czech Jews who distanced themselves from their Jewish roots.[2] Two months after he wrote the entry, Redlich was sent to Auschwitz, where he was killed, together with his wife and their baby.

Terezín offers many similar stories. These seemingly bizarre situations were part of the logic of the forced community. The Nazis fashioned Theresienstadt for their purposes but left the day-to-day administration of the ghetto to Jewish functionaries. Redlich's diary recounts numerous conflicts and controversies among the inmates; the SS (Schutzstaffel) were mostly absent. Other diarists likewise focused much more on their fellow inmates and material conditions than on their persecutors. The people in Terezín created and inhabited different groups and hierarchies. All four participants in this scene—the child, old man, passerby, and diarist—expressed and lived their place in the social structure in the ghetto society.[3] To curse the old man, the child used a slur that combined dirt and Jewishness. It was no accident that the target of the insult was old. Old people occupied the bottom layer of the sharply segmented inmate community. To chastise the child, the passerby used a moralistic notion of Czechness. As the dominant group in Terezín,

The Last Ghetto. Anna Hájková, Oxford University Press (2020). © Oxford University Press.
DOI: 10.1093/oso/9780190051778.001.0001.

2   THE LAST GHETTO

Czech Jews controlled access to status and prestige. Redlich, the diarist, was no mere observer. As head of the Department of Youth Care, he bore some responsibility for the child's behavior; the Zionist Youth Care strove to raise children in the ghetto as conscious Jews. Meanwhile, the shadow of transports—"to the East"—hung over them all. Even the fate of the vignette is telling. Whether because it implied pedagogical failure or because it showed the dearth of solidarity among inmates, this entry was not included in the published Hebrew or English editions of Redlich's diary.

Terezín was a victim society in the Holocaust; it is necessary to go to the eye of the horrors, to observe with an empathetic eye, and then ask what it means. This book examines the world in which the inmates of Terezín lived: the beliefs, mentality, and dynamics of the forced community. Terezín was a ghetto, established by German authorities to constrict the people they confined there. Although deprivation and suffering shaped the society that emerged, these factors did not entirely define it. Prisoners communicated, formed groups, and created rules. A close examination of the society in Theresienstadt helps us understand how people adapted to and worked in an extreme society.[4]

Studying the prisoners' social relations shows that Nazi victims should be understood beyond the dynamic of the perpetrator-victim binary and should not be read through victims' deaths alone. For a long time Holocaust studies focused on the perpetrators. Works that examine the victims, especially those that look at society in camps and ghettos, have often been judgmental or descriptive, as scholars struggled with how to address and account for the conflicts and inequalities among Holocaust victims. However, victims should not be defined by their imminent murder, nor should they be ennobled by their impending fate. We need to tell the history of the society of victims, while occasionally integrating, wherever pertinent, the perpetrators' role. This focus allows us to highlight the issues of responsibility, agency, and powerlessness, as well as the human tendency to understand through judgment.[5]

Among the ghettos Terezín was distinctive, notably because it was the transit point for all Czech Jews; a designated ghetto for the elderly; international with respect to its population; and long-lasting, surpassing even Lodz. Nevertheless, Terezín was part of an interlocking system and merits integration in the wider history of Nazi ghettos and places of detention. With that idea in mind, *The Last Ghetto*, though not explicitly comparative, offers a road map for how to think about and analyze prisoner societies in the Holocaust.

INTRODUCTION 3

Every camp and ghetto had a different social field: the prisoner population, the particulars of the perpetrators' persecution, the distribution of resources, and chronology. Rather than focusing on what made each camp and ghetto unique, we should approach the study of prisoner society with a theoretically informed, unified, analytical framework. Moreover, studying society in Theresienstadt provides insights not only into prisoner society specifically, but more important, into human society at large. Even if many of the events of the Holocaust would not happen in the "outside world," whether because of their violence or scale, society during the Holocaust is one of the many versions of what human society can be.

One goal in this history is to place Holocaust and Jewish history into the wider context of modern history. Another is to argue for combining empirical Holocaust research with relevant theories. Perhaps because this European genocide in the midst of the twentieth century was so horrible, historians often tend to view it outside of the European context. As a result, much is lost. The Holocaust was connected to the context and society it came from and thus needs to be viewed in this perspective. Similarly, the way that middle-class Jews from Central and Western Europe viewed and acclimated themselves to the ghetto contributes to our understanding of their social, cultural, and gender histories. For an entire civilization of Central European Jews, Theresienstadt was a final station on the way to murder. These people's lives were artifacts of a previous European world, whose last traces we can find in Terezín; it was not another planet but a site where Central European cultures continued, albeit under duress. The same rules that underpinned society in the ghetto structured the societies outside it. Examining people in the ghetto tells us more about the Central and Western European middle class, both before and after the war.

A cultural history of Terezín sheds light on the societies from which prisoners came and to which they went after the war. Culture is not static; Norbert Elias and others have pointed out its slow transformations, the development and perpetuation of habits and beliefs.[6] We can discern that cultures have a half-life; they develop and exist for decades, even centuries. When certain factors that produced the culture change, the old culture wanes, but it does not disappear all at once. One such example is tropes of sentimentality and irony, present in Czech culture since the early nineteenth century.[7] We find the same tropes in Czech films of the 1930s and in the diaries of Czech inmates in Theresienstadt, and Jan Svěrák's popular films owe their success with Czech audiences to the fact that they employ these tropes. Being able

4   THE LAST GHETTO

to read culture backward (and forward) is especially valuable because cultural, social, and gender histories and histories of sexuality are scarce for the interwar era for those countries from which Jews were sent to Terezín.[8] Even where we do have excellent cultural histories (mostly for German Jewry), information about culture from Terezín offers valuable insights for reflecting on Jewish societies long before the ghetto.[9]

The prisoner society operated on the basis of categorization. Ethnicity, culture, language, habitus, and social capital determined inmates' status and shaped their access to resources, translating them into class. Historians have pointed out the stark social stratification in ghettos and camps, but what is often missed is that the category of class itself had changed. Unlike in the "civil" world, economic capital—access to resources—was less important in constituting class. Similarly, ethnicity took on new meanings in Theresienstadt among prisoners who nominally shared Jewishness. What was identified as ethnicity changed as well; it depended on culture, nationality, and language. Habitus defined people's behavior in unfamiliar surroundings, but unlike social theorists' conceptualization of it as defined only by culture and class,[10] in Theresienstadt it was largely determined by one's ethnicity. In this society, even more interestingly, class and ethnicity were intersectionally linked and translated into one another. Ethnicity became in Terezín the most prominent category in how prisoners made sense of each other. It also became a hierarchical statement, as most of the social elite were young Czech Jews.[11]

In order to appreciate how these social categories changed, we need to put them into historical context.[12] Before the war, Czech-German relations were negotiated according to categories fixed differently; language, for instance, was a defining category of belonging (Czech versus German), whereas class, culture, and kinship were secondary (there were many mixed Czech German families). However, Czech Jews in Theresienstadt could no longer define their ethnicity via language or class. As a result, they renegotiated the categories of ethnic belonging: culture and kinship became central, while their understanding of language changed, given the presence of many German-speaking "foreigners," as Czech Jewish inmates regarded the inmates from outside the Czech countries. Now those prisoners who spoke local German (Böhmisch) were recognized as Czech, while German-speaking prisoners from Germany or Austria were seen as Germans. Thus the Terezín inmates came to understand the categorization of language either as ethnic and salient (when designating non-Czech prisoners) or as cultural and secondary

INTRODUCTION 5

(in the case of Czech prisoners). Remarkably, "foreign" prisoners adopted this categorization as well. The linguistic social practices in the ghetto thus enhance our understanding of the workings of nationalism.

Although nationalism is a principal topic in the modern history of East and Central Europe,[13] studies of Czech German nationalism do not engage with Terezín. This disregard is another example of separating the Holocaust from history, as if Czech Jews—albeit frequently acknowledged as assimilated and intermarried—were a society apart.[14] But we need to incorporate Holocaust history in general, and Theresienstadt in particular, into the histories of Central Europe. In the ghetto, stratification was usually expressed in ethnicized terms, and that ethnicity had a class indication, for instance when the German or Austrian prisoners depicted the social elite of young Czech Jews as athletic and beautiful. Constructionist anthropologists have shown that society creates, constructs, and employs ethnic, cultural, and social differences and belongings.[15] However, scholars have not addressed the link in the construction of stratification and ethnicity. The interdependent working of class and ethnicity in the newly emerging society of Terezín contributes significantly to our understanding of societal processes, beyond solely Holocaust history.

Terezín, though part of Jewish history, was not very Jewish, and in that sense it is part of what Isaac Deutscher called "non-Jewish Jewish history."[16] The ghetto did not engender a common sense of Jewishness, even though all its inhabitants, including a sizable Christian minority, were confined there because of their Jewish background. Rather, the inmates were shaped by the countries they considered home; they self-identified, or were ascribed an ethnic belonging, according to the place where they had lived before the deportation. Jewishness in Theresienstadt was always a strategy of demarcation. The members of each of the national units considered themselves Jewish in the correct way, while they considered the others too assimilated, too intermarried, or too religious. These assertions were socially constructed, national stereotypes, connected to the observer's sensibilities rather than to what the person observed.

Popular and academic opinion alike has often put forward the notion that the camps destroyed people and atomized society. Most notably, Hannah Arendt argued that the totalitarian regime in the camps stripped individuals of all characteristics of their humanity until the prisoners were no longer moral persons.[17] However, stripping people of their citizenship, social, and individual rights does not efface humanity, nor does it suspend

6 THE LAST GHETTO

society. The forcibly incarcerated, suffering, and heterogeneous people developed and lived in a society. Building on research by Erving Goffman on "total institutions"[18] and prison history more generally,[19] the society in Terezín, and by extension society in camps and ghettos, can be seen as a form of what human society can look like, rather than a deformation.[20] For instance, kinship continued; families tried hard to stay together when they faced deportation. Familial bonds changed and usually were limited to two generations, however, which is why the elder generation of grandparents was much more vulnerable than the younger inmates. Touching on the limits of familial solidarity necessitates an overdue critique of redemptive, sentimentalizing Holocaust narratives. There is a need for explanations of the ways people behaved, even if at times we find them less than palatable. Studying the Holocaust victim society needs to take on long-marginalized topics, be it Jewish informers, prostitution, or same-sex conduct.

The agency of Holocaust victims—whether they had any, and whether it is ethical to discuss it, limited as it was—is a central topic in Holocaust studies and even more so in public perceptions of the Holocaust.[21] By studying prisoner society as one in its own right, we gain key insights into the agency of Holocaust victims in recognizing seemingly small acts as serious instances of choice. This approach contradicts Lawrence Langer's argument of "choiceless choices" that came to dominate the field.[22] Langer's aim was to surpass the moralization of life in the death camps, yet his concept is often used to deny the victims agency broadly speaking. In a more general context, Michel Foucault, immensely influential in prison historiography, rejected the idea that inmates exercised agency. Yet dismissing prisoners' agency because their actions were only rarely "successful"—that is, because they did not survive—is an erringly linear view. A number of cases—from food sharing over sexual barter to the decision of whom to send on a transport—illuminate what the agency of Holocaust prisoners looked like and what decisions it entailed. Many who survived Terezín in fact did so due to their behavior.

Terezín numbers among those historical locations that many people believe they know well. Some aspects of its history—the visit of the International Red Cross, the propaganda film, and the cultural productions—dominate perceptions of the ghetto. Of more immediate concern here is another set of issues about Terezín: its purpose and organization within the Nazi system, the number of people sent there, the origin and destination of transports, and its chronology.[23]

INTRODUCTION 7

The site itself was not new. Austrian emperor Joseph II built Terezín in the mid-eighteenth century as a fortification against the Prussian army. Located sixty kilometers northwest of Prague, halfway to Dresden, the Vaubanian fort was completed in 1780. It was never attacked and served as a military town. Terezín comprises the Great Fortress (the actual town and later the ghetto) and the Small Fortress, a lesser fortification to the east, used after 1939 as a transit prison by the Prague Gestapo. Shaped like a star with multiple points, the large fortress included twelve multistory barracks and more than a hundred small houses. Later, the SS had built various huts (*Baracken*), largely for forced labor, but some also housed prisoners. Before the war, Terezín garrisoned members of the Czechoslovak army and fewer than 4,000 civilian inhabitants.

The Nazis used Terezín to serve four overlapping functions. It was a transit ghetto, an advantage ghetto (that is, a destination for groups deemed exceptions, such as the elderly), a propaganda ghetto, and eventually a camp to hold Jews for exchange. Each of these functions linked Terezín to larger processes of confinement and destruction. "Transit" signaled that Terezín would not be the final destination for the people sent there, even if initially planners had not yet determined where that would be. The concepts of "advantage" and "exception" implied that those sent to Terezín would receive different treatment from what the Nazis accorded most Jews—that is, direct transport from their residence to the East for forced labor and killing. The propaganda and exchange functions reflected Nazi concerns with domestic and international affairs.

Altogether, the SS sent more than 143,000 Jews to Terezín. Among them were 74,000 Jews from the Protectorate of Bohemia and Moravia, 600 from the Sudeten area, 1,400 Slovaks, 42,000 German and 15,000 Austrian Jews, 4,900 from the Netherlands, 466 from Denmark, and 1,150 from Hungary. About 34,000 people died in Terezín, most of them elderly.

Terezín started operations on November 24, 1941, as a transit camp for Jews from the Protectorate of Bohemia and Moravia. It was located near the frontier with the Sudetengau, where the Protectorate bordered on Germany. Two months earlier, in September 1941, the Central Office for Jewish Emigration had ordered the Jewish Community of the Protectorate to set up department G (for ghetto).[24] The small department had to prepare draft plans for places in the Protectorate where the Czech Jews could be concentrated. In November the SS suggested Terezín. The first Jewish men brought from Prague formed the construction detail (*Aufbaukommando*), followed

8   THE LAST GHETTO

by thousands of Czech Jews in the next months. Beginning in June 1942, the SS also sent to Terezín Jews from Germany and Austria who fit certain categories: those over sixty-five years of age, decorated war veterans, and functionaries of the Reich Association of German Jews. Later they added *Geltungsjuden*, people of mixed background whom German law considered to be Jewish, and spouses from mixed marriages that had ended by either divorce or death.

In April 1943 the first Jews from the Netherlands arrived, along with further groups categorized as exceptions: people with certain distinctions in civil life, prisoner functionaries from Westerbork, and Dutch Sephardic Jews. Half a year later, Adolf Eichmann's Department IVB4 of the Reich Security Main Office (RSHA) added 466 Jews from Denmark who, unlike the majority of Danish Jews, had not been able to escape to Sweden. Finally, in winter and spring 1945, as the Germans evacuated Slovakia and Vienna before the advancing Red Army, the SS consigned groups of Slovak and Hungarian Jews to Terezín. The latter had worked as forced laborers in and around Vienna. At the same time, Czech and German Jewish partners from existing mixed marriages, until then protected, were also sent to Terezín. Theresienstadt was the last ghetto to remain until the end of war; the First Ukrainian Front of the Red Army liberated the ghetto on May 9, 1945, one day after V-E Day.

That is an overview of when different Jewish populations were sent to Terezín. The planning and founding of Terezín did not happen in isolation, but rather as leaders of the German state were finalizing their decision about what to do with the Jews from across continental Europe. On October 10, 1941, Reinhard Heydrich, deputy Reich Protector of Bohemia and Moravia and head of the RSHA, raised the subject of isolating the Jews of the Protectorate in a ghetto on former Czech territory. Hitler wished to remove as many Jews as possible from Greater Germany, Heydrich stated, and complaints from Nazi authorities in Lodz made a ghetto on Czech territory the next best option. Later, the plan was that after all Jews had been dispatched to the East, the area would be repurposed as a German settlement.[25]

Plans to send German Jews to Terezín were already formulated in mid-November 1941, although it took nine months to implement them.[26] While Heydrich was debating where to situate the transit ghetto, Eichmann's office dispatched the first mass transports of Jews from Greater Germany to Lodz. Plans at that time were to remove Jews from Central Europe, if not yet to kill them. On December 12, three weeks after the first Czech Jews arrived in Terezín, Hitler confirmed that all Jews would be killed during the war rather than expelled to the East or murdered after the war ended.[27] Terezín played a role in the way that decision was implemented; on January 8, 1942, Department IVB4 ordered the first of sixty-three transports from the ghetto to the East. The second transport to Riga followed a week later, where an auxiliary security police commando murdered all the women and children and most of the men in a forest near Bikierniki.[28]

For the next two years and ten months, Terezín served as a transit point, and for the entire population of Czech Jews, Terezín was *the* transit ghetto. Personnel in IVB4 determined where transports of Jews were to be sent and assigned the number of people to leave from each place. Terezín belonged to the same area as Berlin and Vienna, distinct from other parts of Central and Western Europe.[29] Altogether, more than 87,000 people were sent from Terezín to the East. About 4,000 of them survived.[30]

During its first eight months of existence, the ghetto consisted of only a few barracks. Inmates had to stay inside, families were separated, and women and men were not allowed to meet. Over time, more barracks became available as the gentile population was expelled. By July 1, 1942, the entire town, including the little houses, was incorporated into the ghetto. The entire terrain was then open, and prisoners could move around freely until the curfew. The ghetto covered 0.52 square kilometer, of which only 0.16 square kilometer was usable space. In terms of population density, if the same population statistics were applied to Berlin of that era, the city would have had a population of over 100 million inhabitants—more than all of Greater Germany.[31] Unlike other ghettos, Theresienstadt was placed in the entire town, using the fortification architecture as a wall. Compared to Lodz ghetto, it was relatively easy to smuggle food or people in and out, whether by agricultural workers or through the casemate tunnels. Relatively few prisoners escaped, though, due to fear of reprisals against their families left behind; difficulty in finding help among gentile Czechs, who were terrified after the imposition of two brutal martial laws; and finally the fact that the border with Germany, the Sudetengau, blocked the logical escape route to the mountainous region in the northwest (see map Terezín Ghetto and surroundings).

With the transports of German and Austrian Jewish older people to Terezín, Eichmann added a new function: Terezín became a ghetto for the elderly (*Altersghetto*). The Nazis needed this preferential alternative if they were to maintain the illusion among Germans that the other transports were indeed intended for workers. Old people could hardly be expected to work, so they were sent to Terezín. Some arrived expecting a spa town, but all found

10   THE LAST GHETTO

a desolate place where they received the worst accommodations. With the incoming German Jews, the population of Terezín increased dramatically. Mortality rose accordingly, primarily affecting older people.

The propaganda and exchange functions of the ghetto emerged in the last two years of the war and still somewhat overshadow public perception of it. After the defeat at Stalingrad, Heinrich Himmler, Reichsführer of the SS, decided to expand Terezín's role as an advantage ghetto in order to appease the Allies, with whom he hoped to negotiate. On May 1, 1943, Terezín was relabeled a "Jewish settlement area" (rather than a ghetto); the SS headquarters were dubbed the "office" (*Dienststelle*); and the streets, previously known by abbreviations (such as "L" [Lang] and "Q" [Queer]), received names (see map Terezín Ghetto). A delegation from the German Red Cross spent two days, June 27 and 28, 1943, in Terezín. The visitors, apparently shown around freely, were shocked by the dire conditions, lack of food, and crowded accommodations.[32]

To prepare for a more successful site visit, the SS sent 17,500 Jews in three waves from Terezín to Auschwitz. In February 1944, the third and last commandant, Karl Rahm, arrived to oversee the "beautification" of the ghetto. Inmates repainted facades, cleaned streets, and placed banks and a music pavilion in the park. Delegates of the International Red Cross arrived on June 23, 1944, and their highly orchestrated visit was deemed a complete success.[33] Hitler did not participate in the preparations, nor is there evidence that he knew about them. Eichmann was absent, organizing transports of Hungarian Jews to Auschwitz. Ten months later a second delegation from the International Red Cross, on April 6, 1945, was much more critical. On May 2, the Swiss delegate, Paul Dunant, effectively took over the ghetto from the SS.

German authorities made two films about Terezín. The first, shot near the end of 1942, depicted the transport of a Jewish family from Prague to Terezín. It is not clear who commissioned the film.[34] The second film, one of the best known depictions of the ghetto, was the brainchild of Hans Günther in the Central Office for Jewish Emigration in Prague.[35] Two Czech gentiles, Ivan Frič and Karel Pečený from Aktualita, a Prague firm, and one prisoner, Kurt Gerron, a German actor and director, directed the film. Titled *Theresienstadt: A Documentary from the Jewish Settlement Area*, it was shot in January and late summer 1944. Many misconceptions surround this film. It was not in fact titled *The Führer Gives a City to the Jews*, as is often claimed. The leading Nazi authorities neither commissioned the film nor were informed about it. And in fact, the quotidian life of the prisoners was not much influenced by these propaganda activities.

To a limited extent, inmates of Terezín participated in work for German industry and the army. German officials closed a deal with the commandant and the Economic Department of the Terezín SS, who received the payments.[36] The two largest enterprises were the "K-production," which built boxes (*Kisten*) for the Wehrmacht, and the mica workshop. In summer 1942, the Reich Office for electrotechnical products set up the mica workshop, in which female workers split mica into thin blades for use in airplane production.[37] Processing of mica halted in 1943 but resumed in September 1944. The 1,200 women who worked on this project were protected from the large transports that followed.

There is often confusion about whether Theresienstadt was a ghetto or a concentration camp. This debate dates to the aftermath of the war, when the camps came to signify the Nazi cruelty. Few people recognized ghettos as sites of Nazi atrocities, even though the ghettos had a higher mortality rate and, with their double function as transit and labor sites, were loci of intense suffering. Survivors framed Terezín as a concentration camp in order to have their accounts accepted.[38] But Terezín was indeed a ghetto.[39] Such a distinction is always blurred, because many ghettos were similar to concentration camps, and some camps were like ghettos.[40] In addition, Nazis did not provide a clear definition of the term and used it only rarely in their official communications.[41] One definition of "ghetto" described it as "resettlement and concentration of the Jewish population into an area only for Jews and [with] severe restrictions on entering and leaving."[42]

Terezín, however, was already named a ghetto before its foundation and carried this designation until the end of the war. Only for propaganda reasons did the SS change the label to "Jewish settlement area" in May 1943. The prisoners themselves used "ghetto" and "Theresienstadt" synonymously. The relevant German authorities were the Prague Central Office, commander of the Sipo and SD (Sicherheitsdienst) in the Protectorate, and IVB4, but significantly, not the Inspectorate of Concentration Camps. Other factors affirm the classification of Terezín as a ghetto. Unlike in most of the camps, but similar to most ghettos, there was no selection upon arrival, so Terezín's population included children and the elderly. Men and women encountered each other during the day and in some cases could live together. Prisoners did not have to wear uniforms, and they were housed in existing buildings rather than newly constructed barracks. Ghettos were only for "racial" Jews (with

12 THE LAST GHETTO

the exception of Romas in Lodz), whereas camps could contain prisoners of any kind from any country under German control. The topography and life in the camps were usually more regimented than in the ghettos; only rarely were there German or other non-Jewish guards in ghettos.

This book is a transnational, cultural, social, gender, and organizational history of the Theresienstadt ghetto. Like many other camps and ghettos, Terezín constituted a significant transnational moment, a fact usually neglected by Holocaust histories; there is still a tendency to write the Holocaust as national history. Even though nation-oriented works on the Holocaust present important insights, they have missed fundamental features, shielding from our view the transnational forces that shaped the cultural and social history of the prisoner community.[43] Albeit forced, Terezín was a site of transnational encounters, with Czech, German, Austrian, Dutch, Slovak, and Hungarian Jews living there side by side. The internationality of the prisoner society influenced its shape, logic, and culture, and we cannot grasp it if we observe it from the point of view of only one nationality or another.

I have been profoundly influenced in this work by microhistory and the history of everyday life.[44] Focusing on "small" historical actors allows us to discern power in everyday actions, as well as their political dimensions.[45] The history of everyday life has roots in social history but is different from social history in its method and line of inquiry. Unlike social historians, who focus on collectives and statistics, the historian of everyday life examines rituals, culture, and humor, and thus the meaning of a society. This approach is of particular significance if we want to grasp the short-lived prisoner society from memories that are marked by dominant and politically charged master narratives.

Microhistorians believe that by examining one incident or event in great detail in a methodologically consequential way, we can draw conclusions about the larger society of which it is a part. An example is the teenage siblings Charlotta and Karel Weinstein, who were deported to the ghetto without their parents and separated from each other upon arrival there. Within a short time they had established a pattern wherein Charlotta washed her brother's laundry and Karel brought her gifts of food. The siblings established in the unfamiliar surroundings a new kinship unit with a pointedly gendered labor division; possibly it was its gendered character that for them defined family. The analysis of everyday stories like these always suggests a larger point, compelling us to ask: What does it mean?

INTRODUCTION   13

This account offers a cultural history of Theresienstadt, drawing on the methods of the new cultural history.[46] Cultural production is not just a source but an event in its own right, showing the network of meaning within which people of a given place and time lived; it encompasses aesthetics, values, and how gender is lived.[47] Therefore, it is more suitable to use gender analysis throughout rather than singling it out as many studies do. Gender is such a pervasive, basic societal category that we need to look at any aspect of human relationships in history using gender analysis.[48]

Records reflect power hierarchies of the society they document.[49] Just as E. P. Thompson presented a plea to restore the experience of the "forgotten people,"[50] here I aim to recover and give voice to those Theresienstadt victims who so far have been left out. The goal is not only a political intervention; it is simply good historical practice, for which it is key to integrate all participants' perspectives.[51] Studies of Czech German Jewry and concentration camps alike have often been based on sources generated by a small number of intellectuals, almost all of them male, thus producing an elitist bias.[52] What do Max Brod's articles in the *Prager Tagblatt* tell us about a German-speaking, Jewish, female owner of a leather shop, who at best used the *Tagblatt* to stuff her wet shoes? What do Bruno Bettelheim, Eugen Kogon, and Viktor Frankl tell us about the myriad conflicts, connections, and loyalties among, say, Greek Jewish and Polish gentile women in Auschwitz? Similarly, Terezín has been largely narrated from the perspective of young Czech Jews; using sources produced by only one victim group cements their perspective into official history. One of the aims of *The Last Ghetto* is to contextualize, analyze, and overcome this interpretive dominance.

To write such a representative history, it was crucial to collect as many testimonies as possible, representing perspectives corresponding with the various experiences and groups in the ghetto. This book is based on sources collected in seventy-six public and twenty-three private archives from ten countries and three continents, written in nine languages. Years of research made it possible to detect what had been left unsaid in the histories of Terezín. Many narrators never name key phenomena because they were inherent to their everyday lives. To recognize such blind spots, I deliberately contrasted documentation from different vantage points. I examine how a matter was perceived by young and old, people of various ethnic backgrounds, men and women, the childless and parents. I have also stayed attuned to the period and context in which sources came into being, reading wartime diaries and letters, as well as texts written shortly after the war, witness depositions, and

14 THE LAST GHETTO

late oral histories, viewed in print and as audio and video recordings.[53] The core of the material consists of thousands of self-testimonies produced by the inmates and occasionally also by perpetrators and bystanders, recorded between 1945 and 2016. However, no documentation of the SS headquarters remains, and I have had to resort to perpetrators' statements at legal proceedings for that information.[54]

Even with the gaps in written records (for instance, the records of the Jewish self-administration survived only in fragments, scattered across archives on two continents) and archival materials that have been lost, this enterprise amassed a wealth of sources. One question that arises when working with self-testimonies is their trustworthiness. I usually cite one representative source, and only when the statement is potentially controversial have I included more. When discussing a point made by one witness, the text makes clear who the narrator is and his or her perspective. In working through the material, this study applied clustering, looking for themes and patterns. I analyzed the language of the sources, paying attention to figures of speech and examples people used, humor, tone, drama, and emotionality.

These frameworks help to make sense of much that was happening in the prisoner society and to represent their experiences and self-understanding. Returning to Redlich's diary entry, where we started, it is just as important to remember that these were people, almost all of them slaughtered. While analyzing, I tried most of all to encounter its protagonists with empathy. May the readers do the same.

A Note on Names and Images

I use "Theresienstadt/Terezín/ghetto" synonymously. Theresienstadt is the German name of the place, Terezín the Czech one. I also rotate the expressions "inmates/prisoners/people." Unless I know that they signed their names otherwise before the war, I use the Czech version of Czechoslovak women's names if they lived before 1933 in Czechoslovakia (and thus were not German or Austrian refugees, such as Susanne Eckstein rather than Zuzana Ecksteinová). I also use the Czech version of Czech place names that were located in the Protectorate (and Polish for those in the General Gouvernement). For those in the annexed Sudetenland, I use both the Czech and German versions, such as Ústí nad Labem/Außig. For places that have an

INTRODUCTION 15

established place name in English, I use those: Prague, Auschwitz, and Lodz, rather than Praha, Oświęcim, and Łódź.

The images printed in this book are black and white. For originals, large version of maps, and many further materials, you can either visit www. thelastghetto.org or read the book digitally in Oxford Scholarship Online.

1

The Overorganized Ghetto

Administering Terezín

Among the ghettos, Terezín stands out for its effective Jewish self-administration and the massive apparatus that went with it. Previous historical accounts have explained the inflated organization within the frame of the ghetto as a showplace, that is, as an aspect of Nazi authorities' efforts to delude the inmates and inmates' wishful thinking.[1] However, the ghetto's organization was very much part of its reality and was symptomatic of the place. The organizational history of Theresienstadt explains its hierarchies, how its departments functioned, and its administrative dynamics, and helps to explain the mentality of the forced community.

Terezín's self-administration was operational. First, Jewish functionaries strove to improve conditions by organizing, and the self-administration's organization shaped the face of the ghetto. Second, the inmates' backgrounds, both before and during the war, proved central to the self-administration. The particular mixture of inmates created an administration of their own, though under circumstances determined by the SS.

The SS were only nominally interested in the day-to-day management of the ghetto and intervened sporadically to control, punish, or enforce their purpose: Terezín was a transit ghetto, a ghetto for the elderly, for exceptions, and for propaganda. Even though the self-administration in Terezín was planned by the SS, its development unfolded organically. Various institutions and departments in the Jewish administration gained and lost influence over time, and new leadership and alliances emerged. The self-administration expanded due to patronage and also the belief among inmates that a familiar, bureaucratic system could control the looming threats of deprivation and transports. In this way, Jewish functionaries acquired agency. As much as they shaped and organized Terezín, however, Jewish functionaries could not influence the Nazis' ultimate goal: the ghetto was a gateway to the East, a stage in the process of destruction.

The Last Ghetto. Anna Hájková, Oxford University Press (2020). © Oxford University Press.
DOI: 10.1093/oso/9780190051778.001.0001.

The SS: Hierarchies and Lines of Communication

Personal ties defined the relationships among the members of the SS who ran Terezín. From the very beginning, they belonged to the grouping known as "the Eichmann men": a collective of younger men, born between 1907 and 1911, who had experienced the post–World War I dismantling of the Habsburg Empire and the interwar economic crisis.[2] Eager to create an empire of their own, they shared a habitus of rabid Austrian antisemitism and ready violence. Moreover, all three commandants came from Lower Austria, and two of the three began their careers at the Central Office for Jewish Emigration in Vienna. The commandants all worked closely with Hans Günther and Adolf Eichmann and were deployed with Eichmann to Salonica in 1943 and to Hungary a year later.

The general camaraderie among the Eichmann men did not extend to everyone who worked in the team, especially as the enterprise changed from an adventure to a competitive bureaucracy. In 1939 Eichmann founded the Central Office for Jewish Emigration in Prague, a copy of his Viennese creation.[3] In 1940 he moved to Berlin and named Hans Günther his successor in Prague. Rolf, Hans's younger brother, followed Eichmann to Berlin and became his deputy.

From the viewpoint of the SS, responsibility for SS headquarters in Terezín was divided between Adolf Eichmann's Department IVB4 in the RSHA in Berlin; the commander of the SiPo and SD in the Protectorate (BdS) under Erwin Weinmann; and the Central Office in Prague, led by Hans Günther. (See Figure 1.1.) These institutions were administratively and personally entangled. The BdS, Weinmann's office in the Protectorate, was a subdivision of the RSHA.[4] Hans Günther's Central Office in Prague was a subdivision of Weinmann's BdS, yet for the most part it reported directly to IVB4 in Berlin. The last commandant, Karl Rahm, described the division of labor as straightforward: BdS was responsible for administrative affairs, IVB4 for political matters.[5] However, almost everything in Terezín was political. The BdS participated in the Red Cross visits and also managed the somewhat difficult communication with the nearby Small Fortress, the transit prison for political prisoners of the Gestapo.[6]

Berlin was responsible for all incoming and outgoing transports, including setting up the categories for selection, logistics, and any decision-making. Authorities from IVB4 in Berlin also chose the Jewish leadership; organized the Red Cross visits; handled special groups such as Jews with foreign

18 THE LAST GHETTO

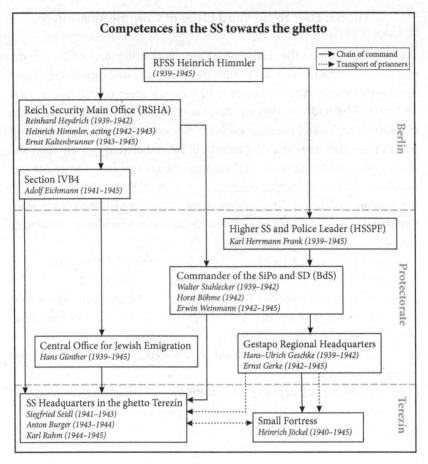

Figure 1.1 Competences in the SS toward the Ghetto

citizenship; sent inmates to the Small Fortress; and checked in during crises, including the typhoid epidemic in winter 1943. Rolf Günther, Ernst Moes, and Eichmann periodically visited the ghetto to monitor larger transports or accompany visitors.

The Prague Central Office was IVB4's local representative. Moes, Eichmann's man for Terezín and Bergen-Belsen, would travel to Terezín via Prague rather than directly from Berlin.[7] Moes did not get along with Karl Rahm, Terezín's third commandant.[8] Rahm was *Obersturmführer* and commandant of the ghetto but Moes, as *Hauptsturmführer*, outranked him. However, Moes did not head an institution, nor did he, a German, unlike Rahm, have a long history with Eichmann. Moes came to Terezín

THE OVERORGANIZED GHETTO 19

regularly—sometimes once a month, sometimes every three months. He passed on orders (in particular with regard to transports), checked on Jewish functionaries, and generally oversaw the ghetto. There was another reason for Moes's frequent visits: his lover, a German gentile woman named Hanna Walter, worked in the RSHA archive in the Sudeten barracks.[9]

By December 1942, with the removal of the Czech Jews from the Protectorate nearly completed, the Central Office's tasks diminished. The SS still had to catalog the looted Jewish property and decide how to categorize people of mixed descent, but these matters required far less effort than the mass emigration, registrations, and deportations during the preceding three years had entailed. Hans Günther began working on pet projects such as the Central Jewish Museum, an idea that art historians from the Jewish Community had successfully pitched to him.[10] He also commissioned a propaganda film about Terezín.[11] Persistent myths about links to the Nazi leadership notwithstanding, both projects were local and pushed forward single-handedly by Hans Günther who, as master of his domain, could afford such extravagant behavior.

Günther's ambitious projects are relevant because they suggest that supervising Terezín constituted the bulk of his work. It was probably Günther, possibly following an order of the RSHA, who ordered the first commandant, Siegfried Seidl, to make an example of sixteen prisoners who were executed in winter 1942.[12] Günther also undertook preparatory visits for Eichmann. For instance, he summoned the Council of Elders and department leaders to prepare for the beautification process prior to the Red Cross visit.[13] Günther supervised the Terezín SS; the commandants submitted intelligence and other reports to him.[14] The SS in Terezín sent the purloined money and jewelry to Prague, where the money was funneled to the Emigration Fund,[15] and jewelry was handed over to the Central Office representative.[16] When Commandant Rahm beat up Paul Eppstein, the second Elder of the Jews, Eichmann informed Günther, who reprimanded Rahm.[17]

Siegfried Seidl was the first commandant, from November 1941 to July 3, 1943. Of the three commandants, Seidl, with a PhD in history from the University of Vienna, was the most educated.[18] Before he was posted to Terezín, he had organized the forced migration in the "annexed Eastern territories" and in Slovenia. In the fall of 1941 he started working at the Central Office in Prague, helping to organize the second wave of Jewish registration and the transports to Lodz that followed. As the first commandant, the organizationally gifted Seidl established a process that transformed people

20 THE LAST GHETTO

swiftly into inmates of the ghetto. He manipulated the Jewish functionaries with a combination of blunt, public violence and lies. In July 1943 he left to direct Bergen-Belsen. It is not clear whether his departure was because of internal conflicts or because his experience suited him for the delicate task of running a camp for exchange of Jews.[19]

Anton Burger was commandant at Terezín for the shortest period, between July 1943 and February 1944. Rough and violent, even by SS standards, Burger was unpopular with his subordinates.[20] After a brief career in the military, he worked in the Central Office in Vienna. In spring 1941 he went to direct the Brno branch of the Prague Central Office. Burger's brief rule at Terezín was marked by some exceptionally brutal orders: forced abortions of pregnancies conceived in the ghetto, shooting sick children from the Bialystok transport, disorderly counting of the entire ghetto population in the meadow of Bohušovice in November 1943, and several particularly vicious interrogations of prisoners accused of smuggling.[21] Even if any other SS colleague probably would have done the same things, the sheer brutality of the implementation, combined with his poor organization of the ghetto, made Burger unsuitable for the increasingly complex job of commandant.

Burger's successor from February 8, 1944 was a former electrician from Klosterneuburg, Obersturmführer Karl Rahm. Along with the job Rahm got the tricky assignment of preparing the ghetto for the International Red Cross visit. Rahm, who came from a working-class family, had the least education of the commandants. He also had an ideological disadvantage: his Communist brother Franz was incarcerated in Rodgau (Dieburg) prison for many years. Perhaps for these reasons Rahm's career was slow to take off; he was Hans Günther's trusted deputy and replaced him during his travels. Rahm's assignment in Terezín, a step up the career ladder and an independent position, came only after four years. By the standards of the Eichmann men, who moved from one exciting location to another, that was a long time.

With his organizational and technical experience, Rahm turned out to be an effective commandant. "Theresienstadt is a nice task," he once told Benjamin Murmelstein.[22] Rahm was well known for his high-handed leadership style; Terezín was his sphere of influence and he disliked others' interventions. Rahm would tease his junior colleagues by putting their favorite prisoner functionaries on transport.[23] In keeping with his choleric temperament, he beat up a Jewish Elder for accepting orders from his subordinate, without his approval or knowledge.[24]

THE OVERORGANIZED GHETTO 21

Rahm organized the massive transports of fall 1944, which reduced the population by 62 percent. In late winter 1945 Rahm, who even more than his predecessors saw the inmates as a resource, attempted to use them to dig fortification trenches for the Wehrmacht. The BdS intervened and pointed out that Terezín had a strictly political purpose and was not to be mixed with other affairs.[25] In the chaotic final weeks of war, Rahm passed on the rule of the ghetto to Paul Dunant of the Swiss Red Cross. Apparently he did not want to liquidate Terezín, "his" ghetto and the fruit of his labor. According to Benjamin Murmelstein, before Rahm left the ghetto, he handed over to him a violin he had borrowed and a savings book for the ghetto at the bank in Bohušovice.[26]

Aside from the commandants, there were at most twenty-eight SS men at any one time working at the SS headquarters. Their tasks, apart from acting as drivers, cooks, secretaries, and electricians, were twofold: political and administrative. There was a high turnover among SS in the ghetto; only a few of the men stayed throughout the ghetto's existence.[27]

The camp inspector, Untersturmführer Karl Bergel, in some respects the deputy commandant, and his representative, Scharführer Rudolf Haindl, were directly in touch with the ghetto population. They were considered the "police" of the SS. Fritz Baltrusch, adjutant to the commandant, and the men from the economic department also had direct contact with the inmates. Rolf Bartels, head of the economic department, was responsible for supplying food and for shopping for the ghetto population.[28] Heinrich Scholz worked for a long time in cash management and was the last head of the economic department. In addition, two civilian Sudeten Germans worked for the SS, Otto Kursawe, who oversaw the Agriculture Department, and Josef Bobek, head of the power plant. Finally, a group of women from nearby Leitmeritz/ Litoměřice, nicknamed by the prisoners "berušky," came in regularly to check inmates' belongings for prohibited items, which they also used as an occasion for theft.[29]

Almost all of the higher-ranking SS men were married, and their wives lived in Prague. The commandants encouraged this arrangement.[30] Often accommodated in "aryanized" Jewish apartments, the wives were given furniture formerly owned by Jews from the collection sites, provided by the Central Office. This practice assisted the SS men who could not afford the cost of living.[31] The men would go every two weeks to Prague for a visit. Some of the SS men had extramarital relationships with the secretaries and telephone operators in the headquarters.[32] Together with frequent drinking,

22   THE LAST GHETTO

these liaisons strengthened the cohesion of the collective and increased the men's dedication to work onsite.

Though the SS viewed Jews as human beings of lesser value, they were happy to use them as a resource. They had Jewish gynecologists perform abortions on their lovers,[33] and they found Jewish doctors equally useful when it came to other ailments. Inmates grew their food, produced honey and silk, took care of their horses and dogs, built furniture, and repaired their shoes.[34] Extant memos from winter and spring 1944/1945 documenting the commandant's orders for the Elder of the Jews show a long list of repairs and demands to supply new clothes, including shirts, trousers, ties, blouses, and winter coats.[35] As the last Elder, Benjamin Murmelstein observed: "Really, they could live very comfortably in the Terezín SS quarters."[36]

Czech gendarmes did the actual guarding of Terezín. The gendarmes numbered between 120 and 150 and came from the Special Department of Gendarmerie, a subunit of the Protectorate Police in Uniform, who followed the organization of the SS.[37] The men were relatively well paid so that they would not take bribes (though some of them did anyway). Only men without any Jewish relatives could be transferred to service in the ghetto. Married members rotated out every three months, single ones every six months. The gendarmes' tasks were to guard the ghetto at each of the five gates, escort inmates working at external job sites or in agriculture, make sure the inmates did not steal produce, accompany the transports from Bohušovice, and supervise the arrival of luggage. For the inmates, the gendarmes were a frequent source of news, food, medications, and cigarettes. They also helped gentile relatives establish contact with their incarcerated families.[38] Some of them were engaged in resistance; Karel Salaba secretly photographed the executions in winter 1942 and smuggled these photos out.[39] A small group was antisemitic,[40] including the unit's directors: Theodor Janeček, who held office between November 1941 and July 1943, and his successor, Miroslav Hasenkopf.[41]

In some instances, the SS and other men guarding the ghetto subjected women prisoners to sexual and sexualized violence. Haindl and several men from the rank-and-file SS and the Slovak ethnic Germans watched Jewish women undressing.[42] Sudeten German Josef Bobek, a civilian and head of the power plant, was considered one of the "nice" Germans; he took advantage of the women prisoners who worked for him. Doris Donovalová recalled that Bobek groped her.[43] For the most part, however, the SS did not view the inmates as objects of desire. Some memoirs suggest there were

THE OVERORGANIZED GHETTO   23

sexual relationships between the SS and Jewish women. However, there is no evidence that such relationships took place, and the claims appear to be the product of postwar sexualized stereotypes.[44] The SS were unlikely to take Jewish women as sexual partners when there were young gentile German female assistants at the SS headquarters. Moreover, Außig/Ústí nad Labem and Roudnice, towns close to the ghetto, had regulated prostitutes, as Leitmeritz/ Litoměřice probably also did.[45]

Unlike the SS, gendarmes sometimes engaged in sexual barter with the prisoners. Probably in some instances the gendarmes directly coerced the inmates, while others, the Jewish women initiated the encounters.[46] As the gendarmes controlled workers returning from Agriculture who often smuggled in fruits and vegetables, they had leeway to threaten smuggling women into having sex with them. Both prisoners and gendarmes recalled that some gendarmes were particularly helpful to attractive women prisoners. One man who worked as the cleaner for the gendarmes, remembered that Karel Salaba kept three or four lovers in the ghetto and funded parties there. The cleaner acted as a go-between and believed that the commandant actually knew about the relationships Salaba had with women prisoners.[47] Usually, if gendarmes were caught having sex with the prisoners, they were sent to the Small Fortress.

The nearby Small Fortress had no direct connection with the ghetto; its administration answered to the Gestapo in Prague,[48] and it served as a transit site for political prisoners from the Protectorate on their way to concentration camps or prisons.[49] However, the two institutions shared a transmitter system: the ghetto had the telephone exchange and the Small Fortress the cable.[50] When the Small Fortress needed to phone, the phone worker in the ghetto had to connect them. Conversely, the SS headquarters in the ghetto had to send someone to collect and dispatch cables, which, given that every incoming transport was accompanied by a cable, was several times a week. The Small Fortress served as a destination for inmates whom the SS wanted to punish or have killed. Conditions in the Small Fortress were similar to a concentration camp, and Jewish prisoners were particularly maltreated. Inmates in the ghetto told stories about the horrible destination; the SS may have spread these stories to discourage contact with the outside.[51] We do not know exactly how many people were transferred from the ghetto to the Small Fortress, but the number was probably about five hundred prisoners.[52]

The main job of the SS headquarters was to ensure the ghetto functioned well for their purposes. It was the Jewish self-administration who ran the

24 THE LAST GHETTO

ghetto. The SS maintained control and dealt out punishments. The SS did not seek to administer the ghetto; the lack of logic in their orders is indicated in the fact that often they prohibited things they had formerly allowed.[53] What went on in the ghetto itself or what the Jews thought did not concern the SS. The commandant was responsible for keeping the inmates in the ghetto; escapes were taken very seriously.[54] The SS had to ensure that the transit ghetto worked smoothly, with transports arriving and leaving. Also important was to keep the ghetto population quiet; there should be no sign of revolt, nor were inmates to have contact with the outside world. SS headquarters was in charge of the treatment of certain groups of prisoners: *Geltungsjuden* who may have been recategorized as *Mischlinge* (people of mixed background) because they were not members of the Jewish community, some prominent individuals, and people with designated foreign citizenships. The SS also supervised production of goods destined for the outside world.

Inmates, unless they were in leadership positions or worked outside the ghetto, had minimal contact with the SS. Emanuel Herrmann, an attorney from Jindřichův Hradec, remembered: "Often three weeks passed without meeting a German."[55] The SS men did not like to spend time in the ghetto itself, and if they had to pass through, they did so in pairs.[56] They exerted their control by spot checks in the accommodation and offices, often tipped off by Jewish informers.

Instances of extreme physical violence inside Terezín were rare. Without a doubt this relative absence of violence was a product of the particular place the ghetto occupied within the SS system. Violence almost always was "constructive"; it had a meaning, a message that the SS wanted to convey to the prisoners.[57] The best-known example occurred early in the ghetto's existence: the executions in winter 1942. On January 10, 1942, the SS hanged nine young men, then seven more on February 26.[58] The men were arrested for made-up reasons: one had written to his mother; another left the Jewish part of the town to buy gingerbread. The Jewish administrators had to attend the hangings; Edelstein could not bear to see the murders and sent Leo Janowitz and Otto Zucker in his stead.[59] The prisoners were shocked by the injustice and brutality of the executions. Günther did not order the executions to punish anyone in particular but rather to set an example. Public staging of violence was a practice that the SS frequently applied early on.[60] These public executions were to demonstrate that the SS had absolute control over the inmates. Günther deemed the executions so important that he was present at the first of them, and Franz Abromeit from IVB4 attended the second.[61] For the SS this brutal performance was a success: the hangings became a crucial part of the master narrative of the ghetto.[62]

Other occurrences of physical violence followed a similar pattern. The SS applied full force against those who organized smuggling with the outside world, particularly when the smuggling might have a political dimension. There was considerable smuggling of letters and cigarettes; mail was allowed only through the official censored channels, and the Germans prohibited smoking. It seems that the SS aided the smuggling of cigarettes because the excessive prices brought about by the prohibition made for a lucrative side income. But mostly, the camp inspector, Bergel, and his deputy, Haindl, focused their investigations on inmates who broke the "political" rules. In June 1944 four painters were brutally beaten up and dispatched with their families to the Small Fortress because their drawings, smuggled out to an art dealer, documented the misery inside the ghetto. This incident took place near the time of the International Red Cross visit.[63]

One of the men the SS tortured was the furrier Julius Taussig, who worked in Shipping, a department that transported materials from the Bohušovice station. Taussig smuggled mail for those with gentile relatives, but also newspapers, in particular the illegal Communist paper *Rudé Právo*. Haindl and Bergel interrogated Taussig to find out whom he worked with, tortured him, and eventually sent him to the Small Fortress. Taussig survived to tell the tale.[64] Evžen Weiss, another smuggler, did not.[65] Bergel and Haindl had a routine for their torture: they would make the prisoner sit on a hot oven, knock out his teeth, make him lick his own blood, and stick objects into his anus. Although other prisoners were not present during these sessions (the torture usually took place in the SS prison, located in the basement of the SS headquarters), stories about such brutalities leaked out and served as a deterrent. These methods were always executed on male prisoners. If the victims survived their abuse, they were sent to the Small Fortress, where physical violence, especially for Jews, was a daily occurrence.[66] Altogether, there were no more than twenty cases of torture in Terezín.

However, not all violence in Theresienstadt fit into the constructive mold; occasionally it was cruelty. When Bergel or Haindl, during interrogations, wildly beat up the prisoner or applied sexually coded violence, causing excessive pain to the victim, the mistreatment was not meant to extract information or to set an example; both had already taken place. Rather, it was an orgy of violence by perpetrators without any control mechanism—an act of total power and self-assertion.[67] Cruelty served to dehumanize the victim, turning

26 THE LAST GHETTO

the victim into an object, providing pleasure to the perpetrator.[68]The fact that the surviving victim provided this information undoes that total power. Julius Taussig, for instance, made a point of speaking against his tormentors in various trials and investigations. After the war, Taussig worked again as a furrier and lived to be seventy-two. When he was interviewed for the Terezín Memorial's oral history collection, he produced a fur coat for his interviewer, an attractive woman.[69]

The Three Elders of the Jews

An Elder of the Jews (Judenältester) and a Council of Elders (Ältestenrat) led the Terezín self-administration (see Figure 1.2). The Elder usually had two deputies, with the exception of the first eleven months, when Otto Zucker was Edelstein's only deputy, and the last nine months, when the last Elder, Benjamin Murmelstein, held office without deputies.

The SS appointed the Elders of the Jews; the orders came from IVB4. Ernst Moes brought the sudden announcement of Paul Eppstein as the new Elder in January 1943.[70] The commandant likely had an advisory function in the appointment. The last appointment, of Murmelstein in September 1944, was probably Rahm's suggestion; the two men had good rapport. Eichmann, by contrast, had had only marginal contact with Murmelstein since 1940. The Elder's deputies were also appointed from Berlin, but the Elder could influence the designation. Edelstein brought his closest associate and deputy, Otto Zucker, from Prague.

Jakob Edelstein, the first Elder of the Jews, led the ghetto from its beginning until the end of January 1943. He then became Eppstein's deputy until November 1943, when he was arrested; six weeks later he was sent to Birkenau. Edelstein, born in 1903 in Galician Horodenka, came to Brno in 1915 as part of the Jewish evacuations; his family stayed behind. He later moved to Teplice, where he married and was active as an ardent Zionist of the socialist Poalei Tsion group; he was fluent in German and spoke decent Czech. He became the director of the Palestine Office and later helped organize the forced emigrations. Edelstein's charismatic personality ensured him a large circle of fellow Zionist friends.

Edelstein remains the best-known Elder of the Jews, contributing much to the master narrative of the ghetto. His idea was that although everyone was sent there against their will, Terezín would prove to be a Jewish

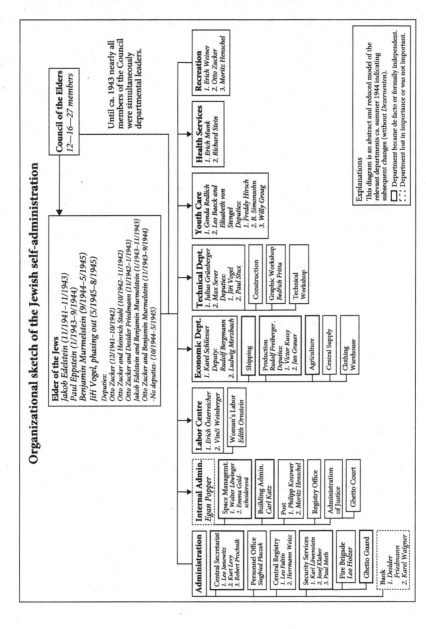

Figure 1.2 Organization of the Jewish Self-Administration

28   THE LAST GHETTO

accomplishment. Edelstein himself became part of the legend: an Elder of the Jews who was humane, idealist, brave, beloved by the inmates, and did not allow himself to be broken by the SS.[71] His dream was to create a place where young and healthy Jews could live until the end of the war. In some sense he viewed the ghetto as a site of an extreme *hachshara* (preparation for Palestine), and he was genuinely proud of his team's achievements.[72]

Edelstein—like his successors—did not know the extent of the destruction of the Jews. He worked to ensure that a younger remnant of inmates survived in Terezín in order to guarantee "the continuity of the Jewish nation." To achieve this goal, he continually strove to fashion Terezín as a labor ghetto, negotiating with Seidl and producing reports that confirmed the ghetto's productivity. Edelstein probably had the strongest team of coworkers. He selected twenty-four people who had arrived with him in one of the first transports (Stab), and others whom he knew from the Hechalutz youth movement, the Palestine Office, and the Prague Jewish Community. It was a tight-knit community not particularly open to outsiders.[73] Edelstein's people led most of the departments. Having Edelstein's trust and knowing one belonged to the inner network, in combination with considerable power within the ghetto itself, eventually led to extensive corruption, so much so that the level of graft surprised the new German Jewish functionaries. By November 1942, power struggles among the leaders began to surface.[74] To consolidate his influence, Edelstein insisted that everyone must follow his authority and departments should limit their autonomy.[75] His tenure ended just a month later, in late January 1943.

On January 30, 1943, Paul Eppstein from Berlin was named the new Elder of the Jews. Eppstein was an ideal type of German academic; born in 1901 in Ludwigshafen, he studied in Heidelberg and from 1929 directed the *Volkshochschule* in his hometown. After he was dismissed in 1933, he began working in the Reich Representation of German Jews (*Reichsvertretung*). By 1939 he had made a career for himself, becoming head of the Reich Association of German Jews, the umbrella organization of German Jews that the Nazis forced all German Jews to join. Among Terezín functionaries, Eppstein had the most experience negotiating with the perpetrators. Unlike other Elders, he had been imprisoned several times, which made him both more experienced and more apprehensive.

Eppstein too arrived in Terezín with a team of trusted co-workers, whom he installed in positions in the ghetto administration. The SS had ordered that every department of the Jewish self-administration have either a German or an Austrian head or a deputy.[76] Burger ordered Eppstein to come to the daily meetings alone; later Eppstein did not allow other functionaries to go to the SS headquarters without him. He was used to going alone from his time in Berlin and did not want to share power with his predecessor.[77] Edelstein, in the meantime, did not take his dismissal well and started fighting with his closest colleague, Zucker.[78]

Eppstein started meeting with Moes alone, playing Moes off the commandant.[79] Eppstein's approach was legalistic; he worked closely with the SS, overfilling the commandant's orders in a way that served Jewish interests while making sure he would not be held liable.[80] Walking a tightrope between his desire to make decisions alone and his fear of doing something wrong, Eppstein left matters unresolved.[81] In the first year he made several mistakes, putting incompetent people into leadership positions.

By 1944, after Edelstein was sent to Auschwitz, Eppstein understood the ghetto better, and his administrative professionalism grew.[82] Still, the face of the ghetto did not change much under him, and his changes were additions rather than adjustments. The administration was a working mechanism, and in many respects, the change of the Elder of the Jews did not impact how the middle ranks functioned. Eppstein dealt with the pressure by escaping into cultural and intellectual events and relationships with his lovers.[83] To play the role of scholar and lover of life and the arts helped him maintain the belief that he was the same person. In fact, the office and its associated responsibilities changed the personality of each of the Elders.

Eppstein was possibly the only Elder informed about the fate of the Terezín prisoners who had been deported to Auschwitz.[84] Therefore, when Rolf Bartels informed him in mid-September about preparations for the fall transports,[85] Eppstein gave a speech. He wanted to assure the inmates of his leadership, and he hinted that liberation was near but inmates had to stay calm and rely on him to help them make it to the end of the war alive. Eppstein assumed that the upcoming transports would be large but did not know they would include two-thirds of the ghetto population. Ten days later, the SS had Eppstein arrested and shot at the Small Fortress, on September 27, 1944. While some scholars attributed his execution to the daring speech,[86] it seems likely that Eppstein's death had already been decided, in connection with the fall transports, preparation for which had started in July 1944.[87] As an experienced Elder of the Jews, Eppstein would have posed much more risk during the transports than Murmelstein, a functionary without a clique.

30   THE LAST GHETTO

Murmelstein's promotion was hinted at the previous month, when the commandant refused to approve Murmelstein's planned hernia operation.[88]

Murmelstein became de facto Elder of the Jews in late September 1944, de jure in December. Born in 1905 in Lemberg/Lwów, he went to Vienna as a young man to study to become a rabbi. Murmelstein was intelligent and disciplined; if he had not been a first-generation immigrant, he would probably have become an academic.[89] One of the more liberal rabbis in the city, Murmelstein lectured and wrote popular interest books. With the Anschluss, he became active in the Jewish Community; as a skilled organizer, he became head of its Emigration Department and then its deputy director. Vienna provided the first model of a Jewish Council; many of the painful decisions the Viennese Jewish Council made anticipated similar decisions elsewhere.[90] For example, the Jewish Council decided that it was more humane if the Jewish functionaries put the transports together and also brought the deportees from their homes to the transport site.

Murmelstein was not an easy character; he was ambitious, choleric, and authoritarian. He was the perfect person onto whom others could project all things negative. Eventually he became widely criticized as a "collaborator."[91] People spread rumors that he zealously put people on transports and blackmailed women into providing sexual favors.[92]

Before he became Elder, and in addition to his role acting as the Elder's deputy, Murmelstein took charge of two central departments: Health Services and the Technical Department.[93] The new job in working with the doctors was highly political; a typhoid infection reached its peak in February 1943, and the SS feared an epidemic. These two departments constituted the backbone of Edelstein's Terezín and had been built up from scratch by veteran Czech prisoners. Murmelstein demonstrated an understanding of the social field, respected the existing effective structures, and learned rudimentary Czech. His new subordinates grew to respect him for his common sense and diligence. In December 1943, after Edelstein's deportation, Murmelstein became the head of two different departments: Internal Administration and its factually independent subdepartment, Space Management. In spring 1944 he was also responsible for the "beautification" preparations undertaken for the visit by the International Red Cross.[94] Murmelstein led the ghetto through the devastating fall 1944 transports; this time, the SS assembled the deportation lists. After October 1944, he consolidated the emptied ghetto.

Murmelstein probably had the best rapport with his commandant, Karl Rahm. The two men shared several qualities: both were German-speaking, were Austrians or Austrian-socialized, came from poor backgrounds, were short-tempered, and liked to outsmart others. Most important, Murmelstein was a strategist and possessed years of experience in dealing with Eichmann's men. Murmelstein believed in top-down meritocracy, in which he had decision-making responsibility but left details to the professionals. After the fall transports in 1944, the self-administration existed only in fragments; almost everyone had been deported.

Murmelstein did not respect the Council of Elders, and he discussed at the meetings only what suited him. Moreover, he energetically opposed discussing the responsibilities of Jewish functionaries in front of the SS. Murmelstein picked a Council of well-known, old men, whom he did not expect to contradict him but who also would not be endangered by this exposure. Jiří Vogel believed that Murmelstein did so not only because of his despotic character but because others could not denounce what they did not know. Murmelstein redistributed the food rations and homeless parcels among the reduced population. He allocated new accommodations for the workers, assigned women to "hard labor jobs," and introduced a seventy-hour workweek. In this way he succeeded in running the emptied ghetto despite the fact that most people of a productive age were already gone. One of his secretaries, Marie Schelerová, recalled Murmelstein as a strikingly intelligent, ugly man whose position was so difficult because his predecessor was well-liked.[95]

Where Murmelstein did not succeed—and he did not care about this at the time—was in public relations. His leadership style included eighteen-hour workdays, often with no sleep. The irritable Murmelstein, apprehensive that he would be killed before the war was over, grew nervous and unjust.[96] Afraid they would be killed before the end of the war, other leading Jewish functionaries kept a low profile; Murmelstein could not.[97] He stepped down on May 5, 1945, after Rahm left the ghetto, and passed the job to Jiří Vogel. A month later, prompted by the Terezín Communist Party, the Czechoslovak police arrested him, and he spent the next year and a half in pretrial custody.

The exact relationship between the Elder of the Jews and the Council of Elders was never fully defined. The early statutes of the ghetto proclaimed that the Council of Elders would stand in an advisory capacity at the side of the Elder of the Jews.[98] Hermann Strauß, a Berlin gastroenterologist and a member of the Council of Elders, described the relationship of the Elder to the Council as that of the city council to the mayor. Eventually, the triumvirate of the Elder and his deputies, represented solely by the Elder, made the decisions.[99]

32 THE LAST GHETTO

The SS commandants who had to approve nominations to the Council, and who at times probably also nominated people, did not leave behind any useful narratives. In his interrogations, Seidl denied everything. He claimed he had only been responsible for the somewhat opaque "very top leadership"; the Central Office or the Jews themselves had decided everything else.[100] Rahm spoke about the Jewish functionaries who reported to him, the Elder of the Jews and his two deputies who, together with the sixteen members of the Council of Elders, accounted to him for the ghetto. However, Rahm did not remember details about the Council of Elders: "I do not exactly know what the task of the sixteen advisors was," he claimed.[101] Rahm's condescending remark does not mean that the Council was superfluous. Rather, it meant that to the SS, the Council was of no importance. Even though the commandant sometimes attended its meetings, the Council's sphere of influence did not interact with that of the SS. All the members were men.

Members of the Council of Elders were usually nominated at the suggestion of the Elder or other members; the technician Jiří Vogel was nominated by his former acquaintance Karel Schliesser from the Economic Department.[102] Schliesser was a Zionist, but he knew that Vogel, a gifted organizer with a technical mind, could take care of what needed to be done. Alfréd Meissner, a former Czechoslovak minister of justice, social democrat, and Czecho-Jew, became a member of the Council in the fall of 1944; the departing Czecho-Jews Rudolf Bergmann and Herbert Langer recommended him to Murmelstein.[103] Others, like František Weidmann, former head of the Jewish Council in Prague and a prominent Czecho-Jew, received their nomination to the Council of Elders as a consolation prize from Hans Günther upon being put on a transport to Theresienstadt.[104]

Members of the Council of Elders were in an exposed position; approved by the commandant, they could become influential and as such could be removed when the perpetrators saw fit. This vulnerability became obvious in September 1943 when the first two functionaries, Leo Janowitz and Fredy Hirsch, were sent to Auschwitz.[105] Some members chose to remain oblivious to this situation, taking pride in their new importance. Others, like Vogel, chose to remain inconspicuous, which was one of the reasons he survived in the ghetto until the end of the war.

Council members were supposed to represent major political and ideological streams in the ghetto, including Zionists and Czecho-Jews. In October 1942, four months after the arrival of German Jews, the SS rearranged the Council's membership to add six German and two Austrian Jews. The change

THE OVERORGANIZED GHETTO   33

took place four months after the arrival of the first transport from Germany. Only later were representatives of other nationalities invited to join the Council: two Dutchmen—David Cohen, later replaced by Eduard Meijers—and Max Friediger from Denmark were invited to join in September 1944, although their groups had been in Theresienstadt since April and October 1943, respectively.

Friediger and Cohen's position was symptomatic of another Council function, which was to accommodate and appease. Although most executive influence belonged to the Elder of the Jews and his clique,[106] there were still influential posts to be claimed. The Council was a site where political power was staged, where opinions could be expressed and one's symbolic capital put on display. Some of the Council's discussions occurred just to prove a point; Walter Löwinger of Space Management complained to Redlich that arguments in the Council were mostly about members showing off their importance.[107] Karel Fleischmann, who headed the Welfare Department of Health Services, documented one meeting of the Council in March 1943 as a display of conceited, chatty men who staged replayed, ongoing arguments.[108]

However, the Council of Elders also made significant decisions, especially for midranking functionaries. The only surviving minutes from winter and spring 1945 reflect several crucial developments: accommodation for workers' forces, distribution of packages sent to those no longer in the ghetto, the change of the code of law, and food distribution.[109] Given that there were still departmental leaders with assigned responsibilities, plus the fact that Murmelstein liked to decide alone, the Council of Elders certainly did not function in name only.

Of all of the Theresienstadt inmates, the Elders of the Jews had the most intense contact with the SS. Every morning at 8:00 a.m. the Elder had to report to the commandant to communicate happenings in the ghetto, provide the number of inmates, and receive orders. These meetings established the power asymmetry between them: the commandant often let the Elder wait for hours in the cold hallway.[110] Occasionally the SS beat the Jewish functionaries.[111] In Theresienstadt as in other ghettos, this physical transgression clearly demonstrated that the perpetrators dictated the rules.

As in the Jewish Councils in Vienna, Amsterdam, and Berlin, the SS always gave the orders in person, never in written form; the Jewish functionaries had to put the orders into writing. After these meetings, the Elder would go to his office and dictate a memo. These memos were then sent to the commandant to be acknowledged.[112] It may be that the SS deliberately did not want to leave

34 THE LAST GHETTO

any traces, or perhaps they could not be bothered with written communication. Summoning the Jewish functionaries took less time and exercised the symbolic power of the SS. It also kept the Jewish functionaries dependent. The Elders passed on this dependency; even if they were supposed to inform their deputies and the Council of Elders about the discussion with the commandant, the practice was much more selective.[113] Edelstein and Eppstein shared delicate information only with their inner circle, Murmelstein with no one.

The Elders' room for maneuver is apparent from two examples about how they dealt with the SS arresting prisoners who had contact with the outside: the Bělov siblings and Herbert Kain. The leeway was minimal, but the way the three Jewish Elders used the influence they had is instructive. In April 1943 the teenagers Hana and Arnold Bělov escaped from the ghetto. They were *Geltungsjuden* from a mixed marriage; their two younger brothers still lived at home. In the fall, Hana and Arnold were caught and on November 9, sent back to Theresienstadt. The siblings first stayed in the SS prison in the ghetto and were later sent to the Small Fortress. In April 1944 they were sent to Auschwitz; both died there.[114]

This family catastrophe was symptomatic of the situation of inmates with mixed parentage and at the same time highly political. The *Geltungsjuden*, who were usually in the ghetto without their parents, were the most likely to escape. The second largest group were members of an external resistance movement. Both groups were alike in that they were separated from their kinship unit.[115] The Bělovs' escape was one of several that took place between January and April 1943. Seidl, who did not quite trust the new Elder, Paul Eppstein, on account of the latter's communication with Moes, became anxious. Seidl introduced draconian measures to prevent further escapes: he switched off electric lights, banned all cultural activities, and introduced an absolute curfew.[116]

In September 1943 Eppstein found out that Edelstein's administration had concealed the actual number of prisoners. During the transport on October 26, 1942, several dozen people did not present themselves, a mistake that became obvious only after the transport departed. Edelstein and Leo Faltin, the head of Central Evidence, which supervised the population statistics, concealed the total numbers by having the Dresden barracks daily report fifty-five inhabitants more than were really living there. Edelstein also obscured the population count by including people who had passed away on a recent transport to Terezín in the evidence as if they were alive. When he wanted to save people from the transport, he included the names of the dead in their stead.[117]

In September 1943 Alfred Goldschmid, high ranking functionary of the Central Registry, was put on a transport; trying to save himself, he revealed this fraudulent reporting of prisoners to Eppstein.[118] Eppstein did not want to take responsibility for his predecessor's mistake, so he told Moes about Edelstein's deception. He did not, however, tell Edelstein that he had done so. Moes most likely passed on the information to Eichmann, who then complained to Burger, the new commandant, about the chaos he was tolerating in the ghetto. For some time Burger had Edelstein observed, waiting for a suitable moment to strike.[119] The moment came when the Prague Gestapo caught the Bělov siblings and returned them on November 9. When the Gestapo, a related yet different body of the RSHA, in competition with the SD, returned the escaped teenagers, it was an affront to Burger, who was reminded of the disarray in which his predecessor had left the ghetto. Burger decided to act and had Edelstein arrested the next day. The following day, November 11, Burger forced the entire population to gather in the Bohušovice meadow for a census. In his handling of this, Eppstein proved himself to the commandant and, taking no chances, delivered his unpopular predecessor to the SS. The seemingly private tragedy of a mixed family was thus linked to a critical decision in Eppstein's leadership that brought about Edelstein's removal.

Murmelstein experienced a comparable crisis in January 1945, but handled it very differently. Haindl, tipped off by a Jewish informer, found out that Herbert Kain, a German emigrant to Denmark, along with Arthur Busch, the dog trainer for the SS, and one Oskar Taussig were smuggling cigarettes, letters, and newspapers into the ghetto. Rahm imposed harsh measures, including banning cultural events, providing no heating, and implementing an 8:00 p.m. curfew.[120] Moreover, he ordered the smugglers interrogated. Taussig was the first to be tortured; he gave the names of the inmates whom he had supplied but not the name of the outside supplier. Afraid that he could not stay silent, he committed suicide.[121] Rahm promised Murmelstein that if he got the name of the supplier from Kain, there would be no further consequences for the culprits.[122] In the meantime, Murmelstein warned those who had contacts with the smugglers.[123] He agreed to Rahm's suggestion, and the punitive measures were lifted.[124] Together with Max Friediger, representative of Danes, Murmelstein persuaded Kain to give up the name of the supplier. Rahm, however, broke his promise and sent Kain to the

36 THE LAST GHETTO

Small Fortress.[125] Busch was replaced as the head of the dog kennel for three months and then got his job back. Everyone else was released.[126]

Murmelstein made the most of his connection with the commandant. He allowed Rahm to feel that he was master of the situation. Only then did Murmelstein negotiate. Perhaps he let the SS have Herbert Kain because, as a Danish Jew and thus protected, Kain was less likely than the other inmates to be harmed. Murmelstein also talked to Kain, rather than delivering him to the SS and cutting his losses. Most important, Murmelstein correctly assessed the danger. The SS saw the smugglers as a possible cell of resistance—perhaps an entry point for weapons. Murmelstein was concerned that, threatened with a revolt, the SS would liquidate the ghetto. He did not rely on others and saw everything as too important not to get involved.

Over time a number of SS men developed a symbiotic relationship with the functionaries. The Jewish functionaries learned that the Germans were not monolithic: some were more influential than others, they had differences of opinion, and many were corrupt. Eppstein had a special relationship with Moes and tried to gain some advantage from the conflict between Moes and Rahm. Other functionaries learned to utilize the corruption among the SS for the sake of the ghetto. Murmelstein, for instance, bribed Haindl into addressing rumors about a possible transport by providing him with new boots for his lover.[127] Often the Theresienstadt SS were no better informed than the Jews, and they too were surrounded by rumors. However, for the SS rumors were harmless; for the Jews they were matters of life and death.

The symbiosis of the SS with some Jewish functionaries did not change the functioning of the ghetto as a whole, but it did structure its everyday existence. Karel Schliesser, head of the Economic Department, had a good relationship with Rolf Bartels, his counterpart on the SS side.[128] Schliesser aided Bartels in stealing some of the food in exchange for information, extra supplies, and turning a blind eye to Shipping's illegal activities.[129] In turn, Bartels sold some of the food intended for inmates for his own profit.[130] When Rahm once found out that Bartels had ordered furniture to be made for him without asking for approval first, Rahm ordered Bartels's house arrest and beat Eppstein and Schliesser, the responsible Jewish functionaries, bloody.[131]

Bartels acted unusually in that he followed through with information for the Jewish functionaries. In early September 1944 he even tipped off Schliesser and Erich Munk about the upcoming fall transports. He told Schliesser that the recently enlarged mica-splitting workshop could save its workers from future transports.[132] Schliesser arranged for Bartels to meet with Eppstein in the mica workshop. Rudolf Freiberger, the head of Production, kept the workshop's supervisor, Hauptscharführer Kurt Ulbrichts, busy while Schliesser and Eppstein spoke with Bartels.[133] Soon afterward, Schliesser was put on the first fall transport. Freiberger fought for "his" women, and indeed twelve hundred mica workers were protected from deportation.[134] The decision to enlarge the mica workshop came from Ulbrichts and Bartels, who wanted to avoid being sent to the front. Moreover, additional industry gave them more opportunity for fraud.

This incident indicates that Jewish functionaries had limited leverage with the SS. It also points to several aspects of their mentality. The functionaries usually thought in the present. By September 1944, transports seemed the exception in the ghetto and improved living conditions the norm. Based on their "good" communication with the perpetrators, the functionaries assumed the status quo would continue. Something similar happened in other ghettos, where leading functionaries believed they had "working relationships" with perpetrators.[135] They felt they had had an impact, which they had, but it did not last. In Bremen, where Carl Katz and his Gestapo counterpart were on a first-name basis and drank together, Katz was eventually deported.[136] When the large fall deportations started, some SS men tried to keep "their" Jews off the lists. They would not go to any particular trouble to do so, however.[137]

The timing of arrival in Terezín was crucial in determining the sort of job a functionary received. From January 1943 onward, as the Reich Association in Germany and the Jewish Communities in the Protectorate and Vienna were being closed, the SS sent the remaining functionaries to Terezín.[138] It was a contradictory situation: because of their importance, these individuals had not been sent out earlier. When they arrived in Terezín, they found the important jobs taken and had to fight to get decent positions.[139] Richard Friedmann, a Jewish functionary from Prague (and previously Vienna), used to be just as important as Otto Zucker or Karel Schliesser, but he came to Terezín thirteen months after they did. Friedmann received a position in the Central Labor that was high ranking but had limited influence.[140]

There was also a gender factor for the late arrivals; most of the men succeeded in getting relatively good positions. None of their female colleagues (even those who arrived early) received positions that corresponded to their former importance. In Terezín, Martha Mosse, former head of the Reich Association's Accommodation Advice Center, became a rank-and-file

38   THE LAST GHETTO

detective under her former colleague, Eppstein. Hana Steinerová, who was a key organizer of Jewish emigration from 1930s Czechoslovakia and later head of the Emigration Department of the Jewish Community, received no official position in the self-administration.

The functionaries who arrived later appealed, with a sense of entitlement, for better positions. To placate their respective cliques, veteran leaders usually assigned them posts. As a result, the already complex Terezín administration expanded. A thirty-seven-page overview of the organization from summer 1944 listed dozens of subdepartments.[141] Construction, for instance, had forty-nine sub- and sub-subdepartments, including its own Accounting Department. Making space for newly arrived functionaries meant displacing veteran Zionists. Such decisions led to bad blood within the self-administration.[142]

Procuring jobs for one's clique was not only about power for power's sake; it also meant better classification in terms of food rations and protection from transports. These patterns were so obvious that some Viennese inmates complained about the absence of Austrians in leading positions. Indeed, there were only a few Austrian Jews among the leading functionaries: Benjamin Murmelstein, Desider Friedmann, who led the bank, and Heinrich Klang, head of the Ghetto Court. Some of the Austrians were not pleased to see that Czech and German Jews held most of the influential positions. They told Murmelstein he should do more to help Viennese functionaries, but Murmelstein, who believed in meritocracy, rebuffed them.[143] Julius Boschan, Murmelstein's colleague from Vienna, who worked in Theresienstadt in the Central Secretariat's Financial Department, was angered and went so far as to complain to another old Viennese acquaintance, the SS man Rudolf Haindl. Boschan's contact with Haindl led other prisoners to believe that he was informing.[144]

Ethnicity was very important to loyalties in the self-administration. The SS was aware of the friction between the Czech and German and Austrian Jews and issued orders with an ethnic dimension. Several of the Treblinka transports in fall 1942 included only elderly German and Austrian Jews. Two large waves of transports in September and December 1943 were exclusively Czech. In a series of orders issued between fall 1942 and winter 1943, the SS placed German and Austrian functionaries in leadership positions. The real push in naming "foreign," that is, non-Czech, prisoners to positions came from Eppstein. In January 1944 Eppstein ordered that if the head of a department was not German or Austrian, the deputy had to be German.[145] Some departments received a German leader, such as Kurt Levy, who replaced Leo Janowitz as head of Central Secretariat. Others had a German Jew as second-in-command, for instance Berthold Simonsohn in Youth Welfare.

The veteran Czechs eyed their new colleagues with mistrust. Some of the new German and Austrian officials proved themselves through skill and empathy; others simply expected their colleagues to follow them.[146] Sometimes Czech functionaries tricked the system; for example, Victor Kussy was named Freiberger's deputy in Production. Freiberger selected Kussy because he knew Kussy came from a Czech Jewish family from Plzeň that in the 1920s had moved to Dresden and later emigrated before the Nazis to the Netherlands.[147] Kussy acted as a pro forma deputy; the real second-in-command was Jan Grauer. To Eppstein, Kussy was German, whereas the Czech prisoners knew that "actually," Kussy was Czech. Grauer remembered his colleague as a decent person, partly due to his Czechness: "The only thing German about him was his factory in Dresden."[148]

January 1943 brought the additional system of *Dezernent* (political director, as opposed to a practical director, *Leiter*). Members of the Council were assigned to the political leadership of a department as *Dezernenten*, an additional position to the *Leiter*. Often the *Dezernent* was German or Austrian and the *Leiter* Czech.[149]

The ethnic undertone to SS orders convinced the inmates (as well as later scholars) that the SS were trying to drive a wedge between Czech Jews on the one hand and German and Austrian Jews on the other. Such orders did add to the spitefulness and ethnic stereotypes that already existed. Was it deliberate? Miroslav Kárný believed so. During a visit to Mussolini in October 1942, Himmler spoke about the deportation of German Jews and mentioned the conflicts in Terezín.[150] Himmler's statement came just a week after non-Czech Jews were appointed to the self-administration, but it is the only documentation pointing to the intentions of the SS. We should be cautious about drawing conclusions about intentions based on outcomes. It was not because the Germans did not trust "Czech Jews" that Eppstein replaced Edelstein. Rather, the Germans needed to "reward" Eppstein. By winter 1943, Edelstein had successfully set up the ghetto, and the German authorities could let him go. Perhaps the SS installed German Jews in leading positions because they could not communicate in Czech, a foreign language. Perhaps they wanted German Jews to have "their share" of influence.

Under Edelstein's leadership, Jewish administration was influenced by an attitude of functionaries who believed they were pioneers doing something

40   THE LAST GHETTO

new, bold, and special. This belief was an extension of the Edelstein team's mentality. Many of the administrative workers under Edelstein did not have corresponding experience from their earlier careers; often they had done something entirely different. For instance, Otto Zucker, a key functionary, born in 1892 in Prague, had been an architect in Berlin and was part of the team of architects who built the Ullsteinhaus, Berlin's first skyscraper with a steel framework.[151] After 1933 he returned to Czechoslovakia and became deputy chairman in the Jewish National Party and worked for the Palestine Office. However, his day job, in which he was successful, was as a modernist architect.[152] Others in Edelstein's team were young, such as Janowitz, born in 1911, and Robert Vinči Weinberger, born in 1913, from the Central Labor, or really young, as was Harry Tressler, born in 1922.

The sense of exceptionality continued with Eppstein's people. Yet their profile was different: they were older and had worked for Jewish organizations or in social work their whole professional lives or at least since 1933. Murmelstein's administration included elements of the previous group, many of them skilled clerks who had been promoted. One of them was Martha Mosse, who in November 1944 was named director of the Detective Department.

Many functionaries were united in the belief that the self-administration was instrumental to the self-reliant, Jewish city.[153] This pioneering mentality gave rise to a feeling of self-importance. Many of the functionaries took themselves very seriously and were proud of their decisions and offices.[154] This pride partly explains why many sought to be on the Council of Elders and why its deliberations became increasingly drawn out. By January 1944, the Council of Elders had become so large that its twenty-four members had to divide into committees in order to make decisions.[155] Discussions became contentious and bureaucratized; departmental heads feared loss of influence. The functionaries believed that holding office brought real power. Not only did they structure the everyday and tasks of their subalterns, but with regard to the transports, they decided who in their department was marked "dispensable" and who "indispensable." Heads of departments themselves were protected and could shield several dozen family members and friends with their personal protection lists. As the head of the Ghetto Guard, Karl Loewenstein, put it, a leading position in the administration was life insurance.[156]

There were also issues of seniority and age. Many of the high-ranking Czech functionaries were younger than their German Jewish colleagues,

THE OVERORGANIZED GHETTO   41

and their prior experience in Jewish community organizing was shorter or nonexistent. Yet the Czech functionaries had more extensive experience in Terezín; they felt they had built Terezín from nothing into a livable community. Many of the Czech functionaries had arrived with one of the first three transports, Stab, or as part of one of the Aufbaukommandos. In Terezín, seniority and, in connection with it, ethnicity, trumped pre-ghetto experience. Erich Munk from Health Services resented Karl Loewenstein and Rolf Grabower because they tried to exercise control over his domain.[157] Hence Munk's irritation when Loewenstein, who was not Czech and who arrived nine months after him, questioned his authority. Loewenstein and Grabower, both German Jews, failed to recognize the veterans' status.

The ghetto had eight main departments: Administration, Internal Administration, the Central Labor, the Technical Department, the Economic Department, Youth Welfare, and Health Services; Recreation was added later. The Administration was the main executive organ of the Elder of the Jews. It had two important subdepartments—the Central Secretariat and Central Evidence—as well as the less important but highly visible Security Services and Bank.

The head of the Central Secretariat was in a political and influential position, someone extremely well informed about events in the ghetto.[158] Leo Janowitz, Edelstein's confidante, was the first to hold this office. He was replaced in September 1943, eight months into Eppstein's tenure; possibly his removal was connected to the false registry numbers. His successor was the Berlin lawyer Kurt Levy, who later followed Eppstein as head of the Reich Association. Levy was killed in the liquidation transports in fall 1944.[159] The last Central Secretary was Robert Prochnik, Murmelstein's co-worker from Vienna, who was sent to Theresienstadt in summer 1942.[160]

The Central Secretariat gained in influence throughout the ghetto's existence. It collected information and made decisions related to all things bureaucratic as well as matters concerning citizenship and "Aryan" papers, complaints and clemency pleas, and applications for prominent status. The Central Secretariat controlled the house elders and issued the *Tagesbefehle* (Orders of the Day), checked on construction, and supervised appointments of the less important leaders.[161] Its Transport Registry put together the lists for departing transports. Siegfried Placzek from Southern Moravia, believed to be a long-standing Zionist, headed the Personnel Office, which also oversaw a central index of affiliations that informed many hiring decisions. Placzek, who in the 1930s emigrated to Palestine, became disappointed by

42 THE LAST GHETTO

Zionism and turned to communism instead. His communist allegiance in Theresienstadt was secret; first, the Communist Party in Terezín operated illegally, and second, the party made use of Placzek's position. He planted several Communists in influential positions, including Zucker's secretary, Klára Lindtová, and Vilém Cantor in the Transport Registry.[162]

Central Evidence had the task of supervising and keeping the population statistics—a demanding job in Theresienstadt, where people constantly arrived, departed, and died. The SS headquarters demanded periodic reports about the number of prisoners and sometimes required special statistics concerning, for instance, Geltungsjuden or World War I veterans. The code the Central Secretariat received from the SS for each transport served in combination with other information as an identity number for each inmate. Moreover, Central Evidence also kept indexes on families, gentile relatives, foreign citizenship, women pregnant at arrival, and more.

Internal Administration has been described as a ministry of the interior because it united the subdepartments of Space Management, the Legal Department, Building Administration, Post, and Registry. Egon Popper, a Czecho-Jew from Slaný and head of the first Aufbaukommando, was the director. Internal Administration moved in the opposite direction of the Central Secretariat,[163] in that it lost responsibilities and departments (many to the Central Secretariat) rather than gaining new ones. When Edelstein redistributed tasks among himself, Zucker, and Desider Friedmann in early January 1943, he assigned Friedmann the Financial Department, Bank, and Internal Administration, with the exception of Space Management—all lesser departments.

Edelstein also confirmed the independence of the Space Management Department.[164] This department was directed by a young Zionist lawyer, Walter Löwinger of Teplice, with the addition of Murmelstein as its political leader (*Dezernent*) from December 1943.[165] Murmelstein made the Space Management and Building Administration Departments independent from one another. In November 1944, Emma Goldscheiderová of Plzeň became the director of Space Management and thus the highest-ranking woman in the self-administration.[166] Carl Katz, the former head of the Reich Association in Bremen, led the Building Administration Department. Internal Administration mostly supervised the house elders and registered births, marriages, and deaths. Murmelstein, always the pragmatist, eventually abolished Internal Administration altogether, establishing the subsidiary departments as independent.[167]

Central Labor was the stronghold of Zionist influence.[168] It was headed by Erich Österreicher until fall 1944, when he was sent to Auschwitz, and after that by his subordinate, Vinči Weinberger. There was general labor duty for everyone in the ghetto; the minimum age varied from twelve to sixteen and the maximum from sixty to seventy.[169] Central Labor assigned individuals to jobs, kept an overview of what work was needed, monitored the staffing of each department, and matched experience to demand. Central Labor also decided what jobs were categorized as heavy labor; these people then received higher food rations. Central Labor was Edelstein and his team's idea. They viewed the Terezín population as in need of care, education, and training in the harsh conditions. The functionaries were truly proud of their accomplishments and judged the ghetto, a year later, to be a success. To celebrate they produced an album for Edelstein, complete with illustrations and stories.[170]

Another bastion of Zionism was the Youth Welfare Department. Codirected by Fredy Hirsch, a German refugee to Czechoslovakia and Egon (Gonda) Redlich of Olomouc, both from the Stab transport, it was set up early in the ghetto's existence.[171] The separation of the sexes, horrible accommodations, and labor duty for women were reasons for the functionaries to set up youth homes. There were youth homes for babies and children up to the age of eighteen, separated by age and language. Youth Welfare was allocated several buildings, usually houses (many of them on the L4, later Hauptstrasse), and at times rooms in the barracks. Educators were selected from among other Zionists or picked on someone's recommendation. Getting a job as an educator was very difficult for non-Zionists, especially in the beginning.

Youth Welfare was organized in local units of relative autarky. Each home was separated into rooms, and each room was a collective of its own, led by an educator who kept the children busy during the day and made sure they were clean and the food was distributed equally. To some degree activities were Zionist influenced. Some non-Zionist parents protested that Zionist education was misusing their children.[172] Redlich tried to appease the parents, who in any case had little alternative. If they removed their children from the homes they had to take them to the crowded rooms and leave them there alone during the day.[173] Compared to other ghettos, the level of care for children in Theresienstadt was exceptional; even if, like the Bialystok ghetto, some had schools, there was no special accommodation for the youth.[174]

44   THE LAST GHETTO

The Economic Department, the largest department in the ghetto, was hugely influential.[175] It controlled the income and distribution of food, administered the production of goods for the SS. The chief of the Economic Department, Karel Schliesser, was one of Edelstein's men and a long-term Zionist.[176] His deputy was a representative of the Czech Jewish movement, Rudolf Bergmann.[177] Schliesser was the only functionary beyond the Elder who regularly met the commandant, reporting about production and taking orders for the furniture demanded by the SS. After Schliesser was sent to Auschwitz, his replacement was Ludwig Merzbach from the Reich Association.[178] One subdepartment was Agriculture, run by the Sudeten German civilian Otto Kursawe, which cultivated the land belonging to the ghetto and grew produce for the SS in Terezín and Prague (see map "Terezín Ghetto and surroundings", where the agricultural property that belonged to the ghetto is marked in horizontal hatches). The Economic Department also housed Production, led by Rudolf Freiberger, the only large sector in which inmates conducted forced labor for the financial profit of the SS. Activities included the production of the boxes in 1943 and later, the mica-splitting workshop.

Production was largely independent, and after October 1944 it received independent status. This department also oversaw Central Supply and Shipping. Central Supply kept an inventory of food for the tens of thousands of inmates. The Shipping Department was responsible for bringing in supplies from the Bohušovice station; Shipping was the central source of smuggled mail and newspapers.[179] Staffed by young, strong men, the detail was a center of the Czecho-Jews.[180]

The Technical Department was the backbone of the ghetto. Its workers made the desolate old town halfway habitable for the tens of thousands of new inhabitants. They set up a new water supply system, installed water pipes, repaired sewers, built the crematorium and two delousing stations, installed 150 cooking cauldrons and dozens of new toilets, and expanded the electricity plant's output.[181] Technicians ran the delousing stations and exterminated the vermin that persistently plagued the inmates. The Technical Department was also responsible for a railway extension between Bohušovice and the ghetto.[182] It worked closely with the Central Secretariat, Central Evidence, Health Services, and the Economic Department.[183]

The Technical Department was the apex of the Terezín master narrative, proof that Jews could be manually and physically able.[184] Numerous Czech engineers and architects worked there, many of whom had volunteered for the two Aufbaukommandos.[185] The Technical Department was not ideological; Zionists, Czecho-Jews, and Communists worked alongside each other.[186] Julius Grünberger, a Zionist from Třešť, was the head at least until summer 1943.[187] Murmelstein was the first *Dezernent* and later became the full-time department head. Max Sever, a Zionist technician from Teplice, took over from him in summer 1944.[188] Sever concentrated on the sewer and water lines and left political decisions to his deputies, Paul Stux and Salomon Süß of Vienna.[189] Otto Zucker keenly participated in the department.[190] Another major influence was Jiří Vogel, who served as deputy and also the head of the Installation and Heating subdepartment.[191]

Health Services was the last of the central Theresienstadt institutions and, after the Economic Department, employed the most workers.[192] Erich Munk, a Zionist from Uherské Hradiště and one of Jakob Edelstein's closest cooperators, headed this department. His deputy from January 1944 on was Adolph Metz of the Reich Association.[193] Munk was an excellent doctor and organizer who, far more than other colleagues, was sensitive to intervention issues. After the SS sent Munk to Auschwitz in fall 1944, Richard Stein, a Prague Zionist and ophthalmologist, succeeded him.[194]

Well known, although with fewer workers, the Recreation Department (*Freizeitgestaltung*) was established after the other departments.[195] Singing, acting, and lecturing took place from the beginning of the ghetto's establishment, but initially under prohibition. Only later were they tolerated, and the full bloom of cultural activities and Nazi instrumentalization of them did not begin until 1943. In March 1942, Fredy Hirsch and the young Plzeň rabbi, Erich Weiner, had initiated the establishment of Recreation, which started as a subdepartment of Internal Administration.[196] Weiner also became the first head and directed the department until January 1943, when the newly unemployed Otto Zucker took over. Zucker was a great art lover; his sister-in-law Tamara was an opera singer. The department blossomed during the ten months of Zucker's leadership. He was able to ensure better conditions for the performers and often could keep them off the transport lists.[197] It was also probably under Zucker that Recreation became an independent department.

After Zucker was reinstalled as deputy Elder, Moritz Henschel from the Reich Association became his successor. Under Henschel, Eppstein's influence on the Recreation Department intensified. Eppstein attended more cultural events than the other two Elders, partly because he liked to boost his reputation as an art lover, but also because he wanted to make sure there would not be any political incidents outside of the approved script. After

46 THE LAST GHETTO

October 1944, Recreation lost its independent status again and rejoined Administration, this time falling directly under the authority of the Elder of the Jews.[198] (Henschel now headed the Postal Department.) Murmelstein had a keen interest in the department not only because he wanted to control what would be performed and avoid provocations, but also because his lover in the ghetto was the Czech actress and director Vlasta Schönová. She was prominent within the Recreation Department.

The Ghetto Guard became a controversial institution, as in other ghettos.[199] Unlike Jewish police in other ghettos, however, it was not responsible for organizing the deportations or bringing people to the transport site. The Ghetto Guard was relatively unimportant. The Ghetto Guardians deterred theft and checked prisoners at certain exits; sometimes they were seen as helpful, but more often as self-important and forming an obstacle. Nominally, Security Services belonged to Administration. In August 1942, Siegfried Seidl named Karl Loewenstein as its head, who professionalized the Ghetto Guard, introduced uniforms, military greetings, rehearsals, marching, and collective accommodation. The Security Services gained in influence, commanding the Fire Brigade, Detective Department, and the Office of Economic Supervision. By spring 1943, the Ghetto Guard reached its highest personnel level, with some five hundred people. Loewenstein wanted the Ghetto Guard to fulfill policing and state-building functions; he used the guardians to deter theft and graft. He did not notice that the SS felt threatened by the presence of a quasi-military, trained unit. In September 1943, almost the entire Ghetto Guard was put on transport. Eppstein used the opportunity to dismiss and arrest Loewenstein.[200]

His successor (and predecessor), Josef Klaber of Prague,[201] led the reduced and aged Ghetto Guard until fall 1944, when Paul Meth of Vienna replaced him. Meth's renamed Community Police was staffed almost entirely by women.[202] The Ghetto Court, headed by the Viennese jurist Heinrich Klang, sentenced those prisoners who were detained by the Ghetto Guard.[203] Criminal law represented the bulk of the work of the court, in addition to some guardianship (for orphans) and probate (for belongings of prisoners who passed away or were deported) issues. The sentencing could lead to prison sentences up to three months in the ghetto prison, based in the Magdeburg barracks. Unlike in the Vilna, Lodz, or Warsaw ghettos, however, the SS had no influence on the sentencing.[204] Instead, the Central Secretariat oversaw the verdicts and clemency pleas.[205]

THE OVERORGANIZED GHETTO   47

What do we learn from this organizational overview? The five departments described by Zucker and Lederer (Internal Administration, Economic, Financial, Technical, and Health Services) were not necessarily the mainstays of the administration. Two of the departments on the list were not that influential (Internal Administration and Financial Department, which was in fact only a section of Central Secretariat), and there were many more important divisions as the self-administration branched out.[206] Some of the subdepartments gained in importance and became quasi-independent; several sections were assigned very similar work, but effectively one department did the work.

This organizational outline also enables an overview of changes; there was a relatively straightforward assignment of offices in Edelstein's time. As new colleagues and specialists came in, the organization grew. Departments became even more complex following the arrival of the German and Austrian functionaries, after which it was only the Central Labor and Youth Welfare that remained strongholds of the predominantly Czech Zionists. From January 1943 onward, bureaucratization increased, as did the complicated communication between department heads. Departments increasingly became separate entities. In November 1944 Murmelstein reworked the dramatically reduced ghetto's administration, closing several departments and making others independent.

The dense organization meant that many people were not aware of their workplace structure. Quite a lot of work was done outside of the formal organization, yet some departments had a strong presence in the lives of their workers. The identities of employees from Youth Welfare, Health Services, and Recreation were closely bound up with their work. In the end, the ghetto administration, though overgrown, was viable. Heads of departments had to justify their existence to the deportation commission during each round of deportations, a brutal control mechanism. In part bureaucratization reflected an effort to appease the SS. For a long time, Edelstein tried to showcase Theresienstadt as a labor ghetto, and functionaries meant their reports and statistical overviews as a means of presenting the ghetto as a viable workplace whose population was worth keeping.[207] The purpose of such reports changed when the SS began to refashion Theresienstadt into a privilege camp. The SS always insisted on daily reports about the population, frequently demanding statistics.[208]

At the same time, the bureaucratic mentality in Terezín was a form of agency among mid- and high-ranking Jewish functionaries, who tried to

48   THE LAST GHETTO

make the ghetto a livable space, "their" ghetto. Affection for paper was a permanent feature of the self-administration;[209] it generated thousands of memos from each department about every detail of their activity; minutes of the Council of Elders; *Tagesbefehle* and *Mitteilungen* (Messages, a later name of the Orders of the Day); and elaborate annual, quarterly, and monthly activity reports prepared for the SS. The self-administration's communication with the inmates took on a similar form. It summoned individuals for labor or sent the dreaded pink slips for transports in dry, formal language, always in the passive voice.[210] The satirical samizdat journal *Šalom na pátek* (Shalom for Friday) poked fun at the ubiquitous bureaucracy and proclivity for bulletins in mock circulars.[211]

Theresienstadt's self-administration operated on two levels: one administration went through the departments and another through accommodation. In July 1942, after all the non-Jews had to leave the town, Theresienstadt was separated into four districts, each headed by a District Elder. Each district had several blocks, separated into single houses, either as much larger barracks (of the total twelve, two were seized for RSHA archives in July 1943) or small houses (195 houses, 174 of them habitable). Several houses constituted one block; barracks were blocks of their own. The smallest spatial administrative unit was a room.[212]

Each of the administrative units had its Elder, who was responsible for the population count and enforcing the orders of the SS. The room and house elders checked the curfew and daily passed the inhabitant count to their superior. They also distributed food; assigned sleeping spaces; passed the calls for transports; were the point of contact for newcomers about the infrastructure of the ghetto; reported names of the sick; and from July 1943, passed on information about pregnant women who had conceived in the ghetto.[213] House, block, and district Elders were full-time jobs within the Building Administration. The position offered several bonuses: house Elders had a small room of their own, they were usually protected from the transports, they had an opportunity to steal food, and their limited responsibilities meant that they were offered bribes.[214] At the same time, the house elders were everyone's contacts at any time, and their work was perceived as a service.[215]

This parallel administration via housing mattered, as many of the inhabitants who were over sixty-five years of age, as well as the weak and sick, did not work. These people were not organized via the Central Labor (as was the working population), by Youth Welfare (children), or by Health Services (the ill, including the long-term patients). The Building Administration and Space Management thus provided a possibility to keep these people in the system. In addition, the daily count of house elders was the central checking system that no one escaped.[216] This closely supervised living arrangement recalled a camp, while the self-administered, relatively autarkic departments aimed at creating a self-sufficient town.

Indirect Power

In addition to the work of the Jewish functionaries run through official offices, there were several instances of indirect power that existed within the Jewish self-administration

In September 1942, the SS introduced a new category of prisoners, the "prominents."[217] The idea was that people who were outstanding in their previous lives—scholars, inventors, writers, or relatives of important people—would be protected from the harshness of ghetto life.[218] The decision was connected to the SS goal to establish Theresienstadt as an "advantage camp," to mollify the German Jews and soothe public opinion. The prominents, who did not number more than three hundred,[219] received better accommodation in several separate houses in L1 Street, later renamed Seestrasse. They were also given better food rations, did not have to work (even if many did), could shower daily, received tickets to cultural events of their choice, and were protected from transports until further notice.[220] Compared to their prewar lifestyle, it was a humble life. Else Countess Goertz asked her children to send her soap, a fur vest, and boots.[221] Martha Mosse, herself prominent, observed: "They live like a poor maid, who saved her entire life for a few thousand marks, and who spends her remaining years in a senior home for the poor."[222] And yet, in contrast to the other prisoners, being able to wash in hot water on a daily basis or send clothing for mending put them in a very advantageous position.

There were two ways to become a prominent: through the Jewish self-administration or the SS. Inmates could apply to become prominent—often their house elders informed them about the possibility—and submit their credentials to the Central Secretariat. Leo Janowitz and later Kurt Levy reviewed these and passed the "worthy ones" on to the Elder of the Jews, who then introduced select cases to the commandant.[223] The SS suggested some individuals, including Alfred Philippson, a geographer from Bonn,

50 THE LAST GHETTO

and Georg Gradnauer, minister of the interior in 1921.[224] Some of the prominents may have been nominated even before their arrival. Eppstein had his colleagues from the Reich Association named prominent.[225] In addition, the SS named informers to the list.

Interestingly, although the prominents had substantial advantages in terms of resources, they never became prestigious. Many of the younger inmates had no idea that such a designation existed, and at best, they perceived them as old people. The prominents hinted at the essence of social and political leadership; namely, the elites were twofold. There were the political elite of the Magdeburg barracks, where the self-administration resided, and the social elite, the young Czech Jews.[226] The social elite had the best access to good jobs and accommodation. They secured jobs as cooks or in Agriculture, as craftsmen, or in Shipping. It is telling that Edelstein did not make his team prominent, while Eppstein did.[227] Edelstein's veteran associates had much better access to resources, utilizing their social and symbolic capital. The main reason Eppstein named his team "prominent" was material: like most German Jews, they simply suffered from hunger to an extent that their Czech colleagues did not. Kurt Levy's secretary Erna Goldschmidt suffered long-term consequences from her malnutrition in Terezín. Her colleague, Hilda Hahnová, who was Murmelstein's secretary, was connected to cigarette smuggling into the ghetto, representing a very wealthy position.[228] In addition, there was the symbolic message when the former functionaries had a better standard of living than the new leadership.[229] Finally, starving functionaries would open the way for graft, and Eppstein was trying to fight the corrupt structure left by his predecessor.

Leo Baeck

Leo Baeck is the best example of someone being able to establish unofficial power within the ghetto. The many stories told about Leo Baeck in Theresienstadt depict a moral force in the face of corruption and folly, a man who led the prisoners during difficult times. These stories, however, tell us little about the real person and his position in the ghetto. Baeck left almost no direct testimonies about his time in Theresienstadt.[230] The fact that he did not write a concrete memoir about the ghetto left room for the legend to take hold.

THE OVERORGANIZED GHETTO   51

Baeck was the chief rabbi of Berlin and also the chairperson of the Reich Association. Sent to Theresienstadt in January 1943, the seventy-year-old Baeck quickly became a prominent.[231] He received two rooms, where he lived with his Berlin housekeeper, Dora Czapski, who also became a prominent and thus had the time and means to take care of Baeck.[232] Baeck did not mention the woman who enabled his work in the ghetto, who after the war was too shy to bother her former employer to confirm her incarceration when applying for reparations.[233] Very few inmates in Theresienstadt were in a position to have a housekeeper.

Baeck had several relatives in Theresienstadt; several branches of the Baeck family lived in Czechoslovakia. There are discrepancies in Baeck's memories of his siblings; he stated that three of his sisters died in Theresienstadt before his arrival and that one died shortly afterward.[234] Two of his sisters did die in the summer of 1942,[235] but Elisa, the third, died fourteen months after Baeck's arrival—a long time by Theresienstadt standards.[236] Moreover, Anna Fischerová, Baeck's fourth sister, survived.[237] Baeck was in touch with his niece, Nelly Sternová, a medical doctor, who took care of her dying aunts, and three grandnieces, Ruth Baecková and Dorothea and Eva Sternová, all of whom survived.[238] Dorothea and Eva were sent to Auschwitz in fall 1944; Nelly and Ruth survived in the ghetto.[239]

Accounts that Baeck at first cleaned the streets and refused to become prominent are highly improbable.[240] Prominents did not have to work unless they wanted to; moreover, Baeck arrived with Eppstein, constituting the top functionaries. According to Werner Neufliess, an emigrant from Germany, who was friendly with Baeck, he worked at the post office, checking incoming packages for German newspapers.[241] Baeck also received many packages from his gentile friends.[242] He worked in spiritual guidance, preaching to prisoners and conducting wedding ceremonies.[243] He also connected with other scholars and gave lectures in the Recreation Department. His lectures on Judaism, Jewish history, philosophy, and religion were enthusiastically attended.[244] Philipp Manes, an experienced organizer of lectures, pointed out that Baeck's public speaking had improved since his sermons in Berlin; he found Baeck "facile and fluent, pleasant to listen to. He speaks in a quiet pose, without pathos, convincingly, insistently, memorably."[245] However, Vítězslav Braun, a middle-aged Czech inmate working in the ghetto library, had a more critical response: "Baeck's lectures are very scholarly, but he avoids having any actual content."[246]

52   THE LAST GHETTO

Baeck also worked with the Catholic community.[247] The position of the Catholics in the ghetto was not easy; some inmates, in particular the Zionists, confronted their Christian fellow prisoners with antipathy.[248] Nevertheless, the Catholic community, thanks to excellent organizational work and growing numbers of incoming Christians, established itself as one of the ghetto institutions. The Catholics invited Baeck to give a lecture,[249] and later Baeck successfully supported Catholic inmates' efforts to perform Catholic marriages and baptisms.[250]

Baeck became the honorary head of the Council of Elders, and within a month of his arrival he was active in decision-making processes, lobbying for the welfare of elderly inmates—an undesirable topic for the administration, since distribution of food and other resources was skewed in favor of the young.[251] Baeck also criticized the role of the administration in the beautification that preceded the visit of the International Red Cross.[252] The scholarship has nevertheless portrayed Baeck as "forced" to join the Council, where he was quiet.[253] After October 1944 he became the new head of the Youth and Elderly Welfare Department, a job in which he excelled.[254] He continued as a member in the restructured and reduced Council of Elders. At this point Baeck became, apart from Murmelstein, the most regular and active participant in Council discussions.[255]

Baeck invested considerable energy in getting along with other inmates; almost everyone remembered him in an extremely positive light.[256] Repeatedly, he was described as wise and friendly, but aloof. It is remarkable that Baeck got along with people who had opposing opinions and were very critical of each other.[257] Almost everyone admired him: the Czecho-Jews; Zionists; German, Austrian, and Czech Jews; Christians; observant Jews; and atheists. Indeed, all his life Baeck was described as a tolerant and pluralist personality.[258]

There were very few people who did not get along with Baeck: Heinrich Stahl, Paul Eppstein, and Benjamin Murmelstein.[259] These three men had one thing in common: they were in official positions of power over Baeck or competed with him in this respect. This conflict points out the nature of Baeck's position in Terezín. Leaning on decades of experience in religious and political community work, he positioned himself as a moral authority and accumulated symbolic capital, which enabled him to secure a symbolic leadership role. Active leadership, especially in times of persecution, with all its compromises and necessary decisions that were bound to disappoint elements of the population, would not have allowed him to be a charismatic, spiritual leader. Rudolf Bunzel, who was in charge of finances in the Central Secretariat, described Baeck as very selfish, and not pulling his weight.[260] Baeck, who understood his authority and knew how to use it, grasped the rules of the Theresienstadt social landscape.[261] His particular attitude of friendliness, inspiring yet unspecific talks, and aloofness from the compromises of the self-administration, was exactly the message the alienated inmates in Theresienstadt craved. The fact that he was a rabbi, a spiritual leader, and thus could code the message in religious terms, constituted the key ingredient of his success.[262]

Baeck employed a kind of social contract: those who sought him out as such acknowledged him as a moral authority. In exchange, those people could make a claim about their own integrity and prestige because they were associated with him.[263] The root of the conflict with Stahl, Eppstein, and Murmelstein was that they did not recognize—and did not legitimize—his claim to power. Baeck did not forget these conflicts. It was in response to Baeck's pressure that Murmelstein stepped down on May 5, 1945.[264] On the day Baeck left Theresienstadt by plane for Britain, he left behind a note denouncing Murmelstein, who had just been arrested for "collaboration."[265]

A well-known incident further demonstrates the mechanism at play. According to Baeck, in August 1943 he was approached by a Czech engineer, Grünberg, who told him about his friend, a Mischling who was sent to Auschwitz (although not from Theresienstadt). That man escaped, visited Grünberg in the ghetto, and told him about the gas chambers. Baeck and Grünberg considered what to do, and Baeck decided not to tell anyone, because life with the expectation of death would only be harder for the inmates.[266] Baeck's account is widely accepted, so much so that Hannah Arendt criticized his decision.[267]

This account has several problems. Even though successful escapes from Auschwitz have been extensively researched, there is no mention of any Czech who escaped in 1943.[268] It is also odd that apart from Baeck, no one has ever heard about this fugitive. There was also no engineer named Grünberg in Theresienstadt.[269] A well-known case was Vítězslav Lederer, who escaped Auschwitz and came to the ghetto in April 1944.[270] If a person had undertaken the dangerous escape and snuck into Theresienstadt to warn the inmates, why would the fugitive or Grünberg be content with Baeck's decision not to tell anyone?

There is a simple explanation: there was no escapee in August 1943. Baeck did meet with Vítězslav Lederer, along with two dozen other people. Lederer

54   THE LAST GHETTO

told them about Auschwitz and tried to warn them.[271] According to Leo Holzer of the Fire Brigade, Lederer's main contact in the ghetto, it was decided that Lederer should include Baeck among the people he met. Baeck was chosen because he was a member of the Council of Elders and "very reasonable and very influential. Decent, too."[272] Lederer reportedly convinced Baeck about his experience: "When they told him, he was blown away. Just like us he said that we have to deal with the report very carefully, to avoid some horrible catastrophes."[273] Eppstein's information about Birkenau also came from Lederer.

Why did Baeck change the story? Historians have pointed out that were other cases in which Baeck blurred the facts.[274] The last weeks of the ghetto brutally demonstrated to the veteran prisoners what had happened in the death camps, as thousands of emaciated and dead prisoners arrived on death marches, among them Theresienstadt prisoners deported earlier. For many prisoners, including Baeck, this was a crushing experience.[275] After liberation, the story of Lederer's escape and warning became public. Perhaps Baeck did not want to be known as one of the twenty people who had met with Lederer; he wanted his own fugitive. Fashioning the escapee as someone who was not deported from Theresienstadt made the story impossible to confirm.[276]

Baeck's conduct in Theresienstadt reflects that of a weathered functionary. Foremost, Baeck excelled in being recognized and revered as a leader. He was well aware that the position of Jewish functionaries was not only ethically compromising but also simply dangerous; most of his colleagues were murdered by the Nazis. Baeck skillfully stayed out of responsible positions, and if he could not avoid it, he succeeded in hiding his role from the public record. In those positions he held, he did well, demonstrating organizational talent and an ability to compromise and bring people together. The fact that Baeck was critical, sometimes backstabbingly so, of his opponents, reveals a shrewd player. Finally, his "forgetting" of dead sisters created a narrative showing Baeck as a suffering victim—similar to other German Jews—rather than an active, informed, and decision-taking functionary who could navigate Theresienstadt so skillfully because he was comparably well off and had the help of a servant.

One reason the SS could afford to devote relatively little supervision to the ghetto was that it had a network of Jewish informers. Informers prepared reports for the SS about the atmosphere in the ghetto and about various violations, most often smoking and smuggling.[277] Based on these reports,

Bergel and Haindl undertook spot checks. Successful, probing controls were a strong deterrent. Some informers would also approach gendarmes and ask for a favor; if the gendarme helped, they would pass on his name to the SS. The SS had photographs of all the gendarmes so that informers could point them out more easily.[278] SS headquarters also wanted to be informed about eminent Jewish functionaries and their relatives and friends. This came to the fore when putting together the liquidation transports in the fall of 1944: On the list for Ev, the last transport from Theresienstadt, were Edelstein's secretary, Josefina Steifová; Eppstein's lovers; and prominent individuals in the Czech Jewish bloc.[279]

Bergel, Haindl, and the commandant gathered the reports and then passed on the relevant ones to Hans Günther.[280] The informers' reports, with one exception, have not survived.[281] Murmelstein believed that informers were behind the demise of at least one of his predecessors. He believed he had tackled the matter by writing scathing reports about himself and submitting them anonymously to Rahm, who dropped the issue.[282]

It seems that informers volunteered for their positions. They came from different countries, were both male and female, and were often younger. Their job came with several advantages: they were protected from transports, did not have to work, and received better food and accommodation. To this end, several of them were named prominent by the SS.[283] In the end, the profit informers drew from their service rarely outlasted the war; the SS sent almost all of their informers to Auschwitz with the last transports.[284] After October 1944, Haindl had to build a new network.

There are obvious challenges to writing about Jewish informers in the ghetto, starting with their identification. Inmates freely labeled other prisoners as traitors. It sufficed that someone was seen entering the SS headquarters more than once and without an obvious reason. Many accused Karl Loewenstein of acting as an informer.[285] However, Loewenstein, as head of the Ghetto Guard, went daily to SS headquarters. Such accusations came not only from "simple" prisoners who misunderstood the context, but also from surviving functionaries, who left similar statements about other prisoners.[286]

Marianne Meyerhoff, a young woman from Bremen, almost certainly worked as an informer in Terezín. Survivors mentioned Meyerhoff as a denouncer. She had already worked in such a capacity for the Gestapo in Bremen[287] and had blackmailed those Jews that she spied on into paying her large sums.[288] In April 1942, when Jews could no longer move around freely, Meyerhoff and her mother moved to Berlin; in July 1943, they were sent to

56   THE LAST GHETTO

Terezín. In the ghetto, Meyerhoff became prominent, although her resumé was comparably "thin": she was thirty-one years old and had studied chemistry but not graduated. [289] Her late, gentile teacher father had been a member of the National Socialist German Workers' Party (NSDAP) and the German Labor Front.[290] Viktor Kende, head of Transport Management, marked her as a denouncer; moreover, she was included on a list of *Weisungen* by the SS.[291] Marianne Meyerhoff was sent to Birkenau on October 28, 1944. Together with the overwhelming majority of that transport and all those whom Kende marked with a *denunc*, she did not survive.

The prisoners loathed the denouncers, and if they felt they could afford to do it, sometimes attacked them physically. Robert Mandler helped organize transports first in Prague and later in other towns.[292] When he was sent to Theresienstadt at the end of January 1943, he was beaten up so badly that he needed to be hospitalized.[293] Beating up informers became an expression of the inmates' control: former victims could now demonstrate that they were veterans in position of power. Fifteen years after the war, in East Germany, having beaten up an informer was one element an individual could use to apply for a higher category of award and compensation.[294] In cases where informers survived, after liberation they faced the fury of other survivors.[295] Jadwiga Weinbaumová, a young woman originally from Tarnopol who was deported without her family, had acted as an informer since fall 1943.[296] After the liberation, she hid, infected with typhus, under a false name in a hospital, where she was found and arrested. Real and assumed informers and "collaborators" were arrested and investigated, often for months and years. After eighteen months in custody, Benjamin Murmelstein, Rudolf Freiberger, and Karl Loewenstein were released. Jadwiga Weinbaumová was expelled to the Soviet Union but made her way to Austria, where she married a Japanese American soldier and emigrated with him to the United States; she died in 1998 in a suburb of Washington, D.C.[297]

We do not consider informing an ethical activity, and the same applied in the ghetto. What are we to make of informing during the Holocaust? More than anything else, the Theresienstadt informers offer an important lesson in human agency in extreme situations: whereas the *Greifer*, the Jew catchers, in Berlin were given the choice between their own deportation and hunting for others,[298] and men from the *Sonderkommandos* faced the choice between immediate death and complying,[299] the informers in Theresienstadt volunteered. The denouncers tried to improve the desperate living conditions in the ghetto; to protect themselves from transport to the

East; and, similarly to the Jewish policemen in Warsaw ghetto, to have power over other prisoners.[300] The last motivation is particularly important, as the Theresienstadt informers, like most informers in general, had informed before.[301]

The SS did not administer Terezín; rather, they exerted control via constructive violence. The commandants, who demanded information about the decisions of the self-administration, did not participate in the decision-making, nor did they care how the lives of prisoners were administered. The SS's central tool of control was spot checks, facilitated by information from Jewish denouncers. The spot checks and ensuing punishments demonstrated that the SS had the sole access to violence and thus were the sovereign.

Scholars have pointed out the particular position of the Jewish functionaries who, while caring for the Jewish population, had to fulfill the perpetrators' orders that led to their murder.[302] But rather than reducing the Jewish functionaries' relations with German perpetrators to "collaboration," we learn more by asking about their mentality, expectations, and loyalties. Jewish functionaries tried to make sense of the persecution, believing that if orders were fulfilled, the perpetrators would let the remaining Jewish community be; believing in annihilation did not make sense.[303]

For many leading Jewish functionaries, the good opinion of the victims' community was part of being "good at the job." The inmates liked Edelstein and to a lesser extent Eppstein.[304] Edelstein, who represented the veterans and the largest inmate group, signaled that he sought people's approval, which he received in turn. Murmelstein, the despised Elder, used his social capital with the perpetrators to maximize his room to maneuver. He was able to improve the conditions and to survive, yet his disregard for popular opinion made him deeply unpopular. This analysis of Murmelstein demonstrates a model of Jewish leadership distinct from previous assessments of other ghetto Elders like Moshe Merin and Mordechai Rumkowski.[305]

The Theresienstadt self-administration was political, but not in the conventional understanding of politics and parties; moreover, the meaning of politics kept evolving. In the first period, the ideological streams among the Czech Jews defined "politics" alongside social belonging and networks. Later, when the SS and Eppstein installed German and Austrian Jews in leading positions, ethnicity acquired a political note. After spring 1943, when departments became increasingly autonomous, association with a department took on a political identity of its own: as a clerk in the Health Services, or working under Erich Munk. These political belongings worked alongside

58 THE LAST GHETTO

one another. However, not all of these political relationships were relevant for everyone; for instance, the competition between Zionists and Czecho-Jews did not apply for the German and Austrian functionaries.

Status connected the social with the political elite. The social elite of Terezín were associated with the first charismatic Jewish Elder, Edelstein's, team of young Czech Zionists. The young Czech men and women became the "jeunesse dorée," bright young people, a group with immense status, defined both socially and economically. In turn, they acknowledged the Zionist leadership. This implicit connection affirmed both groups' status and power: one social, the other political. When Paul Eppstein took office, the structures were so entrenched that he did not change them. Unlike his predecessor, Eppstein was not charismatic, and in order to be accepted as the leader, he recognized the position of the social elite. Young Czech Jews thus retained their status, which perhaps even rose when the Elder of the Jews was "foreign."

The inflated bureacratization of Terezín reflected prewar Central European practices of governmentality. The continuity of bureaucracy could express a sense of order in the horrible new conditions and was hence a means of control. When Jewish functionaries redefined Terezín as a Jewish settlement, they intended to make something good out of something bad; administrative structure was a way to assert control, indeed, to redefine the social space in their own terms. The argument of self-organizing as a form of agency holds true for other ghettos and camps as well, as these often also had a complex system of departments. It is telling, though, that Theresienstadt, which never became a labor ghetto, had by far the most complex organization. The functionaries could not determine everything in the ghetto, but bureaucracy, paperwork, and a formal tone were ways to express agency. And so Theresienstadt became the most organized ghetto of the Holocaust.

2

A Society Based on Inequality

"Then, after the horrible rupture of fate and life, the worms, crammed into the unprepared barracks, began to work, hate, remember, and love; to bend their backs and to rule."[1] So wrote a young Prague author, Mirko Tůma, in his early postwar account of Theresienstadt. Tůma's account portrayed the early stages of Terezín as the onset of a new society. But that new society, in his depiction, worked much like the old one. What changed, and what remained the same in the ghetto society? This chapter discusses the social organization of the society in Terezín. What constituted social class in the ghetto, and what factors determined a person's position? Which networks—familial, romantic, or others—were important? What did it mean for the society that formed in Terezín that everyone who was incarcerated was there because they were identified as "Jewish" by the Third Reich? How did this "Jewishness" shape the prisoner society?

Terezín produced a complex society in which ethnicity, social networks, age, gender, and other factors created diverse yet interconnected groups. People of various geographic and cultural backgrounds were thrown together and interacted on a daily basis at work, on the streets, in food lines, and in their accommodations. Inmate society was based on inequality; although everyone was a prisoner, even the smallest differences became extremely important. Factors that influenced social hierarchy (and at the same time, served as its yardstick) in Terezín included the job one held, lodgings, protection from transport, and whether one could have an intimate life. These differences permeated the entire prisoner society. Ethnicity emerged as the most salient method of categorization, producing social asymmetries among the prisoners. Ethnic differences also served to exclude and sometimes to stigmatize other groups, often in conjunction with gender and sexuality.

From the Shock of Arrival to the Master Narrative

Arrival at Terezín was a traumatic experience. Contemporaneous narrators devoted many pages to describing their leave-taking, the collection sites in

The Last Ghetto. Anna Hájková, Oxford University Press (2020). © Oxford University Press.
DOI: 10.1093/oso/9780190051778.001.0001.

60   THE LAST GHETTO

their hometowns, their journeys, and their arrival in the ghetto.[2] The journey and chaotic arrival served as a rite of passage—a liminal period of shock transporting deported Jews from home to the new environment of Terezín. The process of being registered in the ghetto stripped the newly arrived of their expectations and acted as an opener for settling into the new order.

Deportation to Terezín was the final step in dispossessing Jews of their rights as citizens.[3] The transports mostly took place in third-class train cars and arrived in Bohušovice (Bauschowitz in German).[4] From there people had to walk the remaining mile carrying their luggage; the sick and weak rode on a wagon. After June 1943, the trains arrived directly in the ghetto via a spur line built by the prisoners. One or two SS men, gendarmes, and prisoners from the Shipping detail accompanied the march. Whereas the SS men screamed at and browbeat the inmates, the gendarmes frequently tried to cheer up the Czech deportees. The Shipping employees often explained to the new arrivals what was awaiting them and sometimes even offered to smuggle their belongings past the checkpoint upon arrival.

The whole process was a long and disorienting experience. One or more halls of the barracks were designated as *Schleuse* (literally, water navigation lock), the building where the newly arrived were registered and checked for prohibited items. The Ghetto Guard supervised this process. Workers of Central Evidence took down the inmates' names, birthdates, professions, family members, and religion. They asked if the new arrivals had close gentile relatives, if the women were pregnant, and whether they had participated in the First World War, and inquired about citizenship. At the end of the procedure, the new arrivals received their Terezín IDs and food cards and became inhabitants of the ghetto.

The code the SS provided to the Central Secretariat for each transport served, in combination with other information, as an identity number for each inmate. The Protectorate transports were given a letter combination; transports from outside the area received a Roman numeral code. The IDs given were in consecutive order. Berlin was the first area from which a non-Czech transport arrived, and it was assigned I; Vienna was fourth and was given IV. An Arabic numeral, indicating the order of the transports from the respective area, followed the code for non-Czechs. The last Arabic numeral indicated the individual's number in his or her transport. The departing transports from Theresienstadt received alphabetic codes.[5]

The veterans of Transport Help went through the new inmates' luggage.[6] They confiscated everything that was prohibited along with other things, including medications, thermoses, bottles, flashlights, and even the 50 Reichsmarks German Jews were allowed to bring.[7] New inmates generally received their luggage weeks later, often with many items missing; some never received it at all. The stolen items were sorted: the SS took what they wanted, other items were sent to the Winter Relief program, and what remained went into the Clothing Warehouse. Two SS men were usually present: Rudolf Haindl from the political and Heinrich Scholz from the economic departments.

The arrival procedures, which included the violation of one's material belongings and body, shocked and disoriented the new inmates.[8] In this way, the *Schleuse* served as the first step in an inmate's integration into ghetto society. The harassment of the arrival violated physical boundaries: the newly arrived were subjected to physical inspections, and women had to undergo gynecological examinations to establish whether they had hidden valuables or if they were pregnant. Haindl and some lower-ranking SS men liked to watch the disrobed women.[9] After 1943, people were immunized against typhoid.[10] Those who arrived in the first four months of Terezín, as well as some who arrived later, had their hair cut. In later years, people were sent to showers, and their clothing was steamed.[11] Sometimes the newly arrived had to spend their first night or longer in the *Schleuse* before they were directed to their lodging.

Getting used to life in Terezín posed many challenges. Inmates were assigned a room where, in the first months, people slept on the floor, or if they were lucky on a mattress. By summer 1942, three-level bunk beds were built, which were viewed as a huge improvement. Living quarters became more orderly, and every inhabitant had a small space. For the most part men and women were separated. Pavel Fischl, a young Czech poet, described how one got used to the new life:

> Not for nothing is it said that one even gets used to the gallows. We have all gotten used to the noise of steps on the barracks' hallways. We have already gotten used to those four dark walls surrounding each barracks. We are used to standing in long lines, at 7am, at noon, and again at 7pm, holding a bowl to receive a bit of heated water tasting of salt or coffee, or to get a few potatoes. We are wont to sleep without beds, live without radio, record player, cinema, theatre, and the usual worries of average people. We have gotten accustomed to greet every uniform and not to walk on the sidewalk and then to walk on the sidewalks again, we have gotten used to being hit

62   THE LAST GHETTO

in the face without reason but also groundless executions, we have gotten accustomed to see people die in their own dirt, to see the sick in filth and disgust. [. . .] We are habituated not to read the newspaper and to wear one shirt one week long; well, one gets used to everything.[12]

The Germans and Austrians who began arriving in June 1942 were worse off than the veteran Czech prisoners because they were housed in the barracks' attics.[13] The attics were the only empty places left, and they increased space in the ghetto by 25 percent.[14] But they had been empty because they were not habitable: there was no water, toilets were located on the lower floors, and there was no electric lighting and no beds.[15] The majority of the German and Austrian Jews were elderly, seventy, eighty, and even ninety years old. They could not walk well and were unable to manage the stairs. The hygiene situation became catastrophic, as people lay soiled in their excrement.[16] The new inmates were disoriented and upset. Some cried, others lost their minds, and some simply died.[17] Sometimes Health Services assigned newly arrived elderly inmates a nurse who stayed with them at night, brought water, and helped people use a bucket as a makeshift bathroom.[18]

Berl Herškovič, a Hechalutz member who inspected one of the attics, was shocked: "Inhabitants of the attics faced the problem of how to get to the lavatories and access water. People defecated in their clothes although they had nothing to change into. There were not enough mattresses. It was horrendous, horrendous!"[19] It seems the Protectorate transports that arrived during summer 1942 were not relegated to the attics, at least not all of them.[20] Space Management ranked the inmates in terms of "human material"; elderly individuals were on the bottom.[21] Accommodation, similar to food and medical care, was a moment of assigning value, a triage mechanism.

The rooms accommodated between eight and two hundred inhabitants. People changed, bathed, ate, met with their families, and slept in front of each other. Curfew began at 8:00 p.m. in the early years and later at 10:00 p.m.; sometimes the SS prohibited the lights being on after a certain time. Inmates acquired a blanket or sleeping bag, made a stool, built a shelf, and drove nails into the wall as part of their unpacking, thus creating a home, Terezín style. Margaret Pedde from Mühlheim remarked, "For two months I have been eating on the floor like a Turk."[22] The ghetto was crowded, and people were never alone; there was no privacy in the bathrooms or bedrooms, which added to the psychological pressure.

A SOCIETY BASED ON INEQUALITY 63

Inmates described the surreal experience of arrival in Terezín. Truda Sekaninová, a Communist lawyer from Prague, remembered: "I had the feeling that abstract art became the reality there. [. . .] Each square centimeter was used [. . .] and so people lived in grocery stores, in former shops. In the old shopping windows were those ancient German women, and over them hung a sign saying, 'fresh meat.' "[23] Two mechanisms helped inmates cope: distancing themselves by perceiving Terezín as absurd and mourning. Some new arrivals attempted to take their lives.[24] Health Services, aware of the extreme shock among the recently arrived, established a welcoming committee, who offered psychological help for the suicidal.[25]

Friends, relatives, and acquaintances gave a helping hand.[26] Arnošt Klein from Prague, who was almost sixty-five when he arrived, fell ill soon afterward. He met a "good acquaintance," V.S., who had arrived with the second Aufbaukommando: "Here I could find out what a great and fine guy he was, and we became good friends. VS tows me . . . into the infirmary, softly pats the behind of the nurse, and as if it was the most natural thing in the world, places me into the best spot in an immaculate bed."[27] Every familiar face was perceived as a friendly messenger; existing social ties gained in importance. An inmate's readiness to help was particularly salient when a new arrival was looking for a job or housing. Regional ties, provided one did not come from a metropolis like Prague or Berlin, were also binding. František Kollman from Plzeň received a position as a cook because a friend told him to contact Ruth Hoffeová, who was also from Plzeň. Hoffeová was an influential functionary during Edelstein's tenure.[28]

The barracks were the first buildings to be inhabited. When the ghetto was opened in July 1942, newcomers were placed in small houses.[29] The infrastructure in the houses lagged behind the barracks, where conditions had improved. By this stage the barracks had electricity, toilets on every floor, and opportunities for washing. The small houses had only a water pump and latrine in the courtyard. It seems that the clerks of Space Management often assigned younger Czech Jews accommodations in the barracks, where the infrastructure was eventually improved; they installed non-Czechs, along with the elderly, in the small houses.[30]

The rooms produced a heterogeneous encounter: people who had never before met now lived in close quarters. Louis Salomon from Berlin lived with roommates from Vienna, Berlin, Prague, Breslau, and Bonn, who came from diverse ideological and religious backgrounds.[31] Sometimes men and women were assigned to one room. Since there was nowhere else to go,

Karel Fleischmann, *Motiv z Terezína (všední život v ghettu)* (Everyday life in the ghetto, 1943). Fleischmann's drawings depicted everyday life in the crowded, stifling conditions of Theresienstadt. Courtesy of the Jewish Museum, Prague.

daily life took place in front of everyone: some went without delicate bodily functions, while others washed their feet, used a chamber pot, or took an enema.[32] One's bunk bed was the only exclusive place of one's own.[33] Many compared their lodgings with Maxim Gorki's *The Lower Depths*,[34] a play about a Russian homeless asylum, with social norms, and ties, falling apart. Still, rules regulating conduct emerged and allowed for minimal privacy.[35] Those in mixed-gender rooms established that women would change behind a curtain or a coat or men would look away; hygiene time was to be kept short.[36] There were even rules for toilet usage. Because of the long lines, pants were to be pulled up outside.[37]

Prisoners had to move often, as many as ten times. Whatever routines people had established, they then had to recreate them in their new lodgings. People could apply to move if they found out there was an available spot; Czech Jews often tried moving in with friends or relatives, especially if they were of the same generation.[38] When Czech prisoners had to share a room with "foreigners," they often saw it as an indignity.[39] Elderly inmates did not stay in the attics longer than a few months.[40] Due to the poor conditions, those who remained there died. As the ghetto's infrastructure improved, carpenters were dispatched to improve the attics and construct windows in the roofs.[41] Bedřich Hoffenreich, a craftsman sent to the attic of the Magdeburg barrack to build dry toilets, discovered that the attics were located too high to dispose of the waste, so the bathrooms would not work. "There was shit all over the place," he commented laconically.[42] In these conditions ended an entire generation of German, Austrian, and Czech Jewish bourgeoisie.

A room of one's own was a luxury in the ghetto. In 1942 only a few dozen functionaries had their own rooms, and house elders occupied only very small rooms.[43] By the end of the year, when the population sank to forty thousand, inmates with access to resources and good social networks constructed tiny rooms in the attics. The attics had become empty again; the elderly prisoners had moved elsewhere within the ghetto, died, or been sent to Treblinka and Maly Trostinets. These attic rooms were called *kumbáls*, meaning cubbyholes in Czech. Built from thin wood, kumbáls measured between sixty and one hundred square feet and were usually furnished with a narrow bed, a desk, and folding chairs.[44] In the context of Terezín, they represented what a villa in Prague-Střešovice or Berlin-Grunewald had once meant. Their inhabitants were nearly always young, Czech men, living alone, with roommates or with a partner. Women did not live in a kumbál alone but rather with a man or another woman.[45]

Terezín prescribed general labor duty for everyone between the ages of sixteen and sixty. Over time those age boundaries changed; after October 1944, when most of the younger inhabitants had been removed, labor duty was extended to prisoners between twelve and seventy. Teenagers were often allotted to Agriculture; Youth Care viewed these jobs as an opportunity for youth to get out of the ghetto and, when unobserved, eat some fruits or vegetables.[46] The working day was usually ten hours, although the length and shifts differed. Saturday afternoons were free.

Every new arrival (with the exception of eminent functionaries) had to undergo a period of general work—the so-called *Hundertschaft*—for what was usually one hundred hours: they cleaned the streets, shoveled coal, and pushed loaded wagons. Afterward, the Central Labor assigned newcomers a permanent job, or they could apply for a job, especially if they could point to an opening. People often began in less advantageous positions and worked their way up.[47] One example of what such a Theresienstadt career represented was Leopold Neuhaus, a Frankfurt/Main rabbi deported at sixty-three years of age, who worked as a rabbi for the Magdeburg barracks and eventually became head of the Welfare Section for the elderly.[48]

66 THE LAST GHETTO

Jobs in the kitchens, bakeries, Central Supply and Agriculture Departments, Post Office, and showers, and as physicians were in high demand. People usually secured these positions through networks; as members of the Hechalutz, Šimon Kopolovič and Sam Berger received jobs in the bakery.[49] Central Labor looked for technicians, electricians, and artisans because they were underrepresented; often they were assigned directly from the *Schleuse*. Most positions, however, were not in high demand. The lower part of the labor hierarchy was inhabited by thousands of inmates who worked as cleaning staff or toilet attendants, in the mica workshop, and mending clothes or mattresses.

Several factors influenced the symbolic capital of certain positions. In part, the status of a profession depended on access to material resources and protection from the transports. But the prestige of a job was also tied to the ghetto's master narrative. Certain kinds of work were understood to be of crucial service to the community.[50] Bakers, butchers, and cooks were admired and much sought-after romantic partners; their jobs provided them with economic and symbolic capital. In contrast, people who worked in Central Supply or the Criminal Police, even though they too had access to food, had no comparable standing; the Ghetto Guard had little control over the inmates. Physicians and technicians received better rations but had no extra access to food through their jobs. These jobs had decent economic capital but high status.

Work was a key site of social interaction between various ethnic groups. Whereas dormitories sometimes placed people of the same ethnic background together, especially the younger and middle-aged Czech Jews, in most jobs the workers came from diverse countries and were of different ages. Norbert Buchsbaum, a young Dutchman of Polish background, was directed to the wood workshop, where his boss was fifty-nine-year-old Norbert Hoffenberg from Vienna. The Czech engineers in the Technical Department were condescending to Hoffenberg, Buchsbaum noticed, but Hoffenberg and his team befriended Buchsbaum.[51] In certain jobs, especially where the overwhelming majority of workers were Czech, ethnic boundaries persisted. Ida Süß, a nineteen-year-old Viennese, worked in Agriculture, which had a strong Czech presence. In 1946, testifying against Rudolf Haindl, she stated: "I do not know the names of my colleagues, because to a large part, they were Czech."[52]

Employment in Terezín had a pronounced sexist bias. For many of the women who had been housewives, the ghetto was the first time they worked outside the home. Edelstein's self-administration made a point about work duty as representing a break in the life experience of presumably spoiled, bourgeois women.[53] This perception of the challenges women faced when working is not confirmed in the testimonies of women from such backgrounds. Indeed, if any women experienced a significant change with regard to work experience, it was the professionals. In interwar Germany, Austria, and Czechoslovakia, women had become clerks, teachers, physicians, and attorneys.[54]

Although many experts struggled to find a position within their profession in Terezín, it was much harder for women. Women only gained such positions after October 1944, when most younger people had been deported. But even then, inmates disapproved of female superiors: When Martha Mosse was appointed head of the women's section of the Criminal Police in November 1944 under Murmelstein, her women colleagues told her that they did not like having a female boss; it gave their position less status.[55] Camilla Hirsch enjoyed her work in the administration of house L 223. Although she did the job of deputy house elder, caring for 340 inhabitants, her boss resisted providing her with the formal title because she was a woman.[56]

Although heterogeneous, the community in Terezín was surprisingly cohesive; the togetherness operated through a master narrative, to which a great majority of the inmates subscribed. This means, as Eric Hobsbawm has demonstrated, a story that connects a body of people by interpreting their past or present in a meaningful way. Such a story ties various events together so that people can become a group with positive characteristics. Nationalism, for instance, employs historic, heroized legends to create a national group.[57]

The prisoners of Terezín produced a master narrative that enabled inmates to endow their experience with meaning. It was functioning by November 1942, toward the end of the large transports into the ghetto, with the production of Smetana's operas and the onset of the celebrated cultural life in the ghetto. This master narrative interpreted Terezín as a success story, in which Jews whom the Nazis stigmatized created something good out of something bad. In Terezín, according to the master narrative, Jews demonstrated they could be more than businessmen or intellectuals and excelled at manual labor. In fact, labor was portrayed as a moral activity, with everyone contributing to the community to the best of his or her ability. Although people suffered and were hungry, the prisoners took care of children and produced outstanding cultural events, demonstrating that even in the depths of misery, Jews were amazing artists.[58]

68 THE LAST GHETTO

Menasche Mautner, an elderly Viennese inmate, related how the Aufbaukommando constructed the ghetto out of desolation and delivered "amazing accomplishments."[59] Prisoners depicted Terezín as a place outside time and space.[60] By this account, Terezín's prisoners were the best and the brightest—scholars, politicians, writers, and virtuosos—and its inmate community never experienced murder and only rarely theft. The ghetto population recalled the SS executions of sixteen young men in early 1942 as a key moment of suffering.

The legend of Terezín had a normative function: it told a moral story prescribing appropriate conduct and dictated the prestige of certain groups.[61] One of the purposes of a master narrative is to create a corporate identity, a sense of groupness.[62] The legend helped people overcome the negative experience of the ghetto. In the same entry, diarists would complain about the dirt and injustice of the ghetto and simultaneously remind themselves of the exceptional place in which they were living.[63] They depicted Theresienstadt as a place without violent criminality, even though at least one murder did take place.[64] Nearly everyone subscribed to the legend of Terezín, including the elderly, the group that lived in the worst conditions. Subscribing to the story enabled them to feel like equal members of a community rather than the abandoned. In exchange, the elderly population, often the former intellectual elite, acknowledged the social elite of young Czech Jews.

Only two groups did not subscribe to the master narrative, which in turn corresponded with their overall failure to integrate into the ghetto: Dutch Jews and the Czech spouses from mixed marriages who arrived in winter 1945. Neither group integrated into the Terezín community. The native Dutch among the transports from the Netherlands (a majority of these inmates were German and Austrian emigrants, who integrated well) came from a different sociohistorical background than most Terezín Jews.[65] Dutch society was separated into pillars, which also influenced the low number of intermarriages. This habitus influenced the reaction of Dutch gentiles and Jews alike to the new, threatening surroundings: passive withdrawal.

Within six weeks in winter 1945, 3,654 Czech Jews arrived; they were Czech Jewish spouses from still intact intermarriages, sometimes accompanied by young children. They knew the war would be over within a few months, and they missed their families.[66] The much-reduced community of Terezín veterans could no longer integrate a large contingent of newcomers. Veterans complained that the newcomers failed to see the virtue of labor for the ghetto.[67] When forty-three-year-old Pavel Herz from Prague was

A SOCIETY BASED ON INEQUALITY   69

assigned his first job, towing buckets filled with ashes, he left and went to Robert Weinberger of the Central Labor to ask for a different assignment. To Weinberger, a functionary from Edelstein's team, Herz's refusal came across as insolence. Herz was reported to the Ghetto Court, where he was sentenced to a twenty-four-hour prison sentence after a twenty-four-hour workday. The labor judge, Rolf Grabower, reproached Herz for his poor work ethic and pointed out that he was the brother "of an artist who demonstrated her art just yesterday."[68] That artist was the pianist Alice Sommer Herz, the centerpiece of the Terezín master narrative, who played Beethoven and Chopin until the very end.

A World in a City

The inmates of Terezín were a skewed reflection of Central and Western European society; some groups were underrepresented and others were overrepresented. For instance, young men were underrepresented because they had been the most likely to emigrate. Elderly individuals were overrepresented because they had had the least chance to leave. Age aside, the demographics of the ghetto reflected the urban, liberal, assimilated, middle- and upper-middle-class individuals, who had worked as attorneys, tradesmen, physicians, journalists, civil servants, and engineers.

Many people in the ghetto had gentile relatives. This was true of nearly every Czech Jew in Terezín, which is not surprising, given that by 1930 about 40 percent of Jewish marriages in Prague (24 percent in Bohemia) were with a gentile.[69] Benjamin Frommer pointed out that many Czech intermarried couples opted for a "fake divorce," in order to save their property or their jobs, but remained living together.[70] Because these mixed marriages were now dissolved, the now divorced Jewish partners were no longer protected by the mixed marriage and were deported. Throughout the research for this book, I came across many divorced Czech Jews in Theresienstadt, whose marriages came to an end after the occupation. The evidence is anecdotal, but it seems that even though in 1937 many Czech Jews were intermarried, by 1943 a large portion of them were in Theresienstadt. There were also many *Geltungsjuden*, people with one Jewish parent who were categorized as Jewish.[71]

Several dozen inmates were released from Terezín.[72] Most of them could successfully claim that they were *Mischlinge* rather than *Geltungsjuden*, and

70 THE LAST GHETTO

they often owed their release to outside pressure by someone with influence. Elsa Bernstein recalled that Gisela Countess Kolowrat, a widowed Viennese Catholic of Jewish background, was a kind, modest woman: "I thought she was a Bohemian cook. She may have been, before her marriage." Kolowrat was released and returned to Vienna, arrested again, and murdered in Auschwitz.[73]

The mix of inmates in Terezín reflected the heterogeneity of the Jews in prewar Europe. Ghetto inhabitants included the magician Herbert Nivelli, who had emigrated from Germany to Czechoslovakia in 1933;[74] citizens of various South American countries, Turkey, and the Soviet Union; and three French Jews, former minister Léon Meyer, his wife Suzanne, and their daughter Denise, who were noticeable by their stars of David with the inscription *Juif.*[75] In addition to a sizable Catholic and Protestant minority, there were twelve Adventists, four Christian Scientists, and even three Muslims.[76]

Categorization and Stratification

Categorization is one of the central ways a society operates. In the inmate community, categorization was informed by several factors that shaped the prisoner society: ethnicity, age, gender, and social capital. When encountering someone new, people in Terezín most often pointed out their ethnicity. The comments touched upon perceptions of the geographic, ethnically coded cultural, ethnically coded religious, or national background. Inhabitants described others' differences, their language, and syntax in terms of ethnicity. They applied what I call an ethnic gaze, categorizing people according to their looks, pointing out "racial" signifiers such as skin, hair color, and facial and bodily features. Cultural and linguistic characteristics—accent, tone of speech, attire, and the makeup and hairstyles of women—were observed and assessed as part of the ethnic gaze.

Ethnicity came to be a crucial tool of differentiation because Terezín was so international and the community it produced was transnational. Czech, German, Austrian, Dutch, Danish, Slovak, and Hungarian Jews used ethnicity to make sense of their surroundings. To an extent such ethnic categorization was probably due to the widespread mentality of the "folk community" in interwar Europe. But in Terezín, a place of constant enforced ethnic encounters, ethnicity acquired a new salience. Previously, people had primarily met foreigners during holiday travel. Tourists, however, travel in a liminal space; their sojourn is an exception and thus they react to people of another ethnicity differently than they would at home.[77] Yet Terezín was "home," a constant, to which people became accustomed.

Framing and stereotypes are key tools of ethnic categorization. Both are mechanisms people use to make sense of new surroundings, ways to interpret based on existing knowledge.[78] For instance, German and Austrian inmates employed framing to describe the ghetto. They depicted the Czech Jews as strikingly non-Jewish looking, a "far-reaching, assimilated," and "beautiful race." This "assimilated" look was sometimes interpreted as Slavic, for instance by Otto Bernstein from Berlin: "A beautiful race. Splendid boys—well-built young women. A pasture for the eyes. The Slavic type was prevalent; assimilation in Czechoslovakia seems to be far advanced."[79] But others classified the same looks as "Germanic." Rosa Salomon from Berlin noted: "The Czechs are an entirely different sort of people than we are. The women are of a proud posture and astonishing height, true Valkyries; the men Siegfrieds and Gunthers. I haven't seen such people even in Sweden." The characterization as Slavic/Germanic served here as a frame; "Valkyrie" was a stereotype within this frame.

In making sense of the Czech Jews, elderly Germans and Austrians explained them as a kind of superior people, spirited, perhaps a little arrogant, yet tremendous.[80] Narrators viewed the "locals" in markedly ethnic and physical terms, as tall, athletic, and "non-Jewish." Whether the perceived lack of Jewishness was explained as Germanic or Slavic, it was always interpreted as beautiful; non-Jewish looks were positively coded. The characterization of Czech Jews had nothing in common with stereotypes of Eastern Jews, which would have been the obvious stereotype to fall back on. German Jews had had little contact with Czechoslovakia (perhaps with the exception of those from Dresden), and Terezín was their first encounter with anything Czech.

When talking about German Jews, the Czech prisoners, particularly Czecho-Jews, utilized stereotypes based on Czech history, in which the German is a negative figure. The opinion of thirty-six-year-old Jiří Borský serves as an example of what many Czechs thought about German Jews: "Unpleasant news was the arrival of the first transport from Berlin on June 2, 1942. It was a strange and foreign element, speaking in a foreign language, very different in its Kraut habits."[81] The treasured novelist Karel Poláček expressed a similar notion during a 1944 lecture: "Germans and the German Jews whom they educated do not talk but they order; they do not

72   THE LAST GHETTO

walk but they march; Prussian grandmothers are better in standing in a line-up than our active soldiers."[82]

Many Czech Jews reproached the German Jews for their presumed identification with Nazi Germany. Hana Munková, a young actress from an eminent Czecho-Jewish family, performed in the theater organized by the Berliner Philipp Manes.[83] Fifty years later, Munková claimed that the German Jews were unhappy about the defeats of the Wehrmacht. An elderly German woman reportedly complained about the Czechs: "If only the Führer saw how the Czech Jews treat us!"[84] Munková's recollection was biased; German Jews felt much the same about Hitler and the Wehrmacht as their Czech fellow prisoners did.

Czech perceptions of German Jews operated with established Czech, anti-German stereotypes and prejudices: Prussianism, militarism, lacking fantasy and individuality, but also a mistaken loyalty to Germany. The last reproach ignored the fact that German Jews were equally thrilled about Allied successes. Additional stereotypes—connected with ideas of the socially underprivileged, dirt, and Eastern Jewry—were general prejudices applied to demarcate one's self from a lesser other. Czech Jews often depicted elderly German inmates as dirty, less to describe a state of cleanliness than to connote a lower class and hence to demarcate themselves.[85] Arnošt Klein's complaint about his boss, Carl Katz, head of the Building Administration, made use of these stereotypes and added on prejudices against Eastern Jews:

> Katz is a prototype of a German Jew in the worst meaning of the word. He is in his 40s, well-fed and dressed tip-top, even though they took all of his belongings. He portrays himself as an uncompromising, tyrannical despot. Yet, he is incapable, arrogant, and vulgar. Karl is the canaille's name! In Bremen, he was an employee in the Jewish Community, and his Bremen dialect smacks of Poland.[86]

But most often the younger Czechs did not mention the German inmates at all. When Czech narrators needed to portray German Jews, their lack of knowledge was fixed through the use of stereotypes. In the first historical account of Terezín, Zdeněk Lederer used stock images that showed he knew nothing about Jews from Northern Germany:

> The Jews from Hamburg, Bremen and Kiel, most of them wearing blue sailors' caps worn by shipping and dock clerks in Germany, used to sit

quietly and solidly in the courtyards. With their blue eyes they watched the confusion around them; their faces were crisscrossed by small reddish veins and their upper lips were adorned by handlebar moustaches. Like sailors, they spat at regular intervals and seemed to long for their tobacco and their pints.[87]

Hamburg Jews in Theresienstadt, who were represented by the older diarist Martha Glass or the young Esther Jonas, who fell in love with a Czech cook, would never have recognized themselves in this image. Lederer's Hanseatic clichés were as far from the reality of Hamburg Jews as were the Czech Jews' general stereotypes about Jews from Germany in Terezín.[88]

Portrayals of Slovak Jews offer another illustration of stereotyping. The 1,447 Slovak Jews arrived during the last five months of the ghetto.[89] For the adults among them, Terezín was only the last and relatively uneventful chapter in their wartime odyssey.[90] In February 1945, the Prague actress and director Vlasta Schönová put together a children's theater performance based on an adaptation of Jan Karafiát's *The Fireflies*. Karafiát's beloved book deals with a community of fireflies whose work it is to come out at night and carry the light so that travelers can see. Schönová staged the children's tale as a statement of Czechness. To achieve a particularly folkish quality, she chose Slovak children as dancers and singers because, as she remembered, they were especially gifted in dancing and singing.[91]

One of the dancers was Eva Berner, a nine-year-old from Topoľčany. Berner believed she was selected because she had attended ballet classes,[92] which she attended because, like many other Slovak Jews, her family was bourgeois. For Schönová, however, the children's dancing was something inherently Slovak. The Czech perception operated with a certain orientalization of the "ethnic," more saliently Czechoslovak, simple, rural Slovaks, who were assumed to be close to nature.[93]

Ethnic categorization in Terezín brought about marked hierarchies. This asymmetry was indicative of the social hierarchy of the inmate community: the younger Czech Jews, who arrived first, generated the master narrative and established hegemony. Many German Jews lamented the condescension of the Czechs, their dislike of German Jews, and the unjust distribution of jobs and resources.[94] Yet the "foreign" prisoners also tacitly accepted the prevailing order of Theresienstadt and thus carried this power structure. We can see it in the knowledge disparity: the German Jews were open to new knowledge, and their depictions of Czech Jews were detailed.

74 THE LAST GHETTO

However, the opposite was the case with the Czech Jews' perceptions of "foreign" Jews; who remained in Czech depictions as clichés or most often, a gap.

Jeunesse Dorée

Young Czech Jews had the highest status in the ghetto and were the social elite. The foremost claim for prestige of the Czech Jews was rooted in the two Aufbaukommando transports of November 24 and December 4, 1941 (the construction detail, abbreviated as AK and J, also AK1 and AK2). They were the first and fourth transports, including altogether 1,342 men from Prague between eighteen and fifty years of age. They had volunteered or had been selected by the Jewish Community to prepare the town for its soon-to-arrive population. Although the men from the Aufbaukommando were in the ghetto only a few weeks, sometimes only days longer than the new arrivals, that was long enough to lay the basis for differentiation. They were perceived as being informed about the infrastructure, having good humor, and being a source of strength. Specialists from the Aufbaukommando acquired leading positions as cooks, physicians, and technicians in the emerging infrastructure, as well as functionaries in the self-administration. The Jewish Community promised that members and their families would be protected from transports, and for a long time members of the Aufbaukommando were indeed spared.[95]

As more and more people arrived, the Aufbaukommando members' importance grew; they were the most senior among the inmates, and most had very good positions, which meant better access to food. They were friends with one another and built solid social networks. Esteem for the Aufbaukommando was an inherent part of the master narrative. Franz Hahn, a young Viennese physician, recalled:

> Theresienstadt was built up by the Czechs from Prague. There was the so-called AK1 and AK2, Aufbaukommando 1 and Aufbaukommando 2. These were the people who built it up under the most difficult conditions. Well, these people were privileged. . . .Well, when someone from the AK1 came, for us, he walked on water. People from AK held such and such important positions. They had it better, they had a small room, and if one had even the tiny hole of one's own, that was already.[96]

The Aufbaukommando always kept its special position, but other young, Czech men shared some of its status because they were part of the same cultural, generational, and geographic group—and in many cases friends with its members.[97] Aufbaukommando veterans helped their friends find good positions or better accommodations. This tie between the Aufbaukommando and other young Czech men was strengthened from June 1942 onward with the arrival of non-Czech Jews. The influx of what were perceived as masses of sick and old people incapable of hard manual labor who were, for the first three months, protected from transports, consolidated the position of the Czech social elite. Their younger age, in contrast to the German and Austrian Jews, added to their prestige.

The social elite led what was, by the standards of the ghetto, a comfortable life: they had "good" jobs as cooks, butchers, or bakers and thus had access to sufficient food; lived in a kumbál or a room shared with friends; were well-dressed; and had access to sought-after cultural events. The young men played soccer, which was admired by thousands of onlookers. Young Czech women were also part of the social elite, yet their membership was defined relationally. They were someone's partners, friends, or sisters. or they were members because their behavior was gender-appropriate for young Czechs.[98] The men flirted, had girlfriends, and had access to a space where they could be intimate with their partners. Their privileged position was legitimized in the master narrative, even if many noticed the blatant social inequalities. The contemporaneous description "jeunesse dorée," depicting a golden youth in the time of uproar and social insecurity, showed that the social elite was viewed with humor and only a touch of criticism.[99]

Political belonging in Theresienstadt was negotiated according to ethnic boundaries. The Zionists in Terezín were a movement of young Czech Jews. The overwhelming majority of Hechalutz were young people who had joined the movement after the occupation or after arriving in the ghetto. Even though the Zionists in Terezín demarcated themselves from the Czecho-Jews, they shared all of the important ethnic, social, cultural, and linguistic markers; the Zionists were part of the social elite. Differentiation among Czech Jews was about the struggle for symbolic capital, and conflicts were not ideological per se. The Shipping Detail, Office for Technical Issues, and Butchers were influential departments of Czecho-Jews.[100] The Zionists controlled large parts of the Youth Care Department and Central Labor, and many parents complained about Zionist propaganda in the youth homes.[101] Controlling the children's education, given the high symbolic capital of children in the

76 THE LAST GHETTO

Terezín legend, was symbolic capital, a power statement. The Zionist youth movement Hechalutz placed its members in advantageous positions and protected them from transports.[102] Patronage among the Zionists was so strong that some nicknamed the organization "protektsionismus."[103]

The members of Hechalutz shared their aesthetic values and sense of friendship with other Czech groups of their generation. The Czecho-Jewish engineers from the Technical Department produced for their head, the Zionist Julius Grünberger, a birthday album drawn by Leo Haas. The aesthetics of this album were identical to the *AZ Album* the Zionist stronghold Central Labor had produced half a year earlier as a keepsake for Jakob Edelstein.[104] The much-loved, Terezín-produced magazine *Šalom na pátek* poked fun at the Aufbaukommando, the Zionists, their opportunist membership, the jeunesse dorée, and other Terezín-specific groups. Tellingly, the three hundred readers of *Šalom na pátek* were nearly all Czech Jews but of various ideological factions, including Zionists, Czecho-Jews, and apolitical people.[105]

The Zionists in Terezín had hardly any "foreign" members. This exclusion applied to large parts of the social life of Czech Jews in Theresienstadt. Individuals who had emigrated to Czechoslovakia in the 1930s were accepted as part of the in-group; the boundary of belonging was drawn at the origin of the transport to Theresienstadt: only those deported here from the Protectorate could become part of the Theresienstadt Zionists. In fact, young Czechs redefined the membership of the Zionist group. Paul Eppstein was actually Zionist, but no one in the Terezín Zionist group perceived him as such.[106] Only those of the "foreign" inmates who were "originally" Czech, like some of the Danish Czech Youth Aliyah youngsters, could be integrated. Two German Jews who were considered members, Berthold Simonsohn and Sonia Okun, were accepted only thanks to their considerable social effort.[107] One of the few Austrian members, Aron Menczer, who had formerly organized the Youth Aliyah, was accepted because the Hechalutz leadership knew and liked him from before. There were many young German, Dutch, and Danish Hechalutz members, but they were not accepted into the movement in Terezín.[108] Leo Säbel, a young Danish German member of the Youth Aliyah, described the Hechalutz members in the ghetto: "No, you could not be a part of it, they kept apart."[109] Eva Fränkel was a German emigrant who was active in a Hechalutz resistance group in the Netherlands. Later she was sent to Terezín, but she only learned about the strong Zionist presence in the ghetto from me in 2001.[110]

Similarly, membership in the Communist group in Terezín consisted only of Czech Jews and a few German and Austrian emigrants.[111] Miroslav Kárný, the only surviving member of the leading triumvirate, remembered that the group attempted in vain to solicit members among non-Czech prisoners. Kárný attributed this failure to the apolitical character of the bourgeois German Jews, broken after years of persecution and too assimilated to grasp the necessity to fight against Germany. Kárný's assessment of German Jews followed the stereotypes with which most Czech Jews viewed the German inmates. Perhaps the Czech Communists' behavior was so coded in Czech culture that it was inaccessible to members of other ethnic groups. Kárný did mention one "Dutch comrade," who, however, remained anonymous because no one remembered his name, a memory lapse that was confirmed when I interviewed the former members of the Terezín Communist Party.

The Elderly Inmates

The disproportionate number of old people in Terezín lived in the worst conditions. Nazi authorities designated Theresienstadt as a destination for people over sixty-five years of age from Germany and Austria, and a large majority of the fifty-seven thousand deportees from those regions were old. Even the groups from the Protectorate, Netherlands, and Denmark were older than the general demographic; younger people were more likely to have emigrated or, in the case of Denmark, had managed to flee during the organized escape in October 1943. Only the Slovaks and Hungarians who came at the end of the war had a younger demographic.

The desperate living conditions for the elderly in Terezín were defined by several decisions of the self-administration. Nowhere did the self-administration define the elderly as less worthy than others, but it did define laborers and children as particularly important.[112] Jakob Edelstein's team established food rations according to worker status.[113] Nonworkers—most of them people over sixty who did not have to work—received the smallest rations. The elderly also had worse accommodations, in the beginning in the attics of the large barracks and later, when the barracks were repaired, in the small houses where the infrastructure was worse. These differences had an impact on the mortality rate: 84 percent of those over sixty years of age who were not transported out died in Terezín.[114] No other group (defined by age or ethnicity) had more than a 11.5 percent likelihood of dying in Terezín.

78 THE LAST GHETTO

Table 2.1 Prisoner Mortality According to Age and Ethnicity

Year of birth	Percent mortality: Czech Jews	Percent mortality: German Jews	Percent mortality: Austrian Jews
1890	3.12	11.50	10.60
1900	1.23	10.90	6.98
1910	0.88	0.00	4.41
1920	0.98	0.35	4.00
1930	0.92	0.00	0.00

There was also no significant difference according to gender. Table 2.1 shows the mortality rates of Czech, German, and Austrian Jews born in 1890, 1900, 1910, 1920, and 1930.[115]

The mortality rate of Czech Jews was significantly lower than that of German and Austrian Jews of the same age; the mortality rate of German Jews was the highest. The younger the inmates were, the less probable it was they would die in Terezín; teenagers had the best chance of survival. This ratio only changed for very young infants.[116] Viktor Kosák, a thirty-one-year-old physician, had just arrived from Prague when he observed generational differences: "It is pleasant when you see your lost friends in front of you healthy and smiling. Of course the acquaintances from the generation of our parents are having a hard time. Thin, tired, white or yellow in the face, suffering. They are dealing with it badly."[117]

If the young paid attention to the seniors, it was often in the very first months, when someone noted how the old people looked out of place or how odd it was to see old women with short hair.[118] Pavel Fischl remarked on the appearance of the elderly:

Now in the only habitable room [. . .] there are 18 grand papas living and seven who are actually already dead from pneumonia and enteritis. Over 40 others live in the remaining uninhabitable holes. They have a water pump and a toilet. In the courtyard . . . behind the pump, there are four tiny flowers. They get the little bit of sunshine that reaches just this spot at noon every day. Then the grand papas go out and they bathe in the sun with their wrinkles, beards, and worried foreheads.[119]

The elderly were treated the worst of all ghetto inhabitants. The seventy-year-old Czech Viennese writer and translator Anna Auředníčková described an incident in which a physician came to her room to visit one of the inhabitants. He entered while the old women were washing themselves; one of them, "entirely naked and wet," became upset and cried. When Auředníčková reprimanded the visitor, he screamed at her: "Who do you think you are, you are only an old woman," using the Terezín slang word, *síchka*. Coming from German *siech* (sick or ailing, usually elderly), the word was used in Terezín to describe the elderly, who were frequently ill. Fischl's unwitting use of the phrase "actually already dead" captured the position of the elderly. In the eyes of the community, they no longer counted.[120] This disregard for the elderly was by no means something that occurred automatically in all ghettos; for instance, in Lodz, Chaim Rumkowski tried to protect the seniors until the September 1942 deportation, when the Germans deported those "unfit to work."[121]

Youth and Children

The status of children in Terezín was the polar opposite to that of the elderly.[122] In February 1942, when men and women still lived in different barracks, the self-administration decided to place children in youth homes. Most parents did bring their children into the homes.[123] The homes were separated according to age, gender, presence of parents (if they were *Geltungsjuden*), and language, that is, Czech and German.[124] Infants under four lived in homes run by the Health Services.[125] The youth homes were rooms in houses that were designated only for children.[126] Danish, Slovak, and those few Dutch children who attended were sent to Czech or German homes. Children received better food from separate kitchens, their rooms were less crowded, and they had better access to washing facilities. Girls sang in Raphael Schächter's choir, and youngsters received music lessons from some of the most admired musicians in the ghetto.[127]

Working for the Youth Care Department was considered prestigious, and new care workers were picked with great scrutiny. There were differences between the homes as well as the children; homes competed with each other to be considered the best. Accordingly, there were "bad homes."[128] Similarly, youth care workers spoke about "interesting children" and "uninteresting children," the latter being the offspring of people in the mica workshop or others considered "Terezín plebs."[129]

80 THE LAST GHETTO

It is frequently and erroneously claimed that only one hundred children survived Terezín.[130] In fact, 2128 children survived Terezín. This mistake goes back to a sloppy reading of a report by Willy Groag, deputy director of the Youth Care Department. Groag stated: "From those 15,000 children who passed through Terezín, in winter 1944/5 only 1,086 children remained. After the end of the war, fewer than 100 children up to the age of 14 [that is, younger than 15] came back from the concentration camps."[131] Margita and Miroslav Kárný criticized this misreading, in which the 1,086 surviving children were left out. They also showed that Groag's calculations were off. They counted 242 children under fifteen who were sent to the East but survived.[132] The Kárnýs also showed that the total number of Terezín children was 9,000 rather than 15,000.[133] Another 800 arrived before April 20, 1945, and yet another 998 children, Jewish and gentile, came with the evacuation transports.[134]

The miscalculated number of young survivors has become part of the postwar master narrative, the legend of Terezín, that depicted the ghetto within the framework of the triumph of the human spirit and thereby reduced the ghetto community to its cultural activities and children.[135] This juxtaposition of care and death had a redemptive effect.

The legend of Terezín conceals the complexities of the reality in which the children lived. Youth care workers and the children themselves employed categorization, ethnic stereotypes, and racism toward their fellow inmates. Czech, and to some extent also German, *Geltungsjuden* were sent to Terezín when they were fourteen years old; their parents stayed behind, protected in mixed marriages. Many children excluded *Geltungsjuden*, and the Youth Care eventually established homes exclusively for them.[136] Other children projected their resentments and fears onto the *Geltungsjuden*. Boys claimed that Jindřich Kolben, whose mother was gentile, had been a member of the Hitler Youth.[137] Others called the *Geltungsjuden* dirty.[138] What is significant about this process of exclusion is not simply that the children othered the *Geltungsjuden*, but rather that they othered those who arrived later. Unless they disposed considerable social capital or were assigned to atypically welcoming collectives, children who arrived after 1943 found it difficult to integrate into the youth homes; the community was already established, and the boundaries were closed.[139] Like all categorizations, the mechanism of exclusion was not connected to a "real" category; the actual gentile parentage was irrelevant. Instead the mark of *Geltungsjuden* was used to differentiate those who did not fit in, whether because of their late arrival or because they came without their families.

Social capital enabled three young women from Prague, Alisa Ehrmannová, Irena Seidlerová, and Hanna Schicková, whose mothers were gentile, not only to fit into the prisoner community but also to participate in othering *Geltungsjuden* and spouses of mixed marriages.[140] All three women, who arrived at Terezín relatively late (July and March 1943 and December 1942, respectively), were, unlike the people whom they criticized, Zionists, or were dating within the in-group. Their kinship group and ideological networks enabled them to fit in.

One stereotype used in the othering of German children and their supervisors was the standard Czech, anti-German prejudice. Hana Fischlová, a young Zionist Czech, youth care worker, depicted the German children as bedraggled, uneducated, unimaginative, and illiterate. In her view they came from poor classes and moved in herds. They would sing only German, Nazi songs, and even when they sang Jewish religious songs, she complained, they used Nazi rhythms and melodies.[141] Rather than providing information about a group, Fischl's portrayal was part of the ethnic gaze, or what anthropologists have termed "ethnicity as seeing as."[142] Irena Seidlerová, a youth care worker, remembered how her Czech pupils put on a show presenting countries of the world. For Poland, they showed the introduction of a new rabbi:

> They staged it and kept bowing and singing. They gave him the task to sing the main prayer and then he sang, completely out of tune, *Baruch atah adonai*.... They kept bowing, it was simply a burlesque. Then they told him, "But, brother, you have to sing to a melody known to God and the people." And then the boy, he started singing to the melody of a German tune sung often in Terezín, Es klappen die Mühlen [*sic*; Es klappert die Mühle]. So he started singing that *Baruch atah adonai* to this tune and they kept bowing and saying "Klip klap."[143]

Avi Fischer, Irena's superior, complained about the mix-up. Fischer worried about criticism from the leaders of the Youth Care Department had an inspector been present. The anecdote has an additional layer: Irena did not know that "Die Mühle," a romantic song by Carl Reinecke, had been appropriated by the *völkisch* movement. It is not clear whether Avi Fischer reprimanded Irena because of the mix-up about the religious content and German tune, or whether he was aware of the song's associations. When German children sang a song from the *völkisch* movement, it was used to

82 THE LAST GHETTO

mark them as German; when Czech children did the same thing, it was seen as the instructor's mistake. When Czech children were uneducated and could not read, it was attributed to the Nazi persecution; illiteracy among German children was viewed as a sign of their German backwardness.

Although children lived in a world somewhat separated within Terezín, they were both objects and subjects of the same categorization processes as everyone else. The coding of children as inherently positive was valid in the eyes of the Czech elite only for Czech children. The "foreign" children were often seen as German first and children second.

German youth were depicted positively only when associated with Czechness, such as in a recollection of the Kolín rabbi Richard Feder:

> Their [Czech youngsters'] singing attracted the German youth and infected them. They also started singing but for obvious reasons they sang only Hebrew songs. And so the Czech and Hebrew singing followed one another. And then someone brought a harmonica, played a waltz, and Czech boys asked the German girls to dance, and so did the German boys, and so they became friends. They had a mutual fate. The German and later the Dutch youth learned a lot of Czech, and I met girls from Berlin and Amsterdam who were fluent in Czech. They liked the Czech songs and they particularly loved singing "Kolíne, Kolíne!"[144]

In this lyrical passage, Feder described a common destiny of the international Jewish youth of Theresienstadt. He used the word "infected" to denote the influence of Czech singing and dancing on the German youth. Significantly, to describe the German youngsters in a positive light, Feder chose a moment of dancing and courting that allowed the German youth to become Czech, later confirmed by their learning Czech.

The constructionist school has argued that ethnicity is "a way of seeing, a way of talking, a way of acting."[145] In this understanding, ethnicity is related to Bourdieu's concept of habitus: ethnicity, culture, and habitus are various expressions of the same category. Indeed, belonging to the Czech group was expressed through culture and language. Language was understood culturally: speaking Czech, or Bohemian or Moravian German, using a specific accent, vocabulary, and syntax. For Czech Jews in Terezín, culture encompassed a plethora of expressions, including forms of gendered behavior, humor, a way of friendship, clothing, conduct, aesthetics, and cultural production.

One important way to express Czech cultural belonging was to evoke rituals and symbols associated with Czechoslovakia. Inmates carved little wooden lions, which were very popular; a double-tailed lion is the Bohemian coat of arms.[146] At the first Christmas in Terezín in 1941, people read out from the Bible of Kralice, the sixteenth-century Bohemian Brethren translation renowned for being anti-Habsburg and pro-Masaryk Czechoslovakia. Reading the Bible of Kralice placed the ghetto in the context of the Czech national struggle. Most Czech Jews in Terezín celebrated Christmas, Easter, and St. Nicholas Day. These holidays played a much more emotional role than Passover and Yom Kippur, although those were also observed.

On St. Nicholas Day in 1943, Arnošt Klein observed a group of boys going around as Nicholas with an angel and the devil. They wore the stars of David on their costume hats.[147] Such ties to Christian holidays sometimes alienated those German inmates who were observant Jews.[148] But these holidays had a cultural rather than a religious meaning; they were connected to notions of home and Czech culture. Some inmates wore sheepskin furs from Moravian Wallachia.[149] Inmates sang songs from the Liberated Theater, the left-oriented modernist theater of Jan Werich and Jiří Voskovec. The first boy born in Terezín, like many after him, was named Tomáš, after the first president of interwar Czechoslovakia, Tomáš Masaryk.[150]

Czechness was often negotiated by way of humor, friendship, and aesthetics. Humor is culturally coded, making some jokes untranslatable to a different culture. Making such jokes, and thus stressing the difference between one's own group and outside people, was a means of maintaining the boundaries in the transnational prisoner society. Czech humor is wry and operates with the notion of the absurd, irony, and the laconic. These traits come to the fore in the certificate of good conduct for Mirko Tůma published in *Šalom na pátek*. Tůma was a writer, friend, and roommate of the journal's editor, Evald Bauer.

> Mirko T ů m a, Ghetto-Goethe, profession: poet,
> marital status: single,
> born: yes, in: bed,
> living in: Terezín BV/125,
> is ~~completely~~ partly law-abiding, has not been sentenced by
> a court and we know of nothing that would contradict his
> ~~good~~ bad reputation.
> This check is issued as an attachment for the change of the
> surname "Tůma" to "T a u s s i g."[151]

84   THE LAST GHETTO

The irony worked with the seemingly banal form of a certificate of good conduct, an absurd thing in the ghetto, where inmates were no longer citizens who needed such confirmations, but where the self-administration overwhelmed inmates with paperwork. Moreover, like some Czech Jews, Tůma's father had changed his surname from the original Taussig, a stereotypically Czech Jewish surname.[152] The response "born in: bed" offered in passing a particularly wry punch line.

Young Czech Jews gathered in a close group of friends, a so-called *parta*.[153] Being a member of a parta meant belonging to a kinship unit. A parta could be mixed-gender or single-sex. The term "parta" originally meant a group of mine workers or a work collective and was adopted during the interwar years by Czech youth to denote a group of friends engaged in scouting and tramping.[154] Inmates often invoked the sportsman ideal, the embodiment of the free Czechoslovak man: athletic, congenial, loyal, cheerful, and easygoing.[155] The enduring self-image of the young Czech Jews in Terezín incorporated humor and a sporting spirit. One tried to cut a good figure, made jokes, did not reflect about the difficult circumstances, and supported the parta.

Indeed, parta was such an important part of belonging it sometimes surpassed familial bonds. In this way, Theresienstadt sometimes recreated kinship groups. Many young people stressed the importance of staying together with others of their age. Scholars have shown how, in the concentration camps, prisoners often created "non biological families."[156] Theresienstadt shows that people had reshuffled and redefined kinship beforehand.[157] Relationships between children and parents were still close, but familial solidarity usually did not extend across three generations. The social elite provided for their parents but not for their grandparents.

Notably, the ideal of a young Czech was a man, not a woman; men were represented as the unmarked part of the gender binary, women as the marked part. In a drawing by the painter Lotka Burešová, a female figure evoked cultural and ethnic belonging.[158] Burešová painted the watercolor in December 1944 as a birthday gift for František Feigl, a framemaker colleague in the Graphic Workshop. The inscription says "Calm and prudence—breathe deeply!," which may have related to the approaching liberation or hinted at the songs of the avant-garde leftist Liberated Theater. But it is the female figure jumping through a frame that draws the viewer's attention. She wears a simplified Czech national costume, and the ribbons on the flowers are the Czech national colors of red, blue, and white. The

Lotka Burešová's watercolor *Klid, rozvahu—z hluboka dýchat!* (Calm and prudence—breathe deeply!) shows a woman in a red skirt, black bodice, and white shirt holding a bouquet with blue and red ribbons. The figure is jumping through a frame, and the skirt is up, showing her entire legs. Courtesy of the Leo Baeck Institute.

woman, who may signify hope, spring, or the Czech nation, is beautiful but also very corporeal. She is nearly naked, exposing arms, cleavage, and legs. The skin has a "healthy" color. Many of these features corresponded with the German Jewish characterizations of Czech Jews. To the Czech viewer, the figure was not naked; rather, her body signified her beauty. Burešová's drawing helps us discern salient values about the Czech self-perception and esthetics: the figure is beautiful because she is corporeal, daring, and very much present. The belonging in the picture was emotionally coded; to this end, Burešová used the female figure, gendered in her beauty and nakedness.

Language

How did language reflect the social field of Terezín? Language is crucial for defining ethnic groups, and how it is used depends on the conditions of the specific social field. Terezín presents an interesting contradiction of power asymmetry: Czech Jews, who stocked the ghetto elite, used German to speak with non-Czech Jews. Czech was used as well and was negotiated as an inside language of the elite. However, the short span of time, not quite three years, in which Czech and other Jews lived together in Terezín was too short a period for non-Czech speakers to acquire Czech. It was long enough for "foreign" inmates to learn some Czech, which is a difficult language, but it was not sufficient for a new linguistic situation to take form. While scholars studying other ghettos, particularly Lodz, have often pointed out the different languages prisoners used, how social hierarchies influenced language praxis has largely remained a lacuna.[159]

It is a much-quoted assumption that in the interwar period, the Czech Jews, especially those in Prague, were bilingual.[160] My findings show that the older generations and the urban population spoke both Czech and German equally well or spoke German as their first language. But younger people, the offspring of mixed marriages in which the gentile parent was Czech, and Jews from the countryside (though not in the western or northern border regions), usually spoke German as a second language or not well enough.[161] Indeed, many young people did not speak German at all.[162] The prevalence of Czech speakers among young Czech Jews was increased after the occupation, when many young German speakers switched to Czech.[163] In Terezín, this tendency became even more pronounced; fifteen-year old Eva

Mahrerová from Troppau/Opava, who spoke only German at home, learned Czech proper in Terezín.[164] Using Czech was often encouraged as something appropriate. Jiří Borský wrote with chalk on a wall of the accommodations of a newly arrived and largely German-speaking Brno transport: "Brno folks, speak Czech!"[165]

But even the use of German could be interpreted, in the correct setting, as Czech, because the meaning of the language in the ghetto changed. Before the war, Czech Jews expressed their groupness but also were seen as German or Czech depending on the language they spoke. Culture and class were secondary. Kinship was not determinative, either; there were families whose members spoke two languages or in which one member spoke one of the languages badly. In Theresienstadt, how these factors played out changed: German-speaking Czech Jews strongly identified and were categorized as Czech. The important shift was the presence of German speakers from Germany and Austria, viewed as "foreigners." Culture, which was expressed in markedly ethnicized terms, class, and age, defined whether one was seen as Czech or "foreign." The defining feature of language thus changed: it was no longer important whether one spoke Czech or German; that is, the language per se was irrelevant. What mattered was the speaker's inflection: the Czech native speaker's accent or the Böhmisch German of Czech German native speakers.

How did the use of language in Theresienstadt play out in everyday life? The common language was German, but Czech was the language of power. Czech Jews spoke both Czech and German with the clerks but switched to German only when prompted to do so.[166] Rolf Grabower, the sixty-year old former permanent secretary of the German Ministry of Finance who worked for the Central Secretariat, complained that during the hectic preparations of the three large transports in May 1944, his "tactless" colleagues spoke only in Czech. Annoyed as he was, he conceded that for many it was a matter of convenience rather than bad manners. Otto Zucker tried to set Grabower at ease, telling him that eventually, Grabower too would learn Czech.[167]

Šalom na pátek was published in a mix of Czech and German, and much of its humor worked with absurd interjections of Czech into German and vice versa. The Czech diarists used words and sentences of the other language than the one in which they were writing when quoting others; Bedřich Kohn even switched from Czech to German after one year.[168] Some non-Czech inmates noted that Czech Jews spoke exclusively Czech among themselves and German only to the foreigners.[169] Many of the younger "foreign" Jews

88 THE LAST GHETTO

learned some Czech.[170] Even older inmates picked up phrases and used them in their diaries, often unintentionally.[171] Who learned which language often reflected the power situation; Willy Mahler made his girlfriend, the Berliner Gertrud Hirsch, learn Czech.[172] In contrast, Karel Fried, a cook from Prague, dated the teenaged Viennese Lucie Drachsler, who did not speak a word of Czech and was glad that Karel's German was excellent.[173]

Boundaries, Connections, and Networks

Terezín was a place of parallel factions; many, if not most, people had little contact outside of their ethnic group. Networks were created according to place of origin.[174] At the same time, there were many ties connecting people across ethnic and class differences. Some people were more likely to have such connections: functionaries, physicians, cooks, attractive women—in general, people with high social capital.

Etta Veit Simon provides a good example of interconnecting networks and how the international prisoner society produced a transnational community.[175] A young, attractive *Geltungsjüdin* woman from an eminent Berlin Jewish family, Veit Simon was sent to Terezín with her older sister Ruth in July 1942; her grandmother and two speech-impaired aunts came later. Etta, who had trained in graphic design, worked in the Graphic Workshop. Introduced by her boyfriend, Bedřich Lerner from Brno, she acted in and produced stage designs for Philipp Manes's theater productions, with their predominantly older bourgeois audience. Her sister Ruth, who was already suffering from tuberculosis before she arrived, was admitted to the Terezín TB clinic directed by František Löwit of Nymburk, a distinguished specialist in pulmonary diseases. Ruth died in July 1943.

Etta lived with her Czech boyfriend in his kumbál; she learned a little Czech, as her boyfriend came from Brno and his first language was German. She was also in touch with Leo Baeck, who had presided over her bat mitzvah. Etta befriended her in-laws, the orthodox Eastern Jewish Smuk couple from Essen. In January 1944, the Smuks' teenaged daughter Mirjam was sent to Terezín from the Dutch transit camp Westerbork; she had spent the previous five years in the Netherlands. Etta took the girl under her wing. Etta's integration into the inmate community bore notes of both her old and new surroundings.

Former Class

In Terezín the old classes collided with a new order. People formerly from the higher classes managed life in the ghetto by creating their own Terezín milieu: a class of the "formerly important." This "former class" accepted the legitimacy of the Terezín elite, confirming their merits in constructing the ghetto. The elderly, formerly important bourgeois prisoners held up the ideal of the athletic, healthy, Jewish youth of the future. Reduced to the lowest jobs (or no positions) in Terezín, this former class confirmed their worth by validating the same core values they had always held: self-possession, good manners, and education—that is, cultural capital and habitus.[176] Thus, the former, upper class strove to demonstrate refinement in the Terezín quotidian.

They exercised their class in terms of old codes of conduct. The old class was also expressed through self-control, for example by not resorting to theft as others in the ghetto did.[177] For the elderly, adapting to Theresienstadt while holding onto their habitus could present in specific forms; Max Rosner was deeply impressed by the "noble decorum and quiet greatness with which the spouse of *Kommerzialrat* Julius Berger carried her difficult fate. Once, when greeted by a fellow inmate with 'Madam *Kommerzialrat*,' she answered: 'Please just call me Mrs. Berger. All of us here are just suffering Jews.'"[178] What for some younger people could be a laughable insistence on an honorific, for many of the older bourgeois inmates represented key social codes that prescribed manners and thus rank.

For members of this class, their former status translated into their current, Terezín status. People who used to be important talked about their accomplishments and positions. Former bankers, attorneys, journalists, civil servants, professors, and physicians told stories from their past, which in retrospect appeared particularly illustrious. Such storytelling was one of the cornerstones in the making of this Terezín class; narrating one's important past was an act of belonging. Former notables surrounded themselves with the same, confirming one another's past status as "better" people. Tales of the past gave birth to a notorious Terezín joke: "A dachshund in Terezín says: back in the day I was a St. Bernard in Prague."[179]

While there were few Eastern Jews in Theresienstadt, the way they were imagined sheds light on how the Terezín inmates struggled to come to terms with the anti-Jewish persecution. The Eastern Jews were the opposite of the Jewish Central European bourgeoisie. There were deep prejudices on the part of the old Germans toward the arriving Eastern Jews.[180] Inmates portrayed

90   THE LAST GHETTO

the Eastern Jews in Terezín as cunning, primitive, unreliable, and not com-radely. They were accused of shady dealings; dressed differently; had dif-ferent names and conspicuous, nonrefined bodies; and spoke with an accent, and they were viewed as having poor hygiene.[181] Supposedly, the Eastern Jews were unrefined and without taste,[182] implying that they came from the lowest classes and were bad characters, unpleasant, or simply criminals.[183]

Many of these resentments resonated in a note by Arnošt Klein, complaining of unethical easterners: "Eastern Jews, of course, so pious and orthodox, they make people who are dying promise incredible sums (in food, clothing, money, watches, and much more) against daily praying of the 'Kaddish' for them for up to eleven months after their passing. Whether the prayers for the dead are even offered is more than questionable."[184] Klein also brought up their lack of local roots and predilection for "the murky waters of cronyism. I have never known that among the Jews there are such incredible plebs. I have never loved them, the dear Yids, those folk comrades coming [hergekommen] from the East via Vienna or Berlin!"[185] The narrators never specified where the Eastern Jews came from (there were no transports from Poland to Terezín) or if they came from the narrator's own country. Manfred Strassburger cataloged the ethnicities present in Terezín ending with the Eastern Jews: "Let's not talk about the Polish chapter. We may talk about it elsewhere. After all, there were some fairly decent people among the Poles, but as they say, you would need a lantern to find them."[186]

The ascription "Eastern Jews" in Terezín was an imagined type. Some leading members of the Hechalutz were young men from Poland, Subcarpathian Rus', and Eastern Slovakia.[187] Although people around them were aware of their accent and "Jewish" looks, the former was not brought up, and the latter were interpreted as beautiful and Jewish in a good way.[188] The beloved first Elder of the Jews, Jakob Edelstein, grew up in Galicia; he had an accent and unlike most Czech Jews, was Orthodox. This feature was somewhat off-putting to some, and to resolve the "stigma," Edelstein was usually depicted as "Czech" or "from Teplice"; his Polish or-igin was downplayed and equated with being religious, Zionist, or "loving the Jewish people."[189]

In contrast, the Eastern Jewish background of Benjamin Murmelstein, the detested last Elder, was employed to exclude him from the community. As a rabbi, Murmelstein was observant, but he was far more liberal than Edelstein. Murmelstein was portrayed as cunning; speaking with an Eastern accent; and possessing a bad character, an unnatural sex drive, and an unrefined body.[190]

The positive figure, Edelstein, was not interpreted as an Eastern Jew, but in describing the negatively marked Murmelstein, people stressed his Eastern Jewish traits. This description of Murmelstein's Jewishness enabled prisoners to frame him negatively.

In Terezín, Eastern Jews were construed as the ultimate other. Eastern Jews constituted the "real" Jews, the marked part of the binary: assimilated Jew (unmarked, normal) versus Eastern Jew (marked, negative). Antisemitic prejudice fed the negative image. By using the Eastern Jews as a counter-group, the Central or Western European Jews could appear non-Jewish, or Jewish in a good, unmarked way.

Gender and Categorization

Gender is a key tool in the functioning of ethnic, social, or other groups. However, sociological and anthropological scholarship on nationality has only rarely engaged the category of gender, which is kept in "a 'separate sphere,' removed from what count as the big questions in the field," mirroring the situation in Holocaust studies.[191] Yet gender operated in Terezín as an expression of core identity, an ethnic and social opener, marker of boundaries, and expression of othering.

Gender and sexuality are a key element of basic human connections. This holds true independently of the sexual potential of the spectator: nubile young people, especially women, attract attention and provide an opening for interaction. Non-Czech Jews almost always commented on the attire and looks of young Czech women: their hair, clothes (they wore pants), and activities (they sunbathed partially undressed). There was a Terezín fashion: skirts and dresses sewn together from blankets, playing with the patchwork, a certain way of wearing a headscarf, necklaces and amulets produced in the ghetto workshops. The fact that the Czech women wore makeup, in particular lipstick, was most often commented upon by nearly all "foreign" prisoners.[192]

Gender identity was central for the inmates, in particular due to the incarceration, but the definition differed culturally. Czechoslovak women had not been the only ones in the interwar period to wear makeup. But to other ethnic groups, makeup was not as intrinsically connected to femininity. Appearing made up, coiffed, and well-dressed was an affirmation of self and provided women with a sense of control. The younger Czech men validated their masculinity through a form of friendship, humor, sports, and being

92 THE LAST GHETTO

sportsmanlike, and also through certain patterns of dating and sexuality. These behaviors demonstrate the immense importance of gender identity, particularly in extreme, dehumanizing situations.[193]

Female or female-coded figures can be used to express positive or negative features of a group. To describe Eastern Jews, Zdeněk Lederer used gendered figures: "There were prolific Polish Jewesses with large families who had made Vienna their home during the First World War and Viennese spivs, smelling of haircream and scent, obliging and up to all sorts of tricks, always on the make."[194] In addition to the characteristics of homelessness and cunning, the Eastern Jews in Lederer's example were othered by their deviant gender: they had large families, coded as proletarian by the middle class. Their men were perfumed, thus marked as female, their masculinity further undermined by their deviousness and lack of backbone.[195] In contrast, rabbi Richard Feder's positive memory of the dancing and singing "foreign" youth was linked to their sexual potential.

Love, Dating, and Sexuality

Love and sexuality were important in the ghetto, intrinsically linked to its societal hierarchies. Intimacy and attachment were central coping mechanisms. Sex functioned both as a normalizer and a validation of prestige. People dated, fell in love, and sought protection and emotional comfort; they did not want to be alone in the ghetto. This free take on sexual mores was on a continuum with prewar Czech practices.[196]

In order to be intimate, most couples sought a place of their own. Some couples never had sex because they had no privacy. Erika, then a twenty-four-year-old from Prague, voiced her frustration; she and her husband, who did not survive, were among those who did not have this opportunity: "[B]ecause when women are fighting for their men and for the happiness to experience marital life on a bunk bed, then they are fighting for their dream. Of course, some people like the cooks had various advantages, they would meet with their wives in the attics [kumbáls], but in the ghetto, Jirka and I probably never had sex, not once. Sometimes we made out, but there were people everywhere, so nothing else was possible."[197]

The man nearly always provided the place for a sexual encounter. Some male rooms had rosters indicating when any of the inhabitants could have the room for himself; some men rented a room from someone.[198] Others had sex in the room while roommates were present, building walls from blankets around the bunk bed.[199] The kumbál was the ideal solution, giving birth to a Terezín hit, *Mit Dir in einem Kumbal, zwei Herzen und ein Raum*: (To be with you in a kumbál, two hearts and a room).[200] A man with a kumbál gained prestige in the eyes of his friends; he could invite women to be intimate and thus had a sexual life.[201] Not every sexual encounter took place in the context of a relationship, and not every romantic relationship was sexual. There were various ways to confirm the seriousness of the relationship: the couple could give each other presents or introduce their friends to the partner, or the man might walk the woman to her accommodation after a night together. We know these habits from our society; in Terezín, these patterns reflected the ethnic and gender asymmetries. How serious a relationship grew to be and whether it became sexual, how the man treated the woman, and how his friends perceived her depended on ethnicity and thus on power relations.

Most Czech Jews dated within their ethnic group. Many young people became couples before the deportation, marrying so as not to be deported alone.[202] In the ghetto, young people were often introduced to their partners through the parta. Dina Gottliebová met her fiancé Karel Klinger through her best friend Růžena, who was invited by Karel's brother to have chocolate pudding.[203] Among the friends of Eva Mändlová, a young Czech woman who took care of the sheep, many couples emerged.[204] People married in Theresienstadt so that, if they were deported, their family unit would be defined with the spouse, rather than with parents.[205] Others divorced, because they met someone else or because they did not want to be tied to their spouses. Eighteen-year-old Margot Lifmann, a German emigrant to the Netherlands, remembered that in Theresienstadt, her father Alfred met and fell in love with another woman, and her parents separated.[206] However, it seems that most Terezín relationships among Czech prisoners, if both survived, resulted in lasting postwar marriages.

Interethnic relationships in Terezín were frequent, and interethnic sexual encounters were even more numerous. Quite a large number, if not the majority, of young, single, non-Czech women dated Czech Jews.[207] Esther Jonas, a young woman from Hamburg, met her boyfriend, the Czech cook Hanuš Leiner, soon after arrival. Seventy years later, she recalled with a twinkle in her eye that the Czech men were "great charmers." They also made fun of the young foreign woman; the first word they taught her in Czech was *hovno* (shit).[208]

94 THE LAST GHETTO

In most interethnic relationships, the man was Czech and the woman "foreign." Interethnic relationships were a poignant imprint of power hierarchies and represented a trade-off. The Czech men invested symbolic and economic capital. The "foreign" women invested social capital in the form of attractiveness and a readiness to fit in within the social field of their partners. The women were often very attractive or in some other way particularly feminine, and they were often depicted as weak and dependent.[209] The relationships between Czech men and non-Czech women were nearly always sexual.[210] The only known relationship between a Czech woman and a "foreign" man demonstrates this pattern in reverse. The Zionists Truda Guttmannová from Olomouc and Berthold Simonsohn from Berlin met in the Youth Care Department, where Guttmannová was a care worker and Simonsohn the deputy director. Simonsohn used his charm to get into the Zionists' good graces. Simonsohn and Guttmannová became a couple; their relationship, however, remained platonic.[211]

An exception in these interethnic relationships was Danish men who dated Czech women and other non-Danes.[212] The material conditions of the Danish prisoners improved significantly after March 1944, when the Danish government started sending food parcels.[213] Compared with the other inmates, the Danes were regarded as wealthy; their packets gave rise to the nickname "bacon Danes."[214]

Being on the lower rank of the Terezín hierarchy marked the "foreign" women for the Czech elite as sexually available, while their inferior status did not create expectations to legitimize the connection. Many Czech men flirted aggressively with "foreign" women. One of the first Czech sentences the non-Czech women learned was the catcall "Slečno, dejte mi hubičku" (Miss, give me a kiss).[215] Hilde Nathan was a nineteen-year-old from Cologne; a shy teenager, she was "young" for her years. She started working as the secretary of Mr. František from the Central Supply Department, who was sixteen years her senior. When they went to pick up groceries, the cooks treated her as fair game, calling her "Du schönes Kind vom Rhein" (you pretty child of the Rhine).[216] She did not know how to react, until her boss chastised the cooks and told them Hilde worked for him and they ought to let her be. He later suggested he would walk her home, where he kissed her, also addressing her as pretty child of the Rhine. Nathan was upset and overwhelmed; František let go of her, remarking that it was too bad she was still so young. She continued working for František and eventually developed a crush on him. She then found out that her boss was no longer interested—and in fact, had had a lover all the while.[217]

If the relationship between a Czech man and a "foreign" lover became serious, she was often integrated into his social circle and expected to learn Czech.[218] Moreover, the material benefits that the German or Austrian women derived from these relationships did not always reach their parents. The young Hamburger Esther Jonas was able to profit from the cultural life in Theresienstadt, while her mother, a doctor, never went to any concerts. Esther had access to the cultural events through her Czech boyfriend's friends, but that was for her, not her mother.[219] The Czech friends were not always accepting of their friends' choices. Valtr Weiss, a twenty-one-year-old from Prague, met and fell in love with a young woman from Saarland. "My relatives did not want to see it; they said she had a bad reputation. She was a frightfully nice girl. I had her registered as my fiancée, to protect her against transports and so that no one would say anything."[220] If one's own ethnic group criticized one's choice of the "foreign" partner, this critique was framed as the woman's lack of sexual integrity. Tellingly, the criticism was always directed against the woman, even if she was of the same ethnic group.

Queer Conduct

Same-sex desire in Terezín was stigmatized, and the community exhibited considerable homophobia.[221] In September 1944, Gonda Redlich discharged a youth care worker because she was lesbian: "Two youth care workers worked together. The one loved the other with a pathological love. I was forced to dismiss her," he noted.[222] In March 1945 the head nurse, Marianne, was expelled because she was caught with a lover. The story was reported by her acquaintance, the young Dane Ralph Oppenhejm: "I have not seen Marianne. Poor thing, she is thrown out from the hospital because she had [sexual] relations one night with a woman in there. A patient passed by and saw it, and surprise, surprise. Yes, it does not come as a surprise to me."[223] Oppenhejm was gay himself; a charming young man, he was the only homosexual whose sexual orientation was accepted. Ralph put considerable energy into ingratiating himself with those around him, especially women. In Terezín, he was alone; his boyfriend was in Sweden. By employing his social capital—being nice and charming, and not being sexually active—Oppenhejm became an "acceptable" homosexual.

96 THE LAST GHETTO

Another gay man from the Danish group was not accepted: the clown Harry Hambo Heymann, a German emigré to Denmark. Hambo's specialty was female impersonations. People bringing up Hambo's sexual orientation did so negatively, questioning his masculinity and describing him as unpleasant and tacky. Finally, Fredy Hirsch offers an example of the double stigmatization as homosexual and foreign. Hirsch was a gay, charismatic, German Jewish athletics teacher who had immigrated to Czechoslovakia in 1936. He was a prominent Zionist and deputy director of the Youth Care Department.[224] Although he was revered, in some instances his foreignness and/or sexual orientation were brought up as criticism.[225] Inmates gossiped that Hirsch was sexually attracted to children; one boy recalled that Fredy groped him before the deportation.[226] Children would sometimes make fun of Hirsch's accent and effeminate ways.[227] One particularly deep-rooted homophobic resentment is the presumed pedophilia of all homosexuals. The denouncement of pedophilia served to stigmatize Hirsch's sexual orientation, akin to marking him as feminine.

Homophobia in Terezín presented a certain rupture of prewar developments. There had been a lively gay scene and active Czechoslovak and German movements for the decriminalization of homosexuality. Acceptance was growing, and many of the activists were Jewish.[228] This development weakened in the 1930s, with the Nazi takeover in Germany and the economic and Sudeten crises in Czechoslovakia.[229] The prisoner society in the camps and ghettos generated a brutal homophobia that interpreted transgressive sexuality as a symbol of everything that was distorted. The homophobia was so stigmatizing that none of the queer inmates who were sexually active in the ghetto ever gave postwar testimony. Through 2018, Ralph Oppenhejm has been the only gay prisoner from Terezín who has done so.[230]

The Holocaust Experience and Jewishness

The heterogeneous prisoner experience of Theresienstadt did not produce a sense of common Jewishness. But how did Theresienstadt influence the inmates' perceptions of the meaning of being Jewish? There was a wide array of opinions, partly contingent on the various Terezín groups, factions, and milieus. Nevertheless, there were three main opinions: pride in the Jewish nation, realization that the Jewish nation was a construction, and shame.

The first sentiment, building on the master narrative of the ghetto, interpreted Terezín as a Jewish triumph. Petr Lang, a young, ardent Zionist, noted: "Terezín meant for me the significant success of the Zionist movement because people behaved there in a good way. In Auschwitz, they turned into monsters."[231] Several older inmates who were not Zionists reached a similar conclusion: the experience of expulsion and Terezín reinforced the inmates' Jewishness. This interpretation would persist in the postwar period as part of the larger Zionist master narrative that interpreted the Holocaust as meaningful because it led to the founding of the State of Israel.[232]

Another group of inmates believed that Terezín revealed there was no such thing as Jews. People pointed out the differences in culture and in "ethnic appearances." Czech Jews were different from German Jews; those from the North Sea were different from those from the Rhine and yet again from the Viennese.[233] Some concluded there was no "Jewish race."[234] German Jews were keen to point out that the inmate community showed hardly any "Jewish features."[235] Bedřich Hoffenreich set out to find the "Jewish looking people" and found none. Yet some inmates with fair hair occasionally found themselves distrusted by those around them or even accused of being informers: looks did work to draw lines of ethnic and social demarcation.[236]

The Communists' view went even further. Miroslav Kárný believed that "it was absurd to speak about a unified Jewish nation."[237] The Communist group in the ghetto published a brochure discussing their position on Zionism, which offered a more tolerant interpretation, informed by Stalin's view on nationalities. Kárný remembered: "We did not deny the existence of the Jewish nationality, recognized by both Czechoslovakia and the Soviet Union, though we did not understand it in the Zionist sense of the word, the mystically racist character of which we analyzed."[238] The Communists Karel Reiner and Kárný placed their experience outside of the confines of the ghetto and saw themselves as participants in the Second World War.

A small number of usually older inmates were disappointed by behavior in Terezín and saw the ghetto as a human failure. Bedřich Kohn lamented:

> There is nothing new, only "průser" [Czech colloquialism for that something went very wrong]. Otherwise, politically inside the ghetto the mood is quite wretched, the Czecho-Jews against the German Jews, against the Zionists and contra and Zionists among themselves. If you ask someone for something, they only help you if you belong to the same "party."

98   THE LAST GHETTO

Otherwise all pleas are in vain, unless you can pay. How can there be so many differences, injustices and indecencies in a ghetto![239]

A former Prague high school teacher, Artur Pollak, sighed: "Our people are the salt of the earth. But so much salt at once?"[240] Some inmates were afraid that inmates' behavior had confirmed antisemitic prejudices. In October 1943, Arnošt Klein proclaimed, "When this is over, we will have to cut off all things Jewish."[241] Rolf Grabower repeatedly declared that Terezín would lead to a "second antisemitism" and observed that the Ghetto Court pursued antisemitic insults for pedagogical purposes.[242]

Thinking about Jewishness revealed the heterogeneity and differences of opinion, and the Terezín inmates were well aware of it. Describing the summer of 1942, the singer Bedřich Borges remembered: "When they moved the people—I don't want to say the Jews, but people—from the barracks into the town [. . .]."[243] This aside demonstrates the foremost conclusion of Terezín inmates: theirs was a human experience. People realized that Jews, a perpetual minority, who "always had to pay attention to not waking antisemitic resentments," were now among themselves. They could and did behave as a normal society, with all of the ups and downs of a forced community. Thus, arriving in Terezín because they were Jewish, many realized that Terezín made them, in the last instance, human rather than Jewish— an observation that may apply to most Holocaust victims. The diversity of opinions was an inherent part of it.

Conclusion

Inmate society in Terezín was both deeply divided and interconnected, based on ethnicity, time of arrival in the ghetto, age, and social capital. At the same time, the community was remarkably coherent and subscribed to a master narrative that endowed incarceration with a meaning. Young Czech Jews were the social elite; elderly and non-Czech prisoners, especially the German and Austrian Jews, were the lowest class. Kinship shifted; many younger people identified with groups of same-age friends as their new kinship unit.

Ethnicity was the most important categorization in Terezín. Inmates employed the ethnic gaze, examining members of different groups in a way that interpreted all traits as fundamentally ethnic. The inmate community expressed belonging in cultural terms, in modes of conduct, rituals, and how gender was expressed. To exclude others, inmates employed stigmatization that connected to notions of an underclass, Eastern Jews, inappropriate gender roles, and deviant sexuality. Sexuality is particularly revealing of the social stratification and gender roles in Terezín; gender roles became more conservative, especially for women. The Terezín prisoners employed a binary vision that differentiated between Czech and "foreign" prisoners. This view was put forward by the "local" Czechs and came to be shared by many of the German, Austrian, and Danish prisoners. Class in the ghetto became ethnicized, and ethnicity linked to class. This interplay in Theresienstadt is germane for further research on both these categories, usually viewed separately.

3

The Age of Pearl Barley

Food and Hunger

When I observe the times going by
I ask myself, what keeps people alive?
As from the helpings they let us have
You may well die, but cannot live.

Corned beef we're fed quite often just now
Yet seeing so tiny crumbs in my bowl
I must keep asking myself full of guilt
Why for such helping an ox was killed?[1]

Food was extremely scarce in the Nazi ghettos, noted Hans Hofer, a cabaret artist from Brno and Vienna. Amid wartime shortages, German authorities allocated the least sustenance to Jews. Hunger became a defining experience for the inmates. The starvation of Jews in the ghettos in the General Government (a German-occupied zone of the former Polish state) was a product of deliberate Nazi food politics, which marked Jews as "useless eaters," allotting them the least amount of food.[2] Yet beyond this assertion, we know little about how hunger and access to food shaped ghetto society.

In a society characterized by a shortage of food, nourishment gained in importance, and access to food translated into power. Most inmates experienced hunger; for many it became a central aspect of their imprisonment biographies. At the same time, however, distribution of food varied widely, and it separated inmate society into three groups. A large number of inmates were rarely hungry. A somewhat larger group experienced hunger but not to a degree that affected their health. A similarly sizable part of the prisoner population had far smaller food rations, and most people in this group died. How food was distributed reflected the priorities of the institution that did

The Last Ghetto. Anna Hájková, Oxford University Press (2020). © Oxford University Press.
DOI: 10.1093/oso/9780190051778.001.0001.

the distributing, whether it was a German authority or an office of the Jewish self-administration.

A close reading of access to food, perceptions of the hungry, and cultural notions of diet offers new insights into inmate society in Terezín. With respect to food distribution, the self-administration categorized prisoners according to their working status. Nonworkers—mostly people over sixty to sixty-five years of age (the boundaries moved over time and differed with gender)—received so little that most of them died of diseases related to lack of food. These people made up the overwhelming majority of the thirty-four thousand deaths in Terezín. How food was distributed indicated how people were valued in the ghetto's self-understanding; the elderly were placed at the bottom. In contrast to "normal" twentieth-century social beliefs, elders were no longer figures to be respected and revered. Moreover, people viewed those who appeared hungry and deprived as repulsive and not belonging to the community. Sharing food established and defined relationships between individuals as well as kinship groups. Food sharing was deeply steeped in gender, and the newly grown importance of food made such gendered exchanges particularly meaningful. How people dealt with food revealed the new codes of conduct: it was significant how and what people ate, which foods they viewed as delicacies, what eating behaviors became the "new normal," and how and under what circumstances stealing became acceptable.

Current thinking about famines rests on the findings of Amartya Sen. In his study of the Bengali famine, Sen pointed out that famines are only rarely caused by failed harvests.[3] Rather, they are human-made: failed distribution, war, occupation, and conflicts among the distributing parties in combination with rumors of a possible food shortage can lead to an accumulation of problems, areas cut off from food, and increasing distribution challenges. Sen's observation that famine is caused by only a slightly lower level of food lends a discerning view to the reasons behind the elderly population's high mortality rate in Terezín. In addition, for a long time there has been a tradition of perceiving the hungry as somehow morally flawed and not fully human.[4]

Famine scholars, physicians, and nutritionists have based much of their research on observations from the ghettos and concentration camps.[5] According to their findings, most famine victims die from a mixture of factors: reduced calorie intake and decreased food variety, which leads to vitamin deficiency and, consequently, susceptibility to various diseases. Women deal better with starvation because their normal nutriment intake is

102 THE LAST GHETTO

already smaller, due to their lesser weight and body mass. With correspondingly reduced rations, women fare better than men. Such findings coincide with the conclusions of scholars who study gender and the Holocaust.[6] Children, on the other hand, infants in particular, are the first to die. Their deaths are not necessarily a consequence of food misdistribution, such as parents eating their children's food; rather, they have weaker immune systems than adults.[7]

Centralized Food Distribution

Food in Terezín was distributed by the self-administration. Inmates received lunch and dinner from centralized kitchens, each of which cooked for several thousand people. One or several blocks in the ghetto included a kitchen where, based on one's address, inmates went to pick up their food.[8] Every prisoner was given a food card, and upon collecting his or her food, the card was stamped. In addition, prisoners received bread, margarine, and sugar from their house or room elders and later, from central distribution points.[9] People made their own breakfasts from their assigned domestic rations. This centralized system in Theresienstadt was both similar to and different from those of other ghettos: Bialystok, Lodz, and Warsaw also relied on prisoner registration with the Jewish Council. In Bialystok, the provisions also came from the Germans, while in Warsaw food came via smuggling, and in Lodz by barter.[10]

In November and December 1941 the food came from the confiscated and collected provisions that people had brought in for themselves. Over the next few months, the SS arranged for bakeries in the surrounding area to deliver bread and other goods. The external bread was often of poor quality and could not be stored for long or it would become moldy; it is likely that suppliers took advantage of the prisoner clients and delivered low-quality goods.[11]

Throughout 1942 one of the central transformations that took place in the ghetto was the establishment of its autarky: establishing the delivery chain, building and installing kitchens, finding cooks and bakers among the prisoners, and organizing food distribution. By May 1942 the Technical Department had rebuilt the old military kitchens, using bricks from the fortress walls, and installed stoves and ovens.[12] The Jewish Community in Prague supplied sufficient cooking utensils; now the ghetto was better suited

THE AGE OF PEARL BARLEY 103

to supply the tens of thousands of inmates. Bakeries in the ghetto started producing their own bread that could be stored for longer periods—a crucial advantage when people received bread once every three days. Bread soon became a central item for trade.[13]

Almost all of the costs of the ghetto were paid for by the Central Office in Prague, and all the food was bought from the outside. Those Theresienstadt inmates who worked for the Economic Department earned the SS some funds, but these covered just a fraction of the costs. The ghetto was largely maintained by stolen Jewish money; the Emigration Fund of the Prague Central Office opened an account at the Böhmische Escompte-Bank, an affiliated company of the Dresdner Bank, and transferred into it money from the confiscated Jewish property. Moreover, money from the Heimeinkaufsverträge flowed here. The Reichsvereinigung transferred funds, altogether about 109 million Reichsmark, to the account of the Emigration Fund at the Böhmische Unionbank (an affiliated company of the Deutsche Bank).[14] The Austrian counterpart of the Emigration Fund also transferred looted capital to the Böhmische Escompte-Bank, which was according to the last Elder of the Jews, Benjamin Murmelstein, about 8 million Reichsmark.[15] Other income came from selling goods stolen from the new arrivals (jewelry, watches, money), which Heinrich Scholz then transferred to the savings bank in nearby Roudnice, which regularly passed it on to Böhmische Escompte-Bank in Prague. Every three months, Scholz took the stolen jewels to a jewelry expert in the Central Office, who then passed them on to the bank.[16] Apart from the looted money, the Jewish Community in Prague collected among the provincial communities all kinds of equipment for the ghetto, such as mattresses and furniture.[17] The Reich Association also sent utensils, albeit less often. The ghetto also owned lands that were worked by the people in the Agriculture; the harvested goods went to the SS (see map "Terezín Ghetto and surroundings," with lands belonging to the ghetto in horizontal hatches).

Orders and shopping for food and supplies were never done directly by the self-administration, but always via the SS. Schliesser, head of the Economical Department, met daily with the commandant and Rolf Bartels, his counterpart, and discussed the ghetto's needs with them in minute detail. Bartels then sent out the mail orders. The ghetto was an enormous customer, ordering from dozens of firms in Roudnice, Kladno, Prague, and elsewhere: food, wood, components for building, sanitary pads, and much more.[18] Two Jewish functionaries, Jiří Vogel and Rudolf Bergmann, regularly went to buy technical supplies in Roudnice.[19]

104   THE LAST GHETTO

In this respect Theresienstadt differed from Warsaw, where the Jewish Council had to raise the funds themselves.[20] The prescribed amounts were supposed to be the same as those of the population in the Protectorate. However, the quality was much worse, as were the food deliveries to the Warsaw ghetto; the gentile suppliers usually brought supplies they could not sell elsewhere.[21] Moreover, certain nutrients were not supplied at all: there were no eggs or butter, and very little meat.[22] Unlike Protectorate inhabitants, inmates could not eat at restaurants. In addition, Rolf Bartels of the Economic Department in the SS headquarters, assisted by the Jewish functionary Karel Schliesser, sold part of the food deliveries on the side, in particular the meat; Bartels kept the money and in exchange gave the Economic Department some advantages.[23] A small amount of vegetables came from Vienna, where the Jewish Community had grown them at a cemetery.[24] Although more than one thousand prisoners worked in the Agriculture Department—the ghetto had a large farming enterprise—the produce was destined for Germans, eaten by members of the SS headquarters, or sent to Prague or Germany. Only later, in 1944, were inmates allowed to grow produce on small allotments on the outskirts of the ghetto near the Stabsgarten (former military garden). They set up tiny gardens wherever the fortification architecture allowed. However, only a small group of inmates succeeded in gaining access to land.

The kitchens carried out the largest part of food distribution. Prisoners were assigned a kitchen to pick up their food according to their residence; some kitchens had a better reputation than others. There were altogether eleven kitchens; the Kavalier barracks held the largest one.[25] In March 1944 alone, the kitchen distributed more than 1.1 million meals. Food was distributed between 11:00 a.m. and 2:00 p.m.; everyone had to bring their own containers and utensils. People waited in lines, easily for hours since, on average, a kitchen was responsible for feeding four thousand people. The wait times caused problems, especially during the winter months. Once one's turn came up, the next in line presented his or her food card and received a portion according to his or her category. People ate lunch on the street, in their accommodations, and later, in the park or on the wall lamps. Those who ate their meals on site could wait—and many did—for second helpings.[26] Dinners were more often eaten reheated in their rooms.

Compared with other ghettos or most of the concentration camps, Terezín was an exception with regard to the nature of the food distribution. There were two warm meals a day, and two courses for lunch. Moreover, the cooking was apparently quite lovingly done, and meager as the food was, inmates often noted that it tasted good.[27] The cuisine was mainly influenced by Czech cuisine and featured dishes such as watery lentil soup, buns with chodeau (sabayon) sauce, semolina dumplings, and pearl barley.[28] The meals were heavy in starch and low in fats and proteins, provided very little fiber, and included almost no fruits or vegetables. The fats were all saturated, fatty acids: margarines produced in the 1940s did not yet contain "healthy" unsaturated fats. Potatoes were a consistent menu item.[29] Because of the long cooking times owing to the numbers who had to be served and the long—and frequently poor-quality—storage, vitamin C, otherwise present in potatoes, was severely reduced.

In addition to the centralized kitchens, the accommodation often offered a small room or a stove that served as a kitchen for the preparation or warming up of "private" food, overseen by an appointed cook. Some houses, however, did not have this option. Residents of these houses tried to acquire a small stove, cooked at a family member's who had access to cooking facilities, or had to make do without cooking. Cooking facilities were a central social point in the house; people had to agree about time and space for cooking as well as whose wood or coal would be used. Often these rooms also served additional functions as washrooms or as accommodation.[30]

Just as the cooks prepared a selection of Czech cuisine that became part of Terezín tradition, the inmates created recipes of their own, which could be prepared with the limited options for cooking and required almost no ingredients: toasted bread; toasted sliced potatoes; egg- and milk-free pancakes; and tarts prepared from bread, sugar, ersatz coffee, and margarine. Color became an important feature in lieu of other characteristics: white (margarine) and black (surrogate coffee) layers in the tart, or sliced bread decorated with caraway seeds, paprika, and mustard (a surrogate for the beloved Czech *chlebíčky* or canapés).[31]

Food Categories

On May 17, 1942, the self-administration introduced the central feature of the Terezín food distribution: ration categories. The population was divided into three categories of bread distribution: S, N, and K, which denoted (respectively) *Schwerarbeiter* (hard laborers, 500 grams of bread a day), *Normalarbeiter* (normal workers, 375 grams), and *Kranke* (nonworkers,

106   THE LAST GHETTO

333 grams). It was possible for men as well as women to be classified as hard laborers. This categorization had been in the planning stage for quite some time; it was implemented two weeks before the arrival of elderly Jews from Germany and Austria.[32] We can only speculate about whether the proximity of the dates was coincidental; by early May, the Czech Jewish functionaries knew that German Jews would arrive.[33] People over sixty years of age (this was later changed to sixty-five for men and sixty for women, and in November 1944 to seventy) did not have to work and hence were categorized as nonlaborers. Therefore, I define "elderly" as individuals over sixty. Later on, a fourth category was added: L (*Leichtarbeiter*), for short-term workers.[34] One month later, the same categorization was applied to meals distributed from the kitchen.[35]

The division of food affected more than just the food rations and cooked meals. Whether one was categorized as S, N, L, or K could also determine additional access to food and one's ability to procure extra rations either daily, twice a day, or weekly. For instance, men from the Shipping unit and bakers received extra portions, as did children or members of the Council of Elders.[36]

In 1943 or 1944, the self-administration assessed daily nourishment: hard laborers received 2,141calories, normal workers 1,630, children 1,759, and nonworkers 1,487.[37] However, these rations were only the ideal amounts. The nonworkers also received the smallest variety of food: they were given no meat, milk, flour, potatoes, or barley. (Admittedly, the official weekly assignments of milk, meat, and barley were microscopic.) Access to additional food rations changed over time.[38] There were also bonuses for hard laborers, children and mothers, and convalescents, though they did not come automatically.[39] These overviews are not entirely reliable, however: the last Elder of the Jews Murmelstein assessed the pre-fall 1944 daily rations at 2,500 calories for hard laborers, 1,800 for short-term workers, and 1,700 calories for nonworkers.[40] For example, Martha Glass, a sixty-five-year old woman from Hamburg, received one kilogram of bread every third day. As a normal worker she should have received more, but it is likely that as an elderly person, her portion had been reduced.[41]

The Central Labor Department (the top administration for all work within the ghetto) and its six deployment offices organized the food categories; a seventh office was responsible for the children's portions. The recipients of bread category N were those who worked at least forty-eight hours a week or, if they were over sixty years of age, twenty-four hours (or four hours of

THE AGE OF PEARL BARLEY   107

work a day). Children between the ages of seven and fifteen and mothers with infants under three years of age were also placed in category N.[42] Nonworking mothers whose children were older than three belonged to category L. Authorities in the place where one worked determined whether one qualified for category N, L, or K; the most advantageous category, S, was allocated by the Central Labor Department. Accordingly, applications for a change in the bread category to which one belonged were directed to one's boss; an application for S status went to Central Labor. Central Labor also kept a centralized bread index, with everyone's name, address, age, work, and bread status; a copy was given to house and room elders and the head of each workplace.

The sick were the object of complex regulations: normal laborers were subjected to different rules than hard laborers, and distinctions were yet again made between youth and the elderly. If people fell sick, after a week (or two, if they were among the elderly), they lost their bread status and were recategorized as K or N. The sick received benefits according to the duration of one's employment: thirty days' worth of extra rations for the ill who had worked up to three months and sixty for those who were employed for up to six months; the illness had to last at least twelve days to receive extra rations.[43] The permanently sick were categorized as "unable to work" and received K rations. The recategorization was passed through Central Labor and the accommodation.

In the beginning, the number of those classified as hard laborers was relatively limited; the administration downplayed it even further.[44] However, by mid-1943 this category contained more than fifty-two hundred people and included—in addition to the more than one thousand kitchen staff—members of the Council of Elders, butchers, bakers, and staff in Central Supply.[45] The number of hard laborers increased for several reasons. As the population grew and the ghetto became more organized, the community needed more workers. Also, several groups and individuals managed to lobby successfully for their inclusion in the S category. At the same time, the S and N rations, and the larger kitchen food helpings, were directly linked to the reduction of the nonworker's rations. For some time, normal workers received double helpings (*Doppelmenage*) in the kitchens. As the elderly starved, however, there was less food to redistribute toward the second kitchen helpings. Eventually, the "double" helpings only consisted of an additional 43 percent.[46] In fall 1944, Benjamin Murmelstein improved the food distribution. For several weeks, the food deliveries provided triple rations for

108   THE LAST GHETTO

the remaining population. Murmelstein, moreover, confiscated the parcels whose intended recipients had been deported or had passed away and shared them among the inmates, with special meals going to the elderly, the sick, and children.[47]

Those manual laborers who received S category rations were mostly younger Czech Jews; by 1943, they made up between 5 and 10 percent of the overall population. These people—cooks, bakers, men in Shipping detail, or those working as electricians or craftsmen—were the social elite of Terezín. Many of them were members of the Aufbaukommando, the construction detail. Their jobs brought them double the advantages of other positions in the ghetto: this group received the largest food portions and supplementary rations. For instance, in addition to their category S food rations, bakers received a loaf of bread each day, because the job was difficult. The administration took this step to stop them from stealing food.[48]

The social elite—the young Czech Jews—was made up of both men and women. Both genders could be categorized as hard laborers.[49] A majority of the agricultural workers were young women who smuggled in most of the fruit and vegetables—a rare and valuable commodity. Many of these women provided for their entire families.[50] Women in the Agriculture Department were often as well off as those employed in the kitchen. However, society perceived only the men as prestigious. Cooks were regarded as all-powerful; Valerie Kohnová remembered Jiří Nalos, the head of the potato storehouse, as the "potato king."[51] Erich Lichtblau, the ironic chronicler of the ghetto, drew a picture called *The Three Magi of Terezín*, depicting cook, baker, and pastry baker.[52] On the other hand, his drawing of a young woman who worked in Agriculture portrayed a fresh, apprehensive, attractive girl smuggling a bouquet into the ghetto.[53] Remarkably, the smuggled material was flowers, a beautiful and quite impractical item, decisively feminine. When women had access to surplus food, the prisoner society still expected them to help their families, but it did not change their status.[54] This perception was diametrically different from the attitude toward men, whose wealth fellow inmates saw as socially relevant.[55]

Everyday Life and Access to Food

Alisa Ehrmannová, a seventeen-year-old Zionist and a *Geltungsjüdin*, worked in the kitchen and later in Agriculture. In 2001, she told me how she had smuggled eggs, hidden in her bosom, into the ghetto. I asked her, whether as a teenager and prisoner, she had a bust large enough to do so. Oh, she did, she told me, laughing; she had not been hungry. "Every time we went through the kitchen, we would dip our arm deep into the pot with roux, and lick it clean."[56]

Anna Nathanová was a twenty-five-year old woman from Prague; her husband, a German emigré architect, was deported to Terezín with the second Aufbaukommando. Anna followed with one of the next transports. In the ghetto, she distributed milk and thus could take care of several of her relatives. She was able to have an intimate life with her husband and was so well nourished that she was able to conceive twice in the ghetto. "I was never hungry in Terezín," she told an interviewer.[57]

Hana Rutarová was another young Czech married woman. She worked in the mail office; her husband, Karel, was well connected and helped her obtain this advantageous position. In March 1944, Karel was sent with two hundred other men to the Wulkow labor detail near Berlin. In a letter Hana wrote him, she noted: "Kájíšku [diminutive for Karel], I just ate and I am hungry yet again. It's horrible. Wait until you come home, I will eat you after dinner!" But Hana's hunger was very different from the hunger experienced by the starving, elderly inmates: she described her menus, which included cauliflower, onion, and tea, food she bartered or received as gifts from friends.[58]

It is no coincidence that all three examples were provided by young Czech women. Women tend to recollect their time in Terezín in more detail, paying attention to the social networks and access to resources; men, on the other hand, focus more on how things were organized, issues around competition, and important people they knew. Therefore, women's testimonies more frequently mention individual access to food. Almost everyone within the economic elite was a member of the social elite, although the reverse was not necessarily the case. Many people who were part of the Terezín jeunesse dorée were not always as well fed as those who were a part of the economic elite. Miloš Pick, a young Communist, recalled how members of his group shared food from one large bowl. It was never enough, he remembered, and sharing it meant an additional loss due to the group dish, yet eating together was a ritual to boost the morale of their group.[59]

For the social and economic elite, eating was also a social occasion. The extra food also allowed for a more varied social life. The "rich" in the ghetto received visitors more regularly and could host dinners. Some were even able to secure a prized luxury, a kumbál of one's own. Two of the women

110   THE LAST GHETTO

mentioned lived in a kumbál. Having a private space and a surplus of food—enough to feed not only oneself and one's spouse, but also family and friends—allowed for a richer social life, modeled on prewar habits. Anna came from a farmer's family in Sušice; her family was killed before the deportation. She married a friend, Karel, who proposed by telling her that she should not go on a transport alone. In the ghetto, Anna eventually worked in Agriculture, and she described herself as a smuggling daredevil. Her husband built a kumbál in the Hohenelbe barracks where the young family made their home: "We had a tiny cooker there, and I always cooked vegetables and sometimes potatoes. Things were easier to bear in the summer. Every evening someone came for dinner so we still had some sort of life."[60] This "some sort of life" described by Anna was a social feast in comparison with the situation of most inmates. Those who had very little food could not host such parties and led significantly poorer social lives.

Depending exclusively on the kitchen for food (or not) was an important marker of divisions in class within the ghetto. For a small but significant number of inmates, their sole access to food was what was issued by the ghetto. The majority of these inmates were nonworkers, mostly elderly Jews. Many jobs allowed for additional access to food outside of what the ghetto issued; kitchen staff or people in the Agriculture and potato peelers, as well as clerks, physicians, and functionaries in positions of power, received benefits. People in these jobs were part of the social elite, which translated into various further privileges.[61] Josef Solar received S portions thanks to his work, first in railway construction and later in Shipping. In both jobs, Solar was able to establish relationships with the outside world, which enabled him to smuggle out mail and valuables. In exchange, he brought in food, especially treats that could not be obtained in the ghetto. For his wife Franci's birthday, for example, he presented her with pork ribs, a luxury in the ghetto.[62]

Danish Jews, who started receiving regular food parcels after February 1944, still ate the kitchen food, or used it for barter, including for services.[63] Sven and Corrie Meyer, a Dutch Danish couple, purchased washing and ironing services. When they published their memoir decades later, Hana Friediger, a Czech woman who had dated another Dane, was angered: "It sounds like they were on some kind of holiday. She writes that she had someone who came and ironed their laundry. That simply did not exist. But maybe it did exist."[64] The class differences in Theresienstadt could be so stark that inmates did not know, nor could they imagine, the situation of others. Moreover, the seemingly banal act of purchasing services signified in the ghetto an enormous luxury: to have the resources to pay for someone's time, when everyone was very busy, and to have the sheer need.

Access to food was an important factor in child rearing and the entire youth home system. Women with children above three years of age had an additional incentive to send them to youth homes, because it made work much easier. The women who kept their children with them usually had well-earning spouses who supported the family, or they were able to live off of food parcels sent by gentile friends and relatives. In addition, they often worked part-time and received L category portions. [65]

For the "poorer" ghetto population—those who depended on the distributed food—the food category in which they were classified was very important. Almost all of the nonworkers were people who were too sick or weak to work; everyone else attempted to hold a job in order to receive workers' rations. Martha Glass's husband had died of enteritis in January 1943. Also known as dysentery, it is a generic intestinal inflammation, resulting in diarrhea; it was widespread in Theresienstadt and for the elderly, often deadly. Glass struggled to keep her job as a sock darner. She needed to work reduced hours (four hours a day) because she was over sixty years of age. Still, the work was exhausting, her eyes were not good, and she felt too weak to work. Glass needed the job to keep her N rations; otherwise she would have starved.[66]

Those who did not have anyone who could help them secure additional food had an extra incentive to file applications to improve their food category. For instance, Alice Randt, a middle-aged head nurse from Hannover, filed an application for bonus rations for all of the nurses on her team. The application was successful. But even with the bonus food, Randt was so thin that her Czech colleagues commented on her appearance.[67] Regina Oelze from Essen was somewhat worse off than Martha Glass. Sixty-five years old upon her arrival, Oelze struggled to obtain a job in order to receive N or L rations.[68] Many elderly inmates were given the jobs that nobody else wanted to do, including toilet service, which consisted of standing and cleaning in cold hallways.

Many elderly inmates searched through garbage for anything that was edible.[69] Camilla Hirsch, a seventy-five-year-old Viennese widow, picked up moldy food that her neighbors threw out. Even though Hirsch worked in the administration section of her house and received parcels, she weighed only 101 pounds, half of her former weight.[70] In April 1943 Hirsch had to step down from her job due to exhaustion. From that point forward she had to live on nonworker rations. Two weeks later, she noted: "It is a hunger

The architect Norbert Troller documented the street scenes in the ghetto. This 1942 pen-and-ink sketch, *Pro šlupky* (For the peels), depicts a group of elderly men and women searching for discarded fruit peels. They are completely absorbed in this task, and their backs are to the observer. Courtesy of the Leo Baeck Institute.

that can tear out one's stomach. Never in my life had I imagined that hunger could hurt so badly!"[71] Many young Czech survivors remembered the elderly Germans begging for soup—the starter was usually a thin lentil soup that those better off did not like to eat. But unlike many others, the old inmates did not resort to stealing. Upsetting as these accounts are, they also draw our attention to the remarkable resourcefulness of the elderly in procuring food and flexibility of their habitus.

The "poorest" in the ghetto—the elderly or permanently sick inmates who did not work—lived on K rations. There are very few protagonists who left testimonies about living on K rations because almost all of them starved. The surviving elderly often had relatives in the outside world who sent them regular food parcels. Hulda Schickler, a seventy-four-year old widow from Hamburg, did not work; for some time, she received monthly parcels from a friend. Her diary mirrored her food situation; Schickler wrote in it when she had more food. There are few entries in her diary during the last months of the ghetto's existence, when the parcels stopped arriving, and none in the months prior to her death in January 1945.[72] In one of her last entries, Schickler noted that she had always bartered jam from her rations for more bread: this exchange shows her focus on essential items: food, especially bread and potatoes.[73] The elderly prisoners were the most likely to die.

First-person accounts from the poorest inmates are rare. But in those accounts that do survive, two stages are evident: in the first period, discussion of food and ration categories take prominence in the diaries. The "rich" hardly ever thematized their categories, but those dependent on the issued food often did so. The elderly noted how they had swiftly lost weight, about two-thirds or even half of what they had used to weigh. Louis Salomon, a seventy-four-year-old Berliner, was amazed that he could lose 106 pounds and still be alive.[74] The elderly observed that sleeping became uncomfortable because they could feel their bones.[75] In the second stage, the very hungry and weak stopped keeping diaries altogether. The representation of those close to death comes almost exclusively from the perspective of others—those who were better off. In spring 1943 Karl Loewenstein, the head of the Ghetto Guard, visited Pathology. He was shocked: "The corpses of those who died, whom I got to see here, were only bones covered by skin. These dead had literally starved to death. I saw corpses who were no heavier than a small child."[76] When he inquired about the situation, the physicians confirmed that such corpses were the norm.

The way individuals experience hunger depends on whether it is a voluntary choice and the nature of the surroundings. We often think of fasting as having a higher spiritual or political purpose. Fasting medieval religious women experienced enlightening visions and much clearer thinking than before; their extreme hunger was an enriching spiritual episode.[77] But the elderly population in Terezín did not choose their malnourishment. They starved surrounded by dirt, insects, overcrowding, and perhaps most important, neglect. Their starvation was anything but enlightening; the weaker they were, the more silent they grew.

In the testimonies of those who were well off, elderly inmates are consistently described as "the others": ill fated, hungry, and undesirable. Hana Schicková, a young Czech Zionist in Terezín (an old woman when she told the story), described two old roommates in a tone of disgust: "They were the poorest. They cooked with their mouth: 'Sauerkraut won't shine if you don't add three spoons of goose lard.'"[78] Giving one's soup to the begging elderly was usually described as donating to someone vaguely disgusting, like giving

114   THE LAST GHETTO

a few coins to a homeless man.[79] The same trope of disgust is prevalent in portrayals of the elderly population's accommodations. Many of the weakened seniors died in the houses, lying in their own excrement—a fact that the younger inmates often interpreted as a sign of dirtiness or weakness.[80] However, most frequently the hungry elderly population is mentioned only in passing or not at all. This pattern was true despite the fact that many of the seniors had children or grandchildren in Terezín who may have been the ones making the observations. Renée Friesová remarked that apparently all of the elderly were hungry, but they inhabited a different world from hers. Miloš Pick recalled in one sentence that his grandmother died shortly after her arrival.[81]

To the younger prisoners, the elderly inhabitants were "the others," whom they perceived with disgust. People stressed their otherness, dirt, and "unhuman" features, without empathy or differentiation. This phenomenon is closely related to that of the *Muselmann* in the concentration camps.[82] Muselmann denotes the emaciated, exhausted prisoners, resigned to their death. Indeed, those Terezín prisoners who were eventually deported to Auschwitz, where they met the Muselmänner, realized that these corresponded with what they knew as the sick elderly in the ghetto.[83] Like the Muselmann, the elderly usually did not leave a recorded testimony, and other inmates rarely spoke to them. Because of their weakness, they were no longer able to observe basic hygiene and could not control their bodily functions. In the eyes of fellow inmates, the sick elderly individuals had crossed the line to a bare existence.

Giorgio Agamben's concept of *homo sacer* is useful here to understand the societal mechanism at hand. Building on Roman law, Agamben's *homo sacer* is a human stripped of all social markers, barely living, no longer communicating.[84] This concept has been used to analyze the Muselmann in the concentration camps. But whereas in the camps anyone could become the Muselmann, in the Terezín ghetto, age was the crucial factor. This use of *homo sacer* shows the similarities between the prisoner population in ghettos and concentration camps. Furthermore, the example of the elderly in Terezín suggests a new insight about *homo sacer*: they are silent because their surroundings no longer communicate with them. This is how *homo sacer* becomes "the other." The Theresienstadt elderly were keenly aware of their social exclusion and how much they had to do to stay alive. Malnourished, weakened, elderly individuals in Terezín often communicated until their death, even if their physical appearance and habits crossed the line of what was thought to be "civilized."[85] *Homo sacer* is bare life from the perspective of "normal," social individuals, who want to reassure themselves of their normality in exceptional circumstances: It can thus be the very narrator who tells us about the Muselmann who enacts the social exclusion that made him. Similarly to historians' application of the concept of social death to American slavery and German Jews prior to their deportation,[86] the mechanism at hand aids in understanding social marginalization in extreme circumstances.

When people receive severely insufficient nutrition, they do not actually die of hunger.[87] Energy intake is directed to four main functions: immunity, metabolism, reproduction, and brain activity. In the camps and ghettos, immunity was particularly important because it is adaptable to new surroundings. The body can compensate for the lack of nutrients and even vitamins for quite a long time, although some functions do not operate well, for instance reproduction. Hunger is not indicative of a malfunction; rather, it is adaptable, sensory, and diminishes over time. Moreover, energy is lost more by physical activity than by food reduction. But passive individuals have a weaker immune system than those who are active. After some time, which could be months or even years, of compensating for the reduced food intake, the genetically weaker organs and functions start to fail.

For instance, a starving person can have a weakened immune system or a failing heart. In addition, lack of vitamin B1 (thiamine) was a contributing reason for starvation-related death.[88] This finding was replicated by Soviet historians and physicians in the Warsaw ghetto, who documented frequent cases of avitaminosis B1, beriberi. This disease leads to hunger edema,[89] well known from the images of Holocaust victims.[90] Theresienstadt patients in later stages of enteritis showed beriberi, as bodies affected by chronic diarrhea have difficulty absorbing B1. Thiamine is central for synthesis of glucose, which feeds the heart muscle; without it, the heart will stop. The avitaminosis B1 had progressed so far that even though the kitchens occasionally distributed yeast, it had no impact.[91] Starving people thus die of a combination of factors caused by hunger, but they do not die of energy "shutdown" or hunger. In Terezín, elderly inmates died of feverish enteritis and/or heart failure. Almost every prisoner became infected with enteritis; indeed, the illness was so frequent it was named *terezínka*. The disease was widely spread in other ghettos and camps; in Lodz, it was just called "ghetto illness."[92] Many of the elderly Jews had heart problems prior to Terezín but did not die of them alone. Only in combination with extreme food shortages did such ailments become deadly.

116   THE LAST GHETTO

Given these conditions, it is striking how long many of these individuals managed to live. When we look at when the deaths occurred, we observe important differences: most people over sixty-five years of age (24.7 percent) died between 100 and 199 days after their arrival. The second largest group (20.4 percent) died between 200 and 499 days after their arrival.[93] In addition, while elderly men and women died proportionally equally often, women died somewhat earlier, after 109 days, while men died after 120; old Czech women died the quickest, after 98 days.[94] The elderly population did whatever it could to obtain extra nutrition: they scavenged for garbage and traded little favors with their richer neighbors. In fact, for an elderly individual, begging for soup was one of the few ways they could improve their food intake. Overcoming shame in asking strangers for food that they would not have eaten showed a great deal of agency. If additional food sources were not sufficient, or when a person had no access to them, most of the elderly who were not deported elsewhere died in Terezín. Thus 84 percent of the elderly population died in Terezín. The overwhelming majority (92 percent) of the 33,600 dead of Terezín were people over sixty years of age.[95] Most of their deaths were related to a lack of nutrition. Only 2.7 percent of the dead were people younger than forty-five years of age.

The self-administration in Terezín, and even more often in postwar narratives, often made the claim that the asymmetrical food distribution was structured in favor of the children.[96] Indeed, the children, including teenagers, received better food rations than adults. According to an overview from 1943, youth received 1,759 kcal, and between 5 and 20 percent more bread, potatoes, sugar, and margarine than the nonlaborers. Unlike any other groups of prisoners, they also received milk.[97] These rations are not significantly higher; the actual difference lay in the establishment of special children's kitchens in summer 1943 with better deliveries from the Youth Welfare Department, frequent extra food, better and cleaner spaces, and less theft among the staff.[98] One of the central expectations in the Terezín community was to take good care of the children. Therefore, stealing from them was not tolerated. Moreover, the children's kitchens received various benefits: they were provided with unexpected deliveries, parcels without addressees, or the few fruits and vegetables that came into the ghetto. Finally, many of the people working in agriculture were teenagers from the youth homes; these much-desired jobs were preferably given to youngsters so that they had access to fresh air and vitamins.[99] In addition, there were at least 13 children's gardens.[100]

THE AGE OF PEARL BARLEY   117

Therefore, the real food rations for children probably consisted of more than 1,759 kcal. If the children had had to subsist only on those small food rations, their mortality and illness would have been much higher. Almost all of the children in Terezín survived in the ghetto; if they died, they died after deportation. This apparent contradiction in the statistics points out the flaws within the entire system of calorie overviews established by the self-administration. The children's good health is exceptional in the context of a starving society; it is usually children, particularly infants under three years of age, who die first. In the Lodz and Warsaw ghettos, the Bengal famine, and elsewhere, infants always died first.[101] Their bodies were not developed enough to manage with the shortages and lack of crucial nutrients; they had no immunity to disease. However, most of the Terezín infants lived, that is at least until their further deportation. Of the children born in 1940 and deported to Terezín (altogether 248), 7.26 percent died there; in 1941 (243 infants), 9.05 percent died; in 1942 (291 infants), 18.21 percent died; in 1943 (172 infants), 11.63 percent died; and in 1944 (82), 7 percent died.[102]

Over the ghetto's duration, the infants' survival rate actually improved, as did their care. By 1943 small children were fed at nurseries, where the food was so plentiful that it sufficed not only for the infants but also for their mothers.[103] The number of children in the ghetto was smaller than the number of elderly people, although still sizable: by December 1944, 1,036 children born in or after 1940 had passed through the ghetto. Yet the number of children is not small enough to explain the low infant mortality in Terezín; the number of infants in the ghettos was also very low, but in Terezín most of the children survived.

Terezín contradicts typical starvation patterns: small children—generally the most endangered group—survived while the elderly population, also at risk but not as much as the children, was destroyed. These contradictions show that the starvation of the elderly inhabitants was engendered by a specific misdistribution, often rigged against the elderly, and not by an overall lack of food. The master narrative of Terezín and popular representation today have presented this difference as a manifestation of humanity. It is impossible to accurately reconstruct the amount of food brought into the ghetto. Although supplies were not sufficient to allow for normal food intake, many more people could have survived despite suffering a certain amount of hunger.[104]

118   THE LAST GHETTO

Food as a Social Event

Food defined social encounters; it became a backdrop to most interactions among the Terezín inmates: meetings of friends, rendezvous, parties, weddings, and even sexual encounters. Eating is typically a social event. In Terezín, where food was scarce and family members usually lived apart, the social importance of meals increased.

Strangers made each other's acquaintance while standing in the line for food from the kitchen. Indeed, old colleagues and friends often recognized each other in these lines. Apart from encounters in the street, food lines were the most important meeting place. During the warmer seasons, inmates often organized picnic lunches, taking their food to the wall lamps, where they could enjoy the sunshine and view of the mountains.[105] Eating lunch outside with colleagues, friends, or one's partner; sunbathing; and taking a brief nap became a routine part of ghetto life by the summer of 1944. Such lunches were an attempt to establish normal, pleasurable activities that served as a way to normalize the new everyday.

Dinners were usually more domestic and intimate. Inmates usually ate in their rooms, together with their closest circle. This group might be one's core family but could also consist of friends if they had become more important than one's actual family, or if the inmate had no relatives in the ghetto. Families (men and women were assigned different accommodations) often met at the mother's accommodation, or wherever the conditions for gathering were the most suitable. Greta, a twenty-five-year old married woman from Prague, customarily went to her father's place for dinner: "I visited my husband only rarely, because we met as a family at my Dad's. My father lived on the main street in one of those tiny houses; in particular, he lived in the kitchen. He made himself a wooden bed and lived there with another man. Mum went there in the evenings to cook some so-called dinner. My sister first worked in the workshop complex and then she managed to get a position in the bakery and made yeast pastries."[106] Therefore, the meeting place for Gerta and her husband was her parents' quarters.

Yet another form of social dinner developed among roommates who did not have any close relatives in Terezín. Gerty Spies, a forty-seven-year old writer from Munich, was alone in Terezín; she was divorced from a mixed marriage, her daughter was in Germany, and her mother had died in February 1944. Spies arranged parts of her social life together with her flatmates and friends, with whom she shared food from her daughter's parcels.

THE AGE OF PEARL BARLEY   119

Alexandr Schmiedt was a twenty-three-year old ardent Hechalutz Zionist youth member from Prague. He and other comrades organized their own room in the Sudeten barracks, the *bet chaluc* (house of the Hechalutz), in room 53. Forty men, most of them young, the majority of them Zionists, lived together and created their own commune: they set up a Hebrew language circle, sang Yiddish songs, listened to lectures about Zionism and Palestine, and shared food.[107] Sharing food in the *bet chaluc* became another ritual of group belonging; even if food was not as coded as many of the other Hechalutz activities, sharing was equally, if not more, coded in terms of togetherness. Regular food sharing within a group of inmates denoted the lines of a group, demonstrating that members of the group could trust one another. In a report written in the ghetto, Schmiedt stressed that the food magazine of *bet chaluc* never experienced any theft. This situation was quite unlike anywhere else. The *bet chaluc* even granted extra food to sick members, confirming the loyalty and care within the group.

In the ghetto, the people with whom one shared food signified kinship groups.[108] The members of the kinship groups were not always biologically related, demonstrating once more that "kinship is not always already heterosexual."[109] With a kinship group, some individuals had better access to material resources than others; often, it was just one person who could secure resources. Thanks to the separate accommodations, people often could not choose where, and with whom, they lived. To keep the group together, the inmates had to organize their meeting place and decide who to include. This Theresienstadt-caused spatial separation was another moment that reshuffled traditional families: With whom did one meet regularly, and where did one meet? For many, it was the biological family. Yet for others—the young and single, or those deported without their families—ideological and generational proximity, as well as friendship, became equally if not more important than biological relations. For example, Miloš Pick and Alexandr Schmiedt became part of "families" made up of their friends.

These kinship groups had fairly hard boundaries, depending on how long they had known each other. These were people who shared food, trust, care, affection, and sometimes accommodations. Of course new friends and partners came in, just as other members died or left with a transport. Yet it was regular food sharing that denoted the group boundaries. They bartered or occasionally gave food to those outside the circle, but not on a regular basis.

The ritual of eating together in younger, tight-knit groups sometimes had another form—the so-called *žranice* or binge. This activity was particularly

120   THE LAST GHETTO

popular among boys and teenagers. They would save until they had enough food and eventually have a feast, at which all participants could eat as much as they wanted.[110] Binges were prevalent only among children or young adults; older inmates dealt with food in a more rational, planned way. Yet adults also liked to celebrate with a larger and more elaborate meal; when Gerty Spies received a parcel from her daughter in September 1944, the first thing she did was take the food to her friend and prepare a multi-course meal.[111] The binges suggest that although children were better nourished than the elderly, they were not well fed; otherwise they would not have needed to experience a lavish meal. The feasts—both the binges and the adult parties—were acts that allowed one to finally eat one's fill without having to painfully save food for the next day. They were both a form of pleasure and an expression of agency. Similarly to Soviet society in Stalinist years, in the ghetto, the meaning of lavish differed from what it had meant before deportation.[112]

The feasts would take place for a number of reasons: birthdays, weddings, or just because. Social functions were almost always accompanied by food; food became the most important aspect of a meeting. Of course the quantity and kind of food served differed from host to host. One of the reasons elderly inmates rejoiced when they received a parcel was that they would now be able to host friends. As in the normal world, hosting a party was a way not only to enjoy company but also to raise one's social capital—to be popular. In a society based on scarcity, a rare item gains symbolic value; in Terezín, it was food. In normalized Czechoslovak society of the 1970s it could be books, films, or theater.

Food became a form of symbolic capital in the ghetto; it became a symbol that allowed one to express status, respect, and power. Eli Friedrich, a thirteen-year-old boy from Ostrava, lived in a boys' home. When he received a baked goose for his bar mitzvah, Eli shared it with his forty-two roommates. For several days afterward he was the most popular boy in the room.[113] Siegmund Hadra, a sixty-seven-year-old gynecologist from Berlin, had an infected boil that needed to be surgically removed. The hospital, however, had hardly any laughing gas; the operation had to be conducted without anesthesia. Hadra was told (and as a doctor, knew very well) that it would be quite painful. He stayed quiet throughout the operation to prove himself, his masculinity, and his status as a German Jew, in an environment that denigrated his culture and his age. Hadra experienced triumph: the nurses were in awe of him, and the head nurse sent him a piece of garlic bread.[114]

THE AGE OF PEARL BARLEY   121

Else Dormitzer, a sixty-six-year old former Nuremberger active in the Jewish community and the Central Verein, had immigrated to the Netherlands in 1939. Like many unsalaried associates, Dormitzer drew a sense of self-importance from knowing many interesting and important people, and she liked others to take notice. She was deported to Terezín in 1943. Later, living in London, she recalled that upon her arrival, the ghetto had immediately begun to talk about her. Leo Baeck had personally taken care of her and sent her food and raisin bread.[115] In various ways, food—both the giving and receiving—served as a symbolic instrument of prestige. Eli bribed his roommates so that he would be well liked; Hadra was given a treat to demonstrate that he was respected; and Dormitzer mentioned Baeck's gift to prove her special status, which had continued even after her arrival in Terezín.

Ema Friedmannová, a twenty-one-year old nurse from Prostějov, met her future husband, František, in the kitchen line in Terezín. He was a cook, and Ema, who was well aware of her good looks, employed her Moravian dialect and charm to cajole František into giving her a larger portion of coffee for her patients.[116] He asked her out, they started seeing each other, and eventually they married. Ema procured elaborate treats for the festivities: "My uncle was a baker and he gave me a pound cake (*bábovka*) that I gave to the rabbi for the ceremony; and I also got normal salty rolls (*rohlíky*)—that was a treat—and we also had canapés, canapés with margarine. It was very pretty, because one line was sprinkled with caraway seeds, another with paprika, and yet another with mustard."[117] For Ema, the story of her great love was intertwined with her ability to obtain food, her organizational talent, and her power. She began the story in a slightly ironic tone, pointing out in retrospect that the reception consisted of simple salty rolls. But in the next sentence, she recounted how she resourcefully set up a pretty and tasty buffet.

Tipping, expressed in food, was another component of social interactions: Ema gave the rabbi a whole pound cake, not because he needed to be paid, but to show that she could afford it.[118] Tipping was a gesture to cement a happy moment, appreciation of everyone who contributed.[119] Ema's tipping, moreover, was a continuation of gestures at bourgeois weddings prior to the war. However, at that time the parents of the bride or groom would have provided the tip, indicating a further shift of generational roles. Finally, tipping in a moment of happiness seems to have been a method to assure the good will of others; similarly, Gerty Spies tipped the postman who delivered her daughter's parcel.[120]

122   THE LAST GHETTO

The practice of feeding one's nearest and dearest reveals an interesting form of double genderedness. Men wooing future partners brought them food, just as brothers and fathers who had better access to food provided for wives and sisters.[121] Cooks and bakers brought their sweethearts little specialties or extra food rations.[122] Apart from being an expression of affection, these items also reinforced the men's status as providers. A related habit accompanied sexual encounters; Norbert Troller, a forty-six-year old architect from Brno, described the pattern of his lady friends' visits to his kumbál. The woman first received a snack, which the couple devoured together, followed by a cigarette; then the couple proceeded to the intimacies.[123]

However, once a romantic relationship was established, the woman provided for her male partner. Edmund Hadra was the doctor for his transport from Berlin; there he met Josefa Ruben, an attractive nurse more than thirty years his junior. Edmund recalled how he and Josefa became close, especially after Josefa's mother passed away. Edmund courted Josefa, who at first did not accept him. But Edmund persevered and gave Josefa a silver spoon for her birthday. Some time later, Josefa's chief doctor molested her, which made her change her mind about Edmund. Having a partner would mean protection from harassment. Once Josef and Edmund became a couple, the arrangement changed: Edmund came twice a day for a visit and was entertained with a meal, for which his roommates envied him. Josefa also took on a large part of Edmund's care, including washing his clothes.[124] Similar patterns took place among many couples (whether romantic partnerships, relationships between a father and a daughter, or siblings), even if the man had better access to food than his female companion.[125] In such cases, women still cared for their partners in compensatory ways. Teenager Charlotta Weinsteinová was a *Geltungsjüdin* living in a youth home with her older brother Karel. They had no other family in Terezín. Karel brought her food that he had bought by selling the wooden pendants he produced in the workshop where he was employed; Charlotta washed his socks.[126] The siblings established in the unfamiliar surroundings a new kinship group with a pointedly gendered division of labor that helped define family.

Food in the ghetto was thus doubly gendered. Men were expected to feed their women when they were in a significantly weaker position or when entering a romantic relationship. Once the relationship became established—such as when Ema Friedmannová got married—women fulfilled a gendered function by providing for their men, although it was sometimes in terms of care, such as doing their laundry, rather than with material goods.

Food Reflecting the Everyday

Due to the scarcity of food in the ghetto, perceptions about nutrition and its place in the everyday changed along with other aspects of everyday life, including the social value of jobs. Manual jobs, which were once viewed as belonging on the bottom of the social ladder, were now catapulted to the top of the social hierarchy because of their connection to food. Edgar Krása, an eighteen-year-old cook from a petit bourgeois family, was one of the few cooks who arrived with the Aufbaukommando. Thanks to the support of Karel Schliesser, who knew him when he was an apprentice cook in the Jewish Community in Prague, Krása soon made a career as the head of an entire kitchen, describing himself as "a big shot."[127] White-collar jobs, in contrast, if not connected with direct access to power, became uninteresting. These social shifts were reflected in a running joke. A weeping young woman at the Ghetto Court charges a man with marriage fraud: he claimed to be a cook, but turned out to be a bank director.[128]

Eating habits changed, too. Those for whom dining manners used to signify crucial social distinctions, wherein much of taste and class belonging was expressed in china, linen, and cutlery, now lived and ate with one bowl and spoon. An August 1944 sketch by the Viennese cabaret artists Myra and Leo Strauss depicted an imagined future. A former inmate has difficulties reintegrating into the "civilized" world. In a farewell letter, his lover complains, "But I began to have serious doubts for the first time about the possibility of living together with you, when, at the *table d'hôte* at the Hotel du Lac in Montreux, you tried to eat the steak with the spoon and afterwards suddenly jumped up, took the plate in your hand, ran to the kitchen window, and demanded in a loud voice, 'seconds.'"[129] Jokes like this showed that the new eating habits were a bitter pill for the former bourgeoisie, even after two years in the ghetto. Some inmates endeavored to keep, or rather develop, good manners. The Communist lawyer Truda Sekaninová worked as a youth care worker. Her colleague observed with fascination how Sekaninová brought her potatoes, sat down, spread a white napkin over her knees, peeled the potatoes, and ate them with a fork and knife.[130]

Many dishes and ingredients were things that people had never eaten before. Some foodstuffs were quite unknown to the urban middle class or were things they had only heard about: pearl barley, millet, and turnips. Pearl barley, in particular, became a staple menu item. Käthe Breslauer, a sixty-six-year old high school teacher from Berlin, spoke deprecatingly about how

124   THE LAST GHETTO

she lived for three months solely on lentil soup. These meals were followed by "the age of pearl barley."[131] Indeed, for several months there was a potato shortage, and cooks tried to replace the side dishes with dumplings and pearl barley.[132] Breslauer, who worried about the lack of vitamin C and who collected sorrel from the wall lamps, did not know that pearl barley was a significant source of fiber and protein. The population may have preferred millet, which was served less often. Richard Ehrlich from Berlin wrote in his diary that he first discovered millet in Terezín and could eat it every day.[133]

The bourgeoisie had not considered domestic fruits, and especially vegetables, to be delicacies. But in Terezín, where there was no fresh fruit, inmates stared longingly at the nearby pear trees.[134] Cucumbers and plums smuggled in by inmates working in Agriculture were bartered at a high rate.[135] Food that had been considered cheap and part of a countryman's diet now became gourmet items. This trend also applied to other rare treats, such as charcuterie or lard.[136] Foreign prisoners learned Czech cuisine: the sixty-six-year-old Berlin cookbook author Elsa Oestreicher, in Theresienstadt working in a warming kitchen, copied recipes for *kolaches* and *perník*, Czech gingerbread.[137] Fans of the tenor Alexandr Singer, who was raised as an orthodox Jew in Subcarpathian Rus' and later moved to Prague to study at the conservatory, brought him salami and pork cracklings; in the ghetto, these were truly magnificent gifts.[138]

Theft

The distribution of food in Terezín—a confusing system in its own right—was even more complex due to widespread theft. The moral code in the ghetto stated that stealing from communal property for one's own need was all right; stealing from an individual was not.[139] It was considered acceptable, for instance, to take some potatoes during one's work in a potato storehouse. Thefts from individuals did occur, although they were much less frequent than robbery from general resources. Upon his arrival, a friendly young woman offered to help Hanuš Bader, a twenty-eight-year old former shop assistant in Pacov, in the *Schleuse*. She suggested that he hide his money in his hat and give it to her. Bader was indignant when he later found out that she had no intention of returning his money. What made matters worse was that during the first few days in the ghetto newcomers did not receive food, and Bader was hungry. He described robbing his neighbors to get food: "My friend, Paul Meller, and me lay beside each other and watched each other's things when the other had to go out. At night we carefully crawled to the sleepers, carefully stuck our hand into their luggage to feel if there was edible inside. Mostly it was a cookie or a piece of sausage. We pulled out these delicacies and shared them like brothers."[140] In his telling, Bader justified his theft; indeed, he did not refer to his actions as theft, instead concentrating on the "brotherly sharing."

First-person narrators who gave accounts outlining how they took from individuals presented their narratives in ways that justified their actions, told the story as an adventure, or depicted it as proof of their inventiveness. Charlotte Guthmann, a young care worker from Wiesbaden, recounted how she stole someone's piece of charcuterie: "[W]e saw that some fortunate inmate has used his second story sill as a food storage space. [...] There sat all kinds of incredible delicacies in the cold night air, including a large piece of bologna the size of half a grapefruit. [...] We instantly decided that anyone who had access to such treasures and was foolish enough to leave them sitting out in the open didn't deserve to keep them."[141]

Bedřich, a forty-year-old chemical engineer, worked in the hygiene station. He organized the delousing and washing of the infected, which consisted mostly of elderly individuals. The delousing station was a huge shock for these people; for the first time in their adult lives, they had to be naked in front of others, their hair was shorn, and their pubic hair and armpits were disinfected with a special liquid. Often the personnel were of the opposite sex. After the disinfection, people had to wait several hours until their cleaned clothes were free of prussic acid (a component of Zyklon B, supplied to Theresienstadt from Auschwitz). Many older people developed severe colds from waiting in the chilly room and died.[142] While waiting, the disinfected were served food. Some of the elderly population were so shaken that they could not eat. Bedřich took their food home and shared it with his family.[143] In his account, the well-being of elderly inmates was not his concern; rather, he viewed them as a resource.

Most people stole for themselves and their kinship unit. However, those who were in positions related to distribution stole food in quantity and then sold it for valuables. Ernst Michaelis, a seventy-two-year old Berliner who left Terezín for Switzerland in February 1945, condemned the situation: "People steal in order to deal in cigarettes and then they hoard golden watches and jewels and they have the prettiest girlfriends. People from bakeries get two or three loaves a day and even boast about it."[144] The bakers showed off because

126   THE LAST GHETTO

boasting is also a way of proving one's status. Michaelis was upset because he nearly starved.

An extraordinary example of graft survived thanks to a unique combination of sources. The head of the butchers, Bohumil Benda, came from a family of butchers. His father had a kosher butcher shop in Pařížská, one of Prague's best streets.[145] Benda, born in 1911, was deported to Terezín with the Aufbaukommando. He stole meat and sold it for jewelry, which, with the help of gendarmes, he arranged to send to his gentile fiancée in Prague.[146] He also may have sent valuables to his sister, Ludmila Perseinová, who lived in a mixed marriage; she and her husband were arrested on November 11, 1942, and sent to Auschwitz.[147] Karl Loewenstein, the head of the Ghetto Guard, suspected that the butchers stole about fifty kilograms of meat daily. When the head of the gendarmes accused the inmates of stealing animals from Agriculture, Loewenstein seized the moment and had the ghetto searched. The meat was found at Benda's.[148] The butcher lost his position and in March 1944 was sent to the Wulkow detail. Here he clashed with the kapo, Paul Raphaelson, a former attorney from Mönchengladbach. Raphaelson sent him back to Terezín; Benda was deported to Auschwitz during the fall 1944 transports. No one from the Benda family survived; his fiancée, whose name is not known, most likely held onto the gold.[149]

Terezín did not have a respected institution that could encourage inmates not to steal; prisoners held the Ghetto Guard in little regard. For a while the Kitchen Guard and Economic Police functioned well and carried out their duties, which included checking the weight of the servings issued. Yet some members of the Economic Police could be easily bribed for a dish of potatoes with margarine and three cigarettes.[150] The Order Service police in the Lodz ghetto were similarly unsuccessful in fighting theft.[151] The cases tried at the Ghetto Court were frequently food-related. For example, an inmate had used another's ration cards or stole food from the community. Punishments for these transgressions varied over time; sometimes the culprit was sentenced to two weeks without extra rations, other times to three days in the ghetto prison.

The prisoners mostly despised the court and did not respect its authority or its sentences. At the same time, many believed that the SS kept a list of all sentences and that those individuals would be included on the next transport.[152] In this practice of the SS, called *Weisung* (literally instruction), prisoners were personally named for inclusion on a transport. A Weisung for the convicted was not a stringent practice, but some of those sentenced were indeed placed on the next deportation list.[153] In September 1943,

Commandant Burger included all inmates who had been incarcerated for more than two weeks.[154] Larceny from the community was tolerated. With the dynamic among hungry people who often had free time and little to keep them busy, theft of food became a popular activity. Many inmates were hungry, and when they had access to extra food, they simply took it.

This analysis of theft and graft provides two conclusions about the inconstant food rations and the mortality of the elderly. First, the administration's information about the number of calories in the rations was not very reliable. The kitchen food that was distributed varied in quantity depending on what remained after theft by those working in Central Supply and the kitchen staff. Food distributed at the accommodation offers more dependable information about consumption patterns. Bread was not as easily stolen because it was distributed directly by the house or room elder; only a minority enriched themselves at the expense of others.[155] More important, theft offers an additional explanation for the asymmetry of food distribution and the high mortality of elderly inmates. Nonworkers suffered the most from the reduced portions. Unlike other prisoners, they had almost no chance to compensate for small portions. They did not work and thus had little access to additional food. Most were too weak to pursue other avenues for increased nourishment.

The decisions made by the self-administration and the community's moral code had a direct impact on the mortality rate in the ghetto and resulted in the death of most of the elderly population—or at least of those who were not sent farther east. Of course, at the root of starvation in the ghetto was the Nazi anti-Jewish policy, which brought about the deportations to Terezín as well as the deliberate decision to supply insufficient quantities of food. But the Nazi policy was fatally intensified by the grouping of the population into food categories, corruption, and the quest for individual enrichment among some inmates. Together, these processes caused the erasure of an entire generation of German, Austrian, and Czech Jewish elderly. The malnutrition that caused these deaths was triggered by a food shortage that in turn engendered misdistribution. Famine in Theresienstadt was man-made, caused by the prisoner society, and the famine victims were defined by its triage rules.

Bartering

Everyday life in Terezín became an economic matter.[156] The ghetto developed a barter system; inmates bartered their surplus food from parcels, smuggled

128 THE LAST GHETTO

fruit and vegetables from Agriculture, smuggled in foodstuffs via gendarmes, and stole edibles in the magazines or kitchens. People traded food for money or in exchange for other items; the two primary items for barter in the ghetto were bread and cigarettes. The nature of the bartered goods varied widely and included food, clothes, makeup, artwork, jewelry (both conventional and Theresienstadt-made), and sexual services. There is a belief that the black market is connected to criminal activity and networks,[157] which is then applied automatically to all informal barter economies. However, the barter system in Terezín does not conform to this description of a black market. There was no legal market, and bartering was never prohibited. In contrast, illegally selling goods to and from Theresienstadt indeed represented the black market.

Prohibited treats, the most important being cigarettes, became coveted goods.[158] Smoking was strictly forbidden, and the SS imposed draconian punishments if someone was caught with cigarettes.[159] Nevertheless, cigarettes were smuggled in great quantities. Individuals brought them from the locals. Benjamin Murmelstein believed that the SS was behind the smuggling; by enforcing the prohibition, the SS earned good money because it pushed cigarette prices sky high.[160] Cigarettes were sold for about eight Reichsmarks apiece; during transports, when the deported tried to sell their savings, the price dropped.[161] Surprisingly, many people smoked out of habit and also because, if they were wealthy, they could afford to.[162] When young Arnošt visited his friend Lilly "the Elder," generally acknowledged to be the most attractive nurse in the entire hospital, he found her living in her own furnished room, smoking a cigarette with a member of the Aufbaukommando.[163] Arnošt was disgusted and considered the act obscene; such opulence was misplaced in the overcrowded, starving community. Some people were able to buy themselves off of transports out of the ghetto. The Berlin physician Adolph Metz, the deputy of Health Services, mentioned it took "twenty to fifty cigarettes" to bribe the Transport Commission to remove a person from the deportation list.[164]

In the first few weeks after their arrival, the new prisoners often traded their clothes and jewelry for food in an effort to come to terms with the shock of scarcity.[165] They also exchanged items for things they needed to get by in the ghetto, such as suitable clothing and bowls in which to pick up the kitchen food. Often their suitcases arrived only weeks later or not at all, and they had usually been looted. With the departure of transports, the price of foodstuffs that could not be transported well, such as potatoes, dropped, while tinned

THE AGE OF PEARL BARLEY   129

food and bread became more expensive.[166] There was no standard meeting place where inmates could sell their goods; rather, they sold to people they knew, building a network from their roommates, friends, friends of friends, or work colleagues.[167]

With the increasing size and heterogeneity of ghetto society, the goods bartered became increasingly varied. The young diarist Eva Mändlová remarked: "Everything is being bartered here, bathing tickets, laundry passes, linen and underwear, as well as theatre tickets."[168] Tickets for leisure-time activities were supposed to be sold for ghetto crowns, which were used for little else and hence remained low in buying power. However, if a performance was particularly popular, such as Rafael Schächter's beloved production of Verdi's *Requiem*, it was accessible only to those who were very influential or could afford to pay for the tickets. Drawings, especially by well-known artists, were also valued. Erich Lichtblau bartered one of his watercolors for two kilograms of flour from a Danish inmate.[169] Once the Danes began receiving regular parcels from late February 1944 on, Danish food played a significant role in the bartering process. Some Danes bought services from others, such as cleaning or working in their place.[170] Barter eventually included various services such as massages and haircuts.[171] Several older German women produced flowers from felt—hair decorations that Czech women liked to wear.[172] People also paid for favors, such as rewarding helpers who carried heavy items for them.

Another form of barter was the trading of romantic, social, and sexual favors for resources and protection. These exchanges could become lasting relationships or one-time affairs; the barter could also include care and affection. The range of exchanges was wide and could be initiated by women or men, although only female sexual favors were sought. The exchange varied from encounters that were deliberately rational to romantic relationships. One facet of the sexual barter is particularly relevant in the context of this discussion: trading sex for food.

Šimon Kolský, a baker in Terezín, recalled how each baker was issued one loaf of bread as a reward at the end of each day. In the courtyard of the house, where his bakery was located, women they did not know were occasionally waiting for him and his colleagues. These women offered sex in exchange for food. Šimon remembered a Dutch woman who told him where she lived and invited him to come and sleep with her, in exchange for bread. He claimed that he refused because he had a girlfriend, whom he adored, and because of his Jewish orthodox upbringing. His colleagues, however, would say, "I can

130 THE LAST GHETTO

have a girlfriend and I can manage this on the side, too."[173] Sex was also a proof of status.[174]

Several women earned income by routinely offering sex in exchange for food.[175] These cases were more "institutional" because these women were known within the inmate community, and men would visit them in their lodgings. Zdeněk Ornest recalled that before he was deported to Auschwitz, he and his friends visited a woman who they knew offered sex in exchange for goods. Their goal was to lose their virginity before deportation.[176] Bedřich Hoffenreich, a thirty-eight-year-old craftsman from Brno, spoke about sexual barter with great frankness: "People did it for three cigarettes, for a dish of potatoes. When a woman saw that someone was receiving a package, she went to that person." Sexual barter in particular and sexuality in general became a social and political statement about social hierarchies in the ghetto.

In contrast with the black market, the barter economy in Terezín was not immoral or criminal.[177] The participants developed their own rules, with value placed on courteousness, favors, and tipping, thus affirming a "correct" way of exchange. In comparison, those prisoners who sold food from the prisoners to the outside were never spoken about, and in fact remain unknown. Similarly, sexual barter was scarcely spoken about. When it was mentioned, the women who bartered sexual services (never men) were described as young, naïve girls who gave up on themselves and did not know what they were doing. Their prostitution was a reaction to their loss of status as Jews.[178] Not only are conclusions about the perceived immorality of bartering drawn only in retrospect; they also reflect the contemporary context of the person making the claim and are hence ahistorical by definition.

Conclusion

Like so many matters in Terezín, pregnancies and babies were intricately tied to the social and ethnic hierarchies of the inmate community. Access to food dictated the fates of two documented Terezín twin pregnancies. Lily Fantlová was the wife of a cook. She was one of the few women who gave birth in Terezín. Not only was Fantlová the only one who gave birth to living twins, Jana and Soňa, but the girls survived infancy.[179] Only men with good access to food had sexual drive. Although women did not need to be well fed to engage in sexual activity—hunger was a key reason for sexual barter—they needed to be in good shape in order to conceive and give birth to a healthy baby. Contrary to Fantlová, Inge Hirschfeld, a twenty-two-year-old caregiver from Berlin, arrived in Terezín in summer 1943, already five months pregnant. Due to malnourishment, she went into premature labor two months later and gave birth to twin girls. Both died hours later.[180] Which women were in a position to carry a pregnancy to term is relevant; it demonstrates who had access to food. Hirschfeld, a German Jew married to another German, did not belong to the social elite and soon became malnourished. Fantlová could carry to term because her husband was a cook. He was even able to purchase a pram.[181] Conversely, as soon as they were outside of the jurisdiction of the Jewish self-administration and at the mercy of the SS, mothers with infants were the least protected group. On October 23, 1944, the Fantls were placed on the penultimate transport to Auschwitz. Fantlová begged Rahm to allow her to take the pram on the transport, but he refused. At the selection in Auschwitz, the meaning of babies shifted drastically: all mothers with young children were sent to the gas chamber, including Lilly Fantlová. Inge Hirschfeld and other mothers whose children had died, on the other hand, had at least a chance at survival. The physical condition and intimate lives of prisoners reflected their position on the social field in Terezín.

The starvation of the elderly in Terezín exemplifies what Amartya Sen found in his study of famines: in situations of shortage, many more people die than is proportional to the food shortfall. Shortages lead to maldistribution, which increases rates of hunger and death. It was the German authorities who consigned Jews to Terezín and restricted the supply of food. But maldistribution, caused by the food categories and corruption, was a consequence of inmate society. Patterns of starvation in Terezín contradicted other situations of scarcity; it was not infants but the elderly who had the highest rate of mortality. The prisoners saw hunger, deprivation, and dying as markers of exclusion, and this view reinforced the process that further relegated the elderly to the lowest level.

4

Medicine and Illness

In 1979, looking back at her imprisonment in Theresienstadt, former nurse Emilie Valentová remembered her boss, the ophthalmologist Richard Stein: "He was a scientist, a specialist, he was operating on, in Theresienstadt, in the conditions there, he was even operating on strabismus, which was then by far not as frequent as today. After the war I realized, he was actually operating on people who were designated to die. But above all, he was a physician."[1] Stein, who survived and emigrated to Israel, becoming one of the key founding physicians of the country, was emblematic of many among the physicians in Theresienstadt.[2]

The doctors in the ghetto tackled the medical conditions as a job, making Health Services probably the best functioning department of the Jewish self-administration.[3] After transports and hunger, illness was the defining experience of Theresienstadt; in this regard it was similar to other ghettos and concentration camps. Because of the conditions created by the Nazis, nearly all prisoners fell ill, and many died. But most of the patients who were treated by the medical department, especially if they fell sick after 1942 and were not old, could regain their health. The prisoner physicians could increasingly provide top-notch medical care, securing decent equipment and a wide range of modern medications. The SS supported medical care because they feared the spread of infections, particularly among the large German population in the proximity of Theresienstadt.[4]

In the Nazi concentration camps, the infirmary represented a central place in the social landscape of camp life, as it embodied both life and death.[5] At times it was the only place where prisoners could seek refuge from forced labor and violence, where they could receive food, rest, and sometimes also medical care.[6] However, at other times it was the place where patients were killed; in other camps, the sickbay became the site of forced medical experiments. This Manichean nature of the sickbay represents the concentration camps in microcosm.

The medical staff viewed Theresienstadt through the framework of public health and saw themselves as having a task to perform within that framework;

The Last Ghetto. Anna Hájková, Oxford University Press (2020). © Oxford University Press.
DOI: 10.1093/oso/9780190051778.001.0001.

MEDICINE AND ILLNESS   133

to the doctors, medicine was a central element in managing Theresienstadt. The healthcare mirrored the general power hierarchies of the ghetto. These power structures were apparent in the medical staff's determinations concerning those "important" patients who were deemed worthy of receiving care and those "unimportant" patients who were not deemed worthy of receiving care, which affected the odds of a patient's survival. This chapter connects Theresienstadt to the wider field of medical history by showing the links between the outside medical world and that of the prisoner physicians. The Terezín doctors were considered modern professionals, and they applied and adapted the same procedures, drugs, and interpretations as their gentile German counterparts. The manner in which prisoner doctors held onto their professionalism and reacted to the persecution foremost as doctors was one of the reasons medical care in Theresienstadt was excellent. It also allowed the physicians a measure of agency.

The Structure of Health Services

The Jewish physicians in Theresienstadt came from a specific world and place, a fact that was reflected in the ways they approached their roles in the ghetto. Jews had been overrepresented in the Central European medical profession since 1900. About 15 percent of physicians in Germany, Austria, and Bohemian lands were Jewish.[7] German doctors were preeminent in the field of medicine worldwide; their research was pathbreaking, and the social and medical insurance introduced in Germany in the 1880s eased access to medical care for many German citizens. In Czechoslovakia, the medical faculty of the (Czech-speaking) Charles University in Prague was progressive and innovative, training many young doctors, while the German University's medical school was a part of the German and Austrian medical network.[8] It also trained many Polish, Romanian, and Russian Jewish medical students, who studied abroad because of antisemitism in their home countries.[9] Many of these students stayed in Czechoslovakia after completing their studies; one such student was the later Communist politician František Kriegel, who left Prague for Spain during the Spanish Civil War. Others were eventually deported to Theresienstadt.

After the Nazi takeover, Jewish medical experts were expelled from universities and state hospitals.[10] In 1938, German Jewish physicians lost their licenses, but some Jewish doctors were allowed to continue practicing among

134   THE LAST GHETTO

Jews as "Krankenbehandler (sick treaters)."[11] In the Czechoslovak Second Republic (1938–1939), Jewish professors were encouraged to resign from medical faculties. Already then, and following the occupation, Czech medical organizations expelled their Jewish members, so most doctors lost their ability to practice.[12] One year later, Prague's hospitals separated their Jewish patients onto isolated floors; later, Czech Jews were allowed to enter only the Jewish hospitals. In Austria, where the ratio of Jews among physicians was even higher—65 percent in Vienna and about one-third Austria-wide—the removal of Jewish physicians took place in the course of only a few months.[13]

The Gesundheitswesen, or Health Services, was one of the first departments established in the ghetto. The department was initially set up in Prague ahead of the first deportations and was to be headed by the Brno-based radiologist Erich Munk.[14] At thirty-seven years of age, Munk was quite young for a leadership position; in addition, radiologists rarely become chief physicians. Munk's youth corresponded with the overall youthful Zionist leadership recruited by Jakov Edelstein and Otto Zucker; in 1941 the latter led the Brno Jewish community and likely met Munk there.[15] The thirty-three-year old surgeon Erich Springer, who had worked at the Prague German University, was assigned to lead the surgery department in the Fair Palace collection camp in December 1941 as part of the Aufbaukommando. Erich Klapp, a thirty-four-year-old TB specialist from Prague, became the head of internal medicine.

With the arrival of the first transports in November and December 1941, people fell sick and became injured; the situation was appalling. The physicians could not help, as they had no medication or instruments. One man who fell ill with appendicitis died after six days.[16] Another patient was operated on with scissors.[17] The three founding doctors of the department, Springer, Munk, and Klapp, set up medical rooms in the first two barracks, Sudeten and Dresden, and collected whatever the newly arrived physicians had brought with them to use as medications and instruments. At the end of 1941 the group set up the bathroom of the Dresden barracks as a second sickbay, which was turned into the surgery in April 1942. The SS then ordered the old military hospital, in the Hohenelbe barracks, to be used as the ghetto hospital.[18] In December 1941 a small outbreak of scarlet fever broke out, which led to the creation of the first department, the isolation ward, led by the nurse Minna Wolfensteinová of Brno.

Hohenelbe barracks became the central location of Health Services. Over the course of the next months, the backbone of the medical services developed: the hospital was set up and doctors and nurses were sought among the prisoners. The medical staff went out in search of medical furniture; in the beginning, there were no beds, tables, or chairs, and operations took place in temporary spaces with patients lying on the ground. With the closing of Jewish hospitals in the Protectorate and Germany, the ghetto received shipments of medications and instruments.[19] Furthermore, prisoners themselves constructed hospital furniture. Each barracks had its own medical unit, infirmary rooms, and equipment.[20] By January 1942, Munk could have his pick from the 563 physicians present in the ghetto.[21] On March 5, 1942, the first radiology office opened, led by Lilly Pokorná.[22] She was an eminent figure in her field (which was then quite new), she was the only woman physician to have presented at interwar radiology conferences, and she had published several articles.[23] Pokorná was divorced from a mixed marriage, and her two children were in England. Her Sudeten German ex-husband Adolf Pokorny later gained notoriety at the Nuremberg trials; in 1942, he suggested to Heinrich Himmler a procedure to sterilize three million Soviet POWs.[24]

Beginning in May 1942, Health Services was run as a central organization headed by a chief physician, with four separate "blocks" (sections of the ghetto) each having its own internal administration. All physicians reported to the office of the Health Services' directorate, which also decided about hiring.[25] Health Services continued to grow. At the end of June 1942, before the ghetto became "open," that is, became a Jewish area only, it had eight specialized walk-in clinics, thirty-four infirmary rooms, and a central hospital. By the summer of 1943, Health Services was the most effectively run department in Theresienstadt. It was also the second largest unit (after the Economic Department), with 4,066 workers, eight hospitals with 2,500 beds, five large senior homes with over 3,000 beds, 635 physicians, and 1,432 staff members.[26] The ratio of physicians to the population was unusually high for the time, almost as high as it is today in Western countries: one doctor for 500 to 600 ghetto residents, or 1.82 physicians for every 1,000 people.[27] (One prisoner-medical statistician calculated that if Czechoslovakia had as many physicians as the ghetto, there would have been 275,000 doctors.) The ghetto also had many more hospital beds per capita, while the average duration of the treatment was the same as in civilian times, nineteen days. Nevertheless, there was a longer wait for treatment.[28]

This large apparatus was much needed, because at any given time throughout the existence of Terezín, the percentage of ill residents was very

136 THE LAST GHETTO

high. In February 1943, 31 percent of the total population was ill.[29] Between the spring and summer of that year, the number of ill individuals rose to between 12,000 and 15,000; more than half were chronically ill seniors.[30] For a town of approximately 46,000, this was an extremely high number. Echoing the overall developments in the ghetto, the elderly were the group with the highest mortality rate: by mid-1943, 25,882 people had already died, and the elderly would account for 77 percent of deaths throughout the duration of Theresienstadt's existence.[31] In fact, the majority of the Terezín dead (20,582 people) perished within a single nine-month period: between August 1942 and March 1943.[32] The result was a brutal kind of attrition of the elderly; in addition to those who died, 16,000 seniors were deported to Treblinka and Maly Trostinets in September and October 1942. By March 1943 the proportions had reversed, as most of the elderly were no longer alive; 64 percent of the treated ill patients were now younger, able-bodied individuals. The number of patients fell accordingly, to only 5,000 bedridden a day in September 1944.[33]

After the initial period, the supply of medications was surprisingly good.[34] One reason was that the Germans were afraid of the spread of infectious diseases, and Theresienstadt was in the immediate proximity of a gentile German population: within half a kilometer of the ghetto was a Wehrmacht military hospital, while the district town of Leitmeritz/Litoměřice was only two kilometers away. In addition, Nazi propaganda about the "advantage ghetto" required the SS to ensure the ghetto looked presentably healthy. Moreover, supplying medication was cheaper than supplying sufficient food, which would have prevented most of the illnesses.[35] These factors help explain the exceptional provision of medical supplies; in Warsaw, Germans were panicking about epidemics but did not provide drugs to ameliorate the situation.[36]

Benno Krönert, the chief physician of nearby Leitmeritz/Litoměřice, was responsible for the medical supplies in the ghetto. He came to make regular checks and turned out to be a good and helpful companion to his Jewish colleagues. After the war he was arrested, but he was later acquitted as a result of the positive testimonies of the former prisoners.[37] Erich Munk traveled regularly to a Roudnice pharmacy.[38] Another reason for the good supply of medications stemmed from a deal Jewish functionaries struck with SS officer Rolf Bartels.[39] At one point a pharmaceutical firm threatened to denounce Bartels for allowing overly large drug deliveries for Jews; it is likely they were resentful at not getting the order themselves. The Jewish functionary Richard

MEDICINE AND ILLNESS 137

Friedmann put them in their place: he asked the firm if it wanted to take on responsibility for Theresienstadt itself—including dealing with epidemics.[40]

Further supplies were delivered from the Gold Crown pharmacy in nearby Budyně nad Ohří. This pharmacy belonged to Jarmila Saicová, the gentile divorced wife of the Theresienstadt doctor Viktor Pentlář.[41] During the anti-Jewish persecution, both he and his sister Emilie Valentová were divorced, as were many other intermarried Czech Jews. The Pentlářs must have remained on good terms, because Health Services likely persuaded the SS to use this small pharmacy in order to receive the best possible deliveries using the Pentlář connection. The surviving delivery lists of medications from the summer of 1944 list all the essential medications used between 1940 and 1945, including pain, dysentery, paratyphoid, and heart medications, as well as sulfa drugs.[42]

Sulfonamides were then new, modern antibiotic drugs, first discovered in 1932 and developed in Germany to fight infections;[43] with the wide use of penicillin after the war, the less effective sulfa drugs became less important. The twenty-six-year-old medic Jindřich Flusser focused on sulfa drugs for the first time in 1943 in Theresienstadt; he even wrote an article about the modern, expensive drug, which he lost upon arrival in Auschwitz in May 1944.[44] Like Flusser, many continental physicians were fascinated by the sulfa drugs. At the same time, to perform research on them, German doctors conducted forced experiments on female Polish prisoners in Ravensbrück.[45]

We do not know how often the drug deliveries came, so it is unclear what quantities the Theresienstadt doctors received, but deliveries included many modern drugs, and the monthly bill ran up to half a million crowns.[46] In 1942 insulin was scarce, and some diabetics died as a result. The Danes who came with the visit of the International Red Cross in June 1944 brought a vast supply of insulin, and apparently more supplies of insulin arrived in general deliveries.[47] In addition, the Shipping detail and some gendarmes smuggled in specialized medications.[48] The ghetto also received deliveries of medical instruments and specialized furniture, which was either delivered from former Jewish practices or purchased. As the war progressed, the availability of medical supplies in Germany worsened; the Reich was cut off from imports, and medications were needed at the front. In 1943 Lilly Pokorná had to accompany a visiting Wehrmacht officer on a tour of the ghetto. He inquired whether she had any photographic material for taking X-rays. She had little, she answered, and often had to make do with X-ray paper. The

138   THE LAST GHETTO

officer was amazed; in Vienna, there had been no X-ray photographic material to be had for months.[49]

The surviving surgical notes of Erich Springer offer insight into the operations performed in the ghetto.[50] Springer's operations were complex, heterogeneous, and state of the art. The most frequent surgery was on hernias (thirty-four), followed by ileus operations. Intestinal obstruction is a rare condition, but in Theresienstadt, with changes in diet, avitaminosis, and the sudden lack of food, intestinal obstructions occurred frequently.[51] The ileus patients were urgently X-rayed, sometimes even in the middle of the night, and then operated on.[52] Other surgeries were performed on patients with perforated stomach and peptic ulcers, appendicitis, tumors, TB, and gall bladder infections. Most of the patients were over sixty years of age, one-third over seventy, but only 4 percent over eighty. The operations occurred quite late after the initial appearance of the symptoms, probably because the patients were not transferred to Health Services immediately; they were also often undernourished. Both circumstances led to high postoperative mortality. The poor state of patients was the main reason Springer often did not opt to perform more extensive operations.

The SS was keen to take advantage of the prisoner physicians and the ghetto's medical infrastructure. The SS was aware that there were excellent doctors in Theresienstadt, and they occasionally sought them out for their own medical treatment.[53] Moreover, the medical services were a frequent point of inspection for external visitors, including SS, Wehrmacht officers, and German physicians. These visits were motivated by the Germans' fear of "Jewish infections," as well as the assumption that the camp was as good, or as bad, as its hospital. But the German physicians also liked to take advantage of Theresienstadt. Werner Kirchert, the chief physician of the RSHA, visited in September 1944 and asked to speak with experts on nicotine acid and criminological literature.[54] Germans taking advantage of prisoner physicians' knowledge also led to one set of medical experiments taking place in Theresienstadt: the Heilgas (healing gas) experiments. An influential physician with good contacts in the SS wanted to prove that his discovery, the treatment of inflammation by medications delivered in gas, was effective. In the summer of 1944, Health Services set up a special department with twenty patients to experimentally treat phlegmons (inflammation of soft tissue that spreads under the skin or inside the body) and abscesses with the healing gas. A camera, albeit always in the hands of an SS man, was used to document the experiments.[55] Most patients found the treatments, which went on until winter 1945, beneficial at best or harmless at worst.[56]

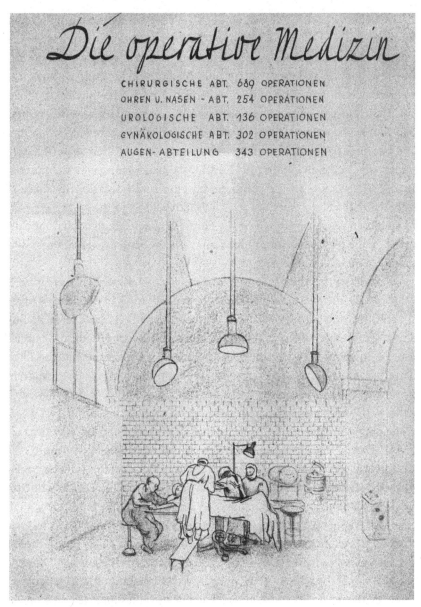

Jo Spier's *Die Operative Medizin* (Surgery) depicts four doctors, three surgeons, and one anesthesiologist, all of them men, operating on a patient. The operating room is modern; there are lights and medical machines, and the surgeons wear masks. The vaulted high ceiling reveals the architecture of the Theresienstadt barracks. The drawing is part of a report on Health Services that provides statistics on its five surgical departments. Courtesy of the Jewish Museum, Prague.

140   THE LAST GHETTO

Health Services also had several specialized departments. One of the eight hospitals was a children's hospital with about a hundred beds, run by the Mikulov doctor Hanuš Schaffa.[57] All patients in this hospital were under fifteen years of age, and they could stay in the hospital for up to a year; most were either battling an infectious disease, during one of the epidemics, or had TB. The children's hospital was outstanding, in large part because the best and youngest doctors and nurses were assigned to take care of the children, and because the medical staff saw their work with children as particularly important.[58] Like all children in Terezín, the patients received preferential food.[59] The doctors in the children's hospital could occasionally successfully lobby the SS for special food and medications. In the spring of 1943, night blindness, caused by a lack of vitamin A, affected both adults and children. Yet the physicians were able to persuade the SS to deliver vitamins and carrots to the children's hospital.[60]

By contrast, the department of Welfare was not viewed as a priority; it was overwhelmed with a high number of patients and had poor access to resources. The only exception was the subsection of infants' welfare: all infants and their mothers lived in infants' homes run by the Medical Services. Mostly, however, the department was in charge of the permanently disabled and the nonworking, including the physically and mentally ill, little children, prisoners in the ghetto prison, invalids, the blind and deaf, and the feeble elderly. The Welfare Department was set up during the summer of 1942, coinciding with the arrival of thousands of elderly German and Austrian Jews.[61] Karel Fleischmann, a forty-five-year-old dermatologist from České Budějovice, was in charge of the department.[62] Fleischmann, who had a deformed back, was a man of many talents. In addition to his work as a doctor, he drew pictures and wrote fiction. In October 1943 his department took care of 11,515 people, and the number remained high until the fall transports in 1944.[63] Welfare differentiated between "closed" and "open" care—that is, between people who were institutionalized (such as the elderly in homes for the old) and those who lived in "normal" accommodations. This separation removed the most vulnerable from the public eye and supported the impression that life in Theresienstadt was not only about suffering. This spatial division made it easier to sever the ties between the disabled and the healthy. The disabled were often too weak to leave their accommodations to look for help. There are no numbers to examine the impact of such separation on mortality, but it seems likely that living in closed care often translated into living, and dying, out of sight.[64]

MEDICINE AND ILLNESS   141

H. G. Adler, survivor historian and widower of an outstanding doctor, argued that while Fleischmann was well meaning and attempted to improve these sad conditions, he failed organizationally.[65] Fleischmann's testimony demonstrates his horror and disgust at some of the people in his care: "the crippled girl with the spirit of a 12 year old who has never left her wheelchair"; "the 94-year old human spider. [. . .] The nurse lifts this 30kg something from the wheelchair. A wizened, little, evil face [. . .] and make it go away now."[66] He further described the elderly in the senior homes as troglodytes.[67] At Fleischmann's side were two German colleagues who were in charge of the chronically ill elderly. The Frankfurt rabbi Leopold Neuhaus led Welfare for the Elderly Department and endeavored to provide individual care. The internist Hermann Strauß trained twelve older nurses to take care of the sick elderly. Fleischmann, however, ridiculed the work of both.[68]

On the bottom of the Terezín medical care class structure was the insane asylum, placed in a section of the Kavalier barracks. The ghetto asylum was exclusively custodial rather than therapeutic, thus returning to the standard methods of care used prior to 1917.[69] The conditions in the asylum stood in stark contrast to much of the Terezín Health Services. Erich Springer compared the situation in the asylum to those of mental institutions in the eighteenth century.[70] The dark, wet, and strictly isolated Kavalier, built into the town walls and positioned opposite the hospital in Hohenelbe, housed the chronically ill elderly. Those Jewish mentally disabled individuals who were not murdered through euthanasia (Jewish mentally ill were the most decimated group in the Nazi euthanasia killings) were deported to Theresienstadt in the spring and summer of 1942. The Prague Bohnice asylum had already separated its Jewish patients into a separate wing two years before.[71] The asylum in Terezín accommodated women and men together. The dirty and hungry patients suffered in the unhygienic, claustrophobic conditions; patients were never allowed to leave their rooms. There were about 240 patients, most of whom either perished in Theresienstadt or were deported to Auschwitz.[72] For the nurses, the work was particularly exhausting, and there were no bonuses.[73]

Other prisoners spoke of the mentally ill with dread and disrespect. When Trude Neumann, the mentally ill daughter of Theodor Herzl, was deported to Theresienstadt in the fall of 1942, she asked Edelstein for help. He dismissed her, saying that all her life she had been an assimilationist, and now she would opportunistically use her father's efforts for Zionism. Edelstein's biographer, Ruth Bondy, related the story and depicted Neumann

142   THE LAST GHETTO

as ludicrous.[74] A further story illustrates the difficult position of the inmates in the asylum: in November 1943, the SS sent a closed transport of twenty-three German Jews from Berlin, all of whom were apparently mentally ill *Geltungsjuden* and partners from mixed marriages. One of these individuals was Hanna Erdmann, a forty-eight-year-old divorced Cuxhaven mother of two small boys who was arrested in 1938, became depressed in prison, and attempted suicide. She spent the next eighteen months locked in a room with four men and three women, taking care of a little girl, Margot Raphael, who developed TB in the dreadful conditions.[75] After much effort by the Jewish functionaries, Margot was allowed to be X-rayed and transferred to the children's hospital.[76] Unlike most mentally ill people in Terezín, Hanna, Margot, and most of their transport survived. Hanna was reunited with her children. In 2010, Margot was living in assisted living in Ahlen.[77]

Irma Goldmannová, one of the three leading women doctors in the ghetto, headed the Pathology Department. From February 1943, Pathology was housed in the newly constructed crematorium situated outside of the ghetto walls, toward Bohušovice. Goldmannová had the task of performing autopsies on certain categories of deaths, such as those individuals who died of infectious diseases, imprecise diagnoses, and tumors, as well as the deaths of all young people; altogether, between 15 and 23 percent of the dead had postmortems. After the initial difficult conditions—Goldmannová and her staff had to work in a room without running water, gloves, or suitable autopsy tables—the SS had two marble tables delivered from Hannover, as well as various instruments.[78] The postmortem analysis was, however, limited to bacterioscopy (that is, observing bacteria with a microscope), as the Jewish physicians were not allowed to work with bacteria strains. The samples were instead sent to Herwig Hamperl, the new head of the Pathology Institute of the German University in Prague.[79] Writing his memoirs in the 1970s, Hamperl, who liked to see himself as "the decent German" among the occupiers, claimed that he had learned about Theresienstadt only in 1944.[80] In this denial of his Nazi past, Hamperl was very much part of a trend among German academics at the German Charles University.[81] It is impossible that Hamperl, as the director, would have not known about the samples from Terezín; his institute was small. The samples from Theresienstadt represented an uncomfortable reminder of his complicity in genocide.

Hamperl's Terezín colleagues were proud to remark that their autopsies—altogether about eight thousand—were conducted according to the rules and that their minutes were in Latin.[82] The postmortem records, together with

MEDICINE AND ILLNESS 143

the diagnoses, were entered into the death certificates, which were apparently filled out truthfully.[83] None of the prisoner doctors ever remarked that according to Jewish law it is prohibited to conduct autopsies on the Jewish dead. In Western and Central Europe, Jewish hospitals had conducted autopsies since 1900, an unthinkable act for Orthodox Jews. Eastern European medical faculties of the 1920s and 1930s were shaken by a scandal when Jewish medical students were ordered to dissect Jewish rather than gentile cadavers— an impossible task, as the Orthodox law, prohibiting the Jewish dead to be opened, was upheld.[84] This scandal, together with *numerus clausus* (a cap on the number of Jewish students), ultimately led many Eastern European Jewish students to study at the German University in Prague.

In the summer of 1942, faced with skyrocketing mortality, the SS ordered the building of a modern crematorium, where four ovens burned day and night. The SS ordered the physicians to look for dental gold. Sometimes the bodies arrived with broken jaws; after they died, other prisoners removed their gold teeth. One inmate had half a kilogram of gold in his luggage when he was deported to Auschwitz. Sometimes the crematorium also burned the bodies from the Small Fortress, and in the last months of the war it also burned bodies from Richard, a nearby auxiliary camp of Flossenbürg.

Another part of the sanitary facilities was Disinfection, housed in the former brewery. Headed by the chemist Josef Pacovský, the Disinfection Department had the task of removing insects from both the inmates and the Terezín buildings. With the crowded conditions of the ghetto, first lice and later bedbugs became rampant. The unit disinfected houses, which entailed relocating the inhabitants, isolating all openings, and using Zyklon B to gas the building. The inmates had no idea about the other, far wider use of the disinfectant; Zyklon B was used in the gas chambers. The Zyklon B used in the cleaning was provided by the firm Draslovka from Kolín and came from the Department of the Extermination of Vermin, under the control of the Waffen SS and the police from Auschwitz.[85]

Newly arrived prisoners were subjected to disinfection: they were undressed, were checked, and their hair was often cut short. Meanwhile, their clothing was gassed. After a shower, the people were touched up with Lysol. The same procedure was repeated as soon as an inmate became infected with lice. This procedure was often distressing: standing in front of others, often people of opposite gender, naked, had a dehumanizing effect.[86] Women were particularly upset at having their hair cut. Lilly Pokorná remembered that one of her nurses who fell ill with ileus was shorn of her hair after the operation

144 THE LAST GHETTO

and had to wear a kerosene bandage. The nurse was more anguished as a result of being bald than by the painful postoperative symptoms.[87] The seniors, who were frequently infected and generally perceived as dirty, often died in the aftermath of the disinfection. After the hot bath, the weakened elderly waited for hours in an unheated room for their cleaned clothing.[88] The disinfection was of limited effect, as the insects always came back.

In sum, Health Services was remarkably robust in terms of personnel numbers and qualifications. By 1943 there were relatively decent numbers of beds and a steady supply of medications. The main challenge was the number of patients who were disproportionately elderly and physically weak, making it exceedingly difficult to administer effective medical treatments. Furthermore, the elderly patients suffered both because they were less sturdy overall due to age and because they were neglected and discriminated against within Theresienstadt. The only group who were treated with even more severe neglect were the mentally and physically disabled. By contrast, as everywhere in the ghetto, children were a privileged category.

Illnesses

In the unhygienic, crowded conditions of Theresienstadt, disease spread quickly. People fell prey to illnesses they would not have had in normal life and died of infections that would be easily combatable elsewhere. Moreover, most prisoners were weakened by starvation, and a deficit of vitamins resulted in organisms being more vulnerable to illness; patients in advanced stages of enteritis also showed avitaminosis B.[89] Nearly all prisoners in Terezín were affected by enteritis. For the elderly, the disease often had deadly consequences.[90] Enteritis is a generic intestinal inflammation, resulting in diarrhea, which in extreme cases leads to dehydration and cardiac failure. Enteritis claimed the majority of those who died in Terezín. It was the main cause of death until October 1943; after that, most deaths were caused by pneumonia, TB, intestinal obstruction, and blood poisoning.[91] But while the other diseases were treated, enteritis rarely was.[92] We can speculate whether the treatment—which includes saline drips, careful diet, and good care—would have been possible in Theresienstadt. Health Services had saline drips and about twenty-five hundred beds. Yet using these spaces for old prisoners affected with enteritis would have meant having far less space for other patients. The conditions in Theresienstadt, created by the Nazis,

MEDICINE AND ILLNESS   145

fostered disease, and accordingly, the physicians faced a large percentage of ill residents. In this situation, Health Services applied a triage mentality, in which the most frequent disease, enteritis, which was usually dangerous only for the elderly, was seen as unimportant. This triage mentality in medical care echoed that of the self-administration in food distribution. This categorization of illnesses, alongside incarceration, hunger, and dirt, contributed to the extremely high mortality rate among older patients.

In the 1930s, tuberculosis was a widespread, often fatal, disease usually associated with the working class and poor living conditions. But since the end of the nineteenth century, it had also been seen as a Jewish disease, attributable to the poor Eastern European Jewish migrants.[93] The prevalence of TB thus represented a fitting marker of the prisoners' social descent. By spring 1943, the Terezín physicians realized the illness had become pandemic; Lilly Pokorná remembered that initially, she and her colleagues spotted so many shadows on X-rays that they thought they were seeing sulfonamides residua rather than TB. In the crowded conditions and poor food, the percentage of people infected with TB rose to 7.8 percent.[94]

Terezín physicians opted for a wide range of treatments, dispatching entire barracks' populations for X-ray checks and sputum analysis.[95] The Genie barracks housed a separate TB hospital, led by František Löwit, the former chief pulmonary doctor of the Czechoslovak railways.[96] Divorced by his gentile wife and separated from his teenaged daughter, Löwit was remembered as a dedicated, outstanding physician.[97] The Terezín treatment of TB was that of the outside world: quiet, good diet, and a pneumothorax procedure, in which the surgeons collapsed part of or the whole lung to enable it to stop working and heal; only after the war, with the administration of antibiotics, did TB become a disease of the past. The SS headquarters ordered the numbers in the official reports to be lowered, and in 1944, purposefully deported the TB patients to Auschwitz.[98] Still, some patients got better, so much so that they survived the selection in Auschwitz and the subsequent camps.[99] TB was indeed a widespread illness in Nazi ghettos; by 1944, it accounted for almost two-thirds of the fatalities in Lodz.[100]

In spite of the enforced density in which people lived, Theresienstadt experienced only one full-blown epidemic, which occurred at the end of the war. The prisoners who arrived on the death marches brought with them typhus. The disease killed more than 1,200 people, with most of victims among the approximately 14,000 newly arrived inmates. Fewer than 126 among the 16,777 veteran inmates died, among them dozens of nurses and

146 THE LAST GHETTO

doctors, including Minna Wolfensteinová, the founding nurse of the isolation ward.[101] However, the medical staff spoke of four epidemics: scarlet fever in December 1941 and January 1942, typhoid in January–March 1943, encephalitis in summer 1943, and the typhus epidemic in April and May 1945.[102] The way Terezín doctors categorized these epidemics demonstrates the triage mentality of Health Services.

The typhoid outbreak in the winter of 1943 epitomizes the way Terezín doctors categorized patients. This epidemic started in January 1943 when a sewage pipe that led to a kitchen in a youth home burst.[103] Typhoid spread quickly, infecting 444 prisoners, both children and adults,[104] with an overall mortality rate of 9.63 percent.[105] Gonda Redlich, the head of Youth Care, and other leading physicians were dismayed that the illness was killing children. At that time, five transports made up of seven thousand people were departing for Auschwitz. Munk lobbied for the exemption of 113 individuals from the medical staff from Transport Cs, pointing out: "We are at the border of a calamity that I cannot really describe."[106]

However, the number of children who died of typhoid from January to March was very low: twelve in February and one in March.[107] Even the overall numbers of children's deaths were low: twenty, twenty-eight, and twelve, respectively. This information comes from death certificates; it is improbable they were underreported. In the same period, the total mortality in the population was 2,506 in January, 2,271 in February, and 1,653 in March. The great majority of those who died were older inmates who died of enteritis. Even though there were far more elderly people than children in Theresienstadt (about fifty-five thousand elderly to nine thousand children),[108] this huge disparity shows that the prisoner physicians barely registered the six thousand deceased elderly people in the same period, instead focusing on thirteen dead children. In their conception of noteworthy deaths, the doctors reiterated the triage mentality.

The medical staff in Theresienstadt often viewed the ghetto as an issue of public health; that is, everyone's health was their responsibility.[109] They saw it as their goal to develop a preventative health system reaching beyond illness treatment. While medical leaders in other ghettos like Lodz and Warsaw also displayed a pronounced emphasis on public health, it seems that Theresienstadt doctors, making use of the well-functioning Health Services, took it the furthest.[110] The ghetto administration documents, as well as physicians' postwar testimonies, demonstrate the view that medicine was the central element in the running of the ghetto. The Jewish functionaries and prisoner doctors used medicine as a tool to come to terms with the challenges of living in a crowded prison; this is why they instituted area-wide X-rays to test for tuberculosis and made it obligatory to report infectious diseases. Similarly, after the typhoid epidemic, Health Services introduced obligatory immunization for all new arrivals. Fifty years later, the Viennese doctor Franz Hahn celebrated the hands-on approach of vaccinators:

> We dealt with the typhoid epidemic, the hygienic measures were intensified, typhoid is, after all, a question of hygiene. [...] Mind you, how we treat typhoid today, with antibiotics, that hadn't existed yet. And so we treated typhoid only in the traditional way, attend to the heart, attend to the circulation, lower the temperature, yes? Prevent the epidemic, for heaven's sake, wash hands, wash hands, disinfect, yes? Look after the nurses, so that it does not spread. [...] Vaccinate, of course, there has always been the typhoid serum, not 100% effective or at least by far not as effective as the one we have today, which you take orally, back then we injected it, which hurt, but without mercy, the entire camp was vaccinated lock stock and barrel, there was no other way.[111]

This comprehensive approach to mass prevention and the key role of Health Services, extolled by the doctors, was a classic moment of social hygiene. Even if the vaccination was not entirely effective, it still worked and thus saved the lives of thousands of Terezín veteran prisoners during the epidemic at the end of the war. After the war, Viktor Kindermann claimed that he had ordered the typhoid immunizations,[112] while the surviving Jewish physicians made the same claim, continuing the trend of describing the medical care in the ghetto as their responsibility and accomplishment.

One reaction to incarceration in Theresienstadt was suicide. Those who took their lives did so most often by taking poison or jumping from windows. Suicide usually occurred either shortly after their arrival or during departing transports. Historians have discussed whether suicide in the camps was an act of free will, a response to extreme pressure and hence part of the persecution, or a persecution-related reaction akin to mental illness.[113] The suicides in Theresienstadt can be interpreted as being in all of these categories. It seems that for most, taking one's own life represented a last act of free will, a decision to die a quick and more dignified death than the slow and dirty dying of enteritis and malnutrition. The Ulm nurse Resi Weglein viewed with admiration the new arrivals who had the resolve to take their own lives.[114]

148   THE LAST GHETTO

However, newcomers needed several weeks to integrate into the ghetto, and the staff of Health Services actively prevented people from taking their own lives. A "reception committee," based in the Welfare Department and led by Berliner Regina Jonas, the first woman rabbi, together with the Viennese psychologist Viktor Frankl, offered psychological support to the new arrivals. By 1943, when the arrivals had decreased, the committee was dismantled, and Jonas and Frankl were reassigned to take care of the mentally ill and the neurological clinic in the Hannover barracks, respectively.[115]

Between 1941 and 1943, a total of 430 inmates committed suicide. According to the statistician Rudolf Löwith, the age distribution of those attempting suicide corresponded to the ghetto population as a whole but included disproportionately more women than suicides in the outside population. Of those who attempted to kill themselves, 57.2 percent were successful.[116] Among the people who committed suicide was sixty-eight-year-old Max Cohen from Cologne, who committed suicide by poison in May 1944, as he was facing transport to Auschwitz.[117] Another suicide was an unnamed man who in January 1943 tried to rob an old woman and broke her arm. He committed suicide in the ghetto prison.[118]

With the exception of the first months of the ghetto duration, much of being sick, even for the elderly, was a social affair. Their roommates or family members fetched their food; after two weeks, their food rations were recategorized into those of nonworkers, unless a doctor prescribed convalescence food rations. Some elderly went to the doctor because of their loneliness: "They go to the doctor as they would have gone to a café," remarked a medical statistician in summer 1943.[119] Others went to a walk-in clinic because in Theresienstadt the medical care was free, and in civil life, they would have had to pay for the same service, not to that medical care for Jews in the years before the deportation had been very limited.[120]

If they succeeded in receiving care, the Terezín inmates enjoyed being ill, because in the ghetto environment, the hospitals were a safe place, even a nice experience overall. The ill were excused from labor duty with a doctor's note and stayed "home." The patients received better and richer food, delivered to their beds; slept in individual, clean beds; and had a nurse caring for them. This experience of care and attention was particularly vital for the elderly. The sixty-nine-year-old Berliner and former teacher Käthe Breslauer remembered her stay in the hospital warmly: "Those six weeks that I spent in the hospital were the nicest time of my stay in Theresienstadt: Clean beds, kind nurses, better food, far from the misery of the accommodation."[121] The hospitals were also a positive experience for the younger prisoners: twenty-four-year-old Ilse Fuchsová from Ostrava spent most of her time in Terezín sick and then recovering from jaundice and encephalitis. She was deported to Auschwitz and Lenzing once she was healthy.[122] Remarkably, there were only a few instances of faking illness to be exempt when people were called for transport.

Benjamin Murmelstein's operation provides a good example of how a prominent patient was treated. In August 1944 the deputy Elder of Jews was waiting for an operation on a hernia that had ruptured during the deportation to Nisko in 1939.[123] Murmelstein's surgery caused great commotion in Health Services: the hospital relocated patients in order to set him up in a pleasant, spacious room fitted with good furniture and a silk blanket. A particularly competent nurse who was supposed to have that day off was called in to work.[124] But because operations on the Jewish leadership had to be approved by the SS headquarters, Murmelstein did not have his surgery; Rahm rejected the request.[125] The SS was already planning the large fall transports, which would start six weeks later, and apparently Murmelstein had been chosen to become Eppstein's successor as the next Elder.

In the second half of the nineteenth century there was a widespread medical notion that Jews were more susceptible to certain illnesses.[126] By the 1930s and 1940s, that view had lost most of its power; today we see this mentality as a product of the antisemitism of the time. However, some physicians in Terezín still gave this theory some credit. Even Lilly Pokorná, the forty-eight-year-old modern physician, kept an eye out to see if she could observe a higher level of cancer, a presumably Jewish illness, among her patients in Terezín, and she was relieved that the levels were those of the average population.[127] Quite different was the judgment of the eminent internist Hermann Strauß, twenty-six years Pokorná's senior, who had published extensively on "Jewish diseases." He wrote, lectured, and continued his medical observations in Terezín.[128] Strauß was of the older generation, and his medical socialization was intertwined with certain antisemitic stereotypes. In August 1943, twelve hundred Jewish children from Bialystok arrived in Theresienstadt; Himmler planned to exchange them with Jewish organizations for money. The children were frightened, dirty, and hungry; they had experienced the liquidation of the Białystok ghetto. The Jewish administration convened a meeting of the Youth Care and Health Services. Willy Groag recalled that to the shock of other functionaries, Strauß expressed the opinion that the

150 THE LAST GHETTO

Bialystok Jews were always dirty and hence it was no wonder that this was the children's condition when they came to Theresienstadt.[129]

Abortions were performed frequently in Theresienstadt. Since April 1943, all women who became pregnant in Theresienstadt had to undergo an abortion, following an order of the second commandant, Anton Burger.[130] Any woman who did not follow the order was to be deported with her child. It is not clear why the SS enforced this prohibition. Theresienstadt served in their eyes as a transit ghetto, from which all prisoners were to be sent elsewhere to be murdered. Burger may have acted on a whim, and Karl Rahm, his successor, upheld the rule. The direction was strictly implemented until December 1944 and was then softened to a certain degree during Murmelstein's tenure. Both the father and the doctor who failed to report the pregnancy could be punished. The house elders had to keep track of the menstrual periods of all women inhabitants born between 1889 and 1928.[131] The newly arrived women prisoners were checked for pregnancy; in September 1944, Pokorná had to X-ray the women of childbearing age in the large Dutch transport.[132]

Many younger prisoners, especially those with access to food, could be sexually active. There was little access to contraceptives; only a few prisoners were able to get condoms smuggled in from the outside.[133] A substantial number of women did not menstruate or did not get their periods regularly in Theresienstadt. Sexually active women found themselves in an impossible situation: they were without any possibility of controlling whether they would conceive while also unable to decide to deliver their children.[134] While it is difficult to estimate numbers, at least a thousand abortions were performed, a number that could be higher.[135] Surgically speaking, an abortion is an easy operation. Růžena Ranschburgerová, who worked in the ghetto as a nurse, recalled that "they did abortions like on a conveyor belt, pregnancy was a criminal offence, there was nothing to be done."[136]

Hilde Pohlmann, a young Berlin nurse who was dating the much older physician Otto Šťastný, was one of those who found themselves pregnant: "Suddenly, I felt restless and nauseous. I visited a gynaecologist to be certain. [. . .] The self-administration provided a barrack where they performed abortions, assembly-line style. I immediately registered and stayed there for two days."[137] However, other women were mortified by the public nature of their condition and the gossip; the pregnancy had to be reported and the abortion had to be rubber-stamped by Munk.[138] Interestingly, while many physicians and other chroniclers described abortions as particularly wrenching, using terms of genocide, many of the women in question described their pregnancy and abortion as Pohlmann did, as an inconvenience to be got over.[139] Yet other women were forced to undergo abortions late in their pregnancies, in the last term or even during birth. These operations were far more difficult; some patients nearly bled to death and later were unable to have children.[140] For the physicians, participating in delivering a healthy fetus and killing it during delivery was traumatizing.[141]

Overall, illness in Theresienstadt was not only a specific physiological, immunological reaction to the ghetto. It could also be a psychological mechanism indicating the powerlessness of Holocaust victims. Many of the new arrivals contracted a disease in the first months of their stay.[142] In her first twelve months in Theresienstadt, twenty-four-year-old Etta Veit Simon from Berlin contracted dysentery, typhoid, scarlet fever, jaundice, and heart weakness, and she lost fifteen kilograms.[143] In testimonies, the period of illness was often represented as a narrative gap standing in for a loss of control. For many of the newly arrived, becoming ill was a coping mechanism when things became too difficult. The shock of the arrival signified a crisis caused by the extreme experience of powerlessness that affected all Holocaust victims.[144] People loathe being powerless, and this is why becoming ill, stepping aside from the responsibility to manage coping, was such an obvious and socially acceptable way of excusing oneself from taking control. The overwhelming experience of powerlessness bred by the dirt, hunger, and injustice could be put on hold when one was ill. But prisoners rarely remembered much about this initial instance of falling ill because it involved the feeling of being overpowered. For the elderly, whose friends could only rarely bring extra food or bribe officials for reliable medical help, the first disease often became fatal. For the younger inmates, it was an episode usually narrated as an aside.

Physicians, Nurses, and Power

For Jewish physicians, Terezín represented a possibility of agency after the years during which they had been stripped of their licenses, been barred from treating non-Jews, and faced other humiliations. They saw the ghetto as both a medical problem and a challenge that they had the knowledge and power to solve. Unlike most other prisoners, even the Jewish functionaries, physicians continued in their jobs, and the jobs they had to perform were

152 THE LAST GHETTO

immensely important in Theresienstadt, a site marked by hardships. They could make a real difference, alleviate pain and suffering, and cure illnesses. In addition, working as a doctor was a source of esteem: in Central Europe during the 1930s and 1940s, being a physician was a prestigious profession, which is why vocational continuity was for them so crucial.

Addressing physicians with their title expressed people's respect for them and their profession; physicians are the only strangers who possess knowledge about our bodies. We can observe physicians' symbolic capital at work in Theresienstadt, where nearly all physicians registered with their title.[145] An anecdote shows how the Hungarian Dutch dentist couple Elisabeth and Hendrik Egyedi asserted the significance of their status as doctors. The Egyedis arrived with the large transport from Westerbork in September 1944; at registration, they failed to register their title. Elisabeth practiced in Theresienstadt as a doctor caring for a group of elderly Hungarian women.[146] On May 5, 1945, the day the SS handed over control of Theresienstadt to the International Red Cross, and while the typhus epidemic brought by thousands of prisoners from death marches was reaching its peak, the Egyedis applied to have their title included on their ghetto IDs.[147]

Theresienstadt doctors keenly stressed their work ethic,[148] which was also linked to the medical profession as a whole, known for long working hours and absolute dedication. Erich Munk worked twenty-hour days and expected the same dedication from his doctors; Springer passed this on to the nurses.[149] Both nurses and doctors were devoted to their jobs, especially the hospital staff and to a lesser degree the doctors in walk-in clinics or the Welfare Department. The nurse Minna Wolfensteinová experienced Terezín as a sort of liberation: after living through decades as a socially rejected divorcée, she ran the isolation ward and was well-liked and well-known.[150]

The entire medical system was simplified in Terezín: there were no (real) salaries, no taxes, and no telephones, and while the orders for drugs and instruments had to be approved by the SS, most doctors did not have to worry about financial matters. The ghetto was a dream come true for the physicians' planning mentality. Springer's recollection that "the cooperation of the departments was exemplary, certainly much better than in civilian hospitals, perhaps because we had no long distances and then the physicians shared the same fate; for us, there were only moral duties and successes, in no way financial ones" indicated how much the doctors saw the ghetto as a drawing board.[151]

MEDICINE AND ILLNESS 153

The Theresienstadt physicians described their work in terms of achievements that would be valid in the outside world. The physicians worked in a collegial yet competitive atmosphere; doctors worked hard to have the "best" station and better instruments, to be more successful and hence envied by colleagues.[152] Depicting "his" hospital, Springer spoke about "the best possible care" and "incessant improvements," emphasizing how difficult it was to achieve success. In their postwar testimonies, they brought up illnesses, deaths, and epidemics in order to portray Theresienstadt as having been rescued by medical personnel.[153] Similarly, the TB specialist Evžen Kraus spoke of the treatment of tuberculosis patients in terms of accomplishments, stressing that the Terezín hospitals could be compared to those outside.[154] Lilly Pokorná was immensely proud of "her" X-ray station and pointed out that her work resulted in two postwar publications.[155] Prisoner physicians' postwar articles published in medical journals are a special subgenre of testimony. In these the doctors, like Jewish functionaries, described their careers in Theresienstadt as an item in their CVs.[156] Indeed, in general people take pride in their accomplishments, and this tendency continued in the camps and ghettos.

In addition to performing medical services, playing and enjoying music was another form of performing status in Theresienstadt, where music was a particularly beloved activity.[157] Erich Munk was one of the very few prisoners with a record player.[158] Erich Klapp, the head internist, was a keen cellist and organized string quartet concerts in his room.[159] Playing music at home was a sign of belonging to the Central European educated bourgeoisie. For physicians, playing music was moreover a means of cultivation, beyond solely the medical craft.[160] After the Viennese Franz Hahn had spent a few months among the internists, Klapp invited him to join his quartet; they played a string version of Mozart's flute concerto.[161]

For the older doctors, who only rarely practiced in Theresienstadt, the situation was very different. Munk's medical team represented the youth, those of the first generation of Jewish functionaries who built up the ghetto.[162] Because Munk led Health Services until October 1944, there was little generational change. Physicians over sixty-five years of age who applied for medical jobs were usually rejected, a situation that changed only after October 1944.[163] Before that time, Health Services only employed a few older, usually well-known physicians. Perhaps the best known among them was Hermann Strauß, born in 1868, an eminent internist and one of the founders of gastroenterology. In 1910 he had joined the staff of the Jewish hospital in Berlin,

154   THE LAST GHETTO

which he eventually came to direct.[164] Strauß and his wife Elsa, a noted social worker, were deported to Theresienstadt in July 1942. Strauß's reknown saved his life; Heinrich Stahl, upon hearing about his imminent arrival at Theresienstadt, arranged for Strauß to receive a preferential room and better than usual food rations.[165] When Hermann and Elsa Strauß became ill with acute enteritis, they survived thanks to the care of Erich Klapp and Viktor Hahn, the medical head of the Hamburg barracks. At the same time, both of Strauß's siblings perished. In October 1942, Strauß joined the Council of Elders and put Hahn's entire family on his protection list.[166] Strauß did not practice as a physician in Theresienstadt, but he often accompanied Klapp as a consultant; in addition, he led the medical research seminar. Other doctors of advanced years who were able to secure positions in Health Services included Emil Klein, one of the founders of homeopathy; the surgeon Jan Levit of Charles University; Hans Hirschfeld, the eminent German hematologist who worked under Gertrud Adlerová; and Ota Morgenstern-Říkovský, a sanitarian and epidemiologist.

Terezín was the final station for many older, once eminent Central European doctors. Among the forgotten, formerly distinguished doctors was Martha Wygodzinski, a well-known Weimar social democratic politician and antiabortion activist who was deported to Theresienstadt when she was seventy-three; she died there of severe malnutrition and enterecolitis in February 1943.[167] In 1949 in Detroit, Hermann Bohm looked back at his once well-known Hamburg colleagues, none of whom had returned: "Among the Hamburgers in Theresienstadt, in addition to me, there were 13 male and 3 female physicians; I am the only survivor. These people ended either there or in Auschwitz: Korach, Adam, Sarason, Zacharias, Stern, Peltersohn, Lehr, Mendel, Majuhl, de Castro, Fränkel, Glaser, Borgzinner, Schindler, Jonas, Meyer-Arends. Not even their ashes are left. All boxes with ashes were thrown into the Eger River once the bandits saw that their cause was going awry."[168]

The medical community in Theresienstadt was simultaneously transnational and representative of stark ethnic power structure differences. The social elite of young Czech Jewish prisoners was replicated among the doctors. The Essen nurse Regina Oelze, a widow from a mixed marriage, remarked: "Almost all nurses and physicians [. . .] were Czech. It is their country too and they were in the first transport."[169] Indeed, the physicians in Health Services, in particular those in leading positions, were mostly Czech Jews.[170]

MEDICINE AND ILLNESS   155

The "foreign" physicians often intrinsically felt the camp's ethnic hierarchies, which could be overcome, to a point, depending on their social capital. When he arrived in Theresienstadt in October 1942, the twenty-nine-year-old Viennese Franz Hahn was first assigned to the *Hundertschaft*, the newcomers' hundred hours of labor duty. Assigned to shoveling coal, Hahn was annoyed that his medical skills were going to waste; in addition, the manual job did not reflect his status as a doctor. Hahn marched into Munk's office and demanded an assignment; Munk, impressed by his self-assertiveness, gave him a job. Eventually, Hahn was promoted to an internist position and worked under Erich Klapp in the Central Hospital.[171] Hahn was the only non-Czech physician among his nine colleagues, and he recalled that he was to some degree kept as the token foreigner. Starting in January 1943, Paul Eppstein's administration required every department to have a German or Austrian director or vice director. Benjamin Murmelstein was named the political director (*Dezernent*) of Health Services.[172] Similarly, Martha Müller, a Viennese pediatrician, was able to continue in her profession in Theresienstadt. Müller, born in 1906, was a dedicated pediatrician.[173] She worked for the Viennese Jewish Community as a resident physician of the Jewish children's home at Untere Augartenstraße; in September 1943 she was deported with the last fourteen children to Theresienstadt. Soon afterward, Müller worked as a pediatrician in the Hamburg barracks.[174]

The Russian, Romanian, and Moldavian Jewish physicians among the Czech doctors were perceived as part of the "native" Czech group, even if the people did take note that they were originally "Russian" or "Polish." Eva and Šalomoun Racenberg came from Kishinev and Berdychev, respectively, and emigrated to Czechoslovakia in the early 1920s to attend the medical faculty of the Czech-language Charles University.[175] The Racenbergs, who were excellent physicians, were members of the illegal Communist Party in Terezín.[176]

Many "foreigners" among the medical staff were able to use their strong work ethic to bridge the camp's ethnic divides. Resi Weglein from Ulm was a middle-aged, German-trained nurse who was deported to Theresienstadt in summer 1942.[177] Immediately after arrival, she was given a nursing job in the Dresdener barracks. In April 1943 she was able to move into a nurses' room, where she lived with twenty-eight other nurses: fourteen Austrian, thirteen German, and one Czech. Weglein greatly enjoyed living there. However, the other nurses' rooms had exclusively Czech inhabitants. After the deportations in fall 1944, at which time she was working in a new TB station,

156　THE LAST GHETTO

Weglein was moved with four of her old roommates to one of the "Czech" rooms, where ophthalmologist Julie Pollaková lived with her mother and the nurse Gertruda Thierfeldová. At first the Czech women were unpleasantly surprised that they had to live side by side with five "foreign" women. But after they got to know them, the women developed a cordial friendship.[178] Similarly, Věra Kolářová, a young nurse from Pacov who worked in the phlegmon station, recalled her Viennese colleagues with warmth: "They were terribly kind, warmhearted friends and colleagues and I have the best memories of them."[179]

Another important factor in a doctor's standing was seniority as a prisoner. Those physicians who were deported after Theresienstadt had already been in operation for a year struggled to find a position. Viktor Kosák, who was deported at Christmas 1942, was only able to get a position thanks to the help of his acquaintance Marta Grünhutová-Reinischová, the wife of the transport physician Otto Reinisch. It is possible, of course, that Kosák was neither a good nor charming doctor like Hahn; he was assigned to a hospital for the elderly, which was a position considered neither prestigious nor interesting. The task entailed visiting the elderly in their accommodations: "So I walk with my box through the town and take blood which is then examined in the lab. It's a bad job. I have to climb into all kinds of caves, crowded, dark, and often full of lice. I often have to work by candlelight and I can only put watch glasses and flasks on foot stools. I even have to go to the Infection department, where there is diphtheria and scarlet fever, even to the typhoid departments, and there typhoid is already certain. Never in my life have I washed my hands this often."[180] Descriptions like Kosák's remind us of the immense differences in the Terezín Health Services between the "civilized" hospitals on the one hand, where the medical elite could work, and the quotidian assignments of those physicians who worked with the elderly or in the housing blocks, on the other hand.

A crucial factor dictating a physician's work in Terezín was age. Doctors over sixty years of age were allowed to work only as medical examiners, not as doctors.[181] Older doctors were largely not allowed to work in their profession at all, which distressed many among the cohort of older medical experts. Edmund Hadra, a Berlin gynecologist who was sixty-five when he arrived in Theresienstadt in the summer of 1942, initially fell ill with enteritis. When he recovered, he went to Health Services to inquire about a job, but an "arrogant young Prague physician" sent him back to get better first. When Hadra went a second time, a Viennese transport with fifty young physicians had filled all openings.[182] Hadra ended up overseeing toilets; his much younger partner, Josefa Ruben, whom he married in Theresienstadt, worked as a nurse. There are indications that the older doctors were often quite old-fashioned in their medical views and thus not as good as the younger Czech physicians. The treatment Hermann Strauß received during his fatal heart attack during the transports in October 1944 can be interpreted as a symbol of the different medical generations: Strauß asked for bloodletting and camphor; Erich Klapp gave him strophantin and morphine, which was then a state-of-the art treatment, and indeed is still used today.[183] In the Lodz ghetto, the arrival of Czech physicians was seen as a marked improvement of the health situation.[184]

An comparison can be made of the age and ethnicity of Theresienstadt doctors for patients in two groups who died in January 1943: the very young and very old, that is, patients considered "important" and "irrelevant," respectively. The experiences of these two groups offer further insight into the ways doctors' age and ethnicity played out in connection to their Theresienstadt careers.[185] The attending physicians for the elderly patients were on average forty-six years old, and the coroners (this job was performed in Theresienstadt by physicians) were on average fifty-two years old. The doctors were a more heterogeneous and larger group, which included nine Czechs, four Austrians, and one German.[186] The physicians who had treated the deceased seniors also included relatively few women, indicating that women physicians, in spite of sexism, secured good positions.

The physicians who took care of infants were a small group.[187] The doctors whose names appeared on the death certificates for children were relatively young: forty-five (attending physicians) and forty-two (coroners). The children's physicians were all Czech, with the exception of the Viennese Martha Müller. Müller was also the only woman doctor who was a children's attending physician, whereas female doctors appear seven times as children's coroners. Overall, most of the physicians who signed the death certificates, both the attending physicians and coroners, were Czech and born between 1890 and 1910. The children had somewhat younger doctors who were nearly exclusively Czech and often specialists and thus the most highly ranked in the medical hierarchy of the ghetto. Doctors for the elderly inmates were slightly older and included some "foreigners," although it appears that the doctors for the elderly also included excellent physicians.

Conducting research was another way Theresienstadt physicians were able to stay connected to the medical profession and thus come to terms with

158   THE LAST GHETTO

Theresienstadt and exercise agency. Physicians could research, discuss with colleagues, write about, and so by extension master this horrifying, deadly place. They organized talks, trained doctors, and conducted research on the medical phenomena they observed in the ghetto. Munk and his team considered medical research and the training of medical students in Theresienstadt part of their jobs. A German émigré to the Netherlands, Henriette Louise Blumenthal-Rothschild, worked for the surgical department on anatomical drawings.[188] In the 1930s and after the war, she played a decisive part in the preparation of Martinus Woerdeman's anatomical atlas and the overall development of the study of anatomy in the Netherlands.[189] Hermann Strauß organized medical lectures and formed seminars for various specializations to serve as continuing education. The talks, held in German, Czech, and Dutch, were well attended.[190] Doctors lectured about their prewar experiences as well as about their findings in Theresienstadt. There were also smaller, unofficial afternoon and weekly get-togethers at which doctors discussed particularly difficult or interesting illnesses, then dictated the appropriate protocol to a nurse.[191] Doctors welcomed colleagues from among the new arrivals to Theresienstadt and inquired about medical developments in the world outside. When in September 1944 a Dutch physician brought a copy of a Swiss medical journal with an article on the new drug, penicillin, the Terezín doctors enthusiastically discussed the discovery.[192]

Erich Munk's medical library became the basis for the Central Medical Library in Theresienstadt. The library's first head was Marta Weinwurmová-Löwyová; in December 1943 she was deported to Auschwitz.[193] Her position was filled by Felix Meyer, a sixty-eight-year old Berlin physician. In his memoir, Meyer described his staff, giving everyone's names and the places they came from, ending with an aside describing the only female colleague: "and a Danish woman."[194]

The medical research undertaken in Theresienstadt included the work of gynecologist František Bass and his research on amenorrhea, addressing the frequent cessation of women's menstruation in Theresienstadt. For most women prisoners, who had no sanitary napkins, having no period came as a relief.[195] Lecturing on the topic in December 1943, Bass argued that rather than malnutrition, amenorrhea was connected "to a psychological shock of incarceration."[196] After liberation, Bass wrote up his research and went on to direct a gynecological clinic in Prague.[197] In his Theresienstadt research, Bass, who was a dedicated, warm physician, followed a long-lived medical praxis. Medicine has a tradition of pathologizing women's bodies, in particular their reproductive system.[198] Until the late eighteenth century, physicians recognized female orgasm and saw it as key for conception. However, nineteenth-century doctors saw women as passive, rejecting the notion of female sexual excitement. Freud reintroduced the clitoris and female climax, setting out the path to the subsequent "rationalization of sexuality" in Weimar Germany that dictated that a woman needs to orgasm to conceive.[199] But crucially, it was always female sexuality that was being addressed and women who were reduced to their reproductive organs.[200]

It is within the framework of this more general professional and societal context that Bass's research should be viewed. Simultaneously with Bass's Theresienstadt observations, the Berlin anatomist Hermann Stieve dissected the bodies of women executed at Plötzensee prison and examined how chronic stress, in this case, women's imprisonment and impending execution, affected female reproductive function. Among the executed women were resistance fighters, women whose last wish was to have their bodies returned to their families. Stieve was thus not only dissecting Nazi opponents but doing so against the wishes of the dead.[201] Stieve did help to establish that stress is a key factor for why women stop menstruating, proving Bass right. The issue at hand, though, is that these doctors treated women's bodies as objects. Women were reduced to their reproductive function. This mentality stretched across countries and centuries, indeed even from a German physician to a Jewish prisoner doctor.[202]

Material Advantages

Theresienstadt's medical personnel had various material advantages over the general population. Physicians and nurses could be accommodated in separate rooms with colleagues, which meant that their roommates had similar working times and showed consideration for those who worked night shifts and slept during the day. The leading physicians even had their own rooms; Erich Munk, Erich Klapp, Viktor Hahn, and Karel Fleischmann each lived with his family in a single room. In the emptied ghetto after the fall transports in 1944, most doctors, including women physicians, received a room of their own.[203] Both physicians and nurses eventually received better food rations; some physicians were categorized as hard laborers, and those who were categorized as even harder working, such as the TB doctors, had triple rations.[204]

160 THE LAST GHETTO

The nurse Alice Randt was able to acquire better food rations and baths for her team of seventy nurses.[205]

Similarly, Health Services offered preferential food for patients; when an inmate was recognized as sick, he or she could receive convalescence rations. To Martha Glass and many other older prisoners, these rations were the crucial nourishment that kept them alive.[206] The Central Hospital had baths and a laundry, so the staff living in the hospital could wash and change their clothing daily, a major perk in Theresienstadt, where most people washed in cold water at sinks and had only rare access to showers.[207] Some patients brought the medical staff food. Anna Auředníčková remembered that old people presented their nurses with gingerbread.[208] Surpassing these humble gifts, the cooks brought the medical personnel copious quantities of food. In a drawing, Erich Lichtblau depicted a waiting room full of patients with a cook walking straight in: "Because doctors are hungry too, the cook always has right of way!"[209] Pokorná and Fleischmann stressed that they did not take bribes and that they encouraged their staff not to do so either.[210]

Finally, Health Services was represented by its soccer team, Aeskulap; soccer was an immensely popular sport in Theresienstadt.[211] Aeskulap, including medical orderlies as well as physicians, was one of the weakest teams, placing ninth out of eleven in the spring league in 1944. Still, the fact that the medics played and were invited to participate indicated that the nourishment of the medical staff were good enough to participate in this strenuous physical activity—and more important, that they belonged to the social elite.[212]

The ultimate material advantage in Theresienstadt was protection from transports, and Health Services could offer such protection only to some. The SS asked for several physicians and nurses to accompany every departing transport, to support the belief that at the destination, the departing would live and hence need medical care. Because Health Services was a large department and the transports were filled from every department according to the department's size, for each transport many medical workers were called up. The medical supervisors then fought for "their" workers to protect them. It seems that the petitions for auxiliary staff were relatively often successful.[213]

Before the transport, a medical committee headed by Otto Reinisch decided who from the drafted prisoners was too ill to go. This was not a feature specific to Theresienstadt; the *Krankenbehandler* in Germany were forced

MEDICINE AND ILLNESS 161

to decide who could leave on transport.[214] The medical committee was susceptible to bribes, and Reinisch became despised. Rolf Grabower, a former high-ranking clerk in the German Ministry of Finance, worked in 1944 for the personnel office of the Elder of the Jews. Grabower, who believed in transparency and fighting corruption, began an investigation of the medical exemptions at transports, which then led to a major scandal.[215] The doctors Viktor Hahn and Bedřich Berl offered Grabower inside information.[216] Erich Munk understood these outside interventions into the work of Health Services as a personal attack and covered for Reinisch. Grabower noted that the subsequent meeting with the chief physicians "was one of the most unpleasant hearings I have ever had."[217] The investigation was never concluded; during October 1944, nearly all of the physicians and clerks of the Personnel Office were deported to Auschwitz, where most of them were murdered.

During the selection for transports, the physicians sometimes induced high fever to protect their friends and family, who were then proclaimed too ill for transport. In December 1943, Pokorná's seventeen-year old niece Alena Neumannová was listed for transport. Pokorná, who was Grabower's close friend, gave her a fever-inducing shot, and Alena was ruled too ill to go on the transport.[218] In a similar turn of events, when the twenty-three-year old Hana Ledererová was called for transport in January 1943, her admirer, the cook Antonín Utitz, helped save her: "Tonda [...] threw himself into an action with which he wanted to save me: with flour, sugar, dumplings, and God knows what else he bribed doctors and got them to agree to take me in to the hospital, my artificial illness [...] and he made them promise that should I receive the transport slip, they will write 'unfit for transport' and so I will be saved, for this time."[219] In the hospital, Ledererová made friends with her attending physician, Gerhard Aron from Pelhřimov, who made sure that she was registered as ill until the transport wave passed.

Medical protection ended during the fall 1944 transports. The SS deported all of the leading physicians, including Munk, Klapp, Fleischmann, and Reinisch. Klapp left his cello in Theresienstadt; he knew he was going to his death. The ophthalmologist Julie Pollaková and the gynecologist Pavel Klein were among the few doctors who were allowed to stay, after Murmelstein told Rahm that he could not run a ghetto without doctors.[220] In November 1944, only 120 of 600 practicing doctors remained.[221] Lilly Pokorná, Erich Springer, and Richard Stein were allowed to stay. Stein headed Health Services during the last six months of its existence.

162 THE LAST GHETTO

Sexism in Power Structures

Medical power in Theresienstadt was gendered: Health Services was a starkly sexist institution. In this respect, too, Theresienstadt was a product of the contemporary medical world. Many physicians slept with their nurses. Some of these relationships became serious, while others were casual. Ella Roubíčková-Cabicarová remembered how pediatrician Dr. Hardt became enamored with a German nurse named Lieschen from a different department. Hardt "bought" Lieschen from his colleague with a "payment" of sugar so she could work for him in his department.[222] Being accompanied by a young, attractive woman was also a way for the physicians to demonstrate their high status. Similarly, Karel Fleischmann from the Welfare Department, a hunchback whose wife was also a physician, had a young lover.[223]

Otto Šťastný was a fifty-two-year old general practitioner from Prague; he and his gentile wife divorced in order to keep the family house, planning to remarry after the war. In summer 1943, no longer protected by the status of being in a mixed marriage, Šťastný was deported to Theresienstadt. Here he worked in the infirmary of the West barracks, where his nurse was twenty-seven-year old Hilde Pohlmann from Berlin. Pohlmann too was alone; her mother had been deported to Riga, and her gentile father refused to acknowledge her. On one night shift, Šťastný invited her for dinner, and the famished Pohlmann joined him for canned goulash with dumplings. The dinners became routine, and Otto and Hilde became a couple. For the first time in Theresienstadt, Pohlmann was happy; in the fall of 1944 they married.[224] To the retired Berlin gynecologist Edmund Hadra, whose wife Josefa Ruben also worked for Šťastný, the relationship was a confirmation of the arrogance of the Czech physicians. Hilde was "young, blond, and vivacious"—and distinctly younger than Šťastný, who was not even separated from his wife, as Hadra noted.[225] The older German doctor was angry at his Czech colleague because he recognized the doctor's pattern of expressing power by employing the frame of the married physician dating a younger nurse.[226] In his envy, he even described the brunette Pohlmann as blonde in order to validate her trophy status. In fact, Šťastný's relationship with Pohlmann mirrored Hadra's with Josefa: both women were significantly younger and worked as nurses.

In interwar Bohemian countries, women worked as physicians; at Brno and Prague medical faculties, 20 percent of the students were female (11 percent at the Prague German University).[227] In Theresienstadt, there were only three leading female doctors (who were all friends with one another): the radiologist Lilly Pokorná, Irma Goldmannová of Pathology, and Gertrud Adlerová of Bacterioscopy (whose husband H. G. Adler became an eminent historian of the ghetto).[228] In her memoir, Pokorná repeatedly brought up her status, including the fact that her salary was ranked just after that of the Elder of Jews. However, a quarter was subtracted; women were paid only 75 percent of the men's Theresienstadt wages. The ghetto currency had almost no buying power, but Pokorná was still frustrated.[229] The team of women in Radiology was celebrated in a poem by Lucie Auerbach, a thirty-four-year old Breslauer refugee to Czechoslovakia. The first stanza demonstrates that Pokorná and her team were aware of their exceptional situation in the men's world of Health Services:

> We are the republic of women
> the place that works without males
> we just look right through every man
> and trash him as well as his tales.[230]

Not everyone appreciated Pokorná's work; the Viennese Franz Hahn went to see a different, male, radiologist outside of the building, whom he trusted more.[231] But even though Pokorná, an accomplished scientist, researched and published about TB in Theresienstadt, she received no mention in the work of her colleague Evžen Kraus, one of the few surviving doctors of the TB unit.[232]

Finally, women doctors found it difficult to work in their profession in the ghetto. Some male medical students worked in Theresienstadt as doctors.[233] The twenty-eight-year-old Pilsner Gertruda Freundová was a more advanced female medical student—she had finished her studies but as a Jew could no longer pass the second *rigorosum*—who worked in Theresienstadt for two years as a nurse.[234] In the last months, facing a serious shortage of medical staff, doctors who previously had not been accepted on the basis of being too old, new arrivals, or foreigners were employed.[235] There were many more "foreign" doctors in these final six months of Theresienstadt's existence, including Dutch, German, and Austrian prisoner doctors. Nevertheless, even then it was easier for men to work as physicians than for women; of the Rotterdam dentist couple Lion Jacques Frenkel and Carolina Wiener Frenkel, only Jacques could work as a dentist in Theresienstadt, whereas Carolina cleaned toilets.[236]

164   THE LAST GHETTO

Although there were many more doctors than were needed, there was a nursing shortage. [237] Some nurses were trained before the deportation, while others were trained in Theresienstadt. Several women prisoners were appointed nurses even though they had no prior training, among them Minna Wolfensteinová, the head nurse of the isolation ward.[238] Springer recalled that in the beginning there were only two nurses with diplomas, so Health Services had to train the nurses and later recruit trained personnel deported from Austria and Germany.[239] Murmelstein confirmed the lack of Czech-trained nurses; he remembered that the only large group of trained nurses came from the Viennese Rothschild hospital.[240] A large segment of the medical caregivers came from medical families; they were the wives or daughters of physicians. Other women had studied or intended to study medicine or pharmacology.[241] But this trend did not apply to women only; most of the Terezín medical staff were members of medical families, a trend that continued after the war.[242]

One of the Rothschild hospital nurses was thirty-one-year old Federica Spitzer, who worked in the hospital of the Sudeten barracks for the Prague internist Max Gutmann. Her colleague, a single, older Czech nurse, Etelka, felt threatened by the presence of the younger, well-liked Spitzer; the younger nurse had also learned Czech. "I think Etelka had a hard life behind her," remembered Spitzer.[243] The tense situation ended after a few months when Etelka was directed to take care of the Białystok children.[244] In October 1943, Etelka was part of the team of fifty nurses and physicians who accompanied the children on a transport reported to be going to Palestine; however, the transport was sent to Auschwitz and everyone was murdered. Etelka's had indeed been a hard life: Spitzer's colleague was in fact Ottla Davidová, the youngest sister of Franz Kafka.[245] The Czech diminutive of Otilie is Otilka (Ottla being the German one), which the Viennese Spitzer changed into the more familiar Etelka. Davidová had been married to a gentile, who divorced her in 1940 in an acrimonious divorce in order to keep his job as director of an insurance company.[246] No longer protected by a mixed marriage, Ottla was thus delivered to the persecution. Both her daughters remained in Prague, and she missed them bitterly, as documented in letters that a friendly gendarme smuggled to her children. Ottla once looked back at her long-dead brother and noted: "Uncle Franz would love it here."[247]

Nurses took on an important amount of work with Theresienstadt's patients. The ratio was between twenty and thirty patients per nurse.[248] Many patients had enteritis, and the nurses struggled to keep them clean;

the sanitary facilities were rudimentary. Nurses described how they struggled with fecal matter, a lack of clean bedding, and long working hours.[249] The nurses also had to clean the rooms. Radiology nurses even waxed the floor when the SS wanted to show the department to outside visitors.[250] In spite of extensive responsibilities, nurses did not have the power to decide to hire more colleagues; that decision was in the hands of the doctors.[251] Bringing food for the patients was a moment that gave nurses a measure of power; some nurses stole food from the portions of the elderly.[252] Nurses often stressed that they experienced the medical conditions as a challenge, learning new techniques and enjoying being part of the medical collective.[253] Twenty-four-year-old Illa Loeb from Wuppertal had worked as a nurse in the Dutch Westerbork transit camp; after her deportation to Theresienstadt in February 1944 she was given a position in the surgery. Several months later, she was transferred to the new *Heilgas* department and after the war recounted with ardor how her work helped the patients.[254]

However, physicians saw nurses as aides rather than colleagues. Franz Hahn even recalled the nurses as his own creation: "From us, there were some nurses in the Central Hospital, among them my future wife, and they had an excellent education. They had namely been seamstresses, not nurses, but already during Hitler's time in Vienna we trained them into perfect nurses. And the Czechs were enthusiastic, especially in the Central Hospital: 'What, Viennese nurses? Oh my god.' And one of the people, who trained the Viennese nurses, was I. And people would ask them, where do you know this from? Oh we were taught this by Dr Hahn." Hahn, Springer, and most of the male doctors saw the nurses' skills as an extension of their own accomplishments, rather than as the women's own. Many of the doctors did not even know their full names; when Arthur Lippmann asked the Hamburger Hermann Bohm about the nurses from the Eckernförde hospital, Bohm replied that he would not know the answer to his question, as he knew only their first names.[255] Erich Springer devoted only a few side remarks to the nurses, saying he was sorry that he occasionally was impatient, but that all nurses had to work as long as they could stand—and look presentable and pretty.[256]

Notably different was the attitude of the female physicians: Lilly Pokorná, describing her team, gave her nurse colleagues character and names, expressed gratitude for their support and help, and corresponded with those who survived after the war.[257] She remembered the radiology nurse Alžběta Schönhová, who survived Auschwitz and Birnbäumel and after the war

166   THE LAST GHETTO

became head nurse in the radiology unit of a Prague hospital. Schönhová was appreciated for her work, with the most modern equipment at her disposal: "[A]nd yet she likes to reminiscence of the beginnings of the x-ray unit in Theresienstadt." Pokorná described Schönhová's professional success as her own genuine achievement. In this case, it was the former nurse's memories that confirmed the value of her doctor's work.

Conclusion

Because of the conditions that the SS engendered in the ghetto, the prisoner population was much weaker and sicker than under "normal" living conditions. However, the medical personnel in Theresienstadt developed good medical care. One reason they were able to do so was that the SS were afraid of infection, but an even more important factor was that prisoner doctors came to see Health Services as having the power to fix all the ills that could be fixed within Terezín. The mentality behind their approach to social hygiene had a distinctly political undertone. Medical care in Theresienstadt was characterized by asymmetries for physicians and patients. Among the doctors, non-Czech, older, and women doctors had fewer opportunities to continue to work in their chosen professions as medical practitioners in the ghetto. Struggling to deal with the enormous volume of patients, the doctors developed a triage system. Younger patients or those who were ill after fall 1942 were far more likely to be treated. Enteritis, the main disease leading to fatal mortality among the elderly, was not seen as a significant disease.

The Terezín doctors believed, that the ghetto was good for medicine and medicine good for the ghetto.[258] To the medical personnel, healthcare in Terezín, and by extension their incarceration, was a success story. Their attitude was chiefly informed by the doctors' mentality. Physicians saw their medical work in terms of professional continuity and therefore stressed the legitimacy of their work in Theresienstadt. Their position echoed that of Jewish functionaries who were catapulted into fraught positions of power. More than 90 percent of the doctors and nurses were deported to Auschwitz and died, yet as long they were in Theresienstadt, they made an enormous difference.

The study of medicine in Theresienstadt demonstrates the role medical care and hospitals play in society at large: as long as they work, there is a measure of a working society in effect. But when they stop, it is a sign

MEDICINE AND ILLNESS 167

that that everything has fallen to pieces. The medical staff in Theresienstadt worked so well for two reasons: first was the efforts of medical staff to make the best out of a terrible situation, and second was that they were relatively well supplied. In April 1945, as the Red Army was taking over Berlin, doctors were still working in the hospitals, taking care of the wounded and delivering babies, as the conditions allowed. Sixty years later, when in the aftermath of Hurricane Katrina the New Orleans levees broke, Memorial Hospital was evacuated. The physicians in charge triaged the patients, leaving the "hopeless" patients behind but also administering them drugs that effectively euthanized them.[259] In the days after the evacuation, Memorial Hospital became a scene of utter chaos, of corpses left behind. The decision to triage was ethically fraught, raising difficult questions about doctors' responsibility. This comparison shows that medical staff in extreme situations can make very uncomfortable decisions, even if they see themselves as trying to save as many as possible in a dire situation. More important, the situation in Memorial Hospital became desperate because resources were absent. Once a situation is beyond doctors' control—for lack of resources or support from above—the result is chaos and neglect. Medicine is a measure of humanity. As long as it works, we are a functioning society; when it fails, all else already has.

5

Cultural Life

One of the best-known aspects of Terezín is its rich cultural life. But what is often neglected is that art does not stand alone. The prominence of art in the ghetto is linked to the particular value that art held, and holds, in our society. High culture is tied to access to status and power, and these factors influence the negotiation of power.[1] Terezín's cultural life was bound to the social hierarchy of the inmate community and the making of legitimacy. The art produced in Terezín offers salient insights about the power structures and values held by society in the ghetto.

Art does not exist in a vacuum; it reflects the society in which it originates. Prisoners came from the Central European middle class, for whom art was a key expression of their habitus. For this reason, in Terezín they continued to make music and attend the theater, and they bartered food for drawings. Cultural life in Terezín reflected the ethnic and social variations within inmate society. Different ethnic groups considered different art beautiful and meaningful. The SS took note of the ghetto's rich cultural life and used it to showcase Terezín for propaganda, but the German authorities neither participated in nor cared about the art.

The Recreation Department

Contrary to popular belief, Terezín was not a special destination for Jewish artists. The Nazis sent almost the entire Czech Jewish population and later several "exceptional" groups from Greater Germany and the Netherlands to Terezín. The regime defined none of these groups as artists. A smaller number of people were sent to Terezín because the SS designated them as "meritorious," and this group did include a small number of artists. In general, deportees came from all segments of the population: clerks, housewives, children, the mentally ill, and university professors.

Cultural life in the ghetto began with spontaneous singing evenings held in the men's quarters.[2] When thirty-six-year old Prague conductor Rafael

The Last Ghetto. Anna Hájková, Oxford University Press (2020). © Oxford University Press.
DOI: 10.1093/oso/9780190051778.001.0001.

CULTURAL LIFE   169

Schächter arrived in early December 1941, the events were reorganized into a more professional setting with the formation of men's choirs. Other prisoners spent their spare time reciting the poems of beloved Czech authors. People had brought musical instruments with them that they could play at the musical evenings. Later that month, however, the SS prohibited the use of musical instruments; parties now needed to be approved ahead of time.[3] In February 1942, Otto Zucker asked Fredy Hirsch to set up a department called "Recreation" (Freizeitgestaltung) to organize cultural activities. The department belonged to Internal Administration. Its first director was a thirty-year old Plzeň rabbi, Erich Weiner. Aided by a team of female assistants, Weiner organized activities that soon grew to include theater pieces, lectures, and musical events.

In July 1942, when the ghetto became "open" (that is, all of the town became the ghetto), cultural activities were permitted officially and cultural life gained a new momentum. By August the majority of the Czech Jews, as well as many German and Austrian Jews, had been sent to Terezín. An increasing number of professional actors, musicians, and interested laypeople arrived, and cultural life became increasingly heterogeneous and professionalized. Hans Hofer from Brno and Vienna, Vlasta Schönová from Prague, and Philipp Manes from Berlin put on a cabaret, Jean Cocteau's play *The Beloved Voice*, and a series of lectures, respectively. These three individuals, who each in their distinct way became a regular of the Recreation Department, exemplify the quantitative and qualitative change in cultural activities that took place in the summer of 1942.

Inmates brought with them their best-loved books and musical instruments; some came with musical scores. When one prisoner arrived with a piano arrangement of Bedřich Smetana's *The Bartered Bride*, Rafael Schächter decided to stage Terezín's first opera. After attending the premiere on November 28, 1942, Bedřich Kohn, a middle-aged inmate from Prague, wrote in his diary: "It was the first moment in the ghetto when you felt human." Kohn voiced his admiration for "the Jewish nation" that was able to rehearse and put on an opera in such conditions.[4] The performance of *The Bartered Bride* was a smashing success. The audience wept to the notes of this beloved Czech opera.[5] Indeed, music held a distinctive position in the self-understanding of Czech inmates. Many Czech Jews, like other Czechs, made music at home, were members of a choir, and attended local concerts. Much of the Czech national revival had been negotiated through musical channels. *The Bartered Bride* was and is considered the

170   THE LAST GHETTO

central musical piece of the Czech "national struggle" in the second half of the nineteenth century.

The production of *The Bartered Bride* marked the professionalization of cultural activities in the ghetto; an opera, with its complex staging, numerous singers, and minimum two-hour time frame, challenged the possibilities and redefined the standards of productions. Two months later, Otto Zucker became the new director of Recreation. Zucker, the brother-in-law of the opera singer Tamara Zuckerová, was keenly interested in music and other cultural activities. As a former deputy of the Elder of the Jews, he also knew about the control of the SS, and especially the danger of informers; therefore he insisted on caution during rehearsals regarding statements critical of the SS.[6] He managed the censorship single-handedly, often without consulting the Elder, Paul Eppstein. All programs needed to be handed into Recreation a week ahead of time. Otto Zucker passed them on to the commandant, who returned them several hours later. Rudolf Reichmann, who compiled the programs in fall 1943, believed Burger never actually read them.[7] Under Murmelstein's tenure, the Council of Elders discussed Recreation's weekly programs.[8]

Recreation decided what pieces would be produced, assessed their quality, and determined which pieces should continue to be performed. The department also discussed where performances could take place, whether certain plays would be put on in Czech or German, and what needed to be censored and how far. Recreation had to approve every piece first. If a piece was not accepted, production became much more difficult; inmates then had to find a performance space on their own and figure out how to sell tickets and advertise. Philipp Manes, a sixty-seven-year old former furrier from Berlin, organized a series of lectures and readings of plays. "The Manes Group" did not always get along well with Recreation; Manes had strong ideas about pieces he wished to produce, among them Goethe's *Faust* and *Iphigenia on Tauris*, and how he wanted to stage them. The Recreation commission perceived this preference as too old-fashioned and conservative for overall taste.[9]

Zucker, who was head of the deportation commission, could often take performers off the transport list and was also able to secure better rations for them.[10] Moritz Henschel of Berlin, who succeeded Zucker in November 1943, also had an artistic bent. He directed *Die Fledermaus* and wrote a satirical short play, *The Island of Robinson*, that dealt with themes of exile and survival. His work included a frank discussion of the dynamics of triage in the ghetto.[11] Unlike Zucker, who did not promote his sister in law Tamara,

CULTURAL LIFE   171

who was an opera singer, to better roles, Henschel ensured that performers in the *Fledermaus* received additional extra rations and bumped the staging of *Robinson* ahead of other plays.[12] Zucker remained active in Recreation until his transport to Auschwitz in September 1944. At that point Recreation became a subsection of Murmelstein's mandate as Elder, belonging to the Central Secretariat.

By 1944 cultural activities were a fixture of the ghetto: more than half a dozen events took place every day, about half of them lectures.[13] One reason inmates attended was that everyone else did; in addition, the community considered cultural activity beautiful and meaningful. The master narrative that was shared by most of the Theresienstadt inmates made a huge point about art. [14] Newcomers learned that artistic accomplishments were part of the Terezín set of values.

Inmates often emphasized that the productions were as good as if not better than anything done in the normal world. Bedřich Kohn wrote that the Terezín version of *The Bartered Bride* should be staged in the Prague National Theatre after the war.[15] In this view, the arts in Terezín expressed and added to the understanding of Czechness and therefore deserved to be memorialized in the center of Czech high culture.[16] It was not only the nature of the piece but also the quality of the show that inspired this redefinition of Czech high culture. Indeed, inmates welcomed and praised most of the performances; they expressed negative opinions only rarely. Criticism was conveyed by professional music critics, such as Kurt Singer, former head of the German Jewish Culture League; the deputies of Recreation, who discussed the performances at weekly meetings; and actors, who discussed the works of their colleagues.[17] Audience members conveyed direct criticism when the performances somehow hurt their cultural sensibilities, such as when a German singer sang a role in a Czech opera, or when a Czech audience attended a show of German cabaret.

Terezín produced a canon that defined crucial artists, musicians, actors, and directors and largely continues to this day. Certain pieces came to carry emotional value in capturing the essence of imprisonment. Inmates turned to specific poems—among them Ilse Weber's "A Suitcase Speaks," Leo Strauss's "The Town As If," and the anonymous "I Saw Today a Thousand People," which predated Theresienstadt—which they copied, learned by heart, and passed on.[18] The canon included works such as the 1938 children's opera *Brundibár*, Schächter's production of Verdi's *Requiem*, and the drawings of Fritta and Leo Haas. After liberation, the canon shifted; some new works

172 THE LAST GHETTO

were added, most crucially children's drawings and poetry, including Pavel Friedmann's poem "Butterfly." Zeev Shek, the leader of Documentation Action, along with Hana Volavková, the postwar director of the Prague Jewish Museum, set out to collect and document works from the ghetto, thus further defining Terezín art.[19]

This early postwar definition of Terezín art influenced what a broader audience came to understand as important and central art production. Shek in Israel and Volavková in Czechoslovakia both focused on children's art and the drawings of Leo Haas, Bedřich Fritta, Otto Ungar, and Ferdinand Bloch. These artists had been arrested in July 1944, and most of them were murdered. This selection enabled Shek and Volavková to combine a redemptive narrative of the realistic, even horrifying depiction of everyday Terezín drawn by the arrested artists with a sentimentalized interpretation of children's drawings. Therefore, children's art is often viewed outside its initial context, which was art education in the youth homes, led by the Bauhaus artist Friedl Dicker-Brandeis.[20]

The SS were not greatly concerned with cultural life in Terezín. Thus it is unclear why they prohibited instrumental music in the first months of the ghetto's existence.[21] Probably they allowed musical performances in the summer of 1942 because Adolf Eichmann's Department IVB4 wanted to boost the notion of a "privileged" ghetto. When the German Red Cross visited for the first time in June 1943, the itinerary, which did not include any cultural activities, revealed a face of the ghetto that shocked the visitors, Walther Hartmann and his deputy Heinrich Niehaus, who were accompanied by Eberhard von Thadden of the German Ministry of Foreign Affairs.[22]

The SS knew about cultural activities in the ghetto and were happy to utilize them for their own purposes. Through one of their propaganda efforts, the film *Terezín: A Documentary from a Jewish Settlement Area*, ordered by Hans Günther, and the two visits by the International Red Cross on June 23, 1944, and April 6, 1945, the German authorities highlighted the arts. The impact of the first Red Cross visit was by far the strongest;[23] the propaganda film was never screened. The itineraries of both Red Cross visits were arranged in close cooperation between the SS headquarters and the Jewish self-administration; Benjamin Murmelstein organized the preceding "beautification" in winter and spring 1944 and winter 1945.

Murmelstein, who was the Elder at the time of the second Red Cross visit, incorporated the play *Fireflies*—directed by his lover, Vlasta Schönová— into the program.[24] It is possible that Eichmann or Rahm had made the

CULTURAL LIFE   173

suggestion to include a theater play in the visit because such activities were deemed "safe." Moreover, the play would be perceived as proof of good conditions in the ghetto. It was the Jewish functionaries who prepared these propaganda events; the SS had no idea about the details of the ghetto's cultural life. Karl Rahm's disregard for culture in Terezín is exemplified by an incident that took place on October 28, 1944. When putting together the list for the last of the liquidation transports, Rahm, as forty-two-year old Prague alto Hedda Grabová recalled, decided to let the last seven remaining female singers, pianists, and actresses stay in the ghetto with the words: "So what. They might as well stay. Then they can play and sing again."[25]

But the use of the arts for propaganda purposes did not mean the SS fostered or cared about Terezín's cultural life. In June 1944, when von Thadden, Erwin Weinmann, and Rolf and Hans Günther attended the rehearsals of *Requiem*, *Tosca*, and *Brundibár* and a soccer match for about fifteen minutes each, they were not affected. In his novel *The Terezín Requiem*, the writer and survivor Josef Bor claimed that Eichmann was deeply impressed by the Jews staging a mass for the dead.[26] But this was Bor taking poetic license: Eichmann was not in Terezín at the time; he was in Hungary organizing the transports to Auschwitz. Many witnesses criticized Bor for the liberties he had taken, realizing that readers would take his descriptions for fact. In fact, many people have done so, with unfortunate effects.[27]

Some SS men attended soccer games, concerts, and dance performances.[28] But only one member of SS headquarters took advantage of the cultural offerings more systematically, the Sudeten German Josef Bobek, a civilian and head of the power plant. Bobek was often described as a "nice" German, perhaps also because he spoke Czech. He attended some of the Czech performances; helped the set designers with material for the stage; and complimented the director, Ota Růžička, for his production of Erben's *Kytice*.[29] Rahm and Bergel attended the celebration for the opening of the Sokolovna hall on May 5, 1944, yet their presence was owing to the fact that the event was part of the final stage of beautification.[30] The SS used the artists for profit in the graphic workshop they set up; some of the artists working there produced commercial copies of the old masters or portraits of SS officials.[31] Another source of SS income was the "Lautscharna," an arts and crafts workshop that was part of the Prague firm Lautsch. The firm employed several dozen inmates as artists from spring 1942 until fall 1943. Lautscharna was the idea of Oskar Perschke, who wanted to support his Jewish relatives in

174   THE LAST GHETTO

the ghetto, and, it seems, at simultaneously make an income on the free labor of the incarcerated artists.[32]

The only times that high-ranking members of the SS showed a deep interest in the inmates' art was when the artists broke one of the central prohibitions: contact with the outside world to disseminate information about the ghetto. At the height of the beautification campaign, the SS intercepted dozens of smuggled drawings that dramatically illustrated the misery of the ghetto. Fritta, Leo Haas, Otto Ungar, Ferdinand Bloch, and Norbert Troller, who were considered some of the finest painters in the ghetto, drew pictures depicting everyday life and the atmosphere of deprivation, fear, and terror. An elderly collector originally from Náchod, Leo Strass, whose daughter Valerie Bayerlová lived in a mixed marriage and thus was not deported, bought some of their paintings. Strass smuggled the drawings to his son-in-law Václav, who sold them further afield, allegedly as far as Switzerland. At one point in spring 1944, the SS man Rudolf Haindl found Strass, beat him up, and located additional drawings. Rahm sent the drawings to Eichmann. On July 17, 1944, Eichmann ordered that the artists, together with their families, be arrested and sent to the Small Fortress; the men were sent on to Auschwitz I, in "protective custody." Among the men, only Leo Haas and Norbert Troller survived.[33]

Beyond Spiritual Resistance

"Culture as resistance" has become something of an automatic phrase in Holocaust studies. This simplistic reading neglects the fact that people in Terezín engaged in cultural activities for various, often differing reasons. Art had many functions for those in the ghetto and represented the inmates' critical characteristics, motives, and mentalities. Many of these purposes were specific to Terezín, while others could be found in other ghettos and concentration camps. Inmates noted that the ghetto's cultural life "made them feel better."[34] This uplifting feeling can be connected to several aspects of culture. Art is by no means an extra; it is an anthropological constant, and people engage in some form of cultural activity unless reduced to a bare existential minimum, when any communication stops. Art is a basic human need, a pleasurable experiencing of self, similar to sexual intimacy.[35]

Art also offered a solution to the problem of what to do with spare time. Many of the activities that people had previously enjoyed were no longer available: one could not go to the cinema or a pub, eat out, go shopping or dancing, travel, go hiking, listen to the radio, or relax at home.[36] One's "home" in Terezín—the crowded quarters with the allotted space on the bunk bed that also acted as chair, sofa, table, and living room, in short the entire apartment—was not an easy place to rest. Cultural activities provided one of the few options for what to do with spare time.

A principal characteristic of Terezín culture was the distinction between high and low culture; they carried different functions.[37] What was understood as high and valuable culture often depended on one's class or national background. Vlasta Schönová directed several conversational comedies. Czech theater connoisseur Willy Mahler deemed her production of Edmond Rostand's *The Romancers* a brave artistic accomplishment, while Philip Manes interpreted her staging of František Langer's play *Velbloud uchem jehly* (Camel through the needle's ear) "light amusement."[38] Manes probably did not know that Langer was a socially critical, modern playwright. Manes was not privy to the Czech tradition that would have enabled him to appreciate certain details of the production. His habitus, class, and generation determined his taste, and with it his artistic judgment.

For inmates, listening to Alice Herz Sommer play one of Viktor Ullmann's compositions served a different purpose than attending a concert by the jazz band Ghettoswingers or viewing Hanuš Jochowitz's production of *Bastien and Bastienne*. There was an important difference in what books readers checked out of the library, whether by Karel Čapek, Karl May, or Goethe. Although lectures on Jewish philosophy or excavations in Mesopotamia may better correspond with conventional expectations about Central European Jewry, there were many people who enjoyed the controversial (some argued vulgar) operetta *Das Ghettomädel* (The girl of the ghetto). Different groups sought out low and high culture for different purposes. For instance, elderly German Jews often attended theatrical productions of German classics, and Czechs watched soccer matches. Yet for both groups, these activities served as a confirmation of their ethnic affiliation: the holiday activity that people would attend in their Sunday best.[39] In contrast, if Czech Jews attended a Czech play, it could often serve as a vehicle to help them make sense of their new surroundings. For others, perhaps those who were not intellectuals, theater provided a moment of escape and distraction, a safe place where they could withdraw.[40]

The act of producing art also confirmed one's sense of individuality; considering how to stage a play, interpreting a musical piece, or drawing were

176   THE LAST GHETTO

ways of expressing a distinct sense of self.[41] Cultural activities can be understood as a life strategy, a reminder of individuality,[42] a more convincing argument than the idea that art served as a strategy for survival.[43] "Survival" is a problematic concept, coming from an ahistorical postwar expectation that everyday life in the Holocaust consisted of surviving. Moreover, the concept of survival is out of place in Terezín, where younger people were in no immediate danger of dying.[44] Others have proposed that culture and religion could serve as what the sociologist Erving Goffman has called the "territory of the self."[45] This line of thought addresses life in the concentration camps rather than the ghettos; in the extreme and regulated conditions of the camps, which stripped prisoners of their individuality, culture was often the only means to remind people of their background and value. Conditions in Terezín differed from those of a concentration camp in the sense that people had a better chance of keeping some of their individuality. However, the situation of many inmates, especially the elderly, was extremely difficult. The impoverished elderly who had belonged to the educated bourgeoisie used (high) culture to confirm their value and cultural and class membership.

The pursuit of pleasure was an important element of cultural life in the ghetto. Inhabitants used culture to improve their mood and provide a distraction. Indeed, the majority of plays performed in the ghetto were comedies and farces.[46] Humor, such as cabaret sketches written in the ghetto,[47] offered the audience a space in which to calm down and forget where they were. Beyond the element of pleasure, some cultural activities enabled prisoners to process the Terezín experience and make sense of their surroundings. Art was a medium that provided some continuity with pre-ghetto life; maintaining former habits (especially when perceived as "extra" or unnecessary for sheer survival) helped ease one into the much-changed daily life in the ghetto.[48] In addition, theater and cabaret, especially pieces that referred to the world of the ghetto, offered a framework of interpretation and a catharsis. Performances helped individuals organize and process the scattered, confusing, and threatening Terezín experience, where inmates feared the unknown future, into a linear narrative with a (positive) outcome and message.[49]

Music fulfilled a related purpose. It is also a pleasurable activity, an emotional and physical pursuit for musicians and listeners. Music sends a powerful but not always substantial message; listeners endow the music with individual meaning, although the listener may not know this.[50] Similar to theater, music was a medium that helped the inmates organize and understand their environment. However, unlike theater, music served as a facilitator, an organizer. For the prisoners it could establish a connection to the past, giving them a sense of agency, meaning, or self-assurance. Music, moreover, is an activity that feels deeply intimate and familiar, a pursuit in which people can reconnect with their sense of individuality, humanity, and dignity.[51] These characteristics explain why music was so immensely important in Terezín. Survivors have repeatedly stated that "music helped us make it through."[52]

What, then, is the problem with spiritual resistance?[53] Scholars have criticized this concept,[54] arguing that it is a simplistic, redemptive narrative stemming from the postwar inability to come to terms with the absence of meaning in mass murder. This inability led to the search for a positive message, one that endowed cultural activities with a higher, ennobling meaning. The concept of spiritual resistance is both vague and flattening. It diverts attention from the complex and overlapping purposes that art served in the ghettos and concentration camps. Postwar expectations shaped the memories and the selection of what inmates remembered about Terezín into prefabricated chunks divorced from the reality of social life in the ghetto.

How can we apply resistance as a useful category of historical analysis? Resistance should be understood as criticism or even struggle against hegemonic power. The SS stood outside of the inmate community's social field and was generally absent from their everyday life. Therefore the Germans did not figure in the resistance tropes of the inmates, apart from a few exceptions, such as Hans Hofer's production of *Die Fledermaus*.[55] Here, citing Adele's "Laughing Song"—a moment when a disguised maid points out the ridiculousness of her master—Hofer made fun of SS plans to "beautify" the ghetto. But such instances were rare.

More often, prisoners employed resistance to question or even condemn the new Terezín habits or the old elites. Examples include the cabarets of Karel Švenk, Pidla Horpatzký and Felix Porges, and Josef Lustig.[56] Porges and Horpatzký's show *Why We Laugh* poked fun at the Terezín aristocracy, first the Aufbaukommando aristocracy of the ghetto founders and then the French aristocracy—that is, functionaries of the Prague Jewish Community who arrived much later than everyone else: "It is not a 'von,' but a 'De:' D-h, D-e, D-c," noted the cabaret artists, playing on the letters that denoted late transports of the functionaries of the Prague Jewish Community, who arrived in summer 1943. They elaborated: "First I thought this D stood for 'dlouho držet' [stay long] oder 'dlouho doma' [long at home]—but then it turned out

178   THE LAST GHETTO

that when someone is De, it means 'nejede.' " The last word, meaning "does not go," referred to the long-standing protection from transports out of Terezín.[57] But this satire poked fun at the formerly powerful functionaries of the Prague Jewish Community. Their power, like that of the ancien régime, had come to an end. To make that clear, the comedians made fun of the old elite, drawing attention to their lack of seniority in Theresienstadt while avoiding the common fate. Indeed, some forms of irony crossed into a cruel form of social criticism, when the object of parody was not in a position of power. Some shows portrayed the formerly patrician German Jews begging for food.[58]

An important theme in Terezín art was continuity and the connection to home. Art served as a connection to one's belonging, to some extent cultural, but more importantly national, identity. For some inmates, especially German and Austrian Jews, class and education were particularly significant: they came from a background in which education and cultural capital were prized. In addition, for German Jews the connection to home and idea of return were very difficult, if not impossible, because their fellow Germans had redefined Germanness and belonging. In the new definition of belonging to the German folk community, high culture played a central role. The new German community successfully appropriated classic German culture, excluded the German Jews, and nullified Jews' connection to German culture. Exclusion applied not only to performers but also to the audience, to those who could claim to understand German culture and hence "claim" cultural capital in the new community. For German Jews deported to Terezín, this claim, expressed through lectures, Kleist, Goethe, and poetry, were essential to prove their former cultural and symbolic status. At the same time, in the new social field of Terezín, classic German culture became a new form of home for Jews from Germany.

The situation for the Czech Jews was different because they still had a home. Many, whether consciously or unconsciously, exercised their sense of belonging in connection with matters they understood as fundamentally Czech: reciting the poetry of Karel Hynek Mácha and František Halas, listening to the music of Smetana and Mozart (whom Czech tradition adopted as a Czech composer), relating to Czech places of memory such as the Prague Castle or Tomáš Masaryk, and finally, in having a distinct aesthetic sense. A refrain among Czech cultural activities was the (triumphal, happy, wise) return home, in theater plays, children's drawings, and even graffiti. Under a map of Czechoslovakia pinned on a wall, someone scribbled, echoing a poem by Josef Sládek, "We have been and we shall be, we came and we shall go."[59] These markedly Czech projects gave the inmates emotional comfort—explicitly in the case of the Czecho-Jewish or Communist prisoners, more implicitly for those with a Zionist affiliation. This sense of home and belonging is reflected in the many poems that have home as their theme.

Another principal function of cultural life was substantiating the legitimacy of "their" culture. Prisoners used high culture to confirm the validity of their habitus as educated bourgeoisie. The mechanism involved the fact that culture, as well as religion, could serve as a territory of self.[60] Expressing a particular taste, which identified one as a member of the educated bourgeoisie, was a way to affirm one's value, establish continuity with pre-ghetto life, and even assert intellectual superiority. Some cultural events, such as scholarly lectures or even poetry writing, directly served these purposes. For instance, in his opera *Emperor of Atlantis*, Viktor Ullmann cited Luther's chorale *A Mighty Fortress Is Our God*. The allusion to the central hymn of Protestantism, sung in moments of extreme hardship, served as a link to the tradition of the Reformation and thus also as a connection to the European cultural canon. The music composed in Terezín (by Pavel Haas, Karel Berman, Gideon Klein), modern classical music, was never as popular as the performances of established classical music such as Mozart and Smetana; it was not as accessible, especially to elderly people with conservative tastes.

Cultural capital can translate into symbolic capital, prestige, and power in a correct place where others share our notion of artistically valuable matters. It served as a means to situate oneself in the new surroundings of Theresienstadt and express there one's value and dignity. In Terezín it continued to be effective because the prisoners came from a background that highly valued cultural capital. High culture was so central to deported Central and Western European Jews because it confirmed their status. Only the educated bourgeoisie had access to these forms of culture. Even if all economic or habitus-related markers of class were removed, taste and a sense of culture still defined who they were.

Each faction of the inmate society had its legitimate cultural capital; what its members considered meaningful art depended on the culture from which they came. For German Jews, legitimate forms included works of high art, in particular classics of German culture from the late eighteenth and early nineteenth centuries; *Faust* and Lessing's *Nathan* were particularly popular.[61] Czech Jews enjoyed reading authors well-liked in interwar Czechoslovakia, focusing on the Anglo-Saxon writers John Galsworthy and Irving Stone, as

180 THE LAST GHETTO

well as Karel Čapek. Younger people liked the avant-garde, often leftists poets Jiří Wolker, František Halas, and Vítězslav Nezval, and the playwrights Jan Werich and Jiří Voskovec. German Jewish legitimate cultural capital was related to a notion of habitus and class and the Czech Jewish variety to ethnic connection. Both Czech and German definitions had shifted from the prewar standard, becoming more conservative, in a way cultural "comfort food." They did not include pieces the audiences knew and liked but perhaps did not consider core to their sense of belonging; for instance, Germans did not include Hauptmann, Büchner, or Wedekind in what counted as important, meaningful literature. Cultural events sometimes also served to reconstruct the former world. Oskar Fein, once editor-in-chief of *Neue Freie Presse,* the liberal newspaper of the educated bourgeoisie, lectured for Manes's program about old Austria, his newspaper, and the old Parliament.[62] Performances like Fein's transported the audience to bygone places and times.[63] Such lectures often staged a desired past, a world people wished they had inhabited.

Material Aspects of Cultural Life

Art in Terezín became both beautiful and valuable. People who in their normal lives would probably not have cared much for certain forms of art developed a taste for them because of how art was discussed in their social circles and linked to prestige. Seventeen-year-old Edgar Krása, who came from the lower middle class, arrived in Terezín with the Aufbaukommando. He became a cook and later head of one of the kitchens. He was, as he described himself, a "big shot" and functioned as a patron for Leo Haas and Fritta.[64] Krása brought them food from the kitchen. The artists gained food—both were in Terezín with their families, and Fritta had a little boy—and Krása gained cultural capital, which in the ghetto translated into symbolic capital. A closer look at the drawings Fritta made for Krása shows a very different aesthetic from that in their iconic drawings. Fritta and Haas were experienced artists who could draw and paint in a wide array of styles.

In the drawing for Krása, Fritta portrayed a much-beloved site in Prague: the Charles Bridge and the Vltava River. Unlike Fritta's much better known drawings of Terezín, which were expressive, terrifying, and examples of "high art," or his humorous pictures for his son Tommy's third birthday, which have several layers, the drawing for Krása is flat. It is a depiction of Prague, without further complexities. For Fritta, it was a bread-and-butter

CULTURAL LIFE 181

This watercolor by Fritta shows a classic Prague scene of the Charles Bridge and Vltava River, observed from the Lesser Town. The peaceful, simple picture is devoid of people and rendered in washed-out colors. Fritta gave this simple drawing to the cook Edgar Krása, who acted as patron for many Theresienstadt artists. Courtesy of the United States Holocaust Memorial Museum.

sketch. For Krása, the drawing was a token of high art, which was preserved for decades and eventually donated to an archive.

Drawings were an established item of barter. Willy Mahler, the house elder of the Hannover barracks, had his portrait drawn by the Viennese painter Rewald in return for a hard-laborer bread portion.[65] Drawings were also given as gifts, a gesture that confirmed the quality of the relationship. Many inmates kept or were given an autograph book, called a *památník*, in which friends and colleagues wrote entries about the owner or the ghetto, poetry, drawings, or songs. *Památníky* became a Terezín custom and were kept by many prisoners, young and old, men and women, Czech, Danish, and German.[66] Fritz Janowitz, the house elder of the Magdeburg barracks, had in his *památník* songs composed by Viktor Ullmann and Franz Eugen Klein.[67] The entry was a matter of special care and energy when the owner was important. Ullmann lived in the Magdeburg barracks; Janowitz was his landlord in the building that housed the self-administration and the brother of Leo Janowitz of the Central Secretariat.

182 THE LAST GHETTO

The status of art was further affirmed in another symbolic exchange at performances: high-ranking clerks of the self-administration, members of the Council of Elders, and the heads of departments received front-row seats.[68] Their visits set up complex staging and exchanges of power. The presence of the functionaries endowed the performance with importance and the stamp of political approval. The opposite applied in their absence.[69] For their part, sitting in the front row at a well-liked, popular performance gave functionaries access to high cultural and social standing in addition to the pleasure of the performance.

The medium of the cultural performances was a place endowed with symbolic capital. All three Elders of the Jews gave talks in the lecture series. Their jobs kept them extremely busy; participating in a lecture was something they did only because it allowed them to boost their presence in the public and gain status.[70] The Elders also spoke at official events, including anniversaries related to the ghetto.[71]

To a large extent material conditions shaped performers' activities. Very few artists were actually employed in Recreation; most had day jobs elsewhere and rehearsed and performed in their spare time. Many painters, especially those with an artistic education, worked in the Graphic Workshop producing technical drawings and reports for the self-administration. Actors, singers, and composers often worked in unrelated jobs: Ota Růžička, the theater director, produced boxes, and the actress Vlasta Schönová was a youth care worker. The musicians Gideon Klein and Raphael Schächter and the director Karel Švenk were eventually hired by Recreation and were able to rehearse and compose full-time.

The alto singer Hedda Grabová was one of the few recognized women artists. Grabová's pioneering position as a female artist was so unusual that it was mentioned in the annual report about the Hamburg barracks.[72] Alice Herz Sommer had a full-time position outside of Recreation, although for a time this job was in name only.[73] Still, she was lucky; her colleague was assigned to break stones, a job that jeopardized her fingers and thus her ability to play the piano.[74] With decisions like these the administrators of Recreation, many though not all of whom were performers themselves, assigned hierarchies to the women and men artists.

Conductors, actors, directors, lecturers, and musicians became the darlings of the public, who expressed their admiration with treats, usually food. The young tenor Alexandr Singer had fans who brought him salami and pork cracklings—a lavish gift by Terezín standards.[75] Singer, who originally came from Subcarpathian Rus', was one of the few observant Jews among the young Czech group. After the war he became cantor of the Prague Jewish Community. Anna Nathanová, who distributed milk to infants, gave Karel Ančerl's baby boy, born in the ghetto, a triple allotment.[76] Edgar Krása brought food to a group of painters with whom he was acquainted.[77] In June 1944, he and two colleagues were caught stealing margarine, sugar, and roux.[78] Rolf Grabower discussed his case with Karel Lagus from the Post Office; Lagus thought Krása was too young to be a group leader. In his later years Krása became proud of his patronage of Theresienstadt artists; when we talked in 2012, he had completely forgotten about his arrest.[79] Solidarity and patronage have become part of the master narrative; theft and corruption have not.

The gifts bestowed corresponded with the position of the patron, and patrons reflected the nature of the audience. Virtually all of the cooks were young Czech men who were primarily interested in music and Czech-language theater; they rarely attended lectures.[80] To a large extent, the audience for lectures was made up of the elderly and middle-aged and people with bourgeois backgrounds. The speakers here had fans, too. However, they were often among the least wealthy of the ghetto's inhabitants. Else Dormitzer received pieces of bread from sick and elderly listeners who were too weak to move.[81] In contrast to the cooks, who gave gifts made up from other's portions, Dormitzer's fans gave far more modest presents. They also gave away their own food—a loss they felt deeply.

Further material differences were evident in accommodations. Some young artists, most of them Czech men, were eventually able to secure a kumbál, where they had space to write and think. Susanne, wife of the young Austrian composer Franz Eugen Klein, shared a kumbál with Františka Solarová. Edgar Krása, the cook, invited his friend Schächter to live with him in his room. Later, Schächter moved to his own kumbál, designed by the Brno architect Norbert Troller.[82] Somewhat later, in June 1944, the forty-seven-year old Viennese cabaret artist Leo Strauss applied to the Space Management Department for a kumbál: "I work in the Financial Department as an accountant," he wrote, "and additionally I set the program for Blockveranstaltungen [cultural events for the residential block], work as master of ceremonies, and head the Ensemble Strauss and the literary Strauss-Brettl; moreover, I am the author of numerous chansons, poems, and sketches written and published here."[83] They would soon stage their 2000th event, Strauss pointed out, and they had no place to rehearse or prepare. His

184   THE LAST GHETTO

wife lived in a tailor shop that was simultaneously a walk-through room (as in a railroad apartment). It is unclear whether the application was successful. Four months later, the couple were sent to Auschwitz.

Applications like Strauss's demonstrate that the artists' material conditions in Terezín depended on their age, their ethnicity, and the type of art they produced. Schächter, Singer, Fritta, and Gideon and Franz Eugen Klein received better food and housing because they were young and Czech or were identified as Czech. Franz Eugen Klein was a musician, and music was a form of art particularly well liked by the Czech Jews. Although Leo Strauss was popular among the older, German-speaking audience, his popularity did not translate into patronage by those with access to material resources.

Many artists in a relatively good economic situation also belonged to the ghetto's social elite: the young (in most cases male) Czech Jews. Some of the musicians and artists had arrived with one of the Aufbaukommandos, including Bedřich Borges, Gideon Klein, Alexandr Singer, Ota Růžička, and Karel Švenk. Rafael Schächter came with the first transport from Prague. These artists and their companions from the early transports were often friends; they went on to make careers in Terezín as cooks, bakers, butchers, or craftsmen. Švenk worked in the Shipping detail with Josef Taussig and Gustav Schorsch. This labor group, which included Josef Bondy (who after the war changed his name to Bor and wrote *Terezín Requiem*) was composed of Czecho-Jews and Communists. Inclusion in this group provided hard-labor food rations as well as the possibility of establishing connections outside of the ghetto.[84]

It was not easy to gain access to a performance. Initially tickets were distributed for free; later they were sold for Terezín crowns, ghetto currency that had little purchasing power. Tickets to many performances, in particular operas, were highly sought after and became an item of barter. Bartering the tickets was a "huge business," remembered the actress Vlasta Schönová, with cooks able to acquire them easily.[85]

The second performance of Schächter's *Requiem* took place in January 1944, with representatives of the Council of Elders in attendance. The show was so popular that most interested people did not get in. The fact that one of the less fortunate hopefuls was Eva Mändlová, a popular young Czech woman with a good position as a shepherdess and among those most likely to secure tickets, demonstrates the immense popularity of the event.[86] Other events were also in high demand, including lectures by Karel Poláček, the popular Czech writer. Esther Jonas from Hamburg attended many musical events: the *Ghettoswingers, Requiem,* and *Brundibár.* Her boyfriend, the Prague cook Hanuš Leiner, got the tickets from his roommate, the musician Fricek Fleischmann. However, Esther's mother, the physician Marie Jonas, did not see any of these performances; the favor of tickets reached only the girlfriend, not her mother.[87] The inability to secure tickets left many hopefuls unsatisfied.[88] Purchasing a theater ticket by lining up at the office at the Magdeburg barracks became so laborious that it inspired Hans Hofer to write a long, comic poem.[89]

Performances faced thousands of organizational difficulties: there was a dire shortage of space for rehearsals and performances, instruments, scores, music paper, and material for stage design. All of the operas were accompanied by a piano only; there was no orchestra.[90] By 1943 the Council of Elders in Prague occasionally supplied instruments, many of them from Germany.[91] The first operas were held as concerts, without stage design or costumes. The first piano was located when the gentile population left in the summer of 1942. The instrument had no legs and was placed on two vaults. After František Mautner tuned and repaired it, the piano could once again be played.[92] Later there were more pianos; Gideon Klein and Alice Herz Sommer played on a Förster.[93] Otto Zucker and Paul Eppstein, both art lovers, had their own private instruments in their apartments.[94] There were no batons, so conductors directed with their hands. In the summer of 1943, František Zelenka, stage designer and architect, who had previously worked at the exhibition of the wartime Jewish Museum, was sent to Terezín. Zelenka redefined stage design for the plays; for Norbert Fried's play *Ester,* he created costumes by maximizing the available resources, working with papier mâché and dyed bed linens.[95]

Social and cultural differences influenced the material conditions of a production. One important factor was access to space. In order to put on a performance, the organizers needed space, which was administered by the Recreation Department and Space Management. For a long time, no extra space was allocated for cultural events. Instead performances took place in attics, the worst type of accommodation.[96] Manes's performances were held for some time in a room that was a workshop during the day and became dormitories for women in the evening; the show had to fit into less than two hours in between those uses.[97]

Popular shows received advantages. Rudolf Freudenfeld, the conductor of *Brundibár,* was a good friend of Rudolf Reichmann, who always assigned the production the best space.[98] Rehearsing was also difficult. With only a

Norbert Troller's watercolor depicts the functionalist building of Sokolovna, a former sports club that was the site of cultural events in Theresienstadt. On the far left is the outline of the water tower. Courtesy of the Leo Baeck Institute.

few instruments to be shared among many musicians, not everyone had access. The German conductor Karl Fischer, who put on *La Serva Padrona* and a selection from *Aida*, complained that he lacked a venue to rehearse.[99] Fischer was not as popular as some Czech conductors. Milan Kuna suggested Fischer was a weaker conductor than his colleagues and that the audience preferred productions closer to Czech taste—those based on Czech composers and Mozart.[100] Kuna assumed that quality was related to taste and ignored the opinions of non-Czech prisoners. At the same time, musical performances that catered to the tastes of the Czech elite enjoyed better production conditions and as a result could achieve higher musical standards.

The space situation improved somewhat with the beautification effort. In March 1944 the SS widened the area of the ghetto to include a new building, a facility that previously had housed the Czech athletic association, Sokol. The Sokolovna, built in the interwar period and visually different from the predominant classicist architecture, had two halls and was suitable for cultural and religious events. Most of these events, when not musical, used the German language. The building is mostly mentioned in non-Czech testimonies (with various spellings): Sokolowna, Sokolhalle, sokolowne, and

Sokulouska.[101] Perhaps because the building housed events for "foreign" prisoners, Czech Jews did not often mention it.

Ethnicity and Exclusion

There were major disparities between the audiences who attended different performances. In addition to the various class backgrounds and habitus, perhaps the strongest indicator of difference was taste, marked by national and generational lines. The great majority of the young and many of the middle-aged Czech Jews attended Czech theater, cabaret, and operas; only occasionally did they attend German and Austrian dramatic productions. Jiří Borský, a Czecho-Jew, attended and enjoyed Viennese cabarets; his Austrian girlfriend, Helene, encouraged him in this pursuit.[102] Borský was in his late thirties; other middle-aged Czech Jews also attended Austrian cabarets.[103] But when fifty-year-old Bedřich Kohn visited Hans Hofer's cabaret, he was put off by what he called "the stupidest kind of burlesque."[104]

Music was popular among almost all inmates and offered a platform for interethnic encounters. Most groups attended both concerts and operas, especially Mozart's. German Jews tended to go to chamber music concerts but also occasionally attended Czech musical productions, even though tickets were hard to get.[105] Encounters among performers were rare. Hana Munková was a Czech Jewish actress born in 1916. She had studied acting and had been in a film. In Terezín, as one of the more experienced actors, she performed in Schönová's productions of *Camel through the Needle's Ear* and *The Romancers* and Karel Švenk's cabaret, and she advised younger colleagues. Her father was a veteran of the Czechoslovak Legion, a volunteer foreign Czechoslovak military that fought against the Central Powers, and a prominent Czecho-Jew; her husband's mother was a gentile; and her lover in the ghetto was a Communist Czech five years her junior.[106] Munková, introduced to Manes by her colleague Jiří Běhal, was one of the few who reached across ethnic barriers. After the original German actress became ill, she played Margarete in Manes's production of *Faust*.[107] However, in her testimony fifty years later, she did not speak about her German acting at all and described German Jews as annoyingly Prussian.

Munková's experience was an exception. Vlasta Schönová spoke in dismissive terms of the artistic quality of the German cabaret.[108] Her view was symptomatic of the attitude of Czech Jews; claims that German theater

188 THE LAST GHETTO

lacked quality, innovation, and political dimensions were almost omnipresent in the narratives of the Czech actors and directors.[109] An eminent Czech actress displayed this attitude when she spoke about the non-Czech theater as "the Germans," as if it were one group, and even referred to Hans Hofer as German.[110] Hofer, however, was a Czech who had moved to Vienna and there married Lisl Steinitz. In Terezín, Lisl and Hans put on the Hofer-Cabaret.[111] Attempts at appropriation from the non-Czech side were not always welcome; when Leo and Myra Strauss included a Czech chorus in their cabaret, it was received quite negatively.[112] This attitude toward demarcation, based mostly on language, was the result of two factors: ethnic self-definition and professional competition.

The ethnic gaze and ways in which inmates expressed ethnic belonging and its boundaries became more intense in matters related to the arts. Often the "othering" focused on women. *The Bartered Bride* remained one of the best-liked opera productions throughout the duration of Terezín. In the first performance, Josefa Klinkeová played the main female role, Mařenka. Born in 1895, Klinkeová had been a singer and singing teacher in her native German-speaking Teplitz/Teplice. Anna Nathanová, who was married to a German émigré architect and attended the dress rehearsal in November 1942, recalled: "Mařenka was a German Jewess, perhaps 42 years old; she could not speak a word of Czech and looked terrible. An old hag playing Mařenka, that was quite unforgettable."[113] Klinkeová did speak Czech, but likely with a German accent. In her depiction of Klinkeová's rendition, Nathanová stressed her older age and unattractive appearance but did not comment on Klinkeová's singing.

The cast of *The Bartered Bride* varied; later Marion Podolier and Gertruda Borgerová took the role of Mařenka. In 1943 Hana and Lea Blánová, two young Czech *Geltungsjuden* women, attended another performance of *The Bartered Bride*. They recalled "a Viennese woman singer whose Czech, nevertheless, was excellent."[114] Vlasta Schönová also reminisced about a Viennese singer: "Mařenka was a German Jewess [. . .] who had a beautiful voice and who had learned Czech for this role: a lovely woman with a beautiful voice. There was no other Czech soprano, and so this woman, I believe she was Viennese, sang the part."[115] The singer in question was probably Podolier. Born in 1906 in Berlin, Podolier immigrated to Prague after 1933 and worked there with Schächter. The confusion of Podolier's German for an Austrian background was typical of ethnic categorization. In the eyes of

Czech inmates, Austrians were ethnically closer and more adaptable than the Germans.[116]

Schönová's comment shows that Podolier's exact origin was irrelevant—she was German or Austrian, German being shorthand for non-Czech. Although they described Podolier as a beautiful soprano, the narrators stressed her foreignness. Podolier's beautiful voice gained relevance only in the context of a Czech opera in which she was able to perform only because there were, supposedly, no Czech sopranos (although Borgerová and Klinkeová were both Czech) and because she had learned the language. This mechanism of exclusion prompted Hedda Grabová, originally from the German-speaking borderlands, to take Czech elocution lessons.[117]

For German Jews, Czech dramatic production remained linguistically inaccessible, even if many of them had learned rudimentary Czech. In the spring of 1944, Recreation ordered that Czech plays must begin with a plot summary in German.[118] Some Germans may have attended these performances, perhaps for the visual and dramatic experience. In July 1944, Rahm prohibited all Czech-language cultural activities.[119] Murmelstein claimed that Eppstein was behind this ban. Eppstein was invited to a memorial service for the poet and functionary of the Prague Jewish Community, Hanuš Bonn, who was murdered in Mauthausen in 1941. There was no translation from Czech into German, and Eppstein was upset. He suggested to Rahm that Czech productions might be politically subversive, and they were then prohibited until November 1944, when Murmelstein took over.[120] But this story does not hold completely true: this moratorium on Czech cultural activities was not enforced; numerous Czech plays and lectures were presented throughout August 1944.[121] The Czech premiere of *Romancers*, directed by Vlasta Schönová, was presented late that month. Since the director was Murmelstein's lover, it is highly improbable that Murmelstein did not know about it. Possibly Murmelstein made up the story to discredit Eppstein.[122] Eppstein attended the memorial service for the Czecho-Jewish writer Edvard Lederer. This service was an homage to the Czech Jewish movement and included a speech by Alfréd Meissner, a former Czechoslovak minister of justice.[123] This story illustrates how politically charged for the Jewish functionaries language use in the cultural events was.

The way inmates made sense of visual arts also had ethnic aspects. Some of the features are evident in a drawing by Markéta Fröhlichová, an academically trained artist from Prostějov. This drawing is part of an album assembled for the thirty-first birthday of her friend Edith

Markéta Fröhlichová, *Bilderbuch für Dittl* (Picture Book for Dittl). Fröhlichová's watercolor, part of an album, depicts a young farm woman in red skirt and scarf and blue shirt harvesting grain. Behind her are a mountain and the setting sun. Inside the sun are the inscription "Theresienstadt" and a star of David with a J. Courtesy of Friedrich Psenicka.

Orstein,[124] who was head of the Women's Labor Department and a close associate of the Zionist leadership. The artists Leo and Erna Haas, who contributed to the album, called the short Ornstein *la petite corporale*, after Napoleon. Like the *památníky*, birthday albums were a prized item in Terezín. The album consists of a series of scenes depicting the inmates of Terezín as childlike, cute figures. The album employs similar aesthetics to Fritta's well-known birthday album for his son Tommy. However, because the album was not targeted to an audience of children, its tone is ironic rather than cute.[125]

CULTURAL LIFE 191

The drawing shows a young woman from Agriculture harvesting wheat. Agricultural manual labor was a familiar theme for young Zionists, many of whom had attended a *hachshara*, Zionist agricultural training. However, the scene in this picture is situated in the ghetto; the mountain in the background has a sunset with the Star of David and the label "Terezín." Similar to the aesthetics that Lotka Burešová employed in her drawing of a young woman jumping through a frame, the features and attire of the peasant girl are markedly non-Jewish: she has blonde hair and red cheeks and is dressed in white, red, and blue—traditional Czech colors. The attire mirrors the clothes worn by Czech rural workers. Finally, the mountain in the background, even though it has two peaks, is redolent of Mount Říp. That mountain, a symbol of Czech statehood, is eleven miles away from Terezín and visible from the town walls. The birthday album ends with the wish that everyone may soon go wherever they desire.

Ornstein kept the album in her papers, which supported the Zionist master narrative of Terezín that she helped create.[126] Key elements of "Czechness" are implicit in the work. For instance, the cuteness of the figure is expressed in a way that appeals to the viewer's emotions. Unlike Zionists in Palestine, Zionists in Terezín did not have their own established visual aesthetics; they often used Czech aesthetics to express emotional messages. As in Burešová's drawing, the fact that the figure is female is significant; symbols of emotional national belonging are often represented as female.

The prisoner society closely observed the ethnicity of women in public roles, and cultural productions were a particularly public role. When inmates criticized Josefa Klinkeová for her lack of Czechness, the critique addressed her lack of womanliness. When Marion Podolier was accepted as Mařenka in *The Bartered Bride*, narrators stressed her loveliness, the beauty of her voice, and her ability to integrate linguistically, thereby linking her appropriate femininity to her ethnic inclusion as Czech. All the major male singers were Czech, but they were not scrutinized as the women were. No one singled out Alexandr Singer for his Carpathorussian roots or Rafael Schächter for his Romanian background.

Nor were male performers criticized for their ambition. The two women directors, Vlasta Schönová and Irena Dodalová, by contrast, were attacked for being outspoken and assertive. These same qualities were praised in male colleagues, including Norbert Fried and Karel Reiner. Criticisms of Schönová and Dodalová did not necessarily address their directorial skills. Dodalová, who shot the first Terezín propaganda film in 1942, was disparaged for "collaboration."[127] Schönová was condemned for her sexual conduct

192   THE LAST GHETTO

because of her relationship with Benjamin Murmelstein. Many other women had relationships with unpopular functionaries, but people spread rumors about Schönová because in Terezín, the norms of female behavior were defined more conservatively, especially when in combination with power and ambition.

In order to become an active performer in Terezín, musicians, especially those who played an instrument, needed ambition. People had to put themselves forward to secure access to instruments and time to rehearse. Rehearsal time was allotted to those musicians who were considered the best. In order to be viewed as the best, it was necessary to belong to the right networks. For women singers the situation was easier, since female parts were not only indispensable but were often considered particularly beautiful. Many inmates active in musical life were laypeople, for whom music was a hobby. Anna Krasová, a fifty-year-old ENT doctor and gifted pianist, could rehearse only early in the morning because this was the only time she had access to a piano.[128] However, Franz Hahn, a young Viennese internist, could join his Czech boss's string quartet due to his colleague's sense of male camaraderie and as a sign that Hahn had proven himself.[129]

Women musicians who had families often spent their spare time taking care of them. Eliška was six years older than her brother Gideon Klein, a celebrated pianist and composer in the ghetto. An established musician in her own right, she, unlike Gideon, had completed her music degree. Yet she never played in Terezín. She arrived eight months after her brother and spent most of her time taking care of him and their mother.[130] The gendered expectation of nurturing, supportive women was one of the factors that explained why Gideon became a celebrated performer. Gender bias meant that some women never, or only rarely, attended cultural performances; they needed the time after work to take care of their children.[131]

As in the normal world, competitiveness was an aspect of performance. Indeed, rivalry was one of the factors that made cultural life in Terezín so dynamic and appealing. Many of the Czech performers strove for a quality that would stand outside of the context of Terezín—to be as good as they would be on the outside.[132] Conductors tried to present new, more difficult, and emotionally appealing operas. Schächter started by putting on *The Bartered Bride*, later following with Mozart's *Marriage of Figaro*, Smetana's *Kiss*, and Mozart's *Magic Flute*. Jochowitz staged Mozart's *Bastien and Bastienne*; Franz Eugen Klein conducted Verdi's *Rigoletto*, Puccini's *Tosca*, and Bizet's *Carmen*, and Karel Berman directed Vilém Blodek's *In the Well*. Viktor Ullmann put

CULTURAL LIFE 193

on *The Emperor of Atlantis*, which he wrote in Terezín. These conductors were friendly, but at the same time they wanted to be admired by the public and experts alike. Starting with relatively easy pieces, musically and technically, the conductors moved toward more challenging works.

This competitive spirit gave birth to Raphael Schächter's production of Verdi's *Requiem*. Born in 1905 in Romania, Schächter studied at a prestigious music school in Brno founded by Leoš Janáček. After he graduated from the conservatory in Prague, he directed music at the leftist theater D34 and later started a chamber orchestra. In Terezín he organized male choirs that performed Czech national songs. Schächter aimed to become a leading figure in Terezín's music scene, producing meticulous, professional performances. He also worked to push music beyond what was considered possible in the ghetto.[133] During a six-month break in the transports in the summer of 1943, he decided to stage the *Requiem*.

The *Requiem*, a Catholic mass for the deceased, was one of Verdi's later works, a classical piece indicative of the highly emotional wave of late romanticism. From the start it was viewed as an operatic piece as opposed to church music. Hans von Bülow called it "an opera dressed up in church clothes." By the 1930s, the *Requiem* was considered one of the most difficult pieces one could present. It experienced a renaissance from the 1920s onward and became a popular piece in the 1930s.[134] Schächter knew that vocal music, especially in such an enormous production, would be a powerful emotional and physical experience. This fact is even more significant for a large, romantic piece that Verdi wrote in the age of overwhelming mass productions—the same era as Wagner (not a composer one would stage in Terezín).

Of the well-known performers, more women than men survived the war, including Marion Podolier, Hedda Grabová, Josefa Klinkeová, Gertruda Borgerová, and Alice Herz Sommer. Yet men rather than women became the official chroniclers and canonized part of musical life in Terezín. Karel Berman, Karel Ančerl, Martin Roman, and Coco Schumann from the jazz band Ghettoswingers were often interviewed after the war, and some of them wrote autobiographies.[135] Something similar applies to those who were murdered: The alto Magda Spiegel, whose prewar career was probably the most distinguished of the musicians in the ghetto (born in 1887, she had been a prima donna in the Frankfurt opera), continued to sing in Theresienstadt and performed in the *Requiem*.[136] Yet her name comes up only on the margins of accounts of Terezín musical life, in contrast to Gideon Klein or Raphael Schächter. Those female musicians who spoke of their participation

194 THE LAST GHETTO

in Terezín cultural activities offered a markedly emotional narrative, devoid of statements concerning issues of organization or competition. Moreover, traces of these women usually disappeared in the immediate postwar period; what they did and where they lived afterward is not known. Surviving male performers, in contrast, described their work, noted that they had organized something meaningful, emphasized how they were envied and respected by colleagues, and proclaimed how objectively good their performances had been. Indeed, male performers described Terezín as a defining moment in their careers.[137]

Soccer

Soccer was an important part of the Terezín world, one of the most be-loved leisure activities in the ghetto.[138] Like all sports, soccer was organized by Recreation.[139] The SS was wary of athletic activities among the inmates, fearing that they might be preparing for a revolt. They allowed ball games, however.[140] Although other ball games, including volleyball, were also pop-ular, no sport achieved the popularity of soccer. In 1943 there were spring and fall leagues with corresponding lower divisions and a summer and winter cup. There were also youth games.[141] That year, the matches held at the Dresden barracks alone had 300,000 spectators. Representatives of the Council of Elders attended the games, and Otto Zucker presented a ceramic cup to the winners.[142]

There were more than thirty teams, each with seven rather than the usual eleven players.[143] Matches were held in the courtyard of the Dresden bar-racks and also at times in the Magdeburg barracks and the third bastion (as a former fortress, Theresienstadt had bastions). The pitch was reduced to about eighty by forty meters (rather than the regulation minimum, ninety by forty), goal posts were smaller and game times shorter, and there were two periods of thirty-five rather than forty-five minutes. The teams came from select departments, including the clothing warehouse, electricians, and butchers. The butchers, cooks, and clothing warehouse were the favorites. The latter won the 1943 spring league, a match observed by seven thousand spectators.[144] Several of the butchers' and cooks' players were deported in September 1943, and those remaining were merged into a new team named the Economic Department. They went on to win the fall league. The Clothing Warehouse eventually changed its name to Sparta, based on the name of a popular Prague team. There were also exhibition games: teams of the Aufbaukommandos 1 and 2 played on the one-and-one-half- and two-year anniversaries of their arrival. The second anniversary game, on November 27, 1943, was one of the most attended matches in the history of the ghetto, drawing six thousand spectators.[145]

The majority but not all of the players were Czech. Non-Czech inmates joined the FC Wien team. Some of the players on this team came from Vienna, such as Kurt Ladner and Ignatz Fischer, a professional soccer player who had played for Baník Ostrava.[146] Others, including Abraham Lau and Simon Director, were Danish Jews of German background.[147] Prague, supported by its goalkeeper, young pro Jiří Taussig, won against Vienna. The Viennese team had a particular fan in Scharführer Rudolf Haindl.[148]

A player's relationship to a team was not exclusive. Fischer played not only for the Vienna team but also for Sparta. He was also chosen in the "ghetto selection" to play against the Aufbaukommando "all stars" at the second anniversary of the foundation of Terezín. The Aufbaukommando won that match. Lau from Denmark joined the Cooks' team immediately after his deportation to Theresienstadt on October 5, 1943, because the player Jan Fried had been deported to Auschwitz one month earlier. The exhibition games also included teams from several barracks, such as Sudeten or Hannover, or selections of players who played against each other, such as Bohemia and Moravia. Bohemia, considered the favorite, lost 2 to 5.[149]

It is no surprise that the Butchers and later the Economic Department were the best teams; their players had excellent access to food. All players, however, had easier access to food than did others in the ghetto. After a match players received a special meal.[150] Jan Burka, who played for the Youth Welfare team, worked in the kitchen in the Dresden barracks. He arranged for two or three extra lunches for his teammates on the days when they were playing.[151] Burka related the team's extra meals to the contemporary example of soccer players earning millions. The story omits the fact that the extra lunches were taken from someone else's food allowance, usually from the elderly nonworkers.[152] This was part of the cost of having young, charismatic sportsmen, who needed to be fed. When talking about soccer in Theresienstadt, we ought to take into account those thirty-four thousand dead, most of them old, who died from starvation-related diseases.

The special meals for players were significant. All the Czech players belonged to the social elite, and many had arrived with one of the Aufbaukommandos. Soccer and soccer players were the darlings of the

Alfréd Kantor, *Soccer Game as Entertainment on Sunday*. Kantor made this drawing of a soccer game inside the Dresden barracks soon after the liberation as part of his picture memoir about his imprisonment. Huge crowds cheer from the sidelines and the windows of the building's three floors, and some spectators have even climbed up to the roof. Courtesy of Jerry Kantor and Monica Churchill-Kantor.

ghetto. Miloš Gut, who came to Terezín with an Aufbaukommando, worked in the Butchers Department and played on its team. As an old man, he mentioned that he remembered only "all the brilliant moments" in the ghetto: meeting his wife, Zuzana, and playing soccer.[153] Viktor Kende, head of Transport Management in Terezín, as an old man passionately exclaimed, "Of course I rooted for soccer." He was a great fan of the brothers Vilém and František Petschau, who played "fantastic soccer."[154]

Soccer became such a favorite pastime in Terezín because it had been hugely popular before the war. In interwar Czechoslovakia and Austria, soccer was all the rage; men and women, working and middle class, went to watch the matches on Sundays, listened to games on the radio, and scrutinized the sports sections of the newspaper.[155] Jews participated fully in this passion; in 1932 Karel Poláček, a well-known Czech Jewish writer, even wrote a soccer novel, *Men Offside*, which was made into a successful eponymous film. Czechoslovakia was an established force in soccer; the Czech Alley, a maneuver of passing the ball through the opposition defense, made the Czechoslovak team a success. There was a division between the Czech- and German-language sections, which both had Jewish players. However, just as later in Terezín, there were many connections between the two. Pavel Mahrer had played for the German Soccer Club in Prague, for the Czechoslovak Olympic Team in 1924, and for the Viennese Hakoach. In Terezín, Mahrer was the best-known professional player and played for the Butchers.[156]

Soccer spectators in Terezín were men and women, young and old, Czech, Austrian, and Slovak.[157] Old Austrian and Czech ladies cheered at games when their grandsons played but also if they were in the ghetto without family. One group, however, did not attend the matches: elderly Germans. Almost none of this group's testimonies mention soccer, or if they do, it is only as a phenomenon rather than an event they attended.[158] Soccer did become popular in interwar Germany, as in Czechoslovakia and Austria, and many German Jews played or watched the game.[159] But we ought to ask whether bourgeois Germans born before 1880, as were the typical German prisoners in Theresienstadt, were interested in soccer. For the typical German Jews of Terezín, a generation born between 1860 and 1880, soccer was a working-class activity. Despite the fact that FC Bayern had Jewish sponsors and that there were many German Jewish soccer players, soccer was not popular among the bourgeoisie. It was a matter of class and taste.

Soccer in Terezín reveals new insights about the cultural history of interwar Central European Jewry. The popularity of the game among Czech

198 THE LAST GHETTO

Jews demonstrates the values held by the young Czech Jewish elite: living with a sportsman's attitude, good humor, hard work, decency, straightforwardness, and loyalty to the parta. It was a sign of this attitude that, when their lives were relocated to the ghetto, they had to make the best of it. In summer 1945, Ota Klinger eulogized his friend Jan Hermann, a cook in Terezín who died in Schwarzheide, as "a sportsman in body and soul."[160]

The overwhelming enthusiasm for soccer, with players playing for various teams, crossing any sense of boundary or belonging to a faction, raises questions about the importance of divisions between Zionists, Communists, and Czecho-Jews that the camp's conventional wisdom insists divided Czech Jews in Terezín. Playing soccer, reading *Šalom na pátek*, and visiting Švenk's and Taussig's performances, were in some respects more important than ideological differences. Hard-liners may have been few in number, and the social elite lived beyond such distinctions. In this respect cultural life sheds light not only on "culture" but on loyalties within ethnic groups.

At the end of September 1944, with the large transports in progress, the Terezín cultural scene ebbed away until it nearly ceased to exist. The SS sent away two-thirds of the population, including nearly all of the performers, the soccer players, and their audience. Most performers and players, those who had become famous in the ghetto and those who had not, those prisoners who had attended the performances and those who had not, did not live to see liberation. Rafael Schächter, Karel Švenk, and Magda Spiegel did not return. Others, who had been young, healthy, and childless, survived. In Auschwitz and in the camps afterward, cultural life lost its spell of defining prestige and power. Karel Berman remembered that at the ramp in Auschwitz, he stood together with his musician friends František Weissenstein and Karel Reiner. He observed the selection, with the "bleak, thin, and sick looking people on the left and the tanned, athletic ones on the right." Reiner got a sense of what was going on, and as they approached the SS doctor in the selection line, whispered, "Say you are a laborer." When the doctor asked Weissenstein, the first of the three, for his profession, Weissenstein said that he was an opera singer. He was sent to the left. Berman and Reiner claimed to be laborers and were sent to the right.[161]

The well-liked, attractive couple Vilém and Nita Petschau provide another example of the special position culture had in Terezín. Vilém and his brother František arrived with the early transports; they became the soccer darlings of the ghetto. Vilém led the incoming transport command. Nita, born in

CULTURAL LIFE 199

1921 in Prague, was active as a youth care worker and actress. The couple lived a privileged life; not only was Nita able to get pregnant, she was also able to avoid a forced abortion.[162] In the third month of her pregnancy, she was sent to Auschwitz, later to Bergen-Belsen and then to Raguhn, an auxiliary camp of Buchenwald, and eventually back to Terezín on a death march. She arrived, exhausted and in an advanced stage of pregnancy, on April 22. A few days later she gave birth to a boy, who died within a week. Nita was the only surviving member of the Petschau family.[163] The world of Auschwitz and other camps had no regard for soccer players and well-liked, pretty actresses, for the jeunesse dorée of Terezín. In Terezín the social elite could live in a bubble. Their ghetto experience offered relatively decent food, friendships, romantic relationships, music, theater, and soccer. The special position of the Terezín social elite ended in Auschwitz—but the bubble did not burst. It lives on in memories of Terezín.

Conclusion

The arts occupied a highly important position in Terezín. Rather than being an expression of spiritual resistance, they reflected the specific Terezín inmate society. Art confirmed people's former status and displayed their national loyalties. Artistic production was connected to inequalities and ethnic differences. For the social elite in Terezín, legitimate art was that which reinforced their Czechness, such as drawings that appealed to the Czech sense of aesthetics or Smetana's *The Bartered Bride*. In Terezín, culture in the right form was what the social circle admired, a way to secure cultural capital, status, and by extension dominance. Taste dictated positioning on the social field; while German, Austrian, and Czech prisoners enjoyed different productions, for them the right kind of culture could affirm their habitus and hence their standing.

Class position in Theresienstadt profoundly shaped the cultural life there. It influenced who would be able to purchase the most desired theater tickets, which performers received gifts and who these came from, and the conditions for artistic work. Gender was defining for cultural production in the ghetto; one of the functions of art is to engender emotional ties, often confirming a sense of national belonging. To this end, artists routinely used female figures, whose genderedness established the salient connection to an ethnic entity. Czech Jews criticized the performances of "foreign" women in

200 THE LAST GHETTO

Czech-coded theatrical productions much more readily than those of their male counterparts, as women's ethnicity was more critical.

The art that was produced in the ghetto was connected to prewar and postwar art production. Most of the artists within Terezín had written, created, and performed before the war; those who survived continued to be active afterward. The performers in the ghetto were as ambitious as they had been before the war, and they achieved remarkable things. What distinguishes these works is not their quality but their origin. Artistic testimonies capture a perspective of the Holocaust experience that eludes other genres.

6

Transports from Terezín to the East

Transports to sites of annihilation—the core function of a transit ghetto—shattered the status quo into which Terezín's inmates had arranged themselves. And yet inmates managed to compartmentalize their danger.

The Jewish self-administration was responsible for organizing departing transports and selecting individuals to be included on them. The role of the Jewish Councils in preparing the transports has sparked heated discussion.[1] Examining Terezín shows that Jewish functionaries strove to do the best job possible, to send people out as families, with supplies and in good shape, to be fair, and to protect their own. The transports out of Terezín triggered reactions of exclusion and inclusion and revealed to whom people felt connected. During the transports inmates experienced crippling panic and powerlessness. Yet they still exercised choice, however limited. Inmates in Terezín feared the transports most of all the dangers they encountered. Until the end of the war, the small fraction of prisoners who were never deported did not know what had happened in the East. This lack of awareness was fed by, among other factors, an uneasy conscience at being spared.

Organization

The SS did not assemble the names on the transport list; this was the task of the Jewish administration. The self-administration organized the entire process of transports up to the point where the inmates boarded the train. The SS provided only the orders, threat of violence, and trains. In this respect, Theresienstadt was similar to other ghettos, including Warsaw and Lodz: for a long time, transports were organized by the Jewish functionaries. This system lasted until fall 1944, when the SS took over, beginning with the fourth of the fall transports, En, which almost entirely cleared out the ghetto population.[2] Similarly to the incoming transports, the outgoing were given codes, a combination of letters. Once the self-administration could no longer

The Last Ghetto. Anna Hájková, Oxford University Press (2020). © Oxford University Press.
DOI: 10.1093/oso/9780190051778.001.0001.

202   THE LAST GHETTO

believe that people would be spared, or the prisoners would not follow orders, the Germans took over.[3]

Before October 1944, transports were often preceded by Ernst Moes coming to the ghetto to bring the IVB4 transport directives. Inmates noticed his arrival and realized the connection between his appearance and future transports. Soon there were rumors that Moes was the bearer of bad news.[4] The commandant announced the departing transport, usually several days before the impending event, to the Elder of the Jews. Sometimes the commandant attended a meeting of the Council of Elders.[5] The commandant passed on the outline dictated from Berlin, which included the date and size of the transport, the categories that were to be selected and those that were to be protected, as well as the nationalities and their ratios to be included. These categories were in flux: a group that was protected at one time could be marked for transport the next. Categories included, among others, those sick with TB, a certain nationality, elderly or younger inmates, and orphans. For instance, until fall 1944, most members of the Aufbaukommando and nearly all Geltungsjuden were protected.

There was, however, one exception to this rule: the commandant listed and passed on the names of the Weisungen—individuals who were personally named for inclusion on a transport. Weisungen were often those who, for whatever reason, knew too much about the SS. They had acquired this knowledge either in Terezín or during the period before their deportation when they had worked for one of the Jewish Communities.[6] In May 1944 there was a large number of Weisungen.[7] Sometimes they were those who had been sentenced in the Ghetto Court.[8] For instance, in September 1943, Anton Burger ordered all individuals whose sentences were longer than two weeks to be put on a transport.[9] However, not all convicts were deported as Weisungen.[10] People marked in this manner carried a "W" sign; inmates believed that these people were likely going to be killed. Inmates thus designated were usually put into a separate car.

The Elder passed on the instructions to Vilém Cantor, the head of Transport Registry within the Central Registry from the Central Evidence department.[11] The Large Commission, consisting of the heads of the departments and presided over by Otto Zucker, selected the names for the transport list. One of the members was Edith Ornstein, head of the Women's Labor Department, responsible for decisions about which working single women would be included on a transport. A married woman's status was usually defined by her husband's.[12] Occasionally women tried to protect their families and succeeded, but these cases were few.[13] Throughout most of the ghetto's existence, the self-administration honored the unity of families (a rule called *Familienzerreißung*). The Technical Committee within the Transport Registry protected families from being torn apart; couples and parents with children up to eighteen years of age were considered a unit.[14]

The Commission read the names of all prisoners destined for transport, and Cantor reported who was to be protected. The departmental leaders brought their card indexes with their workers ranked in the order of their importance to the department. This ranking was termed "indispensability." During the reading, these departmental leaders listened for the names of their people and claimed their indispensability.[15] Since the Aufbaukommando members were protected, their names were not included at such readings for a long period of time.

After the first reading, the remaining list was usually not long enough. Zucker then noted the number of individuals that each department still needed to put forward.[16] The Large Commission discussed names until the final list was established—a process that often took all night.[17] The Large Commission paid attention to those on various protection lists to be preserved from transports when putting together the deportation list. It also discussed people's age, illness, political activity, and merits in civil life when establishing the lists.[18] The Elder of the Jews and his deputies were absent from these meetings, intervening only when the Commission could not agree—a situation that rarely arose.

Unless the SS explicitly ordered otherwise, the list was compiled according to a nationality key. For instance, if the transport was to include one thousand people, and at that point 45 percent of the inmates in Terezín were Czech Jews, then 450 Czechs were put on the transport.[19] In addition to the Large Commission, there were also National Commissions (*Landsmannschaftkommissionen*) representing the various groups in the ghetto (Czech, German, Austrian, and Dutch), who suggested individuals who should and should not be included on the lists.[20] The Czech Commission consisted of veterans of the self-administration: Leo Janowitz, Otto Zucker, Erich Österreicher, Karel Schliesser, Siegfried Placzek, Egon Popper, Rudolf Bergmann, and František Weidmann. These individuals represented the two main ideological groups: Zionists (the first five) and Czecho-Jews (the remaining three).[21] The National Commission kept a so-called objective list of people with cultural, civil, or other merits; for the Czech Jewish community, this list consisted of writers and composers or relatives of important Jewish

204 THE LAST GHETTO

political representatives. In addition to the National Commissions, there was also a Departmental Commission that produced so-called qualification lists, defining people who were "indispensable" for their department.[22]

The only objective list that survived the war was from summer 1943 and included about eight hundred names. A close look at the list reveals that most of the people were functionaries in the local Jewish communities, and sometimes their relatives—family of respected Zionists and occasionally writers.[23] Yet also listed were Zdeňka Vochočová (sister of the poet Richard Weiner and the first wife of the Czechoslovak consul in Marseille, Vladimír Vochoč) and the Communist lawyer Truda Sekaninová.[24] In addition, members of the Council of Elders and departmental leaders had their personal protection lists (*Schutzlisten*), which included several dozen names.[25] None of the lists were static. They changed over the course of time as people were taken off for various reasons: they wanted to leave on a transport with someone important to them, they had an alternative source of protection, they had died, or they were simply removed from a list.[26] The personal protection lists were perhaps the most consistent. For instance, the protection list of Rudolf Bergmann, deputy head of the Economic Department, in August 1943 totaled seventy-seven people, all of them Czech Jews. The large majority of this group was still in Terezín one year later, before the large fall transports began.[27]

It is not clear whether the objective and qualification lists were created on the occasion of a transport that was due for departure or whether they were updated every so often, such as after a transport left. The surviving lists from August, September, and October 1943 appear to have been updated throughout those months, that is, before transports Dl and Dm, and afterward. For instance, the mathematician Ota Fischer, who headed the Statistical Department in the Prague Jewish Community and had to organize the registrations and departing transports, was deported to Theresienstadt with the Do transport on September 11, 1943.[28] He had previously been included on the objective list.

When time was limited, the Small Commission, rather than the Large Commission, met to discuss the transport list. The Small Commission consisted of the Council of Elders; the Elder of the Jews; the head of Central Labor, Erich Österreicher; and the head of the Personnel Office of the Central Secretariat, Siegfried Placzek. The latter two could speak to the "usefulness" of the workers, since the members of the Council of Elders eventually stopped acting in a double capacity as department leaders.[29] Eventually the Large or Small Commission agreed on a transport list and, because the

TRANSPORTS TO THE EAST   205

SS required that there be 20 percent extra names in case individuals needed to be replaced, an additional list called the *Reserve* (standby list). For every person from the original list who did not leave with the transport, someone from the standby list was included. Once the list was agreed upon, the Jewish functionaries submitted it to SS headquarters. From this point forward, only the Elder (with the commandant's permission) could replace names on the list.[30]

The typed lists, sorted by accommodation, were passed on to the house and room elders, who informed the inhabitants. Every deportee received a slip of paper summoning him or her for transport. It was the responsibility of the house and room elders to ensure that those called up for transport came forward. Individuals selected for transport had a day—sometimes less—to pack. Transport Management prepared an outline of recommended goods to pack: sleeping bag, medications, eating utensils, sweater, two shirts, working outfit, six handkerchiefs, and two sets of underwear.[31]

Inmates often managed to accumulate many things that made life in the ghetto easier, including books, clothes, blankets, and a stool, as well as items of emotional value such as diaries, poems, and autograph books (památníky). Just before their scheduled departure, some deemed many of these articles impractical and either sold or gave them away. Others, however, left with so much luggage they needed a wheelbarrow to carry everything. Some inmates approached those leaving on transports and volunteered to "inherit" their belongings or their mail authorizations, which entitled them to pick up whatever parcels arrived for the deportees.[32] Inmates considered certain food, including lard, sugar, canned goods, and potatoes, useful to take along, and those destined for transport bartered to get them.[33] Friends and colleagues who came to say goodbye brought farewell presents and helped with the packing. Close friends or family helped the deportees carry their luggage to the collection point.

The deportees had to report to a building, designed as a *Schleuse*, for departure. The self-administration usually emptied one of the barracks (or several of its floors) to serve as a *Schleuse* and had the inhabitants temporarily move elsewhere. At the collection point, deportees, including those on the standby list, were registered and waited for the transport. The SS was present during this process to oversee the transport's departure. In December 1943, after the SS found out that the first Elder, Jakob Edelstein, had falsified population numbers, Anton Burger personally controlled the deportation list. Eva Mändlová remembered the scene in the Jäger barracks: "There sat Burger

206 THE LAST GHETTO

with headlights and two coal ovens at either side of him. He had an entire staff of people waiting for a cue from the lord and master."[34] At the collection point, people had one last chance to apply to be removed from the transport, report as too sick to leave, or save themselves in some other way. As soon as the deportees were entered on the transport list, their cards were taken out of Central Evidence.

The Transport Management Department, headed by Hanuš Eisler and later Viktor Kende, organized the technical side of the departure. Initially the transportees had to walk to the town of Bohušovice. However, in June 1943 Jewish workers connected the railway line to the ghetto through a spur line so that the deportees, starting with Dl and Dm in September 1943, boarded the train in Terezín. Workers from Transport Management helped people board the train, stored their luggage, and made sure families stayed together. They also brought in food and medications supplied by the self-administration.[35]

Travel to the final destination usually took several days; Auschwitz was a three-day journey. One or two SS men, Karl Bergel or Rudolf Haindl—sometimes both—and two lower-ranking colleagues from Prague, Walter Aschenbrenner and Johann Fidler, accompanied the transports; once, Otto Kursawe from Agriculture was sent along.[36] Moreover, about sixty members of the German police (*Ordnungspolizei*) from Prague, Außig/Ústí nad Labem, or Teplitz/Teplice accompanied the train.[37] Bergel or Haindl was present in Auschwitz when people debarked; sometimes they also made sure that some of those marked as Weisung, or those whom they wanted to dispose of, were sent to be killed at the selection point.[38]

To the Jewish functionaries, the transports were an arduous, exhausting, and sad chore. However, they believed that in doing their job well—ensuring that everything happened in an orderly fashion, that everyone had their family and luggage with them, that people could say their goodbyes, and that the transport left with supplies—a piece of Terezín was sent out. In their perspective, it was a job that needed to be organized and accomplished.[39]

The prisoners' views were quite different: they believed that the administration could save their friends and relatives. Eva Mändlová described Otto Zucker during the September transports: "Wherever Zucker walked or stood, he had a trail of six or seven people behind him, all of them talking at him simultaneously and shouting over each other. He'd throw them out one door and they'd come back in the other one."[40] The Jewish functionaries' inability to help and their words, "I cannot help you," meant that the prisoners blamed them for the deportation of their friends and families. The ordinary prisoners had little authority in the ghetto; hence they begged for help. But after liberation, the power shifted; most of the Jewish functionaries lost their authority, and many of them faced harsh criticism or even prosecution, accused of "collaboration" with the Germans. Accordingly, the self-perception of the functionaries changed; whereas in the ghetto they pointed out their responsibilities and accomplishments during the organization of the transports, after the war they depicted their task as "purely technical."[41] Responsibility for transports was a very public position, in which it was impossible to win accolades.

Chronology of the Transports

Six weeks after the establishment of the ghetto, transports began leaving Terezín. The destinations of Terezín transports were consistent with the transports from Germany and Austria.[42] The first transports left for the Riga ghetto. In the spring and summer of 1942, the destinations were labor camps and ghettos in the Lublin District. During these transports, the SS ordered the protection of elderly and ill inmates as well as skilled workers. The percentage of younger people in the ghetto quickly sank. Indeed, some of the veteran Zionists were deported with these early transports.[43] The self-administration, at this time consisting solely of the Zionists, was overwhelmed by the arrivals and departures; in spring 1942, the population was much smaller, about ten thousand inhabitants. The deportation of one thousand people had a large impact.

At that time the Jewish functionaries put nearly everyone from the transport that came into Theresienstadt onto the next departing transport.[44] Many of such incoming (and immediately outgoing) deportees were from rural Jewish communities. One such community, Kolín, was well known for its Czecho-Jewish orientation. Many of the Kolín Jews were sent to Terezín and then directly to the East. Out of the three Kolín transports that arrived in Terezín in the second week of June 1942, more than half of the transportees were deported within a month of arrival.[45] Some of the Czecho-Jews understood that shipment further East meant liquidation and accused the Zionists of saving their own kind at the expense of others.[46]

During spring and early summer 1942, while half of the ghetto was still non-Jewish, transports streamed in from the Protectorate, and later Germany and Austria, and the inmate population grew. The SS continued

208   THE LAST GHETTO

the established pattern and directed the incoming transports further East. The June 10, 1942, transport Aah did not even stop in Terezín; it passed by Bohušovice and went directly to the Ujazdów labor camp in the Lublin district.[47] Only six transports left, headed to Riga, Baranovichi in Belarus, and Raasiku in Estonia, in summer 1942, and the ghetto became critically full. By late August the population had reached nearly sixty thousand. The mortality rate rose drastically, peaking in September with 3,976 dead.

The SS solved the overpopulation crisis in its own way: IVB4 ordered the transport of first the German and Austrian and later the Czech seniors, people over sixty-five years of age who previously had been protected.[48] Jakob Edelstein, the first Elder of the Jews, reportedly called the deportation of those sixteen thousand elderly inmates in September and October 1942 "cold pogroms."[49] In August 1942, Eichmann's deputy Rolf Günther arrived in Terezín along with several colleagues and ordered the selection of all German and Austrian elderly inmates; it is not clear whether the seniors filled out a questionnaire or were assessed according to their physical condition. Divided into two groups, O (East) and T (Terezín), the former group was sent on a series of transports to the death camps in Treblinka and Maly Trostinets.[50]

The rule of honoring family units was broken for the first time; members of the older generation were no longer defined as a part of the family and were thus deported on their own. Younger Czech Jews filled several of this series of transports (Bp, Bn, Bt, and Bu). Unlike the transports of the older group, which included two thousand people each (altogether over sixteen thousand), each transport of the younger inmates included only one thousand people. The sight of the weak, old, helpless people being carried to the transport shook the population, even if most viewed the deportees as "only Germans." In her diary, Eva Mändlová wrote: "Now Polish transports of Germans from the Reich, whose deportation has so far been out of the question, are leaving. But because the mortality rate is so high the order came to deport the Germans from 65 to 90 years of age, that is if they are alive by Bohušovice."[51]

None of the elderly inmates who had been sent to Treblinka or Maly Trostinets survived. During the transports that took place between September 8 and October 22, 1942, another five thousand seniors over age sixty-five died. Otto Zucker remarked that after October 1942, the proportion of seniors over age sixty-five remained at 33 percent.[52] Terezín was no longer in fact a ghetto for the elderly.

TRANSPORTS TO THE EAST   209

From the end of October 1942 onward, Auschwitz-Birkenau was the final destination for all Terezín transports. The first transport to Auschwitz, By, left on October 26, 1942, with 1,866 people. About 55 people did not report for the transport. In the chaos of the large transports, those in charge had not noticed that many were missing. When the escapees came forward after the transport's departure, Leo Faltin, head of Central Evidence, and Edelstein decided to conceal the evidence. They had the head of the Dresden barracks, Alfred Goldschmid, falsely report that an additional 55 inhabitants were living in his barracks, and they put their cards back into evidence in exchange for those who had died. These 55 people were to become fateful for Edelstein in November 1943.

Following Himmler's order to boost the labor capacity in the concentration camps, between January 20 and February 1, 1943, the SS ordered another five transports, with a total of 7,000 people under the age of sixty. Himmler had asked for 5,000 people, and IVB4 had sent 2,000 more.[53] For the first time, younger German and Austrian inmates were also included on the transports (886 and 528 people, respectively). At the end of January, incidentally at the same time that Paul Eppstein replaced Jakob Edelstein as the Elder, Terezín experienced a typhoid outbreak.[54] The SS stopped the transports, possibly due to fear of an epidemic. The next eight months marked the longest period in the history of the ghetto in which no transports took place. Inmates began to believe that the deportations had ended.

The year 1943—a long stretch of time without any regular transports— was a period in which the ghetto "normalized": the population was lower, at about forty thousand inhabitants. A more stable everyday life developed, allowing the inmates to build or repair infrastructure. In June, the spur line connecting Bohušovice and Terezín was completed. In September 1943, the SS ordered a new wave of transports. The deportations after winter 1943 differed from the preceding ones: they were now large transports leaving in clusters of several thousand people. In September 1943 (5,007), December 1943 (5,007), and May 1944 (7,503), transports were directed to Auschwitz-Birkenau. There they were sent to the new Family Camp in the BIIb section.

The first two transport groups were made up almost exclusively of Czech Jews (and filled up with about three hundred stateless inmates as well as several of those Viennese deportees who had Czechoslovak citizenship);[55] the May cluster included other national groups, including Jews from the Netherlands. IVB4 wanted to create a Jewish labor camp that could be shown to an international commission, similar to the plans the SS had for

210 THE LAST GHETTO

Terezín.[56] By this time the ghetto population had reached forty-six thousand. Transports out of the ghetto also helped to reduce the population. In order to decrease the possibility of an uprising, the SS included solely Czech and mostly younger prisoners on the transports.[57] Unlike other arrivals in Birkenau, these three transport groups did not undergo selection; they all went to the Family Camp. However, the entire September transport—with the exception of several dozen prisoners—was killed half a year after arrival. The other two transports were sent to a selection in early July 1944. The Dl and Dm transports that left the ghetto on September 6, 1943, differed even more significantly from their predecessors. The preparation for these transports began at least five weeks before their departure, near the beginning of August.

This was the only wave of transports in which the commandant demanded that the Aufbaukommando be systematically called forward for transport registration. Burger selected all those among the Aufbaukommando who did not appear to be actively working, a total of 101 men.[58] Until then, the Aufbaukommando members were largely all protected. Before these transports, altogether 188 members of the Aufbaukommando had been deported in the previous forty transports. Some were included directly by the SS, but most probably volunteered to go with their families.

This change was dramatic for the Aufbaukommando members, who had become the established elite within the ghetto. Although many of them worked in pivotal jobs within the kitchen or Shipping Department, or as physicians or technicians, others had secured positions that required little work but supplied them with sufficient resources. During the transport registration, several dozen Aufbaukommando members appeared elegantly dressed, showing no indication of having performed manual labor; Burger included them on the transport.[59] Burger also restructured the Ghetto Guard. The previous leader, Karl Loewenstein, had been dismissed just days before. Burger ordered that only those over forty-five years of age could remain in their jobs. Those younger than forty-five were to leave with the transports.[60]

In addition to these large transports, there were another half dozen different deportations. On August 24, 1943, the SS had sent twelve hundred Jewish children from the previously liquidated Bialystok ghetto to Terezín.[61] Himmler had hoped to exchange them with Jewish organizations in Switzerland and North America for goods and to send the children to Palestine. However, the exchange negotiations were not successful; the Jewish aid organizations did not pay; and six weeks later the children, together with fifty-three caretakers, were sent to Auschwitz and killed.[62] In March 1944, the SS had a group of mentally ill and three caretakers deported to Auschwitz on the transport Dx, where all of them were killed.[63]

In May and September of the same year, two small transports, Eg and Ej, consisting of inmates with certain foreign citizenship or valid Palestine certificates, left for Bergen-Belsen. Eleven transports left Terezín between September 28 and October 28, 1944. Finally, on February 5, 1945, the last transport, Ew, left Terezín. However, this was a very different transport: twelve hundred people were sent to Switzerland as the result of a transfer of funds from the former Swiss president, Jean-Marie Musy, to Himmler. Altogether, over eighty-seven thousand people were deported from Terezín to the East. About four thousand of them survived.

Transports and Belonging

The transports sparked worry about one's nearest family members. Reactions and feelings toward those on the transports and those saved reflect mental patterns of belonging: To whom did people in the ghetto feel related, and who were the "others"? The comments about who was put on the transports reveal a lot about Terezín categories and merits of belonging. The main factors in these differentiations were ethnicity, seniority, generation, ideology, and social networks.

The perceptions of ethnicity were the strongest until January 1943. When the self-administration prepared the transport list on June 12, 1942, and included German and Austrian Jews, the SS stopped them and pronounced these groups protected.[64] Both the inmates and the functionaries expressed resentment that the Czechs were the targets of the transports while the German Jews were spared.[65] In January 1943, Arnošt Klein, house elder of Q314, expressed these feelings in his diary when the deportation slips were distributed for the first transport, Cq, which unlike the following four consisted solely of Czech Jews:

Tomorrow they will carry out the transport orders for 2,000 men, for people from the Protectorate under 65 years of age. The inhabitants of the Protectorate are very stricken while the Jews from the Reich gloat a bit and carry their heads high. There is a certain animosity between the Czech Jews and those from Germany; one cannot get along very well with their gnarly,

212 THE LAST GHETTO

always patronizing character. In the house, the women are lazy, demanding and unclean and unhappy because they did not take along their Aryan maids. The men, with few exceptions, are unintelligent, nonchalant, uppity, and quarrelsome. They were not pleasant before the ghetto, but here they turn nauseating. At the same time, they are orthodox and bigoted and they get offended when we smile over it.[66]

Klein's portrayal of the Reich German Jews was a veritable diatribe. His attack was inspired by the perceived injustice of Czech Jews leaving on the transport while the German Jews were spared. In the next transports, German and Austrian Jews were also included, but Klein did not comment on this. Two days later, he mentioned that only younger Czech Jews were leaving.[67]

During the large transports of elderly inmates in September and October 1942, many Czech Jews remarked upon the fact that now the German Jews or "foreigners" were leaving. Significantly, hardly anyone mentioned that many Czech seniors were among the elderly transportees. By September 1943, the nationally coded criticism "why us and not them?" decreased. Although Eva Mändlová complained that it was only Czech Jews who were included in these transports, she did not blame the German Jews. She still depicted them as more appropriate to go, though: "How come it is only people from the Protectorate who always keep going? The Germans are desperately unhappy here, the old people are here completely alone, they are frightfully hungry, and yet we, who have grown somewhat used to things here, are being forced to leave."[68]

People's seniority at Theresienstadt was the second most important aspect in thinking about transport. Inmates stressed the length of their imprisonment or, even more often, cited the code of their transport to Terezín, which indicated the date of arrival. In the middle of the transports of October 1942, Bedřich Kohn complained that his transport, W (which arrived on February 8, 1942), had no protection and that all safeguarding went to the early "single letter transports."[69] Six weeks later, Kohn's attitude changed, and he began to identify with all of the "single letter transports."[70] These transports—H to Z, from Prague, Brno, Pilsen, and Kladno—were the first sixteen transports to arrive in the ghetto, between early December 1941 and late February 1942. Mändlová, a veteran of the ghetto, remarked at the same time, "They still take people from the old transports and the protégé children from the new ones stay here. That's an injustice."[71] In their petitions for exemption from transport, inmates often pointed out their seniority status as a reason they should be removed from the list. In August 1943, Eugen Jellinek, a forty-nine-year-old World War I veteran from Moravian Ivanovice, complained about being harassed early in the morning for an erroneous second registration: "I am a severe war invalid with a gold medal for bravery and I am also an old Ah transport, not a young D-transport."[72] Jellinek's transport had arrived in Terezín in April 1942; transports starting with the letter D began arriving in May 1943.

Ideological ties became a less important component in the transports, perhaps because of the charged struggles between the factions. The accusation that in spring 1942 the Zionists sacrificed the Czecho-Jews to save their own, as voiced by Jiří Borský, resonated for a long time. Zeev Shek, a prominent Zionist and youth care worker, remarked in internal correspondence that people in the Youth Care Department must watch out that non-Zionist children were not disproportionately put on transports.[73]

Finally, age was an important category that differentiated two main groups: the children and the elderly inmates. Most inmates perceived the deportation of elderly inhabitants as tragic but somehow destined; younger and older inmates often described them as nearly dead at the time of their deportation. Even Hermann Strauss, a seventy-six-year old physician and member of the Council of Elders, subscribed to this notion.[74] Departing children were, however, described as lively and looking forward to the trip.[75]

The idea that children were excited about the travel underlined the catastrophe of the deportations. Travel had been the essence of middle-class leisure time, a ritual of childhood and family time.[76] Benjamin Murmelstein disregarded the established rules of protection of children, or rather, certain kinds of children, during the May transports of 1944.[77] The SS ordered the removal of all orphans between ages three and sixteen; however, *Geltungsjuden* children (in Theresienstadt often called *Mischlinge*) were still protected at this point.[78] Murmelstein attempted to keep some of the orphans in the ghetto by adjusting their status. In response to the protest of Youth Care worker Tekla Placzek, Murmelstein proclaimed: "I decide who is a Mischling!"[79] He violated the custom concerning how children's deportations were handled. It may appear that Murmelstein did nothing wrong; he simply tried to save the orphans, the least protected among children. Yet because the deportation of the children was so traumatic for everyone concerned, the functionaries established certain practices concerning which children were sent. Anyone who questioned this routine was perceived as actively deporting children.

214 THE LAST GHETTO

Petitions

To be removed from a transport, inmates often submitted petitions to the Jewish self-administration. These petitions are a unique source that has never previously been analyzed. Indeed, they have never been mentioned in literature about the ghetto. But they offer valuable quantitative data on the prisoner conduct and coping mechanisms, which are otherwise not available. They present a precious window for observing the mentality and values of the people in the ghetto, as recorded in the moment.

About 3,500 pages of petitions have survived, all of which are related to the transports to Family Camp BIIb.[80] Most of these petitions (3,205) are related to the September 1943 transports; 287 are related to the December 1943 transports and 502 to the May 1944 transports.[81] We do not know if they survived in their totality—though it is unlikely—or what part of the entire petition remains. They are not sorted according to date—the petitions start four to two weeks before transports and are chronologically mixed—or according to success. It does not appear that the formality of a petition affected its success.[82] The correspondence of Otto Zucker is mixed in with the petitions, which suggests that the collection came from his files.

Most of the petitions came from individuals, but an inmate's department or subdepartment also filed a number of them—the so-called reclamations (*Reklamationen*).[83] A few people also applied to join a transport to join their families or loved ones. Some inmates filed more than one petition; for others, more than one department applied. The majority of applicants requested exception after they were registered for a transport, although a significant number of people who had not been registered applied preventively. Some of these lists were qualification lists, indicating the order of indispensability for the department; these lists were often kept separately according to nationality.[84]

There are almost no petitions from non-Czech prisoners. Such a bias is self-evident because the September and December 1943 transports were made up almost exclusively of Czech Jews. This fact, however, is striking with regard to the May 1944 transports, especially since other ethnic groups did use the petitions. Ada Levy, a Bonn nurse, saved her parents through these petitions. Her father died of malnutrition in Terezín in February 1944, but her mother survived in the ghetto.[85] With the exception of the smallest group, the Dutch, all non-Czech groups had a somewhat lower rate of success than the Czech Jews.

My analysis includes 1,317 names.[86] Proceeding in the order of the files, I analyzed the first 1,198 and then took a sample (every tenth application) for the next 120 names. Comparing the petitions with the prisoner database of the Terezín Initiative Institute, I listed the names, birth dates, gender, nationality (in this context defined by their transport code), arrival transport, language of the petition, and success of the petition. I also listed when they were submitted, the applicant's address, job in Terezín, the reason(s) the inmate listed for removal from the transport, the date, and other people's—usually Otto Zucker, Paul Eppstein, or individuals from the Transport Registry— handwritten evaluations. The petitions were addressed to the transport commission, the Elder of the Jews, or the more oblique "leadership," and inmates listed why they felt they should be taken off the list.

I also coded who applied on behalf of whom. Finally, I clustered the reasons and the seniority of the arrival transports.[87] There were more than twenty reasons people gave for requesting removal from a transport (they often listed two or more). The most important were one's job in Terezín, family unit, experience on the front or other merits gained during the First World War, illness, protection by a functionary, old or young age, mixed background or mixed marriage, seniority in Terezín, and important status in civil life or in the Jewish Community.

I characterize "seniority" by the transport on which an individual arrived (rather than subjective seniority given in any statement). Following the logic of the ghetto's chronology, I have categorized the arrival transports into eight main groups:

1) the first veteran transports (Ak [Aufbaukommando], Stab [transport of the first Jewish functionaries], J [Aufbaukommando 2])
2) the "single letter transports," until February 26, 1942 (H–Z)
3) late winter and spring 1942 until the arrival of the first non-Czech transports, June 1, 1942 (Ac–AAa)
4) arrival of the first Berlin transport on September 21, 1942 (I/1–I/66)
5) fall 1942, September–December 21, 1942 (Bi–Ci)
6) winter 1942–1943 (Ck–I/90)
7) spring 1943 (Cx–V/9)
8) summer 1943 (II/29–Ez-St_64, *Einzeltransport*, very small transport).

Altogether, a clear majority (75 percent) of those who filed a petition were successful. It is not clear whether the petitions that have survived were

216 THE LAST GHETTO

somehow considered more important, hence explaining the large ratio of success. Since we cannot answer any of these questions, we should conclude that petitions were a successful strategy to avoid deportation.

More women than men (700 to 616) applied to be removed from a transport, or rather, someone included them on their application; the applications were often written for entire families, and Terezín had a surplus of women. (I did not analyze the gender of the chief applicant.) There is no difference in success according to gender.

There are some smaller differences in success according to age (see table 6.1). Among the petitioners, the age distribution was quite a bit younger than that of the overall Terezín population. Also, disproportionately few elderly, and disproportionately many young people between ages thirteen and twenty three, applied. The oldest inmates—those older than sixty-four—were the least likely to succeed (70 percent) with their applications; those between twenty-four and thirty-four years of age were 10 percent more likely to succeed (80 percent). Those younger than twenty-four were probably still successful, but less so.

The distribution of the petitions according to the applicant's seniority was not consistent with the demographics of the ghetto population at the time of the petition. There were relatively few applicants from the "single letter transports" and quite a number from winter 1942/1943, and in particular, from summer 1943. Either the veterans of winter 1941/1942 were protected in a different way and hence did not apply, or they were significantly underrepresented because most of them had already been deported, as Arnošt Klein and Eva Mändlová had complained. The recent arrivals from summer

Table 6.1 Success of Petitions to Be Removed from Transport (Based on Age Group)

Age group (range of birth years)	Total number	Average success rate (%)
1850–1879	67	70
1880–1889	207	71
1890–1899	276	72
1900–1909	260	75
1909–1919	187	80
1920–1929	251	78
1930–1943	64	77

1943 expressed fear that they would be included on a transport (and indeed they were), confirming that those arriving on the last transports were often included on the departing ones. Another possibility is that the new arrivals had not had time to secure jobs that might have protected them from deportation.

Seniority had a surprisingly small impact on a petition's success (see table 6.2). Most of the groups had a 78 percent probability of succeeding. Only those who applied for removal from the winter and summer transports in 1943 had a lower success rate, 68 percent. Thus, those who arrived in summer 1943 were not only deported disproportionately but were also somewhat less successful in their applications. The only pronounced difference was 23 percent, between the least successful group (the Aufbaukommando, with 61 percent) and the most successful one, in spring 1943 (84 percent). The most and the least successful groups in the sample were also the smallest ones.

Burger followed a hard-line approach in his selection of the workers among the Aufbaukommando, which explains why their applications had a relatively low success rate. The petitioners needed to overturn a direction from SS headquarters. The high petition success rate from those who arrived in spring 1943, however, is difficult to explain. One possible explanation is that when the Prague Jewish Community was being closed down, it happened in two phases: one large transport in March, and then three in July 1943. Those who arrived with these late transports strove to get good positions in the ghetto comparable to those they had had in Prague.[88] The petitions suggest that those who arrived in March 1943 succeeded in getting

Table 6.2 Success of Petitions to Be Removed from Transport (Based on Seniority)

Seniority	Total number	Average success rate (%)
1 (Aufbaukommandos)	31	61
2	180	78
3	107	76
4	350	78
5	236	78
6	210	68
7	56	84
8	142	68

218 THE LAST GHETTO

jobs that protected them from transports, and those who arrived four months later did not.

Although most who were deported with the September transports were Czech Jews, there were 295 German, Austrian, and Dutch individuals among the deportees. The fact that these people had been deported although the transport specified Czech Jews has never been explained; indeed, it has been addressed only rarely. Only a few of these non-Czech Jews were sent as Weisungen. Some volunteered to go with their new Czech partners.[89] The petitions, however, reveal that many of these people were stateless or could be marked as such, because the applicants stressed that they had German or other citizenship.[90] By deporting them, the Large Commission could protect 295 Czech Jews and replace them with the stateless.

Among the deported stateless were the Viennese widow Rosa Katz and her twenty-two-year-old daughters Anna and Gusti.[91] In Auschwitz, Josef Mengele selected the girls, who were identical twins, for his experiments, thus shielding them from the gas chamber in March 1944. Anna, who was a nurse, survived the war. This story shows one of the devices the Jewish self-administration used to protect people they considered more valuable, replacing them with a group who did not have a champion. Moreover, it indicates the continued importance of ethnicity expressed as citizenship.

We can draw a related conclusion from the language in which the petitions were written: nearly all (thirteen hundred) were submitted in German, but those nineteen that were submitted in Czech had a slightly higher success rate, 79 percent. Those who felt comfortable enough to submit their applications in Czech were probably familiar with the evaluating functionaries. Or perhaps by writing in Czech they could create an impression of acquaintance. It is also worth noting that nearly

Table 6.3 Success of petitions to be removed from transport (based on ethnicity of the applicant)

Ethnicity	Total number	Average success rate (%)
Austrian	23	70
German	36	69
Dutch	8	75
Czech	1,250	75

all petitions were written in good German, even those from individuals we know did not speak it well. These petitioners probably had help writing their submissions.

Finally, the reasons for requesting a stay of deportation expressed in the petitions had varying rates of success. Indications of family unit as a reason for exemption were successful in 69 percent of the cases (287 mentions), illness in 67 percent (162), Jewish close relatives outside of the ghetto in 69 percent (52 cases), former mixed marriage in 66 percent (105 cases) compared to 94 percent for existing mixed marriages (16 cases), reference to a Mischling offspring in 71 percent (48 cases), own mixed (most often *Geltungsjude*) background in 88 percent (69 cases), protection of an important Jewish functionary in 90 percent (89 cases), age in 56 percent (55 cases), First World War experience in 52 percent (50 cases), and finally, recent family tragedy in 67 percent (42 cases).

What conclusions can we draw from this analysis? First, it shows us the categories in which the ghetto population thought and how valuable these were in negotiating a stay of deportation. The most successful factor in avoiding deportation was a functionary's protection; nearly all who mentioned someone's patronage were exempted from transport. However, petitions that mentioned both the former and current Elder of the Jews, Eppstein and Edelstein, had the lowest success rate, 67 percent. Mixed background and existing mixed marriage (although quite rare) offered an effective protection from transports, as opposed to former mixed marriages, and this trend was only slightly improved if the applicant mentioned Mischling offspring back home. The latter is a surprising result, as scholars have argued that most people with gentile relatives were protected until fall 1944.[92]

One's job was also not particularly effective as a reason, although success depended on the kind of work. Citing the family unit was not a very powerful way of securing exemption, probably because the remaining core family often volunteered to join the person in question. Such questions illustrate that the petitions can tell us only a fragment of the history of the transports; they captured the events at one particular point, and it is impossible to track what followed.[93] With regard to the less frequent reasons mentioned in petitions submitted very close to the time of transport, it is also not certain whether they were pivotal to the decision-making process; it could be that the petitions were not successful and the applicants were exempted only at the last minute for a different, unrelated reason.

220 THE LAST GHETTO

Institutional Protection

There were several ways inmates could receive institutional protection from the transports. One possibility stemmed from the SS and the other from the Jewish self-administration; the former applied to few inmates but was very reliable, and the latter applied to many more but was less effective. For instance, Otto Kursawe, the Sudeten German civilian who headed Agriculture, protected his core workers throughout the duration of the ghetto, including through the fall transports—more so than his colleague Josef Bobek.[94] One such case involved the workers at a small labor detail that farmed silkworms. The inmate who headed the silkworm production, František Pick from Prague, was the only known prisoner who knew how to deal with silk production. He was liberated in Terezín.[95] Similarly, professional craftsmen, repairmen, and electricians were protected because they ensured that the infrastructure continued to function, not only for the ghetto but also for SS headquarters.[96] This reliable protection provided by the SS only applied to approximately one hundred inmates.

A far more frequent, albeit less reliable, form of protection was provided by the self-administration, through either the qualification, objective, or protection lists. The most controversial among these lists were the protection lists, which in May 1944 included one thousand individuals.[97] The only surviving lists belonged to Czech Jewish functionaries, and they included exclusively Czech Jews. None of the protection lists of non-Czech Jewish functionaries have survived. The Berlin gastroenterologist Hermann Strauss, a member of the Council of Elders, put Viktor Hahn and his family on his protection list.[98] Hahn nursed Strauss back to health when he became seriously ill shortly after Strauss's arrival in summer 1942. Strauss was not the only German functionary to include Czechs, and the Czech functionaries also included "foreign" Jews on their protection list.[99]

Several of the survivors remembered that they were able to remain in Terezín because they were put on a protection list. These claims are most often impossible to verify. For instance, some people may have interpreted the promise of protection as the actual placement of their names on the protection list. Františka Solarová remembered that her friend and the cousin of her husband, the actress Vlasta Schönová, made her lover, Murmelstein, protect Solarová during the transports in May 1944. In this account, Murmelstein's protection did not work out, and Solarová was deported in May 1944.[100] However, Schönová's parents and younger sister were deported in September 1943 (when she and Murmelstein were already seeing each other; Schönová was protected because of her position in Recreation).[101] Why would Schönová protect her more distant relative when she did not ask for this protection for her own parents and sister? Although we cannot get to the root of Solarová's deportation, it is unlikely that she, or Schönová's parents, had been on someone's protection list. These lists became legendary because they were a fairly reliable source of protection and moreover a form of protection that was achievable for some ghetto inmates. They also inspired stories because they were intrinsically linked to the thorny issue of Jewish functionaries and their control over deportations.

Several groups were fairly consistently protected until fall 1944: the majority of the members of the Aufbaukommando; nearly all of those working in the Shipping detail; and many of the medical workers in Health Services and caretakers in Youth Care.[102] It is not clear how these groups were protected. For example, a group of workers mostly associated with Youth Care were protected through the objective lists until August 7, 1943, when Otto Zucker canceled their protection in preparation for the large transports in September 1943.[103] Nearly everyone on this list, however, stayed in Terezín not only through September but indeed until fall 1944, indicating that Zucker's cancellation was made because of an alternative source of protection. Were these people placed on qualification lists from their departments? Or were they protected in yet another way? We cannot know for certain. Yet these layers of protection, surviving in fragments of lists and contradictory memories of how protection worked, suggest that the boundaries between the objective and qualitative lists, as well as other sources of protection, were fluid. In their quest to save their people, the departmental heads and representatives of the national and ideological groups tried to save their own and, up to a point, bent the self-created lists in ways that suited this purpose.

None of the objective lists of non-Czech groups have survived, and they are never mentioned in the testimonies of the German or Austrian functionaries, indicating that there were likely no objective lists for non-Czech Jews. Their absence would offer an additional explanation for the prominents, often given to German and Austrian Jews. But whereas there were nearly eight hundred Czech inmates on the objective lists, there were fewer than three hundred prominents, many of whom were Czech Jews. This asymmetry further illustrates the elite position of the Czech Jews within the administration.

Individual Protection

Once they were put on a transport list, the inmates developed several ways to get themselves removed. One was petitions. Yet another method was a medical exemption: until fall 1944, those who were considered too sick to survive the transport were released (and not counted automatically for the next transport). The decision about who was too ill to travel was in the hands of the transport physicians. Some inmates induced temporary illness in order to get a physician's agreement to have their names stricken from the list. A frequent method, also used elsewhere in occupied Europe, was to inject milk into the muscle tissue, after which the patient got an extremely high fever.[104] It was a gamble; if the physician did not exempt the sick person, he or she was deported with a high fever, making the chances of surviving the selection—and surviving to tell the story—much smaller.[105]

The foremost of the transport physicians, Otto Reinisch, was one of the most despised prisoners. He was a Jewish doctor who had not completed his medical degree.[106] He arrived in Terezín on an early transport and worked as one of the first, most trusted physicians.[107] Later, Reinisch became the transport physician. He had the confidence of the SS, who not only trusted his call during the transports but also let him take care of the prisoners they mistreated during the interrogations and to whom no one else had access.[108] One of the torture victims, the smuggler Julius Taussig, who had been bringing Reinisch medical supplies, remembered that Reinisch nursed him after the mistreatment. A young Czech nurse expressed a typical sentiment: "that asshole Reinisch."[109] She was influenced by the fact that her parents were deported in May 1944, when her status as medical worker no longer protected people's families.

During the same transports, Reinisch confirmed several people as sick. He accepted bribes for the confirmation of sick status.[110] In June 1944, he was charged with fraud by the control judge, Rolf Grabower, the former secretary in the German Ministry of Finance who tried, and failed, to reorganize the ghetto according to his idea of Prussian administration.[111] Nevertheless, Reinisch was in a nearly unassailable position: he was in good standing with the head of Health Services, Erich Munk. Munk mentioned him and his partner in his correspondence with Zionist friends in Palestine and fought over him with Grabower.[112] Reinisch even spent time as a guest of the Council of Elders. On October 28, 1944, the SS placed Reinisch and his partner, Marta, on the last transport as a Weisung; neither of them survived.

Reinisch was not the only person who took bribes to exempt people from transports. Adolph Metz, the German deputy head of Health Services, stated that the Transport Registry practiced human trafficking. People would buy themselves out for a bribe of twenty to fifty cigarettes.[113] Such an amount was a fortune that only a few could afford.

The last resort to escape a transport was to hide. People usually hid in the building of the *Schleuse*. In December 1943, Eva Mändlová's fiancé's mother, to whom she was very close, was on the standby list. Eva accompanied her to the *Schleuse*: "Poor Mama! It was dark farther back. The bushes were crawling with people hiding to escape their fate. People in the Jäger barracks hid under beds, behind beds, under planks, on the toilet. There were entire families hiding, and if they were called, they simply didn't come. Mama didn't hide for sure. Mama would go immediately if they called her just once."[114] One of those people who escaped the December transports was the cook František Kollman; his girlfriend, Ema Friedmannová, hid him under a large kettle in the basement.[115] For every person missing, someone from the standby list was placed on the transport. Marie Roubíčková, Mändlová's mother in law, was deported a week before her seventy-third birthday.

Hiding during the transports brought challenges beyond the technicalities of concealment; the records of people on the transport were taken out of Central Evidence, so they had neither IDs nor food cards. Thus, those who managed to hide had to then legalize their presence in the ghetto after the departure of the transport and be put back into the population registry, a tricky enterprise, especially after fall 1943.[116] The administration had no incentive to be lenient toward those who avoided the transport by hiding. It was rumored that those people who came out of hiding after a transport departed were sent to the Small Fortress.[117] Kollman was placed on the next transport in May 1944; Ema, who had married him in the meantime, went along. Those who hid in fall 1944 had a better chance: if they remained concealed until the end of the transports, they could survive in the ghetto.[118] Eva and Kurt Vyth, a couple who had been German refugees in the Netherlands, arrived three weeks before the fall transports and hid in one of the attics.[119]

Transport Psychology

The transports generated various forms of behavior, including conduct that people had hardly ever experienced. Men cried and fainted as they watched

224   THE LAST GHETTO

their families being deported.[120] Panic took hold of people who experienced emotions in quick sequence; they ceased to pay attention to the good opinion of others and focused solely on themselves. The people who hid in December 1943 often did not do so according to premeditated plans; they were simply looking for any way out. Some were passive and unresponsive, not realizing what was happening to them. Others did not fall prey to panic, kept a clear mind, said their farewells, and observed people around them.

Benjamin Murmelstein recalled the story of a young Czech man with whom he was friendly.[121] This man was put on one of the transports in fall 1944 and asked Murmelstein for help; Murmelstein had already saved him once, in December 1943.[122] Later the man appeared, radiant with joy, and proclaimed: 'Doctor Murmelstein, it is not me, it's my dad!' The young man was the novelist Mirko Tůma, whose certificate of bad conduct was printed in *Šalom na pátek*. His father Rudolf was deported with the Er transport. Tůma had no control over whether his father would be deported; his choice consisted of volunteering to join him or not. Murmelstein's witnessing of Tůma's panicked reaction left an impression on Tůma. After the war, Tůma treated Murmelstein in a markedly ambivalent way. In his eminent early account, Tůma depicted Murmelstein as a corrupt, Macbethian character. At the same time, he spoke in his favor at the postwar investigations of Murmelstein's actions.[123]

The transports defined kinship by presenting the choice: Whom would people follow on a transport? Whom were they expected to follow, and whom did they want to follow? This decision-making revealed a new sense of kinship, similar to the food-sharing networks, yet even more pronounced. There was a general anticipation that unmarried offspring would join parents if they were called for transport.[124] But children over the age of eighteen were increasingly counted outside of a family unit, so they were not called to go along. Marriages (for members of the Jewish community), spousal unions (for those outside, especially Christians), and divorces in the ghetto were introduced, most importantly, to define the familial unit: people married to define the person with whom they would go on a transport, rather than their parents. Divorces were introduced to the same end.[125]

Some of the issues of kinship and connectedness with "one's group of belonging" can be illustrated by two examples of young men deciding between their families, lovers, and ideological group. All of these represented a kinship group with its own codes of conduct.

Miloš Pick was a teenage member of the Communist Party in the ghetto. The party decided that the members should do all they could to stay in the ghetto "because their lives belonged to the resistance." At one point, Pick's mother asked him whether he would join should she and his father be put on a transport. Pick answered that he would not:

> Until today I see how shocked my Mom was. I see her sad eyes. I was actually quite afraid that this was something that could happen, that my parents would fall into a transport and I would follow the order of the organization and wouldn't volunteer. In the end, it came up just the other way around, I fell into a transport and they did not. I cannot say that I was enthusiastic to go to Auschwitz but I was greatly relieved that it took this end and I did not have to solve a conflict of my conscience.[126]

In May 1944, Luděk Eckstein, a young actor and a fellow Communist, was in a similar dilemma. His Communist girlfriend was placed on the transport list, while his family remained in the ghetto. He wanted to volunteer for the transport, to the disappointment of his parents. But when his brother was selected later, his parents told Eckstein he should not let his brother go on his own. Eckstein volunteered. In the meantime, the Communist faction was able to pull the girlfriend out. Now what should he do? Eckstein asked his mentor, Gustav Schorch, for advice. "He looked into the distance, just like he always did. He told me a sentence which I shall not forget to my death: 'You know, once in one's life you get into a situation in which you yourself have to find a solution, and this situation will show who you actually are.' He gave me his hand and left. And I went voluntarily to Auschwitz."[127]

In addition to stressing their responsibility and choice, Pick and Eckstein also demonstrated the idea that the transports could be a moral test. Both told the story as having chosen in favor of the core family rather than the party friends; this may be because both told the story sixty years later, after they had raised families, and moreover, at that point, after 1989, communist narratives were no longer valid, indeed not even acceptable.

To return to Schorsch's advice: Is it truly human behavior in the moment of judgment that defines who we are?[128] Was the panicked Mirko Tůma, whose first reaction to his father's deportation was relief, the real Tůma? Schorsch's answer was an invitation to keep a clear mind, try to remain free of panic, and find solace in the ability to act morally. However, the incident with Mirko Tůma demonstrates that extreme stress does not reveal someone's

226 THE LAST GHETTO

"true nature." Rather, it shows how transports broke people, who then often struggled their entire lives to come to terms with what they perceived as their moral lapses. The reactions encompassed blaming the Jewish functionaries, never telling the story, telling it differently, or telling it with gaps. What the inmates had experienced was radical powerlessness.[129] As long as the inmates lived in a society they themselves defined, they could exercise an influence over their fate. Transports represented a severe limitation of their ability to exercise agency. This powerlessness is one of the key moments of the experience as a victim of the Holocaust.[130]

Miroslav Kárný and Berl Herškovič offer a contrasting decision regarding kinship. They were leading personalities in the Communist and Hechalutz movements, respectively, and both were deported with the first two transports in fall 1944. In their testimonies from the 1990s, when speaking about their deportation they expressed a primary identification with the political community.[131] Kárný stated that even though there was some leeway to save some of their members, he did not consider staying: "With the first two transports practically half of the organization went and so it was a question of honor to go along."[132] Thus, even though their decision concerning which of their networks was their defining kinship unit differed from the earlier example of Miloš Pick, Kárný and Herškovič also viewed the transports as a moral choice: to join fellow members of the political organization. This moralizing about voluntarily joining one's kinship group on a transport demonstrates how the groups kept their boundaries and membership: going along was good; not joining was bad.

How does this notion of morality fit in with the experience of powerlessness? This question brings to mind Lawrence Langer's concept of "choiceless choice." Langer argued that the Holocaust victims could not make true morally informed choices "because whatever you choose—somebody loses, shorn of dignity and any of the spiritual renown we normally associate with moral effort."[133] As influential as Langer's notion has become, it is inherently problematic. The present analysis of mentality during the Terezín transports is a suitable opportunity to re-evaluate Langer's concept. Although during transports many of the inmates experienced powerlessness, that did not mean they had no agency or choice.[134] They had a very limited choice, and they loathed being in such a position, as all people do. The experience of limited agency sometimes boosted the later focus in narratives on decision-making and choice.[135] The decision-making particularly addressed the choice of one's kinship group: the biological family—and in that case, parents or spouse; friends; or the political organization. The decision with whom to go on a transport, alongside sharing food and accommodation, very much represents choice.

In this situation and many others, moreover, we should recognize this choice as genuine agency rather than *Eigensinn* (literally, self-will). Fearing a sentimentalized overuse of the category of agency, Alf Lüdtke proposed the *Eigensinn* concept.[136] *Eigensinn* denotes maintaining the self vis-à-vis greater power while allowing for participation: workers grumbling or making jokes. Yet there are crucial moments when we need to recognize that the motivation driving the protagonist is genuine agency: when the protagonists recognize the weight of their decision, the choice is larger, there is more at stake, and it is more deliberate. Deciding with whom to go on a transport is decisively a moment of agency.

Morality came into the picture as a part of the interpretative framework. Enforced situations are artificial and hence by definition confusing. Moreover, it was only at a later point, in 1945, that the inmates realized that the deportees were sent to a site of mass murder. Both aspects characterized the situation as a catastrophe. An unknown, exceptional, or confusing situation is interpreted within a familiar, applicable framework or a framework that has already been established as the interpretative one. It is customary to describe catastrophes as tragedies.[137] Tragedy has become the trope in which the Holocaust and Second World War have been told and interpreted—a framework that is also often integrated in survivor testimonies. In this particular setup, morality serves as the catharsis in the story; it offers a sense of solace, endows the experience—limited choice, powerlessness, the eventual realization that everyone was sent to their death—with a redemptive meaning.

Holocaust as a morality tale offers an emotional and meaningful climax. Therefore, Luděk Eckstein, an actor whose job was to involve the audience in meaningful, dramatic stories, placed the story in the context of Gustav Schorsch—the moral role model who did not survive—engendering a redemptive framework: in this way, the transport did not lead to meaningless slaughter but was a cleansing way to a better, moral self.

The people in Terezín facing transports had limited choices, but these were still choices. We should not deny them the responsibility for these choices; rather, we should analyze the notions of morality they used. These constructions of morality, for what end, and how they fit into the perception of self represent a key part of inmates' mentality and choices. It is particularly

228 THE LAST GHETTO

important to grasp because the choices in the ghetto were different, more limited, new, and unknown. In analyzing the choices Theresienstadt prisoners made in their last days, we learn more about the decision-making of ordinary people in extremis.

Transports in Fall 1944

Between September 28 and October 28, 1944, eleven transports involving a total of 18,402 people left Terezín for Auschwitz. They were frequently called "liquidation transports" due to the dramatic change they created within the ghetto; these transports carried away the majority of the ghetto population. Afterward, only 11,068 people remained.[138] Yet Terezín was not liquidated in a literal sense; Himmler was interested in keeping the ghetto for exchange and camouflage purposes.[139] Terezín was the only ghetto to survive until the end of the war. The SS apparently arranged the transports because they were afraid of a Czech insurrection, which could follow from the Slovak uprising. The failing German war industry also needed the additional manpower provided by camp prisoners.[140]

The fall transports were signaled on July 18, 1944, when the SS ordered all former army officers to be registered.[141] These men were to be put on the first two transports, together with four thousand men between the ages of eighteen and fifty, in order to remove the danger of resistance during the subsequent transports. The general population had no idea that the transports were to commence and instead expected the war to end shortly; after learning of the D-Day landings, people chose not to terminate pregnancies but rather to carry them to term, expecting the babies to be born in freedom.[142] However, around September 10, the SS officer Rolf Bartels informed Karel Schliesser, Rudolf Freiberger, Erich Munk, and Paul Eppstein that the SS headquarters was planning large transports from Terezín. Bartels indicated that only a few people would be able to remain in the ghetto; only jobs in the enlarged mica workshop would be safe. Eppstein believed that if he acted prudently, he could maneuver through the situation. He offered some hints of what was to take place during his speech for Rosh Hashana.[143] His hope did not materialize. The SS let Eppstein announce and prepare the first two transports, then had him arrested and killed on September 27, 1944. Benjamin Murmelstein became the next Elder.

As unexpected and massive as they were, the first transports departed quite smoothly. The SS headquarters described them as labor transports for work in factories near Dresden, similar to the auxiliary camp in Wulkow. They also deported Otto Zucker and Karel Schliesser as the designated leaders of the new camp. The following transport, Em, included five hundred women. The wives and partners of the men who had departed a week earlier fought to be included. The trust ended with the next transport, which left three days later, on October 4. The first three of the fall transports were organized by the self-administration.[144] Afterward, the SS took over the compiling of the lists for the next, and last, eight transports.

These transports were the image of utter horror, a Boschian apocalypse. They signified the end of Terezín and its old world. Seventeen-year-old Alisa Ehrmannová wrote in her diary, "Swarms of six- to seven-year-old children alone on the transport. Cretinous children. Professor Lieben with open tuberculosis. Hans Steckelmacher completely lamed with enteritis. There are no uniforms. It is too desolate."[145] Lily Fantlová, the mother of eight-month-old twins, begged Rahm in vain to let her take the baby carriage on the train.[146] The task of the Jewish administration was reduced to ensuring that the Central Registry was working and that people appeared at the collection site. Murmelstein spent days and nights at the departure site, having to indicate to Rahm and Moes who was absolutely indispensable for the further existence of the ghetto. After much begging, he succeeded in keeping one gynecologist and an eye specialist.[147]

The few exceptions spared included all of the Danish Jews, women who worked in the mica workshop, Dutch prisoners from the Barneveld and Protestant groups,[148] many of the prominents, inmates over sixty-five years of age, and those with certain decorations from the First World War.[149] The SS demanded the lists of all workers in a department, and everyone who did not qualify for any of these exceptions was put on the transport. The function of the standby list changed, too: rather than being released after a transport was sent off, these 20 percent were put on the next one. The functionaries were not informed about how many transports were leaving. There were three or four days between the transports, and people hoped that each of the transports that had just left was the last. Categories that had previously been protected were no longer: Rahm, Moes, Bergel, and Haindl subjected *Geltungsjuden*, spouses from former mixed marriages, and decorated First World War veterans to several selections, and those in the first two categories had to prove they were in touch with their Gentile relatives.[150]

230 THE LAST GHETTO

At this stage the SS became directly involved, interviewing and categorizing the inmates. The high-ranking SS men spent entire days setting up transports. The SS inspected everyone in the ghetto, first according to the departments, then alphabetically.[151] The Jewish functionaries—Murmelstein and his team—had to prepare, inform, and implement the SS plans. Moes spent the entire month in Terezín; Hans Günther came from Prague toward the end of the month. The penultimate transport arrived with more cars than announced, and the standby list did not suffice. Haindl simply pulled those standing nearby, who had accompanied the departing inmates to say their farewells, into the train.[152] One of them was the much-loved Communist youth care worker Irena Krausová, whose gentile partner had managed to visit her in the ghetto throughout.[153]

For the last transport (though only the SS knew it would be the last), the Ev, the SS men did not announce the number of deportees. By this point, compiling the list was critical for the ghetto, as nearly everyone who had not been deported yet was protected by one of the "hard" criteria. Murmelstein was fighting to keep the ghetto viable and struggled to keep the last dozens of technicians, craftsmen, and physicians. After a day of negotiations and two phone calls with Berlin, a list was agreed upon, and 2,036 people were sent to Auschwitz. Murmelstein succeeded in negotiating to hold onto some seventy workers and their families, altogether more than four hundred people. Ev left with several empty cars.[154]

Even more than during the previous transports, people increasingly lost their nerve.[155] They begged those whom they believed to have influence to help them; hysterical scenes took place at the departing platform and in Murmelstein's office.[156] The old bonds of solidarity often fell apart; by the second to last transport, Es, nearly all of the indispensable workers had been deported. Egon Redlich, the head of the Youth Care department, had to rank his few last workers in order of indispensability, including two youth home leaders, Siggi Kwasniewski and Willy Groag. Kwasniewski, who had been in the ghetto eight months longer, pressed Redlich to rank him higher on account of his seniority.[157] Redlich kept Groag because Kursawe protected Groag's pregnant wife. In the next transport, Redlich, along with his family, was deported as a Weisung.[158]

The SS used the last two transports, Et and Ev, to dispose of all inmates whom they wanted to get rid of. After October 20, 1944, Moes handed Murmelstein long lists of Weisungen, consisting of nearly all Jewish functionaries still present (who were so important that they had not been deported), their closest friends, secretaries, lovers, and also informers.[159] Weisungen now had a pronounced political character.[160] These lists were probably compiled by informers and someone in the Reich Association who had been asked to compose a directory of Terezín inmates associated with it.[161] This informational background would explain some apparent mistakes: the list included Eppstein's former servant, Bruno Abraham, and a boy who ran Eppstein's errands.[162]

The "simple inmates" hardly ever asked Rahm for mercy; when they pleaded for help, they turned to Jewish functionaries. Murmelstein had a highly public role during the fall transports: his methods of negotiating with the SS and to let off tension were dramatic, loud scenes, grimaces, and shouting.[163] Unlike during earlier transports, Murmelstein had hardly any room to maneuver at this stage. He was narrowly able to keep three specialist physicians, whereas Kursawe, a low-ranking German overseer, was able to keep two dozen of his workers.[164] The inmates, however, rarely realized this difference, and blamed the Jewish officials for lack of support.[165]

Knowledge of Mass Murder

The large majority of people in Terezín did not know what would happen to the outgoing transports, but they suspected that the destination would be much worse than Terezín. People thought the seniors and sick would probably die or would die even more quickly, that food was very scarce, that people had to work very hard, and that the mortality was high even among the younger people. But these were only guesses and rumors.[166] Many people had no idea whatsoever; one girl, leaving on transport, put her hair into curlers, expecting to meet her boyfriend, who had been deported earlier.[167] Finally, people knew Auschwitz was a deadly concentration camp but did not know that Birkenau was identical. They assumed the latter was a labor camp.[168]

Although there were several instances when the inmates could have found out what was happening, or at least establish some facts, the people in Terezín developed an elaborate psychological means to alternatively explain away these implications. This practice was not particular to Terezín; we can find its variations among nearly all Holocaust victims.[169] The Terezín inmates, however, were unusual because theirs was the only ghetto that survived until liberation. The relatively large distance from the ghetto to the

232   THE LAST GHETTO

annihilation camps allowed for few messengers bearing news. In this respect, Theresienstadt was different from other ghettos such as Lodz, Warsaw, and Vilna, which were closer to the killing sites, so that news or even eyewitnesses trickled in on a regular basis.[170] In Terezín, the SS took precautions to prevent the inmates from figuring out the truth; one of the few measures they exercised was to keep up the image of the preferential ghetto.[171] Yet there were envoys, and Terezín's long existence offered a stretch of time in which the news about slaughter could have sunk in. This slow realization, in combination with the large majority of the people who had been deported, generated telling psychological coping methods.

Those who were deported wrote to their families. Keeping in touch was one of the central concerns of the deported. Much of the mail consisted chiefly of greetings to various relatives and the assurance that one was well, that is, alive. However, some concealed warnings in their letters; they mentioned long dead relatives or a person named "death" in Czech or Hebrew (*smrt* or *mavet*), or marked letters in the text resulting in "gas tod" or "Giftgas" (gas death and poisonous gas, respectively).[172]

Independently from what was in the letters, inmates perceived the mail as reassurance. Letters arriving was a good sign. If no letters arrived, that was a bad sign. When the letters included allusions to something threatening, such as "gas," recipients came up with explanations for such references, including the belief that the deportees had to work in mines with poisonous gas. If a card mentioned meeting an uncle who had been deported in 1940 and subsequently murdered, readers concluded that the uncle was apparently not dead after all. The inmates compartmentalized the bad news so that it fit with the notion of the departed still being alive.

A relatively late episode from fall 1944 demonstrates the ambivalence with which inmates received bad news. In October 1944 the inmates noticed that the train of wagons during the transports was always the same. The transport Es from October 19, 1944, brought in a secret letter, addressed to Rudolf Bergmann, hidden in one of the wagons by a transport participant, describing the killings at the destination and noting that Otto Zucker and Karel Schliesser were dead. Bergmann, a leading figure of the Czecho-Jewish movement in the ghetto, shared the news with some of his nearest friends, among others Herbert Langer, a fellow representative, and Bedřich Berl, a dentist. They talked about gas chambers, still not aware that Birkenau and Auschwitz were identical; Berl did not believe the news. Bergmann had a gentile wife living in Prague, whom he was able to meet during his shopping trips to Roudnice.[173] Bergmann and other people from the Czecho-Jewish organization had prepared a way to escape. Yet Bergmann, when called as a Weisung on the last transport, went, saying that he did not want to endanger his friends and that he would manage to survive the last few months.[174] Willy Groag claimed that Bergmann left without any luggage, knowing that he would not survive.[175] Indeed, Bergmann did not return. Two years later, Marie Bergmannová applied to have her husband recognized as dead.[176]

Berl also remembered that Langer, one of the believers of what he called the "gas theory," was afraid to be deported as a Weisung. He came to Berl and asked him to fix his teeth before the deportation. "I told him then: listen, if you are so certain that you will no longer be alive by Saturday, why do you bother me?"[177] Langer became overwhelmed by pessimism. After receiving the news that he indeed would be deported as a Weisung in what was the last transport, Langer wrote a letter to his sister Elly: "Tomorrow I leave, separated from my other family. After tomorrow, you shall probably never hear from me again. I shall disappear in the infinity of all those who paid for what they knew and found out, what the entire world spent years observing with arms crossed. We are at war, being enemies, we must be able to fall as soldiers."[178] Before the departure of the transport, Herbert and Greta Langer committed suicide.[179] Bergmann, Langer, and several others in similar situations waivered until their departure, saying conflicting things to people around them. Even in his last letter, Langer used the word "probably." Only upon his arrival in Auschwitz did Berl find out that the "gas theory" was correct. Recalling this story fifteen months later, he declared that the only mercy the Terezín inmates ever experienced was their ignorance.[180]

Even before the fall of 1944, there were several instances when reports about mass killing were brought into the ghetto. The auxiliary mining command of Terezín in Kladno was staffed by several dozen young Czech men who had frequent contact with other, civilian, pitmen. One of the gentile miners listened to the Czech broadcast of the BBC. At one point, in June 1943, he announced that the reporters spoke about Jews being killed by gas in concentration camps in Poland. Ervín Bloch, a young Communist, did not believe him. Three months later the Kladno detail had been closed and he was back in Terezín. Bloch became part of the small Trotzkyist group around Wolfgang Salus, who received a copy of a letter from one of the earlier Terezín deportees via their Prague comrades.[181] This time Bloch and his friends believed the report, probably because the news was addressed to them directly. They kept the news to themselves. When Bloch was deported

234   THE LAST GHETTO

in September 1944, he trusted the announcement of the SS that the destination was Riesa, as opposed to Auschwitz.

There were several other instances of reports, but by far the most important is that of Vítězslav Lederer. Lederer, a former member of the Czech resistance, was deported to Auschwitz in December 1943. On April 6, 1944, he escaped from Family Camp together with an ethnic German SS man, Viktor Pestek. In spring and summer 1944, Lederer sneaked into Terezín four times to warn the inmates. On his first visit, in early or mid-April, he contacted his former boss, Leo Holzer, the head of the Fire Brigade. Holzer brought several other people, mostly young Czech Jews, to meet with Lederer, among them the actress Nita Petschauová and her the soccer-playing husband and brother in law.[182] Lederer's news included the information that the entire transport of September 1943, five thousand people, had been killed on March 8, 1944. Most of the participants in the meetings believed Lederer.[183]

Holzer also brought Lederer to meet Leo Baeck, and some of the participants informed Karel Schliesser.[184] Holzer assumed that Baeck later informed Paul Eppstein. Historians differ about whether Eppstein believed the news, some indicating that he alluded to his knowledge of mass murder in his speeches in July and September 1944.[185] In any case, if Eppstein did allude to anything, other inmates did not understand his message. Those who had met Lederer believed him and when later deported were certain about the fate that was awaiting them.[186] This attitude was a distinct shift from earlier, perhaps because Lederer was a real person and an articulate eyewitness who, moreover, had met with his friends.

In December 1944 and January 1945, Slovak Jews from the Sered' camp arrived in Terezín. These were the very last of the Slovak Jews who had managed to avoid the two large deportation waves in 1942 and 1944. Some of them were connected with the Jewish Council (Jewish Center); others had survived in hiding or in the Tatra mountains, living with the partisans.[187] Many of the Slovaks had met, or heard about the report of, the two Auschwitz escapees, Rudolf Rosenberg (later Vrba) and Alfréd Wetzler.[188] Several Slovak Jews in Terezín passed on the news to the veteran inmates.[189] When several Slovak women told Blanka Haasová, a middle-aged Czech nurse, about Auschwitz, she asked them to be silent.[190] Even though many of the inmates had similar reactions, the Slovaks' report was the first moment when a small part of the ghetto population had begun to realize what was taking place at Auschwitz.[191] At the same time, more postcards arrived that hinted about the gassings.[192]

TRANSPORTS TO THE EAST   235

In winter 1945, the beliefs of the veteran Terezín inmates about their fate changed. People had believed that they would survive, together with many or at least a significant part of their deported friends and families. But as the bad news added up, the inmates started rumors about impending plans to execute all of them. What were the reasons for this shift? The inmates were heartbroken by the earlier fall transports. Winter 1945 also brought, in addition to the Slovak Jews, large deportations of Czech and German Jewish spouses from existing intermarriages. The intermarried Czechs did not integrate well; the old order of things proved difficult to re-establish. For the veteran inmates, the old Terezín was over; nearly all their friends had been deported. Those who remained felt uneasy about not having been deported, too.

This feeling of uneasiness, which could be described as close to remorse, translated into an expectation that everyone in Terezín was going to be killed. In February 1945, the SS ordered the reconstruction of three sites. There were two underground spaces, near ravelin XVIII (a ravelin is an outwork of a fortification) and the Leitmeritz gate, that belonged to a tunnel system under the fortress. Inmates insulated these to make them airtight. These spaces were also provided with ventilation, which some believed could be used for blowing air in (rather than out). Moreover, the basin in ravelin XV (the one between the river Ohře and nearer Bohušovice) was fenced in with barbed wire; the only connection was reduced to a little bridge.[193] Hans and Rolf Günther visited both of the sites. Inmates calculated that the two tunnel spaces could hold five thousand people and the hollow in ravelin XV perhaps fifteen thousand.[194] The technicians and craftsmen at the construction sites concluded that these would be used for killing: the former two as gas chambers and the latter as a space that could be attacked using firearms and flamethrowers. According to some accounts, other people also mentioned gas chambers.[195] For the first time in the history of the ghetto, the inmates doing the construction questioned their task. Erich Kohn, the head of the Construction subdepartment in the Technical Department, and Murmelstein asked Rahm the purpose of the construction; they pointed out that the prisoners were anxious and that there was danger of mass disruptions. Rahm claimed that the sites were meant as a grocery storage (tunnels) and a duck farm (ravelin XV). Soon after the inquiries, Rahm ordered the sites abandoned. Many of the prisoners interpreted the abandonment of the sites as a result of their courageous questions.[196]

It is impossible to find out with certainty the goal of these construction projects. There are indications that in February 1945 the German

236 THE LAST GHETTO

authorities were planning alternative ways to continue the mass annihilation in Mauthausen.[197] Terezín might have been considered as an additional location.[198] Yet it is improbable that it was the ghetto inhabitants who were to be killed. Given Rolf Günther's visits and the fact that two months later many death marches were directed to Terezín, it is plausible that the IVB4 or the Business Administration Main Office wanted to secure a site to conduct mass killing of prisoners from concentration camps. At his trial, Rahm mentioned that prisoners from Bergen-Belsen were supposed to be relocated to the newly constructed Southern barracks.[199] Another possibility is that the SS intended to kill the prisoners in the Small Fortress, at this point about fifteen thousand. Even though several of the inmates, among others Murmelstein, did think that it was the inmates of the Small Fortress and not the ghetto inhabitants that the SS intended to kill, most assumed that it was the ghetto inhabitants who were supposed to be murdered, an assumption that later found its way into the Theresienstadt literature.[200]

The real question of interest here, though, is why the inmates concluded that the construction sites were gas chambers when just a few weeks earlier they had not believed that gas chambers existed.[201] The Terezín inmates came to believe that they were going to be murdered because of their uneasiness about remaining in Terezín. As the bad news trickled in, they had gradually realized that all their friends and family members who had been deported to the East had been killed, while they had struggled to remain in the ghetto. The assumption that one's death was impending was a means to come to terms with this realization, combined with the feeling of uneasiness about remaining in the ghetto. Dramatic descriptions of the duck farm and the plans to kill everyone in the ghetto were nearly omnipresent in the testimonies of those liberated in Terezín. These stories accounted for survival, endowed it with meaning, and made the veterans' story unique and exceptional. For those who remained in Terezín and later described their experiences, the story of the duck farm provided the proof and drama in their own tragedy and helped them avoid a narrative moment in which they remained in "boring" Terezín while most were deported to dramatic and deadly camps.

On April 20, 1945, the last victims of the camps arrived at Terezín. For three weeks, prisoners from death marches streamed into the ghetto.[202] Fourteen thousand arrived by train and on foot, reeking, dirty, and dying; the ghetto inhabitants had never seen people in such conditions. Even the Slovak

Jews who had previous knowledge of the atrocities were upset by what they witnessed.[203] Martha Mosse was shaken: "Completely exhausted, starved, and savage. Men and women who had been on the road for four to six weeks. The corpses travelled along in the trains: Those who had died of exhaustion or who had been killed by their fellow travellers. Another 87 people died here during the day. It is a gruesome misery. The women weep when they see children because theirs have died. Nearly all of the men wear striped pyjama, convicts' clothes."[204]

Among the people on the evacuation transports were not only eyewitnesses—hundreds and thousands of them—but many former Terezín inmates.[205] One of the first evacuation transports included eighty women who had left with the fall deportations, including the actress Nita Petschauová. A large majority of those who arrived living were nursed back to health, and as they got better, they told about their experiences.[206] The diarists, upset and horrified, then recorded what is today the classic account of these marches. Now everyone saw and understood. The transports, the essence of the liquidation of humans, gave the people of Terezín no choice but to realize the enormity of the atrocities.

Conclusion

The transports marked the end of Terezín society. But in many ways the conduct they triggered reflected the values of the ghetto society. Inmates volunteered to be deported with those who had become their kinship unit in the ghetto. Although people were shocked and panicked during the transports, afterward they quickly returned to everyday life. Most of the characteristics of belonging that structured how people thought about the deportees overlapped with the stratification of the ghetto: nationality, seniority, and age. Observed from the ethnic point of view, many Czech Jews, unlike their German, Austrian, or Dutch counterparts, were quick to draw conclusions about injustice. Recent arrivals were the most likely to be placed on an outgoing transport. For the most part the social elite—young Czech Jews—was protected until September 1943. For young, healthy, and childless Theresienstadt prisoners, a realistic, if small, chance to survive came with the transports in December 1943. Many of the young Czech inmates stayed in Theresienstadt until fall 1944, when the SS took over and removed nearly everyone.

238 THE LAST GHETTO

The transports caused unprecedented distress among the prisoners. People experienced panic and powerlessness, but even though their options were severely limited, they still had choices that we need to recognize as moments of agency. Survivors often remembered the extreme emotions they felt during transports as a morality lesson, which turned into a narrative strategy. Until the last weeks of the war, prisoners did not know what had happened to those who were deported and refused to acknowledge messages that informed them of the destruction. Still, a wave of panic, based on scant information, surrounding two eventually abandoned projects of the German authorities morphed into the belief that the SS were going to kill everyone in Terezín. This hysteria was a manifestation of the remaining prisoners' slow recognition of the Holocaust.

Conclusion

Terezín was a place where the last generations of Central and Western European Jewry spent the final weeks, months, or years of their lives—lives cut short and ended by Nazi persecution. It was a society in extremis, a story that sheds light on broader issues of ethnicity, stratification, gender, and the political dimension of the actions of "little people."

In observing the victim society outside the focus of the perpetrators and beyond a total focus on violence, we can discern that as important as violence was, it was not omnipresent, in particular not in its physical form. While conditions—hunger, growing mortality, and fear—were created by Nazi persecution, the prisoner society was decisively not a specific Nazi creation. Rather, the society in Theresienstadt was a very human one, albeit one created and lived in extreme circumstances, with pronounced power asymmetries that had lethal consequences. The prisoner society that emerged was characterized by stark social hierarchies, uneven allocation of resources, injustice, and ethnic and generational stereotypes. At the same time, the prisoner community fashioned a code of conduct and master narrative about Theresienstadt that most prisoners followed.

Prisoners in some measure became accustomed to the ghetto; it became a constant, for some even a home. This does not mean that people were not aware of, or influenced by, their environment, hunger, dirt, transports to the East, homesickness, or being separated from their loved ones. However, as long as they were alive, the inmates explored their surroundings, formed new social relations, and in short, produced a society. The society in Theresienstadt diverged from what we know of our society, but by no means did it mean society ceased to exist, nor did social relations and people become atomized. These findings contribute to our understanding of society in camps and ghettos in particular and to extreme society in general.

Prisoner society as viewed through the prism of everyday life brings victims' mentality and decisions to the forefront. We need to take their agency and experience of powerlessness seriously. Incarceration greatly limited people's possibilities, but there still were options. Perhaps because

The Last Ghetto. Anna Hájková, Oxford University Press (2020). © Oxford University Press.
DOI: 10.1093/oso/9780190051778.001.0001.

240   THE LAST GHETTO

the prisoners' decisions were restricted and enforced, they wielded large power: with whom to share food, whether to live in accommodation with friends or parents, and whom to accompany on transport. Indeed, because Holocaust victims often experienced profound powerlessness, instances of control and decision-making were immensely important to them. Therefore, it is timely to critically reconsider the blanket application of Lawrence Langer's concept of "choiceless choices." Recognizing the choices of the Holocaust victims as valid allows us to recognize them as the acting, thinking people they were until the end. These decisions were often a matter of great deliberation; *Eigensinn*, a concept developed by historians of everyday life, does not capture their essence. Decisions such as volunteering to leave with someone for the East were not about affirmation of self, but rather a deliberate, albeit enforced, choice.

The victim society in Theresienstadt underwent changes. Families and group loyalties shifted: while some inmates chose to share food or volunteered for transport to remain with their families, others found nonbiological kinship with friends (*parta*), political groups, or lovers. But kinship remained a basic feature of society. In Terezín, many of the habits of "normal life"—falling in love, envy, gossiping, competition, and striving for higher status—reflected the world in which they took place and were connected to social, gender, and ethnic asymmetries. The social inequalities in the ghetto contributed to the extreme mortality of the older prisoners. Of course, the fact that people died there was caused by German persecution. But who died, how, and when was determined by the prisoner society.

In Terezín, a forced site with a fluctuating population of different ethnic backgrounds and ages, the nexus of ethnicity, age, and class emerged as particularly important. Being in the ghetto, where everyone was a prisoner and at least nominally Jewish, produced pronounced ethnic and social differences. Class remained a powerful category in the forced community, but the social hierarchies were starkly different from the time before the ghetto; old class structures almost entirely lost validity. The social elite consisted of young Czech Jewish prisoners; the elderly, especially from Germany and Austria but also from the Protectorate, were on the bottom. In addition, ethnicity became the main categorizing marker in Theresienstadt; it was linked to social hierarchies, while class differences were expressed in ethnicized terms. Ethnicity and class are usually conceptually separated; my work suggests we should think about the social construction of both categories in connection. Gender and sexuality offers a sagacious means for discerning the changing habits of prisoner community, to mark both proper and inadmissible conduct. In particular, female behavior was negotiated far more conservatively, and space for leading female roles was diminished in comparison to civilian life.

Theresienstadt was a transnational community, but interestingly, the prisoner community embraced a binary view of the "locals" and the "foreigners"—that is, the Czech Jews and the prisoners deported from elsewhere. In addition, the ethnic boundary most often perceived was between Czech and German prisoners, in spite of the presence of various other groups. This binary view had a wide impact on how ethnicity played out. For instance, this constellation erased the difference between Czech-speaking and German-speaking Bohemian Jews, who acted as one, Czech, group. The hegemony of the Czech Jews in Theresienstadt presented in multiple ways; we can observe it from the fact that many foreign prisoners, even the elderly, learned (some) Czech. The prisoner society was at the same time hierarchical, segmented, but also interconnected: everyone was part of the community through their ties to the self-administration—through housing and food, and for many through work. Some inmates succeeded in a professional career or building a network of new friends. Kinship could transcend ethnic and generational boundaries, when a young Czech Jewish cook provided for his grandparents or fell in love with a much "poorer" woman from Vienna.

Seniority was another decisive category in the ghetto: the longer people spent in Terezín, the more deserving they were. The status of the veterans could overcome the negative category of "foreignness." In March 1945 Rolf Grabower, a former high-ranking German civil servant, went to get his hair cut. The barber's chair was empty and yet the Czech barber sent Grabower away. Badly in need of a haircut, Grabower insisted. The barber asked how long he had been in Terezín. "Eight months," lied Grabower. "I have been here thirty-nine months," answered the barber, beaming with pride. No less proudly, Grabower pointed out that in fact, he had been there an entire thirty-three months.[1] Three and a quarter years made the hairdresser one of the most senior inmates; Grabower, with half a year less, was nearly his equal. As the inmates lived and worked here, they grew attached to "their pretty ghetto."[2] The sense of seniority reveals people's affinity for Terezín.

The lack of solidarity in Theresienstadt may be surprising, but at the same time, the prisoner society produced new loyalties while keeping some of the old ones. This absence of unity is less a statement about Jewish society and

242   THE LAST GHETTO

more about society in general. Suffering did not heroize people; this is not a redemptive narrative. This conclusion has a melancholy tone but allows us to embrace a more inclusive—and better—history. In particular, this approach makes it possible to discern agency, mentality, and patterns of conduct among the inmates.

In Theresienstadt, Jewishness turned out to be a divisive rather than a bonding factor, indicating that like any other ethnicity, Jewish nationality is constructed rather than given.[3] Unlike the picture that emerges in conventional accounts, where ethnic and cultural differences are minimized, imprisonment did not engender a common sense of Jewishness. Inmates were shaped by the countries they considered home. Jewishness was always a strategy of demarcation. The members of each of the national units considered themselves Jewish in the correct way, while they considered the others too assimilated, too intermarried, or too religious. These assertions were socially constructed national stereotypes, connected to the observer's sensibilities rather than to what the person observed. Thinking through these observations positions the Holocaust as a part of Jewish *and* European history.

Indeed, Holocaust studies need to be read in the framework of wider history. Too often, our field remains exceptionalist. We need to place our research into outside findings, as with the history of ethnicity or medical history. The same applies reciprocally: wider history will benefit from findings of Holocaust studies. Singling out the Holocaust because it is a horrific history is an intellectual loss. The events in Terezín contribute to a wider context, be it the Czech society under German occupation, prison society, or multiethnic societies.

How does one write a history of society in extremis? Holocaust historians need to look beyond canonical accounts, identify and question master narratives, and incorporate diverging accounts. We need to seek to understand what is excluded in the archives and hence recognize the political of what is collected. When writing about suffering, it is crucial not to capitalize on it, nor to portray it in a sentimentalizing light. When analyzing the dynamics of prisoner society, it is critical not to confuse historical analysis with judgment of their actions. Ghetto residents were not heroic when they listened to music, nor were they monsters when they denounced others to the SS. Such judgments obstruct more pertinent questions: Why did they act this way? What do their actions reveal about their society? The task of a Holocaust historian is to apply systematic, unsentimental analysis together with radical empathy, listening to a kaleidoscope of voices, always asking what are the stories that are not told.

Acknowledgments

I enjoyed writing each part of this book, and yet the loveliest part to write is this last one: revisiting those moments with mentors, friends, and colleagues. History can be a lonely job—too lonely with a topic like mine—and people have been the high point.

This book began its life at the University of Toronto, under the supervision of Doris Bergen. Working with Doris is a privilege. She invested considerable mental and other energy to further my doctoral work and my career and I thank her. In Toronto I was also able to work with Lynne Viola, who remains my inspiration for being a scholar, teacher, and human being. Her work on the Stalinist world showed me new ways to think about society, which never ceases to inspire me. Lynne, wry and brilliant, has always been incredibly generous with her time, support, and understanding. Derek Penslar took me on knowing very little about Jewish history—or why it matters—and working with him was transformative. Jennifer Jenkins has become my role model in careful reading, intellectual excitement, and new ways to think about the Germans and their history.

In Toronto, I would also like to thank the Soviet and Russian reading group, which I had the pleasure of co-organizing in 2011/2012—it was fun, engaging, collegial, thought-provoking. Seth Bernstein, my favorite comrade, who has since moved to Moscow, was always willing to help revise and rewrite.

In Pittsburgh, I would like to thank Lara Putnam and Bruce Venarde, whose teaching has shaped my thinking about ethnicity, culture, and class. Nancy Wingfield has been a mentor on matters concerning gender and sexuality and East Central Europe.

My colleagues in the History Department at the University of Warwick have provided a bold and stimulating intellectual atmosphere to work in. I am particularly grateful to colleagues from the Centre for History of Medicine for their encouragement to write a medical history of a ghetto; without Roberta Bivins's enthusiastic and patient support, it would have been so much harder. I am particularly grateful to Sarah Hodges, Laura Schwartz, and Aditya Sarkar for their support.

244 ACKNOWLEDGMENTS

I am indebted to the Alexander von Humboldt Foundation for funding a year and half fellowship at the University of Erfurt, which gave me some much-needed time to revise the manuscript and to develop two new projects, which then in turn found their way into this book. Christiane Kuller, my mentor in Erfurt, has become a role model in work ethic, positivity, and overall human decency. I am also grateful to the Topf & Söhne Museum in Erfurt for hosting my talk on the transports to the East; the subsequent discussion really helped me clarify my argument.

I spent over two and half years researching this work, and I owe much to the help of many archivists who went far beyond the call of duty. In particular, I would like to mention Vlasta Měšťánková from the National Archives in Prague and Marek Poloncarz from SOA Litoměřice, who took extensive time to answer my emails. Jana Šplíchalová from the Jewish Museum in Prague accommodated my many requests and generously opened my eyes to new sources; Pavla Neuner's expertise greatly helped my work with the Museum's Oral History Collection. In Amsterdam, I am indebted to the late René Kruis and would like to thank his colleague, Hubert Berkhout, from the NIOD. At Yad Vashem, Alla Dvorkin, Spartak Arbatov, and Alex Zangin were a source of help and understanding. I would like to thank the entire wonderful team at Beit Terezin, in particular Sima Shachar. Michael Simonsohn from the LBI in New York is a dream archivist.

I was very fortunate to receive generous funding throughout the course of my PhD studies; the extensive international travel this dissertation required would have not been possible otherwise. Thanks are due to the Hamburger Stiftung zur Förderung von Wissenschaft und Kultur, the University of Toronto Connaught Scholarship, the Vanier Graduate Scholarship, the Leo Baeck Fellowship of the Studienstiftung des deutschen Volkes, and the Fondation pour la Mémoire de la Shoah. I would also like to direct my thanks to the Center for Advanced Holocaust Studies of the USHMM for the Ben and Zelda Cohen Fellowship, which continued to support this book in print. This book was made possible (in part) by funds granted to the author through Ben and Zelda Cohen Fellowship at the Jack, Joseph and Morton Mandel Center for Advanced Holocaust Studies of the United States Holocaust Memorial Museum. The statements made and views expressed, however, are solely the responsibility of the author. I am also grateful to the Emerging Scholars Program at the Mandel Center for Advanced Holocaust Studies for its support in the preparation of the manuscript. As a fellow at the Museum, I had a wonderful, stimulating time and met amazing colleagues

ACKNOWLEDGMENTS   245

who became friends, in particular Erika Hughes, Ursula Knoll, and Richard Lutjens. I should also like to thank Michlean Amir, Martin Dean, Krista Hegburg, Emil Kerenji, Jürgen Matthäus, and Rob Williams at the Museum for their discussions and suggestions and for being there at conferences. I would also like to thank the two anonymous reviewers for their comments.

Perhaps the most important emotional and intellectual support came from my friends, who listened; read draft after draft; held my hand; advised over the phone, Skype, and sometimes in person; photographed; copied; and read. My principal thanks go to Maria von der Heydt, who did all of the above and far more. I owe her so much. Justus von Widekind read, commented, corrected draft after draft, translated the tricky Theresienstadt poetry into English, took me out to dinner, and cheered me up when things were dark. Alexandra Garbarini has been a wonderful, supportive friend, and a generous reader; her advice toward the end of the project was crucial. Silvia Goldbaum Tarabini Fracapane has been a wonderful colleague and friend, and she has been generous with everything she knows about Danes in Theresienstadt. Lena Makarova, *the* expert on cultural life and children in Terezín, was extremely generous and passed on materials, information, and contacts. Perhaps most important, she was open to a newcomer's perspective on a topic she has been working on for over three decades. Mike Beckerman was always up for exchanges about music in Terezín and commented extensively on the fifth chapter. Mike has been a great help in many more things, and he is one of the people I am truly sorry I do not see more often. In 2005 Andrej Angrick, a foremost scholar on perpetrators, helped me formulate what I actually wanted to do with this project, and he has remained a dear friend and support ever since. Beate Meyer accompanied this enterprise even longer, and her generous exchange on all matters Reichsvereinigung has made this book much better. Jaroslava Milotová, an eminent historian of the Holocaust in the Czech lands, helped me understand many complicated matters about the Protectorate, the SS, and the Jewish Community, as did Magda Veselská. As a young student, Miroslav Kárný welcomed me to the topic. He passed away on May 10, 2001, fifty-six years and one day after the liberation of Terezín, which he spent the second half of his life researching. I smile when I reflect on what Kárný would think of my work; I believe he would disagree, but he would be curious and fascinated. Martin Šmok, who knows Central European Jewish history in the twentieth century better than anyone, was always up for thinking and speculating and sent me many unique materials no one else even knew existed. Sabine Lachmann very quickly drew and redrew

246 ACKNOWLEDGMENTS

the organizational sketches. Susanna Schraftstetter and Alan Steinweis, my wonderful doctoral aunt and uncle, have offered support, input, and much needed confirmation. They have also introduced me to Christiane Kuller and Winfried Süß who have become mentors and friends, and to Dana Smith, whose approval on the cultural chapter came at an important stage. In addition, she proofread and commented on the entire draft.

In writing about medicine in the ghetto, I moved to a different terrain entirely, and the change from Holocaust to medical history was liberating. I would like to thank Šimon Krýsl and Harro Jenß for their generosity and frequent advice. Susan Grant, Donna Harsch, Rebecca Schwoch, and Astrid Ley helped me find my feet in medical history. Donna very generously commented on the medical chapter twice, and her feedback made it vastly better.

Natalia Aleksiun, Merav Amir, Max Bergholz, Nir Cohen, Belinda Cooper, Elena Demke, Insa Eschebach, Tomáš Fedorovič, Andrea Genest, Christian Gerlach, Judith Gerson, Eva Gilois, Eric Gordy, Daniel Grey, Mirjam Gutschow, Dagmar Hájková, Susanne Heim, Jörn Hasenclever, Christiane Hess, Akim Jah, Jana Leichsenring, Edna Lomsky-Feder, Dominik Maier, Anna Manchin, Richard Pinard, Jennifer Polk, Janine Rivière, Peter Schöttler, Georg Schromm, Jan Seidl, Jan Sternberg, Jiřina Šiklová, Anita Tarsi, Jindřich Toman, Barry Trachtenberg, Corinna Unger, Martina Voigt, Peter Witte, Zbig Wojnowski, and Moshe Zuckermann: all of them helped immeasurably in discussing ideas with me, suggesting new readings, explaining things, and putting me up on my travels. They fed me good food and patted my back when needed. It is with lasting sadness that I note Alfred Gottwaldt, Katja Jedermann, Miroslav Kryl, Sergei Makarov, Shimon Lomsky, Alisah Schiller, Erna Seykorová, and Jakov Tzur will not be able to see this book in print.

Finally, thanks are due to and Meryl and Shlomo Cohen, who in a different way became my family. My brother, Adam Hájek, encouraged me to start writing for newspapers and taught me much about making a punchy argument. I thank my parents, Marie Krausová and Radko Hájek, who did not always understand what I was doing, but backed me and helped me in whatever ways I asked—and they were many. Albane Duvillier drew the maps with enthusiasm. But far more important, she brought me a life outside of academia, a sense of home, and love. Alena Hájková and Pavel Kraus, my paternal grandmother and maternal grandfather, who went through the war, which changed but did not define their lives, knew what I was doing. They both passed away shortly before I defended the dissertation on which this book is based. I think of them often.

Notes

Introduction

1. Egon Redlich, entry for August 16, 1944, in *Zítra jedeme, synu, pojedeme transportem: Deník Egona Redlicha z Terezína 1.1.1942–22.1.1944*, ed. Miroslav Kryl (Brno: Doplněk, 1995), 228. This entry is missing from both the Hebrew and English editions: *As-if Living: A Diary of Egon Redlich from Theresienstadt Ghetto (1942–1944)*, ed. Ruth Bondy (Lohamei Hagetaot: Hakibbutz Hameuchad Publishing and Beit Lohamei Hagetaot, 1982); and *The Terezin Diary of Gonda Redlich*, ed. Saul S. Friedman (Lexington: University Press of Kentucky, 1992).
2. Redlich described the abuse in Czech using Hebrew letters, translating what he wrote into Hebrew in parentheses.
3. When discussing the various aspects of subjective and external belonging, I work with the terminology put forward in Rogers Brubaker and Frederick Cooper, "Beyond Identity," *Theory and Society* 29 (February 2000): 1–47.
4. See also Terrence des Pres, *The Survivor: Anatomy of Life in Death Camps* (New York: Oxford University Press, 1976); Anna Pawełczynska, *Values and Violence in Auschwitz: A Sociological Analysis* (1973; repr., Berkeley: University of California Press, 1979); and Maja Suderland, *Inside Concentration Camps: Social Life at the Extremes* (Cambridge, UK: Polity, 2013).
5. Dan Stone, ed., *Historiography of the Holocaust* (Basingstoke, UK: Palgrave, 2005).
6. Norbert Elias, *The Civilizing Process* (New York: Urizen Books, 1978); see also Isabel Hull, *Absolute Destruction: Military Culture and the Practices of War in Imperial Germany* (Ithaca, N.Y.: Cornell University Press, 2005).
7. Already the writings of the first modern Czech writer, Božena Němcová, reflect this trend—for instance, her *The Grandmother: A Story of Country Life in Bohemia* [*Babička*] (Prague: Alcor, 1999).
8. Melissa Feinberg, *Elusive Equality: Gender, Citizenship, and the Limits of Democracy in Czechoslovakia, 1918–1950* (Pittsburgh: University of Pittsburgh Press, 2006); Marsha Rozenblit, *The Jews of Vienna, 1867–1914: Assimilation and Identity* (Albany: State University of New York Press, 1983); and Lisa Silverman, *Becoming Austrians: Jews and Culture between the World Wars* (Oxford: Oxford University Press, 2012).
9. Marion Kaplan, *The Making of the Jewish Middle Class: Women, Family, and Identity in Imperial Germany* (Oxford: Oxford University Press, 1991); Michal Brenner, *The Renaissance of Jewish Culture in Weimar Germany* (New Haven, Conn.: Yale University Press, 1996); and Till van Rahden, *Germans and Other Jews: Civil Society, Religious Diversity, and Urban Politics in Breslau, 1860–1925* (Madison: Wisconsin University Press, 2008).

248 NOTES TO PAGES 6–10

10. Pierre Bourdieu, *The Logic of Practice* (Cambridge, UK: Polity 1990); and Michael Pollak, *L'expérience Concentrationnaire: Essai sur le maintien de l'identité sociale* (Paris: Métailié, 1990).

11. Pierre Bourdieu, *The Rules of Art: Genesis and Structure of the Literary Field* (Cambridge, UK: Polity Press, 1996); and Bourdieu, "Identity and Representation: Elements for a Critical Reflection on the Idea of Region," in *Language and Symbolic Power*, ed. John B. Thompson (Cambridge: Polity; Stanford, Calif.: Stanford University Press, 1991), 224.

12. Chad Bryant, *Prague in Black: Nazi Rule and Czech Nationalism* (Cambridge, Mass.: Harvard University Press, 2006).

13. For general studies, see Ernst Gellner, *Nations and Nationalism* (Ithaca, N.Y.: Cornell University Press, 1983); and Miroslav Hroch, *Social Preconditions of National Revival in Europe* (1968; repr., Cambridge, UK: Cambridge University Press, 1985); for applied studies, see Bryant, *Prague in Black*; and Tara Zahra, *Kidnapped Souls: National Indifference and the Battle for Children in the Bohemian Lands, 1900–1948* (Ithaca, N.Y.: Cornell University Press, 2008).

14. I use the term "assimilation" rather than "acculturation," aware that both terms can be contentious; I see the former as a category of analysis rather than of praxis. Moreover, my research confirms the far-reaching level of assimilation of Central European Jewry.

15. A classic study is Fredrik Barth, introduction to *Ethnic Groups and Boundaries: The Social Organization of Culture Difference*, ed. Fredrik Barth (Boston: Little, Brown, 1969); see also Rogers Brubaker, Mara Loveman, and Peter Stamatov, "Ethnicity as Cognition," *Theory and Society* 33 (February 2004): 31–64.

16. Isaac Deutscher, *The Non-Jewish Jew, and Other Essays* (Oxford: Oxford University Press, 1968). See also Ezra Mendelsohn, "Should We Take Notice of Berthe Weill? Reflections on the Domain of Jewish History," *Jewish Social Studies*, n.s., 1 (Autumn 1994): 22–39; and Karen Auerbach, *The House at Ujazdowskie 16: Jewish Families in Warsaw after the Holocaust* (Bloomington: Indiana University Press, 2013).

17. Hannah Arendt, *The Origins of Totalitarianism* (New York: Meridian Books, 1958), 483. Giorgio Agamben builds on Arendt in *Homo Sacer: Sovereign Power and Bare Life* (Stanford, Calif.: Stanford University Press, 1998); see also Wolfgang Sofsky, *Ordnung des Terrors: Das Konzentrationslager* (Frankfurt/Main: Fischer, 1993).

18. Erving Goffman, "On the Characteristics of Total Institutions," in *Asylums: Essays on the Social Situation of Mental Patients and Other Inmates* (Garden City, N.Y.: Doubleday, 1961).

19. Charles Bright, *The Powers That Punish: Prison and Politics in the Era of the "Big House," 1920–1955* (Ann Arbor: University of Michigan Press, 1996); and Michel Foucault, *Discipline and Punish: The Birth of the Prison* (London: Penguin, 1991).

20. See Nikolaus Wachsmann, *KL: A History of the Nazi Concentration Camps* (London: Little, Brown, 2015), 16, 18, 497–541 (the chapter on prisoner society is misleadingly titled "Impossible Choices").

21. Eliyana Adler, "Hrubieszów at the Crossroads: Polish Jews Navigate the German and Soviet Occupations," *Holocaust and Genocide Studies* 28 (Winter 2014): 1–30, 16–17.

NOTES TO PAGES 6–10   249

22. Lawrence Langer, *Admitting the Holocaust: Collected Essays* (New York: Oxford University Press, 1995), 46. Similarly, Foucault's *Discipline and Punish* does not allow for agency.

23. Zdenek Lederer, *Ghetto Theresienstadt* (London: E. Goldston, 1953); H. G. Adler, *Theresienstadt 1941–1945: Das Antlitz einer Zwangsgemeinschaft* (Tübingen: Mohr, 1955) in the following when citing Adler, *Theresienstadt*, this book is meant; the English translation H. G. Adler, *Theresienstadt 1941–1945: The Face of a Coerced Community*, ed. Amy Loewenhaar-Blausweiss, trans. Belinda Cooper (Cambridge: Cambridge University Press, 2017) was used to translate Theresienstadt terms; and Karel Lagus and Josef Polák, *Město za mřížemi* (Prague: Naše vojsko, 1964). Lederer's book was co-written with Josef Polák, whose name was removed from the English edition, as the author lived in socialist Czechoslovakia. See Lederer Papers, Wiener Library.

24. Anita Franková, "Die Vorbereitung zur Konzentrierung der Juden im Protektorat: Die 'Vorgeschichte' des Theresienstädter Ghetto," *Theresienstädter Studien und Dokumente* (2001): 49–105.

25. Notes from the Prague meeting on October 10, 1941, in *Deutsche Politik im "Protektorat Böhmen und Mähren" unter Reinhard Heydrich 1941–1942*, ed. Miroslav Kárný, Jaroslava Milotová, and Margita Kárná (Berlin: Metropol, 1997), 137–141, document 28.

26. Entry for November 18, 1941, in *Die Tagebücher von Joseph Goebbels: Diktate 1941–1945*, ed. Elke Fröhlich, part II, vol. 2 (Munich: Saur, 1996), 309.

27. Christian Gerlach, "Die Wannseekonferenz, das Schicksal der deutschen Juden und Hitlers Grundsatzentscheidung, alle Juden Europas zu ermorden," *WerkstattGeschichte* 18 (1997): 7–44; see also Peter Witte et al., eds., *Der Dienstkalender Heinrich Himmlers 1941/42* (Hamburg: Christians, 1999), 289, 293, 294.

28. Andrej Angrick and Peter Klein, *The "Final Solution" in Riga: Exploitation and Annihilation, 1941–1944* (New York: Berghahn, 2009), 220–222.

29. Alfred Gottwaldt and Diana Schulle, *Die Judendeportationen aus dem Deutschen Reich, 1941–1945: Eine kommentierte Chronologie* (Wiesbaden: Marixverlag, 2005).

30. The standard number of survivors, 3,600, does not include people who had been deported to Terezín from the Netherlands and survived. See Anna Hájková, "Poor Devils of the Camps: Dutch Jews in the Terezín Ghetto, 1943–1945," *Yad Vashem Studies* 43, no. 1 (2015): 77–111, 87.

31. Diary of Arnošt Klein, entry for March 18, 1943, AJMP, T, 324.

32. Gerhart Riegner, note, July 8, 1943, in *Verheimlichte Wahrheit: Theresienstädter Dokumente*, ed. H. G. Adler (Tübingen: Mohr, 1958), 304–307.

33. Maurice Rossel, "Besuch im Ghetto," ed. Vojtěch Blodig, *Theresienstädter Studien und Dokumente* (1996): 284–301.

34. Eva Strusková, "Film Ghetto Theresienstadt: Suche nach Zusammenhängen," in *"Der Letzte der Ungerechten" Der Judenälteste Benjamin Murmelstein in Filmen 1942–1975*, ed. Ronny Loewy and Katharina Rauschenberger (Frankfurt/Main: Campus, 2011), 125–158.

250   NOTES TO PAGES 13–17

35. Karel Margry, "Der Nazi-Film über Theresienstadt," in *Theresienstadt in der "Endlösung der Judenfrage"*, ed. Miroslav Kárný, Vojtěch Blodig, and Margita Kárná (Prague: Logos, 1992), 285–306.

36. Rudolf Freiberger, "Zur Geschichte der Produktionsstätten im Theresienstädter Ghetto," *Theresienstädter Studien und Dokumente* (1994): 90–108.

37. Lodz ghetto also had a mica splitting workshop; see Isaiah Trunk, *Łódź Ghetto: A History*, ed. Robert Moses Shapiro (Bloomington: Indiana University Press, 2006), 304.

38. See statements of Pavel Lužický, Edmund Repper, Adolf Beneš, and Rudolf Gerstmann at the trial of Johann Wostrel, Municipal and Provincial Archives of Vienna (hereafter WStLA), Volksgericht Wien, Vr 314/50 gg. Johann Wostrel.

39. See Peter Klein, "Theresienstadt: Ghetto oder Konzentrationslager?," *Theresienstädter Studien und Dokumente* (2005), 111–123.

40. Martin Dean, ed., "Editor's Introduction," in *Ghettos in German-Occupied Eastern Europe*, vol. 2 of *The United States Holocaust Memorial Museum Encyclopedia of Camps and Ghettos 1933–1945*, ed. Geoffrey Megargee (Bloomington: Indiana University Press, 2012), xliii.

41. Daniel Michman, *The Emergence of Jewish Ghettos during the Holocaust* (Cambridge, UK: Cambridge University Press, 2011), 3; and Evgeny Finkel, *Ordinary Jews: Choice and Survival during the Holocaust* (Princeton, N.J.: Princeton University Press, 2016), 22.

42. Finkel, *Ordinary Jews*, 22.

43. Ann Taylor Allen, *The Transatlantic Kindergarten: Education and Women's Movements in Germany and the Unites States* (New York: Oxford University Press, 2017), 2.

44. See Emmanuel Le Roy Ladurie, *Montaillou: Cathars and Catholics in a French Village, 1294–1324* (New York: G. Braziller, 1978); Carlo Ginzburg, *The Cheese and the Worms: The Cosmos of a Sixteenth-Century Miller* (Baltimore, Md.: Johns Hopkins University Press, 1980); Natalie Zemon Davis, *The Return of Martin Guerre* (Cambridge, Mass.: Harvard University Press, 1983); and Alf Lüdtke, ed., *Alltagsgeschichte: Zur Rekonstruktion historischer Erfahrungen und Lebensweisen* (Frankfurt/Main: Campus, 1989).

45. Belinda Davis, *Home Fires Burning: Food, Politics, and Everyday Life in World War I Berlin* (Chapel Hill: University of North Carolina Press, 2000).

46. Aletta Biersack and Lynn Avery Hunt, eds., *The New Cultural History: Essays* (Berkeley: University of California Press, 1989); Victoria E. Bonnell, Lynn Avery Hunt, and Richard Biernacki, eds., *Beyond the Cultural Turn: New Directions in the Study of Society and Culture* (Berkeley: University of California Press, 1999); William Sewell, "Concept(s) of Culture," in *Beyond the Cultural Turn*, ed. Victoria E. Bonnell, Lynn Avery Hunt, and Richard Biernacki (Berkeley: University of California Press, 1999), 35–61; and Clifford Geertz, *The Interpretation of Cultures: Selected Essays* (London: Fontana, 1973).

47. For cultural histories of the Holocaust, see Alexandra Garbarini, *Numbered Days: Diaries and the Holocaust* (New Haven, Conn.: Yale University Press, 2006); Dan Stone, "Holocaust Historiography and Cultural History," *Dapim* 23 (2009): 52–68;

NOTES TO PAGES 13–17   251

and Amos Goldberg, *Trauma in First Person: Diary Writing during the Holocaust* (Bloomington: Indiana University Press, 2018).

48. Joan Scott, "Gender: A Useful Category of Historical Analysis," *American Historical Review* 91, no. 5 (1986): 1053–1075.

49. "In any society, the conditions of access to the production of documentation are tied to a situation of power and thus create an inherent imbalance." Carlo Ginzburg, "Microhistory: Two or Three Things That I Know about It," *Critical Inquiry* 20 (Autumn 1993): 10–35, 21.

50. E. P. Thompson, *The Making of the English Working Class* (London: Victor Gollancz, 1963), 52–53.

51. Ginzburg, "Microhistory," 24.

52. Scott Spector, *Prague Territories: National Conflict and Cultural Innovation in Franz Kafka's Fin de Siècle* (Berkeley: University of California Press, 2000); Dimitry Shumsky, *Zweisprachigkeit und binationale Idee: Der Prager Zionismus 1900–1930* (Göttingen: Vandenhoeck & Ruprecht, 2012); and Sofsky, *Ordnung des Terrors.*

53. On diaries see Garbarini, *Numbered Days*; on the collecting of the historical commissions see Laura Jockusch, *Collect and Record! Jewish Holocaust Documentation in Early Postwar Europe* (New York: Oxford University Press, 2012).

54. There were altogether thirty-five legal proceedings with a main focus on crimes in Terezín, which I studied in their entirety. See also Anna Hájková, "What Kind of Narrative Is Legal Testimony? Terezín Survivors Speaking Before Czechoslovak, Austrian, and Western German Justice," in *Rethinking Holocaust Justice: Essays across Disciplines,* ed. Norman Goda (New York: Berghahn, 2017), 71–99.

Chapter 1

1. Adler, *Theresienstadt*, 223–263.

2. Hans Safrian, *Eichmann und seine Gehilfen* (Frankfurt/Main: Fischer, 1995).

3. Gabriele Anderl, "Die 'Zentralstellen für jüdische Auswanderung' in Wien, Berlin und Prag—ein Vergleich," *Tel Aviver Jahrbuch für deutsche Geschichte* 23 (1994): 275–300; and Jaroslava Milotová, "Die Zentralstelle für jüdische Auswanderung in Prague: Genesis und Tätigkeit bis zum Anfang des Jahres 1940," *Theresienstädter Studien und Dokumente* (1997): 7–30. The Prague Central Office was renamed "Zentralamt zur Regelung der Judenfrage in Böhmen und Mähren" in summer 1943, when the remnants of the Jewish Council in Prague were deported; the Council was then renamed the Council of Elders. I use the name Central Office throughout this book.

4. Michael Wildt, *Generation des Unbedingten: Das Führungskorps des Reichssicherheitshauptamtes* (Hamburg: Hamburger Edition, 2002), 738.

5. Interrogation of Karl Rahm, March 25, 1947, State Regional Archive Litoměřice (hereafter SOAL), LSP 441/47 (the pagination of this trial is confusing and therefore I do not include the page numbers).

252   NOTES TO PAGES 20–22

6. The Small Fortress fell under the responsibility of the Gestapo; the inmates were put in protective custody. Interrogation of Rahm, March 25, 1947, SOAL, LSP 441/47.

7. Interrogation of Rahm, April 2, 1947, SOAL, LSP 441/47.

8. On Moes, see Alexandra-Eileen Wenck, *Zwischen Menschenhandel und "Endlösung": Das Konzentrationslager Bergen-Belsen* (Paderborn: Schöningh, 2000), 243–245.

9. Heinrich Scholz, his own submission to trial of Rahm, no date, SOAL, LSP 441/47.

10. Magda Veselská, *Archa paměti: Cesta pražského židovského muzea pohnutým 20. stoletím* (Prague: Academia, 2012), 53–119.

11. Karel Margry, "Der Nazi-Film über Theresienstadt," in *Theresienstadt in der "Endlösung der Judenfrage"*, ed. Miroslav Kárný, Vojtěch Blodig, and Margita Kárná (Prague: Logos, 1992), 285–306.

12. Karl Loesten, "Aus der Hoelle Minsk in das 'Paradies' Theresienstadt 1941–1945," Leo Baeck Institute NY (hereafter LBI), ME 398, ch. 4.

13. Egon Redlich, entry for February 13, 1944, in *Zítra jedeme, synu, pojedeme transportem: Deník Egona Redlicha z Terezína 1.1.1942–22.1.1944*, ed. Miroslav Kryl (Brno: Doplněk, 1995), 212.

14. Interrogation of Rahm, April 3, 1947, SOAL, LSP 441/47.

15. The Auswanderungsfonds, a branch of the Central Office, was responsible for administering the stolen property of the emigrated Jews, "aryanized" property, and money coming from sales to the gentile trustees.

16. Interrogation of Heinrich Scholz, April 8, 1947, SOAL, LSP 441/47.

17. Scholz, submission, SOAL, LSP 441/47. Scholz also wrote that the SS was prohibited to beat the prisoners, which routinely happened. When Rahm was in a bad mood, he would slap Murmelstein. See also Claude Lanzmann's interview with Benjamin Murmelstein, Steven Spielberg film and video archive, USHMM, RG–60.5009 ("Created by Claude Lanzmann during the filming of 'Shoah'. Used by permission of the United States Holocaust Memorial Museum and Yad Vashem, the Holocaust Martyrs and Heroes' Remembrance Authority, Jerusalem"; hereafter cited as Lanzmann Interview, with tape number), 3174.

18. This passage, if not indicated otherwise, follows Gabriele Anderl, "Die Lagerkommandanten des jüdischen Ghetto Theresienstadt," in *Theresienstadt in der "Endlösung der Judenfrage"*, ed. Miroslav Kárný et al. (Prague: Logos, 1992), 213–222; Erik Polák, "Spravedlnost vykonaná a nevykonaná (Případy bývalých velitelů terezínského ghetta)," *Terezínské listy* 22 (1994): 7–24; and Safrian, *Eichmann und seine Gehilfen*.

19. For the conflict, see Fedorovič, "Seidl," 191–192. Seidl was only Obersturmführer until the fall of 1942, after which he was promoted to Hauptsturmführer; for the exchange, see Alexandra-Eileen Wenck, *Zwischen Menschenhandel und "Endlösung": Das Konzentrationslager Bergen-Belsen* (Paderborn: Schöningh, 2000), 82. This thesis is supported by the fact that Moes suggested to Edelstein that he might be sent elsewhere to direct another ghetto; this could have been Bergen-Belsen, to continue cooperating with Seidl. Margalit Shlain, "Ein neues Dokument zu den betrügerischen Methoden

NOTES TO PAGES 20–22   253

der Nazis," in *Theresienstadt in der "Endlösung der Judenfrage"*, ed. Miroslav Kárný et al. (Prague: Logos, 1992), 223–232.

20. Karla Müller Tupath, *Verschollen in Deutschland: Das heimliche Leben des Anton Burger, Lagerkommandant von Theresienstadt* (Hamburg: Konkret, 1994), 40.

21. Julius Taussig interview, January 9, 1967, and August 26, 1975, APT, Sbírka vzpomínek, 51.

22. Benjamin Murmelstein, "Všeobecný politický směr," SOAL, LSP 441/47. On Franz Rahm, see database of Gestapo victims at www.doew.at.

23. Scholz, submission, SOAL, LSP 441/47; and Murmelstein about Eppstein and Rudolf Freiberger, no date, Archiv bezpečnostních složek (hereafter ABS), 305-633-1, 82, 168.

24. Fedorovič, "Neue Erkenntnisse über die SS Angehörigen im Ghetto Theresienstadt," *Theresienstädter Studien und Dokumente* (2006), 240; and Murmelstein, Lanzmann Interview, 3176.

25. Memo from Ritterhaus (no first name given), Verbindungsführer Stellungsbau, March 17, 1945, and following correspondence, Czech National Archive (hereafter NA), 110-3/54. Thanks to Jaroslava Milotová. See also Interrogation of Rahm, March 25, 1947, SOAL, LSP 441/47, point 26.

26. Murmelstein, Lanzmann Interview, 3186.

27. Fedorovič, "Neue Erkenntnisse," 238. Karl Bergel was the highest ranking SS man who stayed in the ghetto for its entire duration.

28. For an explanation of the funding of Theresienstadt, see chapter 3.

29. Trial of Elfriede Hübsch, SOAL, MLS, 1802/46.

30. Interrogation of Heinrich Scholz, April 8, 1947, SOAL, LSP 444/47, box 136.

31. Max Feldmar's testimony in trial of Haindl, Municipal and Provincial Archives of Vienna (hereafter WStLA), Volksgericht Wien, Vr 1814/56; and police registration file for Karl Rahm, NA.

32. Müller Tupath, 44; Fedorovič, "Neue Erkenntnisse"; Murmelstein ("Rahm 4") recalled that Rahm impregnated a young woman who worked in the SS headquarters. ABS, 305-633-1, 85.

33. Fedorovič, "Neue Erkenntnisse."

34. Eva Noack-Mosse, "Bericht aus Theresienstadt," no date, YVA, O33, 986; on the silk-worm farm, run by František Pick from Prague, see Věra Blábolová interview, APT, A, 124.

35. List of repairs, February 1945, NA, KT OVS, 64, box 45, file 29.

36. Murmelstein, ABS, 305-633-1, 82.

37. Miroslav Kárný, "Die Gendarmerie-Sonderabteilung und die Theresienstädter Häftlinge: Zur Methodologie der kritischen Interpretation von Erinnerungen," *Theresienstädter Studien und Dokumente* (1996): 136–152; and František Fara, *Četnické vzpomínky* (Prague: Codyprint, 2002), 104. See also Hasenkopf to Gendarmerie-Landeskommando, October 18, 1943, NA, ZČV, 926.

38. Fara, *Četnické vzpomínky*, 102; and Max Berger, Yad Vashem Archive (hereafter YVA), O7, 222.

254 NOTES TO PAGES 24–25

39. Rudolf Iltis, "Die unbesungenen Helden," in *Theresienstadt*, ed. Rudolf Iltis (Vienna: Europa-Verlag, 1968), 320–327.

40. Interview of a man, August 28, 1991, Jewish Museum Prague (hereafter AJMP), The Oral History Collection, 69 (born 1919) (The Prague Jewish Museum prescribes that interviewee names be abbreviated and give a birth date, unless the interviewees, or their families, permit otherwise.); Report of Erna Kafková-Bonnová, Beit Terezin (hereafter BTA), 53/I; Irma Lauscherová, Terezín Memorial (hereafter APT), 85; Jan Jícha, APT, A, 116; and Fára, *Četnické vzpomínky*, 100.

41. Both were prosecuted after the war: interrogation of Janeček in his trial, June 11, 1945, State Regional Archive Prague (hereafter SOAP), MLS, LS 428/46; Hasenkopf, SOAL, MLS, LSP 86/48, box 147. Janeček died in custody; Hasenkopf received fifteen years and died in prison in 1951.

42. František Somolík, APT, 602 (interview of a gendarme); and Murmelstein, Lanzmann Interview, 3174.

43. Doris Donovalová interview, AJMP, The Oral History Collection, 580; and testimony of Vilém Kantor, APT, A 4856.

44. Viktor Pollak, *S Davidovou hvězdou peklem Terezína*, trans. Pavel Kříž (Brno: Littera, 2010), 72–78, has a graphic depiction of Haindl raping a young male inmate.

45. File 1934, box 933, Municipal archive Ústí nad Labem, contains "Erhebungsblätter für gewerbsm: Prostituierte" from May 1940. Thanks to Nancy Wingfield for this information.

46. Somolík, APT; Interview of a man, August 28, 1991, AJMP, The Oral History Collection, 69 (born 1919); Irena Rieselová, APT, A, 129; statement of František Albel against František Drahňovský, August 10, 1945, SOAP, MLS, LS 428/46; interview Jiří Žantovský, May 10, 1995, AJMP, The Oral History Collection, 462.

47. Interview AJMP, 69; for "rational relationships" see Anna Hájková, "Sexual Barter in Times of Genocide: Negotiating the Sexual Economy of the Theresienstadt Ghetto," *Signs* 38 (Spring 2013): 503–533, 505–506.

48. This demarcated relationship of two institutions is reflected in the fact that the ghetto was leasing agricultural land from the Small Fortress (see also map "Terezín Ghetto and Surroundings"); interrogation of Siegfried Seidl, June 4, 1946, WStLA, Volksgerichte, Vg 1 Vr 770/46. Only several levels higher both institutions belonged under the BdS Prague and RSHA Berlin.

49. There is an abundance of Czech literature on the Small Fortress; for a short overview, see Marek Poloncarz, "Dosavadní výsledky výzkumu dějin policejní věznice gestapa Malé Pevnosti a perspektivy další výzkumné a dokumentační práce," *Terezínské listy* 27 (1999): 7–19.

50. Interrogation of Hohaus, April 24, 1947, SOAL, LSP 441/47.

51. Otto Schütz, Moreshet Archive (hereafter Moreshet), A, 553; and Murmelstein, "Geschichtlicher Überblick," Wiener Library (hereafter WL), 1073, 3. There are various versions of this document.

52. The Terezín Initiative Institute prisoner database indicates about eighty cases; Adler, *Theresienstadt*, gives 276. The SS did not register all of the arrested inmates as passed to Gestapo, and the records of the Small Fortress are fragmentary.

NOTES TO PAGES 24–25   255

53. Redlich, entry for October 26, 1942, in *Zítra jedeme*, 154.
54. Interrogation of Siegfried Seidl, 4 June 1946, WStLA, Volksgerichte, Vg 1 Vr 770/46.
55. Emanuel Herrmann interview, December 5, 1971, APT, A, 564.
56. Interrogation of Heinrich Scholz, April 8, 1947, SOAL, LSP 444/47.
57. See Walter Benjamin, "Zur Kritik der Gewalt," *Archiv für Sozialwissenschaft und Sozialpolitik* 47 (1920/1921): 809–832.
58. Because these executions were the only ones that took place, they later played a crucial role in the prosecution of the perpetrators. Anna Hájková, "What Kind of Narrative Is Legal Testimony? Terezín Survivors Speaking Before Czechoslovak, Austrian, and Western German Justice," in *Rethinking Holocaust Justice: Essays across Disciplines*, ed. Norman Goda (New York: Berghahn, 2017), 71–99.
59. Statement of Rudolf Freiberger, February 28, 1967, German Federal Archives Ludwigsburg (hereafter BArch), B 162, 1886, fol. 2; and Miroslav Kárný's interview with Vilém Cantor, December 18, 1972, "Komunistická organizace v terezínském koncentračním táboře 1941–1945" (manuscript, 1983), NA, Kárných, ka 16, 7–10.
60. Isaiah Trunk, *Judenrat: The Jewish Councils in Eastern Europe under Nazi Occupation* (New York: Macmillan, 1972), 389 passim; Isaiah Trunk, *Łódź Ghetto: A History*, ed. Robert Moses Shapiro (Bloomington: Indiana University Press, 2006), 14; Barbara Engelking-Boni and Jacek Leociak, *The Warsaw Ghetto: A Guide to the Perished City* (2001; repr., New Haven, Conn.: Yale University Press, 2009), 37; and Sara Bender, *The Jews of Białystok during World War II and the Holocaust* (Waltham, Mass.: Brandeis University Press; Hanover, N.H.: University Press of New England, 2008), 95–98.
61. Fedorovič, "Seidl," 182.
62. Even Jews from Germany or Austria who arrived much later mentioned the executions as a key moment of the history of Terezín. Arnold M. interview, September 5, 1995, Moses Mendelsohn Zentrum, German Yale Fortunoff interviews (hereafter MMZ), Nr. 16; Otto Schütz, Report on Theresienstadt, Moreshet, A, 553 (March 1945) (Schütz's report is a compilation of six Turkish citizens released to Sweden from Bergen-Belsen, whence they came in July 1944 from Theresienstadt); and report by Jacob Plaut, 1945, YVA, M1E, 1942.
63. Norbert Troller, "A Convict in the 'Little Fortress' near Terezín-Bohemia," LBI, AR 7268, 2/4.
64. Julius Taussig interview, APT; interview man, AJMP, The Oral History Collection, Nr. 77 (born 1917).
65. Statement Vilém Hostovský in trial Seidl on September 30, 1946, WStLA, Volksgerichte, Vg 1 Vr 770/46. Cf. also Lenka Šindelářová, "50 Jahre Zentrale Stelle in Ludwigsburg: Strafverfolgung von NS-Verbrechen am Beispiel des 'Lagerinspekteurs' von Theresienstädter Ghetto," *Theresienstädter Studien und Dokumente* (2008): 64–114, 87–89; Loesten, "Aus der Hoelle Minsk," LBI, ch. 4; and Leo Fink to the prosecutor, July 24, 1945, SOAP, MLS, LS 428/46.
66. Marek Poloncarz, "Das Gestapo-Polizeigefängnis Kleine Festung Theresienstadt," *Theresienstädter Studien und Dokumente* (1999): 11–26.
67. On the domination of perpetrators during torture see Jean Améry, *Jenseits von Schuld und Sühne: Bewältigungsversuche eines Überwältigten* (Munich: dtv, 1988), 53.

256 NOTES TO PAGES 30–32

68. Elissa Mailänder, *Female SS Guards and Workaday Violence: The Majdanek Concentration Camp, 1942–1944* (East Lansing: Michigan State University Press, 2015), ch. 11.

69. I would like to thank the late Miroslav Kryl for this information.

70. Aktenvermerk, January 27, 1943, AJMP, T, W720-927.

71. Hedwig Rosenthal, WL, P.III.h, 164; and Heinrich Wolffheim, YVA, O1, 102. Ruth Bondy's biography of Edelstein, *"Elder of the Jews": Jakob Edelstein of Theresienstadt* (New York: Grove, 1989), is an example of this narrative.

72. Edelstein to Fritz Ullmann (Geneva), October 19, 1942, cited in "Jakov Edelsteins letzte Briefe," ed. Miroslav Kárný, *Theresienstädter Studien und Dokumente* (1997): 216–229, 223–224.

73. Interview of a man, December 3, 1990, AJMP, The Oral History Collection, 5 (born 1904).

74. Redlich, entries for December 12, 1942, and January 2 and 3, 1943, in *Zítra jedeme*, 165, 175.

75. Edelstein to all members of the Council of Elders, January 4, 1943, AJMP, Terezín, 49.

76. Manfred Fackenheim, LBI, AR 1281; and Redlich, entry for January 7, 1944, in *Zítra jedeme*, 211.

77. Interrogation of Rahm, April 3, 1947; and statement of Rudolf Bunzel, ABS 305-633-1, 245.

78. Redlich, entries for February 13, 14, and 17, 1943, in *Zítra jedeme*, 176f.

79. Murmelstein's statement in investigations against Karl Rahm, February 7, 1947, ABS 305-633-1, 10254-I, 69; and Murmelstein, Lanzmann Interview, 3174 and 3175. ("Eppstein had more trust in Moes than in his Jewish colleagues.")

80. Beate Meyer, *Tödliche Gratwanderung: Die Reichsvereinigung der Juden in Deutschland zwischen Hoffnung, Zwang, Selbstbehauptung und Verstrickung (1939–1945)* (Göttingen: Wallstein, 2011).

81. Loesten, "Aus der Hoelle Minsk," LBI, ch. 10.

82. Murmelstein on Paul Eppstein, ABS, 305-633-1, 163 (overleaf).

83. On the piano: Beate Meyer, "'Altersghetto', 'Vorzugslager' und Tätigkeitsfeld: Die Repräsentanten der Reichsvereinigung der Juden in Deutschland und Theresienstadt," *Theresienstädter Studien und Dokumente* (2004): 134; on arts: Murmelstein, ABS, 305-633-1, 164; on lovers: Trude Simonsohn, "Erinnerung an Paul Eppstein," *Theresienstädter Studien und Dokumente* (1996): 127–130, 128; and list for the Ev transport with Viktor Kende's handwritten remarks, Kende papers, APT, A, 7854.

84. From inmates who were in touch with the fireman Vítězslav Lederer, who escaped Auschwitz.

85. Interrogation of Rudolf Freiberger, February 1, 1946, ABS, 305-633-1, 322–324; and minutes from March 4, 1947, with Emilie Tausková, ABS, 305-633-1, 197.

86. Meyer, *Tödliche Gratwanderung*, ch. 2.

87. *Denní rozkazy Rady starších a Sdělení židovské samosprávy Terezín 1941–1945*, ed. Anna Hyndráková, Raisa Machatková, and Jaroslava Milotová (Prague: Sefer, 2003); Mitteilung (hereafter MT) 30/2, 453; diary of Arnošt Klein, entry for July 18, 1944, AJMP, T, 324.

NOTES TO PAGES 30-32   257

88. Benjamin Murmelstein, *Theresienstadt: Eichmanns Vorzeige-Ghetto*, ed. Ruth Pleyer and Alfred J. Noll, trans. Karin Fleischanderl (Vienna: Czernin, 2014), 153–154; and Grabower, Vermerke, entries for August 7 and 8, 1944, Grabower papers, Finanzakademie Brühl. (I viewed the Grabower papers here in 2011; they have since been moved to the German Customs Museum (Steuermuseum), Hamburg.)

89. One of the things that distinguished him from colleagues such as Paul Eppstein or Otto Zucker, who came from an assimilated Western background.

90. Thus the subtitle of Doron Rabinovici's study: *Instanzen der Ohnmacht: Wien 1938–1945; Der Weg zum Judenrat* (Frankfurt/Main: Jüdischer Verlag, 2000).

91. Rabinovici was also one of the first scholars to point out that the Jewish community or the community at large generally judged its own members more harshly than the perpetrators themselves.

92. Fritz Fabian, "Erinnerungen an die Hitlerzeit" (July 1965), LBI, AR 7234; Karl Löwenstein's submission to trial of Prochnik, October 18, 1948, WStLA, Volksgerichte, Vg 41/54 gg Prochnik; Beate Meyer's interview with Merzbacher (1999), with thanks to Beate Meyer; and Rabinovici, *Instanzen der Ohnmacht*, 361; see also interview of Marie Schelerová, 14 January 1997, The Visual History Archive of the USC Shoah Foundation (hereafter VHA), 25819.

93. Murmelstein to Josef Löwenherz, March 10, 1943, YVA, O30, 51.

94. Murmelstein, no date, ABS, 305-633-1, 57.

95. Statement of Jiří Vogel, February 28, 1946, ABS, 305-633-1, 162; interview of Marie Schelerová, VHA.

96. Ibid.; and Murmelstein, ABS, 305-633-1, 55 and 144.

97. Interview, AJMP, 5; and Murmelstein, Lanzmann Interview, 3186.

98. Similarly also in December 12, 1944 (#184) "Neugliederung Verwaltung," YVA, O64, 24.

99. Hermann Strauß, "Aufzeichnungen aus dem Ghetto Theresienstadt," in *Der Arzt Hermann Strauß 1868–1944: Autobiographische Notizen und Aufzeichnungen aus dem Ghetto Theresienstadt*, ed. Harro Jenß and Peter Reinicke (Berlin: Hentrich & Hentrich, 2014), 112–139, 123. On Strauß, see Harro Jenß, *Hermann Strauß: Internist und Wissenschaftler in der Charité und im Jüdischen Krankenhaus Berlin* (Berlin: Hentrich & Hentrich, 2011).

100. Interrogation of Siegfriedl Seidl, June 4, 1946, WStLA, Volksgerichte, Vg 1 Vr 770/46.

101. Interrogation of Karl Rahm, March 25, 1947, SOAL, LSP 441/47.

102. Interview #5, December 3, 1990, AJMP. In English names of Theresienstadt institutions, I follow Belinda Cooper's translation. H. G. Adler, *Theresienstadt 1941–1945: The Face of a Coerced Community*, ed. Amy Loewenhaar-Blausweiss (Cambridge, UK: Cambridge University Press, 2017).

103. Alfréd Meissner's testimony, March 1, 1946, ABS, 305-633-1, 198; and Benjamin Murmelstein's own statement, March 11, 1946, ABS, 305-633-1, 138.

104. Minutes from the Council meeting, January 29, 1943, reprinted in H. G. Adler, *Die Verheimlichte Wahrheit: Theresienstädter Dokumente* (Tübingen: Mohr, 1958), 134.

105. See Lucie Ondřichová, *Příběh Freddyho Hirsche* (Prague: Sefer, 2001), 72f.

258 NOTES TO PAGES 35–37

106. Interview #5, December 3, 1990, AJMP.

107. Redlich, entries for October 31 and November 3, 1943, in *Zítra jedeme*, 205f.

108. Karel Fleischmann, "Zápas krabů," March 11, 1943, AJMP, T, Fleischmann papers (326).

109. NA Prague, KT OVS, inv. no. 64, box 45, files 25 and 29.

110. Statements of Edvard Kurz and Ela Becková, March 3 and February 2, 1946, ABS, 305-633-1, 239, 333.

111. Similarly to Rahm's beating of Eppstein, Adam Czerniakow of Warsaw was also beaten: entry for November 4, 1940, in *The Warsaw Diary of Adam Czerniakow: Prelude to Doom*, ed. Raul Hilberg, Stanislaw Staron, and Josef Kermisz (Chicago: Ivan R. Dee, 1999).

112. Statement by Hilda Hahnová (Murmelstein's secretary), February 9, 1946, ABS, 305-633-1, 207.

113. Murmelstein (who shared in his memos only what he wanted to) explained this mechanism in his memoir, Benjamin Murmelstein, *Theresienstadt: Eichmanns Vorzeige-Ghetto*, ed. Ruth Pleyer and Alfred J. Noll (Vienna: Czernin, 2014), 58.

114. Their younger brother Jiří was deported with his siblings in November 1943 to Theresienstadt, escaped in April 1944, was returned to the ghetto, and survived. Their Jewish mother Edita was deported to Theresienstadt in February 1945 with the mixed marriage transports. One brother remained in Prague. Information from the Terezín Initiative Institute's prisoner database and the Terezín Memorial's Small Fortress database.

115. Alena Hájková, "Lebensgeschichte Karel Körpers," *Theresienstädter Studien und Dokumente* (2002): 272–299, 287–288.

116. Tagesbefehl from April 9 and 10, 1943, in *Denní rozkazy Rady starších a Sdělení židovské samosprávy Terezín 1941–1945*, ed. Anna Hyndráková, Raisa Machatková, and Jaroslava Milotová (Prague: Sefer, 2003), 318f watch out, I cited it already in FN87 so here it needs to be abbreviated The prohibition of light was dangerous for the prisoners and played a role in Seidl's trial six years later. WStLA, Volksgerichte, Vg 1 Vr 770/46.

117. Miroslav Kárný's interview with Vilém Cantor, December 18, 1972, NA; and Malka Hahn-Kartagener interview, VHA, 1828.

118. Murmelstein, *Eichmanns Vorzeige-Ghetto*, 104; see also Murmelstein, Lanzmann Interview, 3173. Goldschmid was deported to Auschwitz together with Edelstein. He did not survive.

119. Edith Ornstein's report on Theresienstadt (1945), BTA, 9, IX.

120. *Denní rozkazy*, MT 59 (January 15, 1945), 483.

121. Isidor Reiser about the mistreatments of Oskar Taussig in the Kain affair, January 25, 1947, trial of Rahm, SOAL.

122. Murmelstein to Max Friediger, May 26, 1945, Rigsarkivet, Jewish Community, chief rabbi M. Friediger, correspondence 1911–1947. Thanks to Silvia Tarabini Goldbaum Fracapane.

NOTES TO PAGES 35–37   259

123. Statement by Hilda Hahnová, ABS, 305-633-1, 207.

124. Murmelstein claimed that he threatened Rahm by submitting his resignation. Murmelstein, *Eichmanns Vorzeige-Ghetto*, 192–193.

125. Kain survived in the Small Fortress. Rahm argued in his interrogations that he let Kain go, but Hans Günther intervened. Interrogation of Rahm, April 3, 1947, SOAL, LSP 441/47, 134; and Loesten, "Aus der Hoelle Minsk," LBI, ch. 3.

126. Memo Central Secretariat on Arthur Busch, April 18, 1945, YVA, O64, 24; and Murmelstein, ABS, 305-633-1, 133.

127. Murmelstein, "Rahm 5," ABS, 305-633-1, 102. It is still unknown whether this particular transport of prominents was at all planned. Miroslav Kárný, "Kaltenbrunners Reise nach Theresienstadt und der Prominententransport im April 1945," *Theresienstädter Studien und Dokumente* (1999): 66–85.

128. Karel Lagus and Josef Polák, *Město za mřížemi* (Prague: Naše vojsko, 1964), 122; see also Rolf Bartels's letter to the Jewish administration asking for a *Persilschein*, July 7, 1945, in ABS, 305-633-1 (copy).

129. Deposition of Rudolf Freiberger, addition to his statement of September 24, 1945 on January 1, 1946, ABS, 305-633-1; Murmelstein on Bartels, "Fleischlieferungen für Teresin" [*sic*], no date, ABS, 305-633-1, 65–66; and Loesten, "Aus der Hoelle Minsk," LBI, ch. 5.

130. Murmelstein on Bartels; and Bartels to the former Jewish self-administration, July 7, 1945, both ABS, 305-633-1.

131. Murmelstein on Bartels; Bartels to the former Jewish self-administration, July 7, 1945, ABS, 305-633-1, 82/88.

132. Interrogation of Rudolf Freiberger, February 1, 1946, ABS, 305-633-1, 322–324; and testimony of Emilie Tausková, March 4, 1947, ABS, 305-633-1, 197.

133. Deposition of Rudolf Freiberger, addition to his statement of September 24, 1945, on January 1, 1946, ABS, 305-633-1, 322–324.

134. Ibid.

135. Barbara Engelking-Boni, and Jacek Leociak, *The Warsaw Ghetto: A Guide to the Perished City* (New Haven, Conn.: Yale University Press, 2009), 164, on Czerniakow and Auersbach.

136. Meyer, *Tödliche Gratwanderung*, 421–423.

137. Bartels let Schliesser be deported without protest, Fedorovič, "Neue Erkenntnisse," 239. In contrast, the civilian employee Otto Kursawe from Agriculture fought for his workers.

138. Interview of a man, May 19, 1999, AJMP, The Oral History Collection, 806 (born 1906).

139. Interview of a woman, AJMP, The Oral History Collection, 596 (born 1920). This mechanism did not only apply to the functionaries but also in other professions, such as physicians. Cäcilie Friedmann (Richard's wife and medical doctor), WL, P.II.e, 1068, 48.

140. Freiberger on Richard Friedmann, February 1, 1946, ABS, 305-633-1, 322–324; and Cäcilie Friedmann, WL, P.II.e, 1068, 48.

260 NOTES TO PAGES 42–44

141. YVA, O64, 24.

142. Redlich, entry January 29, 1943, in *Zítra jedeme*, 174.

143. Robert Prochnik, letter to his trial, June 24, 1954, WStLA, Volksgerichte, Vg 41/54 gg Prochnik.

144. Rudolf Bunzel, no date, ABS, 305-633-1, 245. Boschan, who was too familiar with Haindl, was sent to Auschwitz on the Ev transport as Sonderweisung. Murmelstein, "Sonderzuweisung," February 11, 1946, ABS, 305-633-1, 138/128; and Joe Singer, WL, P.II.h, 141.

145. Statement of Jan Grauer, no date, ABS, 305-633-1, 301; betrifft Fall Dr. Kussy, Murmelstein, ABS, 305-633-1, 150; and Redlich, entry for January 7, 1944, in *Zítra jedeme*, 211.

146. For the former model, see Paul Stux, YVA, O1, 288 and Alexander Gutfeld, LBI, ME 744; for the latter, see Grabower, Vermerke, Brühl.

147. Tamara Warren, email message to author, May 21, 2013; and Frank Werner Kussy (Victor's brother), memoirs, private archive of Tamara Warren.

148. Statement of Jan Grauer, no date, ABS, 305-633-1, 301; and betrifft Fall Dr. Kussy.

149. Interrogation of Rahm, April 3, 1947, SOAL, LSP 441/47, 134; and Murmelstein's own submission, no date, ABS, 305-639-5, 55.

150. Himmler to Mussolini, October 11, 1942, in *Akten zur deutschen auswärtigen Politik: 1918—1945*, Series E, vol. 4, ed. Walter Bußmann (Göttingen: Vandenhoeck & Ruprecht, 1975), Nr. 91. See also Miroslav Kárný, "Jakov Edelsteins letzte Briefe," *Theresienstädter Studien und Dokumente* (1997): 217.

151. Otto Zucker, "Die Konstruktion und ihre Ausführung," in *Ein Industriebau von der Fundierung bis zur Vollendung* (Berlin: Bauwelt-Verlag, 1927), 58–119.

152. Bondy, *"Elder of the Jews"*, 99.

153. Among others, Erich Simon, "Theresienstadt als autarkes Stadtwesen," WL, P.III.h, 894.

154. Loesten, "Aus der Hoelle Minsk," LBI, ch. 5.

155. Minutes of the Council of Elders from winter 1944/1945, NA, KT OVS; and Adler, *Theresienstadt*, 253.

156. Loesten, "Aus der Hoelle Minsk," LBI, ch. 5.

157. Grabower papers, Brühl; and Loesten, "Aus der Hoelle Minsk," LBI, ch. 10. On Loewenstein, see Tom Lampert, "Ein seltener Gerechtigkeitssinn," in *Ein einziges Leben*, ed. T. Lampert (Munich: dtv, 2003), 114–193.

158. Report Fritz und Albert Nothmann, YIVO, Czechoslovakia, 1.11.

159. Memo from Council of Elders (about Verrechnungswesen), June, 26, 1944, AJMP, Terezín, box 7, file 48; and Erna Goldschmidt to Ilse Redlich (Levy's secretary to his sister), December 13, 1945, YVA, O33, 76.

160. Prochnik, letter to his trial, June 24, 1954, WStLA, Volksgerichte, Vg 41/54 gg Prochnik.

161. Circulars of the Central Secretariat, YVA, O64, 24; and Erna Goldschmidt to Ilse Redlich, YVA.

162. Kárný, "Komunistická organizace," NA, 36.

NOTES TO PAGES 42–44   261

163. Zdeněk Lederer, *Ghetto Theresienstadt* (London: E. Goldston, 1953), 65.

164. Edestein to Council of Elders, January 4, 1943, AJMP, T, 49.

165. Murmelstein decided on many of the normal applications; see Danish Jewish Museum (hereafter JDK), uncataloged (Space Management applications).

166. Goldscheiderová used to be the head of the Ubikationskanzlei (Office of Accommodation) in the Hamburg Barracks. "Ein Jahr Hamburger Kaserne," BTA, 124. Interestingly, she said little about her work in her memoir, Emma Fuchs, *My Kaleidoscope* (self-published, 1974); reissued as *My Kaleidoscope: Surviving the Holocaust*, ed. Shari J. Ryan (Seattle: Booktrope Editions, 2014).

167. "Gliederung Grabower," February 7, 1945, YVA, O64, 24, and YVA, O64, 29 (the file is actually started as Internal Administration and ends with notes from Building Administration only).

168. Some of the Edelsteins' closest collaborators worked in Central Labor, in addition to Österreicher and Weinberger, also Harald (Harry) Tressler or Edith Ornstein.

169. Murmelstein extended the labor age in the last period of the ghetto because there was not enough manpower.

170. *Working in a Trap: AZ Album*, ed. Margalit Shlain (Givat Haim Ihud: Beit Terezin, 2008).

171. See Redlich, early entries, in *Zítra jedeme*.

172. Redlich, various entries in *Zítra jedeme*; and "Chronik der r.k. Gemeinde Theresienstadt," Bishopric Archive Vienna (hereafter DAW), entry for June 21, 1943, Erzbischöfliche Hilfsstelle für nichtarische Katholiken, box 1. Annemarie Fenzl of the DAW has been preparing an edition of the Chronicle.

173. Ruth Klüger, *weiter leben: Eine Jugend* (Göttingen: Wallstein, 1992), 88–90.

174. Trunk, *Łódź*, 302; and Bender, *Jews of Białystok*, 148–149.

175. Activity report of the Technical Department, August 1944, YVA, O64, 41.

176. See his letter to Nathan Schwalb, July 12, 1943, Hagannah Archive (hereafter HAG), 114.53, Efrain Dekel. Adler erroneously claimed Schliesser was a Czecho-Jew (*Theresienstadt*, 252).

177. Markéta Berlová-Poláčková's submission to the Freiberger investigations, February 5, 1946, ABS, 305-633-1, 303.

178. Merzbach aided Vogel in liquidating the ghetto over the summer of 1945.

179. Julius Taussig interview, APT.

180. Jiří Borský, BTA, 66; and Josef Bor, *Opuštěná Panenka* (Prague: Státní nakladatelství politické literatury, 1961), second part.

181. Max Sever, "Die technischen Einrichtungen Theresienstadts," *Theresienstädter Studien und Dokumente* (1999): 204–216; and Hans Sladký, "Episoden aus dem Leben eines Überlebenden," *Theresienstädter Studien und Dokumente* (1998): 257–276; and Lederer, *Ghetto Theresienstadt*, 69–70.

182. Tagesbefehl, June 3, 1943, 338.

183. Stux, YVA, O64, 44. The Technical Department worked so well that when in May 1945 the SS left Theresienstadt and cut all phone connections, the ghetto technicians connected the phone into their department, hence having the only telephone connection with the outside.

262   NOTES TO PAGES 46–49

184. Willy Mahler, entry for May 10, 1944, APT, A, 5704; Ada Levy, WL, P.111 h, 16; and Jacob Plaut, YVA, M1E, 1942.

185. Stux, YVA, O1, 288.

186. Many of the workers were Czecho-Jews; Grünberger and Sever were Zionists. See also Julius Grünberger's birthday album, made by his team, archive of Petr Hahn (bequeathed by his father, ing. Bedřich Hahn).

187. Adler claimed that Grünberger was head of the department until summer 1943 (*Theresienstadt*, 252). However, Murmelstein noted that he was the head of the Technical Department from his arrival until at least December 1943 or October 1944: his own statements, no date, ABS, 305-633-1, 55/66.

188. Prochnik, letter to his trial, June 24, 1954, WStLA, Volksgerichte, Vg 41/54 gg Prochnik.

189. YVA, O1, 288; see also Stux and Süß to Löwenherz, May 10 and 11, 1945, The Central Archives for the History of the Jewish People (hereafter CAHJP), A/W, 4035.

190. Zucker to Nathan Schwalb, July 12, 1943, HAG, 114.53, Efrain Dekel.

191. Sladký, "Erinnerungen," 262; interview #5, December 3, 1990, AJMP; and outline organization by Holzer, AJMP, T, 39. Adler, *Theresienstadt*, 217 and 252, and Bondy, *"Elder of the Jews"*, 264, erroneously claimed Vogel was a Communist. Vogel was left-leaning and only became Communist after the war. He had no contact with the Communist Party in Terezín.

192. On Health Services, see chapter 4.

193. Erich Munk to Jakov Edelstein, January 23, 1944, in "Edelsteins letzte Briefe," 226; Adolph Metz's testimony in YVA, O33, 3257 and second part (anonymous) in Stadtarchiv Mannheim, NL Paul Eppstein, Zug. 27/2002 Nr. 30; and reparation files Metz, Entschädigungsbehörde Berlin.

194. YVA, O64, 24.

195. The Recreation department is discussed in chapter 5.

196. Erich Weiner on the history of the Recreation, YVA, O64, 65; and Adler, *Theresienstadt*, 588.

197. Kárný, "Komunistická organizace," NA, 44–46.

198. YVA, O64, 24.

199. For histories of the ghetto police, see Calel Perechodnik, *Am I a Murderer? Testament of a Jewish Ghetto Policeman*, ed. Frank Fox (Boulder, Colo., 1996); Isaiah Trunk, *Judenrat: The Jewish Councils in Eastern Europe under Nazi Occupation* (New York: Macmillan, 1972), 475–527; Aharon Weiss, "The Relations between the Judenrat and the Jewish Police," in *Patterns of Jewish Leadership in Nazi Europe 1933–1945: Proceedings of the Third Yad Vashem International Historical Conference*, ed. Yisrael Gutman and Cynthia J. Haft (Jerusalem, 1979), 201–217, 228–233; and Havi Ben-Sasson, "Ghettos: Ghetto Police," in *YIVO Encyclopedia of Jews in Eastern Europe (2010)*, accessed September 12, 2016, http://www.yivoencyclopedia.org/article.aspx/Ghettos/Ghetto_Police; for a differentiated and recent overview, see Katarzyna Person, *Policjanci* (Warsaw: Żydowski Instytut Historyczny, 2018).

200. The arrest and trial were very probably backed by the headquarters; Burger did not get along with Loewenstein. Ironically, his dismissal and arrest probably saved Loewenstein's life: after his release in January 1944, he was isolated and never

NOTES TO PAGES 46–49   263

became a functionary again. For a comparable case in Bialystok, see Bender, *Jews of Białystok*, 134–136.

201. YVA, O7, 237.

202. YVA, O64, 24; and Murmelstein, Lanzmann Interview, 3174.

203. Martha Mosse's diary, entry for November 21, 1944, WL, P.III.h, 1088; Heinrich Klang (?), "Denkschrift ang (?), entry for November 21, 1944, 28–233; and Havi Ben-Sasson, "Ghettos: Ghetto Police," in *YIVO Encyclopedia of Jews in Eastern Europe* (YIVO Institute for Jewish Research, 2010), http://www.yivoencyclopedia.org/article.aspx/Ghettos/Ghetto_Police.

204. Svenja Bethke, "Crime and Punishment in Emergency Situations: The Jewish Ghetto Courts in Lodz, Warsaw and Vilna in World War II—A Comparative Study," *Dapim* 28 (Autumn 2014): 173–189.

205. Erna Goldschmidt to Ilse Redlich, December 13, 1945, YVA, O33, 76.

206. At his trial, Prochnik said that the ghetto was run by eight to twelve departmental heads rather than by the Elder of the Jews or the Jewish Council: Prochnik, letter to his trial, June 24, 1954, WStLA, Volksgerichte, Vg 41/54 gg Prochnik.

207. Edith Ornstein, "Iluse Terezína," 1945, YVA, O7, 291; and quarterly reports of the Technical Department YVA, O64, 41.

208. Noack-Mosse, entry for February 26, 1945; and statement by Eduard Kurz, ABS, 305-639-5, 202.

209. An overview of the copy runs for the many forms is listed in AJMP, T, 55.

210. Adler, *Verheimlichte Wahrheit*, 102–103.

211. Erich Munk, "Rundschreiben an die Zimmerältesten," *Šalom na pátek* [Shalom for Friday, pun on the popular Czech periodical *Ahoj na sobotu*], no. 9, July 2, 1943, YVA, O64, 64.

212. Neuordnung der Gebäudeleitung, November 11, 1944; circular, July 30, 1943, YVA, O64, 29. Adler, *Theresienstadt*, 420 erroneously gives 162 houses.

213. Diary of Arnošt Klein, House Elder in Q 314/14 Badhausgasse, entry for March 19, 1944, AJMP, T, 324; and "Anweisung für den Zimmerältesten," February 15, 1942, and "Instruktionen," end of December 1942, YVA, O64, 29.

214. Diary of Arnošt Klein, AJMP, T, 324; and Pedde, APT, A, 10549. Many of those who survived were house elders.

215. Petition of House Elders to the administration, July 9, 1944, AJMP, T, 51.

216. This is how Edelstein could conceal his numbers: the block elder of the Dresden barracks reported a head count fifty-five people higher than it really was.

217. Redlich, entry for September 29 and 30, 1942, in *Zítra jedeme*.

218. The inventor of aspirin, Arthur Eichengrün, was prominent: Anna Hyndráková, Helena Krejčová, and Jana Svobodová, eds., *Prominenti v ghettu Terezín, 1942–1945* (Prague: Ústav pro soudobé dějiny AV ČR, 1996), 216f.

219. Hyndráková et al., *Prominenti v ghettu Terezín*, 76, 78, give 225 names.

220. Interview of a woman, May 3, 1996, AJMP, The Oral History Collection, 557 (born 1911).

221. Thomas Kurrer, ed., *K.Z.Theresienstadt April 1944–Mai 1945: Briefe und Aufzeichnungen von Else Gräfin v. Schlitz, gen. v. Goertz und Freifrau v. Wrisberg* (Schondorf: Edition Blaes, 2016), 8.

264 NOTES TO PAGES 51–52

222. Martha Mosse's diary, entry for March 15, 1945, WL, P.III.h, 1088.
223. Ruth Bondy, "Prominent auf Widerruf," *Theresienstädter Studien und Dokumente* (1995): 136–154, 137. Parts of the applications survived at two places: Federal Commissioner for the Stasi Archives (hereafter BStU), MfS HA IX/11, AV 11/82, and BTA, 265.
224. Ruth Bondy, "Prominent auf Widerruf," *Theresienstädter Studien und Dokumente* (1995): 141–142, 152.
225. Meyer, "Altersghetto," 135; and Manfred Fackenheim, LBI, AR 1281. Beate Meyer states that it was the SS who made the Reich Association functionaries prominent (because the more important among them were category A), but the sources are not conclusive. The surviving functionaries, often blamed for "collaboration," had no interest in letting the public know that they received better treatment on their own initiative.
226. Anna Hájková, "Die fabelhaften Jungs aus Theresienstadt: Junge tschechische Männer als dominante soziale Elite im Theresienstädter Ghetto," *Beiträge zur Geschichte des Nationalsozialismus* 25 (2009): 116–135.
227. None of the people of the Stab or others close to Edelstein's coworkers were prominent.
228. Statement of Hilda Hahnová, February 9, 1946, ABS, Murmelstein investigations, 305-639-5, 207.
229. Goldschmidt's reparation file, State archive Hamburg (hereafter StAH), 351–411, 25969.
230. Leo Baeck, "A People Stands Before Its God," in *We Survived: The Stories of Fourteen of the Hidden and the Hunted of Nazi Germany*, ed. E. H. Boehm (New Haven, Conn.: Yale University Press, 1949), 284–298. On difficulties with Boehm's interview of Baeck, see Fritz Backhaus and Martin Liepach, "Leo Baecks Manuskript über die 'Rechtsstellung der Juden in Europa': Neue Funde und ungeklärte Fragen," *Zeitschrift für Geschichtswissenschaft* 50 (January 2002): 55–71, 67.
231. Meyer, *Tödliche Gratwanderung*; and Hyndráková et al., *Prominenti v ghettu Terezín*, 84, 125–126, 206–207. See also Kurt Wehle interview, May 25, 1995, VHA, 2859.
232. Dora Czapski, born in 1882 in Breslau, had a transport number close to Baeck's: Murmelstein, Lanzmann Interview, 3172; and Hyndráková et al., *Prominenti v ghettu Terezín*, 215. Baeck never mentioned Czapski: "A People Stands Before Its God," 290.
233. Bavarian Jewish Community to the Bavarian Reparation Office, December 23, 1954, Bavarian Main State Archive, LEA 8575. Thanks to Max Strnad.
234. Baeck, "A People Stands Before Its God," 291.
235. Bedřiška Feldmannová came from Prostějov and died in June 1942. Růžena Mandlová came from Olomouc and died in September 1942.
236. Elisa Sternová, born in 1866, died March 30, 1944. Nelly Sternová signed both of the death certificates as the treating physician.
237. Anna Fischerová, born May 31, 1867, was deported from Brno.
238. We know Baeck was in touch with them because other inmates mentioned these women as Baeck's relatives.

NOTES TO PAGES 51–52   265

239. Dorothea and Eva Sternová were deported on the Et transport; for Dorothea see also Baeck, "A People Stands Before Its God," 295. On Nelly Sternová, see Edith Kramer Freund, LBI, ME 283b; on Ruth Baecková, see George Korper's (Ruth's widower) interview on March 26, 2007, UMD OHA; see also George Korper to author, June 12, 2011.

240. For the former, see Baeck, "A People Stands Before Its God," 291; taken over in Bondy, *"Elder of the Jews"*, 373; Avraham Barkai, "Von Berlin nach Theresienstadt: Zur politischen Biographie von Leo Baeck 1933–1945," in *Hoffnung und Untergang: Studien zur deutsch-jüdischen Geschichte des 19. und 20. Jahrhunderts*, ed. Avraham Barkai (Hamburg: Christians, 1998), 141–166, 162; Leonard Baker, *Days of Sorrow and of Pain: Leo Baeck and the Berlin Jews* (New York: Macmillan, 1978), 286; and Fritz Backhaus, "Ein Experiment des Willen zum Bösen—Überleben in Theresienstadt," in *Leo Baeck 1873–1956: Aus dem Stamme von Rabbinern*, ed. Fritz Backhaus and Georg Heuberger (Frankfurt/Main: Jüdischer Verlag, 2001), 115. For the latter, see Murmelstein, Lanzmann Interview, 3172.

241. Werner Neufliess, "Erinnerungen," Lochamei Haghettaot (hereafter LHG), 1190.

242. Murmelstein, Lanzmann Interview, 3172; and Baeck, "A People Stands Before Its God," 291.

243. Interview of a man, February 2, 1992, AJMP, Vzpomínky, 109 (born 1917).

244. A list of his lectures is in Elena Makarova, Sergei Makarov, and Viktor Kuperman, *University over the Abyss: The Story behind 520 Lecturers and 2,430 Lectures in KZ Theresienstadt 1942–1944* (Jerusalem: Verba, 2004), 188–190; see also Backhaus, "Ein Experiment," 118; and Philipp Manes, *Als ob's ein Leben wär: Tatsachenbericht Theresienstadt 1942–1944*, ed. Ben Barkow and Klaus Leist (Berlin: Ullstein, 2004), 147, 196, 310.

245. Manes, *Als ob's ein Leben wär*, 196.

246. Vítězslav Braun's diary, entry for January 20, 1944, APT, A, 476.

247. On the Catholics in Theresienstadt, see Jana Leichsenring, "Die katholische Gemeinde in Theresienstadt und die Berliner Katholiken," *Theresienstädter Studien und Dokumente* (2004): 178–222.

248. Interview of a woman, March 20, June 26, July 20, and August 26, 1992, AJMP, The Oral History Collection, 113 (born 1921).

249. "Chronik der r.k. Gemeinde Theresienstadt," DAW, entry for August 5, 1943.

250. "Chronik der r.k. Gemeinde Theresienstadt," DAW, entry for March 5, 1944; and Jana Leichsenring, "Die katholische Gemeinde in Theresienstadt und die Berliner Katholiken," *Theresienstädter Studien und Dokumente* (2004): 183.

251. Loesten, "Aus der Hoelle Minsk," LBI, ch. 5; and Karel Fleischmann, "Zápas krabů," AJMP.

252. Barkai, "Von Berlin nach Theresienstadt," 162; interrogation of Rudolf Freiberger, February 1, 1946, ABS, 305-633-1, 322–324.

253. Barkai, "Von Berlin nach Theresienstadt," 153, 162–163.

254. Willy Groag interview, September 15, 1995, AJMP, Vzpomínky, 82; and Loesten, "Aus der Hoelle Minsk," LBI, ch. 4.

266   NOTES TO PAGES 54–56

255. See the minutes from the meetings, NA Prague, KT OVS, inv. no. 64, box 45, files 27 and 29.

256. Loesten, "Aus der Hoelle Minsk," LBI, ch. 4; diary of Martha Mosse, entry for September 22, 1944, WL, P.III.h, 1088; and Redlich, entry for June 12, 1943, in *Zítra jedeme*, 194.

257. Willy Groag and Elisabeth Freifrau von Stengel are such an example. Willy Groag interview, AJMP; and Elisabeth von Stengel, "Aufklärung in Theresienstadt," YVA, O64, 1/III.

258. Barkai, "Von Berlin nach Theresienstadt," 143.

259. Meyer, "Altersghetto"; Loesten, "Aus der Hoelle Minsk," LBI, ch. 5; and Murmelstein, Lanzmann Interview, 3172, 3174, 3184.

260. Interview of Rudolf and Eva Bunzel, 1970s, Leonard and Edith Ehrlich Collection, USHMM, RG.50.862.0002; in thinking about Baeck's role in Theresienstadt, it is useful to apply Pierre Bourdieu's concept of the prophet: "Legitimation and Structured Interests in Weber's Sociology of Religion," in *Max Weber: Rationality, and Modernity*, ed. Scott Lash and Sam Whimster (London: Allen and Unwin, 1987), 119–136.

261. On Baeck's knowledge of how to play the social field, see Barkai, "Von Berlin nach Theresienstadt," 149.

262. Bourdieu, "Legitimation and Structured Interests," 124.

263. Loesten, "Aus der Hoelle Minsk," LBI; Willy Groag interview, AJMP; and Heinrich Liebrecht, *Nicht mitzuhassen, mitzulieben bin ich da: Mein Weg durch die Hölle des Dritten Reiches* (Freiburg im Breisgau: Herder, 1990). See also his play "Requiem: Ein Schauspiel aus dunkler Zeit," in LBI, AR 5215.

264. Rabinovici, *Instanzen der Ohnmacht*, 374.

265. Handwritten letter from Leo Baeck, June 20, 1945, ABS, 305-639-5.

266. Baeck, "A People Stands Before Its God," 292–293.

267. Hannah Arendt, *Eichmann in Jerusalem: A Report on the Banality of Evil* (New York: Penguin, 2006), 119.

268. Henryk Świebocki, *Widerstand* (Oświęcim: Verlag des Staatlichen Museums Auschwitz-Birkenau, 1999), 237–293. Thanks to Joachim Neander for this citation.

269. There is no one with the last name Grünberg.

270. Interview of a woman, AJMP, The Oral History Collection, 382 (born 1921).

271. Erich Kulka interview with Leo Holzer, no date (early 1960s), BTA, 128.

272. Holzer interview, BTA, 2. Holzer was the head of the Fire Brigade, where Lederer had worked prior to his deportation.

273. Holzer interview, BTA, 3.

274. Baeck claimed to have written a manuscript for the German resistance, but eventually scholars found out that it was written for, and on the orders of, the Gestapo. Herman Simon, "Bislang unbekannte Quellen zur Entstehungsgeschichte des Werkes 'Die Entwicklung der Rechtsstellung der Juden in Europa, vornehmlich in Deutschland,'" in *Leo Baeck 1873–1956: Aus dem Stamme von Rabbinern*, ed. Georg Heuberger and Fritz Backhaus (Frankfurt/Main: Jüdischer Verlag, 2001),

NOTES TO PAGES 54–56   267

103–110; and Fritz Backhaus and Martin Liepach, "Leo Baecks Manuskript über die 'Rechtsstellung der Juden in Europa': Neue Funde und ungeklärte Fragen," *Zeitschrift für Geschichtswissenschaft* 50, no. 1 (2002): 55–71.

275. Eric Lipman, "A trip to ghetto Theresienstadt," mid-May 1945, LBI, AR 2275. Lipman visited Theresienstadt just days after the liberation and described Baeck as a broken man.

276. Baeck also knew that Julius Grünberger did not survive. Moreover, the ghetto records were in socialist Czechoslovakia and hence inaccessible.

277. Murmelstein, "Geschichtlicher Überblick," WL, 21.

278. Fara, *Četnické vzpomínky*, 102; and Stanislav Hlaváč's testimony against Karl Rahm, SOAL, LSP 441/47, 89.

279. Benjamin Murmelstein betreff "Sonderzuweisungen," March 11, 1946, ABS 305-633-1.

280. Interrogation of Rahm, April 3, 1947, SOAL, LSP 441/47.

281. It dates from late April 1945 and is reprinted in Adler, *Theresienstadt*, 209–211.

282. Interrogation of Rahm, April 3, 1947, SOAL, LSP 441/47.

283. Tomáš Fedorovič, "Konfidenti v ghettu Terezín," *Terezínské listy* 37 (2009): 134–140, 136.

284. List for the Ev transport with Viktor Kende's handwritten remarks, APT, Kende papers, A, 7854.

285. Statement of Heřman Weiss, February 15, 1946, ABS, 305-633-1, 224; see also Alice Steinerová, October 24, 1945, ABS, 305-633-1, 24. Hyndráková et al., *Prominenti v ghettu Terezín*, 49 erroneously interpreted these statements at face value and marked all the people mentioned as informers.

286. For instance, Murmelstein accused Alfred Cierer of being an informer. Murmelstein's list of the SS men, no date, ABS, 305-633-1, p. 59; Murmelstein, *Eichmanns Musterghetto*, 108; and Hyndráková et al., *Prominenti v ghettu Terezín*, 88. See also Ausreihungsanträge, YVA, O64, 11. Jakov Tsur (né Kurt Cierer), email to author, February 10, 2002, and various conversations.

287. Statement of Ljubow Sachs, October 28, 1950, State Archive Bremen (StAB), 4, 66, denazification file of Wihelm Parchmann. Thanks to Günther Rohdenburg for sending me materials on Meyerhoff.

288. Max Markreich, "Geschichte der Juden in Bremen und Umgebung" (unpublished manuscript), 284n10, personal archive of Günther Rohdenburg.

289. Another probable informer, Ursula Lewin of Berlin, was suggested by the SS, and the documentation survived: notation of Kurt Levy about Lewin's nomination by Bergel, May 23, 1944, BStU, MfS HA IX 11, AV 11 82.

290. Axel Feuss, ed., *Das Theresienstadt-Konvolut* (Hamburg: Dölling und Galitz, 2002), 51. The notations on her file in the Registration Office of Bremen show involvement of the Ministry of Interior and the Reichssippenamt (Reich Kinship Office) debating her application to be recognized as *Mischling*, StAB 4, 82/1-1/986. See also her entry in the 1939 German minority census indicating her as "half Jew," www. mappingthelives.com.

268 NOTES TO PAGES 60–62

291. Murmelstein on Sonderweisung, 11.2.46, ABS, 305-633-1, p. 138; list of *Weisungen* (presumably, the title page is missing), YVA, O64, 46; and list for the Ev transport with Viktor Kende's handwritten remarks, Kende papers, APT.

292. Adler, *Theresienstadt*, 70.

293. Redlich, entries for February 2 and 3, 1943, in *Zítra jedeme*, 175.

294. Arnold Munter to the Bezirkskommission für die Verleihung der Medaille für Kämpfer gegen den Faschismus about beating up a Kapo from a camp at Zeiß-Jena, January 15, 1959, Landesarchiv Berlin (hereafter LAB), C Rep 118-01, 30958.

295. Jadwiga Weinbaumová, ABS, 305-633-1; SÚMV, 302-198-5/21 and 302-204-45/2.

296. Jadwiga Weinbaumová, ABS, 305-633-1, Resi Weglein, *Als Krankenschwester im KZ Theresienstadt: Erinnerungen einer Ulmer Jüdin* (Tübingen: Silberburg, 1988), 101–102.

297. Note from Prague police, February 13, 1946, ABS, 305-633-1, p. 339; Brandenburger and Davis to Hoerner Bank, June 17, 1998, International Tracing Service (hereafter ITS), file on Jenny Watanabe, 109896205.

298. Doris Tausendfreund, *Erzwungener Verrat: Jüdische "Greifer" im Dienst der Gestapo 1943–1945* (Berlin: Metropol, 2006).

299. Eric Friedler, Barbara Siebert, and Andreas Kilian, *Zeugen aus der Todeszone: Das jüdische Sonderkommando in Auschwitz* (Lüneburg: zu Klampen!, 2002).

300. Person, *Policjanti*.

301. Benjamin Frommer, "The Jewish Department of the Prague Police: What Its Czech Directors Did during the War, and How They Escaped Justice Afterwards" (paper presented at the Association for Slavic, East European, and Eurasian Studies, New Orleans, November 15–18, 2012).

302. Dan Diner, "Historisches Verstehen und Gegenrationalität: Der Judenrat als erkenntnistheoretische Warte," in *Zivilisation und Barbarei: Die widersprüchlichen Potentiale der Moderne*, ed. Frank Bajohr, Werner Johe, and Uwe Lohalm (Hamburg: Christians, 1991), 307–321; Rabinovici, *Instanzen der Ohnmacht*; and Meyer, *Tödliche Gratwanderung*.

303. Similarly, functionaries who did survive, such as Murmelstein, always explain the events as part of a logical whole. They could not understand that what was for them a matter of life and death was often decided arbitrarily by Eichmann's department.

304. This feeling is partly due to the fact that they were both murdered by the Nazis, which the prisoners interpreted as a kind of resistance.

305. Philip Friedman, *Roads to Extinction: Essays on the Holocaust* (New York: Jewish Publication Society of America, 1980), chs. 12 and 13.

Chapter 2

1. Mirko Tůma, *Ghetto našich dnů* (Prague: Jaroslav Salivar, 1946), 13.

2. Hermann Strauß, "Aufzeichnungen aus dem Ghetto Theresienstadt," in *Der Arzt Hermann Strauß 1868–1944: Autobiographische Notizen und Aufzeichnungen aus dem Ghetto Theresienstadt*, ed. Harro Jenß and Peter Reinicke (Berlin: Hentrich &

NOTES TO PAGES 60–62   269

Hentrich, 2014), 112–139, 113; Viktor Kosák, "Vzpomínky našeho táty" (1982), archive of Michal Kosák (thanks to Michal for the copy); Philipp Manes, *Als ob's ein Leben wär: Tatsachenbericht Theresienstadt 1942–1944*, ed. Klaus Leist and Ben Barkow (Berlin: Ullstein, 2005), 36–46; and Diary of Paul Scheurenberg, "Traurige Erlebnisse in der Nazi Hölle Deutschland," entry for June 1943 (no exact date), Centrum Judaicum (hereafter CJA), 6.14, 2.

3. I use here he soft concept of citizenship, rather than the hard one; the Eleventh Decree to the Reich Citizenship Law, which stripped Jews of their citizenship when they were deported to the East, did not apply here because Terezín was in the territory of Greater Germany. The deportees also had to sign the "Declaration of Assets" for the chief of finance. The IDs of Czech Jews were stamped *ghettoisiert* (ghettoized), and they were marked as deported in the police registration files.

4. Alfred Gottwaldt and Diana Schulle, *Die Judendeportationen aus dem Deutschen Reich, 1941–1945: Eine kommentierte Chronologie* (Wiesbaden: Marixverlag, 2005).

5. The logic of the order followed the first five transports from Prague and Brno to Lodz and Minsk ghetto in October and November 1941 (A–E).

6. Susanne Fall, *Terezín, ráj mezi lágry* (Prague: Revolver Revue, 2015), 20–29 passim.

7. Max Berger; testimony of Eva Noack Mosse, YVA, O33, 986; Scheurenberg, entry for June 1943, CJA; and Heinrich Scholz's submission to Rahm's trial, SOAL.

8. On the "unimaginable chaos" at the arrival location, see Julius Taussig interview, APT; and Evžen Foltýn, 1966, APT, Vzpomínky, 86.

9. Adolphe Metz, YVA, O33, 3257.

10. Diary of Simon Magnus, entry for ca. April 7, 1944, Westerbork Memorial, RA 995. I thank Guido Abuys for sending me a copy.

11. Diary of Isaac Cohen, entry for September 8, 1944, YVA, O33, 1222.

12. Gabriel Dagan (né Pavel Fischl), "Deník Pavla Bondyho," BTA, 105.

13. Elena Bork interview, July 7, 1993, and November 20, 1998, Forschungsstelle für Zeitgeschichte, Werkstatt der Erinnerung (hereafter FZH/WdE), 112.

14. Paul Stux stated that the usable space included 156,485 square meters (1,684,390 square feet) without the attics and 210,541 square meters (2,266,244 square feet) with them. "Nutzfläche Theresienstadt," September 1942, YVA, O64, 44.

15. Dora Philippson, "Bericht über die Deportation und das Überleben in Theresienstadt 1942 bis 1945" (May 1945), in *Frauenleben im NS-Alltag*, ed. Annette Kuhn (Pfaffenweiler: Centaurus, 1994), 303–320; and testimony of Edmund Hadra, 1945, LBI, AR 1249, 2.

16. David Boder, interview with Friedrich Schläfrig, August 23, 1946, accessed December 28, 2018, http://voices.iit.edu/interview?doc=schlaefrigF&display=schlaefrigF_de.

17. Rosa Salomon, LBI, ME 1083.

18. Philippson, "Bericht über die Deportation."

19. "Der Theresienstädter Hechalutz: Aus den Erinnerungen von Berl Herškovič," *Theresienstädter Studien und Dokumente* (2000): 151–163, 157.

20. Viktor Kosák to friends, "Friends are one's best luck," January 10, 1943, copied in Kosák, "Vzpomínky našeho táty."

270 NOTES TO PAGES 64–68

21. On this role of the administration (assessing "human material" and its worth), see Otto Zucker, "Theresienstadt 1941–1943," *Theresienstädter Studien und Dokumente* (1995): 271–303.

22. Diary of Margarete Pedde, entry for September 14, 1942, APT, A, 10549; on a similar note, see Manfred Strassburger, YVA, O33, 988.

23. Gertruda Sekaninová Čakrtová interview, ca. July 24, 1984, personal archive of Martin Čakrt; I thank Martin for digitizing the record and letting me view it.

24. For the former, see testimony of Edmund Hadra, LBI; for the latter, see Julius Taussig interview, APT. On suicides in Terezín in general, see "Selbstmorde in Theresienstadt 24.11.1941–31.12.1943," YVA, O64, 51a.

25. For discussion of suicide, see chapter 4.

26. Sven Meyer and Corrie Meyer, "Onze belevenissen tijdens de jodenvervolgingen in den tweeden wereldoorlog," 1945, Netherlands Institute for War Documentation (hereafter NIOD), 244, 920; Elsa Bernstein, *Das Leben als Drama: Erinnerungen an Theresienstadt*, ed. Rita Bake and Birgit Kiupel (Dortmund: Edition Ebersbach, 1999), 88; and Viktor Kosák to friends, "Friends are one's best luck," January 10, 1943.

27. Diary of Arnošt Klein, first entry for May 1942, AJMP.

28. František Kollman, "Vzpomínky na březen 1939-květen 1945," 1973, NA, Svaz protifašistických bojovníků (hereafter SPB), 1809.

29. Nava Shan, August 2, 1965, Institute for Contemporary History, Oral History Division (hereafter ICJ OHD), 34, 13.

30. The diaries of Margarete Pedde, Camilla Hirsch, and Arnošt Klein, who worked as house elders, as well as sample evidence, demonstrate that the roommates and newcomers in small houses were nearly always elderly or "foreign."

31. Louis Salomon, 1945, YVA, O33, 1560.

32. Diary of Richard Ehrlich, November 14, 1943, WL, P.II.h, 306; and testimony of Manfred Strassburger, YVA.

33. Rose Scooler, "Ode to my bed in Theresienstadt. My bed—my castle," Wiener Collection Tel Aviv (hereafter WL TAU), 586; and Ann Lewis's papers.

34. Manfred Strassburger, YVA; and diary of Camilla Hirsch, entry for November 23, 1942.

35. Isaiah Trunk, *Łódź Ghetto: A History* (Bloomington: Indiana University Press, 2006), 300, when writing that "sexual modesty weakened," provides a standard example of not paying attention to new behavioral rules among the prisoners.

36. Philippson, "Bericht über die Deportation"; Friedrich Schläfrig interview, August 23, 1946.

37. Jiří Borský, BTA, 66.

38. Susanne Fall, *Terezín, ráj mezi lágry* (Prague: Revolver Revue, 2015), 22; and Roubíčková, March 31, 1943, AITI.

39. Resi Weglein, *Als Krankenschwester im KZ Theresienstadt: Erinnerungen einer Ulmer Jüdin* (Tübingen: Silberburg, 1988), 78.

40. Philippson, "Bericht über die Deportation"; testimony of Edmund Hadra, LBI; and testimony of Louis Salomon, YVA, O33, 1560. Eighty-one-year-old Marta Blairon

NOTES TO PAGES 64–68   271

arrived in 1943 and lived the first four months in an attic. Opfer des Faschismus application (hereafter OdF), October 16, 1945, CJA, 4.1, 163.

41. Ruth Damwerth, *Arnold Munter: Der Jahrhundertzeuge* (Berlin: Neues Leben, 1994), 99, 101, 109, 117.

42. Bedřich Hoffenreich, APT, Sbírka vzpomínek, 1095.

43. Diary of Arnošt Klein, entry for August 8, 1942, AJMP.

44. Petr Erben, *Po vlastních stopách* (Prague: Kalina, 2003); and Jiří Kosta, *Život mezi úzkostí a nadějí* (Prague: Paseka, 2002), 75.

45. Frances Solar-Epstein, "Roundtrip," 1970s, Helen Epstein's archive; Ruth Šmolková interview, November 26, 1993, AJMP, The Oral History Collection, 241; letters of Hana Rutarová, APT, A, 8652.

46. Hans Gaertner interview, May 9, 2003, FZH/WdE, 863; Charlotta Verešová-Weinstein, "Zápisky z ghetta," 1944, BTA, 174; Friedrich Feldmar (pseudonym) interview, ca. 1995, Milan Šimečka Foundation, Slovak Yale Fortunoff interviews (hereafter NMŠ), 48.

47. Interrogation of Rudolf Freiberger, February 1, 1946, ABS, 305-633-1, 322–324.

48. Leopold Neuhaus to Salomon Wolf, May 6, 1946, and Leopold Neuhaus to Anna von Brümmer, December 14, 1945, Das Zentralarchiv zur Erforschung der Geschichte der Juden in Deutschland, B.1/13 A.261. Thanks to Alon Tauber for sending me copies.

49. Šimon Kolsky, né Kopolovič (pseudonym), to the author, January 16, 2009, Haifa; and Sam Berger, *Die unvergeßlichen sechseinhalb Jahre meines Lebens* (Frankfurt/Main: R. G. Fischer, 1985), 58–62.

50. Manes, 136.

51. Norbert Buchsbaum, *Fotograaf zonder Camera* (Amsterdam: Bataafsche Leeuw, 1991), 97–100.

52. Testimony of Ida Süß, November 8, 1946, WStLA, Volksgericht Wien, Vr 1814/56 gegen Rudolf Haindl.

53. *Working in a Trap: AZ Album*, ed. Margalit Shlain (Givat Haim Ihud: Beit Terezin, 2008), 11–13, 25; and to some degree also Richard Feder, *Židovská tragedie: Dějství poslední* (Kolín: Lusk, 1947), 67.

54. Melissa Feinberg, *Elusive Equality: Gender, Citizenship, and the Limits of Democracy in Czechoslovakia, 1918–1950* (Pittsburgh: University of Pittsburgh Press, 2006).

55. Diary of Martha Mosse, November 20, 1944.

56. Diary of Camilla Hirsch, entry for December 14, 1942, and January 27, 1943 (the quote), BTA, not yet cataloged.

57. Eric Hobsbawm, "Introduction: Inventing Traditions," in *The Invention of Tradition*, ed. Eric Hobsbawm and Terence Ranger (Cambridge, UK: Cambridge University Press, 1983), 1–14.

58. Diary of Hana Platovská, entry for March 17, 1944, APT, A, 5248; and Feder, *Židovská tragedie*, 49–50.

59. Menasche Mautner, YVA, O1, 163.

60. Grete Treitel, June 4, 1945, CAHJP, P231, 38; Feder, *Židovská tragedie*, 41; interview of a man, no date, AJMP, The Oral History Collection, 78 (born 1929).

272 NOTES TO PAGES 70–74

61. Cäcilie Friedmann, WL, P.II.e, 1068.
62. Rogers Brubaker and Frederick Cooper, "Beyond Identity," *Theory and Society* 29, no. 1 (2000): 1–47.
63. Diary of Arnošt Klein, entry for November 11, 1942, AJMP.
64. Diary of Arnošt Klein, entry for January 12, 1943, AJMP; and Loewenstein, ch. 6. The perpetrator committed suicide the next day.
65. On the Jews from the Netherlands in Terezín, see Anna Hájková, "Poor Devils of the Camps: Dutch Jews in the Terezín Ghetto, 1943–1945," *Yad Vashem Studies* 43, no. 1 (2015): 77–111.
66. It seems that German Jewish who intermarried integrated better. The reproaches of the veteran prisoners were voiced only against the Czech who intermarried. Testimonies of the German intermarried show the ghetto in much greater detail. See also diary of Eva Noack Mosse, WL TAU; reparation file of Max Munk, Municipal Archive Minden; and Arthur Greifzu interview, August 20, 1984, Bonn Memorial for the Victims of the National Socialism.
67. Weglein, *Als Krankenschwester im KZ Theresienstadt*, 72; and Alisa Shek, "Alisa Sheks Tagebuch (Oktober 1944–Mai 1945)," *Theresienstädter Studien und Dokumente* (1994): 169–206 (April 18, 1945), 186.
68. Grabower's sentence, glued in diary of Arnošt Klein between entries for February 10 and 12, 1945, AJMP.
69. Franz Friedmann, *Einige Zahlen über die tschechoslovakischen Juden: Ein Beitrag zur Soziologie der Judenheit* (Prague: Barissia, 1933), 16, 31.
70. Benjamin Frommer, "Czechs and Germans, Gentiles and Jews: Intermarriage in a Decade of Genocide and Ethnic Cleansing, 1938–1948," in *Intermarriage in Eastern Europe and Eurasia: Ethnic Mixing under Fascism, Communism, and Beyond*, ed. Adrianne Edgar and Benjamin Frommer (Lincoln: Nebraska University Press, 2020).
71. On the Geltunsgjuden, see Maria von der Heydt, "Wer fährt denn gerne mit dem Judenstern in der Straßenbahn? Die Ambivalenz des 'geltungsjüdischen' Alltags zwischen 1941 und 1945," in *Alltag im Holocaust: Jüdisches Leben im Großdeutschen Reich 1941–1945*, ed. Andrea Löw, Doris Bergen, and Anna Hájková (Munich: Oldenbourg, 2013), 65–80.
72. Adler, in *Theresienstadt*, speaks of thirty-one released (47); Karel Lagus and Josef Polák in *Město za mřížemi* (Prague: Naše vojsko, 1964), 351, mention five. The database mentions lists fifty-three people, but these include those arrested and released by the Prague Gestapo, as well as the transport of people with Hungarian citizenship to Bergen-Belsen in March 1944.
73. Elsa Bernstein, 62, prisoner database, Documentation Archives of Austrian Resistance (hereafter DÖW).
74. Herbert Nivelli (né Lewin), WL, P.III.h, 211.
75. Everyone else wore a star that read *Jude* or *Jood* (for Jews from the Netherlands). diary of Richard Ehrlich, entry for October 22, 1944, WL. There were actually other French Jews in Terezín, but they were not deported there from France. Hungarian Jews wore a star without text. Slovak Jews wore a plain star. Thanks to Regina Fritz and Martin Šmok, respectively, for this information.

NOTES TO PAGES 70-74   273

76. "Chronik der r.k. Gemeinde Theresienstadt," February 1943, DAW, 8.
77. See Zygmunt Bauman, "From Pilgrim to Tourist—or a Short History of Identity," in *Questions of Cultural Identity*, ed. Paul Du Gay and Stuart Hall (London: Sage, 1996), 18–36; and Ellen Badone and Sharon R. Roseman, "Approaches to the Anthropology of Pilgrimage and Tourism," in *Intersecting Journeys: The Anthropology of Pilgrimage and Tourism*, ed. E. Badone and S. Roseman (Urbana: University of Illinois Press, 2004), 1–23.
78. Erving Goffman, *Frame Analysis: An Essay on the Organization of Experience* (New York: Harper & Row, 1974).
79. Testimony of Otto Bernstein, YVA, O33, 1549.
80. Testimony of Edmund Hadra, LBI; and Manes, 115.
81. Testimony of Jiří Borský, 1970, 476, A, APT. For a similar tone, see diary of Arnošt Klein, entry for January 19, 1943, AJMP.
82. Jiří Borský, APT.
83. Manes, 135–136.
84. Hanna Pravda interview, British Library/Sound Archive (hereafter BL), C410, 35. On a similar note, see Helga Hošková-Weissová, *Zeichne, Was Du Siehst* (Göttingen: Wallstein, 2001), 72–73.
85. Testimony of Růžena Ranschburgerová, APT, A, 579.
86. Diary of Arnošt Klein, entry for January 23, 1945, AJMP.
87. Zdeněk Lederer, *Ghetto Theresienstadt* (London: E. Goldston, 1953), 54–55.
88. See Dora Lehmann, *Erinnerungen einer Altonaerin 1866-1946* (Hamburg: Dölling und Galitz, 1998); Martha Glass, *"Jeder Tag in Theresin ist ein Geschenk": Die Theresienstädter Tagebücher einer Hamburger Jüdin 1943-1945*, ed. Barbara Müller Wesemann (Hamburg: Ergebnisse, 1996).
89. See Daniel Putík, *Z nouze život, z nouze smrt? Slovenští Židé v Terezíně, Sachsenhausenu, Ravensbrücku a Bergen-Belsenu, 1944-1945* (Prague: Academia, 2018), 89–117; on the wartime events of Slovak Jews, see Nina Paulovičová, "Rescue of Jews in the Slovak State (1939–1945)" (PhD diss., University of Alberta, 2012); and Katarína Hradská, "Vorgeschichte der slowakischen Transporte nach Theresienstadt," *Theresienstädter Studien und Dokumente* (1996): 82–97.
90. See Daniel Weiser and Selma Steinerová (pseudonym) interviews, both ca. 1995–1997, NMŠ.
91. Schönová, "Dětské divadlo v Terezíně," 1945, YVA, O64, 65. For a condescending Czech view of backward Slovaks, see also testimony of Irma Lauscherová, January 30, 1966, APT, sbírka vzpomínek, 85.
92. Eva Berner (pseudonym), interview with author, Shamir, February 14, 2009.
93. On Czech stereotypes of Slovaks, see Lada Hubatová-Vacková, "Folklorisms," in *Building a State: Representation of Czechoslovakia in Art, Architecture and Design*, ed. Milena Bartlová et al. (Prague: VŠUP, 2015), 65–90.
94. Diary of Richard Ehrlich, entry for November 12, 1943, WL; and testimonies of Edmund Hadra, LBI, and Louis Salomon, YVA.
95. Miroslav Kárný's interview with Vilém Cantor, December 18, 1972, "Komunistická organizace v terezínském koncentračním táboře 1941–1945" (manuscript, 1983), NA, Kárných, ka 16, 7–10.

274 NOTES TO PAGES 77-80

96. Franz Hahn interview, May 13, June 2, 11, and 25, 1987, DÖW, Interviews, 510.

97. *Šalom na pátek*, no. 1, December 1942 (front page with the exact date missing); and Arnošt Reiser, *Útěk* (Prague: Academia, 2003).

98. On the gendered perceptions of the social elite, see Anna Hájková, "Die fabelhaften Jungs aus Theresienstadt: Junge tschechische Männer als dominante soziale Elite im Theresienstädter Ghetto," *Beiträge zur Geschichte des Nationalsozialismus* 25 (2009): 116–135.

99. *Šalom na pátek*, no. 4, 1943, YVA, O64, 64; and Irma Semecká, *Torso naděje* (Prague: Antonín Vlasák, 1946), 92. On the term, see Kerrie Holloway, "The Bright Young People of the Late 1920s: How the Great War's Armistice Influenced Those Too Young to Fight," *Journal of European Studies* 45, no. 4 (2015): 316–330.

100. Petr Lang interview, July 22, 1965, and Nava Shan interview, August 2, 1965, ICJ OHD, 34, 3; Josef Bor, *Opuštěná Panenka* (Prague: Státní nakladatelství politické literatury, 1961), second part; and tableau of Czecho-Jewish engineers and architects in the Technical department, in particular the Office for Technical Issues, archive of Martin Šmok.

101. Egon Redlich, entries for May 16, October 10, and December 20, 1942, in *Zítra jedeme*.

102. Šimon Kolsky interview, author's archive.

103. Viktor Kosák to František Reiman, January 10, 1943, private archive Michal Kosák.

104. Birthday album for Julius Grünberger, personal copy of ing, Bedřich Hahn, personal archive of Peter Hahn, Düsseldorf. Many thanks to Peter Hahn for showing me the album. See also *Working in a Trap*.

105. List of *Šalom na pátek* readers, November 26, 1943, YVA, O64, 64.

106. See Beate Meyer, *Tödliche Gratwanderung: Die Reichsvereinigung der Juden in Deutschland zwischen Hoffnung, Zwang, Selbstbehauptung und Verstrickung (1939–1945)* (Göttingen: Wallstein, 2011), 62–68, on Eppstein's background; and Eppstein correspondence 1939–41, Stadtarchiv Mannheim.

107. Trude Simonsohn interview, March 27, 1992, YVA, O3, 7317; and Redlich, entries for April 14 and 15, 1943, in *Zítra jedeme*, 186f.

108. Leni Yahil quoted Zeev Shek that there were Danish members; however, this seems to have been Shek's idealization of an international Hechalutz: Leni Yahil, *The Rescue of Danish Jewry: Test of a Democracy* (Philadelphia: Jewish Publication Society of America, 1969), 296; and Silvia Tarabini Goldbaum Fracapane, "Danish Testimonies about Theresienstadt: Experiences of Deportation and Ghetto Life" (PhD diss., Technical University Berlin, 2016), ch. 3.

109. Leo Säbel interview, January 22, 2010, author's archive.

110. Eva Fränkel, telephone interview with author, May 2001.

111. Kárný, "Komunistická organizace," NA, 13 and 56–57; and Werner Neufließ, LHG, 1190.

112. Anna Hyndráková, Raisa Machatková, and Jaroslava Milotová, eds., *Denní rozkazy Rady starších a Sdělení židovské samosprávy Terezín 1941–1945* (Prague: Sefer, 2003), passim; and Zucker, "Theresienstadt 1941–1943."

113. On food and hunger, see chapter 3.

NOTES TO PAGES 77–80   275

114. For discussion of mortality according to age, see chapter 3.
115. I took the birth years 1890, etc., as samples. I excluded those who died in the Small Fortress or were executed by the SS (four Czech men born in 1920).
116. See chapter 4.
117. Viktor Kosák to František Reiman in Prague, January 10, 1943, copied in Kosák, "Vzpomínky našeho táty."
118. Wolfgang Salus to his anonymous girlfriend, March 23, 1942, AJMP, T, Salus collection.
119. Pavel Fischl, "Deník Pavla Bondyho," entry for October 1, 1942, BTA; also Redlich, entry for May 8, 1942, in *Zítra jedeme*, 117.
120. For a discussion of the concept "already dead," see Doris Bergen, "No End in Sight? The Ongoing Challenge of Producing an Integrated History of the Holocaust," in *Years of Persecution, Years of Extermination: Saul Friedlander and the Future of Holocaust Studies*, ed. Christian Wiese and Paul Betts (London: Continuum, 2010), 289–310.
121. Trunk, *Łódź*, 304.
122. On children in Terezín, see Elena Makarova, *Pevnost nad propastí: Já, děcko bloudící? děti a učitelé v terezínském ghettu 1941–1945* (Prague: Bergman, 2009).
123. The only exception were most of the Dutch children. Anna Hájková, "Die Juden aus den Niederlanden in Theresienstadt," *Theresienstädter Studien und Dokumente* (2002): 135–201, 172–174.
124. Gertruda Sekaninová-Čakrtová interview; Irena Seidlerová interview, February 13, 1995, AJMP, The Oral History Collection, 407 and Seidlerová to the author, January 26, 2013; and Dana Kasperová, *Výchova a vzdělávání židovských dětí v protektorátu a v ghettu Terezín* (Prague: Filozofická fakulta Univerzity Karlovy, 2010).
125. Zeev Sheck, Děti (1946), YV, O7, 290; Willy Groag, "Sociální péče o mládež," 1945, Moreshet, Groag papers, C.1/5.2.
126. Gertruda Sekaninová-Čakrtová interview, private archive Martin Čakrt; and Kasperová, *Výchova a vzdělávání*.
127. Karel Berman interview, February 15, 1993, AJMP, The Oral History Collection, 170; and Eliška K. interview, June 12, 1991, AJMP, The Oral History Collection, 40 (born 1912); see also https://www.holocaust.cz/zdroje/vzpominky/pani-eliska-k-nar-1912/ (published as "Eliška K.")
128. Jiří F. interview, May 6, 1996, MMZ.
129. Irena Seidlerová interview, February 13, 1995, AJMP, The Oral History Collection, 407; Seidlerová to the author, January 26, 2013; and statement of Miroslav Kárný in interview with Berl Herškovič, October 1997, Kárný papers, NA Prague, ka 3.
130. See, among others, Irma Lauscherová, "Die Kinder von Theresienstadt," in *Theresienstadt*, ed. Rudolf Iltis (Vienna: Europa-Verlag, 1968), 96–112; Nora Levin, foreword to *The Terezin Diary of Gonda Redlich*, by Egon Redlich, ed. Saul S. Friedman, trans. Laurence Kutler (Lexington: University Press of Kentucky, 1992), vii; and Caroline Stoessinger, *A Century of Wisdom: Lessons from the Life of Alice Herz-Sommer, the World's Oldest Living Holocaust Survivor* (New York: Spiegel & Grau, 2012), xvii.

276 NOTES TO PAGES 83-88

131. Groag, "Sociální péče o mládež." The statement also made clear how the self-administration differentiated between the "actual" Terezín inmates, those who arrived before winter 1945, and people from mixed marriages, who arrived in the last months.

132. Margita Kárná and Miroslav Kárný, "Terezínští dětští vězňové," Terezínské listy 22 (1994): 25-40. The number was probably a little higher than 242, because the Kárnýs did not have information on the survivors deported to Terezín from the Netherlands.

133. Prochnik, "Juden in Theresienstadt," AJMP, T, 82.

134. Evacuation transports: Terezín Prisoners Database; number of children deportees, November 1944-April 1945, in Kárná and Kárný, "Terezínští dětští vězňové," 27.

135. See, among others, Hannelore Brenner-Wonschick, Die Mädchen von Zimmer 28: Freundschaft, Hoffnung und Überleben in Theresienstadt (Munich: Droemer, 2004).

136. Feder, Židovská tragedie, 61-62; and Gertruda Sekaninová-Čakrtová interview, private archive Martin Čakrt.

137. Hans Gaertner interview, FZH/WdE. See also author's interview with Hana Kolsky on Inge Strauss, January 16, 2009. Only one boy from Hamburg was reportedly a member of the Jungvolk. Ulrike Sparr, "Paul Dieroff," accessed December 28, 2018, http://stolpersteine-hamburg.de/index.php?&MAIN_ID=7&p=47&BIO_ID=1400.

138. Diary of Marianne Elikan, entry for June, 28, 1944, in "Das Leben ist ein Kampf" Marianne Elikan—Verfolgte des Nazi-Regimes: Tagebuch, Briefe und Gedichte aus Trier und Theresienstadt, ed. Thomas Schnitzler (Trier: Wissenschaftlicher Verlag, 2008).

139. Chava Pressburger, ed., Deník mého bratra: Zápisky Petra Ginze z let 1941-1942 (Prague: Trigon, 2004); and Cordelia Edvardson, Gebranntes Kind sucht das Feuer (Munich: Hanser, 1986), 78-83.

140. Alisa Shek, "Alisa Sheks Tagebuch (Oktober 1944-Mai 1945)," Theresienstädter Studien und Dokumente (1994): 169-206 (entry for October 20, 1944, and entries for April 18 and 23, and May 4, 1945); Irena Seidlerová interview, AJMP; and Hana Kolsky (pseudonym), née Schicková, to the author.

141. Hanka Fischel-Hoffman interview, July 9, 1965, ICJ OHD, 34, 17.

142. Rogers Brubaker et al., Nationalist Politics and Everyday Ethnicity in a Transylvanian Town (Princeton, N.J.: Princeton University Press, 2006), 262.

143. Irena Seidlerová interview, AJMP. Irena Seidlerová mentioned to me that the Hebrew classes had a more ritual character; hardly anyone learned in Terezín anything beyond the alphabet and a few songs. author's interview with Irena Seidlerová, January 25, 2013. See also Egon Redlich, entry for October 10 and 11, 1942, in Zítra jedeme, 151.

144. Feder, Židovská tragedie, 52-53.

145. Brubaker et al., Nationalist Politics, 207; for more context see ch. 7 and 8.

146. Jaroslav Bor (formerly Ervín Bloch), October 12, 15, and 19, 1991, AJMP, The Oral History Collection, 64.

147. Diary of Arnošt Klein, entry for December 5, 1943, AJMP.

NOTES TO PAGES 83-88   277

148. Richard Ehrlich, entry for December 23, 1944, WL.
149. Karel Fleischmann, "Terezínský den," YVA, O64, 74.
150. The baby was Tomáš Martin Winkler, deported to Auschwitz in May 1944 and murdered. See also Andrea Orzoff, *Battle for the Castle: The Myth of Czechoslovakia in Europe, 1914–1948* (Oxford: Oxford University Press, 2009).
151. *Šalom na pátek*, no. 1, December 1942, YVA.
152. Carol Lindz to author, February 7 and 8, 2013.
153. Eva Roubíčková, APT, Sbírka vzpomínek, 65–67.
154. Pavel Jirásek, "Český meziválečný tramping," *Živel* 15 (1999); and Marek Waic and Jiří Kössl, *Český tramping 1918–1945* (Prague: Práh, 1992).
155. See also Jaroslav Fried to author, about his brother Karel, March 2013; and Helen Epstein, *A Jewish Athlete: Swimming against Stereotype in 20th Century Europe* (Lexington, Mass.: Plunket Lake Press, 2011).
156. Sybil Milton, "Women and the Holocaust: The Case of German and German-Jewish Women," in *When Biology Became Destiny: Women in Weimar and Nazi German*, ed. Renate Bridenthal, Atina Grossmann, and Marion Kaplan (New York: Monthly Review Press, 1984), 297–333; and Kim Wünschmann, *Before Auschwitz: Jewish Prisoners in the Prewar Concentration Camps* (Cambridge, Mass.: Harvard University Press, 2015).
157. Young people in Westerbork created similar kinship groups. Manfred Schwarz, *Züge auf dem falschen Gleis* (Wien: Apfel, 1996).
158. LBI, artwork collection.
159. Trunk, *Łódź*, 307.
160. E.g., Gary Cohen, "Cultural Crossings in Prague, 1900: Scenes from Late Imperial Austria," *Austrian History Yearbook* 45 (2014): 1–30, 11.
161. Interview of a man, August 28, 1991, AJMP, The Oral History Collection, 69 (born 1919).
162. Schönová learned proper German only in Terezín: Nava Shan, *Chtěla jsem být herečkou* (Prague: Ivo Železný, 1992). Hana, the girlfriend of Leo Säbel, could barely speak German (Säbel interview, author's archive). For people from the countryside, see Bedřich Hoffenreich, APT.
163. Jan Fischer, *Šest skoků do budoucnosti* (Prague: Idea Servis, 1998); Helen Lewis, *A Time to Speak* (Belfast: Blackstaff Press, 1992); and interview of a woman, 2003, AJMP, The Oral History Collection, 1026 (born 1929).
164. Eva Mahrerová-Rohnenberg's (pseudonym) reparation file, Landesarchiv Saarbrücken.
165. Jiří Borský, APT.
166. Testimony of Ota Růžička, APT, Sbírka vzpomínek, 834; Berger, *Die unvergeßlichen sechseinhalb*, 66.
167. Grabower, Vermerke, May 22, 1942, Grabower papers, Finanzakademie Brühl.
168. He was fluent in both, but his Czech had more depth.
169. Rosa Salomon, LBI.
170. Author's interview with Harts Nijstad, May 4, 2001; Susanne Lamberg, VHA, No. 26350; Gertrud Schneider, *Exile and Destruction: The Fate of Austrian Jews, 1938–1945* (Westport, Conn.: Praeger, 1995), 129, on Ignac Mucinic; and Frances Tritt, "Meine Lebensgeschichte: Das Wunder des Ueberlebens 1918–1971," LBI, ME 650.

278 NOTES TO PAGES 91–93

171. See diaries of Camilla Hirsch, BTA and Margarete Pedde, APT; Elsa Bernstein, *Das Leben als Drama: Erinnerungen an Theresienstadt*, ed. Rita Bake and Birgit Kiupel (Dortmund: Edition Ebersbach, 1999), 85.

172. Diary of Willy Mahler, May 1 and August 27, 1944, APT, A, 5704.

173. Lucy Mandelstam, LBI, ME 1472; Jaroslav Fried to author, March 13, 2013; Lucy Mandelstam, email to author, March 14, 2013.

174. Walter Lode to Eric Heinemann, July 1, 1945, LBI, AR 6409.

175. Anna Hájková and Maria von der Heydt, "Dahlem, Westerbork, Theresienstadt, Seattle: The Veit Simon Children, Class, and the Transnational in the Holocaust history," *European History Review* 24, no. 5 (2017): 732–758.

176. On bad jobs: Elena Bork interview, FZH/WdE; testimony of Edmund Hadra, LBI; Clara Eisenkraft, *Damals in Theresienstadt: Erlebnisse einer Judenchristin* (Wuppertal: Aussaat Verlag, 1977), 35; and Manes, 141.

177. Mélanie Oppenhejm, *Theresienstadt: Die Menschenfalle* (Munich: Boer, 1998), 22.

178. Max Rosner, YVA, O2, 64.

179. Emil Blum Grossmannsucht, WL, P.III.h, 716. The same joke is also conveyed from the German Jewish emigré circles in New York. Hannah Arendt, "We Refugees," *Menorah* 31 (1943): 69–77.

180. Jack Wertheimer, *Unwelcome Strangers: East European Jews in Imperial Germany* (New York: Oxford University Press, 1987); and Yfaat Weiss, *Deutsche und polnische Juden vor dem Holocaust: Jüdische Identität zwischen Staatsbürgerschaft und Ethnizität 1933–1940* (Munich: Oldenbourg, 2000).

181. Jiří Borský, APT; Loesten, "Aus der Hoelle Minsk," LBI; Manfred Strassburger, YVA; Joe Singer, WL, P.II.h, 141.

182. When Irena Dodalová put on Jizchok Leib Perez's *The Golden Chain*, she was criticized for being tasteless. Otakar Růžička, APT, Sbírka vzpomínek, 834.

183. Max Fürst, 1946, NIOD, 250d, box 26; and Alisa Schiller to author, 2009.

184. Diary of Arnošt Klein, entry for November 8, 1943, AJMP.

185. Diary of Arnošt Klein, entry for November 13, 1942, AJMP. For a similar note of homelessness, see Jiří Borský, APT.

186. Manfred Strassburger, YVA.

187. Nava Shan, ICJ OHD.

188. Friends on Berl Herškovič and Jany Lebovič (Lebovič was a member of Hashomer Hatzair and later the communist resistance; he went into hiding rather than to Terezín, but there is photographic evidence of how his Jewish friends saw him in 1940 and 1941).

189. Interview of a man, December 3, 1990, AJMP, The Oral History Collection, 5 (born 1904); and Tůma, *Ghetto*, 33; on admiration, see Klara Caro.

190. Testimony of Eva Noack Mosse, YVA; Klara Caro, YVA, O1, 286; Loesten, "Aus der Hoelle Minsk," LBI, ch. 10; and letter Malka Zimmet, November 1, 1945, YVA, O7, 381.

191. Barth, Brubaker, Goffman, and Bourdieu (but not Katherine Verdery) are scholars whose theories provide the theoretical basis for my work, yet they do not treat gender other than in passing or when addressing "women's" topics; Doris Bergen,

NOTES TO PAGES 91–93   279

"What Do Studies of Women, Gender, and Sexuality Contribute to Understanding the Holocaust?," in *Different Horrors, Same Hell: Gender and the Holocaust*, ed. Myrna Goldenberg and Amy Shapiro (Seattle: University of Washington Press, 2013), 16–38, 17.

192. Diary of Dr. Mathyas Farkas, undated fragment from early May 1945, APT, A, 24; Eva Noack Mosse, entry for 26 February, 1945, WL TAU; Illa Loeb to her sister, 1945, NIOD, 250d, box 35; Richard Ehrlich, entry for November 12, 1943; diary of Bernhard Kolb, entry for June 19, 1943, YVA, O2, 387; and Eric Lipman to Rabbi Silver, May 17, 1945, LBI, AR 2275.

193. On gender identity and expressions of femininity in the concentration camps, see also Monika Flaschka, "'Only Pretty Women Were Raped': The Effect of Sexual Violence on Gender Identities in the Concentration Camps," in *Sexual Violence against Jewish Women during the Holocaust*, ed. Sonja M. Hedgepeth and Rochelle G. Saidel (Hanover, N.H.: University Press of New England, 2010), 77–93.

194. Lederer, *Ghetto Theresienstadt*, 55.

195. Women using perfume, on the other hand, interpreted using the scent as a validation of their femininity. Diary of Eva Noack Mosse, entry for March 8, 1945, WL TAU (she was not aware the date was International Women's Day).

196. For Czech history of sexuality, see Karla Huebner, "The Whole World Revolves Around It: Sex Education and Sex Reform in First Republic Czech Print Media," *Aspasia* 4 (2010): 25–48, and Huebner, "Girl, Trampka, nebo Žába? The Czechoslovak New Woman," in *The New Woman International: Representations in Photography and Film from the 1870s through the 1960s*, ed. Elizabeth Otto and Vanessa Rocco (Ann Arbor: University of Michigan Press, 2011); for Czech interwar gender history, see Melissa Feinberg, *Elusive Equality: Gender, Citizenship, and the Limits of Democracy in Czechoslovakia, 1918–1950* (Pittsburgh: University of Pittsburgh Press, 2006).

197. "Erika" interview, May 31, 1994, AJMP, The Oral History Collection, 320 (born 1920).

198. Testimony of Edmund Hadra, LBI.

199. *Eine Nacht mit ihr allein auf Bar Palanda*, drawing by Eli Lesklý, catalog of artworks, LAMOTH; Šimon Kolsky interview, author's archive; and Ruth Weisz, "Und es war keine Lüge," in *Theresienstadt: Aufzeichnungen von Federica Spitzer und Ruth Weisz*, ed. Wolfgang Benz (Berlin: Metropol, 1997), 98–157, 110.

200. Hans Werner Heilborn interview, September 26, 1995, MMZ. A copy is reprinted in Thomas Schnitzler, ed., *"Das Leben ist ein Kampf": Marianne Elikan—Verfolgte des Nazi-Regimes; Tagebuch, Briefe und Gedichte aus Trier und Theresienstadt* (Trier: Wissenschaftlicher Verlag, 2008), 119–120. The lyrics cite several popular songs.

201. Norbert Troller, *Terezín: Hitler's Gift to the Jews* (Chapel Hill: University of North Carolina Press, 1991), 119–121.

202. Author's interview with Hana Friediger, January 17, 2010, author's archive; Ota Kolář and Věra Kolářová interview, AJMP, The Oral History Collection, 101 and 103.

280 NOTES TO PAGES 95–98

203. Dina Gottliebová-Babbitt interview, September 26, 1998, VHA, 46122.

204. Diary of Eva Mändlová Roubíčková, Archive Terezin Initiative Institute.

205. Ruth Elias, *The Triumph of Hope: From Theresienstadt and Auschwitz to Israel* (New York: John Wiley, 1998), 75.

206. Margot Lifman to author, Haifa, May 10, 2017.

207. Not all non-Czech women mentioned a romantic relationship, but this omission can be explained by the social expectations of double standards in female sexual behavior. Also, firsthand experience of casual sex was only reported by men.

208. Esther Bauer to author, January 3, 2015.

209. Interview Arnold M., MMZ, 016; and Ruth Gutmann-Herskovits, *Auswanderung vorläufig nicht möglich: Die Geschichte der Familie Herskovits aus Hannover*, ed. Bernard Strebel (Göttingen: Wallstein, 2002), 133.

210. Lucy Mandelstam, email to author, March 14, 2013; diary of Willy Mahler, APT; and Jiří Borský, APT.

211. Beate Meyer, interview with Trude Simonsohn, April 9, 2003. Thanks to Beate for sharing this with me.

212. Dagmar Hilarová, *Nemám žádné jméno*, ed. Evžen Hilar (Prague: Svoboda Service, 2010), 53. There were at least seven long-lasting marriages between Danish men and non-Danish women in Terezín and in the immediate postwar period; Silvia Tarabini Goldbaum Fracapane, "Danish Testimonies about Theresienstadt: Experiences of Deportation and Ghetto Life" (PhD diss., Technical University Berlin, 2016). One Danish woman married a Czech man: Rachel Schlesinger (née Fingeret) interview, VHA, no. 45085. Another married Danish woman had an affair with a Czech man, which others viewed with criticism: author's interview with Hana Friediger, January 17, 2010.

213. Silvia Goldbaum Tarabini Fracapane, "'Wir erfuhren, was es heißt, hungrig zu sein': Aspekte des Alltagslebens dänischer Juden in Theresienstadt," in *Der Alltag im Holocaust: Jüdisches Leben im Großdeutschen Reich 1941–1945*, ed. Doris Bergen, Andrea Löw, and Anna Hájková (Munich: Oldenbourg, 2013), 199–216.

214. "Speckdänen," Hans Werner Heilborn interview, MMZ.

215. Author's interview with Doris Meyer Stern, April 10, 2001, Beit Yitshak, Israel; and Arnold M. interview, MMZ.

216. Citing a carnival song from the 1920s.

217. Memoir of Hilde Nathan, NS-Dokumentationszentrum Cologne. Thanks to Barbara Jákli for giving me a copy.

218. Esther Jonas Bauer to author, January 3, 2015; and Ruth Gutmann-Herskovits, *Auswanderung vorläufig nicht möglich: Die Geschichte der Familie Herskovits aus Hannover*, ed. Bernard Strebel (Göttingen: Wallstein, 2002).

219. Esther Bauer to author, January 3, 2015.

220. Jiří Vaníček interview, January 30, 1995, VHA, no. 9840.

221. See both articles by Insa Eschebach in *Homophobie und Devianz: Weibliche und männliche Homosexualität im Nationalsozialismus* (Berlin: Metropol, 2012); see also Anna Hájková, "Den Holocaust queer erzählen," *Sexualitäten* 3 (2018): 86–110.

222. Redlich, entry for September 10, 1944, in *Zítra jedeme*, 230. This entry was removed in the English and Hebrew editions. See also entry for June 15, 1943.

NOTES TO PAGES 95–98 281

223. Diary of Ralph Oppenhejm, entry for March 25, 1945, Jewish Danish Museum (hereafter JDK), 207 A 35, 7.

224. For Hirsch's biography, see Lucie Ondřichová, *Příběh Freddyho Hirsche* (Prague: Sefer, 2001); and Dirk Kämper, *Fredy Hirsch und die Kinder des Holocaust: Die Geschichte eines vergessenen Helden aus Deutschland* (Zurich: Orrell Füssli, 2015).

225. The Czechoslovak coverage of the arrest of Heinz Rutha instrumentalized a similar mix of "homosexual deviance" and Germanness. Mark Cornwall, *The Devil's Wall: The Nationalist Youth Mission of Heinz Rutha* (Cambridge, Mass.: Harvard University Press, 2012).

226. Seidlerová interview, AJMP; and interview of a man, August 30, 1995, AJMP, The Oral History Collection, 482 (born 1928).

227. Ondřichová, *Příběh*.

228. Marti Lybeck, *Desiring Emancipation: New Women and Homosexuality in Germany, 1890–1933* (Albany: State University of New York Press, 2014); Laurie Marhoefer, *Sex and the Weimar · Republic: German Homosexual Emancipation and the Rise of the Nazis* (Toronto: University of Toronto Press, 2015); Andreas Pretzel, "Homosexuality in the Sexual Ethics of the 1930ies: A Values Debate in the Culture Wars between Conservatism, Liberalism, and Moral-National Renewal," in *After the History of Sexuality: German Genealogies, with and beyond Foucault*, ed. Scott Spector, Helmut Puff, and Dagmar Herzog (New York: Berghahn, 2012), 202–215; Jan Seidl, Jan Wintr, and Lukáš Nozar, *Od žaláře k oltáři: Emancipace homosexuality v českých zemích od roku 1867 do současnosti* (Brno: Host, 2012); and Robert Beachy, *Gay Berlin: Birthplace of a Modern Identity* (New York: Knopf, 2014).

229. Pretzel, "Homosexuality in the Sexual Ethics"; and Cornwall, *Devil's Wall*.

230. In the sense of adult and sexually active. See author's interview with Margot H., April 2018.

231. Petr Lang interview, ICJ OHD.

232. Dalia Ofer, "We Israelis Remember, But How? The Memory of the Holocaust and the Israeli Experience," *Israel Studies* 18, no. 2 (2013): 70–85.

233. Clara Eisenkraft, *Damals in Theresienstadt: Erlebnisse einer Judenchristin* (Wuppertal: Aussaat, 1977), 34–35.

234. Eisenkraft, *Damals in Theresienstadt*; and diary of Elisabeth Argutinsky, BTA.

235. Diary of Eva Noack Mosse, entry for April 10, 1945, WL TAU; Elisabeth Argutinsky, BTA; and Manfred Strassburger, YVA.

236. Bedřich Hoffenreich, APT; testimony of Anneliese Gutfeld, LBI, ME 744.

237. Kárný, "Komunistická organizace," NA, 53.

238. Kárný, "Komunistická organizace," NA, 58 and 60.

239. Diary of Bedřich Kohn, entry for June 5, 1943.

240. Irena Seidlerová interview, AJMP.

241. Diary of Arnošt Klein, entry for October 25, 1943, AJMP, T, 324.

242. Grabower, memoranda, April 25, May 25, 1944, January 21, 1945, February 19, 1945 passim, Brühl.

243. Bedřich Borges interview, June 16, 1992, AJMP, The Oral History Collection, 137.

282 NOTES TO PAGES 103–106

Chapter 3

1. Hans Hofer, "Die Kuh," 1943, AJMP, T, 2, excerpts translated by Justus von Widekind. Thanks to the Prague Jewish Museum for permission to reprint.

2. Christian Gerlach, "Die Bedeutung der deutschen Ernährungspolitik für die Beschleunigung des Mordes an den Juden 1942: Das Generalgouvernement und die Westukraine," in *Krieg, Ernährung, Völkermord: Forschungen zur deutschen Vernichtungspolitik im Zweiten Weltkrieg*, ed. Christian Gerlach (Hamburg: Hamburger Edition, 1998), 167–254.

3. Amartya Sen, *Poverty and Famines: An Essay on Entitlement and Deprivation* (Oxford: Oxford University Press, 1981).

4. James Vernon, *Hunger: A Modern History* (Cambridge, Mass.: Belknap Press of Harvard University Press, 2007), 2; for a departure from this view, see Christian Gerlach, "Die Welternährungskrise 1972–1975," *Geschichte und Gesellschaft* 31, no. 4 (2005): 546–585, 576–580.

5. Much-cited works include Lucie Adelsberger, "Medical Observations in Auschwitz Concentration Camp," *Lancet*, March 2, 1946, 317–319; and Myron Winick, ed., *Hunger Disease: Studies by the Jewish Physicians in the Warsaw Ghetto* (New York: Wiley, 1979).

6. Sybil Milton, "Women and the Holocaust: The Case of German and German-Jewish Women," in *When Biology Became Destiny: Women in Weimar and Nazi German*, ed. Renate Bridenthal, Atina Grossmann, and Marion Kaplan (New York: Monthly Review Press, 1984), 297–333. On women and starvation during the Ukrainian famine, see Oksana Kis, "Defying Death: Women's Experience of the Holodomor, 1932–1933," *Aspasia* 7 (2013): 42–67.

7. J. P. W. Rivers, "The Nutritional Biology of Famine," in *Famine*, ed. G. A. Harrison (Oxford: Oxford University Press, 1988), 57–106.

8. September 1942 monthly report for the Dienststelle, AJMP, T, 49. The kitchen in the Genie barracks cooked for four thousand people.

9. Gerty Spies, entry for September 20, 1944, in *My Years in Terezín: How One Woman Survived the Holocaust* (Amherst, N.Y.: Prometheus Books, 1997), 135.

10. Sara Bender, *The Jews of Białystok during World War II and the Holocaust* (Waltham, Mass.: Brandeis University Press; Hanover, N.H.: University Press of New England, 2008), 138–139; Isiah Trunk, *Judenrat: The Jewish Councils in Eastern Europe under Nazi Occupation* (New York: Macmillan, 1972), 99–105; and Barbara Engelking-Boni and Jacek Leociak, *The Warsaw Ghetto: A Guide to the Perished City* (New Haven, Conn.: Yale University Press, 2009), 412, 418, 447.

11. List of deliveries and reclamations, AJMP, T, 7.

12. Otto Zucker, "Theresienstadt 1941–1943," *Theresienstädter Studien und Dokumente* (1995): 271–303, 282.

13. Zucker, "Theresienstadt 1941–1943," 285; diary of Arnošt Klein, entry for January 25, 1943, AJMP, T, 324.

14. Jaroslava Milotová et al., *Jewish Gold and other Precious Metals, Precious Stones, and Objects made of such Materials—Situation in the Czech Lands in the Years 1939*

NOTES TO PAGES 103–106 283

to 1945 (Praha: Sefer, 2001); and Beate Meyer, "'Altersghetto', 'Vorzugslager' und Tätigkeitsfeld: Die Repräsentanten der Reichsvereinigung der Juden in Deutschland und Theresienstadt," *Theresienstädter Studien und Dokumente* (2004): 131. "Bericht über den Status des ehemalige Konzentrationlagers Theresienstadt, without author" (probably written by Murmelstein), WL, 1073, 2, gives a higher number, 120 million Reichsmark.

15. "Bericht über den Status des ehemalige Konzentrationlagers Theresienstadt."
16. Statement by Heinrich Scholz at the main hearing, trial of Rahm, April 23, 1947, State regional archive Litoměřice (hereafter SOAL), LSP 441/47.
17. AJMP, AŽM, fond ŽNO Slaný, 102833 and 102068.
18. See diary of bills of delivery, AJMP, T, 3.
19. Interview of a man, December 3, 1990, AJMP, The Oral History Collection, 5 (born 1904).
20. Engelking-Boni and Leociak, *Warsaw Ghetto*, 153.
21. Engelking-Boni and Leociak, *Warsaw Ghetto*, 429.
22. Murmelstein, "Geschichtlicher Überblick," WL, 1073, 3.
23. Murmestein, "Fleischlieferungen für Teresin [*sic*]," ABS, 305-633-1, pp. 65–66.
24. Adolphe Metz, YVA, O33, 3257; and Grabelandaktion, CAHJP, A/W, 2060.
25. Report of the Jewish self-administration for the SS headquarters for March 1944, YVA, O64, 41.
26. Elly and Ernst Michaelis to unknown friends [month illegible] 21, 1945, LBI, AR 11148.
27. Diary of Richard Ehrlich, entry for November 12, 1943, WL, P.II.h, 306; report from Fritz Rothgiesser, NIOD, 250d, box 39.
28. Arnold M. interview, September 5, 1995, MMZ, 016; and Edgar Krása interview, September 9, 2003, USHMM, RG-50.030*0478.
29. "Der Nährwert der Speisen in Kalorien," AJMP, T, 114; and "Zusammensetzung und Kalorienwert eines Abendmahls," table II, AJMP, T, 115.
30. For an example of an agreement between the residents of house L 219 about the hours for washing for women and men, and about cooking, see Karel Fleischmann's papers, YVA, O64, 74.
31. Ema Donathová interview, April 2, 1992, AJMP, The Oral History Collection, 119. For a cookbook produced in Terezin, see Cara DeSilva, ed., *In Memory's Kitchen: A Legacy from the Women of Terezín* (Northvale, N.J.: J. Aronson, 1996).
32. Note 45, Central Book Keeping and Financial Department, May 18, 1942, YVA, O64, 34.
33. Egon Redlich, entry for May 1, 1942, in *Zítra jedeme, synu, pojedeme transportem: Deník Egona Redlicha z Terezína 1.1.1942–22.1.1944*, ed. Miroslav Kryl (Brno: Doplněk, 1995), 115.
34. *Denní rozkazy Rady starších a Sdělení židovské samosprávy Terezín 1941–1945*, ed. Anna Hyndráková, Raisa Machatková, and Jaroslava Milotová (Prague: Sefer, 2003); Tagesbefehl April 12, 1943, 319.
35. Zucker, "Theresienstadt 1941–1943," 283; and Murmelstein, "Geschichtlicher Überblick," WL, 19.

284 NOTES TO PAGES 110–115

36. "Zusätzlicher Lebensmittelverbrauch," AJMP, T, 116.
37. AJMP, T, 115. The caloric assessment tables that the self-administration produced were accurate.
38. See the discussion about changes in December 1944: AJMP, T, 52.
39. Gerty Spies, entry for September 22, 1944, in *My Years in Terezín*, 141f; and diary of Martha Glass, entry for September 3, 1943; Martha Glass, *"Jeder Tag in Theresin ist ein Geschenk": Die Theresienstädter Tagebücher einer Hamburger Jüdin 1943–1945*, ed. Barbara Müller Wesemann (Hamburg: Ergebnisse, 1996), 81.
40. Murmelstein, "Geschichtlicher Überblick," WL.
41. Diary of Martha Glass, entry for March 11, 1943.
42. "Arbeitszentrale über Führung der Brotkartei," January 18, 1943, YVA, O64, 34.
43. Standführung in Krankheitsfällen, August 26, 1943, YVA, O64, 34; diary of Gerty Spies, entry for September 22, 1944, in *My Years in Terezín*.
44. Zucker, "Theresienstadt 1941–1943," 283.
45. Zusätzlicher Lebensmittelverbrauch, AJMP, T, 116. The same list was reproduced, with fifty-eight hundred hard laborers on it, in AJMP, T, 115. (All other numbers are identical; hence one of the numbers of the hard laborers is probably a contemporaneous typo.)
46. Murmelstein, "Geschichtlicher Überblick," WL, 19; see also "Aufteilung der Lebensmittel," AJMP, T, 115.
47. Murmelstein, "Geschichtlicher Überblick," WL, 42. With this decision, Murmelstein made himself additional enemies; previously, parcels could be inherited. Diary of Paul Scheurenberg, "Traurige Erlebnisse in der Nazi Hölle Deutschland," entry for June 1943 (no exact date), Centrum Judaicum (hereafter CJA), 6.14, 2, November 1944 (no exact dates).
48. Jana Renée Friesová, *Pevnost mého mládí* (Prague: Trizonia, 1997); and Šimon Kolsky interview, January 16, 2009, author's private archive.
49. Circular of the Central Labor, January 28, 1944, YVA, O64, 34.
50. Diary of Eva Roubíčková, entry for September 15, 1942, Archive Terezin Initiative Institute (hereafter AITI).
51. Malka Zimmet (postwar name of Valerie Kohnová) to her brother, November 1, 1945, YVA, O7, 381.
52. Erich Lichtblau, "Tři terezínští králové," 1943, catalog of artworks, Los Angeles Museum of the Holocaust (hereafter LAMOTH).
53. Lichtblau, unnamed, 1943, LAMOTH.
54. Doris Donovalová interview, July 25, 1994, Gender Studies Prague.
55. See Edgar Krása interview, USHMM, on his support of the artists.
56. Alisa Ehrmann-Shek to author, April 2001. Moreover, Alisa's gentile mother sold all of the valuables she possessed so she could send them food parcels. Miroslav Kárný, "Ein Theresienstädter Tagebuch, 18. Oktober 1944–19. Mai 1945," *Theresienstädter Studien und Dokumente* (1994): 169.
57. Anna Nathanová interview, December 9, 2006, AJMP, The Oral History Collection, 1090 (born 1917).
58. Hana Rutarová's letters to her husband, April, 30, APT, A, 8652; see also author's interview with Hana Rutarová-Friediger, January 17, 2010.
59. Miloš Pick, *Naděje se vzdát neumím* (Brno: Doplněk, 2010), 37.

NOTES TO PAGES 110–115 285

60. Interview of "Anna," AJMP, The Oral History Collection, 165 (born 1919).
61. Eva Mändlová was supporting seven people throughout 1943 and 1944. Diary of Eva Roubíčková, entry for August, 15, 1943, AITI.
62. Frances Epstein, "The Roundtrip," private archive of Helen Epstein.
63. Silvia Goldbaum Tarabini Fracapane, "'Wir erfuhren, was es heißt, hungrig zu sein': Aspekte des Alltagslebens dänischer Juden in Theresienstadt," in Der Alltag im Holocaust: Jüdisches Leben im Großdeutschen Reich 1941–1945, ed. Doris Bergen, Andrea Löw, and Anna Hájková (Munich: Oldenbourg, 2013); and Sven Meyer and Corrie Meyer, "Onze belevenissen tijdens de jodenvervolgingen in den tweeden wereldoorlog," (1945) NIOD, 244, 920.
64. Hana Friediger interview, January 17, 2010, author's archive.
65. Sven Meyer and Corrie Meyer, "Onze belevenissen."
66. Diary of Martha Glass, entries for July 16 and October 2, 1943, 79f, 82f.
67. Alice Randt, Die Schleuse (Hann. Münden: Chr. Gauke, 1974), 80, 87.
68. Regina Oelze's notes, Alte Synagoge Essen.
69. Diary of Camilla Hirsch, entries for August 23 and September 1, 1944, BTA, uncataloged.
70. Diary of Camilla Hirsch, entry for July 26, 1944, BTA.
71. Diary of Camilla Hirsch, entry for April 29, 1943, BTA.
72. Diary of Hulda Schickler, Leo Baeck Institute Jerusalem (hereafter LBIJ), 512.
73. Diary of Schickler, entry for July 14, 1944, LBIJ.
74. Diary of Louis Salomon (written in May 1945; hence retrospectively), YVA, O33, 1560.
75. Marie Klánová's notes, 1943, APT, A, 344.
76. Karl Loesten, "Aus der Hoelle Minsk in das 'Paradies' Theresienstadt 1941–1945," Leo Baeck Institute NY (hereafter LBI), ME 398, 262.
77. Caroline Walker Bynum, Holy Feast and Holy Fast: The Religious Significance of Food to Medieval Women (Berkeley: University of California Press, 1987).
78. Hana Kolsky interview, January 16, 2009, author's archive.
79. Interview of a woman, AJMP, The Oral History Collection, 679 (born 1929).
80. Der Theresienstädter Hechalutz, "Aus den Erinnerungen von Berl Herškovič Hechalutz," Theresienstädter Studien und Dokumente (2000): 151–163; and Hana Ledererová, entry for April 15, 1943, in Hana Posseltová-Ledererová, Máma a já (Terezínský deník) (Prague: G plus G, 1992), 44–46.
81. Renée Friesová interview, AJMP, The Oral History Collection, 172; and Miloš Pick, Naděje se vzdát neumím (Brno: Doplněk, 2010), 35.
82. Michael Becker and Denis Bock, "Muselmänner und Häftlingsgesellschaften: Ein Beitrag zur Sozialgeschichte der nationalsozialistischen Konzentrationslager," Archiv für Sozialgeschichte 55 (2015): 133–175.
83. Josef Bor, Opuštěná Panenka (Prague: Státní nakladatelství politické literatury, 1961), 295.
84. Giorgio Agamben, Homo Sacer: Sovereign Power and Bare Life, trans. Daniel Heller-Roazen (Stanford, Calif.: Stanford University Press, 1998).
85. Edmund Hadra, Terezín, LBI, AR 1249, 2; Louis Salomon, YV, O33, 1560; diary of Elisabeth Argutinsky, BTA; diary of Hulda Schickler, LBIJ; diary of Richard Ehrlich,

NOTES TO PAGES 117–121

WL, P.II.h, 306; Jakob Geissmar, LBI, ME 182; diary of Eugenie Singer, BTA, 182; and diary of Camilla Hirsch, BTA, uncatagued when viewed.

86. Orlando Patterson, *Slavery and Social Death: A Comparative Study* (Cambridge, Mass.: Harvard University Press, 1982); and Marion Kaplan, *Between Dignity and Despair: Jewish Life in Nazi Germany* (New York: Oxford University Press, 1998).

87. I thank Professor Emerita Magdalena Krondl (University of Toronto, School of Nutrition) for explaining to me the basics of hunger from the perspective of a nutritionist.

88. Stein, "Terezín—zdravotnický úkol," APT, A, 739, 24; Alfred Wolff-Eisner, *Über Mangelerkrankungen auf Grund von Beobachtungen im Konzentrationslager* (Würzburg: Sauer-Marhard, 1947), 20, 38; and Gerty Spies, "Julius Spanier," WL, P.III.h, 1106 (on pellagra, B2 deficiency).

89. Myron Winick, ed., *Hunger Disease: Studies by the Jewish Physicians in the Warsaw Ghetto* (New York: Wiley, 1979), 102–103; and Isaiah Trunk, *Łódź Ghetto: A History*, ed. and trans. Robert Moses Shapiro (Bloomington: Indiana University Press, 2006), 211.

90. Rebecca Manley, "Nutritional Dystrophy: The Science and Semantics of Starvation in World War II," in *Hunger and War: Food Provisioning in the Soviet Union during World War II*, ed. Wendy Goldman and Donald Filtzer (Bloomington: Indiana University Press, 2015), 206–264; Winick, *Hunger Disease*, 103–104. For edema in Theresienstadt, see Margot Lifman to the author, May 10, 2017.

91. Wolff-Eisner, *Über Mangelerkrankungen*, 20.

92. Andrea Löw, *Juden im Getto Litzmannstadt: Lebensbedingungen, Selbstwahrnehmung, Verhalten* (Göttingen: Wallstein, 2006), 156.

93. I thank my father Radko Hájek for his help in analyzing this information.

94. See a more detailed debate in Anna Hájková, "Mutmaßungen über deutsche Juden: Alte Menschen aus Deutschland im Theresienstädter Ghetto," in *Der Alltag im Holocaust: Jüdisches Leben im Großdeutschen Reich 1941–1945*, ed. Doris Bergen, Andrea Löw, and Anna Hájková (Munich: Oldenbourg, 2013), 179–198, 184.

95. Counted at the point of liberation.

96. Zeev Shek, "Děti," 1945, Moreshet, C, 01.

97. Julie Pollak, "Der Anfang der Dresdener Kaserne," AJMP, T, 271b.

98. Luisa Fischerová, "Sociální zpráva," in "One year of L 417," YVA, O64, 57; interview Irena Seidlerová, February 13, 1995, AJMP, The Oral History Collection, 407; Willy Groag, Sociální péče o mládež, 1945, Moreshet, C, 01; Lisa Wurzel and Hana Fischl, "*Terezín*" (Hebrew), ed. Yehuda Reznicenko, trans. Chaim Goldberg (Tel Aviv: Labor Party, 1947), 146; and Dagmar Hilarová, *Nemám žádné jméno*, ed. Evžen Hilar (Prague: Svoboda Service, 2010), 16.

99. Interview of a woman, AJMP, The Oral History Collection, 249 (born 1923); Hans Gaertner interview, The Research Centre for Contemporary History, Werkstatt der Erinnerung (hereafter FZH/WdE), 863 (all names are pseudonyms); diary (undated) of Charlotta Verešová, spring 1944, BTA, 174.

100. Wurzel and Fischl, "*Terezín*," 127.

NOTES TO PAGES 117–121   287

101. J. P. W. Rivers, "The Nutritional Biology of Famine," in *Famine*, ed. G. A. Harrison (Oxford: Oxford University Press, 1988). The infants in Lodz mostly died of hunger before the deportation of children and elderly in September 1942.

102. It is important to note that babies who died hours after birth were not registered by the Central Registry. Infants born in 1945 are not included in the preceding numbers; the numbers are much lower (eighteen babies altogether), and most of the deaths (five out seven) occurred to infants who came with the evacuation transports.

103. Catharina van den Berg Drukker interview, YVA, O3, 11128.

104. For a similar situation in the Lodz ghetto (caused by the corruption and management decisions of German authorities), see Peter Klein, *Die Gettoverwaltung Litzmannstadt 1940 bis 1944: Eine Dienststelle im Spannungsfeld von Kommunalbürokratie und Staatlicher Verfolgungspolitik* (Hamburg: Hamburger Edition, 2009), 163–166.

105. Edmund Hadra, Terezín, LBI, AR 1249, 2.

106. Interview of "Greta," AJMP, The Oral History Collection, 277 (born 1919). See also Miloš Povondra, September 26, 1997, VHA, 36907; and Hugo Heumann, *Erlebtes-Erlittenes: Von Mönchengladbach über Luxemburg nach Theresienstadt*, ed. Germaine Goetzinger and Marc Schoentgen (Mersch: CNL, 2007), 80.

107. Shlomo Schmiedt, "Bet-chaluc v 'třiapadesátce,'" ca. 1944, BTA, 581. This is a grammatical mistake; the correct title in Hebrew should be "beit he-chaluc." For a similar account in a Communist group, see Pick, *Naděje*, 37, and for the German-language L414 youth home see Klaus Scheurenberg, *Ich will leben* (Berlin: Oberbaumverlag, 1982), 158.

108. See J. Overing, "Kinship in Anthropology," in *International Encyclopedia of the Social & Behavioral Sciences* (New York: Elsevier, 2001), 8098–8105.

109. Judith Butler, "Is Kinship Always Already Heterosexual?," *differences: A Journal of Feminist Cultural Studies* 13, no. 1 (2002): 14–44.

110. Jan Bachrich, BTA, 48; interview AJMP, 407; diary of Charlota Verešová, just before her birthday, BTA.

111. Gerty Spies, entry for September 20, 1944, in *My Years in Terezín*. See also interview of a woman, AJMP, The Oral History Collection, 226 (born 1925), on having a feast for her birthday.

112. Sheila Fitzpatrick, *Everyday Stalinism: Ordinary Life in Extraordinary Times; Soviet Russia in the 1930s* (New York: Oxford University Press, 1999).

113. Eli Bachner interview, August 10, 1965, ICJ OHD, 34, 14.

114. Edmund Hadra, LBI, AR 1249, 2.

115. Testimony of Else Dormitzer, WL, P.II.h, 41.

116. Ema Donathová interview, April 2, 1992, AJMP, The Oral History Collection, 119; see also Lucie Drachsler, LBI; and Doris Donovalová interview, Gender studies, Prague.

117. Ema Donathová interview, AJMP.

118. The rabbi, Ernst Reich, was also from Olomouc. Diary of Willy Mahler, entry for January 23, 1944, APT, A, 5704.

288 NOTES TO PAGES 125-128

119. Marcel Mauss, *The Gift: Forms and Functions of Exchange in Archaic Societies* (Mansfield Centre: Martino Publishing, 2011); and Harry Liebersohn, *The Return of the Gift: European History of a Global Idea* (Cambridge, UK: Cambridge University Press, 2010).

120. Diary of Gerty Spies, entry for September 20, 1944, in *My Years in Terezín*.

121. Diary of Charlotta Verešová, late 1943–September 1944, BTA; Jana Renée Friesová, *Pevnost mého mládí* (Prague: Trizonia, 1997), 173–175; and Marion Sapir, October 11, 1995, VHA, no. 7471.

122. Friesová, *Pevnost mého mládí*, 173–175.

123. Norbert Troller, *Terezín: Hitler's Gift to the Jews*, trans. Susan E. Cernyak-Spatz (Chapel Hill: University of North Carolina Press, 1991), 119–121. See also similar stories in his papers, LBI, AR 7268, box 3, folder 4.

124. Edmund Hadra, Terezín, LBI, AR 1249, 2.

125. Diary of Willy Mahler, APT, entries for April, June, and July 1944, on his girlfriend Trude.

126. Diary of Charlotta Verešová, late 1943–September 1944, BTA.

127. Edgar Krása interview, USHMM.

128. Ludmila Chládková, "Karel Poláček v Terezíně," *Terezínské listy* 26 (1996): 55–70, 63n19.

129. Leo and Myra Strauss's cabaret, performed at Philipp Manes's, in Manes, *As If It Were Life: A WWII Diary from the Theresienstadt Ghetto*, ed. Klaus Leist and Ben Barkow, trans. Janet Forster, Klaus Leist, and Ben Barkow (New York: Palgrave Macmillan, 2009), 264. Also recounted in Edmund Hadra, LBI.

130. Interview, AJMP, 407. Sekaninová survived her later deportation to Auschwitz, remarried, and went on to become the only Jewish deputy to a minister to survive the Slánský trials. After she protested the Soviet occupation in 1968, she was frequently arrested with other dissidents, keeping her Terezín attitude. Martin Čakrt, email to author, January 23, 2012.

131. Käthe Breslauer, WL, P.III.h, 215.

132. Diary of Eva Roubíčková, entry for March 1944, AITI.

133. Diary of Richard Ehrlich, entry for November 12, 1943, WL, P.II.h, 306.

134. Gerty Spies, entry for September 19, 1944, in *My Years in Terezín*; and Arnold M. interview, MMZ.

135. Barend Kronenberg, NIOD, 250d, box 32.

136. When Celeste Raspanti mentions a boy giving a sausage to the protagonist, she paints an erroneous picture of Terezín. Raspanti, *I Have Never Seen Another Butterfly* (Woodstock, Ill.: Dramatic Publishing), 39. The Warsaw ghetto also experienced "trendy" foods; see Engelking-Boni and Leociak, *Warsaw Ghetto*, 434–435.

137. Elsa Oestreicher collection, LBI, MF 1085, series II, box 1, folder 4.

138. Alexander Singer interview, VHA, 40047.

139. Thus the interpretation of Ruth Bondy in "*Elder of the Jews*": *Jakob Edelstein of Theresienstadt* (New York: Grove, 1989).

140. Hanuš Hans Bader, "Ich habe es überlebt," BTA, 75.10.

141. Charlotte Opfermann and Robert A. Warren, *Charlotte, a Holocaust Memoir: Remembering Theresienstadt* (Santa Fe, N.Mex.: Paper Tiger, 2006), 132.

NOTES TO PAGES 125–128   289

142. Hedwig Ems, YVA, O33, 91; see also Federica Spitzer, "Verlorene Jahre," in Wolfgang Benz, ed., *Theresienstadt: Aufzeichnungen von Federica Spitzer und Ruth Weisz* (Berlin: Metropol, 1997), 46.

143. Interview of "Bedřich," AJMP, The Oral History Collection, 42 (born 1902).

144. Elly and Ernst Michaelis to unknown friends, LBI.

145. Policejní ředitelství, NA Prague, 42/K, Benda. I thank Zdenka Kokošková for her help.

146. Ota Kolář interview, AJMP, The Oral History Collection, 103.

147. Prisoner database of the Państwowe Muzeum Auschwitz-Birkenau w Oświęcimiu, entries for Franz and Ludmila Persein.

148. Loesten, "Aus der Hoelle Minsk," LBI, ch. 6.

149. Ota Kolář interview.

150. Bedřich Hoffenreich, APT, Sbírka vzpomínek, 1095.

151. Löw, *Juden im Getto Litzmannstadt*, 175–176.

152. In her analysis of the ghetto law codex, Renata Lipková put forward this belief as a fact, but without any documentary evidence: Lipková, "Právo v nuceném společenství," *Terezínské listy* 27 (1999): 20–38, 30.

153. Memo of the Council of Elders, January 26, 1943, AJMP, T, 147. See the petitions to be exempted from transport from Ella Köpplová, Vilém Friedmann, and František Metzker, August 30, 1943, YVA, O64, 17/I. Michael Wögebauer errs when arguing that there was no connection between being sentenced and the deportation lists: Michael Wögerbauer, "Kartoffeln: Ein Versuch über Erzählungen zum Ghettoalltag," *Theresienstädter Studien und Dokumente* (2003): 95–144.

154. Diary of Eva Mändlová-Roubíčková, entry for August 29, 1943, AITI; Murmelstein's petition for workers of the Barackenbau, note on Anne Reisz, September 3, 1943, YVA, O64, 10; and petition of Anton Rosenbaum, no date, YVA, O64, 11/I.

155. Diary of Louis Salomon, YV, O33, 1560; and diary of Margarete Pedde, APT, A, 10549.

156. "Z deníku sedmnáctileté," *Šalom na pátek*, no. 13, December 31, 1943, YVA, O64, 64.

157. See the debate in Paul Steege, *Black Market, Cold War: Everyday Life in Berlin, 1946–1949* (Cambridge, UK: Cambridge University Press, 2007); Malte Zierenberg, *Stadt der Schieber: Der Berliner Schwarzmarkt 1939–1950* (Göttingen: Vandenhoeck & Ruprecht, 2008); Anna Holian, *Between National Socialism and Soviet Communism: Displaced Persons in Postwar Germany* (Ann Arbor: University of Michigan Press, 2011); and Stefan Mörchen, *Schwarzer Markt: Kriminalität, Ordnung und Moral in Bremen 1939–1949* (Frankfurt am Main: Campus, 2011).

158. Letter of Hedwig Ems, 16.7.1947, no. 91, O33; and Adolphe Metz, "Ghetto Terezín," YVA, O33, 3257.

159. Loesten, "Aus der Hoelle Minsk," LBI, ch. 4; and *Denní rozkazy*, Tagesbefehl March 5, 1943, 304.

160. Murmelstein, "Geschichtlicher Überblick, WL, 21.

161. Arnošt Klein recorded a drop to 49 crowns (5 Reichsmark), December 15, 1943.

162. Frances Epstein, "The Roundtrip."

163. Arnošt Reiser, *Útěk* (Prague: Academia, 2003), 89–90.

290 NOTES TO PAGES 132–134

164. Adolphe Metz, YVA; on a similar note, see Loesten, "Aus der Hoelle Minsk," LBI, ch. 6.
165. Anna Stamm, LBI, ME 616; and Hannelore Grünberg, "Zolang er nog tranen zijn," NIOD, 244, 1289.
166. Diary of Arnošt Klein, entry for December 15, 1943, APT, A, 344; and diary of Maurits Frankenhuis, entry for September 22, 1944, NIOD, 250n, 12g.
167. Author's interview with Leo Säbel, January 22, 2010, Charlottenlund.
168. Diary of Eva Mändlová-Roubíčková, entry for November 1943, AITI.
169. Eli Leskly (né Erich Lichtblau) interview, 1965, ICJ OHD, 36, 29. Similarly, an elderly German painter drew customers for a pound of flour or a jar of jam; before the deportation, she had painted portraits of important Germans for the Berlin National Gallery. Eva Noack Mosse, YVA, O33, 986.
170. Fracapane, "Wir erfuhren."
171. Massages: Betty Mannheimer Presser, YVA, O2, 711; hairdresser: Julius Papp, YVA, O15E, 2377.
172. Hedwig Ostwaldt, LBI, AR 11029; and Elly and Ernst Michaelis.
173. Šimon Kolsky interview, private archive of the author.
174. Anna Hájková, "Sexual Barter in Times of Genocide: Negotiating the Sexual Economy of the Theresienstadt Ghetto," Signs 38, no. 3 (Spring 2013): 503–533.
175. Joe Singer, WL, P.II.h, 141; and Valter Kesler, August 12, 1966, APT, A, 134.
176. Elena Makarova, interview with Zdeněk Ornest, ca. 1989. Thanks to Elena for sharing this material. One of the friends was Arnošt Lustig, who incorporated the story in an increasingly sexualized fashion into his fiction.
177. Mark Mazower, Inside Hitler's Greece: The Experience of Occupation, 1941–1944 (New Haven, Conn.: Yale University Press, 1993), 62.
178. Leonard Baker, Days of Sorrow and of Pain: Leo Baeck and the Berlin Jews (New York: Macmillan, 1978), 294.
179. "Dodala více než objednáno," Šnap, no. 15, YVA, O64, 64; see also Anna Nathanová interview, AJMP.
180. OdF application of Inge Hirschfeld, CJA, 4.1, 729; Hans Hermann Hirschfeld [her husband] to Hans Reissner, December 29, 1968, LBI, AR 2275; and Hans Hermann Hirschfeld interview, 1984, Holocaust Center of Northern California (hereafter HCNC), OHP, 8370.
181. Testimony of Josef Klábr, February 25, 1947, SOAL, LSP 441/47, p. 131; Anna Nathanová interview, AJMP.

Chapter 4

1. Emilie Valentová, APT, A, 1279, April 22, 1979.
2. Richard Stein, "Terezín—zdravotnický úkol," APT, A, 739. After the liberation, Stein emigrated with his family to Israel and became one of the founders of Israeli ophthalmology.

NOTES TO PAGES 132–134   291

3. Erich Springer, "Das Gesundheitswesen in Theresienstadt-Ghetto," 1950, YVA, O64, 18, 9. In addition, the medical department has outstanding surviving documentation, making it unique, as the SS ordered all paperwork to be burned in November 1944.

4. The military hospital Theresienstadt was located just outside the water tower on the western side of the town. Springer, "Das Gesundheitswesen in Theresienstadt-Ghetto," YVA, 56a; Miroslav Kárný interview, June 15, 1994, AJMP, The Oral History Collection, 328. For Germans fearing infections in other ghettos, see Isaiah Trunk, *Łódź Ghetto: A History*, ed. and trans. Robert Moses Shapiro (Bloomington: Indiana University Press, 2006), 13; and Isaiah Trunk, Isaiah, *Judenrat: The Jewish Councils in Eastern Europe under Nazi Occupation* (New York: Macmillan, 1972), 143.

5. The literature on medicine and the Holocaust is extensive. See, among others, Robert Jay Lifton, *The Nazi Doctors: Medical Killing and the Psychology of Genocide* (New York: Basic Books, 1986); Michael H. Kater, *Doctors Under Hitler* (Chapel Hill: University of North Carolina Press, 1989); Astrid Ley, *Medizin und Verbrechen: Das Krankenrevier des KZ Sachsenhausen 1936–1945* (Berlin: Metropol, 2005); and Paul Weindling, *Victims and Survivors of Nazi Human Experiments: Science and Suffering in the Holocaust* (London: Bloomsbury, 2014). A useful bibliography is found in Robert Jütte, Winfried Süß, and Wolfgang Eckart, eds., *Medizin und Nationalsozialismus: Bilanz und Perspektiven der Forschung* (Göttingen: Wallstein, 2011).

6. Kim Wünschmann, *Before Auschwitz: Jewish Prisoners in the Prewar Concentration Camps* (Cambridge, Mass.: Harvard University Press, 2015), 196–197.

7. Jütte, Süß, and Eckart, *Medizin und Nationalsozialismus*, 83.

8. Petr Svobodný and Ludmila Hlaváčková, *Dějiny lékařství v českých zemích* (Prague: Triton, 2004), 191.

9. Natalia Aleksiun, "Jewish Students and Christian Corpses in Interwar Poland: Playing with the Language of Blood Libel," *Jewish History* 26 (December 2012): 327–342, 328.

10. Hermann Strauß's obituary for Hans Hirschfeld, September 15, 1944, original in personal archive of Irene Hallmann-Strauß.

11. Rebecca Schwoch, "'Praktisch zum Verhungern verurteilt': 'Krankenbehandler' zwischen 1938 und 1945," In *Jüdische Ärztinnen und Ärzte im Nationalsozialismus : Entrechtung, Vertreibung, Ermordung*, ed. Thomas Beddies, Susanne Doetz, and Christoph Kopke (Munich: de Gruyter, 2014).

12. Petr Svobodný and Ludmila Hlaváčková, *Dějiny lékařství v českých zemích* (Prague: Triton, 2004), 199–201.

13. Daniela Angetter und Christine Kanzler, " 'Eltern, Wohnung, Werte, Ordination, Freiheit, Ehren verloren!': Das Schicksal der in Wien verbliebenen jüdischen Ärzte von 1938 bis 1945 und die Versorgung ihrer jüdischen Patienten," in *Jüdische Ärztinnen und Ärzte im Nationalsozialismus: Entrechtung, Vertreibung, Ermordung*, ed. Thomas Beddies et al. (Munich: de Gruyter, 2014), 58–74; and Michael Hubenstorf, "Vertriebene Medizin: Finale des Niedergangs der Wiener Medizinischen Schule?," in *Vertriebene Vernunft II: Emigration und Exil österreichischer Wissenschaft*, ed. Friedrich Stadler (Vienna: Jugend und Volk, 1988), 766–793.

292 NOTES TO PAGES 136–138

14. Notation by Siegfried Seidl, December 1, 1941, YVA, O7, 85. On Munk, see testimony of Max Rauchenberg, August 8, 1967, APT, A, 220.

15. "Wechsel in der Leitung der Kultusgemeinde Brünn," *Jüdisches Nachrichtenblatt*, December 27, 1940, 8.

16. Erich Springer, "Gesundheitswesen in Theresienstadt," in *Theresienstadt*, ed. Rudolf Iltis (Vienna: Europa-Verlag, 1968), 126–135, 127f.

17. Testimony of Hedvika Svobodová, April 7, 1981, APT, A, 2060.

18. Stein, "Terezín—zdravotnický úkol," APT; and Minna Wolfensteinová, "Die Schöpfungsgschichte der Infektionsabteilung," Peter Barber papers.

19. Springer, "Gesundheitswesen in Theresienstadt," 130; and Erich Munk to Paul Eppstein, May 25, 1943, YVA, O64, 54.

20. Stein, "Terezín—zdravotnický úkol," APT.

21. Stein, "Terezín—zdravotnický úkol," APT, 12.

22. Lilly Pokorny, "Eine Ärztin erlebt das 'Musterlager' Theresienstadt," Institute for Contemporary History Munich, MA 199. Although Pokorny subtitled her testimony a diary, it is a postwar testimony written ca. 1950, which she based on her notes from the ghetto. Thanks to Giles Bennett for sending me a copy. Lilly Pokorny's postwar publications appeared under the Czech version of her last name, Pokorná.

23. Emilie Těšínská, "Kontakty českých a německých rentgenologů a radiologů v českých zemích (do r. 1945)," *Dějiny věd a techniky* 30, no. 2 (1997): 88–96. The Viennese radiologist Nelly Blum was the only female department head in the Rothschild Hospital: Angetter and Kanzler, " 'Eltern, Wohnung, Werte,' " 67.

24. Pokorny to Heinrich Himmler, proposing chemical sterilization experiments, October 1941, Harvard Law School Library, Nuremberg Trials Project: A Digital Document Collection, accessed December 29, 2018, http://nuremberg.law.harvard.edu/documents/94-letter-to-heinrich-himmler?q=heinrich+himmler#p.1.

25. Springer, "Gesundheitswesen in Theresienstadt"; and Stein, "Terezín—zdravotnický úkol," APT, 15.

26. Adolph Metz, "Ghetto Theresiestadt," ca. 1945, YVA, O33, 3257 (Metz gives two thousand as the number of workers); for the lower number, see "Das Gesundheitswesen lädt ein, Juli 1943," YVA, O64, 54. Pokorny has the number of workers at two thousand ("Eine Ärztin erlebt das 'Musterlager' Theresienstadt," 199). Springer, has five thousand ("Das Gesundheitswesen in Theresienstadt-Ghetto," YVA, 5).

27. Stein, "Terezín—zdravotnický úkol," APT, 14. For comparison, in 1936, Czechoslovakia had 0.76 physician per one thousand inhabitants: Svobodný and Hlaváčková, *Dějiny lékařství v českých zemích*, 180. In 2012, Britain had 2.71 physicians per one thousand inhabitants, Czech Republic had 3.58, and Germany had 3.73; report of the European Commission for 2012, http://ec.europa.eu/eurostat/statistics-explained/index.php/Healthcare_statistics.

28. Ota Kolář interview.

29. Stein, "Terezín—zdravotnický úkol," APT, 18.

30. YVA, O64, 54; Karel Fleischmann, "Terezínský den," AJMP, T, 326, 101.

31. "Das Gesundheitswesen lädt ein, Juli 1943," YVA, O64, 54; and "Morbidität in Theresienstadt," YVA, O64, 56.

NOTES TO PAGES 136–138   293

32. Springer, "Gesundheitswesen in Theresienstadt," 132.

33. Stein, "Terezín—zdravotnický úkol," APT, 18.

34. Evžen Kraus, "Boj proti tuberkulose v koncentračních táborech," *Boj proti tuberkulose* 27, no. 8 (1946): 131–133, 131; Springer, "Das Gesundheitswesen in Theresienstadt-Ghetto," YVA, 18.

35. See also Sara Bender, *The Jews of Białystok during World War II and the Holocaust* (Waltham, Mass.: Brandeis University Press; Hanover, N.H.: University Press of New England, 2008), 143.

36. Barbara Engelking-Boni and Jacek Leociak, *The Warsaw Ghetto: A Guide to the Perished City* (New Haven, Conn.: Yale University Press, 2009), 281.

37. Trial of Benno Krönert, SOAL, MLS, 963/46.

38. Erich Springer interview, January 12, 1991, AJMP, The Oral History Collection, 50.

39. Rolf Bartels to the Jewish self-administration, July 7, 1945, ABS 305-633-1, 273–274.

40. Testimony of Cäcilie Friedmann, 1945, WL, P.II.e, 1068.

41. *Seznamy lékaren a lékařů* (1938), 534, 616; Antonín Sismilich, "Stručná historie lékárny v Budyni nad Ohří" (unpublished manuscript, Budyně). Thanks to Ivana Kodlová of the Budyně pharmacy for sending me a scan of this document.

42. Jarmila Saicová, delivery list, August 1, 1944, AJMP, T, 273; and Franz Hahn interview, DÖW, 510.

43. Sulfa drugs were developed by Gerhard Domagk at Bayer, then a subsidiary of IG Farben.

44. Jindřich Flusser, "Ein Rückblick," *Theresienstädter Studien und Dokumente* (1999): 43–75, 48.

45. Volker Roelcke, "Fortschritt ohne Rücksicht: Menschen als Versuchskanninchen bei den Sulfonamid-Experimenten im Konzentrationslager Ravensbrück," in *Geschlecht und "Rasse" in der NS-Medizin*, ed. Insa Eschebach and Astrid Ley (Berlin: Metropol, 2012), 101–114.

46. On May 30, 1944, the pharmacy's bill was for 136,000 crowns. Aktenvermerk W 720 (Economical Department) AJMP, T, 146; for half a million, see Karel Fleischmann, "Jak vznikalo zdravotnictví v terezínském ghettu," AJMP, T, 326.

47. Pokorny, "Eine Ärztin erlebt das 'Musterlager' Theresienstadt," 9; and Silvia Tarabini Goldbaum Fracapane, "Danish Testimonies about Theresienstadt: Experiences of Deportation and Ghetto Life" (PhD diss., Technical University Berlin, 2016)

48. Julius Taussig interviews, January 9, 1967, and August 26, 1975, APT, Sbírka vzpomínek, 51; and Zuzana Mannabergová on František Drahoňovský, September 21, 1945, trial of Theodor Janeček, SOAP, MLS, LS 428/46.

49. Pokorny, "Eine Ärztin erlebt das 'Musterlager' Theresienstadt," 200.

50. Erich Springer's operating notes, 1943, WL TAU, 578. Thanks to Harro Jenß for analyzing the first one hundred operations of 1943.

51. Irma Goldmannová of Pathology died in January 1945 of ileus.

52. Pokorny, "Eine Ärztin erlebt das 'Musterlager' Theresienstadt," 45, 83.

53. Tomáš Fedorovič, Neue Erkenntnisse über die SS Angehörigen im Ghetto Theresienstadt," *Theresienstädter Studien und Dokumente* (2006): 240.

54. Aktenvermerk L 505 (of the Council of Elders), WL, 1073, 4.

294 NOTES TO PAGES 142–145

55. Springer, "Gesundheitswesen in Theresienstadt," 134.

56. YVA, O1, 102; Murmelstein, "Geschichtlicher Überblick," WL, 1073; and Illa Loeb, YVA, O2, 324.

57. There was also a children's dentist; YVA, O64, 56a.

58. See also the entry on Anna Rosenzweig, YVA, O64, 53.

59. Manes, 343; Alice Randt, *Die Schleuse* (Hannoversch Münden: Chr. Gauke, 1974), 105; and Springer, "Das Gesundheitswesen in Theresienstadt-Ghetto," YVA.

60. Stein, "Terezín—zdravotnický úkol," APT, 24–25.

61. Stein, "Terezín—zdravotnický úkol," APT, 16

62. A sympathetic, if uncritical, biography is Leonard J. Hoenig, Tomas Spenser, and Anita Tarsi, "Dr. Karel Fleischmann: The Story of an Artist and Physician in Ghetto Terezin," *International Journal of Dermatology* 43 (February 2004): 129–135.

63. Report of Welfare, October 1943, YVA, O64, 53.

64. Those elderly who survived in Terezín did not live in closed care, and there are very few testimonies of the disabled in closed care. Adler, *Theresienstadt*, 537.

65. Adler, *Theresienstadt*, 534, 536.

66. Karel Fleischmann, "Panoptikum Q 403," June 23, 1943, AJMP, T, 326.

67. Fleischmann, "Terezínský den," AJMP.

68. Karel Fleischmann, "Zápas krabů," AJMP, T, 326.

69. Susan Grant, "Caring for the Mind: Medical Workers in Psychiatric Hospitals, 1930–1950" (unpublished manuscript, n.d.).

70. Springer, "Gesundheitswesen in Theresienstadt," 133.

71. Tomáš Fedorovič, "Jüdische Geisteskranke Patienten aus dem Protektorat," in *Die nationalsozialistische "Euthanasie" im Reichsgau Sudetenland und Protektorat Böhmen und Mähren 1939–1945*, ed. Michal Šimůnek and Dietmar Schulze (Červený Kostelec: Pavel Mervart and AV ČR, 2008), 199–236; on Jews in T4, see Lutz Kälber, "Child Murder in Nazi Germany: The Memory of Nazi Medical Crimes and Commemoration of 'Children's Euthanasia' Victims at Two Facilities (Eichberg, Kalmenhof)," *Societies* 2, no. 3 (2012): 157–194.

72. In March 1944, the SS ordered a small transport (Dx) of the mentally disabled to be sent to Auschwitz.

73. Marie Schnabel, "Als Irrenschwester in Theresienstadt," March 1960, WL, P.III.h, 1189.

74. Ruth Bondy, *"Elder of the Jews": Jakob Edelstein of Theresienstadt* (New York: Grove, 1989), 300–301.

75. Hanna Erdmann interview, July 1988, FZH/WdE, 1153.

76. Memo from Benjamin Murmelstein, March 15, 1945, NA Prague, KT OVS, inv. no. 64, box 45, file 29; and Pokorny, "Eine Ärztin erlebt das 'Musterlager' Theresienstadt," 118–119.

77. "Bilderausstellung von Margot Raphael im St. Franziskus-Hospital in Ahlen," accessed June 30, 2020, https://www.st-vincenz-gesellschaft.de/neuigkeiten/neuigkeiten/nachricht/news/detail/News/bilderausstellung-von-margot-raphael-im-st-franziskus-hospital-in-ahlen.html.

78. Sometimes the pathologists were allowed to use a camera.

NOTES TO PAGES 142-145   295

79. Rudolf Klein, October 25, 1945, YVA, O7, 239; Egon Redlich, entry for April 11, 1944, in *Zítra jedeme*, 217f.

80. Herwig Hamperl, *Werdegang und Lebensweg eines Pathologen* (Stuttgart: Schattauer, 1972), 199.

81. Michal Šimůnek, "Konec 'nenahraditelného muže': Likvidace R. Heydricha v lékařském kontextu. II. část," *Dějiny věd a techniky* 45, no. 1 (2012): 213–250.

82. Pokorny, "Eine Ärztin erlebt das 'Musterlager' Theresienstadt," 132f; Max Rauchenberg; Klein; Fedorovič, "Několik poznámek," 94.

83. Pokorny, "Eine Ärztin erlebt das 'Musterlager' Theresienstadt," 110.

84. This prohibition was part of the background for the controversy surrounding cadavers for use by Jewish medical students in interwar Poland. Natalia Aleksiun, "Jewish Students and Christian Corpses in Interwar Poland: Playing with the Language of Blood Libel," *Jewish History* 26, no. 3–4 (December 2012): 328.

85. Entry of medications, Central Drug Store to the Economic department, September 1, 1944, AJMP, T, 146.

86. L. Stern, "Juden von Giessen im Konzentrationslager Theresienstadt," LBI, AR 11759; and Ruth Weisz, "Und es war keine Lüge," in *Theresienstadt: Aufzeichnungen von Federica Spitzer und Ruth Weisz*, ed. Wolfgang Benz (Berlin: Metropol, 1997), 98,-157 106.

87. Pokorny, "Eine Ärztin erlebt das 'Musterlager' Theresienstadt," 143.

88. Resi Weglein, *Als Krankenschwester im KZ Theresienstadt: Erinnerungen einer Ulmer Jüdin* (Tübingen: Silberburg, 1988), 33.

89. Stein, "Terezín—zdravotnický úkol," APT, 24; and Alfred Wolff-Eisner, *Über Mangelerkrankungen auf Grund von Beobachtungen im Konzentrationslager* (Würzburg: Sauer-Marhard, 1947).

90. Pokorny, "Eine Ärztin erlebt das 'Musterlager' Theresienstadt," 145.

91. Monthly reports of Irma Goldmann, YVA, O64, 50.

92. In a similar vein, Trunk, *Łódź*, 207–209, mentions dysentery (enteritis) as the second most frequent disease in the first phase of Lodz but does not discuss it.

93. Sander Gilman, *Franz Kafka, the Jewish Patient* (New York: Routledge, 1995), ch. 4; on the Nazi perception of Jews as a diseased race, see Robert Proctor, *Racial Hygiene: Medicine under the Nazis* (Cambridge, Mass.: Harvard University Press, 1988), 194–202. Proctor pointed out that the Nazi perception of Jews as a "diseased race" led to the introduction of ghettos in the General Government.

94. Lilly Pokorná, "Die Lungentuberkulose im Konzentrationslager Theresienstadt im Vergleich mit der bei Häftlingen in anderen deutschen Konzentrationslagern," *Tuberkulosearzt* 4 (1950): 406–414, 405–406; and Vojtěch Král, "Nakažlivé choroby v Terezíně" (addenda to Stein, "Terezín—zdravotnický úkol," APT), 33.

95. Pokorná, "Die Lungentuberkulose," 407; and Stein, "Terezín—Zdravotnický úkol," APT, 18.

96. Kraus, "Boj proti tuberkulose," 131.

97. Kraus, "Boj proti tuberkulose," 131; and author's correspondence with Daniel Dražan (Löwit's grand-nephew), March 2013.

98. Stein, "Terezín—zdravotnický úkol," APT, 18.

296   NOTES TO PAGES 148–150

99. Franz Hahn interview, DÖW.
100. Trunk, Łódź, 207–208. Among those who arrived in Theresienstadt with the evacuation transports, the TB infection rate was 48 percent. Pokorná, "Die Lungentuberkulose," 414.
101. We have no numbers for the cause of death for those who arrived with the evacuation transports, and many died of exhaustion and hunger. According to the most recent estimate, 1,665 people who arrived with the death marches died. Marek Poloncarz, "Die Evakuierungstransporte nach Theresienstadt (April–Mai 1945)," Theresienstädter Studien und Dokumente (1998): 242–262, 249.
102. Stein, "Terezín—zdravotnický úkol," APT, 32; see also Aron Vedder, "Bericht über die Gesundheitslage in Theresienstadt mit besonderer Berücksichtigung der Flecktyphus-Epidemie nebst Vorschlägen zu ihrer Bekämpfung," May 15, 1945, YVA, O64, 56a.
103. Stein, "Terezín—zdravotnický úkol," APT, 32; and Springer, "Das Gesundheitswesen in Theresienstadt-Ghetto," YVA, 12.
104. Diary of Arnošt Klein, entries for January and February, 1943, AJMP, T, 324; and Egon Redlich, entry for February 6, 1943, in Zítra jedeme, 175.
105. In 1943, altogether seventy-four people died of typhoid. Annual report of the Health Services for 1944, YVA, O64, 56a.
106. Munk to Edelstein, Janowitz, and Zucker, January 25, 1943, YVA, O64, 23/II.
107. Defining children as fifteen and younger; Data Terezín Prisoners Database and the death certificates.
108. Estimate, calculated at over sixty-five and under fifteen years of age. In February 1943, the inmate statisticians in the Technical Department counted ca. 235 infants under the age of two and 1,921 inmates over the age of sixty-five who died. YVA, O64, 45.
109. On a similar case in the early years of the German Democratic Republic, see Donna Harsch, "Medicalized Social Hygiene? Tuberculosis Policy in the German Democratic Republic," Bulletin of the History of Medicine 86 (Fall 2012): 394–423.
110. Trunk, Łódź, 163; and Engelking-Boni and Leociak, The Warsaw Ghetto, 239–240.
111. Franz Hahn interview, DÖW.
112. Interrogation of Viktor Kindermann, September 17, 1945, SOAP, MLS, LS 591/45.
113. Christian Goeschel, "Suicide in Nazi Concentration Camps, 1933–9," Journal of Contemporary History 45 (July 2010): 628–648; Wünschmann, Before Auschwitz, ch. 1; and Timothy Pytell, "Redeeming the Unredeemable: Auschwitz and Man's Search for Meaning," Holocaust and Genocide Studies 17, no. 1 (2003): 89–113.
114. Weglein, Als Krankenschwester im KZ Theresienstadt, 30.
115. Welfare, monthly report, October 1943; Welfare, monthly report, March 1944, NIOD, 250n; Frankl, 17th monthly report, March 27, 1944, Frankl Institute Vienna.
116. Rudolf Löwith, "Selbstmorde in Theresienstadt," April 22, 1944, YVA, O64, 51.
117. Note of Irma Goldmann, July 31, 1944, YVA, O64, 50.
118. Diary of Arnošt Klein, entry for January 12, 1943, AJMP.
119. "Die Morbidität in Theresienstadt," 5, YVA, O64, 56.

NOTES TO PAGES 148–150   297

120. In Germany in 1938, and in Czechoslovakia in 1940, Jews were only allowed to visit Jewish physicians. In Germany, stripped of their title, a fraction of Jewish doctors were allowed to continue practicing as "Krankenbehandler." Schwoch, " 'Praktisch zum Verhungern verurteilt," 78n12; and Svobodný and Hlaváčková, *Dějiny lékařství v českých zemích*, 200, 202.

121. Testimony of Käthe Breslauer, January 15, 1956, WL, P.III.h, 215.

122. Ilse Porath interview, June 4, 2000, YVA, O3, 11611.

123. Benjamin Murmelstein, *Theresienstadt: Eichmanns Vorzeige-Ghetto*, ed. Ruth Pleyer and Alfred J. Noll, trans. Karin Fleischanderl (Vienna: Czernin, 2014), 153.

124. Grabower, Vermerke, entries for August 7 and 8, 1944, Grabower papers, Finanzakademie Brühl.

125. Murmelstein, *Eichmanns Vorzeige-Ghetto*, 153–154.

126. Sander Gilman, *Franz Kafka, the Jewish Patient* (New York: Routledge, 1995).

127. Pokorny, "Eine Ärztin erlebt das 'Musterlager' Theresienstadt," 81. See also Cancer statistics (1942–44), YVA, O64, 50. The Berlin gynecologist Herbert Lewin, who was deported to Lodz ghetto, in fact established that thanks to the starvation diet, ghetto residents had a lower rate of cancer. Rebecca Schwoch, *Herbert Lewin: Arzt-Überlebender-Zentralratspräsident* (Berlin: Hentrich & Hentrich, 2016), 34–36.

128. Herman Strauß, "Krankheitsdispositionen bei den Juden," AJMP, T, 272. See also Harro Jenß, *Hermann Strauß: Internist und Wissenschaftler in der Charité und im jüdischen Krankenhaus Berlin* (Berlin: Hentrich & Hentrich, 2010); and Harro Jenß and Peter Reinicke, eds., *Der Arzt Hermann Strauß 1868–1944: Autobiographische Notizen und Aufzeichnungen aus dem Ghetto Theresienstadt* (Berlin: Hentrich & Hentrich, 2014).

129. Willy Groag interview, September 15, 1995, AJMP, The Oral History Collection, 82.

130. Munk/Bass, August 21, 1943, YVA, O64, 54. Egon (Gonda) Redlich mentioned this prohibition for the first time on July 7, 1943.

131. Diary of Arnošt Klein, entry for March 21, 1944, AJMP.

132. Pokorny, "Eine Ärztin erlebt das 'Musterlager' Theresienstadt," 67.

133. Hanuš Schimmerling wrote to his Prague friends Jakub Berger and Jany Lebovič asking for condoms. Miloš Hájek, personal communication to the author, September 21, 2008.

134. Katharina von Kellenbach, "Reproduction and Resistance during the Holocaust," in *Women and the Holocaust: Narrative and Representation*, ed. Esther Fuchs (Lanham, Md.: University Press of America, 1999), 19–32, 29.

135. Springer, "Das Gesundheitswesen in Theresienstadt-Ghetto," YVA, speaks of "many hundreds, maybe thousands"; the annual report of Health Services for 1944 gives 196 "curetages." Stein, SOAL Rahm, spoke about three hundred to four hundred abortions. Irma Goldmann mentioned 141 pregnancies for January 1943; YVA, O64, 50.

136. Testimony of Růžena Ranschburgerová, January 29, 1972, APT, A, 579.

137. Hilde Bürger, *Bezwingt des Herzens Bitterkeit: Autobiographie einer jüdischen Krankenschwester* (Waldkirch: Waldkircher Verl.-Ges., 1991), 68.

298 NOTES TO PAGES 153–156

138. Diary of Eva Roubíčková, entries in May 1944, AITI; and diary of Hana Platovská's entries for June 6 and 16, 1944, APT, A, 5248.

139. Doris Donovalová interview, July 25, 1994, Gender Studies Prague.

140. Anna Herrmannová Barker, YVA, O2, 777 (=WL, P.III.h 943); Hedvika Svobodová, née Křiváčková, interview, April 7, 1981, APT, A 2060.

141. Pokorny, "Eine Ärztin erlebt das 'Musterlager' Theresienstadt," 40; and Stein, "Terezín—zdravotnický úkol," APT.

142. Eliška K. interview, AJMP, The Oral History Collection, 40 (born 1912); Jiří Hahn et al., "Die Morbidität in Theresienstadt," YVA, O64, 56.

143. Medical certificate B, December 20, 1954, reparation file Etta Japha (no. 76079), Reparation Office Berlin, B8.

144. Saul Friedländer, *The Years of Extermination*, vol 2, *Nazi Germany and the Jews* (New York: HarperPerennial, 2006), 8–9, 438–443; see also Amos Goldberg, "The Victim's Voice in History and Melodramatic Esthetics," *History and Theory* 48, no. 3 (2009): 220–237.

145. The same applied did not apply to other academic titles, even though these were frequent.

146. Weglein, *Als Krankenschwester im KZ Theresienstadt*, 84–85.

147. Applications from Elisabeth and Henrik Egyedi, May 5, 1945, YVA, O64, 30.

148. Flusser, "Ein Rückblick," 53; and Kraus, "Boj proti tuberkulose," 131.

149. Springer, "Das Gesundheitswesen in Theresienstadt-Ghetto," YVA, 9.

150. Helga Wolfensteinová to Renate Barber, no date (summer 1945), Peter Barber papers.

151. Springer, "Das Gesundheitswesen in Theresienstadt-Ghetto," YVA, 11.

152. Franz Hahn interview, DÖW; and Springer, "Das Gesundheitswesen in Theresienstadt-Ghetto," YVA, 10.

153. Springer, "Das Gesundheitswesen in Theresienstadt-Ghetto," YVA.

154. Kraus, "Boj proti tuberkulose," 131.

155. Laura Jockusch, *Collect and Record! Jewish Holocaust Documentation in Early Postwar Europe* (Oxford: Oxford University Press, 2012); Alexandra Garbarini, "Document Volumes and the Status of Victim Testimony in the Era of the First World War and Its Aftermath," *Études arméniennes contemporaines* 5 (2015): 113–138; and Lisa Leff, *The Archive Thief: The Man Who Salvaged French Jewish History in the Wake of the Holocaust* (Oxford: Oxford University Press, 2015).

156. Beate Meyer, "'Altersghetto,' 'Vorzugslager' und Tätigkeitsfeld: Die Repräsentanten der Reichsvereinigung der Juden in Deutschland und Theresienstadt," *Theresienstädter Studien und Dokumente* (2004): 141–142.

157. Otto Zucker also had house concerts; Fleischmann, "Křivule II," AJMP, T, 326. See also chapter 5.

158. Elena Makarova, Sergei Makarov, and Viktor Kuperman, *University over the Abyss: The Story behind 520 Lecturers and 2,430 Lectures in KZ Theresienstadt 1942–1944* (Jerusalem: Verba, 2004), 245.

159. Jan Rocek to the author, July 22, 2015. (Klapp was Rocek's cousin). Petr Kien's drawing of the doctors' quartet, APT.

NOTES TO PAGES 153–156   299

160. In this respect, music was related to Karel Fleischmann's drawings or the dentist Kurt Kapper's poetry. AJMP, T, 326, Kapper collection.

161. Franz Hahn interview, DÖW.

162. Fleichschmann, "Jak vznikalo," AJMP; and Pokorny, "Eine Ärztin erlebt das 'Musterlager' Theresienstadt," 17.

163. Siegmund Hadra, "Theresienstadt," LBI, AR 1249, 2.

164. The institution moved in 1914 to Wedding, where after 1943 the Gestapo also used the building also as a collection camp.

165. Strauß's notes from Terezín are the only contemporaneous source of a member of the Council of Elders, and one of their few self-testimonies. Jenß and Reinicke, *Der Arzt Hermann Strauß 1868-1944*, 112–113.

166. Interview of Hahn's stepdaughter, January 28, 1992, AJMP, The Oral History Collection, 105 (born 1921).

167. Dietlinde Peters, *Martha Wygodzinski (1869-1943) "Der Engel der Armen": Berliner Ärztin—engagierte Gesundheitspolitikerin* (Berlin: Hentrich & Hentrich, 2008); and Frieda Sington, WL, P.II.h, 186.

168. In November 1944, the SS ordered that the ashes of the dead be thrown into the Ohře. Hermann Bohm to Arthur Lippmann, June 20, 1949, StAH, 622-1/55 Lippmann, B5. See also Anna von Villiez, *Mit aller Kraft verdrängt: Entrechtung und Verfolgung "nicht arischer" Ärzte in Hamburg 1933 bis 1945* (Hamburg: Dölling und Galitz, 2009), 138–144.

169. Notes from Regina Oelze, 1947, Alte Syn Essen.

170. Grabower Vermerke, July 21, 1944, Brühl.

171. Franz Hahn interview, DÖW.

172. Murmelstein to Josef Löwenherz, March 10, 1943, YVA, O30, 51.

173. In medical school, Müller dated her fellow student, the dental surgeon Emmerich Weindling. Over a decade later, in 1938, Weindling left for Britain, and his son Paul went on to become a key medical historian of the Holocaust. Thanks to Karl Bettelheim and Paul Weindling for this information. For Müller in Vienna, see Angestelltenverzeichnis der IKG, CAHJP, A/W 568, 2. Thanks to Michaela Raggam Blesch for this information.

174. "Ein Jahr Hamburger Kaserne," BTA, 124.

175. Application of Šalomoun Racenberg for "presidential exception" to be exempt as Jew after 1940, NA, police registrations. The Racenbergs were among the 2 percent of Jewish doctors who were allowed to practice.

176. Miroslav Kárný's interview with Eva Štichová, in "Komunistická organizace v terezínském koncentračním táboře 1941-1945" (manuscript, 1983), NA, Kárných, ka 16, 7–10.

177. Weglein, *Als Krankenschwester im KZ Theresienstadt*.

178. Weglein, *Als Krankenschwester im KZ Theresienstadt*, 77.

179. Věra Kolářová interview, January 20, 1992, AJMP, The Oral History Collection, 101.

180. Viktor Kosák to friends, February 15, 1943, personal papers Kosák. I thank Michal Kosák for sharing his grandfather's papers.

181. Randt, *Die Schleuse*, 53.

NOTES TO PAGES 160–163

182. Hadra, "Theresienstadt," LBI.

183. Elsa Strauß's notes in Jenß, *Hermann Strauß*, 62–63.

184. Trunk, Łódź, 313.

185. I took a sample of fourteen elderly people (born between 1845 and 1865) and all fourteen children born after 1937.

186. Oskar Weissbrod, block physician and Alice Randt's boss, is named twice, indicating that it was the block physicians who took care of the dying elderly.

187. Attending physicians: three times Felix Weiss and Felix Schwarz; coroners: three times Anna Gans, twice Martha Müller.

188. Erich Springer collection, AJMP, OP, 17; Henriette Blumenthal-Rothschild to Erich Springer, September 1, 1946, personal papers Petra Kristen; and Pokorny, "Eine Ärztin erlebt das 'Musterlager' Theresienstadt," 148–149.

189. Laurens de Rooy, *Snijburcht: Lodewijk Bolk en de Bloei Van de Nederlandse Anatomie* (Amsterdam, Amsterdam University Press, 2011), 280–281; and Martinus Woerdeman, *Atlas of Human Anatomy: Descriptive and Regional* (London: Butterworth, 1948).

190. Pokorny, "Eine Ärztin erlebt das 'Musterlager' Theresienstadt," 203–204; and Stein, "Terezín—zdravotnický úkol," APT, 7–8.

191. Marieta Š.-B. interview, AJMP.

192. Franz Hahn interview, DÖW.

193. Health Services petition to be taken out of transport, YVA, O64, 22.

194. Dr. Felix Meyer, LBI, AR 1437. The books survived the war and are today kept, with the ghetto medical library stamp, at the Jewish Museum in Prague.

195. Ruth Bondy, "Women in Theresienstadt and the Family Camp in Birkenau," in *Women in the Holocaust*, ed. Dalia Ofer and Lenore J. Weitzman (New Haven, Conn.: Yale University Press, 1998), 310–326, 315.

196. Franz Bass, "Amonerrhoe in Theresienstadt," December 12, 1943, AJMP, T, 272.

197. Franz Bass, "L'amour et les camps de concentration," *Theresienstädter Studien und Dokumente* 13 (2006): 343–347; Bass's son Giovanni and his granddaughter Barbara Bass are gynecologists in Zurich.

198. Thomas Laqueur, *Making Sex: Body and Gender from the Greeks to Freud* (Cambridge, Mass.: Harvard University Press, 1990).

199. Atina Grossmann, "The New Woman and the Rationalization of Sexuality in Weimar Germany," in *Women in Culture and Politics a Century of Change*, ed. Judith Friedlander et al. (Bloomington: Indiana University Press, 1986), 153–171.

200. Laqueur, *Making Sex*, 22, 216.

201. Sabine Hildebrandt, "The Women on Stieve's List: Victims of National Socialism Whose Bodies Were Used for Anatomical Research," *Clinical Anatomy* 26 (2013): 3–21.

202. In contextualizing this argument, I follow Robert Jay Lifton's placing of prisoner doctors into his study of Nazi physicians, *The Nazi Doctors: Medical Killing and the Psychology of Genocide* (New York: Basic Books, 1986), chs. 11–14.

203. Pokorny, "Eine Ärztin erlebt das 'Musterlager' Theresienstadt," 215.

204. Franz Hahn interview, DÖW.

NOTES TO PAGES 160–163   301

205. Randt, *Die Schleuse*, 77.
206. Martha Glass, *"Jeder Tag in Theresin ist ein Geschenk"*: *Die Theresienstädter Tagebücher einer Hamburger Jüdin 1943–1945*, ed. Barbara Müller Wesemann (Hamburg: Ergebnisse, 1996), entry for September 3, 1943, 81.
207. Springer "Das Gesundheitswesen in Theresienstadt-Ghetto," YVA.
208. Anna Auředníčková, *Tři léta v Terezíně* (Prague: Alois Hynek, 1945), 61.
209. "Doctors Are Hungry. Too," drawing of Erich Lichtblau, catalog of artworks, LAMOTH (1943).
210. Pokorny, "Eine Ärztin erlebt das 'Musterlager' Theresienstadt"; and Karel Fleischmann, "Jedna ruku druhou myje," AJMP, T, 326.
211. Anna Hájková, "Die fabelhaften Jungs aus Theresienstadt: Junge tschechische Männer als dominante soziale Elite im Theresienstädter Ghetto," *Beiträge zur Geschichte des Nationalsozialismus* 25 (2009): 128–130.
212. František Steiner, *Fotbal pod žlutou hvězdou* (Prague: Olympia, 2009), 23, 41; diary of Willy Mahler, entry for April 29, 1944, APT, A, 5704; poster of Aeskulap, Heřman collection, APT. Thanks to Tomáš Raichl for identifying many of the signatures.
213. Pokorny, "Eine Ärztin erlebt das 'Musterlager' Theresienstadt"; see also chapter 6.
214. Rebecca Schwoch, "The Situation and Ethical Dilemmas of Krankenbehandler (Sick Treaters), 1938–1945: The Example of Hamburg," *Korot* 23 (2015–2016): 173–194, 186.
215. Pokorny, "Eine Ärztin erlebt das 'Musterlager' Theresienstadt," 207.
216. Grabower, Vermerke, September 15, 1944.
217. Grabower, Vermerke, August 16, 1944.
218. Pokorny, "Eine Ärztin erlebt das 'Musterlager' Theresienstadt," 54.
219. Diary of Hana Posseltová-Ledererová, entries for January 14–30, 1943, in Hana Posseltová-Ledererová, *Máma a já (Terezínský deník)* (Prague: GG, 1997), 33–39.
220. Statement of Pavel Klein, February 19, 1946; and statement of Julie Pollaková, both in January 26, 1946, ABS 305-633-1, 232–233 and 260.
221. "Jahresbericht des Gesundheitswesens für das Jahr 1944," YVA, O64, 56a.
222. Ella Cabicarová interview, June 8, 1994, AJMP, The Oral History Collection, 317.
223. Edmund Hadra, memoirs II, LBI, AR 1249, box 2, 87–88; interview of a woman, April 17, 1997, AJMP, The Oral History Collection, 658 (born 1928).
224. Bürger, *Bezwingt des Herzens Bitterkeit*, 64–65.
225. Hadra, memoirs II, LBI.
226. After the war, Šťastný returned to his first wife. Pohlmann attempted to commit suicide, survived, returned to Berlin, married a physician, and had two daughters. Bürger's and Šťastný's descendants have differing interpretations of their parents' parting.
227. Svobodný and Hlavačková, *Dějiny lékařství v českých zemích*, 179.
228. Pokorny, "Eine Ärztin erlebt das 'Musterlager' Theresienstadt," 49f.
229. Pokorná, "Eine Ärztin erlebt das 'Musterlager' Theresienstadt," 197f.
230. Lucie Auerbach, "Zum zwei-jaehrigen Bestehen der Roentgen-Abteilung EVI Maerz 1944," cited in Pokorny, "Eine Ärztin erlebt das 'Musterlager' Theresienstadt," 114–115. Translation Justus von Widekind.

302 NOTES TO PAGES 165-171

231. Franz Hahn interview, DÖW.

232. Kraus, "Boj proti tuberkulose."

233. Statement of Rudolf Klein, YVA, O7, 239; Flusser, "Ein Rückblick."

234. Pokorny, "Eine Ärztin erlebt das 'Musterlager' Theresienstadt," 204–205, does not give her name, but "Seznamy lékařů a zdravotnických zařízení v osvobozeném ghetto," AJMP, T, 262, gives MUC Gertrude Freund as the second doctor in the Surgery in the General Hospital. See also "Grete Freund" in AJMP, OP, no. 17. Vally Scheftel-Fabisch, a young Viennese doctor, was only able to find work as a nurse after her move to Berlin when she started working for the Reich Association. Sarah Wildman, *Paper Love: Searching for the Girl My Grandfather Left Behind* (New York: Riverhead Books, 2015), chs. 8 and 9.

235. Pokorny "Eine Ärztin erlebt das 'Musterlager' Theresienstadt"; Leo Spitzer interview, December 5, 1971, APT, A, 500 (on Salomon Vintura); Vedder, "Bericht über die Gesundheitslage," YVA.

236. Author's interview with Ina ter Beek Frenkel, February 5, 2001.

237. For a history of nursing in this period see, among others, Bronwyn Rebekah McFarland-Icke, *Nurses in Nazi Germany: Moral Choice in History* (Princeton, N.J.: Princeton University Press, 1999); Susan Benedict and Linda Shields, eds., *Nurses and Midwives in Nazi Germany: The "Euthanasia Programs"* (London: Routledge, 2014); Susan Grant, ed., *Russian and Soviet Health Care from an International Perspective Comparing Professions, Practice and Gender, 1880–1960* (Basingstoke, UK: Palgrave, 2017).

238. OdF application of Lucie Salzmann-Lewy, October 8, 1945, LAB, C Rep 118-01, 31041; and Peter Barber (Wolfenstein's grandson) to the author, October 23, 2015.

239. The lack of professional nursing training in interwar Czechoslovakia is mentioned in Joža Bruegel, "Memoirs," 20, private archive of Richard Kuper.

240. Murmelstein, "Geschichtlicher Überblick," WL, 33.

241. Věra Kolářová interview, AJMP; and Felicitas Průšová, "Vzpomínky na okupaci," (June 1984), AJMP, Vzpomínky, 953.

242. For instance, both daughters of Rudolf Klein (later Klen) became medical workers, as did the son and granddaughter of František Bass.

243. Federica Spitzer, "Verlorene Jahre," in Wolfgang Benz, ed., *Theresienstadt: Aufzeichnungen von Federica Spitzer und Ruth Weisz* (Berlin: Metropol, 1997), 9–97, 63.

244. Spitzer, "Verlorene Jahre," 62–63, 67.

245. Anna Hájková, "Die Jahre der Verbitterung: Neues über Otilie Davidová, die 1942 nach Theresienstadt deportierte jüngste Schwester Franz Kafkas," *Süddeutsche Zeitung*, November 24, 2015.

246. SOAP, KSČ Praha, CK VIIIa 95/40, March 1940.

247. Otilie Davidová to Věra and Helena Davidová, family collection. I thank Josef Třeštík and Pavla Neuner for letting me read the letters.

248. Springer "Das Gesundheitswesen in Theresienstadt-Ghetto," YVA; and Weglein, *Als Krankenschwester im KZ Theresienstadt.*

249. Poems of Minna Wolfenstein (esp. "Terezinka im Kinderzimmer"), YVA, O64, 78.

NOTES TO PAGES 165–171   303

250. Pokorny, "Eine Ärztin erlebt das 'Musterlager' Theresienstadt."
251. Helga King's comment on Bruno Zwicker's letter to Minna Wolfenstein, April 24, 1942, Peter Barber's papers.
252. Auředníčková, *Tři léta v Terezíně*.
253. Spitzer, "Verlorene Jahre"; Thea Höchster, YVA, O33, 3534; Trude Groag, Beit Terezin Archives (BTA), 81; and Zdenka Bínová, APT, Sbírka vzpomínek, 68.
254. Ellen Loeb, "Liebe Trude, lieber Rudy" (1945), in *Sisters in Sorrow: Voices of Care in the Holocaust*, ed. Roger A. Ritvo and Diane M. Plotkin (College Station: Texas A&M University Press, 1998), 107–125, 112.
255. Bohm to Artur Lippmann, June 20, 1949, HHStA, 622-1/55 Lippmann, B5.
256. Springer, "Das Gesundheitswesen in Theresienstadt-Ghetto," YVA, 9.
257. Pokorny, "Eine Ärztin erlebt das 'Musterlager' Theresienstadt," 85–89, 214–215.
258. Deborah Dwórk, *War Is Good for Babies and Other Young Children: A History of the Infant and Child Welfare Movement in England 1898–1918* (London: Tavistock, 1987).
259. Sheri Fink, "The Deadly Choices at Memorial," *New York Times*, August 25, 2009.

Chapter 5

1. Pierre Bourdieu, "Social Space and the Genesis of Classes," in *Language and Symbolic Power*, ed. Pierre Bourdieu (Cambridge, Mass.: Harvard University Press, 1991), 229–251.
2. Interview Bedřich Borges, AJMP, The Oral History Collection, 137.
3. Mirko Tůma, *Ghetto našich dnů* (Prague: Jaroslav Salivar, 1946), 15; Ota Růžička, APT, Sbírka vzpomínek, 834; and Erich Weiner's report on the history of the Freizeitgestaltung, YVA, O64, 65.
4. Diary of Bedřich Kohn, entry for November 29, 1942, APT, A, 11891.
5. Interview of a woman, AJMP, The Oral History Collection, 727 (born 1926); and testimony of Heda Grabová, September 28, 1945, YVA, O7, 228.
6. Minutes of Recreation, November 16, 1943, YVA, O64, 65.
7. Elena Makarova's interview with Jakov Rachman (Reichmann's postwar name), in Elena Makarova, Sergei Makarov, and Viktor Kuperman, *University over the Abyss: The Story behind 520 Lecturers and 2,430 Lectures in KZ Theresienstadt 1942–1944* (Jerusalem: Verba, 2004), 333.
8. Minutes of the meetings for March 1945, NA Prague, KT OVS, inv. no. 64, box 45, file 29.
9. Manes, 424–425; Minutes of Recreation, October 26 and November 9, 1943, YVA, O64, 65.
10. Additional list of the artists, August 21, 1943, YVA, O64, 47 (see also ch. 6); and Nava Shan, ICJ OHD.
11. Henschel papers, BTA, 146; and Makarova et al., *University over the Abyss*, 313–314.
12. Minutes of Recreation, March 10, 1944, YVA, O64, 65.
13. Adler, *Theresienstadt*, 596–597.

304 NOTES TO PAGES 173–176

14. Weekly program for theater and soccer, February 14–20, 1944, YVA, O64, 65.

15. Diary of Bedřich Kohn, entry for October 23, 1943, APT, A, 11891, on Smetana's *Kiss* and *Bartered Bride*.

16. Josef Bor, *Opuštěná Panenka* (Prague: Státní nakladatelství politické literatury, 1961), 221, 257, 259.

17. Kurt Singer, "Musikkritischer Brief Nr. 4: Verdis Requiem," YVA, O64, 65; minutes of Recreation; Shan, ICJ OHD.

18. Apparently the poem was written during the early deportations in Munich and brought by Münchner to Terezín. Else Behrend-Rosenfeld mentioned that the anonymous poem circulated among the Jews of Munich: *Ich stand nicht allein: Erlebnisse einer Jüdin in Deutschland 1933–1944* (Munich: Beck, 1988), entry for April 12, 1942. Some give the title as "Transport," others as "1942," yet others as "Ich sah heute tausend Leute." Richard Feder, *Židovská tragedie: Dějství poslední* (Kolín: Lusk, 1947), 36–37; Erich Kessler, "Der Theresienstädter 20. April 1945 und die Tage danach ...," *Theresienstädter Studien und Dokumente* (1995): 306–324, 323.

19. Trude Groag, YVA, O64, 76; and Magda Veselská, *Archa paměti: Cesta pražského židovského muzea pohnutým 20. Stoletím* (Prague: Academia, 2012), ch. 3.

20. Two important contributions to reading the children's art in its original context are Elena Makarova, *Friedl Dicker-Brandeis: Ein Leben für Kunst und Lehre: Wien, Weimar, Prag, Hronov, Theresienstadt, Auschwitz* (Vienna: Brandstätter, 2000); and Nicholas Stargardt, "Children's Art of the Holocaust," *Past & Present* 161 (November 1998): 191–235.

21. Nava Shan [Schönová's postwar name], *Chtěla jsem být herečkou* (Prague: Ivo Železný, 1992), 83.

22. Memo from Gerhart Riegner, July 8, 1943, reprinted in H. G. Adler, *Verheimlichte Wahrheit: Theresienstädter Dokumente* (Tübingen: Mohr, 1958), 304–306.

23. Maurice Rossel, "Besuch im Ghetto," ed. Vojtěch Blodig, *Theresienstädter Studien und Dokumente* (1996): 284–301.

24. Murmelstein believed that as long as the SS was happy with the ghetto, they would not liquidate it—and he did whatever it took to please them. Murmelstein, Lanzmann interview, 3158, 3179, 3183 passim.

25. Testimony of Heda Grabová, YVA: "Aber was, lassenses da. Sollens dann wieder spielen und singen."

26. Josef Bor, *Terezínské rekviem* (Prague: Československý spisovatel, 1963), 73.

27. Karel Berman interview, February 15, 1993, AJMP, The Oral History Collection, 170; and interview of a woman, (1992 and 1993) AJMP, The Oral History Collection, 135 (born 1909). Some scholars take Bor as a reliable source, such as Marjorie Lamberti, "Making Art in the Terezin Concentration Camp," *New England Review* 17, no. 4 (1995): 104–111. See also the production of *Defiant Requiem* by Murray Sidlin, Catholic University of America.

28. Blanka Haasová, APT, A, 392; Fritz Warenhaupt, YVA, O33, 173; interview of a woman, AJMP, The Oral History Collection, 387 (born 1913); and David Bloch's interview with Hedda Grab-Evans, David Bloch's collection, USHMM. Thanks to Michael Beckerman and Vojin Majstorovic for their help.

NOTES TO PAGES 173–176   305

29. Otakar Růžička, APT, Sbírka vzpomínek, 834; see also interview of a man, AJMP, The Oral History Collection, 173 (born 1903).
30. Diary of Willy Mahler, entry for May 5, 1944, APT, A, 5704.
31. Charlotta Burešová to Jiří Lauscher, March 19, 1981, BTA, 11c; author's interview with Anny Wafelman Morpurgo, July 10, 2001.
32. Ivan Salač, "Rodinná kronika," AJMP, DS, VI-260; and Margit Perschke, WL, P.III.f, 954.
33. Norbert Troller, Die Maleraffäre von Theresienstadt, 1981, LBI, AR 7268, 2/7; and Leo Haas, BTA, 125.
34. Irena Rieselová, APT, A, 129; and Benno Leiter, LBI, AR 4448.
35. Doris Bergen made this point in her analysis of the double-edgedness of sexuality: it is particularly coded as intimate and can be a means of assurance but also of particular violence. Music, she argued, has a similar function, hence the alienation of the concentration camp inmates from the music of the camp orchestras. Doris Bergen, "Sexual Violence in the Holocaust: Unique and Typical?," in *Lessons and Legacies VII: The Holocaust in International Perspective*, ed. Dagmar Herzog (Evanston, Ill.: Northwestern University Press, 2006), 179–200, 194.
36. Adler, *Theresienstadt*, 586.
37. For this differentiation, see useful remarks by Celia Applegate, "The Importance of Culture: GSA Presidential Address 2010," *GSA Newsletter* 35, no. 2 (2011): 23–36.
38. Diary of Willy Mahler, entry for August 30, 1944, APT; Manes, 133.
39. Frances Epstein, "The Roundtrip," private archive Helen Epstein.
40. Anna Stamm, LBI, ME 616; and Hana Rutarová to her husband Karel, April 29, 1944, APT, A, 8652.
41. Christiane Hess, *Das Lager im Blick: Zeichnungen aus den Konzentrationslagern Ravensbrück und Neuengamme* (Berlin: Metropol, 2021).
42. Juliane Brauer, *Musik im Konzentrationslager Sachsenhausen* (Berlin: Metropol, 2009).
43. Anne Dutlinger, "Art and Artists in Theresienstadt: Questions of Survival," in *Art, Music, and Education as Strategies for Survival: Theresienstadt 1941–45*, ed. Dutlinger (New York: Herodias, 2000), 1–9.
44. For criticism of the concept of "survival," see Lawrence Langer, *Holocaust Testimonies: The Ruins of Memory* (New Haven, Conn.: Yale University Press, 1991), 175.
45. Maja Suderland, *Territorien des Selbst: Kulturelle Identität als Ressource für das tägliche Überleben im Konzentrationslager* (Frankfurt/Main: Campus, 2004).
46. Diary of Bedřich Kohn, entry for January 1, 1943, APT; Gertrud Grassmann, BStU, ZUV 74 Ga, vol. 19; Makarova et al., *University over the Abyss*, 195.
47. On pleasure and humor, see Lisa Peschel, "Das Theater in Theresienstadt und das Zweite Tschechische Kabarett: 'Geistiger Widerstand'?" *Theresienstädter Studien und Dokumente* (2006): 84–114.
48. Shirley Gilbert, *Music in the Holocaust: Confronting Life in the Nazi Ghettos and Camps* (Oxford: Oxford University Press, 2005), 10.
49. See also David Bloch, "Skryté významy: Symboly v terezínské hudbě," in *Terezín v konečném řešení židovské otázky, ed. Miroslav Kárný* (Prague: Logos, 1992), 113; see

306 NOTES TO PAGES 180–185

also Michael Beckerman and Naomi Tadmor, "'Lullaby': The Story of a Niggun," *Music and Politics* X, no. 1 (2016).

50. David Bloch argued that even if we can connect music to a meaning, for instance to the significance of the lyrics, music is nothing else than itself. Bloch, "Skryté významy," 110.

51. Doris L. Bergen, "Sexual Violence in the Holocaust: Unique and Typical?," in *Lessons and Legacies VII: The Holocaust in International Perspective*, ed. Dagmar Herzog (Evanston, Ill.: Northwestern University Press, 2006).

52. Valter Kesler, APT, A, 134; and Hana Pírková, APT, A, 304.

53. Janet Blatter and Sybil Milton, *Art of the Holocaust* (New York: Routledge, 1981); and Miriam Novitch, *Spiritual Resistance: Art from Concentration Camps, 1940–1945* (New York: Union of American Hebrew Congregations, 1981); see also Murray Sidlin's *Defiant Requiem.*

54. Lawrence Langer, *Admitting the Holocaust: Collected Essays* (New York: Oxford University Press, 1995); Shirli Gilbert, *Music in the Holocaust: Confronting Life in the Nazi Ghettos and Camps* (Oxford: Oxford University Press, 2005); Garbarini, *Numbered Days*; and Peschel, "Das Theater in Theresienstadt .

55. Hofer's text of the Fledermaus, APT, A, 4045.

56. See Peschel, "Das Theater in Theresienstadt," for Horpatský and Porges; diary of Willy Mahler, entry for July 11 and 16, 1944, APT; interview of a man, AJMP, The Oral History Collection, 116 (born 1914); Josef Taussig, "Die Theresienstädter Cabarets," *Theresienstädter Studien und Dokumente* (1994): 207–246; and Nava Shan, ICJ OHD.

57. Taussig, "Die Theresienstädter Cabarets," 235.

58. Walter Lindenbaum's Bunte Gruppe cited in Taussig, "Die Theresienstädter Cabarets," 219.

59. Theater plays: *Ben Akiba lhal* (Ben Akiba lied), diary of Willy Mahler, entry for August 14, 1944, APT; drawings: Helga Weissová-Hošková, "The birthday wish I & II," in Helga Weissová- Hošková, *Zeichne, Was Du Siehst* (Göttingen: Wallstein, 2001), 94–95, 98–99; and testimony of Jiří Borský, BTA, 66 ("Byli jsme a budem, přišli jsme a půjdem."). The last word of the inscription, *půjdem* (we will go), referred to the return home rather than leaving on a transport, endowing the slogan with a heroic rather than an ironic note.

60. Suderland, *Territorien des Selbst.*

61. Raja Engländerová's památník, AJMP, T, 324a; Dagmar Hilarová, *Nemám žádné jméno*, ed. Evžen Hilar (Prague: Svoboda Service, 2010), 14, 42; Norbert Frýd, "Kultura v předposlední stanici," in *Theater—Divadlo. The Oral History Collection českých divadelníků na německou okupaci a druhou světovou válku*, ed. František Černý (Prague: Orbis, 1965), 219; Philipp Manes, *Als ob's ein Leben wär: Tatsachenbericht Theresienstadt 1942–1944*, ed. Klaus Leist and Ben Barkow (Berlin: Ullstein, 2005), 134; Edmund Hadra, LBI, AR 1249; and Anna Auředníčková, *Tři léta v Terezíně* (Prague: Alois Hynek, 1945), 38.

62. Manes, 71–72.

63. Taussig, "Die Theresienstädter Cabarets."

NOTES TO PAGES 180–185   307

64. Edgar Krása interview, USHMM, RG-50.030*0478.
65. Diary of Willy Mahler, entry for April 15 and 19, 1944, APT.
66. There are dozens of surviving *památníky* and *Poesiealben*. See AJMP, Terezin, 324a; BTA, 171; Arnold Munter's personal archive; and Hanne-Lore Munter; *The Terezín Album of Mariánka Zadikow*, ed. Debórah Dwork (Chicago: University of Chicago Press, 2007).
67. Albumblätter, AJMP, T, 324a.
68. Minutes of Recreation, October 20, 1943, YVA, O64, 65; and Hana Rutarová to Karel Rutar, May 8, 1944, APT, A, 8652.
69. Manes on the absence of Moritz Henschel as the head of Recreation (and the presence of Leo Baeck) at the celebration of the 500th lecture: Manes, 352–353.
70. Heinrich Wolffheim, YVA, O1, 102.
71. Makarova et al., *University over the Abyss*, 384, 386, 425. Edelstein presented lectures at official events rather than giving his own lectures, with the exception of a talk on Zionism at the one-hundredth lecture of the Manes group in March 1943. Manes, 146; and diary of Willy Mahler, entry for July 15, 1944, APT, on Eppstein's presence.
72. Article of Einsatzstelle CIII, in "Ein Jahr Hamburger Kaserne," BTA, 124.
73. Otto Zucker to the Labor Center, July 8, 1943, YVA, O64, 23/I.
74. Arnold M. about an anonymous pianist, MMZ, 16.
75. Alexander S., VHA, 40047.
76. Interview Anna Nathanová, AJMP.
77. Edgar Krása interview, USHMM.
78. Diary of Willy Mahler, entry for August, 1, 1944, APT; Mitteilung August 3, 1944. Grabower, Memos from Theresienstadt, July 21, 1944, Finanzakademie Brühl.
79. Author's phone and email exchange with Edgar Krása, September 2012.
80. A rare exception was Karel Arnstein, a literary scholar who worked for a while as a cook. Auředníčková, 40. Edgar Krása never attended lectures; Edgar Krása interview, USHMM.
81. Else Dormitzer, NIOD, 250d, box 25.
82. Epstein, "The Roundtrip"; and Edgar Krása interview, USHMM.
83. Skrapbok, JDK, 207, 28.
84. Nava Shan, ICJ OHD; and Bor, *Opuštěná Panenka*.
85. Nava Shan, ICJ OHD.
86. Diary of Eva Mändlová-Roubíčková's, entry for December 20, 1943 (the entry is probably misdated and is from early January 1944), AITI.
87. Esther Jonas Bauer to author, January 3, 2015.
88. Viktor Kende interview, April 1, 1994, AJMP, The Oral History Collection, 295; see Makarova et al., *University over the Abyss*, 174–176.
89. Hans Hofer, "Die Theaterkarte," in Ulrike Migdal, ed., *Und die Musik spielt dazu: Chansons und Satiren aus dem KZ Theresienstadt* (Munich: Piper, 1986), 90–93; see also Horpatsky's cabaret in Peschel, "Das Theater in Theresienstadt."
90. Bor fictionalized the existence of an orchestra in his depiction of the *Requiem*.
91. Minutes of Recreation, March 21, 1944, YVA, O64, 65; and Nava Shan, ICJ OHD.

NOTES TO PAGES 188–193

92. Testimony of Heda Grabová, YVA; and Weiner, report on the history of the Freizeitgestaltung, 26. (There is a mistake in the reprint in Migdal, *Und die Musik spielt dazu*, 151, mistakingly speaking about ing. Pick.)

93. Irma Semecká, *Torso naděje* (Prague: Antonín Vlasák, 1946), 49.

94. Elena Makarova interview's with Jakov Rachman, private archive Elena Makarova; and testimony of Anneliese Gutfeld, LBI, ME 744. Erich Munk had a record player; Elena Makarova's interview with Avraham Benes, Makarova et al., *University over the Abyss*, 212.

95. Eva Šormová, *Divadlo v Terezíně 1941–1945* (Ústí nad Labem: Severočeské nakladatelství, 1973), 57–59; and Zdenka Fantlová, *Klid je síla, řek' tatínek* (Prague: Primus, 1996).

96. Interview Viktor Kende, AJMP; Věra Hájková-Duxová, "Takový byl život," in *Svět bez lidských dimenzí* (Prague: Státní židovské muzeum, 1991), 77; Manes, 138; and Shan, ICJ OHD.

97. Manes, 130 (on approval), 138 (on the accommodation).

98. Makarova's interview with Jakov Rachman.

99. Minutes of Recreation, complaint of Karl Fischer, November 24, 1943, YV; see also Milan Kuna, *Hudba vzdoru a naděje: Terezín 1941–1945* (Prague: Bärenreiter, 2000), 42.

100. Kuna, *Hudba vzdoru a naděje*, 42.

101. Interview of a woman, AJMP, The Oral History Collection, 195 (born 1920); Manes, 293; Estella Simons, Jewish Historical Museum Amsterdam (hereafter JHM), D5320; Engelina Kronenberg, NIOD, 250d, box 32; Dora Lehmann, *Erinnerungen einer Altonaerin 1866–1946* (Hamburg: Dölling und Galitz, 1998), 121.

102. Jiří Borský, BTA, 66.

103. Diary of Willy Mahler, entry for March 20, and August 22, 1944, APT.

104. Diary of Bedřich Kohn, entry for January 29, 1943, APT.

105. Nava Shan, ICJ OHD; and diary of Martha Mosse, introduction (retrospect, undated, written before September 1944), WL, P.III.h, 1088.

106. Nava Shan, ICJ OHD, 34, 13; and Jan Fischer, *Šest skoků do budoucnosti* (Prague: Idea Service, 1998), 62–63, 129.

107. Manes, 136–137. Hannah Pravda interview, BL/Sound Archive, C410, 35; Hana Pravda, *Kaleidoscope: Snapshots of My Life* (London: Veritas, 2002), 137; and Fischer, *Šest skoků*.

108. Nava Shan, ICJ OHD, 34, 13.

109. Fischer, *Šest skoků* 59f; interview, AJMP, 195; Reiner, APT, A, 4164; Taussig, "Die Theresienstädter Cabarets"; more pronounced are Šormová, *Divadlo v Terezíně*, 83–84, and Adler, *Theresienstadt*, 590.

110. Interview, AJMP, 195.

111. Hannelore Rabe, *Die Hofers: Theresienstadt—Kabarett—Rostock* (Rostock: VVN-BdA, 2013).

112. Minutes of Recreation, October 26, 1943.

113. Anna Nathanová, December 9, 2006, AJMP, The Oral History Collection, 1090. See also Kuna, *Hudba vzdoru a naděje*, 26–27. Klinkeová later worked

NOTES TO PAGES 188–193 309

as a youth care worker; the children in her group sometimes mocked her for her large chest: Charlotte Opfermann and Robert A. Warren, *Charlotte, a Holocaust Memoir: Remembering Theresienstadt* (Santa Fe, N.Mex.: Paper Tiger, 2006), 119.

114. Testimony of Hana and Lea Blánová, APT, A, 330. Borgerová was born in 1903 in Ostrava.

115. Nava Shan, ICJ OHD.

116. Petr Lang interview, July 22, 1965, ICJ OHD, 34, 3.

117. Interview of a woman, May 20, 1991, AJMP, The Oral History Collection, 49 (born 1921).

118. Minutes of Recreation, March 4, 1944.

119. Adler, *Theresienstadt*, 589.

120. Murmelstein, Lanzmann Interview, 3182.

121. Willy Mahler attended several Czech-language events: diary of Willy Mahler, entries for August 2, 14, 24, and 30, 1944, APT.

122. Diary of Willy Mahler, entry for August 30, 1944, APT. One of the central points in the Murmelstein investigation was his presumed anti-Czech activity (in concordance with the jurisdiction in the people's trials).

123. Diary of Willy Mahler, entry for July 14, 1944, APT; and Bor, *Opuštěná panenka*, 255–257.

124. M.F., "Bilderbuch für Dittl," Edith Ornstein, BTA, 9; original in the holding of Dani Singer.

125. Bedřich Fritta, *This Is Not a Fairy Tale—It's Real! To Tommy for His Third Birthday in Terezín, 22 January 1944* (Prague: Jewish Museum, 2000).

126. Ornstein was one of the key witnesses for Ruth Bondy's *"Elder of the Jews": Jakob Edelstein of Theresienstadt* (New York: Grove, 1989). See also Ornstein's "Iluse Terezína," YVA, O7, 291.

127. On Schönová, see Irena Seidlerová interview, February 13, 1995, AJMP, The Oral History Collection, 407; on Dodalová, see Eva Strusková, "Film Ghetto Theresienstadt: Suche nach Zusammenhängen," in *"Der Letzte der Ungerechten": Der Judenälteste Benjamin Murmelstein in Filmen 1942–1975*, ed. Ronny Loewy and Katharina Rauschenberger (Frankfurt/Main: Campus, 2011).

128. Edith Kramer Freund, "As a doctor in Theresienstadt," LBI, ME 283c, p. 6.

129. Franz Hahn interview, DÖW, Interviews, 510.

130. Eliška K. interview, AJMP.

131. Irena Rieselová, APT, A, 129; and interview of a woman, AJMP, The Oral History Collection, 313 (born 1916).

132. Nava Shan on herself and Gustav Schorsch, ICJ OHD.

133. Adler, *Theresienstadt*, 590, 594. Schönová and Schorsch had a similar attitude: Nava Shan, ICJ OHD.

134. David Baruch Rosen, *Verdi: Requiem* (Cambridge, UK: Cambridge University Press, 1995), 14f.

135. Coco Schumann, *Der Ghetto-Swinger: Eine Jazzlegende erzählt* (Munich: dtv, 1998).

136. Claudia Becker, *Magda Spiegel: Biographie einer Frankfurter Opernsängerin, 1887–1944* (Frankfurt: Kramer, 2003).

310 NOTES TO PAGES 196–202

137. Paul Kling interview with David Bloch, October 12, 1989: Kling said that he preferred not to discuss the history and politics of the period. He would rather remember Terezín as a stage in his development as a violinist. "Of course I was self-centered as anybody would be, professionally speaking, so all that mattered to me was that I could practice. And I would practice in basements, and I had friends who made sure I had a place to practice." Quoted in Aleeza Wadler, "Paul Kling," accessed on January 2, 2019, http://holocaustmusic.ort.org/places/theresienstadt/paul-kling/.

138. On soccer in Theresienstadt, see Nicola Schlichting, "'Kleiderkammer Schlägt Gärtner 9:3:' Fußball Im Ghetto Theresienstadt," *Nurinst* (2006): 73–90; Anna Hájková, "Die fabelhaften Jungs aus Theresienstadt: Junge tschechische Männer als dominante soziale Elite im Theresienstädter Ghetto," *Beiträge zur Geschichte des Nationalsozialismus* 25 (2009): 116–135; and František Steiner, *Fotbal pod žlutou hvězdou* (Prague: Olympia, 2009).

139. Structure of the self-administration, YVA, O64, 24.

140. Murmelstein, "Geschichtlicher Überblick," WL.

141. In the League each team played against all others in a round-robin tournament (for example, eight teams needed to play twenty-eight games); the winner was the team with the most points. In Cup competitions, in contrast, only winners played teams that proceeded to the next game by winning, so that there were fewer games (eight teams needed to play seven games to establish the winner) played altogether.

142. "Jahresbericht über die Tätigkeit der Sektion für Sportveranstaltungen im Jahre 1943," YVA, O64/65.

143. Steiner, *Fotbal*, 21.

144. "Jahresbericht Sportveranstaltungen," YVA; Steiner, *Fotbal*, 21; Ludvík Steinberg, YVA, O15E, 20.

145. "Jahresbericht Sportveranstaltungen," YVA.

146. His police registration file stated "profession: soccer player." Hynek Fischer, policejní přihlášky, NA.

147. "Jahresbericht Sportveranstaltungen," YVA; Silvia Tarabini Fracapane's interview with Simon Direktor, April 3, 2008; thanks to Silvia for sharing this.

148. Joe Singer, WL, P.II.h, 141 (Mrs. Singer was Austrian).

149. Ibid.

150. Ibid.

151. Jan Burka, quoted in Steiner, *Fotbal*, 64.

152. See chapter 3.

153. Miloš Dobrý, AJMP, The Oral History Collection, 115.

154. Viktor Kende, AJMP.

155. On soccer in interwar Czechoslovakia, see Stefan Zwicker, "Aspekte der Memorialkultur des Fußballs in den böhmischen Ländern, der Tschechoslowakei und der Tschechischen Republik," in *Die Memorial- und Sepulkralkultur des Fußballsports*, ed. Markwart Herzog and Michael Barsuhn (Stuttgart: Kohlhammer, 2013), 387–408.

NOTES TO PAGES 196–202   311

156. Steiner, *Fotbal*, 73–79; Mahrer papers, Museum of Jewish Heritage; and Stefan Zwicker, "Paul Mahrer, der Nationalspieler, der Theresienstadt überlebte," in *Sportler im "Jahrhundert der Lager" und der Verfolgung: Profiteure, Widerständler und Opfer*, ed. Diethelm Blecking and Lorenz Peiffer (Göttingen: Die Werkstatt, 2012), 322–329.

157. Hana Kolsky interview, January 16, 2009, author's archive (her grandmother watched the matches); Fritz Warenhaupt, YVA, O33, 173; interview with Kurt Zwi Elias, August 2, 1996, Mahn- und Gedenkstätte Düsseldorf; Joe Singer, WL, P.II.h, 141; Lucy Mandelstam; and author's interview of Eva Berner, author's archive.

158. Manes, 63. In early 1945, Esther and Heinold Hirsch, the *Geltungsjuden* children of the first Jew in the German Football Association, Julius Hirsch, were sent to Terezín. Werner Skrentny, *Julius Hirsch: Nationalspieler. Ermordet: Biografie eines jüdischen Fußballers* (Göttingen: Die Werkstatt, 2012), 239.

159. Michael Brenner and Gideon Reuveni, eds. *Emancipation through Muscles: Jews and Sports in Europe* (Lincoln: University of Nebraska Press, 2006); Dietrich Schulze-Marmeling, *Der FC Bayern und seine Juden: Aufstieg und Zerschlagung einer liberalen Fußballkultur* (Die Werkstatt: Göttingen, 2011); and Dietrich Schulze-Marmeling, ed., *Davidstern und Lederball: Die Geschichte der Juden im deutschen und internationalen Fußball* (Göttingen: Wallstein, 2003).

160. Ota Klinger, YVA, O7, 240.

161. Karel Berman interview, AJMP.

162. František and Alžběta Petschau also had a baby born in Terezín, Ladislav, born in February 1944.

163. Statistics on the Czech theater for 1943 are from YV, O64, 65; Nava Shan, ICJ OHD, 34, 13; Hilarová, *Nemám žádné jméno*, 52, 104–106; N. N, "Muži v offsidu v Terezíně," *Vedem*, 12, 1943, APT; diary of Eva Mändlová-Roubíčková, entry for April 22, 1945, AITI; and Michael Petschau, prisoner database; NA Prague, police registrations, file of Nita Petschauová. Petschauová remarried, continued working as an actress, and died in a traffic accident in 1949.

Chapter 6

1. Hannah Arendt, *Eichmann in Jerusalem: A Report on the Banality of Evil* (New York: Penguin, 2006), 117–119; Raul Hilberg, *The Destruction of the European Jews* (New Haven, Conn.: Yale University Press, 2003), 1111–1112; and Isaiah Trunk, *Judenrat: The Jewish Councils in Eastern Europe under Nazi Occupation* (New York: Macmillan, 1972).

2. Testimony of Vilém Cantor, February 13, 1946, ABS, 305-633-1, 192–194.

3. Isaiah Trunk, *Łódź Ghetto: A History*, ed. and trans. Robert Moses Shapiro (Bloomington: Indiana University Press, 2006), 231–245; and Barbara Engelking-Boni and Jacek Leociak, *The Warsaw Ghetto: A Guide to the Perished City* (New Haven, Conn.: Yale University Press, 2009), 163.

4. Murmelstein, "Geschichtlicher Überblick," WL, 1073, 24.

312 NOTES TO PAGES 204–207

5. Statement of Lev Kraus, January 27, 1947, SOAL, LSP 441, box 134.
6. Statement Vilém Cantor, March 5, 1947, SOAL, LSP 441, box 134.
7. Letter diary of Hana Rutarová, May 12, 1944, APT, A, 8652.
8. In her analysis of the ghetto law codex, Renata Lipková put forward this belief as a fact, but without any documentary evidence: Renata Lipková, "Právo v nuceném společenství," *Terezínské listy* 27 (1999): 20–38, 30. For evidence, see diary of Eva Mändlová-Roubíčková's, entry for January 20, 1943; and petitions to be exempted from transport from Ella Köpplová, Vilém Friedmann, and František Metzker, August 30, 1943, YVA, O64, 17/I.
9. Petition for exemption of Antonín Rosenbaum, YVA, O64/11.
10. Michael Wögebauer erred when arguing that there was no connection between being sentenced and the deportation lists, but he showed many cases of people who were sentenced who were not deported with the next transport: Wögerbauer, "Kartoffeln: Ein Versuch über Erzählungen zum Ghettoalltag," *Theresienstädter Studien und Dokumente* (2003): 95–144.
11. Testimony of Vilém Cantor, 1946, ABS, 305-633-1, 192–194. Cantor was a member of the Communist organization in the ghetto.
12. Ghettorecht, YVA, O64, 28.
13. Petition of the Health Services to exempt Beatrix Schulhof (Božena Schulhofová), nurse for the elderly, and her husband Ladislav, YVA, O64, 22/II. (The Schulhofs were put on the transport.) According to anecdotal evidence, the bacteriologist Gertrud Adlerová was able to protect her mother and husband, H. G. Adler, until fall 1944.
14. Adler, *Theresienstadt*, 287; and Prochnik, letter to his trial, June 24, 1954, WStLA.
15. Jan Grauer describes the line of action for Productions: testimony on Rudolf Freiberger, January 5, 1945 ([*sic*], actually 1946), ABS, 305-633-1, p. 289; *Šalom na pátek*, August 13, 1943, explanation of "šuclyste," YVA, O64, 64; and Petr Erben on the monthly indispensability lists in the Youth Care Department in his *Po vlastních stopách* (Prague: Kalina, 2003), 46 and 51.
16. Miroslav Kárný, "Komunistická organizace v terezínském koncentračním táboře 1941–1945" (manuscript, 1983), NA, Kárných, ka 16, 7–10.44–46.
17. Testimony of Markéta Šmolková, March 7, 1946, ABS, 305-633-1, 231.
18. Of particular importance for most of the elderly, who did not work. Testimony of Vilém Cantor, February 13, 1946, ABS, 305-633-1, 192–194.
19. Diary of Willy Mahler, entry for May 14, 1944, APT, A, 5704.
20. Testimony of Vilém Cantor, ABS. The Danes were protected from transports, and Slovaks and Hungarians only arrived at Theresienstadt after the end of transports.
21. Testimony of Vilém Cantor, ABS. Placzek was a Communist, infiltrated into the Zionists by the Communist group. Kárný, "Komunistická organizace," NA, 36 and n72.
22. Prochnik, letter to his trial, June 24, 1954, WStLA.
23. Neue objektive Listen, YVA, O64, 47a.
24. Neue objektive Listen, YVA, O64, August 9, 1943, YVA, O64, 47a. With thanks to Alla Dworkin.
25. For instance, a section of the protection list of the chief rabbi and member of the Council of Elders, Leopold Neuhaus, is in YVA, O64, 15/II.

NOTES TO PAGES 204–207 313

26. Verzichtsliste no. 1 (Youth care), August 7, 1943, YVA, O64, 47; and testimony of a woman, AJMP, The Oral History Collection, 35 (born 1890).

27. Rudolf Bergmann's protection list, YVA, O64, 47. Bergmann lived in a childless intermarriage and was deported with the Aufbaukommando. Bergmann thus could "take care" of relatively many prisoners in lieu of his family. Interview of a woman, 1992 and 1993, AJMP, The Oral History Collection, 135 (born 1909); and František Fuchs, "Die tschechisch-jüdische Widerstandsbewegung in Theresienstadt," Theresienstädter Studien und Dokumente (1997): 141–156.

28. "Fehlende Fälle," October 3, 1943. Otto Fischer's son, Jan, later became Czech prime minister between 2009 and 2010 in a caretaker government.

29. Testimony of Vilém Cantor, ABS, 192–194.

30. Prochnik, letter to his trial, June 24, 1954, WStLA.

31. Diary of Arnošt Klein, entry for January 20, 1943, AJMP, T, 324; and Transportleitung, YVA, O64, 47.

32. Hedwig Ems, July 16, 1947, YVA, O33, 91.

33. Diary of Eva Roubíčková, entry for December 20, 1943, AITI; diary of Arnošt Klein's diary, entry for December 15, 1943, AJMP, T, 324.

34. Diary of Eva Roubíčková, December 20, 1943, AITI; for a similar note on Rahm's behavior in May 1944, see also diary of Ralph Oppenhejm, May 18, 1944, JDK, 207 A 35, 7.

35. Viktor Kende interview, April 1, 1994, AJMP, The Oral History Collection, 295; Kende's private album, archive of Jiří Kende; and Murmelstein's statement, March 14, 1946, ABS, 305-633-1, 152.

36. Interview of Hana Fuchsová, January 9, 1993, AJMP, The Oral History Collection, 175.

37. Interrogation of Siegfried Seidl, June 4, 1946, WStLA, Volksgerichte, Vg 1 Vr 770/46; Heinrich Scholz' own submission to trial of Rahm, no date, SOAL, LSP 444/47, p. 78; statement of Rudolf Gibián, March 27, 1947, SOAL, MLS, LSP 159/48, box 156; and Stefan Klemp, Nicht Ermittelt: Polizeibataillone und die Nachkriegsjustiz—Ein Handbuch (Essen: Klartext, 2005), 168 (for the Batallion 65 that accompanied the Danish transport to Terezín in October 1943) and for the practice of accompanying transports.

38. Affidavit of Emanuel Herrmann, May 14, 1965, BArch, B 162, 1885 fol. 1.

39. Beate Meyer, Tödliche Gratwanderung: Die Reichsvereinigung der Juden in Deutschland zwischen Hoffnung, Zwang, Selbstbehauptung und Verstrickung (1939–1945) (Göttingen: Wallstein, 2011).

40. Diary of Eva Mändlová-Roubíčková, entry for September 7, 1943, AITI; for a similar note, see testimony of Ota Růžička.

41. Prochnik, letter to his trial, June 24, 1954, WStLA; and interview Kende, AJMP.

42. Alfred Gottwaldt and Diana Schulle, Die Judendeportationen aus dem Deutschen Reich, 1941–1945: Eine kommentierte Chronologie (Wiesbaden: Marixverlag, 2005).

43. Egon Redlich, entries for April 25 and 26, 1942, in Zítra jedeme, synu, pojedeme transportem: Deník Egona Redlicha z Terezína 1.1.1942–22.1.1944, ed. Miroslav Kryl (Brno: Doplněk, 1995), 114.

44. Jaroslava Milotová, "Nachwort," in Jan Osers, Unter Hakenkreuz und Sowjetstern: Erlebnisse eines Verfolgten in zwei Diktaturen (Berlin: Metropol, 2005), 165–175, 168–170.

314 NOTES TO PAGES 211–214

45. AAb, 53 percent; Aac, 58 percent; and Aad, 39 percent. In summer 1942, people over sixty-five years of age, who made up between 18 and 22 percent of the incoming transports, were automatically protected.

46. Jiří Borský, BTA, 66; and Josef Bor, *Opuštěná Panenka* (Prague: Státní nakladatelství politické literatury, 1961), 79–91, 118.

47. It was rumored that the Nazis had ordered the transport as retaliation for the Heydrich assassination (hence Aah, Attentat auf Heydrich), but this rumor was an urban legend. The transport also included Judita Halberstamová, the grandmother of Jack Halberstam.

48. Diary of Bedřich Kohn, entry for October 5, 1942, APT, A, 11891. German and Austrian elderly people were deported with transports Bo, Bp, Bq, Br, and Bs; the Czech elderly were sent with Bv, Bw, and Bx.

49. Willy Weber to Oskar Mareni, ca. July 1945, YVA, O64, 72–73.

50. Tomáš Fedorovič, "Der Theresienstädter Lagerkommandant Siegfried Seidl," *Theresienstädter Studien und Dokumente* (2003): 188; Egon Redlich, entries for September 6 and 8, 1942, in *Zítra jedeme* and diary of Eva Roubíčková, entry for October 7, 1942, AITI; and Otto Zucker, "Theresienstadt 1941–1943," *Theresienstädter Studien und Dokumente* (1995): 294.

51. Diary of Eva Roubíčková, entry for October 7, 1942, AITI.

52. Zucker, "Theresienstadt 1941–1943."

53. Ernst Kaltenbrunner to Heinrich Himmler, cable, February 1, 1943, reprinted in H. G. Adler, *Verheimlichte Wahrheit: Theresienstädter Dokumente* (Tübingen: Mohr, 1958), 296–298.

54. Egon Redlich, entries for February 4 and 5, 1943, in *Zítra jedeme*; and Erich Munk to Leo Janowitz, Jakob Edelstein, and Otto Zucker, January 25, 1943, YVA, O64, 23/II.

55. Anne Springer interview, September 27, 1995, VHA, no. 7207.

56. Miroslav Kárný, "Terezínský rodinný tábor v konečném řešení," in *Terezínský rodinný tábor v konečném řešení*, ed. Toman Brod, Kárný, and Margita Kárná (Prague: Melantrich and Terezínská Iniciativa, 1994), 32–43.

57. Kárný, "Terezínský rodinný tábor," 37, 39. Kárný provides no source for this claim.

58. Egon Redlich, entry for August 22–24, 1943, in *Zítra jedeme*, 202; Burger selected 147 members of the Aufbaukommando to be deported. Testimony of Rudolf Bunzel, February 2, 1946, ABS, 305-633-1, 245.

59. Otto Deutsch, "The War Time Experience of Otto Deutsch" (before 1988), BTA, 114; Burka.

60. Loesten, "Aus der Hoelle Minsk," LBI, ch. 6.

61. The children were accompanied by twenty caretakers and parents, who were separated in Theresienstadt and deported immediately to Auschwitz. Sworn deposition of Hadassa Helena Lewkowicz (for the Zentrale Stelle Ludwigsburg), January 28, 1971, YVA, O33, 668.

62. Sara Bender, *The Jews of Białystok during World War II and the Holocaust* (Waltham, Mass.: Brandeis University Press; Hanover, N.H.: University Press of New England, 2008), 269–273 (who overestimates the influence of the Jerusalem mufti); Katrin Stoll, *Die Herstellung der Wahrheit: Strafverfahren gegen ehemalige Angehörige*

NOTES TO PAGES 211–214   315

der Sicherheitspolizei für den Bezirk Bialystok (Berlin: De Gruyter, 2011); Yehuda Bauer, *Jews for Sale? Nazi-Jewish Negotiations, 1933–1945* (New Haven, Conn.: Yale University Press, 1994), ch. 7; and Martin Šmok's interview with Andrej Steiner, October 29, 1995, Martin Šmok's archive.

63. Dx included the only Danish Jew, Schmuel Jonisch, to be sent to Auschwitz, where he was killed. Jonisch was orthodox and somewhat eccentric. He pledged not to cut his hair until the war was over and hence was easily mistaken as mentally ill.

64. Dora Philippson, "Bericht über die Deportation und das Überleben in Theresienstadt 1942 bis 1945, (May 1945)," in *Frauenleben im NS-Alltag*, ed. Annette Kuhn (Pfaffenweiler: Centaurus, 1994), 303–320.

65. Zucker, "Theresienstadt 1941–1943"; and Jiří Borský, BTA.

66. Diary of Arnošt Klein, entry for January 20, 1943, AJMP, T, 324.

67. Diary of Klein, entry for January 22, 1943, AJMP.

68. Diary of Eva Roubíčková, entry for September 13, 1943, AITI. This entry is misdated and mistranslated (omitting the crucial "we") in the English translation of the diary, *We're Alive and Life Goes on: A Theresienstadt Diary*, trans. Zaia Alexander (New York: H. Holt, 1998), 100.

69. Diary of Bedřich Kohn, entry for October 14, 1942, APT.

70. Diary of Bedřich Kohn, entries for November 29, 1942, August 12, 1943, and July 18, 1944, APT; see also *Šalom na pátek*, August 16, 1944, no. 16.

71. Diary of Eva Roubíčková, entry for January 20, 1943, AITI.

72. Eugen Jellinek's complaint to Paul Eppstein, August 14, 1943, YVA, O64, 15/II.

73. Zeev Shek to other youth care workers, no date, BTA, 571.

74. Herrmann Strauss, archive of Irene Hellmann-Strauß.

75. Herrmann Strauss, archive of Irene Hellmann-Strauß; Bedřich Hellmann, BTA, 140; and Therese Klein to Herbert Müller and Yvonne Adler, August 1945, YVA, O5.

76. See Miriam Triendl-Zadoff, *Nächstes Jahr in Marienbad: Gegenwelten jüdischer Kulturen der Moderne* (Göttingen: Vandenhoeck & Ruprecht, 2007).

77. Murmelstein was the political director, *Dezernent*, of Youth Care, in 1944. Statement of Zeev Scheck, January 28, 1946, ABS, 305-633-1, p. 259.

78. Diary of Ralph Oppenhejm, entry for May 14, 1944, JDK, 207 A 35, 7.

79. Cited from Miroslav Kárný to inspector Mužík, no date, 1946, ABS, 305-633-1.

80. Some of the petitions are several pages long; some pages include two or three petitions.

81. September 1943 transports: YVA, O64, 10-21/II, one leaf in 22/II, p. 279; December: YVA, O64, 22/I-II; May 1944: YVA, O64, 22/II (p. 280)-23/II.

82. I defined success by whether the person in question was deported with the September transports, not by what the evaluating remarks said (the remarks are only on a fraction of the petitions).

83. Many more of the petitions for the transports of December 1943 were filed by the departments and nearly all for May 1944, chiefly with the exception of the Security Services.

84. Qualification list of the Health Services for the standby list, May 17, 1944, YVA, O64, 22/II.

316 NOTES TO PAGES 221-224

85. Ada Levy, WL, P.IIIh, 16.
86. I thank my father, Radko Hájek, for technical advice and help with building the pivot table, as well as Gabriel Vogel and Klaus Fiala for their help with analyzing the data.
87. Most importantly, I have clustered various groups of mixed marriage and kinds of work.
88. Interview of a woman, no date, AJMP, The Oral History Collection, 596 (born 1920); see also Cäcilie Friedmann, WL, P.IIe, 1068.
89. Irma Kornfein's volunteering petition (Austrian, no date), even though not successful, suggests that there must have been others. Lucie Drachsler, the Viennese girlfriend of Karel Fried, who was called for the transport, volunteered and married him to be able to join, but the marriage came too late. Lucy Mandelstam, LBI, ME 1472.
90. Petition of Lilly Schatzmann, September 4, 1943, YVA, O64, 13/II, and Kurt Bauer's petition on account of Juer Ginzberg (family unit), YVA, O64, 12/II; Bertha Bondi, no date, YVA, O64/15/I. Delfine Meyer; and diary of Hulda Schickler, entry for December 1943, LBIJ, 512.
91. Anne Springer interview, VHA.
92. Adler, *Theresienstadt 1941-1945*, 282; and testimony of Vilém Cantor, ABS.
93. I have contacted several of the petitioners, or their offspring; no one remembered the petitions. If they did, they often downplayed their agency and characterized the events as a result of a higher, exceptional power.
94. Diary of Eva Roubíčková, entry for September 7, 1943, AITI; Willy Groag interview, September 15, 1995, AJMP, The Oral History Collection, 82; Hana Fuchsová interview, AJMP.
95. Testimony of Věra Blábolová, APT, A, 124.
96. Ruth Damwerth, *Arnold Munter: Der Jahrhundertzeuge* (Berlin: Neues Leben, 1994); and Bedřich Hoffenreich, APT, Sbírka vzpomínek, 1095.
97. Diary of Arnošt Klein, entry for May 21, 1944, AJMP.
98. Interview of a woman, AJMP, 596.
99. Herrmann Strauss, archive of Irene Hellmann-Strauß; Leopold Neuhaus also put the chairperson of the Jewish Community in Jindřichův Hradec, Arnold Fleischer, and his family on his protection list: note of from Space Management, August 15, 1943, YVA, O64, 15/II, and December 14, 1943, YVA, O64, 22/I; and Otto Zucker to the transport commission, protecting the Tropp family from Vienna, January 21, 1943, YVA, O64, 23/I.
100. Frances Epstein, "The Roundtrip," private archive Helen Epstein.
101. YVA, O64, 47; list of the protected members and their relatives, Freizeitgestaltung, August 16, 1943, YVA, O64, 23/I; and "bedingte Meldung" of Vlasta Schönová to her sister Marie, petition signed by Egon Redlich, September 5, 1943, YVA, O64, 10.
102. Shipping: petition for exemption of the Shipping, September 4, 1943, YVA, O64, 10; Reklamationsliste Spedition, May 11, 1944, YVA,O64/23/II; and interview Irena Seidlerová, February 13, 1995, AJMP, The Oral History Collection, 407 and Seidlerová to the author, January 26, 2013. Josef Bondy, later Bor, the head of the Shipping detail, was deported with Ev.

NOTES TO PAGES 221–224   317

103. Verzichtliste 1, Otto Zucker and Josef Beck, August 7, 1943, YVA, O64, 47.

104. Ann Weinstock, Holocaust Center of Northern California, OHP, 3538; and Federica Spitzer, "Verlorene Jahre," in Wolfgang Benz, ed., *Theresienstadt: Aufzeichnungen von Federica Spitzer und Ruth Weisz* (Berlin: Metropol, 1997), 68–70.

105. Milk injections, whether subcutaneous or intramuscular, bring about an immune reaction against casein, a protein not naturally present in our bodies. The reactions usually include high fever, ague, and an acute feeling of sickness, in the worst case even anaphylactic shock and death; it is impossible to predict the reaction. In the 1920s, yatren casein injections were used as stimulation therapy for various diseases.

106. Otto Reinisch's file, police registration, NA. I thank Šimon Krýsl for sharing this information.

107. Ein Jahr Hamburger Kaserne, BTA, 124.

108. Julius Taussig interview, January 9, 1967, and August 26, 1975, APT, Sbírka vzpomínek, 51; the SS did not let Reinisch treat other victims. Statement by Josef Klaber, 1947, ABS, 325-82-2.

109. Interview of a woman, no date, AJMP, The Oral History Collection, 382 (born 1921); on a similar note, including Reinisch's wife Marta, see Spitzer, "Verlorene Jahre," 30.

110. Zdenka Popper Weinberg interview, March 22, 1974, New York Public Library, American Jewish Committee Oral History Collection/Dorot Jewish Division; testimony of Gerda Schild, 1945, YVA, O33, 987; and Grabower notes, September 15, 1944, Grabower papers, Finanzakademie Brühl.

111. Grabower Aktenvermerke, June 5, July 31, August 16, 1944, Brühl, Grabower papers.

112. Erich Munk to Jakov Edelstein, March 13, 1944, reprinted in Miroslav Kárný, "Jakov Edelsteins letzte Briefe," *Theresienstädter Studien und Dokumente* (1997): 226–227.

113. Adolph Metz, Ghetto Theresienstadt, ca. 1945. YVA, O33, 3257; see also interview of Rudolf and Eva Bunzel, 1970s, Leonard and Edith Ehrlich Collection, USHMM, RG.50.862.0002.

114. Diary of Eva Roubíčková, entry for December 20, 1943, AITI.

115. Ema Friedmannová-Donathová interview, AJMP; and author's Skype interview with her son, Michal Donath, January 25, 2013.

116. Benjamin Murmelstein's submission to his investigation, re: Otto Brod, March 14, 1946, ABS, 305-633-1, p. 141.

117. Jaroslav Bor, AJMP, The Oral History Collection, 64.

118. Spitzer, "Verlorene Jahre," 70–75.

119. Author's interview with Sonja Kiek-Rosenstein-Cohen, July 26, 2001.

120. Adolf and Frau [sic, Therese] Haarburger, WL, P.III.h, 111.

121. Murmelstein, Lanzmann Interview, 3189. See also Mirko Tůma, *Ghetto našich dnů* (Prague: Jaroslav Salivar, 1946), 43–44 passim; see also Carol Lidz, email to author, February 7 and 8, 2013. On Tůma, see ch. 2.

122. Statement of Mirko Tůma, January 28, 1946, investigations against Benjamin Murmelstein, ABS, 305-633-1, p. 252.

123. Statement of Mirko Tůma, January 28, 1946, ABS, 305-633-1, p. 252.

124. Interview of a man, AJMP, The Oral History Collection, 111 (born 1920).

318 NOTES TO PAGES 227–230

125. Richard Feder, "Meine erste Trauungszeremonie in Theresienstadt," in *Theresienstadt*, ed. Rudolf Iltis (Vienna: Europa-Verlag, 1968), 66–72.
126. Miloš Pick, *Naděje se vzdát neumím* (Brno: Doplněk, 2010), 38.
127. Luděk Eliáš (formerly Eckstein), VHA, no. 22495, https://sfi.usc.edu/czech/terezin/lesson.php?nid=950&vid=973 (program "Ghetto Terezín: holokaust a dnešek. Volba v životě").
128. See also Jacques Presser, *The Night of the Girondists* (London: HarperCollins UK, 1992).
129. On the powerlessness and agency of Holocaust victims, see Doris L. Bergen, "No End in Sight? The Ongoing Challenge of Producing an Integrated History of the Holocaust," in *Years of Persecution, Years of Extermination: Saul Friedlander and the Future of Holocaust Studies*, ed. Christian Wiese and Paul Betts (London: Continuum, 2010), 289–310; and Bergen, "I Am (Not) to Blame: Intent and Agency in Personal Accounts of the Holocaust," in *New Directions in Holocaust Research and Education: Lessons and Legacies*, ed. Wendy Lower and Lauren Faulkner Rossi, vol. 12 (Evanston, Ill.: Northwestern University Press, 2017), 87–107.
130. Saul Friedländer, *Years of Extermination: Nazi Germany and the Jews, 1939-1945* (New York: HarperCollins, 2007), 8f, 438–443; see also Amos Goldberg, "The Victim's Voice in History and Melodramatic Esthetics," *History and Theory* 48, no. 3 (2009): 220–237.
131. Miroslav Kárný interview, AJMP, The Oral History Collection, 328; and Der Theresienstädter Hechalutz: Aus den Erinnerungen von Berl Herškovič," *Theresienstädter Studien und Dokumente* (2000): 151–163. Kárný's parents were deported after him, as was Herškovič's spouse.
132. Miroslav Kárný interview, AJMP.
133. Lawrence Langer, *Admitting the Holocaust: Collected Essays* (New York: Oxford University Press, 1995), 46.
134. Eliyana Adler, "Hrubieszów at the Crossroads: Polish Jews Navigate the German and Soviet Occupations," *Holocaust and Genocide Studies* 28, no. 1 (2014): 1–30; and Evgeny Finkel, *Ordinary Jews: Choice and Survival during the Holocaust* (Princeton, N.J.: Princeton University Press, 2016).
135. Bergen, "I Am (Not) to Blame."
136. Alf Lüdtke, "Geschichte und Eigensinn," in *Alltagskultur, Subjektivität und Geschichte: Zur Theorie und Praxis von Alltagsgeschichte*, ed. Berliner Geschichtswerkstatt (Münster: Westfälisches Dampfboot, 1994), 139–153. Lüdtke himself touched on *Eigensinn* and Holocaust victims only in passing.
137. Here I build upon Hayden White's suggestion that historical events are emplotted as tropes. There has been some controversy over White's suggestion that the Holocaust was a modernist event and hence did not necessarily need to be emplotted as a tragedy. White, *The Content of the Form: Narrative Discourse and Historical Representation* (Baltimore, Md.: Johns Hopkins University Press, 1987), 76–80. In fact, certain stories do narrate the Holocaust as different tropes, among others Art Spiegelman's *Maus* and Louis Begley's *Wartime Lies*. However, survivors who live in

NOTES TO PAGES 227–230   319

a social field with a dominant narrative framework of the Holocaust (which was the case for all four examples here) do tell the Holocaust as a tragedy. On the controversy, see Saul Friedländer, ed., *Probing the Limits of Representation: Nazism and the "Final Solution"* (Cambridge, Mass.: Harvard University Press, 1992).

138. Miroslav Kárný, "Die Theresienstädter Herbsttransporte 1944," *Theresienstädter Studien und Dokumente* (1995): 7–37, 21; and Karel Lagus and Josef Polák, *Město za mřížemi* (Prague: Naše vojsko, 1964), 349.

139. Kárný, "Herbsttransporte"; Baldur von Schirach, *Ich glaubte an Hitler* (Hamburg: Mosaik, 1967), 64.

140. Kárný, "Herbsttransporte," 24; and Marc Buggeln, *Slave Labor in Nazi Concentration Camps* (Oxford: Oxford University Press, 2014).

141. Testimony of Vilém Cantor, ABS; diary of Bedřich Kohn, entry for July 18, 1944, APR.

142. Willy Groag interview, AJMP; Anna Nathanová even chose to conceive.

143. Berthold Simonsohn, WL, P.I.d.343.

144. Testimony of Vilém Cantor, ABS, 192–194.

145. Alisa Shek, "Alisa Sheks Tagebuch (Oktober 1944-Mai 1945)," *Theresienstädter Studien und Dokumente* (1994): 169–206, 171f entry for October 20, 1944. I follow my translation; Kenneth Kronenberg's translation in Alexandra Zapruder, ed., *Salvaged Pages: Young Writers' Diaries of the Holocaust* (New Haven, Conn.: Yale University Press, 2002), 395–424, 404, misunderstood some expressions.

146. Testimony of Josef Klábr, February 25, 1947, SOAL, LSP 441/47, 131.

147. Testimony Pavel Klein, February 19, 1946, ABS, 305-633-1, 232–233; and Dr. Julie Polaková from January 26, 1946, ABS, 305-633-1, 260.

148. Both groups were stripped of their stateless members, that is, German and Austrian emigrants without Dutch citizenship. Apparently some prominent members of both groups pointed out the presence of the stateless to the commandant. Testimony of Fritz Schönfeld, no date, Louis de Jong's collection of notes for vol. 8, NIOD; and David Simons, "De joodse uitzonderingsgroep 'Barneveld' en de voornaamste schepper daarvan, de Secretaris-Generaal van Binnenlandse zaken, Mr. Dr. K.J. Frederiks" (lecture ms., 1980), NIOD, Doc. II.

149. Murmelstein re: Oktobertransporte, no date, ABS, 305-633-1, 185–186.

150. Hedwig Geng, "Bericht über Theresienstadt: Memoiren," 1963, LBI, AR 1587.

151. Tůma, *Ghetto*, 45.

152. Testimony of Josef Polák at the Haindl trial, SOAL, MLS, 147/48, box 154; Luisa Fischerová et al., *In memoriam Irena Krausová* (Prague: Organisace sociálních pracovnic, 1947).

153. Jiří Žantovský interview, AJMP.

154. Murmelstein, re: Transport vom 28. Oktober 1944, no date, ABS, 305-633-1, 146.

155. Erich Simon, WL, P.III.h, 894; and Hedwig Ems, YVA, O33, 91.

156. Karl Löwenstein to H. G. Adler, April 18, 1960, DLA, HG Adler, A I 17.

157. Willy Groag interview, AJMP.

158. Egon Redlich, entry for October 24, 1944, in *Zítra jedeme*; and YVA, O64, 46.

320 NOTES TO PAGES 234–236

159. This list survived in two copies: Viktor Kende's, APT, A, 7854; and Vilém Cantor's, YVA, O64, 46.

160. Vilém Cantor's statement, March 5, 1947, ABS, 305-633-1, 193.

161. Murmelstein, re: Sonderzuweisungen, ABS, 305-633-1, 138–139.

162. Ibid.

163. Statement of Rudolf Freund, February 1, 1946, ABS, 305-633-1.

164. Testimony of Dr. Pavel Klein, February 19, 1946, ABS, 305-633-1, 232–233.

165. Benjamin Murmelstein, Rudolf Freiberger, and Vilém Lieder-Kolben were arrested after the war and spent months in pretrial custody. ABS, 305-633-1. Robert Prochnik, Murmelstein's secretary, was accused in 1954 and put on trial in Vienna, while he was living in Paris. WStLA, Volksgerichte, Vg 41/54 gg Prochnik.

166. Arnošt Klein, in diary entries for September 17, 1942 and January 20, 1943, AJMP, assumed the transports went to Ostrowo near Poznań/Posen.

167. Interview of a woman, AJMP, The Oral History Collection, 510 (born 1926).

168. Robert Prochnik, letter to his trial, June 24, 1954.

169. Isaiah Trunk, *Judenrat: The Jewish Councils in Eastern Europe under Nazi Occupation* (New York: Macmillan, 1972); Andrea Löw, *Juden im Getto Litzmannstadt: Leben sbedingungen, Selbstwahrnehmung, Verhalten* (Göttingen: Wallstein, 2006); and Samuel Kassow, *Who Will Write Our History? Emanuel Ringelblum and the Oyneg Shabes Archive* (Bloomington: Indiana University Press, 2007).

170. Löw, *Juden*, 289–291.

171. Jaroslav Bor interview, AJMP.

172. Pick, *Naděje*: 39; Willy Groag interview, AJMP; interview of a man, 1992, AJMP, The Oral History Collection, 109 (born 1917); and Hans Sladký, "Episoden aus dem Leben eines Überlebenden," *Theresienstädter Studien und Dokumente* (1998): 257–276.

173. Interview Karolína Hradecká, AJMP.

174. Statement of Bedřich Berl, February 5, 1946, ABS, 305-633-1, 227f.

175. Willy Groag interview, AJMP. Franz Hahn, a Viennese doctor, told a similar story about Erich Klapp, the head of Internal Medicine; Franz Hahn interview, DÖW.

176. Police registration file of Marie Bergmannová, NA Prague, police registration.

177. Statement of Bedřich Berl, February 5, 1946, ABS.

178. Herbert Langer to Elly Weil, October 27, 1944, Simon Wiesenthal Center, 1999-037.

179. Miroslav Kárný's remarks to the Terezínská pamětní kniha, 2000.

180. Statement of Bedřich Berl, February 5, 1946, ABS.

181. Jaroslav Bor interview, AJMP.

182. Miroslav Kárný, "Die Flucht des Auschwitzer Häftlings Vítěslav Lederer und der tschechische Widerstand," *Theresienstädter Studien und Dokumente* (1997): 168–169; and Erich Kulka's interview with Leo Holzer, BTA, 128. Holzer gave varying accounts of his first meeting with Lederer and whether Lederer actually met with Baeck or Holzer approached Baeck about his meeting Lederer. I follow Holzer's first version, as it explains Baeck's inconsistencies; interview Eva and Rufolf Bunzel, USHMM.

183. Interview; and František Kollman, NA, SPB, 1809.

NOTES TO PAGES 234–236 321

184. Erich Kulka, *Útěk z tábora smrti* (Prague: MNO, 1966), 151–153, 158.
185. Kárný, "Die Flucht des Auschwitzer Häftlings," 169; and Miroslav Kryl, "Die Deportationen aus Theresienstadt nach dem Osten im Spiegel des Tagebuch Willy Mahlers," *Theresienstädter Studien und Dokumente* (1995): 69–92, 75. Kárný cited testimony of Holzer's according to which Holzer and Baeck informed Eppstein about the gassings and Eppstein beseeched them to stay silent; Kárný, "Die Flucht des Auschwitzer Häftlings," 168. The Holzer account was supposedly in Kárný's private archive but is not in his papers in NA. Kárný sometimes took liberties with sources, twisting them to fit his interpretation.
186. Interview, AJMP, 382.
187. Diary of Eva Dýmová, Moreshet, D.2, 334; author's interview with Eva Berner (pseudonym), kibbutz Shamir, February 14, 2009.
188. Selma Steinerová interview, ca. 1995, NMŠ, 15; René Glatsteinová, VHF, no. 20201; and Klára Chlamtáčová, *Pramienok života* (Bratislava: SNM, 1995), 202. On Vrba and Wetzler see also Ruth Linn, *Escaping Auschwitz: A Culture of Forgetting* (Ithaca, N.Y.: Cornell University Press, 2004).
189. Sven Meyer and Corrie Meyer, "Onze belevenissen tijdens de jodenvervolgingen in den tweeden wereldoorlog," 1945, NIOD, 244, 920; Erich Springer interview, January 12, 1991, AJMP, The Oral History Collection, 50; Curt Friedmann (1958), YVA, O2, 707; and Murmelstein, Lanzmann Interview, 3176.
190. Testimony of Blanka Haasová, October 1969, APT, A, 392.
191. Lagus and Polák, *Město za mřížemi*, 254.
192. Willy Groag interview, AJMP.
193. Murmelstein, "Geschichtlicher Überblick," WL, 47; and Benjamin Murmelstein, *Theresienstadt: Eichmanns Vorzeige-Ghetto*, ed. Ruth Pleyer and Alfred J. Noll, trans. Karin Fleischanderl (Vienna: Czernin, 2014), 227–231.
194. Murmelstein, *Eichmanns Vorzeige-Ghetto*, 227–231.
195. Murmestein, *Eichmanns Vorzeige-Ghetto*, 206; and Anna Auředníčková, *Tři léta v Terezíně* (Prague: Alois Hynek, 1945), 56.
196. Murmelstein, "Geschichtlicher Überblick," WL, 47–48; and Damwerth, *Arnold Munter*, 121.
197. Bertrand Perz and Florian Freund. "Auschwitz Neu? Pläne und Maßnahmen zur Wiedererrichtung der Krematorien von Auschwitz-Birkenau in der Umgebung des KZ Mauthausen im Februar 1945," *Dachauer Hefte* 20 (2004): 58–70.
198. Kurt Gerstein's report (May 4, 1945), in Hans Rothfels, "Augenzeugenbericht zu den Massenvergasungen," *Vierteljahrshefte für Zeitgeschichte* 1 (1953): 177–194.
199. Interrogation of Karl Rahm, April 3, 1947, SOAL, LSP 441/47, 134.
200. Lagus and Polák, *Město za mřížemi*, 262; and Adler, *Theresienstadt*, 201.
201. Moreover, gas chambers did not need ventilation systems blowing air in, just those that blew air out to clean out the poisonous gas after the killings.
202. In the context of Terezín, the death marches have been called "evacuation transports." On the wider context of death marches, see Katrin Greiser, *Die Todesmärsche von Buchenwald: Räumung, Befreiung und Spuren der Erinnerung* (Göttingen: Wallstein,

322 NOTES TO PAGES 236–242

2008); and Daniel Blatman, *The Death Marches: The Final Phase of Nazi Genocide* (Cambridge, Mass.: Belknap Press of Harvard University Press, 2011).

203. VHA Interviews of Eva Klug, no. 1325; Mária Jarkovská, no. 22679; and Tibor Vidal, no. 34312.

204. Diary of Martha Mosse, entry for April 21, 1945,WL, P.III.h, 1088.

205. For a perspective of a former Terezín inmate, see Petr Lang, June 25, 1991, AJMP, The Oral History Collection, 46; for Polish Jewish participants on the death marches, see report of Jehuda Czarnoczapka, August 31, 1945, 301/786; Dina Emma, no date, 301/2601; and Gizela Lundner, 301/1368, all Jewish Historical Institute (ŻIH).

206. On the evacuation transports, see Marek Poloncarz, "Die Evakuierungstransporte nach Theresienstadt (April–Mai 1945)," *Theresienstädter Studien und Dokumente* (1998): 242–262.

Conclusion

1. Rolf Grabower's Aktenvermerke, 1138, March 10, 1945, Grabower papers, Brühl.

2. *Šalom na pátek*, no. 12, November 26, 1943, YVA, O64, 64.

3. See also Karen Auerbach, *The House at Ujazdowskie 16: Jewish Families in Warsaw after the Holocaust* (Bloomington: Indiana University Press, 2013); and Elissa Bemporad, *Becoming Soviet Jews: The Bolshevik Experiment in Minsk, 1917–1939* (Bloomington: Indiana University Press, 2013).

Archives Consulted

Public Archives

Austria

Diözesenarchiv Wien [Bishopric Archive], Vienna (DAW): Hilfsstelle für nichtarische Katholiken/Aid Agency for Non Aryan Catholics

Dokumentationsarchiv des österreichischen Widerstandes [Documentation Archives of Austrian Resistance], Vienna (DÖW): oral histories "Erzählte Geschichte"

Viktor Frankl Institut, Vienna: private archives Viktor Frankl

Wiener Stadt- und Landesarchiv [Municipal and Provincial Archives of Vienna] (WStLA): Volksgericht Wien [people's court Vienna]

Czech Republic

Archiv bezpečnostních složek [Archive of the Secret Police], Prague (ABS): 425-231-2; 305-633-1; 302-204-45; 302-198-5; 305-639-5; Z-10-976a; 325-15-5 S 6419; 325-90-7; 325-82-2; 325-93-1

Archiv Památníku Terezín [Archive of the Terezín Memorial] (APT): collection of documents (A); sbírka vzpomínek [collection of testimonies]

Archive of the Terezín Initiative Institute, Prague (AITI): Diary of Eva Roubíčková

Gender Studies, Prague: Paměť žen [Memory of women], interviews

Národní archiv [Czech National Archives] Prague (NA): Koncentrační tábory a okupační vězeňské spisy (KT OVS), Zvláštní četnický výbor (ZČV), Svaz politických vězňů (SPB), Miroslav and Margita Kárná papers (Kárných), Policejní ředitelství - policejní přihlášky (police registrations), Hubert Ripka collection

Státní oblastní archiv Litoměřice [State regional archive Litoměřice] (SOAL): Mimořádný lidový soud Litoměřice (MLS) [Extraordinary people's court Litoměřice]

Státní oblastní archiv Prague [State regional archive Prague] (SOAP): Mimořádný lidový soud Prague (MLS) [Extraordinary people's court Prague]

Židovské Muzeum Prague [Jewish Museum Prague] (AJMP): The Oral History Collection; Terezín; Dokumenty perzekuce [documents of the persecution]; Fleischmann collection

Denmark

Dansk Jødisk Museum [Jewish Danish Museum] Copenhagen (JDK): 207; 166; 140A; 207A; uncataloged (space management applications)

Rigsarkivet [Danish National Archives], Copenhagen: Jewish Community, Chiefrabbi M Friediger, correspondence 1911–1947

Germany

Alte Synagoge Essen (Old Synagogue Essen): BR, Regina Oelze

Bavarian Main State Archive Munich: reparation file

324 ARCHIVES CONSULTED

Brandenburgisches Landeshauptarchiv [Brandenburg State Main Archive], Potsdam (BLHA): Rep. 36 A II (Akten des Oberfinanzpräsidenten)

Bundesarchiv Ludwigsburg [German Federal Archives Ludwigsburg] (BArch): B 162, investigations against Karl Bergel, Anton Burger, and Hans and Rolf Günther

Der Bundesbeauftragte für die Unterlagen des Staatssicherheitsdienstes der ehemaligen Deutschen Demokratischen Republik [Federal Commissioner for the Stasi Archives], Berlin (BStU): MfS HA IX, IX/11, XI/11 ZUV X, department X, GStA, ZUV 74 Ga, MfS Zentralarchiv, W/3416/50/303/201, RHE-44-88 DDR, Archiv der Zentralstelle AR3

Bundesfinanzakademie [Financial Academy], Brühl: Rolf Grabower papers (since moved to Bundesarchiv Koblenz)

Centrum Judaicum, Berlin (CJA): Opfer des Faschismus (OdF); diary of Paul Scheurenberg

Deutsches Literaturarchiv [Archive of German Literature], Marbach (DLA): H.G.Adler papers; Sebald papers; Piper publishing house papers

Entschädigungsbehörde [Office for Reparations], Berlin

Forschungsstelle für Zeitgeschichte [The Research Center for Contemporary History], (FZH/WdE) Hamburg: Werkstatt der Erinnerung (oral histories)

Gedenkstätte für die Bonner Opfer des Nationalsozialismus (Bonn Memorial for the Victims of the National Socialism), Bonn (Bonn): Arthur Greifzu collection; Alfred Philippson collection

Gemeindearchiv Minden [Municipal Archive] (Minden): reparation files

Geographisches Institut [Geography Institute] Bonn: Alfred Philippson papers

Hamburgisches Haupt und Staatsarchiv (Hamburg Main and State Archive), Hamburg (StAH): reparation files; Lippmann

Institut für Zeitgeschichte [Institute for Contemporary History], Munich (IfZ): Zeugenschrifttum (ZS)

Landesarchiv Berlin [Berlin State Archive] Berlin (LAB): Opfer des Faschismus, OdF, C Rep 118-01

Landesarchiv des Saarlandes [Saar State Archive] (Saarbrücken): reparation file of "Eva and Filip Rohnenberg"

Moses Mendelsohn Zentrum/Haus der Wannseekonferenz, Berlin (MMZ): interviews of Holocaust survivors (Yale Fortunoff for Germany)

NS-Dokumentationszentrum (Cologne): memoirs of Hilde Nathan

Politisches Archiv des Auswärtigen Amtes [Political Archive of the Foreign Office], Berlin (PA AA)

Staatsarchiv Bremen [State Archive Bremen] (StAB): registry office; denazification papers

Stadtarchiv Mannheim [Municipal archive Mannheim]: Paul Eppstein papers

Das Zentralarchiv zur Erforschung der Geschichte der Juden in Deutschland, Heidelberg: Leopold Neuhaus collection

Israel

Beit Terezin, Givat Hayim Ihud (BTA): various collections

Central Archives for History of Jewish People (CAHJP), Jerusalem: various collections

Hagannah Archives (HAG), Tel Aviv: 31.177, 123.8, 114.53, 114.43

Institute for Contemporary History, Oral History Division, Hebrew University, Jerusalem (ICJ OHD): oral histories

Leo Baeck Institute Jerusalem (LBIJ): 341, 489, 512, 589, 814, 1190

Lochamei Haghettaot (LHG): 2746, 425, 332, 262, 2746, 328, 4870, 1190, 5517, 1236, 1324, 1417, 1467, 1750, 1754, 2162, 2292, 3338, 5507

ARCHIVES CONSULTED   325

Moreshet archive, Givat Haviva (Moreshet): A.228; A.553; A.548; A.1395; C.01; D.1/ 118.1-2, 923, 929, 934, 1105,1284, 1368, 1370, 5644, 5976; D2.215; D.2/334; D.2/789 (poems)
Wiener Collection, Tel Aviv University (WL TAU): 504d, 545, 578, 586, 587
Yad Vashem, Jerusalem (YVA): M1E, M1P, M5, M16, M19, M20, M21, O1, O2, O3, O4, O7, O8, O15E, O27, O30, O33, O64

The Netherlands

Herinneringscentrum Kamp Westerbork [Westerbork Memorial] (HcKW): RA 995
Nationaalarchief [Dutch National Archive], The Hague (NA The Hague): Archief van het Ministerie van Buitenlandse Zaken (Londen)
Nederlands Instituut voor Oorlogsdocumentatie [Netherlands Institute for War Documentation], Amsterdam (NIOD): HSSPF collection; Doc. II; 187 (Red Cross); 244 (diaries); 250d (early testimonies); 250i (Westerbork); 250k (Theresienstadt); 250n (H.G.Adler papers)

Poland

Żydowski Instytut Historyczny [Jewish Historical Institute], Warsaw (ŻIH): reports from the time of the Holocaust (301)

Slovakia

Nadácia Milana Šimečku [Milan Šimečka Foundation], Bratislava (NMŠ): interviews of Holocaust survivors (Yale Fortunoff project for Slovakia)

United Kingdom

British Library, London (BL): sound archive
Wiener Library, London (WL): eyewitness testimonies, 504, 574, 578, 889, 940, 958, 1003, 1016, 1035, 1073, 1169, 1179, 1237, 1308, 1339, 1361, 1365, 1423, 1521, MF Doc 2, G 59.02; Lederer papers; digital archive of the International Tracing Service (ITS)

United States

Holocaust Center of Northern California, San Francisco: Oral History Project
Illinois Institute of Technology, Chicago (online at iit.edu): David Boder interviews
Leo Baeck Institute, New York (LBI): collections: AR, AZ, ME, MM, MS, Wahl Family, Leo Baeck, Austrian Heritage Collection, artwork
Los Angeles Museum of the Holocaust, LAMOTH: Eli Lesklý (Erich Lichtblau) artwork
Museum of Jewish Heritage, New York (MJH): Pavel Mahrer papers
New York Public Library (NYPL): American Jewish Committee Oral History Collection/ Dorot Jewish Division, oral histories
Simon Wiesenthal Center, Los Angeles (SWC): Herbert Langer
United States Holocaust Memorial Museum, Washington, DC (USHMM): oral histories; Steven Spielberg film and video archive; David Bloch collection; Ehrlich collection; Margosches collection; Zwilsky collection; Henschel collection; Jenö Klein; Ruth Knopp-Lebram
University of Michigan Dearborn, Oral History Archive (UMD OHA)
USC Visual History Foundation, Los Angeles (VHA)
YIVO, New York: Czechoslovakia; RG 717

ARCHIVES CONSULTED

Personal Archives

Personal archive Peter Barber, London
Personal archive of Martin Čakrt, Prague
Personal archive of Helen Epstein, Lexington, Ma.
Personal archive Peter Hahn, Düsseldorf
Personal archive Irene Hallmann-Strauß, Munich
Personal archive of the Japha family, New York and Seattle
Personal archive Jiří Kende, Berlin
Personal archive Irena Kodlová, Budyně nad Ohří
Personal archive of Michal Kosák, Prague
Personal archive of Alice Kundrátová, Terezín
Personal archive of Ann Lewis, Wilmslow
Personal archive of Elena Makarova, Haifa
Personal archive of Beate Meyer, Hamburg
Personal archive Hanne-Lore Munter, Berlin
Personal archive of Leo Säbel, Charlottenlund
Personal archive of Martin Šmok, Prague
Personal archive of Maria von der Heydt, Berlin
Personal archive of Tamara Warren, Brooklyn

Author's Interviews

Ina ter Beek Frenkel, February 5, 2001, Amsterdam
"Eva Berner," February 14, 2009, in Shamir
Dorie Birkenhäger Frenkel, February 8, 2001, Rotterdam
Werner Bloch, July 21, 2001, Amsterdam
Ab Caransa, February 1, 2001, in Amstelveen
Greetje Cohen Rooselaar, August 7, 2001, in Amsterdam
Michal Donath, January 25, 2013 (Skype interview)
Marianne Dreyfus, February 23, 2012 in Brooklyn
Eva Fränkel, May 2001 (phone interview)
Jaroslav Fried, March 13, 2013 (phone interview)
Hana Friediger, January 17, 2010, Dyssegaard
Peter Hahn, December 14, 2012 (phone interview) and March 19, 2013, in Düsseldorf
Šimon and Hana Kolský, former Kopolovič, January 16, 2009, in Haifa
Edgar Krása, June 19, 2012 (phone interview)
Doris Meyer Stern, April 10, 2001, in Beit Yitshak, Israel
Marianna Müllerová, March 22, 2006, in Prague
Kitty Nijstad Kok de Wijze and Harts Nijstad, May 4, 2001, in Lochem
Ellen Oppenhejm, January 21, 2010, in Charlottenlund
Liselotte Panofsky Delman, January 24, 2013 (phone interview)
Leo Säbel, January 22, 2010, in Charlottenlund
Irena Seidlerová, January 26, 2013, in Prague
Erna Seykorová-Friesová, December 5, 2012, in Prague
Alisah Schiller, January and February 2009, in Givat Haim Ihud
Renate van Hinte Kamp, July 25, 2001, in Bloemendaal
Anny Wafelman Morpurgo, July 10, 2001, in Amsterdam
Mirjam Weitzner Smuk, December 12, 2012 (phone interview)

Bibliography

Adelsberger, Lucie. "Medical Observations in Auschwitz Concentration Camp." *Lancet*, March 2, 1946, 317–319.

Adler, Eliyana. "Hrubieszów at the Crossroads: Polish Jews Navigate the German and Soviet Occupations." *Holocaust and Genocide Studies* 28, no. 1 (2014): 1–30.

Adler, H. G. *Theresienstadt 1941–1945: Das Antlitz einer Zwangsgemeinschaft.* Göttingen: Wallstein, 2005.

Adler, H. G. *Theresienstadt 1941–1945: The Face of a Coerced Community.* Edited by Amy Loewenhaar-Blausweiss. Translated by Belinda Cooper. Cambridge, UK: Cambridge University Press, 2017.

Adler, H. G. *Verheimlichte Wahrheit: Theresienstädter Dokumente.* Tübingen: Mohr, 1958.

Agamben, Giorgio. *Homo Sacer: Sovereign Power and Bare Life.* Translated by Daniel Heller-Roazen. Stanford, Calif.: Stanford University Press, 1998.

Akten zur deutschen auswärtigen Politik: 1918—1945. Series E, Vol. IV. Edited by Walter Bußmann. Göttingen: Vandenhoeck & Ruprecht, 1975.

Aleksiun, Natalia. "Jewish Students and Christian Corpses in Interwar Poland: Playing with the Language of Blood Libel." *Jewish History* 26, no. 3–4 (December 2012): 327–342.

Allen, Ann Taylor. *The Transatlantic Kindergarten: Education and Women's Movements in Germany and the Unites States.* New York: Oxford University Press, 2017.

Améry, Jean. *Jenseits von Schuld und Sühne: Bewältigungsversuche eines Überwältigten.* Munich: dtv, 1988.

Anderl, Gabriele. "Die Lagerkommandanten des jüdischen Ghetto Theresienstadt." In *Theresienstadt in der "Endlösung der Judenfrage"*, edited by Miroslav Kárný et al., 213–222. Prague: Logos, 1992.

Anderl, Gabriele. "'Die Zentralstellen für jüdische Auswanderung' in Wien, Berlin und Prag—ein Vergleich." *Tel Aviver Jahrbuch für deutsche Geschichte* 23 (1994): 275–300.

Angetter, Daniela, and Christine Kanzler, "'Eltern, Wohnung, Werte, Ordination, Freiheit, Ehren verloren!': Das Schicksal der in Wien verbliebenen jüdischen Ärzte von 1938 bis 1945 und die Versorgung ihrer jüdischen Patienten." In *Jüdische Ärztinnen und Ärzte im Nationalsozialismus: Entrechtung, Vertreibung, Ermordung*, edited by Thomas Beddies, Susanne Doetz, and Christoph Kopke, 58–74. Munich: de Gruyter, 2014.

Angrick, Andrej, and Peter Klein. *The "Final Solution" in Riga: Exploitation and Annihilation, 1941–1944.* New York: Berghahn, 2009.

Applegate, Celia. "The Importance of Culture: GSA Presidential Address 2010." *GSA Newsletter* 35, no. 2 (2011): 23–36.

Arendt, Hannah. *Eichmann in Jerusalem: A Report on the Banality of Evil.* New York: Penguin, 2006.

Arendt, Hannah. *The Origins of Totalitarianism.* New York: Meridian Books, 1958.

Arendt, Hannah. "We Refugees." *Menorah* 31 (1943): 69–77.

328 BIBLIOGRAPHY

Auerbach, Karen. *The House at Ujazdowskie 16: Jewish Families in Warsaw after the Holocaust*. Bloomington: Indiana University Press, 2013.

Auředníčková, Anna. *Tři léta v Terezíně*. Prague: Alois Hynek, 1945.

Backhaus, Fritz. "Ein Experiment des Willen zum Bösen—Überleben in Theresienstadt." In *Leo Baeck 1873–1956: Aus dem Stamme von Rabbinern*, edited by Fritz Backhaus and Georg Heuberger, 111–128. Frankfurt/Main: Jüdischer Verlag, 2001.

Backhaus, Fritz, and Martin Liepach. "Leo Baecks Manuskript über die 'Rechtsstellung der Juden in Europa': Neue Funde und ungeklärte Fragen." *Zeitschrift für Geschichtswissenschaft* 50, no. 1 (2002): 55–71.

Badone, Ellen, and Sharon R. Roseman. "Approaches to the Anthropology of Pilgrimage and Tourism." In *Intersecting Journeys: The Anthropology of Pilgrimage and Tourism*, edited by Badone and Roseman, 1–23. Urbana: University of Illinois Press, 2004.

Baeck, Leo. "A People Stands Before Its God." In *We Survived: The Stories of Fourteen of the Hidden and the Hunted of Nazi Germany*, edited by E. H. Boehm, 287–298. New Haven, Conn.: Yale University Press, 1949.

Baker, Leonard. *Days of Sorrow and of Pain: Leo Baeck and the Berlin Jews*. New York: Macmillan, 1978.

Barkai, Avraham. "Von Berlin nach Theresienstadt: Zur politischen Biographie von Leo Baeck 1933–1945." In *Hoffnung und Untergang: Studien zur deutsch-jüdischen Geschichte des 19. und 20. Jahrhunderts*, edited by Barkai, 141–166. Hamburg: Christians, 1998.

Barth, Frederik. Introduction to *Ethnic Groups and Boundaries: The Social Organization of Culture Difference*, edited by Frederik Barth. Boston: Little, Brown, 1969.

Bass, Franz. "L'amour et les camps de concentration." *Theresienstädter Studien und Dokumente* (2006): 343–347.

Bauer, Yehuda. *Jews for Sale? Nazi-Jewish Negotiations, 1933–-1945*. New Haven, Conn.: Yale University Press, 1994.

Bauman, Zygmunt. "From Pilgrim to Tourist—Or a Short History of Identity." In *Questions of Cultural Identity*, edited by Paul Du Gay and Stuart Hall, 18–36. London: Sage, 1996.

Beachy, Robert. *Gay Berlin: Birthplace of a Modern Identity*. New York: Knopf, 2014.

Becker, Michael, and Denis Bock. "Muselmänner und Häftlingsgesellschaften: Ein Beitrag zur Sozialgeschichte der nationalsozialistischen Konzentrationslager." *Archiv für Sozialgeschichte* 55 (2015): 133–175.

Beckerman, Michael, and Naomi Tadmor. "'Lullaby': The Story of a Niggun." *Music and Politics* X, no. 1 (2016).

Behrend-Rosenfeld, Else. *Ich stand nicht allein: Erlebnisse einer Jüdin in Deutschland 1933–1944*. Munich: Beck, 1988.

Bemporad, Elissa. *Becoming Soviet Jews: The Bolshevik Experiment in Minsk, 1917–1939*. Bloomington: Indiana University Press, 2013.

Bender, Sara. *The Jews of Białystok during World War II and the Holocaust*. Waltham, Mass.: Brandeis University Press; Hanover, N.H.: University Press of New England, 2008.

Benedict, Susan, and Linda Shields, eds. *Nurses and Midwives in Nazi Germany: The "Euthanasia Programs"*. London: Routledge, 2014.

Benjamin, Walter. "Zur Kritik der Gewalt." *Archiv für Sozialwissenschaft und Sozialpolitik* 47 (1920/1921): 809–832.

BIBLIOGRAPHY   329

Ben-Sasson, Havi. "Ghettos: Ghetto Police." In *YIVO Encyclopedia of Jews in Eastern Europe*. YIVO Institute for Jewish Research, 2010. http://www.yivoencyclopedia.org/article.aspx/Ghettos/Ghetto_Police.

Benz, Wolfgang, ed. *Theresienstadt: Aufzeichnungen von Federica Spitzer und Ruth Weisz.* Berlin: Metropol, 1997.

Bergen, Doris L. "I Am (Not) to Blame: Intent and Agency in Personal Accounts of the Holocaust." In *New Directions in Holocaust Research and Education: Lessons and Legacies*, vol. 12, edited by Wendy Lower and Lauren Faulkner Rossi, 87–107. Evanston, Ill.: Northwestern University Press, 2017.

Bergen, Doris L. "No End in Sight? The Ongoing Challenge of Producing an Integrated History of the Holocaust." In *Years of Persecution, Years of Extermination: Saul Friedlander and the Future of Holocaust Studies*, edited by Christian Wiese and Paul Betts, 289–310. London: Continuum, 2010.

Bergen, Doris L. "Sexual Violence in the Holocaust: Unique and Typical?" In *Lessons and Legacies VII: The Holocaust in International Perspective*, edited by Dagmar Herzog, 179–200. Evanston, Ill.: Northwestern University Press, 2006.

Bergen, Doris L. "What Do Studies of Women, Gender, and Sexuality Contribute to Understanding the Holocaust?" In *Different Horrors, Same Hell: Gender and the Holocaust*, edited by Myrna Goldenberg and Amy Shapiro, 16–38. Seattle: University of Washington Press, 2013.

Bernstein, Elsa. *Das Leben als Drama: Erinnerungen an Theresienstadt.* Edited by Rita Bake and Birgit Kiupel. Dortmund: Edition Ebersbach, 1999.

Bethhe, Svenja. "Crime and Punishment in Emergency Situations: The Jewish Ghetto Courts in Lodz, Warsaw and Vilna in World War II—A Comparative Study." *Dapim* 28 (Autumn 2014): 173–189.

Biersack, Aletta, and Lynn Avery Hunt, eds. *The New Cultural History: Essays.* Berkeley: University of California Press, 1989.

Blatman, Daniel. *The Death Marches: The Final Phase of Nazi Genocide.* Cambridge, Mass.: Belknap Press of Harvard University Press, 2011.

Blatter, Janet, and Sybil Milton. *Art of the Holocaust.* New York: Routledge, 1981.

David Bloch. "Skryté významy: Symboly v terezínské hudbě." In *Terezín v konečném řešení židovské otázky*, edited by Miroslav Kárný, 109–115. Prague: Logos, 1992.

Bock, Gisela Bock, ed. *Genozid und Geschlecht: Jüdische Frauen im nationalsozialistischen Lagersystem.* Frankfurt/Main: Campus, 2005.

Bondy, Ruth. *"Elder of the Jews": Jakob Edelstein of Theresienstadt.* New York: Grove, 1989.

Bondy, Ruth. "Prominent auf Widerruf." *Theresienstädter Studien und Dokumente* (1995): 136–154.

Bondy, Ruth. "Women in Theresienstadt and the Family Camp in Birkenau." In *Women in the Holocaust*, edited by Dalia Ofer and Lenore J. Weitzman, 310–326. New Haven, Conn.: Yale University Press, 1998.

Bonnell, Victoria E., Lynn Avery Hunt, and Richard Biernacki, eds. *Beyond the Cultural Turn: New Directions in the Study of Society and Culture.* Berkeley: University of California Press, 1999.

Bor, Josef. *Opuštěná Panenka.* Prague: Státní nakladatelství politické literatury, 1961.

Bor, Josef. *Terezínské rekviem.* Prague: Československý spisovatel, 1963.

Bourdieu, Pierre. *Distinction: A Social Critique of the Judgement of Taste.* Cambridge, Mass.: Harvard University Press, 1984.

330   BIBLIOGRAPHY

Bourdieu, Pierre. "Legitimation and Structured Interests in Weber's Sociology of Religion." In *Max Weber: Rationality, and Modernity*, edited by Scott Lash and Sam Whimster, 119–136. London: Allen and Unwin, 1987.

Bourdieu, Pierre. *The Logic of Practice*. Cambridge, UK: Polity Press, 1980.

Bourdieu, Pierre. *The Rules of Art: Genesis and Structure of the Literary Field*. Cambridge, UK: Polity Press; Stanford, Calif.: Stanford University Press, 1996.

Bourdieu, Pierre. "Social Space and the Genesis of Classes." In *Language and Symbolic Power*, edited by P. Bourdieu, 229–251. Cambridge, Mass.: Harvard University Press, 1991.

Brauer, Juliane. *Musik im Konzentrationslager Sachsenhausen*. Berlin: Metropol, 2009.

Brenner, Michael. *The Renaissance of Jewish Culture in Weimar Germany*. New Haven, Conn.: Yale University Press, 1996.

Brenner, Michael, and Gideon Reuveni, eds. *Emancipation through Muscles: Jews and Sports in Europe*. Lincoln: University of Nebraska Press, 2006.

Brenner-Wonschick, Hannelore. *Die Mädchen von Zimmer 28: Freundschaft, Hoffnung und Überleben in Theresienstadt*. Munich: Droemer, 2004.

Bridenthal, Renate, Atina Grossmann, and Marion Kaplan, eds. *When Biology Became Destiny: Women in Weimar and Nazi Germany*. New York: Monthly Review Press, 1984.

Bright, Charles. *The Powers That Punish: Prison and Politics in the Era of the "Big House", 1920–1955*. Ann Arbor: University of Michigan Press, 1996.

Brubaker, Rogers, and Frederick Cooper. "Beyond Identity." *Theory and Society* 29, no. 1 (2000): 1–47.

Brubaker, Rogers. Liana Grancea, and Jon Fox Margit Feischmidt. *Nationalist Politics and Everyday Ethnicity in a Transylvanian Town*. Princeton, N.J.: Princeton University Press, 2006.

Bryant, Chad. *Prague in Black: Nazi Rule and Czech Nationalism*. Cambridge, Mass.: Harvard University Press, 2006.

Buggeln, Marc. *Slave Labor in Nazi Concentration Camps*. Oxford: Oxford University Press, 2014.

Bürger, Hilde. *Bezwingt des Herzens Bitterkeit: Autobiographie einer jüdischen Krankenschwester*. Waldkirch: Waldkircher Verlags-Gesellschaft, 1991.

Butler, Judith. "Is Kinship Always Already Heterosexual?" *differences: A Journal of Feminist Cultural Studies* 13, no. 1 (2002): 14–44.

Buxbaum, Norbert. *Fotograaf zonder Camera*. Amsterdam: Bataafsche Leeuw, 1991.

Bynum, Caroline Walker. *Holy Feast and Holy Fast: The Religious Significance of Food to Medieval Women*. Berkeley: University of California Press, 1987.

Chládková, Ludmila. "Karel Poláček v Terezíně." *Terezínské listy* 26 (1996): 55–70.

Chlamtáčová, Klára. *Pramienok života*. Bratislava: SNM, 1995.

Cohen, Gary. "Cultural Crossings in Prague, 1900: Scenes from Late Imperial Austria." *Austrian History Yearbook* 45 (2014): 1–30.

Cole, Tim. *Holocaust City: The Making of a Jewish Ghetto*. New York: Routledge, 2003.

Cornwall, Mark. *The Devil's Wall: The Nationalist Youth Mission of Heinz Rutha*. Cambridge, Mass.: Harvard University Press, 2012.

Damwerth, Ruth. *Arnold Munter: Der Jahrhundertzeuge*. Berlin: Neues Leben, 1994.

Davis, Belinda. *Home Fires Burning: Food, Politics, and Everyday Life in World War I Berlin*. Chapel Hill: University of North Carolina Press, 2000.

Davis, Natalie Zemon. *The Return of Martin Guerre*. Cambridge, Mass.: Harvard University Press, 1983.

BIBLIOGRAPHY 331

de Rooy, Laurens. *Snijburcht: Lodewijk Bolk en de Bloei Van de Nederlandse Anatomie.* Amsterdam: Amsterdam University Press, 2011.

"Der Theresienstädter Hechalutz: Aus den Erinnerungen von Berl Herškovič." *Theresienstädter Studien und Dokumente* (2000): 151–163.

des Pres, Terrence. *The Survivor: Anatomy of Life in the Death Camps.* New York: Oxford University Press, 1976.

DeSilva, Cara, ed. *In Memory's Kitchen: A Legacy from the Women of Terezín.* Northvale, N.J.: J. Aronson, 1996.

Deutscher, Isaac. *The Non-Jewish Jew, and Other Essays.* Oxford: Oxford University Press, 1968.

Diner, Dan. "Historisches Verstehen und Gegenrationalität: Der Judenrat als erkenntnistheoretische Warte." In *Zivilisation und Barbarei: Die widersprüchlichen Potentiale der Moderne,* edited by Frank Bajohr, Werner Johe, and Uwe Lohalm, 307–321. Hamburg: Christians, 1991.

Dutlinger, Anne. "Art and Artists in Theresienstadt: Questions of Survival." In *Art, Music, and Education as Strategies for Survival: Theresienstadt 1941–45,* edited by A. Dutlinger, 1–9. New York: Herodias, 2000.

Dwork, Debórah, ed. *The Terezín Album of Mariánka Zadikow.* Chicago: University of Chicago Press, 2007.

Dwórk, Deborah. *War Is Good for Babies and Other Young Children: A History of the Infant and Child Welfare Movement in England 1898–1918.* London: Tavistock, 1987.

Edvardson, Cordelia. *Gebranntes Kind sucht das Feuer.* Munich: Hanser, 1986.

Eisenkraft, Clara. *Damals in Theresienstadt: Erlebnisse einer Judenchristin.* Wuppertal: Aussaat, 1977.

Elias, Norbert. *The Civilizing Process.* New York: Urizen Books, 1978. First published 1933.

Elias, Ruth. *The Triumph of Hope: From Theresienstadt and Auschwitz to Israel.* New York: John Wiley, 1998.

Engelking-Boni, Barbara, and Jacek Leociak. *The Warsaw Ghetto: A Guide to the Perished City.* New Haven, Conn.: Yale University Press, 2009.

Epstein, Barbara. *The Minsk Ghetto, 1941–1943: Jewish Resistance and Soviet Internationalism.* Berkeley: University of California Press, 2008.

Epstein, Helen. *A Jewish Athlete: Swimming against Stereotype in 20th Century Europe.* Lexington, Mass.: Plunket Lake, 2011.

Erben, Petr. *Po vlastních stopách.* Prague: Kalina, 2003.

Eschebach, Insa, ed. *Homophobie und Devianz: Weibliche und männliche Homosexualität im Nationalsozialismus.* Berlin: Metropol, 2012.

Fall, Susanne. *Terezín, ráj mezi lágry.* Prague: Revolver Revue, 2015.

Fantlová, Zdenka. *Klid je síla, řek' tatínek.* Prague: Primus, 1996.

Fara, František. *Četnické vzpomínky.* Prague: Codyprint, 2002.

Feder, Richard. *Židovská tragedie: Dějství poslední.* Kolín: Lusk, 1947.

Fedorovič, Tomáš. "Der Theresienstädter Lagerkommandant Siegfried Seidl." *Theresienstädter Studien und Dokumente* (2003): 162–209.

Fedorovič, Tomáš. "Jüdische Geisteskranke Patienten aus dem Protektorat." In *Die nationalsozialistische "Euthanasie" im Reichsgau Sudetenland und Protektorat Böhmen und Mähren 1939–1945,* edited by Michal Šimůnek and Dietmar Schulze, 199–236. Červený Kostelec: Pavel Mervart and AV ČR, 2008.

Fedorovič, Tomáš. "Konfidenti v ghettu Terezín." *Terezínské listy* 37 (2009): 134–140.

Fedorovič, Tomáš. "Zánik města Terezín a jeho přeměna v ghetto." *Terezínské listy* 32 (2004): 15–43.

332 BIBLIOGRAPHY

Feinberg, Melissa. *Elusive Equality: Gender, Citizenship, and the Limits of Democracy in Czechoslovakia, 1918–1950.* Pittsburgh: University of Pittsburgh Press, 2006.

Feuss, Axel, ed. *Das Theresienstadt-Konvolut.* Hamburg: Dölling und Galitz, 2002.

Fink, Sheri. "The Deadly Choices at Memorial." *New York Times,* August 25, 2009.

Finkel, Evgeny. *Ordinary Jews: Choice and Survival during the Holocaust.* Princeton, N.J.: Princeton University Press, 2016.

Fischer, Jan. *Šest skoků do budoucnosti.* Prague: Idea Service, 1998.

Fischerová, Luisa, et al. *In memoriam Irena Krausová.* Prague: Organisace sociálních pracovnic, 1947.

Fitzpatrick, Sheila. *Everyday Stalinism: Ordinary Life in Extraordinary Times: Soviet Russia in the 1930s.* New York: Oxford University Press, 1999.

Flaschka, Monika. "'Only Pretty Women Were Raped': The Effect of Sexual Violence on Gender Identities in the Concentration Camps." In *Sexual Violence against Jewish Women during the Holocaust,* edited by Sonja M. Hedgepeth and Rochelle G. Saidel, 77–93. Hanover, N.H.: University Press of New England, 2010.

Flusser, Jindřich. "Ein Rückblick." *Theresienstädter Studien und Dokumente* (1999): 43–75.

Foucault, Michel. *Discipline and Punish: The Birth of the Prison.* London: Penguin, 1991.

Fracapane, Silvia Goldbaum Tarabini. "'Wir erfuhren, was es heißt, hungrig zu sein': Aspekte des Alltagslebens dänischer Juden in Theresienstadt." In *Der Alltag im Holocaust: Jüdisches Leben im Großdeutschen Reich 1941–1945,* edited by Doris Bergen, Andrea Löw, and Anna Hájková, 199–216. Munich: Oldenbourg, 2013.

Franková, Anita. "Die Vorbereitung zur Konzentrierung der Juden im Protektorat: Die 'Vorgeschichte' des Theresienstädter Ghetto." *Theresienstädter Studien und Dokumente* (2001): 49–105.

Freiberger, Rudolf. "Zur Geschichte der Produktionsstätten im Theresienstädter Ghetto." *Theresienstädter Studien und Dokumente* (1994): 90–108.

Friedländer, Saul. *Nazi Germany and the Jews.* 2 vols. New York: HarperCollins, 1997–2006.

Friedländer, Saul, ed. *Probing the Limits of Representation: Nazism and the "Final Solution".* Cambridge, Mass.: Harvard University Press, 1992.

Friedler, Eric, Barbara Siebert, and Andreas Kilian. *Zeugen aus der Todeszone: Das jüdische Sonderkommando in Auschwitz.* Lüneburg: zu Klampen!, 2002.

Friedman, Philip. *Roads to Extinction: Essays on the Holocaust.* New York: Jewish Publication Society of America, 1980.

Friedmann, Franz. *Einige Zahlen über die tschechoslovakischen Juden: Ein Beitrag zur Soziologie der Judenheit.* Prague: Barissia, 1933.

Friesová, Jana Renée. *Pevnost mého mládí.* Prague: Trizonia, 1997.

Fritta, Bedřich. *This Is Not a Fairy Tale—It's Real! To Tommy for His Third Birthday in Terezín, 22 January 1944.* Prague: Jewish Museum, 2000.

Frommer, Benjamin. "Czechs and Germans, Gentiles and Jews: Intermarriage in a Decade of Genocide and Ethnic Cleansing, 1938–1948." In *Intermarriage in Eastern Europe and Eurasia: Ethnic Mixing under Fascism, Communism, and Beyond,* edited by Adrianne Edgar and Benjamin Frommer, 47–82. Lincoln: Nebraska University Press, 2020.

Frommer, Benjamin. *National Cleansing: Retribution against Nazi Collaborators in Postwar Czechoslovakia.* New York: Cambridge University Press, 2005.

BIBLIOGRAPHY   333

Frýd, Norbert. "Kultura v předposlední stanici." In *Theater—Divadlo. Vzpomínky českých divadelníků na německou okupaci a druhou světovou válku*, edited by František Černý. Prague: Orbis, 1965.

Fuchs, Emma. *My Kaleidoscope*. Self-published, 1974.

Fuchs, Emma. *My Kaleidoscope: Surviving the Holocaust*. Edited by Shari J. Ryan. Seattle: Booktrope Editions, 2014.

Fuchs, František. "Die tschechisch-jüdische Widerstandsbewegung in Theresienstadt." *Theresienstädter Studien und Dokumente* (1997): 141–156.

Garbarini, Alexandra. "Document Volumes and the Status of Victim Testimony in the Era of the First World War and Its Aftermath." *Études arméniennes contemporaines* 5 (2015): 113–138.

Garbarini, Alexandra. *Numbered Days: Diaries and the Holocaust*. New Haven, Conn.: Yale University Press, 2006.

Gardella, Lorrie Greenhouse. *The Life and Thought of Louis Lowy: Social Work through the Holocaust*. Syracuse, N.Y.: Syracuse University Press, 2011.

Geertz, Clifford. *The Interpretation of Cultures: Selected Essays*. London: Fontana, 1973.

Gellner, Ernst. *Nations and Nationalism*. Ithaca, N.Y.: Cornell University Press, 1983.

Gerlach, Christian. "Die Bedeutung der deutschen Ernährungspolitik für die Beschleunigung des Mordes an den Juden 1942: Das Generalgouvernement und die Westukraine." In *Krieg, Ernährung, Völkermord: Forschungen zur deutschen Vernichtungspolitik im Zweiten Weltkrieg*, edited by Gerlach, 167–254. Hamburg: Hamburger Edition, 1998.

Gerlach, Christian. "Die Wannseekonferenz, das Schicksal der deutschen Juden und Hitlers Grundsatzentscheidung, alle Juden Europas zu ermorden." *Werkstatt Geschichte* 18 (1997): 7–44.

Gerlach, Christian. "Die Welternährungskrise 1972–1975." *Geschichte und Gesellschaft* 31, no. 4 (2005): 546–585.

Gilbert, Shirli. *Music in the Holocaust: Confronting Life in the Nazi Ghettos and Camps*. Oxford: Oxford University Press, 2005.

Gilman, Sander. *Franz Kafka, the Jewish Patient*. New York: Routledge, 1995.

Ginzburg, Carlo. *The Cheese and the Worms: The Cosmos of a Sixteenth-Century Miller*. Baltimore, Md.: Johns Hopkins University Press, 1980.

Ginzburg, Carlo. "Microhistory: Two or Three Things That I Know about It." *Critical Inquiry* 20, no. 1 (Autumn 1993): 10–35.

Glass, Martha. *"Jeder Tag in Theresin ist ein Geschenk": Die Theresienstädter Tagebücher einer Hamburger Jüdin 1943–1945*. Edited by Barbara Müller Wesemann. Hamburg: Ergebnisse, 1996.

Goeschel, Christian. "Suicide in Nazi Concentration Camps, 1933–9." *Journal of Contemporary History* 45, no. 3 (July 2010): 628–648.

Goffman, Erving. *Frame Analysis: An Essay on the Organization of Experience*. New York: Harper & Row, 1974.

Goffman, Erving. "On the Characteristics of Total Institutions." In *Asylums: Essays on the Social Situation of Mental Patients and Other Inmates*, edited by Goffman. Garden City, N.Y.: Doubleday, 1961.

Goldberg, Amos. *Trauma in First Person: Diary Writing during the Holocaust*. Bloomington: Indiana University Press, 2018.

Goldberg, Amos. "The Victim's Voice in History and Melodramatic Esthetics." *History and Theory* 48, no. 3 (2009): 220–237.

334 BIBLIOGRAPHY

Gottwaldt, Alfred, and Diana Schulle. *Die Judendeportationen aus dem Deutschen Reich, 1941–1945: Eine kommentierte Chronologie.* Wiesbaden: Marixverlag, 2005.

Grant, Susan, ed. *Russian and Soviet Health Care from an International Perspective Comparing Professions, Practice and Gender, 1880–1960.* Basingstoke, UK: Palgrave, 2017.

Greiser, Katrin. *Die Todesmärsche von Buchenwald: Räumung, Befreiung und Spuren der Erinnerung.* Göttingen: Wallstein, 2008.

Grossmann, Atina. "The New Woman and the Rationalization of Sexuality in Weimar Germany." In *Women in Culture and Politics: A Century of Change,* edited by Judith Friedlander et al., 153–171. Bloomington: Indiana University Press, 1986.

Gutmann-Herskovits, Ruth. *Auswanderung vorläufig nicht möglich: Die Geschichte der Familie Herskovits aus Hannover.* Edited by Bernard Strebel. Göttingen: Wallstein, 2002.

Hájková, Alena. "Lebensgeschichte Karel Körpers." *Theresienstädter Studien und Dokumente* (2002): 272–299.

Hájková, Anna. "Die Juden aus den Niederlanden in Theresienstadt." *Theresienstädter Studien und Dokumente* (2002): 135–201.

Hájková, Anna. "Die fabelhaften Jungs aus Theresienstadt: Junge tschechische Männer als dominante soziale Elite im Theresienstädter Ghetto." *Beiträge zur Geschichte des Nationalsozialismus* 25 (2009): 116–135.

Hájková, Anna. "Der Judenälteste und seine SS–Männer: Benjamin Murmelstein, der letzte Judenälteste in Theresienstadt und seine Beziehung zu Adolf Eichmann und Karl Rahm." In *"Der Letzte der Ungerechten": Der Judenälteste Benjamin Murmelstein in Filmen 1942–1975,* edited by Ronny Loewy and Katharina Rauschenberger, 75–100. Frankfurt/Main: Campus, 2011.

Hájková, Anna. "Mutmaßungen über deutsche Juden: Alte Menschen aus Deutschland im Theresienstädter Ghetto." In *Der Alltag im Holocaust: Jüdisches Leben im Großdeutschen Reich 1941–1945,* edited by Doris Bergen, Andrea Löw, and Anna Hájková, 179–198. Munich: Oldenbourg, 2013.

Hájková, Anna. "Die Jahre der Verbitterung: Neues über Otilie Davidová, die 1942 nach Theresienstadt deportierte jüngste Schwester Franz Kafkas." *Süddeutsche Zeitung,* November 24, 2015.

Hájková, Anna. "Poor Devils of the Camps: Dutch Jews in the Terezín Ghetto, 1943–1945." *Yad Vashem Studies* 43, no. 1 (2015): 77–111.

Hájková, Anna. "What Kind of Narrative Is Legal Testimony? Terezín Survivors Speaking Before Czechoslovak, Austrian, and Western German Justice." In *Rethinking Holocaust Justice: Essays across Disciplines,* edited by Norman Goda, 71–99. New York: Berghahn, 2017.

Hájková, Anna, and Maria von der Heydt. "Dahlem, Westerbork, Theresienstadt, Seattle: The Veit Simon Children, Class, and the Transnational in the Holocaust History." *European History Review* 24, no. 5 (2017): 732–758.

Hájková-Duxová, Věra. "Takový byl život." In *Svět bez lidských dimenzí.* Prague: Státní židovské muzeum, 1991.

Hamperl, Herwig. *Werdegang und Lebensweg eines Pathologen.* Stuttgart: Schattauer, 1972.

Harsch, Donna. "Medicalized Social Hygiene? Tuberculosis Policy in the German Democratic Republic." *Bulletin of the History of Medicine* 86, no. 3 (Fall 2012): 394–423.

BIBLIOGRAPHY   335

Herzog, Dagmar. *Sex after Fascism: Memory and Morality in Twentieth-Century Germany.* Princeton, N.J.: Princeton University Press, 2005.

Hess, Christiane. *Das Lager im Blick: Zeichnungen aus den Konzentrationslagern Ravensbrück und Neuengamme.* Berlin: Metropol, 2021.

Heumann, Hugo. *Erlebtes-Erlittenes: Von Mönchengladbach über Luxemburg nach Theresienstadt*, Edited by Germaine Goetzinger and Marc Schoentgen. Mersch: CNL, 2007.

Hilarová, Dagmar. *Nemám žádné jméno.* Edited by Evžen Hilar. Prague: Svoboda Service, 2010.

Hilberg, Raul. *The Destruction of the European Jews.* New Haven, Conn.: Yale University Press, 2003.

Hildebrandt, Sabine. "The Women on Stieve's List: Victims of National Socialism Whose Bodies Were Used for Anatomical Research." *Clinical Anatomy* 26, no. 1 (January 2013): 3–21.

Hobsbawm, Eric. "Introduction: Inventing Traditions." In *The Invention of Tradition*, edited by Eric Hobsbawm and Terence Ranger, 1–14. Cambridge, UK: Cambridge University Press, 1983.

Hoenig, Leonard J., Tomas Spenser, and Anita Tarsi. "Dr. Karel Fleischmann: The story of an Artist and Physician in Ghetto Terezin." *International Journal of Dermatology* 43, no. 2 (2004): 129–135.

Holian, Anna. *Between National Socialism and Soviet Communism: Displaced Persons in Postwar Germany.* Ann Arbor: University of Michigan Press, 2011.

Holloway, Kerrie. "The Bright Young People of the Late 1920s: How the Great War's Armistice Influenced Those Too Young to Fight." *Journal of European Studies* 45, no. 4 (2015): 316–330.

Hošková-Weissová, Helga. *Zeichne, Was Du Siehst.* Göttingen: Wallstein, 2001.

Hradská, Katarína. "Vorgeschichte der slowakischen Transporte nach Theresienstadt." *Theresienstädter Studien und Dokumente* (1996): 82–97.

Hroch, Miroslav. *Social Preconditions of National Revival in Europe.* Cambridge, UK: Cambridge University Press, 1985.

Hubatová-Vacková, Lada. "Folklorisms." In *Building a State: Representation of Czechoslovakia in Art, Architecture and Design*, edited by Milena Bartlová et al., 65–90. Prague: VŠUP, 2015.

Hubenstorf, Michael. "Vertriebene Medizin: Finale des Niedergangs der Wiener Medizinischen Schule?" In *Vertriebene Vernunft II: Emigration und Exil österreichischer Wissenschaft*, edited by Friedrich Stadler, 766–793. Vienna: Jugend und Volk, 1988.

Huebner, Karla. "Girl, Trampka, nebo Žába? The Czechoslovak New Woman." In *The New Woman International: Representations in Photography and Film from the 1870s through the 1960s*, edited by Elizabeth Otto and Vanessa Rocco, 231–235. Ann Arbor: University of Michigan Press, 2011.

Huebner, Karla. "The Whole World Revolves Around It: Sex Education and Sex Reform in First Republic Czech Print Media." *Aspasia* 4 (2010): 25–48.

Hull, Isabel. *Absolute Destruction: Military Culture and the Practices of War in Imperial Germany.* Ithaca, N.Y.: Cornell University Press, 2005.

Hyndráková, Anna, Helena Krejčová, and Jana Svobodová, eds. *Prominenti v ghettu Terezín, 1942-1945.* Prague: Ústav pro soudobé dějiny AV ČR, 1996.

Hyndráková, Anna, Raisa Machatková, and Jaroslava Milotová, eds. *Denní rozkazy Rady starších a Sdělení židovské samosprávy Terezín 1941-1945.* Prague: Sefer, 2003.

336 BIBLIOGRAPHY

Iltis, Rudolf, ed. *Theresienstadt*. Vienna: Europa-Verlag, 1968.

Jenß, Harro. *Hermann Strauß: Internist und Wissenschaftler in der Charité und im jüdischen Krankenhaus Berlin*. Berlin: Hentrich & Hentrich, 2010.

Jenß, Harro, and Peter Reinicke, eds. *Der Arzt Hermann Strauß 1868–1944: Autobiographische Notizen und Aufzeichnungen aus dem Ghetto Theresienstadt*. Berlin: Hentrich & Hentrich, 2014.

Jirásek, Pavel. "Český meziválečný tramping." *Živel* 15 (1999): 33–39.

Jockusch, Laura. *Collect and Record! Jewish Holocaust Documentation in Early Postwar Europe*. New York: Oxford University Press, 2012.

Jureit, Ulrike. *Erinnerungsmuster: Zur Methodik lebensgeschichtlicher Interviews mit Überlebenden der Konzentrations- und Vernichtungslager*. Hamburg: Ergebnisse, 1999.

Jütte, Robert, Winfried Süß, and Wolfgang Eckart, eds. *Medizin und Nationalsozialismus: Bilanz und Perspektiven der Forschung*. Göttingen: Wallstein, 2011.

Kälber, Lutz. "Child Murder in Nazi Germany: The Memory of Nazi Medical Crimes and Commemoration of 'Children's Euthanasia' Victims at Two Facilities (Eichberg, Kalmenhof)." *Societies* 2, no. 3 (2012): 157–194.

Kämper, Dirk. *Fredy Hirsch und die Kinder des Holocaust: Die Geschichte eines vergessenen Helden aus Deutschland*. Zurich: Orrell Füssli, 2015.

Kaplan, Marion. *Between Dignity and Despair: Jewish Life in Nazi Germany*. New York: Oxford University Press, 1998.

Kaplan, Marion. *The Making of the Jewish Middle Class: Women, Family, and Identity in Imperial Germany*. Oxford: Oxford University Press, 1991.

Karas, Joža. *Music in Terezín 1941–1945*. New York: Beaufort Books, 1985.

Kárn, Miroslav, Vojtěch Blodig, and Margita Kárná, eds. *Theresienstadt in der "Endlösung der Judenfrage."* Prague: Logos, 1992.

Kárný, Miroslav. "Anmerkungen des Herausgebers." *Theresienstädter Studien und Dokumente* (1995): 264–270.

Kárný, Miroslav. "Die Flucht des Auschwitzer Häftlings Vítěslav Lederer und der tschechische Widerstand." *Theresienstädter Studien und Dokumente* (1997): 157–183.

Kárný, Miroslav. "Die Gendarmerie-Sonderabteilung und die Theresienstädter Häftlinge: Zur Methodologie der kritischen Interpretation von Erinnerungen." *Theresienstädter Studien und Dokumente* (1996): 136–152.

Kárný, Miroslav. "Die Theresienstädter Herbsttransporte 1944." *Theresienstädter Studien und Dokumente* (1995): 7–37.

Kárný, Miroslav. "Ein Theresienstädter Tagebuch, 18. Oktober 1944–19. Mai 1945." *Theresienstädter Studie und Dokumente* (1994): 169–171.

Kárný, Miroslav. "Jakov Edelsteins letzte Briefe." *Theresienstädter Studien und Dokumente* (1997): 216–229.

Kárný, Miroslav. "Kaltenbrunners Reise nach Theresienstadt und der Prominententransport im April 1945." *Theresienstädter Studien und Dokumente* (1999): 66–85.

Kárný, Miroslav. "'Pracovní' či 'zaopatřovací' Terezín? Iluze areality tzv. produktivního ghetta." *Litoměřicko* 25 (1989): 95–107.

Kárný, Miroslav. "Terezínský rodinný tábor v konečném řešení." In *Terezínský rodinný tábor v konečném řešení*, edited by Toman Brod, M. Kárný, and Margita Kárná, 32–43. Prague: Melantrich and Terezínská Iniciativa, 1994.

Kárný, Miroslav. "Zur Typologie des Theresienstädter Konzentrationslagers." *Judaica Bohemiae* 17, no. 1 (1981): 3–14.

BIBLIOGRAPHY 337

Kárný, Miroslav, Jaroslava Milotová, and Margita Kárná, eds. *Deutsche Politik im "Protektorat Böhmen und Mähren" unter Reinhard Heydrich 1941–1942*. Berlin: Metropol, 1997.

Kasperová, Dana. *Výchova a vzdělávání židovských dětí v protektorátu a v ghettu Terezín*. Prague: Filozofická fakulta Univerzity Karlovy, 2010.

Kassow, Samuel. *Who Will Write Our History? Emanuel Ringelblum and the Oyneg Shabes Archive*. Bloomington: Indiana University Press, 2007.

Kater, Michael H. *Doctors Under Hitler*. Chapel Hill: University of North Carolina Press, 1989.

Kellenbach, Katharina von. "Reproduction and Resistance during the Holocaust." In *Women and the Holocaust: Narrative and Representation*, edited by Esther Fuchs, 19–32. Lanham, Md.: University Press of America, 1999.

Kessler, Erich. "Der Theresienstädter 20. April 1945 und die Tage danach ...." *Theresienstädter Studien und Dokumente* (1995): 306–324.

Kis, Oksana. "Defying Death: Women's Experience of the Holodomor, 1932–1933." *Aspasia* 7 (2013): 42–67.

Klein, Peter. *Die Gettoverwaltung Litzmannstadt 1940 bis 1944: Eine Dienststelle im Spannungsfeld von Kommunalbürokratie und staatlicher Verfolgungspolitik*. Hamburg: Hamburger Edition, 2009.

Klein, Peter. "Theresienstadt: Ghetto oder Konzentrationslager?" *Theresienstädter Studien und Dokumente* (2005): 111–123.

Klemp, Stefan. *Nicht Ermittelt: Polizeibataillone und die Nachkriegsjustiz—Ein Handbuch*. Essen: Klartext, 2005.

Klüger, Ruth. *Weiter leben: Eine Jugend*. Göttingen: Wallstein, 1992.

Kosta, Jiří. *Život mezi úzkostí a nadějí*. Prague; Litomyšl: Paseka, 2002.

Kraus, Evžen. "Boj proti tuberkulose v koncentračních táborech." *Boj proti tuberkulose* 27, no. 8 (1946): 131–133.

Kryl, Miroslav. "Die Deportationen aus Theresienstadt nach dem Osten im Spiegel des Tagebuch Willy Mahlers." *Theresienstädter Studien und Dokumente* (1995): 69–92.

Kulka, Erich. *Útěk z tábora smrti*. Prague: MNO, 1966.

Kuna, Milan. *Hudba vzdoru a naděje: Terezín 1941–1945*. Prague: Bärenreiter, 2000.

Kurrer, Thomas, ed. *K.Z. Theresienstadt April 1944–Mai 1945: Briefe und Aufzeichnungen von Else Gräfin v. Schlitz, gen. v. Goertz und Freifrau v. Wrisberg*. Schondorf: Edition Blaes, 2016.

Lagus, Karel, and Josef Polák. *Město za mřížemi*. Prague: Naše vojsko, 1964.

Lamberti, Marjorie. "Making Art in the Terezin Concentration Camp." *New England Review* 17, no. 4 (1995): 104–111.

Lampert, Tom. "Ein seltener Gerechtigkeitssinn." In *Ein einziges Leben: Acht Geschichten aus dem Krieg*, 114–193. Munich: dtv, 2003.

Langer, Lawrence. *Admitting the Holocaust: Collected Essays*. New York: Oxford University Press, 1995.

Langer, Lawrence. *Holocaust Testimonies: The Ruins of Memory*. New Haven, Conn.: Yale University Press, 1991.

Laqueur, Thomas. *Making Sex: Body and Gender from the Greeks to Freud*. Cambridge, Mass.: Harvard University Press, 1990.

Le Roy Ladurie, Emmanuel. *Montaillou: Cathars and Catholics in a French Village, 1294–1324*. New York: G. Braziller, 1978.

Lederer, Zdeněk. *Ghetto Theresienstadt*. London: E. Goldston, 1953.

338 BIBLIOGRAPHY

Leff, Lisa Moses. *The Archive Thief: The Man Who Salvaged French Jewish History in the Wake of the Holocaust.* New York: Oxford University Press, 2015.

Lehmann, Dora. *Erinnerungen einer Altonaerin 1866-1946.* Hamburg: Dölling und Galitz, 1998.

Leichsenring, Jana. "Die katholische Gemeinde in Theresienstadt und die Berliner Katholiken." *Theresienstädter Studien und Dokumente* (2004): 178-222.

Lewis, Helen. *A Time to Speak.* Belfast: Blackstaff, 1992.

Ley, Astrid. *Medizin und Verbrechen: Das Krankenrevier des KZ Sachsenhausen 1936-1945.* Berlin: Metropol, 2005.

Liebersohn, Harry. *The Return of the Gift: European History of a Global Idea.* Cambridge, UK: Cambridge University Press, 2010.

Liebrecht, Heinrich. *Nicht mitzuhassen, mitzulieben bin ich da: Mein Weg durch die Hölle des Dritten Reiches.* Freiburg im Breisgau: Herder, 1990.

Lifton, Robert Jay. *The Nazi Doctors: Medical Killing and the Psychology of Genocide.* New York: Basic Books, 1986.

Linn, Ruth. *Escaping Auschwitz: A Culture of Forgetting.* Ithaca, N.Y.: Cornell University Press, 2004.

Lipková, Renata. "Právo v nuceném společenství." *Terezínské listy* 27 (1999): 20-38.

Louie, Ronald. *Etta at Eighty!* Seattle: Family Press, 1998.

Löw, Andrea. *Juden im Getto Litzmannstadt: Lebensbedingungen, Selbstwahrnehmung, Verhalten.* Göttingen: Wallstein, 2006.

Lüdtke, Alf, ed., *Alltagsgeschichte: Zur Rekonstruktion historischer Erfahrungen und Lebensweisen.* Frankfurt: Campus, 1989.

Lüdtke, Alf. "Geschichte und Eigensinn." In *Alltagskultur, Subjektivität und Geschichte: Zur Theorie und Praxis von Alltagsgeschichte,* edited by Berliner Geschichtswerkstatt, 139-153. Münster: Westfälisches Dampfboot, 1994.

Lybeck, Marti. *Desiring Emancipation: New Women and Homosexuality in Germany, 1890-1933.* Albany: State University of New York Press, 2014.

Mailänder, Elissa. *Female SS Guards and Workaday Violence: The Majdanek Concentration Camp, 1942-1944.* East Lansing: Michigan State University Press, 2015.

Makarova, Elena. *Friedl Dicker-Brandeis: Ein Leben für Kunst und Lehre: Wien, Weimar, Prag, Hronov, Theresienstadt, Auschwitz.* Vienna: Brandstätter, 2000.

Makarova, Elena. *Pevnost nad propastí: Já, děcko bloudící? Děti a učitelé v terezínském ghettu 1941-1945.* Prague: Bergman, 2009.

Makarova, Elena, Sergei Makarov, and Viktor Kuperman. *University over the Abyss: The Story behind 520 Lecturers and 2,430 Lectures in KZ Theresienstadt 1942-1944.* Jerusalem: Verba, 2004.

Manes, Philipp. *Als ob's ein Leben wär: Tatsachenbericht Theresienstadt 1942-1944.* Edited by Klaus Leist and Ben Barkow. Berlin: Ullstein, 2005.

Manes, Philipp. *As If It Were Life: A WWII Diary from the Theresienstadt Ghetto.* Edited by Klaus Leist and Ben Barkow. Translated by Janet Forster, Klaus Leist, and Ben Barkow. New York: Palgrave Macmillan, 2009.

Manley, Rebecca. "Nutritional Dystrophy: The Science and Semantics of Starvation in World War II." In *Hunger and War: Food Provisioning in the Soviet Union during World War II,* edited by Wendy Goldman and Donald Filtzer, 206-264. Bloomington: Indiana University Press, 2015.

Margry, Karel. "Der Nazi-Film über Theresienstadt." In *Theresienstadt in der "Endlösung der Judenfrage",* edited by Miroslav Kárný, Vojtěch Blodig, and Margita Kárná, 285-306. Prague: Logos, 1992.

BIBLIOGRAPHY 339

Marhoefer, Laurie. *Sex and the Weimar Republic: German Homosexual Emancipation and the Rise of the Nazis*. Toronto: University of Toronto Press, 2015.

Mauss, Marcel. *The Gift: Forms and Functions of Exchange in Archaic Societies*. Translated by Ian Cunnison. Mansfield Centre: Martino Publishing, 2011.

Mazower, Mark. *Inside Hitler's Greece: The Experience of Occupation, 1941–44*. New Haven, Conn.: Yale University Press, 1993.

McFarland-Icke, Bronwyn Rebekah. *Nurses in Nazi Germany: Moral Choice in History*. Princeton, N.J.: Princeton University Press, 1999.

Mendelsohn, Ezra. "Should We Take Notice of Berthe Weill? Reflections on the Domain of Jewish History." *Jewish Social Studies*, n.s., 1 (Autumn 1994): 22–39.

Meyer, Beate. "'Altersghetto', 'Vorzugslager' und Tätigkeitsfeld: Die Repräsentanten der Reichsvereinigung der Juden in Deutschland und Theresienstadt." *Theresienstädter Studien und Dokumente* (2004): 124–149.

Meyer, Beate. *"Jüdische Mischlinge": Rassenpolitik und Verfolgungserfahrung 1933–1945*. Hamburg: Dölling und Galitz, 1999.

Meyer, Beate. *Tödliche Gratwanderung: Die Reichsvereinigung der Juden in Deutschland zwischen Hoffnung, Zwang, Selbstbehauptung und Verstrickung (1939–1945)*. Göttingen: Wallstein, 2011.

Michman, Dan. *The Emergence of Jewish Ghettos during the Holocaust*. Cambridge, UK: Cambridge University Press, 2011.

Migdal, Ulrike, ed. *Und die Musik spielt dazu: Chansons und Satiren aus dem KZ Theresienstadt*. Munich: Piper, 1986.

Milotová, Jaroslava. "Die Zentralstelle für jüdische Auswanderung in Prag: Genesis und Tätigkeit bis zum Anfang des Jahres 1940." *Theresienstädter Studien und Dokumente* (1997): 7–30.

Milotová, Jaroslava. "Nachwort." In *Unter Hakenkreuz und Sowjetstern: Erlebnisse eines Verfolgten in zwei Diktaturen*, edited by Jan Osers, 165–175. Berlin: Metropol, 2005.

Milotová, Jaroslava, et al. *Jewish Gold and Other Precious Metals, Precious Stones, and Objects Made of Such Materials—Situation in the Czech Lands in the Years 1939 to 1945*. Prague: Sefer, 2001.

Milton, Sybil. "Women and the Holocaust: The Case of German and German-Jewish Women." In *When Biology Became Destiny: Women in Weimar and Nazi German*, edited by Renate Bridenthal, Atina Grossmann, and Marion Kaplan, 297–333. New York: Monthly Review Press, 1984.

Mörchen, Stefan. *Schwarzer Markt: Kriminalität, Ordnung und Moral in Bremen 1939–1949*. Frankfurt am Main: Campus, 2011.

Müller, Melissa, and Reinhard Piechocki. *Alice Herz-Sommer: "Ein Garten Eden Inmitten der Hölle"; Ein Jahrhundertleben*. Munich: Droemer, 2006.

Müller Tupath, Karla. *Verschollen in Deutschland: Das heimliche Leben des Anton Burger, Lagerkommandant von Theresienstadt*. Hamburg: Konkret, 1994.

Murmelstein, Benjamin. *Theresienstadt: Eichmanns Vorzeige-Ghetto*. Edited by Ruth Pleyer and Alfred J. Noll. Translated by Karin Fleischanderl. Vienna: Czernin, 2014.

Němcová, Božena. *The Grandmother: A Story of Country Life in Bohemia*. Prague: Alcor, 1999. First published 1855.

Novitch, Miriam. *Spiritual Resistance: Art from Concentration Camps, 1940–1945*. New York: Union of American Hebrew Congregations, 1981.

Ofer, Dalia. "We Israelis Remember, But How? The Memory of the Holocaust and the Israeli Experience." *Israel Studies* 18, no. 2 (2013): 70–85.

Ondřichová, Lucie. *Příběh Freddyho Hirsche*. Prague: Sefer, 2001.

340 BIBLIOGRAPHY

Opfermann, Charlotte, and Robert A. Warren. *Charlotte, a Holocaust Memoir: Remembering Theresienstadt*. Santa Fe, N.Mex.: Paper Tiger, 2006.

Oppenhejm, Mélanie. *Theresienstadt: Die Menschenfalle*. Translated by Dietmar Possart. Munich: Boer, 1998.

Oppenhejm, Ralph. *An der Grenze des Lebens: Theresienstädter Tagebuch*. Translated by Albrecht Leonhardt. Hamburg: Rueten & Loening, 1961.

Orzoff, Andrea. *Battle for the Castle: The Myth of Czechoslovakia in Europe, 1914–1948*. Oxford: Oxford University Press, 2009.

Overing, J. "Kinship in Anthropology." In *International Encyclopedia of the Social & Behavioral Sciences*, edited by Neil J. Smelser and Paul B. Baltes, 8098–8105. New York: Elsevier, 2001.

Patterson, Orlando. *Slavery and Social Death: A Comparative Study*. Cambridge, Mass.: Harvard University Press, 1982.

Pawełczynska, Anna. *Values and Violence in Auschwitz: A Sociological Analysis*. Berkeley: University of California Press, 1979.

Perechodnik, Calel. *Am I a Murderer? Testament of a Jewish Ghetto Policeman*. Edited by Frank Fox. Boulder, Colo.: Westview Press, 1996.

Person, Katarzyna. *Policjanci*. Warsaw: Żydowski Instytut Historyczny, 2018.

Perz, Bertrand, and Florian Freund. "Auschwitz Neu? Pläne und Maßnahmen zur Wiedererrichtung der Krematorien von Auschwitz-Birkenau in der Umgebung des KZ Mauthausen im Februar 1945." *Dachauer Hefte* 20 (2004): 58–70.

Peschel, Lisa. "Das Theater in Theresienstadt und das Zweite Tschechische Kabarett: 'Geistiger Widerstand'?" *Theresienstädter Studien und Dokumente* (2006): 84–114.

Peschel, Lisa, ed. *Divadelní texty z terezínskéha ghetta 1941—1945*. Prague: Akropolis, 2008.

Peters, Dietlinde. *Martha Wygodzinski (1869–1943) "Der Engel der Armen": Berliner Ärztin engagierte Gesundheitspolitikerin*. Berlin: Hentrich & Hentrich, 2008.

Philippson, Dora. "Bericht über die Deportation und das Überleben in Theresienstadt 1942 bis 1945, May 1945)." In *Frauenleben im NS-Alltag*, edited by Annette Kuhn, 303–320. Pfaffenweiler: Centaurus, 1994.

Pick, Miloš. *Naděje se vzdát neumím*. Brno: Doplněk, 2010.

Pokorná, Lilly. "Die Lungentuberkulose im Konzentrationslager Theresienstadt im Vergleich mit der bei Häftlingen in anderen deutschen Konzentrationslagern." *Tuberkulosearzt* 4 (1950): 406–414.

Polák, Erik. "Spravedlnost vykonaná a nevykonaná (Případy bývalých velitelů terezínského ghetta)." *Terezínské listy* 22 (1994): 7–24.

Pollak, Michael. *L'expérience concentrationnaire: Essai sur le maintien de l'identité sociale*. Paris: Métailié, 1990.

Pollak, Viktor. *S Davidovou hvězdou peklem Terezína*. Translated by Pavel Kříž. Brno: Littera, 2010.

Poloncarz, Marek. "Die Evakuierungstransporte nach Theresienstadt (April–Mai 1945)." *Theresienstädter Studien und Dokumente* (1998): 242–262.

Poloncarz, Marek. "Dosavadní výsledky výzkumu dějin policejní věznice gestapa Malé Pevnosti a perspektivy další výzkumné a dokumentační práce." *Terezínské listy* 27 (1999): 7–19.

Posseltová-Ledererová, Hana. *Máma a já (Terezínský deník)*. Prague: G plus G, 1992.

Pravda, Hana. *Kaleidoscope: Snapshots of My Life*. London: Veritas, 2002.

BIBLIOGRAPHY 341

Pressburger, Chava, ed. *Deník mého bratra: Zápisky Petra Ginze z let 1941–1942*. Prague: Trigon, 2004.

Presser, Jacques. *The Night of the Girondists*. Translated by Barrows Mussey. London: HarperCollins UK, 1992.

Pretzel, Andreas. "Homosexuality in the Sexual Ethics of the 1930ies: A Values Debate in the Culture Wars between Conservatism, Liberalism, and Moral-National Renewal." In *After the History of Sexuality: German Genealogies, with and Beyond Foucault*, edited by Scott Spector, Helmut Puff, and Dagmar Herzog, 202–215. New York: Berghahn, 2012.

Proctor, Robert. *Racial Hygiene: Medicine under the Nazis*. Cambridge, Mass.: Harvard University Press, 1988.

Putík, Daniel. *Z nouze život, z nouze smrt? Slovenští Židé v Terezíně, Sachsenhausenu, Ravensbrücku a Bergen-Belsenu, 1944–1945*. Prague: Academia, 2018.

Pytell, Timothy. "Redeeming the Unredeemable: Auschwitz and Man's Search for Meaning." *Holocaust and Genocide Studies* 17, no. 1 (2003): 89–113.

Rabe, Hannelore. *Die Hofers: Theresienstadt—Kabarett—Rostock*. Rostock: VVN-BdA, 2013.

Rabinovici, Doron. *Instanzen der Ohnmacht: Wien 1938–1945: Der Weg zum Judenrat*. Frankfurt/Main: Jüdischer Verlag, 2000.

Randt, Alice. *Die Schleuse*. Hannoversch Münden: Chr. Gauke, 1974.

Raspanti, Celeste. *I Have Never Seen Another Butterfly*. Woodstock, Ill.: Dramatic Publishing.

Redlich, Egon. *As-If Living: A Diary/Egon Redlich from Theresienstadt Ghetto (1942–1944)*. Edited by Ruth Bondy. Lohamei Hagetaot: Hakibbutz Hameuchad Publishing and Beit Lohamei Hagetaot, 1982.

Redlich, Egon. *The Terezin Diary of Gonda Redlich*. Edited by Saul S. Friedman. Translated by Laurence Kutler. Lexington: University Press of Kentucky, 1992.

Redlich, Egon. *Zítra jedeme, synu, pojedeme transportem: Deník Egona Redlicha z Terezína 1.1.1942–22.10.1944*. Edited by Miroslav Kryl. Brno: Doplněk, 1995.

Reiser, Arnošt. *Útěk*. Prague: Academia, 2003.

Reznicenko, Yehuda, ed. *Terezín*. [In Hebrew.] Translated by Chaim Goldberg. Tel Aviv: Labor Party, 1947.

Ritvo, Roger A., and Diane M. Plotkin, eds. *Sisters in Sorrow: Voices of Care in the Holocaust*. College Station: Texas A&M University Press, 1998.

Rivers, J. P. W. "The Nutritional Biology of Famine." In *Famine*, edited by G. A. Harrison, 57–106. Oxford: Oxford University Press, 1988.

Roelcke, Volker. "Fortschritt ohne Rücksicht: Menschen als Versuchskanninchen bei den Sulfonamid-Experimenten im Konzentrationslager Ravensbrück." In *Geschlecht und "Rasse" in der NS-Medizin*, edited by Insa Eschebach and Astrid Ley, 101–114. Berlin: Metropol, 2012.

Rosen, David Baruch. *Verdi: Requiem*. Cambridge, UK: Cambridge University Press, 1995.

Rossel, Maurice. "Besuch im Ghetto," edited by Vojtěch Blodig. *Theresienstädter Studien und Dokumente* (1996): 284–301.

Rothfels, Hans. "Augenzeugenbericht zu den Massenvergasungen." *Vierteljahrshefte für Zeitgeschichte* 1 (1953): 177–194.

Roubíčková, Eva. *We're Alive and Life Goes On: A Theresienstadt Diary*. Translated by Zaia Alexander. New York: Henry Holt, 1998.

342 BIBLIOGRAPHY

Rozenblit, Marsha. *The Jews of Vienna, 1867–1914: Assimilation and Identity.* Albany: State University of New York Press, 1983.

Safrian, Hans. *Eichmann und seine Gehilfen.* Frankfurt/Main: Fischer, 1995.

Schirach, Baldur von. *Ich glaubte an Hitler.* Hamburg: Mosaik, 1967.

Schlichting, Nicola. "'Kleiderkammer schlägt Gärtner 9:3': Fußball im Ghetto Theresienstadt." *Nurinst* (2006): 73–90.

Schneider, Gertrud. *Exile and Destruction: The Fate of Austrian Jews, 1938–1945.* Westport, Conn.: Praeger, 1995.

Schnitzler, Thomas, ed. *"Das Leben ist ein Kampf": Marianne Elikan—Verfolgte des Nazi-Regimes; Tagebuch, Briefe und Gedichte aus Trier und Theresienstadt.* Trier: Wissenschaftlicher Verlag, 2008.

Schulze-Marmeling, Dietrich, ed. *Davidstern und Lederball: Die Geschichte der Juden im deutschen und internationalen Fußball.* Göttingen: Wallstein, 2003.

Schulze-Marmeling, Dietrich. *Der FC Bayern und seine Juden: Aufstieg und Zerschlagung einer liberalen Fußballkultur.* Göttingen: Die Werkstatt, 2011.

Schumann, Coco. *Der Ghetto-Swinger: Eine Jazzlegende erzählt.* Munich: dtv, 1998.

Schwoch, Rebecca. *Herbert Lewin: Arzt-Überlebender-Zentralratspräsident.* Berlin: Hentrich & Hentrich, 2016.

Schwoch, Rebecca. "'Praktisch zum Verhungern verurteilt': 'Krankenbehandler' zwischen 1938 und 1945." In *Jüdische Ärztinnen und Ärzte im Nationalsozialismus: Entrechtung, Vertreibung, Ermordung,* edited by Thomas Beddies, Susanne Doetz, and Christoph Kopke, 75–91. Munich: de Gruyter, 2014.

Schwoch, Rebecca. "The Situation and Ethical Dilemmas of Krankenbehandler (Sick Treaters), 1938–1945: The Example of Hamburg." *Korot* 23 (2015–2016): 173–194.

Scott, James. *Weapons of the Weak: Everyday Forms of Peasant Resistance.* New Haven, Conn.: Yale University Press, 1992.

Seidl, Jan, Jan Wintr, and Lukáš Nozar. *Od žaláře k oltáři: Emancipace homosexuality v českých zemích od roku 1867 do současnosti.* Brno: Host, 2012.

Semecká, Irma. *Torso naděje.* Prague: Antonín Vlasák, 1946.

Sen, Amartya. *Poverty and Famines: An Essay on Entitlement and Deprivation.* Oxford: Oxford University Press, 1981.

Sever, Max. "Die technischen Einrichtungen Theresienstadts." *Theresienstädter Studien und Dokumente* (1999): 204–216.

Sewell, William. "Concept(s) of Culture." In *Beyond the Cultural Turn: New Directions in the Study of Society and Culture,* edited by Victoria E. Bonnell, Lynn Avery Hunt, and Richard Biernacki, 35–61. Berkeley: University of California Press, 1999.

Seznamy lékaren a lékařů. 1938.

Shan, Nava. *Chtěla jsem být herečkou.* Prague: Ivo Železný, 1992.

Shek, Alisa. "Alisa Sheks Tagebuch (Oktober 1944–Mai 1945)." *Theresienstädter Studien und Dokumente* (1994): 171–206.

Shlain, Margalit. "Ein neues Dokument zu den betrügerischen Methoden der Nazis." In *Theresienstadt in der "Endlösung der Judenfrage",* edited by Miroslav Kárný et al., 223–232. Prague: Logos, 1992.

Shumsky, Dimitry. *Zweisprachigkeit und binationale Idee: Der Prager Zionismus 1900–1930.* Göttingen: Vandenhoeck & Ruprecht, 2012.

Sidlin, Murray. *Defiant Requiem.* Catholic University of America.

Silverman, Lisa. *Becoming Austrians: Jews and Culture between the World Wars.* New York: Oxford University Press, 2012.

BIBLIOGRAPHY 343

Simon, Herman. "Bislang unbekannte Quellen zur Entstehungsgeschichte des Werkes 'Die Entwicklung der Rechtsstellung der Juden in Europa, vornehmlich in Deutschland.'" In *Leo Baeck 1873–1956: Aus dem Stamme von Rabbinern*, edited by Georg Heuberger and Fritz Backhaus, 103–110. Frankfurt/Main: Jüdischer Verlag, 2001.

Simonsohn, Trude. "Erinnerung an Paul Eppstein." *Theresienstädter Studien und Dokumente* (1996): 127–130.

Šimůnek, Michal. "Konec 'nenahraditelného muže': Likvidace R. Heydricha v lékařském kontextu. II. část." *Dějiny věd a techniky* 45, no. 1 (2012): 213–250.

Šindelářová, Lenka. "50 Jahre Zentrale Stelle in Ludwigsburg: Strafverfolgung von NS-Verbrechen am Beispiel des 'Lagerinspekteurs' von Theresienstädter Ghetto." *Theresienstädter Studien und Dokumente* (2008): 64–114.

Skrentny, Werner. *Julius Hirsch: Nationalspieler Ermordet: Biografie eines jüdischen Fußballers*. Göttingen: Die Werkstatt, 2012.

Sladký, Hans. "Episoden aus dem Leben eines Überlebenden." *Theresienstädter Studien und Dokumente* (1998): 257–276.

Sofsky, Wolfgang. *Die Ordnung des Terrors: Das Konzentrationslager*. Frankfurt/Main: Fischer, 1993.

Šormová, Eva. *Divadlo v Terezíně 1941–1945*. Ústí nad Labem: Severočeské nakladatelství, 1973.

Spector, Scott. *Prague Territories: National Conflict and Cultural Innovation in Franz Kafka's Fin de Siècle*. Berkeley: University of California Press, 2000.

Spies, Gerty. *My Years in Terezín: How One Woman Survived the Holocaust*. Translated by Jutta R. Tragnitz. Amherst, N.Y.: Prometheus Books, 1997.

Stargardt, Nicholas. "Children's Art of the Holocaust." *Past & Present* 161, no. 1 (November 1998): 191–235.

Steege, Paul. *Black Market, Cold War: Everyday Life in Berlin, 1946–1949*. Cambridge, UK: Cambridge University Press, 2007.

Steiner, František. *Fotbal pod žlutou hvězdou*. Prague: Olympia, 2009.

Stoessinger, Caroline. *A Century of Wisdom: Lessons from the Life of Alice Herz-Sommer, the World's Oldest Living Holocaust Survivor*. New York: Spiegel & Grau, 2012.

Stoll, Katrin. *Die Herstellung der Wahrheit: Strafverfahren gegen ehemalige Angehörige der Sicherheitspolizei für den Bezirk Bialystok*. Berlin: De Gruyter, 2011.

Stone, Dan, ed. *Historiography of the Holocaust*. Basingstoke, UK: Palgrave, 2005.

Stone, Dan. "Holocaust Historiography and Cultural History." *Dapim* 23 (2009): 52–68.

Strusková, Eva. "Film Ghetto Theresienstadt: Suche nach Zusammenhängen." In *"Der Letzte der Ungerechten": Der Judenälteste Benjamin Murmelstein in Filmen 1942–1975*, edited by Ronny Loewy and Katharina Rauschenberger, 125–158. Frankfurt/Main: Campus, 2011.

Suderland, Maja. *Inside Concentration Camps: Social Life at the Extremes*. Cambridge, UK: Polity, 2013.

Suderland, Maja. *Territorien des Selbst: Kulturelle Identität als Ressource für das tägliche Überleben im Konzentrationslager*. Frankfurt/Main: Campus, 2004.

Svobodný, Petr, and Ludmila Hlaváčková. *Dějiny lékařství v českých zemích*. Prague: Triton, 2004.

Świebocki, Henryk. *Widerstand*. Oświęcim: Verlag des Staatlichen Museums Auschwitz Birkenau, 1999.

Tausendfreund, Doris. *Erzwungener Verrat: Jüdische "Greifer" im Dienst der Gestapo 1943–1945*. Berlin: Metropol, 2006.

344 BIBLIOGRAPHY

Taussig, Josef. "Die Theresienstädter Cabarets." *Theresienstädter Studien und Dokumente* (1994): 214–246.

Těšínská, Emilie. "Kontakty českých a německých rentgenologů a radiologů v českých zemích (do r. 1945)." *Dějiny věd a techniky* 30, no. 2 (1997): 88–96.

Thompson, E. P. *The Making of the English Working Class*. London: Victor Gollancz, 1963.

Triendl-Zadoff, Miriam. *Nächstes Jahr in Marienbad: Gegenwelten jüdischer Kulturen der Moderne*. Göttingen: Vandenhoeck & Ruprecht, 2007.

Troller, Norbert. *Terezín: Hitler's Gift to the Jews*. Translated by Susan E. Cernyak-Spatz. Chapel Hill: University of North Carolina Press, 1991.

Trunk, Isaiah. *Judenrat: The Jewish Councils in Eastern Europe under Nazi Occupation*. New York: Macmillan, 1972.

Trunk, Isaiah. *Łódź Ghetto: A History*. Edited and translated by Robert Moses Shapiro. Bloomington: Indiana University Press, 2006.

Tůma, Mirko. *Ghetto našich dnů*. Prague: Jaroslav Salivar, 1946.

The United States Holocaust Memorial Museum Encyclopedia of Camps and Ghettos, 1933–1945. Bloomington: Indiana University Press and United States Holocaust Memorial Museum, 2009.

Valfer, Jerry. *Jerry's Story: Sometimes I Did Not Think, I Just Kept on Living; A Heart-Rending Saga*. Coon Valley, Wis.: Aavery Counseling and Press, 2000.

van Rahden, Till. *Juden und andere Breslauer: Die Beziehungen zwischen Juden, Protestanten und Katholiken in einer deutschen Großstadt von 1860 bis 1925*. Göttingen: Vandenhoeck & Ruprecht, 2000.

Vernon, James. *Hunger: A Modern History*. Cambridge, Mass.: Belknap Press of Harvard University Press, 2007.

Veselská, Magda. *Archa paměti: Cesta pražského židovského muzea pohnutým 20. Stoletím*. Prague: Academia, 2012.

Villiez, Anna von. *Mit aller Kraft verdrängt: Entrechtung und Verfolgung "nicht arischer" Ärzte in Hamburg 1933 bis 1945*. Hamburg: Dölling und Galitz, 2009.

Volavková, Hana, and Jiří Weil, eds. *Children's Drawings and Poems: Terezín 1942–1944*. Prague: Státní židovské muzeum v Praze, 1959.

von der Heydt, Maria. "'Sobald ich schreiben kann, wirst du von mir hören': Johanna Larché-Levy." *Theresienstädter Studien und Dokumente* (2006): 162–203.

von der Heydt, Maria. "'Wer fährt denn gerne mit dem Judenstern in der Straßenbahn?' Die Ambivalenz des 'geltungsjüdischen' Alltags zwischen 1941 und 1945." In *Der Alltag im Holocaust: Jüdisches Leben im Großdeutschen Reich 1941–1945*, edited by Doris Bergen, Andrea Löw, and Anna Hájková, 65–80. Munich: Oldenbourg, 2013.

Wachsmann, Nikolaus. *KL: A History of the Nazi Concentration Camps*. London: Little and Brown, 2015.

Waic, Marek, and Jiří Kössl. *Český tramping 1918–1945*. Prague: Práh, 1992.

The Warsaw Diary of Adam Czerniakow: Prelude to Doom. Edited by Raul Hilberg, Stanislaw Staron, and Josef Kermisz. Chicago: Ivan R. Dee, 1999.

Weglein, Resi. *Als Krankenschwester im KZ Theresienstadt: Erinnerungen einer Ulmer Jüdin*. Tübingen: Silberburg, 1988.

Weindling, Paul. *Victims and Survivors of Nazi Human Experiments: Science and Suffering in the Holocaust*. London: Bloomsbury, 2014.

Weiss, Aharon. "The Relations between the Judenrat and the Jewish Police." In *Patterns of Jewish Leadership in Nazi Europe 1933–1945: Proceedings of the Third Yad Vashem*

BIBLIOGRAPHY 345

International Historical Conference, edited by Yisrael Gutman and Cynthia J. Haft, 201–217, 228–233. Jerusalem: Yad Vashem, 1979.

Weiss, Yfaat. *Deutsche und polnische Juden vor dem Holocaust: Jüdische Identität zwischen Staatsbürgerschaft und Ethnizität 1933–1940*. Munich: Oldenbourg, 2000.

Wenck, Alexandra-Eileen. *Zwischen Menschenhandel und "Endlösung": Das Konzentrationslager Bergen-Belsen*. Paderborn: Schöningh, 2000.

Werb, Bret. "Music." In *The Oxford Handbook of Holocaust Studies*, edited by Peter Hayes and John Roth, 478–489. New York: Oxford University Press, 2011.

Wertheimer, Jack. *Unwelcome Strangers: East European Jews in Imperial Germany*. New York: Oxford University Press, 1987.

White, Hayden. *The Content of the Form: Narrative Discourse and Historical Representation*. Baltimore, Md.: Johns Hopkins University Press, 1987.

Wildman, Sarah. *Paper Love: Searching for the Girl My Grandfather Left Behind*. New York: Riverhead Books, 2015.

Wildt, Michael. *Generation des Unbedingten: Das Führungskorps des Reichssicherheitshauptamtes*. Hamburg: Hamburger Edition, 2002.

Winick, Myron, ed. *Hunger Disease: Studies by the Jewish Physicians in the Warsaw Ghetto*. New York: Wiley, 1979.

Witte, Peter, Michael Wildt, Martina Voigt, Dieter Pohl, Peter Klein, Christian Gerlach, Christoph Dieckmann, and Andrej Angrick, eds. *Der Dienstkalender Heinrich Himmlers 1941/42*. Hamburg: Christians, 1999.

Woerdeman, Martinus. *Atlas of Human Anatomy. Descriptive and Regional*. London: Butterworth, 1948.

Wögerbauer, Michael. "Kartoffeln: Ein Versuch über Erzählungen zum Ghettoalltag." *Theresienstädter Studien und Dokumente* (2003): 95–144.

Wolff-Eisner, Alfred. *Über Mangelerkrankungen auf Grund von Beobachtungen im Konzentrationslager*. Würzburg: Sauer-Marhard, 1947.

Working in a Trap: AZ Album. Edited by Anita Tarsi and Dani Singer. Givat Haim Ihud: Beit Terezin, 2008.

Wünschmann, Kim. *Before Auschwitz: Jewish Prisoners in the Prewar Concentration Camps*. Cambridge, Mass.: Harvard University Press, 2015.

Yahil, Leni. *The Rescue of Danish Jewry: Test of a Democracy*. Philadelphia: Jewish Publication Society of America, 1969.

Zahra, Tara. *Kidnapped Souls: National Indifference and the Battle for Children in the Bohemian Lands, 1900–1948*. Ithaca, N.Y.: Cornell University Press, 2008.

Zapruder, Alexandra, ed. *Salvaged Pages: Young Writers' Diaries of the Holocaust*. New Haven, Conn.: Yale University Press, 2002.

Zierenberg, Malte. *Stadt der Schieber: Der Berliner Schwarzmarkt 1939–1950*. Göttingen: Vandenhoeck & Ruprecht, 2008.

Zucker, Otto. "Theresienstadt 1941–1943." *Theresienstädter Studien und Dokumente* (1995): 271–303.

Zwicker, Stefan. "Aspekte der Memorialkultur des Fußballs in den böhmischen Ländern, der Tschechoslowakei und der Tschechischen Republik." In *Die Memorial- und Sepulkralkultur des Fußballsports*, edited by Markwart Herzog and Michael Barsuhn, 387–408. Stuttgart: Kohlhammer, 2013.

Zwicker, Stefan. "Paul Mahrer, der Nationalspieler, der Theresienstadt überlebte." In *Sportler im "Jahrhundert der Lager" und der Verfolgung: Profiteure, Widerständler*

346 BIBLIOGRAPHY

und Opfer, edited by Diethelm Blecking and Lorenz Peiffer, 322–329. Göttingen: Die Werkstatt, 2012.

Unpublished Dissertations and Manuscripts

Fracapane, Silvia Tarabini Goldbaum. "Danish Testimonies about Theresienstadt: Experiences of Deportation and Ghetto Life." PhD diss., Technical University Berlin, 2016.

Grant, Susan. "Caring for the Mind: Medical Workers in Psychiatric Hospitals, 1930–1950." Unpublished manuscript, n.d.

Markreich, Max. "Geschichte der Juden in Bremen und Umgebung." Unpublished manuscript.

Paulovicova, Nina. "Rescue of Jews in the Slovak State (1939–1945)." PhD diss., University of Alberta, 2012.

Index

For the benefit of digital users, indexed terms that span two pages (e.g., 52–53) may, on occasion, appear on only one of those pages.

Tables and figures are indicated by *t* and *f* following the page number

abortions
  antiabortion activists, 154
  avoiding forced, 198–99
  forced by order of Anton Burger, 20, 150
  number of, 150, 297n135
  performed on lovers of SS members, 22
  prisoners' reactions to, 150–51
Abromeit, Franz, 24–25
accommodations
  for artists, 183–84
  assigned based on a triage
    mentality, 62
  attic rooms for elderly inmates, 62
  better for *Aufbaukommando,* 75
  better for informers, 55
  better for Jewish functionaries, 65
  better for prominent prisoners, 49
  better for social elite, 50, 63
  better for young artists, 183–84
  closed versus open care, 140
  collective for Ghetto Guard, 46
  crowding in, 10, 62
  for cultural events, 185
  forced reshuffling of traditional
    families, 119
  inclusion of cooking area in, 105
  less crowding in children's rooms, 79
  limited agency and, 226–27, 239–40
  new for workers, 31, 33
  Reich Association's Accommodation
    Advice Center, 37–38
  separate for men and women, 118
  separate youth homes, 43
  spot checks in, 24
  worse for elderly inmates, 77–78,
    113–14, 156

adaptation
  becoming accustomed to the ghetto, 239
  of elderly, 89
  to insufficient nutrition, 115
  understanding through study of
    Theresienstadt, 2
Adler, H. G., 141, 162–63
Adlerová, Gertrud, 153–54, 162–63
advantage ghetto, 7, 10, 47, 49, 136, 231–32
agency
  acquired by Jewish functionaries, 16,
    47–48, 58
  as central topic in Holocaust studies, 6
  derived from music, 176–77
  downplayed by survivors, 316n93
  of elderly, 116
  expressed through feasts, 119–20
  highlighting issues of, 2
  limits on, 225–27
  of physicians, 132–33, 151–52, 157–58
  recognizing moments of, 238,
    239–40, 241–42
  self-organizing as a form of, 58
  of Theresienstadt informers, 56–57
Ančerl, Karel, 182–83, 193–94
anti-Semitism
  among Czech gendarmes, 22
  among the Eichmann men, 17
  pursued by the Ghetto Court, 98
  stereotypes affecting medical
    care, 149–50
  suffered by Jewish medical students, 133
  towards Eastern Jews, 91
Arendt, Hannah, 53
Aron, Gerhard, 161
art. *See* cultural events; cultural life

348 INDEX

Aschenbrenner, Walter, 206
Auerbach, Lucie, 162–63
Aufbaukommando (construction detail)
  applications for removal from
    transports, 217*t*, 217–18
  arrival transports, 215
  Bohumil Benda's arrival with, 126
  Edgar Krása's arrival with, 123, 180
  Erich Springer's arrival with, 134
  formation of, 7–8
  inclusion in transports, 210
  lead by Egon Popper, 42
  musicians' and artists' arrival with, 184
  preferred status associated with, 40–41,
    63, 65, 74–75, 108
  protection from transports, 202,
    203, 221
  ridicule of, 76, 177–78
  soccer teams sponsored by, 194–97
  volunteers for, 44–45
Auředníčková, Anna, 78–79, 160
autopsies, 142–43, 159, 295n84

Bader, Hanuš, 124–25
Baeck, Leo, 27*f*, 50–54, 88, 121, 234, 266–
  67n274, 267n276
Baecková, Ruth, 51
Baltrusch, Fritz, 21
Bartels, Rolf, 21, 29–30, 36–37, 103–4,
  136–37, 228
bartering
  of drawings, 181
  with and for food, 127–30
  of performance tickets, 184
Bass, František, 158–59
Bayerlová, Valerie, 174
BdS. *See* SiPo and SD
Běhal, Jiří, 187
Bělov, Arnold, 34, 35
Bělov, Hana, 34, 35
Benda, Bohumil, 126
Bergel, Karl, 21, 25–26, 54–55, 173–74,
  206, 229
Berger, Julius, 89
Berger, Sam, 66
Bergmann, Rudolf, 32, 44, 203–4, 232–33
Bergmannová, Marie, 232–33
Berl, Bedřich, 160–61, 232–33
Berman, Karel, 192–94, 198

Berner, Eva, 73
Bernstein, Elsa, 69–70
Bernstein, Otto, 71
Blánová, Hana, 188–89
Blánová, Lea, 188–89
Bloch, Ervín, 233–34
Bloch, Ferdinand, 172, 174
Blumenthal-Rothschild, Henriette
  Louise, 157–58
Bobek, Josef, 21, 22–23, 173–74, 220
Bohm, Hermann, 165
Böhme, Horst, 18*f*
Bohn, Hermann, 154
Bondy, Josef, 184
Bondy, Ruth, 141–42
Bonn, Hanuš, 189
Bor, Josef, 173, 184
Borgerová, Gertruda, 188–89, 193–94
Borges, Bedřich, 98, 184
Borský, Jiří, 71–72, 86–87, 187, 213
Boschan, Julius, 38
Braun, Vítězslav, 51
Breslauer, Käthe, 123–24, 148–49
Buchsbaum, Norbert, 66
Bülow, Hans von, 193
Burešová, Lotka, 191
Burger, Anton, 18*f*, 20, 28–29, 35, 126–27,
  150, 170, 202, 205–6, 210, 217–18
Burka, Jan, 123–24
Busch, Arthur, 35–36

Cantor, Vilém, 41–42, 202–3
Čapek, Karel, 179–80
categorization and stratification
  based on age, 113–14
  based on ethnicity, 59
  based on gender, 29, 91–92, 239
  in prisoner society, 4, 70–74
  with respect to food distribution, 101
Catholic community, 52, 70
Central Evidence, 34–35, 41, 42, 60, 202–3,
  205–6, 209, 223
Central Office for Jewish Emigration, 7–8,
  10–11, 17
Central Secretariat, 27*f*, 41–42, 44, 46,
  49–50, 60, 87
children
  better food and food rations for
    children, 79, 116–17

causes of deaths during famines, 101–2
deaths among newborns, 287n102
plan to exchange Jewish children for money, 149–50, 210–11
role of Jewish functionaries in transporting children, 213
shooting of sick children, 20
survival rate of, 80, 117
treatment of, 77–86
Zionist goal of raising children as conscious Jews, 1–2
"choiceless choices," 6, 226–27, 239–40
class
  as basis of categorization, 4
  "formerly important" class, 89–91, 123
  stark differences in Theresienstadt, 110–11
Cohen, David, 32–33
Cohen, Max, 148
construction detail. See *Aufbaukommando*
Council of Elders (*Ältestenrat*)
  Baeck as honorary head of, 52
  discussion of Recreation's weekly programs, 170
  feelings of self-importance fostered by, 40
  Hermann Strauß as member of, 153–54, 213, 220
  as members of the Small Commission, 204–5
  minutes of, 47–48
  Murmelstein's lack of respect for, 31
  nomination to, 32
  organization of, 26, 27f
  personal protection lists held by members, 204
  preferential treatment of, 106, 107–8, 182, 184–85, 194
  preparations for Red Cross visit, 19
  relationship to Elder of the Jews, 31
  role in Theresienstadt, 31–34
  size of, 40
  vulnerability of members, 32
cultural events
  attended by Jewish Elders, 45–46
  attended by social elite, 75
  banned as punishment, 35–36

as confirmation of educated bourgeoisie, 179
language use in, 189
playing and enjoying music, 153
produced in the depths of misery, 67
serving to reconstruct the former world, 179–80
status gained by playing and enjoying music, 153
tickets to as rewards, 49
venues for, 185, 186f
cultural life
  beyond spiritual resistance, 174–80
  bound to social hierarchy of inmate community, 168
  conclusion of, 198
  culture as basis of categorization, 4
  ethnicity and exclusion, 187–99
  material aspects of, 180–87
  Recreation Department, 168–74
  role of arts in Theresienstadt, 199–200
  soccer, 194–98
culture as resistance, 174
Czapski, Dora, 51
Czech gendarmes
  assistance given to prisoners by, 126, 127–28, 137–38
  informers reporting on, 54–55
  role in Theresienstadt, 22, 60
  sexual barter with prisoners by, 23
Czech Jews
  anti-German prejudice of, 81–82
  arrival in Theresienstadt, 7–8
  definition of ethnicity by, 4–5
  distrust of German and Austrian functionaries, 39
  expressions of Czech cultural belonging, 83–86
  framing and stereotypes of, 71
  generation of master narrative, 73–74
  largest food portions received by, 108
  removal from Protectorate completed, 19
  sense of belonging gained through Czech culture, 178–79
  as social elite of the ghetto, 74–77
  targeted by SS for deportation, 211–12
  understanding of transports as liquidation, 207

350   INDEX

Davidová, Ottla (Etelka), 164
deaths
  among children, 117
  among elderly inmates, 112–13,
    116, 208
  among newborn children, 287n102
  causes of deaths during famines,
    101–2, 115
  due to smaller food rations, 100–1
  due to typhus, 296n105
  knowledge of mass murder, 231–37
  number, origin, and deaths of Jews sent
    to Theresienstadt, 7–10, 101
  of those arriving with evacuation
    transports, 296n101
denouncers. *See* informers
Department IVB4, 8–9, 11–12, 17–19,
    18*f*, 24–25, 26, 172, 202, 205, 208,
    209–10, 235–36
Dicker-Brandeis, Friedl, 172
Director, Simon, 195
Disinfection Department, 143–44
Dodalová, Irena, 191–92
Dormitzer, Else, 121, 183
Drachsler, Lucie, 87–88
Dunant, Paul, 10, 21

Eastern Jews
  exclusions based on origin as, 90–91
  as imagined type, 90
  prejudices against, 72, 89–90
  resentments toward, 90
  as the ultimate other, 91
Eckstein, Luděk, 225, 227
Edelstein, Jakob
  AZ Album produced for, 76
  choice to not make team prominent, 50
  dismisses Trude Neumann's requests for
    help, 141–42
  establishes food rations by worker
    status, 77–78
  falsification of population numbers, 34–
    35, 205–6, 209
  feelings of prisoners toward, 57–58
  inability to watch executions, 24–25
  organization of Jewish self-
    administration, 26–29, 27*f*
  pioneering mentality of, 39–40

  reaction to deportation of elderly
    inmates, 208
  redistribution of tasks and departments
    by, 42–43
  secretary deported in fall of 1944, 54–55
  sexism practiced by, 66–67
  sharing of information by, 33–34
  showcasing of Theresienstadt as a labor
    ghetto, 47
  stigmatized by origins, 90
  youthful Zionist leadership recruited
    by, 134
Edgar Krása, 181*f*
Egyedi, Elisabeth, 152
Egyedi, Hendrik, 152
Ehrlich, Richard, 123–24
Ehrmannová, Alisa, 81, 108–9, 229
Eichmann, Adolf, 8–10, 17–19, 18*f*, 26,
    35, 174
Eichmann men, 17, 20
Eigensinn (self-will), 227, 239–40
Eisler, Hanuš, 206
elderly inmates
  accommodations for, 62, 77–78,
    113–14, 156
  adaptation of, 89
  agency demonstrated by, 116
  appearance of, 78
  deaths among, 77–78, 78*t*, 101, 116, 208
  deportation of 16,000 in 1942, 208
  hunger experienced by, 111–14
  jobs assigned to, 111
  lack of victim testimonies from, 114
  othering of, 113–15
  reason for transport to
    Theresienstadt, 9–10
  smaller food rations assigned to,
    105–7, 112–13
  social organization and, 77–79
  targeted by SS for deportation, 212
  treatment of elderly versus laborers and
    children, 77–86, 101
  widespread gastroenteritis among, 111
Elder of the Jews (*Judenältester*)
  appointees and dates served, 27*f*
  Benjamin Murmelstein, 30–31
  contact with SS, 33–34
  handling of crises by, 34–36

INDEX   351

Jakob Edelstein, 26–28
leeway for maneuvering, 34
Paul Eppstein, 28–30
relationship to Council of Elders, 31–33
role in Theresienstadt, 26–49
Elias, Norbert, 3–4
Emigration Fund, 19, 103
Eppstein, Paul
as art lover, 185
beaten by Rahm, 19
disagreements with Baeck, 52–53
feelings of prisoners toward, 57–58
hopes of maneuvering through large
transports, 228
influence over Recreation
Department, 45–46
installation as Elder, 26, 28–30
knowledge of mass murder, 234
lovers transported in fall of 1944, 54–55
names colleagues from Reich
Association as prominent, 49–50
organization of Jewish
self-administration, 27f
push for naming non-Czech prisoners
to positions, 38–39, 155
reveals Edelstein's deception to
SS, 34–35
rewarded by SS, 39
sharing of information by, 33–34
special relationship with Moes, 36–37
typhoid outbreak under, 209
upset over use of language in cultural
offerings, 189
as a Zionist, 76
Erdmann, Hanna, 141–42
escapes and escapees
alerting prisoners of gas chambers,
92–94, 234
from Auschwitz, 234
of Geltungsjuden of teenagers Hana and
Arnold Bělov, 34
planned, 232–33
SS handling of, 23–24, 34
ethnicity
categorization and stratification based
on, 4, 59, 70–74
in cultural offerings, 171
impact of binary view, 241

importance to loyalties in
self-administration, 38–39
interethnic relationships, 93–95
lack of contact outside of ethnic
group, 88
mortality rates according to, 77–78, 78t
number, origin, and deaths of Jews sent
to Theresienstadt, 7–10
role in cultural life, 187–94
transports and belonging, 211–13
executions
as demonstration of absolute
control, 24–25
inmates reactions to, 19, 61–62, 68,
159, 255n62
key role of in prosecution of
perpetrators, 255n58
photographed by Karel Salaba, 22
See also violence

Faltin, Leo, 27f, 34–35, 209
Familienzerreißung, 202–3
Fantlová, Lily, 130–31, 229
Feder, Richard, 82, 92
Feigl, František, 84–86
Fein, Oskar, 179–80
Fidler, Johann, 206
Fischer, Avi, 81–82
Fischer, Ignatz, 195
Fischer, Karl, 185–86
Fischerová, Anna, 51
Fischl, Pavel, 78–79, 81
Fischlová, Hana, 81
Fleischmann, Fricek, 184–85
Fleischmann, Karel, 33, 64f, 140–41, 159–
60, 161, 162–63
Flusser, Jindřich, 137
food and hunger
access to food and child bearing/child
rearing, 111, 130–31
bartering with and for food, 127–30
better food and food rations for
children, 79, 116–17
better food and food rations for
performers, 170–71
causes of deaths due to famines,
101–2, 115
centralized food distribution, 102–5

352   INDEX

food and hunger (*Cont.*)
  deliberate starvation of Jews by Nazis,
    100, 127
  everyday life and access to food, 108–17
  famines as human-made, 101
  food as a social event, 118–22
  food categories, 105–8
  food reflecting the everyday, 123–24
  food sharing, 101
  food taken along on transports, 205
  power derived from access to
    food, 100–1
  preferential food offered for
    convalescence, 140, 160
  reduced rations for non-working
    elderly, 77–78, 131
  role of food in prisoner society, 101
  theft of food, 124–27
Frank, Karl Herrmann, 18*f*
Fränkel, Eva, 76
Freiberger, Rudolf, 27*f*, 36–37, 39, 44,
    56, 228
Frenkel, Carolina Wiener, 163
Frenkel, Lion Jacques, 163
Freudenfeld, Rudolf, 185–86
Freundová, Pilsner Gertruda, 163
Frič, Ivan, 10–11
Fried, Jan, 123
Fried, Karel, 87–88
Fried, Norbert, 191–92
Friediger, Hana, 110–11
Friediger, Max, 32–33, 35–36
Friedman, Pavel, 171–72
Friedmann, Desider, 27*f*, 38, 42
Friedmann, Richard, 37, 136–37
Friedmannová, Ema, 121, 122, 223
Friedrich, Eli, 120
Fritta, Bedřich, 172, 174, 180–81, 181*f*, 184
Fröhlichová, Markéta, 189–90, 190*f*
Frommer, Benjamin, 69
Fuchsová, Ilse, 148–49

gas theory, 233
Geltungsjuden
  definition of, 7–8, 69
  deportations of, 229
  escapes among, 34
  mentally ill, 141–42

protection from transports, 202, 213
released from Theresienstadt, 69–70
separate accommodations for young, 79
under SS command, 23–24, 42
treatment of by other children, 80–81
gender
  asymmetries in, 92–93, 240–41
  and categorization, 91–95
  categorization and stratification based
    on, 29, 239
  categorization as hard laborers and, 108
  as defining for cultural production,
    199–200
  double genderedness and food, 122
  as factor in attaining positions in
    Theresienstadt, 37–38
  food sharing and, 101–2
  gender bias in attendance of cultural
    events, 192
  gender roles in Theresienstadt,
    98–99, 122
  inequality based on, 59
  medical power and, 162–66
  mortality rates and, 77–78
Gerke, Ernst, 18*f*
German Jews
  considered as foreign by Czech
    Jews, 73–74
  excluded from German culture, 178
  framing and stereotypes of, 71–73
  protected from deportation by
    SS, 211–12
Gerron, Kurt, 10–11
Geschke, Hans–Ulrich, 18*f*
Gestapo, 23, 35, 37, 55–56, 223
Gesundheitswesen. See Health Services
ghettos
  advantage ghetto, 7, 10, 47, 49,
    136, 231–32
  labor ghettos, 28, 47, 58
  privilege ghettos, 7, 47
  Theresienstadt's designation as, 11–12
  transit ghetto, 7, 8–9, 16, 23–24, 150, 201
Glass, Martha, 73, 106, 111, 160
Goertz, Else Countess, 49
Goldmannová, Irma, 142, 162–63
Goldscheiderová, Emma, 27*f*, 42
Goldschmid, Alfred, 35, 209

INDEX   353

Goldschmidt, Erna, 50
Grabová, Hedda, 172–73, 182, 189, 193–94
Grabower, Rolf, 40–41, 68–69, 87, 98, 160–61, 182–83, 222–23, 241
Gradnauer, Georg, 49–50
Grauer, Jan, 27f, 39
Great Fortress, 7
Greifer, 56–57
Groag, Willy, 27f, 80, 149–50, 230, 232–33
Grünberger, Julius, 27f, 44–45, 76
Grünhutová-Reinischová, Marta, 156
Günther, Hans, 10–11, 17, 18f, 19, 20, 24–25, 32, 55, 173, 230, 235
Günther, Rolf, 17–18, 173, 208, 235–36
Gut, Miloš, 124
Guthmann, Charlotte, 125
Gutmann, Max, 164
Guttmannová, Truda, 94

Haas, Erna, 189–90
Haas, Leo, 76, 172, 174, 180, 189–90
Haasová, Blanka, 234
Hadra, Edmund, 122, 156–57, 162
Hadra, Siegmund, 120
Hahn, Franz, 74, 146–47, 153, 155, 165, 192
Hahn, Viktor, 153–54, 159–61, 163, 220
Hahnová, Hilda, 50
Haindl, Rudolf, 21, 22, 25–26, 35–36, 38, 54–55, 60–61, 174, 195, 206
Hamperl, Herwig, 142
Hartmann, Walther, 172
Hasenkopf, Miroslav, 22
Health Services
    Aeskulap soccer team representing, 160
    differences between hospital and housing block care, 191–92
    doctors holding positions in, 153–56
    German deputy head of, 222–23
    as high functioning, 132
    leadership by Erich Munk, 153–54
    leadership by Richard Stein, 161
    planned surgery of Benjamin Murmelstein, 149
    preferential food offered for convalescence, 140, 160
    protection from transports and, 160, 221
    role in ghetto life, 166–67

as sexist institution, 162–66
structure of, 133–44
suicide prevention by, 147–48
triage mentality employed by, 62, 144–47
See also medicine and illness; physicians
Hechalutz, 28, 62, 66, 75–76, 90, 119, 226
Heilgas (healing gas) experiments, 138
Henschel, Moritz, 27f, 45–46, 170–71
Hermann, Jan, 197–98
Herrmann, Emanuel, 24
Herškovič, Berl, 62, 226
Herz, Alice Sommer, 68–69
Herz, Pavel, 68–69
Herzl, Theodor, 141–42
Herz-Sommer, Alice, 175
Heydrich, Reinhard, 8–9, 18f
Heymann, Harry Hambo, 96
Himmler, Heinrich
    attempt to use Theresienstadt to appease the Allies, 10
    competences in the SS, 18f
    mention of Theresienstadt to Mussolini, 39
    order to boost labor capacity in camps, 209
    plan to exchange Jewish children for money, 149–50, 210–11
    plan to use ghetto for exchange and camouflage purposes, 228
    release of prisoners to Switzerland, 211
Hirsch, Camilla, 67, 111–12
Hirsch, Fredy, 27f, 32, 43, 45, 96, 168–69
Hirsch, Gertrud, 87–88
Hirschfeld, Hans, 153–54
Hirschfeld, Inge, 130–31
Hitler, Adolf, 8–9, 10
Hofer, Hans, 100, 169, 177, 184–85, 187–88
Hoffenberg, Norbert, 66
Hoffenreich, Bedřich, 64–65, 97, 130
Hoffeová, Ruth, 63
Holocaust history
    focus on issues of responsibility, agency, and powerlessness, 2
    Holocaust experience and Jewishness, 96–98
    in wider context of modern history, 3, 5

354 INDEX

Holzer, Leo, 27f, 53–54, 234
homophobia, 95–96
homo sacer, 114–15
Horpatzký, Pidla, 177–78
Hundertschaft (hundred hours of labor
  duty), 155
hunger. *See* food and hunger

informers
  cooperation with SS, 24, 57
  danger to cultural activities, 170
  inclusion in "prominent"
    prisoners, 49–50
  as lesson in human agency, 56–57
  network of SS informers, 54–56
  post-war arrest and
    investigation of, 56
  reports of *Weisungen* by, 230–31
inmate society. *See* prisoner society
IVB4. *See* Department IVB4

Janeček, Theodor, 22
Janowitz, Fritz, 181
Janowitz, Leo, 24–25, 27f, 32, 38–40, 41,
  49–50, 203–4
Jellinek, Eugen, 212–13
Jewish functionaries
  accommodations for, 65
  agency acquired by, 16, 47–48, 58
  boundaries, connections, and
    networks of, 88
  criticism faced by after liberation,
    22, 225–26
  difficulties of non-Czech Jews, 38
  difficulty of late arrivals securing
    positions, 37–38
  disposed of by SS, 230–31
  Germans and Austrians preferred by SS,
    38–39, 47
  indirect power exerted by, 49–58
  interactions with Rahm, 32
  interactions with SS, 33–34, 37
  issues of seniority and age
    among, 40–41
  low profile kept by, 31
  manipulated by Seidle, 19–20
  organization of transports by, 30
  pioneering mentality of, 39–40

political aspects of Czech versus
  German language use, 189
preferred status associated with,
  110, 182
propaganda events prepared by, 172–73
protection from transports, 177–78,
  204, 220–21
representation of Theresienstadt as
  viable workplace, 47
resentment over targeting of
  Czechs, 211
role in Theresienstadt, 1–2, 16, 33,
  201–2, 204–5
role in transporting children, 213
shocked by opinions of Hermann
  Strauß, 149–50
surprised by level of graft, 28
symbiotic relationship with SS
  men, 36–37
transports organized by, 206,
  207, 229–30
used as pawns by Rahm, 20
use of medicine to help inmates
  by, 146–47
violence against, 33, 36
vulnerability of, 32
Jewish property
  aryanized Jewish apartments, 21–22
  cataloging of looted, 19
  dental gold confiscated from
    prisoners, 143
  funneled to the Emigration Fund, 19
  looting of suitcases bound for ghetto,
    60–61, 128–29
  responsibility for administering, 252n15
  stolen to maintain ghetto, 103
Jewish self-administration
  barrack provided for abortions, 150–51
  cooperation with SS in propaganda
    film, 172
  development of, 16
  ethnicity, loyalty, and, 38–39
  ethnic undertone to SS orders, 39
  expansion of complex system in, 38, 47
  feelings of self-importance
    fostered by, 40
  food distribution by, 100–31
  fragmentation of, 30–31

gender factor for late arrivals, 37–38
highest-ranking woman in, 42
indirect power existing within, 49–58
organization of, 16, 26–49, 27f
organization of departing transports
by, 201–21
physical organization of, 48–49
proclivity for bulletins, memos, and
minutes, 47–48, 84
purpose of, 23–24
records of, 14
SS order for German or Austrian
heads, 28–29
symbolic capital of artistic performance
and, 182
treatment of elderly versus laborers and
children, 77–86
Jochowitz, Hanuš, 175, 192–93
Jöckel, Heinrich, 18f
Jonas, Esther, 73, 93, 95, 154, 184–85
Jonas, Marie, 154, 184–85
Jonas, Regina, 147–48

Kain, Herbert, 34, 35–36, 259n125
Kaltenbrunner, Ernst, 18f
Kantor, Alfréd, 196f
Kárná, Margita, 80
Kárný, Miroslav, 39, 77, 80, 97, 226
Katz, Carl, 27f, 37, 42, 72
Kende, Viktor, 55–56, 124, 206
Kindermann, Viktor, 147
Kirchert, Werner, 138
Klaber, Josef, 27f, 46
Klang, Heinrich, 38, 46
Klapp, Erich, 134, 153–54, 156–57,
159–60, 161
Klein, Arnošt, 63, 72, 83, 90, 98, 128,
211–12, 216–17
Klein, Emil, 153–54
Klein, Franz Eugen, 181, 183–84, 192–93
Klein, Gideon, 182, 184, 185, 193–94
Klein, Pavel, 161
Kleinová, Eliška, 192
Klinger, Karel, 93
Klinger, Ota, 197–98
Klinkeová, Josefa, 188, 191, 193–94
Kohn, Bedřich, 97–98, 169–70, 171,
187, 212–13

Kohn, Erich, 235
Kohnová, Valerie, 108
Kolářová, Věra, 155–56
Kolben, Jindřich, 80
Kollman, František, 63, 223
Kolowrat, Gisela Countess, 69–70
Kolský, Šimon, 129–30
Kopolovič, Šimon, 66
Kosák, Viktor, 78, 156
Kozower, Philipp, 27f
Krankenbehandler (sick treaters), 133–34,
297n120
Krása, Edgar, 123, 180–81, 182–84
Krasová, Anna, 192
Kraus, Evžen, 23, 153, 163
Krausová, Irena, 230
Kriegel, František, 133
Krönert, Benno, 136–37
Kuna, Milan, 185–86
Kursawe, Otto, 21, 44, 206, 220, 231
Kussy, Victor, 27f, 39
Kwasniewski, Siggi, 230

labor ghettos, 28, 47, 58
Ladner, Kurt, 195
Lagus, Karel, 182–83
Lang, Petr, 97
Langer, František, 175
Langer, Greta, 204
Langer, Herbert, 32, 204, 232–33
Langer, Lawrence, 6, 226–27, 239–40
language
categorization and stratification based on,
4–5, 43, 75, 79, 98, 197
expression of belonging and, 82
formal used by
self-administration, 47–48
language barriers among SS, 39
political aspects of Czech versus
German language use, 189
role in cultural life, 189
social capital categorized by, 4–5
social organization and, 86–88
used in cultural offerings, 170
used in petitions for removal from
transports, 218t, 218
use in cultural events, 186–87, 189
use of Hebrew, 119

356 INDEX

Lau, Abraham, 195
Lederer, Edvard, 189
Lederer, Vítězslav, 53–54, 234
Lederer, Zdeněk, 72–73, 92
Ledererová, Hana, 161
legend of Terezín
    as concealing of complexities, 80
    function of, 68
    as triumph of human spirit, 80,
        97, 117
    See also master narrative
Leiner, Hanuš, 184–85
Levit, Jan, 153–54
Levy, Ada, 214
Levy, Kurt, 27f, 38–39, 41, 49–50
Lichtblau, Erich, 108, 129, 160
Lifmann, Margot, 93
Lindtová, Klára, 41–42
Lippmann, Arthur, 165
Loeb, Illa, 164–65
Loewenstein, Karl, 40–41, 46, 55, 56, 113,
        126, 210
Löwenstein, Karl, 27f
Löwinger, Walter, 27f, 33, 42
Löwit, František, 88, 145
Löwith, Rudolf, 148
Lustig, Josef, 177–78

Mahler, Willy, 87–88, 175, 181
Mahrer, Pavel, 124–25
Mahrerová, Eva, 86–87
Mandler, Robert, 56
Mändlová, Eva, 93, 129, 184–85, 206–7,
        212–13, 216–17, 223
Manes, Philipp, 51, 72, 75, 88, 169, 170,
        · 175, 185
mass murder, knowledge of, 231–37
master narrative
    1942 hangings as significant in, 67
    centerpiece of, 68–69
    cohesiveness gained by, 67, 98, 239
    contributions of Paul Edelstein
        to, 26–28
    creation of, 191
    cultural activities and, 171
    development of, 59–69
    endowment of experiences with
        meaning through, 67

esteem for the *Aufbaukommando*
        members and, 74
    generated by younger Czech Jews,
        73–74, 75
    ghetto as a triumph of human spirit, 80,
        97, 117
    groups not corresponding to, 68
    politically charged, 12
    purpose of, 68
    questioning of, 242
    role of Technical Department in, 44–45
    solidarity and patronage as part
        of, 182–83
    symbolic capital of various
        professions, 66
Mautner, František, 185
medicine and illness
    common illnesses and treatments, 111,
        115, 137–38, 140, 144–51
    material advantages held by medical
        personnel, 159–66
    overview of, 166–67
    physicians, nurses, and power, 151–59
    professionalism of prisoner
        doctors, 132–33
    smaller food rations assigned to sick
        inmates, 107
    structure of Health Services, 133–44
    temporary illness as protection from
        transport, 222–23, 317n105
    use of ghetto's medical infrastructure by
        SS, 140
    See also deaths; Health Services;
        physicians
Meijers, Eduard, 32–33
Meissner, Alfréd, 32, 189
Meller, Paul, 124–25
Menasche, Mautner, 68
Mengele, Josef, 218
Merin, Moshe, 57
Merzbach, Ludwig, 27f, 44
Meth, Paul, 27f, 46
methodology, 13–14
Metz, Adolph, 45, 128, 222–23
Meyer, Corrie, 110–11
Meyer, Denise, 70
Meyer, Felix, 158
Meyer, Léon, 70

Meyer, Suzanne, 70
Meyer, Sven, 110–11
Meyerhoff, Marianne, 55–56
Michaelis, Ernst, 125–26
microhistory, 12, 251n49
Moes, Ernst, 17–19, 26, 29, 34, 35, 36, 202, 229–31
Morgenstern-Říkovský, Ota, 153–54
Mosse, Martha, 37–38, 40, 49, 67, 236–37
Müller, Martha, 155, 157
Munk, Erich
  appreciation for the arts, 153–54
  approval of forced abortions, 150–51
  covers for Otto Reinisch, 160–61, 222–23
  dedication of, 152
  deportation of, 161
  as head of Health Services, 45, 57–58, 134–35
  lobbies for transport exemptions for medical staff, 146
  material advantages held by, 159–60
  organization of Jewish self-administration, 27f
  professionalism of, 157–58
  relationship with Rolf Bartels, 36–37
  as representing ghetto youth, 153–54
  resentment toward Loewenstein and Grabower, 40–41
  travels to Roudnice pharmacy, 136–37
  view of Franz Hahn, 155
Munková, Hana, 72, 75
Murmelstein, Benjamin
  arrest and investigation for collaboration, 53, 56
  assessment of daily calorie rations by, 106
  belief in meritocracy, 38
  belief SS behind cigarette smuggling, 128
  campaigns for medical team protection from transport, 161
  claims Eppstein behind ban on Czech cultural activities, 189
  comments on lack of Czech nurses, 164
  depicted as corrupt by Tůma, 224
  disagreements with Baeck, 52–53

discussion of Recreation's weekly programs, 170
disregards established rules of protection of children, 213
excluded based on Eastern Jewish background, 90–91
handling of smuggler by, 35–36
improves food distribution, 107–8
installation as *Dezernent*, 42, 44–45, 155
installation as Elder, 29–31, 228–29
interest in Recreation Department, 45–46
observations of SS, 22
organization of Jewish self-administration, 26, 27f
organization of Theresienstadt beautification, 172–73
preferences for decision making, 33
questions purpose of construction in 1935, 235–36
reaction to informers, 55
receives special medical treatment, 149
relationship with Rahm, 20–21
reorganization of ghetto's administration by, 47
role in organizing transports, 230–31
sharing of information by, 33–34
softening of forced abortions under, 150
speculates on amount of looted Jewish capital, 103
use of social capital with perpetrators, 57
Muselmann, 114–15
music. *See* cultural events; cultural life
Mussolini, Benito, 39

Nathan, Hilde, 94–95
Nathanová, Anna, 109, 182–83, 188
Neufliess, Werner, 51
Neuhaus, Leopold, 65, 141
Neumann, Trude, 141–42
Neumannová, Alena, 161
Niehaus, Heinrich, 172
Nivelli, Herbert, 70

Oelze, Regina, 111, 154
Oestreicher, Elsa, 124
Okun, Sonia, 76

358 INDEX

Oppenhejm, Ralph, 95
organization and hierarchies
　indirect power within Jewish
　　self-administration, 49–58
　SS hierarchies and lines of
　　communication, 17–26, 18f
　three Elders of the Jews, 26–49, 27f
　unique characteristics of Theresienstadt, 16
Ornest, Zdeněk, 130
Ornstein, Edith, 27f, 189–90, 202–3
Österreicher, Erich, 27f, 43, 203–5

Pacovský, Josef, 143
památníky (autograph book), 181
parta (group of Czech friends), 84, 93
Pečený, Karel, 10–11
Pedde, Margaret, 62
Pentlář, Viktor, 137
Perseinová, Ludmila, 126
Pestek, Viktor, 234
petitions (for removal from transports),
　　214–19, 216t, 217t, 218t
Petschau, František, 124, 198–99
Petschau, Nita, 198–99
Petschau, Vilém, 124, 198–99
Petschauová, Nita, 237
Philippson, Alfred, 49–50
physical violence. See violence
physicians
　agency achieved by, 151–59
　conditions for under Nazi rule, 133–51
　female, 142
　material advantages held by, 159–61
　pre-war conditions for, 133
　professionalism of prisoner doctors,
　　132–33, 166–67
　sexism and, 162–66
　triage mentality employed by, 144–47
　See also medicine and illness
Pick, František, 220
Pick, Miloš, 109, 225–26
Placzek, Siegfried, 27f, 41–42, 203–5
Placzek, Tekla, 213
Podolier, Marion, 188–89, 191, 193–94
Pohlmann, Hilde, 150–51, 162
Pokorná, Lilly, 134–35, 137–38, 143–
　　44, 145, 149–50, 153, 160, 161,
　　162–63, 165–66

Pokorny, Adolf, 134–35
Poláček, Karel, 71–72, 124–25, 184–85
Pollak, Artur, 98
Pollaková, Julie, 155–56, 161
Popper, Egon, 42, 203–4
Popperová, Gertruda, 187–88
Porges, Felix, 177–78
powerlessness
　agency and, 238
　experienced during transports, 201
　highlighting issue of, 2, 239–40
　illness as indication of, 151
　as key moment of victims'
　　experience, 225–26
　notion of morality and, 226–27
Prague Central Office, 18–20, 21–22,
　　32, 103
preferential ghetto, 231–32
prisoner society
　approach to studying, 2–3, 12, 242
　benefits of studying, 2–6, 59
　as both deeply divided and
　　interconnected, 98–99
　brutal homophobia generated by, 95–96
　categorization and stratification
　　in, 70–74
　categorization in, 4
　characteristics of, 239–40
　cultural life as reflection of ethnic and
　　social variations, 168
　determination of who died and how by,
　　239 (see also social organization)
　experience of Jewishness in, 96–98
　factors influencing social
　　hierarchy, 59
　gender expectations in, 108
　handling of food distribution in, 101
　as hierarchical and also
　　interconnected, 241
　loyalties produced by, 241–42
　man-made famine caused by, 127
　method of studying, 13–14
　observations of ethnicity of women in
　　public roles, 191
　shaped by transnational forces, 12
　transnational aspects of, 83, 88
privilege ghettos, 7, 47
Prochnik, Robert, 27f, 41

"prominent" prisoners, 49–52, 54–56, 221, 229
propaganda films, 6, 10–11, 19, 172, 191–92
Protectorate of Bohemia and Moravia, 7–8, 11–12, 17, 18*f*, 22, 23, 37, 60, 62, 76, 77, 104, 134–35, 207–8, 211–12, 240–41

queer sexuality
  double stigmatization of foreigners, 96
  stigmatizing homophobia suffered by inmates, 95–96
  See also sexuality

Racenberg, Eva, 155
Racenberg, Šalomoun, 155
Rafael Schächter, 192–94
Rahm, Franz, 20
Rahm, Karl, 10, 17, 18*f*, 18–19, 20–21, 26, 30–31, 32, 35–36, 55, 150, 161, 172–74, 189, 229, 231, 235–36
Randt, Alice, 111, 159–60
Ranschburgerová, Růžena, 150
Raphael, Margot, 141–42
Raphaelson, Paul, 126
Recreation Department, 168–74
Red Cross
  arts highlighted during visits from, 172
  criticism of Baeck over visit from, 52
  delegates from IRC visit Theresienstadt, 10
  distribution of insulin during visit from, 137–38
  German Red Cross visits Theresienstadt, 205
  Günther's preparation for visit from, 19
  Murmelstein's preparation for visit from, 30, 206
  notoriety gleaned from visits by, 6
  participation of BdS and IVB4 in visit from, 17–18
  Rahm's preparation for visit from, 20
  rule of ghetto passed to Swiss Red Cross, 21
  shock of visitors from German Red Cross, 10
  SS hands control of ghetto to IRC, 185
  violence preceding visit from, 25

Redlich, Egon (Gonda), 1–2, 14, 27*f*, 33, 43, 95, 146, 230, 247n2
Reichmann, Rudolf, 170, 185–86
Reich Security Main Office (RSHA), 8, 17, 18*f*, 18–19, 35, 48
Reiner, Karel, 97, 191–92, 198
Reinisch, Otto, 156, 160–61, 222
RHSA. See Reich Security Main Office
Roman, Martin, 193–94
Rosenberg, Rudolf, 234
Rosner, Max, 89
Roubíčková, Eva, 205–6, 208, 212
Roubíčková, Marie, 223
Roubíčková-Cabicarová, Ella, 162
Ruben, Josefa, 122, 156–57, 162
Rudolf Haindl, 229
Rumkowski, Mordechai, 57
Rutarová, Hana, 109
Rutarová, Karel, 109
Růžička, Ota, 173–74, 182, 184

Säbel, Leo, 76
Saicová, Jarmila, 137
Salaba, Karel, 22, 23
Salomon, Louis, 63, 113
Salomon, Rosa, 71
Salus, Wolfgang, 233–34
Schächter, Raphael, 79, 129, 168–70, 182, 184, 193–94, 198
Schaffa, Hanuš, 140
Schickler, Hulda, 112–13
Schicková, Hana, 81, 113–14
Schleuse, 60–61
Schliesser, Karel, 27*f*, 32, 36–37, 44, 103–4, 123, 203–4, 228–29, 232–33, 234
Schmiedt, Alexandr, 119
Scholz, Heinrich, 21, 103
Schönhová, Alžběta, 165–66
Schönová, Vlasta, 45–46, 73, 75, 169, 172–73, 175, 184, 188–89, 191–92, 220
Schorch, Gustav, 184, 225–26, 227
Schumann, Coco, 193–94
Seidl, Siegfried, 18*f*, 19–20, 28, 32, 34, 46, 252–53n19
Sekaninová, Truda, 63, 204
self-administration. See Jewish self-administration
Sever, Max, 27*f*, 44–45

360 INDEX

sexism
  incidences in cultural life, 191–92
  lack of female artists, 182
  in power structures, 162–66
  work of females in kitchens seen as not
    prestigious, 108
sexuality
  double-edgedness of, 305n35
  ethnic groups and, 93–95
  exclusion and stigmatization
    based on, 59
  intrinsically linked to societal
    hierarchies, 92, 130
  as key element of human condition, 91
  lack of contraceptives and, 150
  love, dating, and sexuality, 92–96
  as means for discerning changing habits
    of prisoner community, 240–41
  pathologization of women's
    bodies, 158–59
  as revealing of social stratification and
    gender roles, 98–99
  scarcity of histories for interwar era, 3–4
  as validation of masculinity, 91–92
  See also queer sexuality
Shek, Zeev, 213
Simon, Etta Veit, 88, 151
Simonsohn, B., 27f
Simonsohn, Berthold, 38–39, 76, 94
Singer, Alexandr, 182–83, 184, 191
Singer, Kurt, 171
SiPo and SD (BdS), 17, 18f, 21
Sládek, Josef, 178–79
Small Fortress, 7, 17–18, 18f, 23, 25, 142–
  43, 223, 235–36, 252n6
smuggling
  assistance of SS for, 25, 128
  as cell of resistance, 36
  of cigarettes, 35–36, 50
  of drawings depicting
    Theresienstadt, 174
  of execution photos, 22
  of flowers, 108
  of food and people, 9, 108–9,
    124, 127–28
  by Hilda Hahnová, 50
  informers reporting on, 54–55
  by Julius Taussig, 25, 222

  of mail and valuables, 110
  of medications, 137–38
  of new arrivals belongings, 60
  of prophylactics, 150
  punishment for, 25, 35–36
  role of gendarmes in, 23, 164
  Shipping Department as central
    source of, 44
  vicious interrogations of prisoners
    accused of, 20
Smuk, Mirjam, 88
soccer, 160, 194–98, 310n141
social organization
  boundaries, connections, and
    networks of, 88
  categorization and stratification
    in, 70–74
  complex society produced in
    Theresienstadt, 59
  elderly inmates, 77–79
  "formerly important" class, 48–51
  gender and categorization in, 91–92
  Holocaust experience and
    Jewishness, 96–98
  language use and, 86–88
  love, dating, and sexuality in, 92–96
  post-arrival assimilation of
    prisoners, 59–69
  as reflection of Central and Western
    European society, 69–70
  social capital as basis of categorization, 4
  social capital categorized by
    language, 4–5
  social elite, 74–77, 184
  transports and belonging, 211–13
  youth and children, 79–86
  See also prisoner society
Solar, Josef, 110
Solarová, Františka, 183–84, 220
solidarity
  among non-family groups, 84, 119–20
  lack of in Theresienstadt, 1–2,
    97–98, 241–42
Sommer, Alice Herz, 182
Sommer, Alice Herz-, 185, 193–94
Sonderkommandos, 56–57
Special Department of Gendarmerie, 22
Spiegel, Magda, 193–94, 198

Spies, Gerty, 118, 121
Spitzer, Federica, 164
sports. *See* soccer
Springer, Erich, 134, 138, 141, 152–53, 161, 164, 165
SS (Schutzstaffel)
  appointment of Elders of the Jews, 26
  attendance at soccer games, concerts, and dance performances, 173–74
  control exerted by violence, 57
  designation of prisoners as meritorious, 168
  ethnic undertone to orders, 38–39
  forced labor for financial profit, 44
  hierarchies and lines of communication, 17–26, 18*f*
  introduction of "prominent" prisoner category, 49–52
  involvement in final transports, 230
  network of informers run by, 54–56
  number, origin, and deaths of Jews sent to Theresienstadt by, 7–10
  order for modern crematorium, 143
  order to lower reports of TB cases, 145
  planning of self-administration in Theresienstadt, 16
  prohibited from beating prisoners, 252n17
  protection of certain prisoners from transport, 220
  symbiotic relationship with Jewish functionaries, 36
  use of ghetto's medical infrastructure, 140
Stahl, Heinrich, 27*f*, 52–53, 153–54
Stahlecker, Walter, 18*f*
Šťastný, Otto, 150–51, 162
Steckelmacher, Hans, 229
Steifová, Josefina, 54–55
Stein, Richard, 27*f*, 45, 132, 161
Steinerová, Hana, 37–38
Steinitz, Lisl, 187–88
Stengel, Elisabeth von, 27*f*
Sternová, Dorothea, 51
Sternová, Eva, 51
Sternová, Nelly, 51
Stieve, Hermann, 159
Strass, Leo, 174

Strassburger, Manfred, 90
Strauß, Elsa, 153–54
Strauß, Hermann, 31, 141, 149–50, 153–54, 157–58
Strauss, Hermann, 213, 220
Strauss, Leo, 123, 183–84, 187–88
Strauss, Myra, 123, 187–88
Stux, Paul, 27*f*, 44–45
suicide
  attempts by Hanna Erdmann, 141–42
  categories of, 147–48
  demographics of, 148
  of Herbert and Greta Langer, 204
  of Max Cohen, 148
  of Oskar Taussig, 35–36
  preventing among new arrivals, 147–48
Süß, Salomon, 44–45
Švenk, Karel, 177–78, 182, 184, 187, 198
Svěrák, Jan, 3–4

Taussig, Jiří, 195
Taussig, Josef, 184
Taussig, Julius, 25–26, 222–23
Taussig, Oskar, 35–36
Terezín. *See* Theresienstadt
Theresienstadt
  building of ghetto, 74
  cultural life in, 168–200
  food and hunger in, 100–31
  as ghetto versus a concentration camp, 11–12
  history of Terezín, 7
  lack of solidarity in, 1–2, 241–42
  liberation of, 8
  medicine and illness in, 132–67
  multiple roles of, 2–3, 7, 9–11, 16
  number, origin, and deaths of Jews sent to, 7–10
  organization and hierarchies of, 1–2, 16–26, 38, 41, 47–48
  physical organization of, 48
  size and density of, 9
  social organization of, 59–99
  survival rates, 9, 249n30
  transports from, 201–38
  work for German industry and army in, 11
Thierfeldová, Gertruda, 155–56

362 INDEX

torture. *See* violence
transit ghetto, 7, 8–9, 16, 23–24, 150, 201
Transport Help, 60–61
Transport Management
  function of, 206
  goods recommended to pack by, 205
  heads of, 55–56, 195–97, 206
Transport Registry
  bribes for removal from, 222–23
  Communists planted in, 41–42
  function of, 41–42
  petitions for removal from, 215
  process of organizing transports, 201–7
  protection of family units by, 202–3
transports
  chronology, destination, and resolution
    of, 207–11
  codes assigned to, 60, 201–2
  conduct surrounding as reflection of
    societal values, 237
  description of arriving, 60–61
  escaping, 209, 223
  in Fall 1944, 21, 228–31
  first and second, 8–9
  individual protection from, 170–71, 222–23
  institutional protection from, 11,
    160, 220–21
  knowledge of mass murder, 231–37
  organization of, 201–7
  petitions for removal from, 214–19,
    216*t*, 217*t*, 218*t*
  powerlessness and agency
    surrounding, 238
  to prepare Theresienstadt for Red Cross
    visit, 10
  responsibility for departing, 201
  responsibility for incoming and
    outgoing, 17–18
  survival rates, 9, 249n30
  transport psychology, 223–28
  transports and belonging, 211–13
Troller, Norbert, 112*f*, 122, 174,
  183–84, 186*f*
Tůma, Mirko, 59, 224, 225–26
typhus, 56, 61, 145–47, 151, 152,
  296n105

Ulbrichts, Kurt, 36–37
Ullmann, Viktor, 179, 181

Ungar, Otto, 172, 174
Utitz, Antonín, 161

Valentová, Emilie, 132, 137
victim society
  benefits of studying, 2–5
  changes underwent by, 240
  method of studying, 13–14
  See also prisoner society
victim testimonies
  lack of among elderly, 112–13, 114
  of prisoner physicians, 153
  of queer inmates, 96
  See also individual names
violence
  adopted by Eichmann men, 17
  beating of Adam Czerniakow, 258n111
  beating of Paul Eppstein, 19
  beatings of smugglers, 25
  "constructive" violence administered
    for control, 57
  control exerted by SS, 57
  as daily occurrence in Small
    Fortress, 25
  against denouncers, 56
  orgy of violence practiced by Bergel and
    Haindl, 25–26
  refuge from in Health Services, 132
  relative absence of extreme physical
    violence, 24–25, 239
  role in human society, 2–3
  sexualized violence against women
    prisoners, 22–23
  shooting of Paul Eppstein, 29–30
  shooting of sick children, 20
  against smugglers, 25
  SS prohibited from beating
    prisoners, 252n17
  threat of by SS, 201–2
  torturing of smugglers, 25,
    35–36, 222
  used by Siegfried Seidl for
    manipulation, 19–20
  See also executions
Vochočová, Zdeňka, 204
Vogel, Jiří, 27*f*, 31, 32, 44–45
Volavková, Hana, 171–72
Vyth, Eva, 223
Vyth, Kurt, 223

Waigner, Karel, 27*f*
Weglein, Resi, 155–56
Weidmann, František, 32, 203–4
Weinbaumová, Jadwiga, 56
Weinberger, Robert Vinči, 27*f*, 39–40, 43, 68–69
Weiner, Erich, 27*f*, 45, 168–69
Weinmann, Erwin, 17, 18*f*, 173
Weinstein, Charlotta, 12
Weinstein, Karel, 12
Weinsteinová, Charlotta, 122
Weinwurmová-Löwyová, Marta, 158
Weiss, Evžen, 25
Weissenstein, František, 198
Weisungen
    convicted by Ghetto Court, 126–27
    Egon Redlich as, 230
    Herbert Langer as, 233
    killed in Auschwitz, 206
    listed after October 1944, 230–31
    listed in May 1944, 202
    listed in September 1943, 218
    Marianne Meyerhoff as, 55–56
    Otto and Marta Reinisch as, 222–23
    Yet Bergmann as, 232–33
Weisz, Herrmann, 27*f*
Welfare Department
    devotion of nurses and doctors, 152
    head of, 33
    prioritization of, 140
    reception committee, 147–48
Wetzler, Alfréd, 234
Woerdeman, Martinus, 157–58
Wolfensteinová, Minna, 134, 145–46, 152, 164
Wygodzinski, Martha, 154

Youth and Elderly Welfare Department
    autarkic administration of, 48–49
    employees' justification based on, 47
    head of, 22–23, 52, 141
    need for, 43
    organization of, 38–39, 41, 43, 47
    origins of, 140
Youth Welfare Department, 79, 116

Zelenka, František, 185
Zionists
    accused of saving their own from
      deportation, 207, 213

    Alexandr Schmiedt as, 119
    Alisa Ehrmannová as, 108–9
    Berthold Simonsohn as, 94
    Central Labor and Youth Welfare as
      strongholds of, 43, 47, 75–76
    commune created by, 119
    Communists' view of, 97
    confrontation of Christian inmates, 52
    deportations of, 207
    displaced by newly arrived
      functionaries, 38
    Edith Orstein as, 189–90
    Erich Munk as, 45
    Fredy Hirsch as, 96
    goal of raising children as conscious
      Jews, 1–2
    hachshara (Zionist agricultural
      training), 191
    Hana Fischlová as, 81
    Hana Schicková as, 113–14
    interpretation of Holocaust as
      meaningful, 97
    Jakob Edelstein as, 26
    Julius Grünberger as, 44–45, 76
    Karel Schliesser as, 32, 44
    loyalty within ethnic groups, 198
    as main ideological group, 203–4
    master narrative of Theresienstadt, 191
    as part of social elite, 75–76
    Paul Eppstein as, 76
    Petr Lang as, 97
    protection from transports, 204
    representation by council
      members, 32–33
    Richard Stein as, 45
    sense of home and belonging
      among, 178–79
    Siegfried Placzek as, 41–42
    in Theresienstadt versus
      Auschwitz, 97
    Truda Guttmannová as, 94
    use of Czech aesthetics for
      expression, 191
    Walter Löwinger as, 42
    young Czech Jews as, 58, 75–76
Zucker, Otto
    ability to protect performers from
      transport, 170–71
    as art lover, 185

364 INDEX

Zucker, Otto (*Cont.*)
  blamed for failure to protect inmates
    form deportation, 206–7
  cancels protection of Youth Care
    workers, 221
  death of, 232–33
  deportation of, 229
  disagreements with Edelstein, 28–29
  organization of Jewish self-
    administration, 26, 27f
  participation in Large Commission, 202–4
  participation in Recreation
    Department, 45–46, 168–69, 170, 194
  participation in Technical
    Department, 44–45
  petitions for removal from transports,
    214, 215
  pre-war career of, 39–40
  relationship with Grabower, 87
  remarks on dwindling elderly
    population, 208
  witnesses executions, 24–25
  youthful Zionist leadership recruited
    by, 134
Zuckerová, Tamara, 170
Zyklon B, 143